Introduction to Simulation
Using SIMAN

Introduction to Simulation Using SIMAN

C. Dennis Pegden
President
Systems Modeling Corporation

Robert E. Shannon
Professor of Industrial Engineering
Texas A & M University

Randall P. Sadowski
Vice President
Systems Modeling Corporation

McGraw-Hill, Inc.

New York   St. Louis   San Francisco   Auckland   Bogotá   Caracas   Hamburg
Lisbon   London   Madrid   Mexico   Milan   Montreal   New Delhi   Paris
San Juan   São Paulo   Singapore   Sydney   Tokyo   Toronto

This book was developed by Systems Modeling Corp. and published under a joint distribution arrangement with McGraw-Hill, Inc.

Order Information:

Text orders should be addressed to:
McGraw-Hill, Inc.
Order Services Department
Princeton Road
Hightstown, New Jersey 08520

Orders may also be placed by calling the McGraw-Hill College Division, 1-800-338-3987 or by contacting your local McGraw-Hill sales representative.

Designer: Peter Kauffman

Library of Congress Catalog Card Number 90-70925

ISBN 0-07-049217-4

Printed in the United States of America

10 9 8 7 6 5 4 3 2 1

Dedicated to
Lisa, Wesley, Kelsey and Whitney Pegden
Marion, Kelly, and Ted Shannon
Charles and Lily Sadowski

Preface

Simulation modeling has become an extremely important approach to analyzing complex systems. In recent years the number of people using simulation as a problem-solving aid has increased dramatically. This increase in use has led to a proliferation of both simulation software and simulation textbooks.

Most of the current textbooks on simulation fall into one of two categories. The first contains books which focus on simulation methodology, independent of a specific simulation language. These books address topics such as fitting distributions to data, verification and validation of a model, and interpretation of simulation output. These books tend to be statistical in nature. The second category contains textbooks which discuss model building using a specific simulation language. These textbooks are often the primary documentation for the language which they discuss. The books in this second category either ignore or only briefly discuss the methodological topics addressed by the books in the first category.

We believe that neither of these two approaches is completely adequate. In our view simulation is both an art and a science. As a consequence, we must study both the science aspects of the topic, and also gain first-hand experience in building and using models. By focusing solely on the methodology of simulation, we miss the knowledge which is gained from the experience of actually building, verifying, validating, and executing simulation models of complex systems. On the other hand, by focusing solely on mastering the intricacies of a particular simulation language, we learn the skills necessary to build and execute models of complex systems, but lack the full understanding of the methodological issues which are essential to the successful application of simulation.

The purpose of this book is to provide an introduction to simulation modeling using the SIMAN simulation language. Our objective is to both present the methodology of simulation, and to illustrate the discussion using a specific simulation language — i.e. SIMAN. Our focus in the text is on presenting the practical aspects of simulation modeling using SIMAN in a way that is easily understood by a beginning student to simulation. We have made extensive use of examples throughout the book and have attempted to limit our use of probability and statistics to basic concepts. We have also provided explanations of terms that may be new to or forgotten by the student. We have emphasized simplicity of explanation over rigorous proofs and technical details.

This book is appropriate for use in a senior level or first year graduate course on simulation in engineering or business. We assume that the student has had a first course in probability and statistics. Although not necessary, it is also useful to have had some experience with one or more programming languages.

This book can also be used by the motivated reader for self-study to learn simulation using SIMAN. This book also serves as a useful companion to the SIMAN Reference Guide to further explain and illustrate many of the features of the SIMAN language.

The simulation methodology topics covered in this book are those which we feel are important in the practical use of simulation in problem-solving. Hence we have deliberately omitted many topics which are theoretically interesting, but of little value to the practitioner. For example, we do not cover the regenerative method for interpreting simulation results, which although theoretically interesting, can only rarely be used in a practical setting. We have also omitted topics which are not directly relevant to the simulation analyst employing a modern simulation language such as SIMAN. For example, we do not discuss in detail the mathematical procedures for generating samples from the various distributions, nor do we discuss the procedures for testing the quality of a random number generator.

Although the book includes several chapters which are devoted to modeling using the SIMAN language, we have not attempted to completely document the SIMAN language within this text. There are modeling features in SIMAN which are not discussed in this book. We have limited our discussion to a subset of SIMAN which we feel is adequate for modeling most systems — and certainly adequate to serve as a vehicle for learning simulation. A complete documentation of the SIMAN language is provided in the SIMAN Reference Guide, which can be used as a companion to this book.

The first two chapters of the book are devoted entirely to methodological topics in simulation. Chapter 1 (Introduction to Modeling) provides a general introduction to the topic of simulation modeling. Chapter 2 (Beginning the Study) discusses the topics related to beginning a simulation study. This includes important preliminary issues such as deciding on the level of detail for the model, as well as the problems of data collection and selection of input distributions for the model.

Chapter 3 (Basic Modeling Concepts) presents the basic modeling concepts of SIMAN. A small subset of SIMAN modeling features which is sufficient to allow the reader to build and execute models of relatively simple systems is presented in this chapter.

Chapter 4 (Verification and Validation) discusses the problems of verifying and validating a model. In addition to presenting a detailed discussion of model verification and validation, this chapter also introduces the SIMAN interactive debugger, a powerful tool for isolating and correcting SIMAN modeling errors.

Chapter 5 (Interpreting the Results) discusses the problem of interpreting the results of the simulation model. This is one of two chapters in the book which requires a basic understanding of probability and statistics. This chapter discusses the approaches to properly interpreting the output from a simulation model, and introduces the SIMAN Output Processor, which can be used to automatically perform the analysis procedures discussed in this chapter.

Chapter 6 (Station Submodels) introduces additional SIMAN modeling constructs which are useful for modeling large systems, particularly those involving complex flow or the use of material handling equipment. By the completion of this chapter, we have covered the essential methodological issues and modeling topics which are sufficient to allow the student to successfully build and use models of many complex real-world systems.

Chapter 7 (Animation using Cinema) discusses the role of animation in simulation modeling and introduces the Cinema system for animating SIMAN models. The use of animation in verification and validation activities is discussed. This chapter includes an overview of a number of real-world Cinema animation examples.

Chapter 8 (Additional Modeling Constructs) discusses some additional SIMAN modeling constructs which are useful in modeling complex systems. Mastery of the material in this chapter further enhances the modeling capability of the student.

Chapter 9 (Advanced Manufacturing Features) discusses some advanced SIMAN modeling features which are useful for modeling systems containing complex material handling devices such as automatic guided vehicles, automatic storage and retrieval systems, multiple interacting cranes, etc. The material in this chapter is particularly relevant for courses in industrial/manufacturing engineering.

Chapter 10 (Interfacing User-Written Subprograms) discusses the procedures for interfacing SIMAN models to user-written subprograms developed with FORTRAN or C. This capability is useful for modeling certain types of complex logic or interfacing the model to external systems.

Chapter 11 (Continuous and Combined Models) discusses the use of simulation for modeling continuous and combined continuous-discrete systems. This chapter includes both a general discussion of the methodology for modeling continuous/combined systems and details for implementing these models in SIMAN.

Chapter 12 (Variance Reduction Techniques) discusses the use of variance reduction techniques to improve on the output analyis methods discussed in Chapter 5. This chapter assumes a basic understanding of probability and statistics. The variance reduction techniques discussed in this chapter include indirect measures, control variates, common random numbers, and antithetic sampling. The practical use of each of these techniques is illustrated with examples.

Although the material in the first six chapters is written assuming that the chapters are covered in sequence, the last six chapters are written to be independent of each other and can be covered in any order. A typical one-semester course would include all of the first six chapters plus selected material from the last six chapters of the book. Courses emphasizing process-oriented modeling skills with SIMAN could augment the first six chapters with material from chapters 8 (Additional Modeling Constructs) and 9 (Advanced Manufacturing Features). Courses emphasizing methodology could augment the first six chapters with material from chapters 7 (Animation using Cinema) and 12 (Variance Reduction Techniques). Material from chapters 10 (Interfacing User-Written Subprograms) and 11 (Continuous and Combined Models) could be covered in courses which have programming in C or FORTRAN as a prerequisite.

Acknowledgements

It is a pleasure to recognize and thank the many individuals who have helped us in the writing of this book.

We would like to give a special thanks to Deborah A. Davis who spent many hours reading early drafts of the material and made numerous editorial, technical, and substantive improvements to the manuscript. The final manuscript has benefited greatly from her critical reading of the material and from her many constructive suggestions.

Professor Byron Gottfried from the University of Pittsburgh also made many helpful suggestions for improving the orignal manuscript. Dave Sturrock and Jim Higley provided a detailed technical review of much of the SIMAN material in the book. We would also like to thank Professor Ben Kleindorfer from the Pennsylvania State University who provided us with a large collection of modeling exercises, and Sherri Conrad, John Meszaros, Dan Quinn, and Tony Vandenberge, who assisted us in the development and running of the examples and exercises for the book.

Finally, we would like to thank Barbara Miller, our technical writer, and Peter Kauffman, our graphics designer.

Software Acknowledgements

Since much of the material in this book is based on the SIMAN/Cinema software, we would like to acknowledge the individuals whom have contributed to the development of the software.

The original version of SIMAN was developed by Pegden. His work in language development began at the University of Alabama in Huntsville where he led in the development of the original version of SLAM and did the initial conception, design, and implementation. Portions of SLAM were based on

Pritsker and Associates' proprietary software called GASP and Q-GERT. Since its original implementation, SLAM has been continually refined and enhanced by Pritsker and Associates.

After leaving the University of Alabama in Huntsville, Pegden joined the faculty at the Pennsylvania State University where he began his work on SIMAN. The SIMAN language was designed to be a general-purpose modeling language — but the design also included many special-purpose manufacturing features to make the language particularly useful in modeling large and complex manufacturing systems. SIMAN was also designed around the logical modeling framework proposed by Zeigler in which the simulation is separated into the model frame, experiment frame, and analysis frame.

Many of the concepts included in SIMAN are based on the previous work of other simulation language developers. Many of the basic ideas in the process-orientation of SIMAN can be traced back to the early work by Geoffory Gordon at IBM who developed the original version of GPSS. Many of the basic ideas in the discrete-event portion of SIMAN can be traced back to the early work by Phillip Kiviat at US Steel who developed the original version of GASP. SIMAN also contains features which Pegden originally developed for SLAM. Some of the algorithms in SIMAN are based on work done by Pritsker and Associates. The combined discrete-continuous features of SIMAN are in part based on SLAM.

Since its initial implementation, SIMAN has been continually refined and enhanced by System Modeling Corporation who markets and distributes the software. A number of individuals have played key roles in the evolution of the SIMAN software over the years. Many of the early enhancements to the language were implemented by Kevin J. Healy, who directed the enhancements to the language between 1984 and 1987.

During 1988 and 1989, the SIMAN language was completely redesigned and reimplemented. Deborah A. Davis played a major role in both the initial reimplementation and in the design of many of the new features which were added to the language. Dave Sturrock, who joined Systems Modeling Corporation during this project, managed the completion of this new version of SIMAN and also designed and implemented many of the new features which were incorporated into the language.

The Cinema software was originally designed and implemented in 1984 by a development team consisting of Deborah Davis, Kevin Healy, John Jackman, Trevor Miles, and Dennis Pegden. Since its initial implementation, it has been refined and enhanced by Rafael Otalora and Jack Poorte.

A number of individuals have also contributed to the development of support packages for use with SIMAN/Cinema. Randy Sadowski designed and implemented the original version of the Blocks editor. Bruno Dindelli and Deb Medeiros designed and implemented the original version of the Elements editor. Trevor Miles and Gustavo Diaz designed and implemented many enhancements to the original Output Processor. All of these support packages (Blocks, Elements, and the Output Processor) were completely redesigned and integrated into a single environment by a development team led by Cheryl Vicinanza and comprised of Steve Frank, Judy Joos, Robb Kipp, and Dave Takus.

In summary, the SIMAN/Cinema software is a blend of ideas from many sources. Without doubt, the design of the software will continue to evolve over the years and be influenced by both the staff at Systems Modeling Corporation and the feedback and advice from the large installed base of SIMAN/Cinema users.

Systems Modeling Corp.
The Park Building
504 Beaver Street
Sewickley, PA 15143
(412) 741-3727
Telex: 865775
FAX: (412) 741-5635

Table of Contents

Chapter 1: Introduction to Modeling 3
Simulation Defined 3
Systems and Models 3
Types of Models 5
Simulation Applications 6
Simulation In Manufacturing 7
Advantages and Disadvantages of Simulation 9
Simulation Example 10
Monte-Carlo Sampling 12
The Simulation Process 12
Problem Definition and Project Planning 13
System Definition and Model Formulation 16
Experimental Design 17
Input Data 18
Model Translation 19
Verification and Validation 20
Experimentation and Analysis 21
Documentation and Implementation 23
World Views 23
SIMAN 25
References 26

Chapter 2: Beginning the Study 31
Definition of the Study Objective 31
Information Collection 32
Boundary Definition 34
Simplification and Reduction 35
Omission, Aggregation, and Substitution 37
Impact of Model Simplification on Results 38
Sources of Input Data 39
No Existing Data 41
    Mean Value Only 41
    Range Only (Largest and Smallest Values) 42
    Range and Most Likely Value 43

Existing Data 44
Distribution Selection 46
    Continuous Distributions 47
    Discrete Distributions 49
Parameter Estimation 49
Goodness-Of-Fit Test 51
    Chi-Square 51
    Kolmogorov-Smirnov 54
Summary 56
References 57

Chapter 3: Basic Modeling Concepts 61
Introduction 61
Process Modeling in SIMAN 62
    The Relationship Between the Model
        and Experiment 62
    Entities, Attributes, Processes 62
    Block Diagrams 62
    Basic Block Types 63
    Block Function Names 64
    Block Operands 65
        Constants 65
        Variables 66
        Attributes 67
        Random Variables 68
        Expressions and Conditions 69
        Symbolic Names 70
    Block Sequence Numbers 71
    Block Labels 71
    Block Comments 71
    Block Modifiers 71
    Entity Flow Between Blocks 72
Sample Problem 3.1: A Single Workstation 73
An Initial Subset of Blocks 74

Entering Entities into the Model: The CREATE
    Block 74
Providing Waiting Space for Entities: The QUEUE
    Block 75
Allocating Resources to Entities: The SEIZE Block . . .77
Representing Time Delays: The DELAY Block 79
Releasing Resources: The RELEASE Block 80
Counting Events: The COUNT Block 81
Constructing the Block Diagram Model 81
Translation of the Block Diagram into Statement
    Form 82
The Block Statement Format 83
The Sample Model's Source File 84
An Initial Subset of Experiment Elements 85
Describing the Simulation Project: The PROJECT
    Element 86
Limiting the Number of Entities: The DISCRETE
    Element 87
Describing Queues: The QUEUES Element 87
Describing Resources: The RESOURCES Element 89
Describing Counters: The COUNTERS Element 90
Controlling Replications: The REPLICATE Element . .91
Using the Experiment Source File 92
Simulation Compilation, Linking, and Execution 93
Compiling the Model and Experiment Source Files . . .93
Linking the Model and Experiment Object Files 95
Executing the Program File 96
Sample Problem 3.2: Two Job Types and a Second
    Workstation 97
Describing the Process .98
Describing General-Purpose Attributes and Variables:
    The ATTRIBUTES and VARIABLES Elements 99
Assigning Values to General-Purpose Attributes and
    Variables: The ASSIGN Block 102
Sampling from a User-Defined Discrete Probability
    Distribution 103
Directing the Flow of Entities Among Blocks:
    The BRANCH Block 103
Solving the Sample Model 105
Sample Problem 3.3: Statistics on Queues, Resources,
    and Time in System 108
Collecting Observational and Time-
    Dependent Data 109
Recording Time-Dependent Data: The DSTATS
    Element 109
Recording Observational Data: The TALLY
    Block 110

Describing the Tally Records: The TALLIES
    Element 112
Describing Storages: The STORAGES Element 113
Solving the Model 114
Additional Sample Problems 116
Sample Problem 3.4: A Restaurant 116
Sample Problem 3.5: A Hospital Emergency
    Room 120
Exercises 125

Chapter 4: Model Verification and Validation 133
Introduction 133
Verifying Model Operation 134
Establishing a Doubting Frame of Mind 134
Incorporating Outside Doubters 135
Conducting Model and Experiment Walkthroughs . .135
Performing Test Runs .136
Tracing the Model's Operation:
    The TRACE Element 137
Isolating and Correcting Errors with the
    Interactive Debugger 139
Starting and Stopping a Debug Session 140
Entering Debugger Commands 140
Controlling Execution: The GO and
    STEP Commands 141
Setting and Canceling Options: The SET and
    CANCEL Commands 142
Showing Current Status: The SHOW and
    VIEW Commands 145
Assigning Values: The ASSIGN Command 146
Redirecting Entity Flow:
    The NEXT Command 147
Saving and Recalling Snapshots: The SAVE and
    RESTORE Commands 147
Obtaining On-Line Help: The HELP Command . . .148
Using Animation as a Verification Aid 148
Correcting Errors 148
Avoiding Some Common Errors 149
Data Errors 149
Initialization Errors 150
Errors in Units of Measurement 150
Flow Control 150
Blockages and Deadlocks 151
Arithmetic Errors 151
Overwriting Variables and Attributes 152
Data Recording Errors 152
Language Conceptual Errors 153

Validating the Model 153
   Defining Validity 154
   Testing for Reasonableness 156
   Testing Model Structure and Data 157
   Testing Model Behavior 158
Building Confidence 159
Exercises 160
References 161

Chapter 5: Interpreting Simulation Output 165
Conducting Statistical Analyses 165
Interpreting Information on The SIMAN
   Summary Report 166
Estimating Unknown Parameters 168
Controlling Randomness 170
   Generating Random Samples 171
   Controlling the Initial Seeds:
      The SEEDS Element 173
Terminating and Non-Terminating Systems 174
Analyzing Terminating Systems 175
   Constructing Confidence Intervals on
      the Mean 177
   Comparing Two Systems 181
Analyzing Non-Terminating Systems 185
   Reducing the Initial Condition Bias 186
   Estimating the Variance of the Mean 187
      Replication 188
      Summing Covariances 188
      Batching Observations 190
Using The SIMAN Output Processor 191
   Graphics Commands 194
      Creating Plots: The PLOTS Command 194
      Creating Bar Charts: The BARCHART
      Command 195
      Interpreting the Distribution of Data:
      The HISTOGRAM Command 195
      Interpreting the Correlation Structure:
      The CORRELOGRAM Command 197
   Statistical Commands 198
      Smoothing the Response:
      The MOVAVERAGE Command 198
      Batching and Truncating:
      The FILTER Command 199
      Generating Confidence Intervals on the Mean:
      the INTERVALS Command 201
      Comparing Two Systems:
      The COMPARISONS Command 203

Other Useful Statistical Commands 204
Transferring Data 204
   Listing Data: The TABLES Command 205
   Moving Data Between Systems:
      The IMPORTS/EXPORTS Commands 205
Performing an Analysis with the Output Processor:
   A Step-by-Step Summary 206
   Making Pilot Runs 207
   Making Production Runs 208
   Preparing the Data for Analysis 208
   Performing the Analysis 208
Examples 209
   Analyzing the Results of the
      Restaurant Model 209
   Analyzing the Results of the Hospital Emergency
      Room Model 211
Exercises 214
References 216

Chapter 6: Station Submodels and Entity Transfers . . . 219
The Need for Station Submodels 219
Sample Problem: Three-Workstation Flow-Line 219
The Station Concept 220
   Moving Between Stations: The Transfer
      Block 221
   Transferring Entities: The ROUTE Block 221
   The Station Attribute M 222
   The Sample Flow-Line Model Frame 222
   Defining Information about Stations:
      The STATIONS Element 224
   The Sample Flow-Line Experiment Frame and
      Summary Report 225
Control of Entity Transfers Between
   Station Submodels 227
   The Modified Flow-Line 227
   The Concept of Visitation Sequences 228
   Station-Visitation Sequences:
      The SEQUENCES Element 228
   Sequence Control: The NS and IS Attributes 229
   The Modified Flow-Line Model 231
Transfers Between Stations: Using Transporters 234
   The Modified Flow-Line with Transporters 234
   The Concept of a Transporter 235
   Allocation and Movement of Empty Transporters:
      The REQUEST Block 236
   Transfer to the Destination:
      The TRANSPORT Block 238

The Freeing of Transporters: The FREE Block 239
Model Frame for the Transporter Example 240
Definition of Transporter Characteristics:
    The TRANSPORTERS Element 243
Definition of Travel Distances: The DISTANCES
    Element 244
SIMAN Transporter Variables 246
Experiment Frame and Summary Report for the
    Transporter Example 247
The Enhanced Example: A Narrow Aisle and
    Failures 249
The Allocation of Transporters: The ALLOCATE
    Block 249
Transporter Movement: The MOVE Block 250
The Enhanced Example: The Narrow-
    Aisle Logic 251
Modeling Failures: The HALT and ACTIVATE
    Blocks 256
Summary Report for the Enhanced Transporter
    Example 258
Transfers Between Stations: Using Conveyors 258
The Modified Flow-Line with Conveyors 259
The Concept of a Conveyor 259
Non-accumulating Conveyors 260
Allocation of Conveyor Cells:
    The ACCESS Block 261
Transfer to the Destination:
    The CONVEY Block 262
Exit from the Conveyor Cells:
    The EXIT Block 262
Model for the Non-accumulating Conveyor
    Example 263
Definition of Conveyor Characteristics:
    The CONVEYORS Element 265
Definition of Conveyor Segments:
    The SEGMENTS Element 266
SIMAN Conveyor Variables 267
Experiment Frame and Summary for the
    Non-accumulating Conveyor Example 268
The Modified Flow-Line with Finite Buffers and
    Conveyor Failures 270
The Stopping and Starting of Conveyors:
    The STOP and START Blocks 270
The Model and Experiment Frames for Finite Buffers
    and Conveyor Failures 271
Accumulating Conveyors 275

The Modified Flow-Line with Accumulating
    Conveyors 277
Accumulating Conveyor Constructs 278
Model Frame for the Accumulating Conveyor
    Example 278
Experiment Frame and Summary Report for
    the Accumulating Conveyor Example 281
Additional Sample Problems 283
Sample Problem 6.8: A Circuit Board Assembly
    System 283
Sample Problem 6.9: A Power-and-Free Conveyor
    System 289
Exercises 295
References 301

Chapter 7: Animating the Simulation by
    Using Cinema 305
The Need for Animation 305
Model Verification 305
Model Validation 306
Dynamic Interactions.....................306
Presentation of Model Results 307
Animation's Limitations in Interpreting Model
    Results 307
The Small-Sample Problem 307
Trends Over Time 308
Overview of Cinema 308
The Animation Layout and its Relationship to
    the Model 309
The Static Component 310
The Dynamic Component 311
Symbol Libraries 311
Entity Symbols 312
Queues 313
Resource Symbols 314
Storages 315
Variables 316
Levels 317
Global Symbols 317
Frequencies and Plots....................318
Dynamic Colors 318
Transfers 319
Execution of the SIMAN Model with Animation ...323
Preparing the Model for Animation:
    The LAYOUTS Element 323
Running the Simulation with CSIMAN 324

Controlling the Time Advance 325
Sample Animations 326
  Westinghouse Just-In-Time Metal Fabrication
    Shop 326
  General Motors Truck Assembly (Body and
    Chassis) 327
  United Parcel Service Hub Shifter Simulation 328
  LTV Flexible Machining Cell 329
  Department of Energy Nuclear Waste Handling
    Facility 330
References 332

Chapter 8: Additional Discrete Modeling Concepts . . . 335
Introduction 335
Generic Station Submodels 335
  The Need for Generic Station Submodels:
    The Modified Flow-Line 335
  The Use of Numbers in Place of Names 336
  Station Ranges and the Station Attribute M 336
  Indexed Resources 337
  Sample Problem 8.1: The Modified Flow-Line
    Revisited 338
Resources Revisited 341
  Selecting among Parallel Resources: The SELECT
    Block 341
  Changing Resource Capacities: The ALTER Block
    and SCHEDULES Element 343
  Preempting a Resource: The PREEMPT Block 345
Queues Revisited 348
  Selecting Among Parallel Queues: The PICKQ and
    QPICK Blocks 349
  Manipulating Entities in Queues: The SEARCH and
    REMOVE Blocks 352
  Matching Queued Entities: The MATCH Block 354
Entity Sets 355
  Temporary Entity Sets: The GROUP, SPLIT,
    PICKUP, and DROPOFF Blocks 356
  Permanent Entity Sets: The COMBINE and
    DUPLICATE Blocks 360
Input/Output 362
  Defining an Input/Output File:
    The FILES Element 363
  Reading Data from a File: The READ Block 366
  Writing Data to a File: The WRITE Block 367
  Closing Files: The CLOSE Block 368
Conditional Holds 368

Waiting for an Event to Occur: The WAIT and
  SIGNAL Blocks 369
Waiting for System Status to Change:
  The SCAN Block 370
Evaluating System Status: The FINDJ Block 371
Some Additional Experimental Controls 372
  Creating External Arrivals:
    The ARRIVALS Element 372
  Experimentally Defining Block Operands:
    The DISTRIBUTIONS Element 374
  Experimentally Defining Decision Rules:
    The RULES Element 374
  Defining Table Functions: The TABLES Element 375
  Experimentally Defining Parameters:
    The PARAMETERS Element 376
Additional Sample Problems 378
  Sample Problem 8.1: The Jobshop Problem 378
  Sample Problem 8.2: Highway Toll Booth 382
  Sample Problem 8.3: The Bank Teller Problem 384
  Sample Problem 8.4: A Production
    Scheduling System 389
Exercises 394
References 400

Chapter 9: Advanced Manufacturing Features 403
Introduction 403
Guided Transporters 403
  The Modified Flow-Line with Guided Transporters . . 404
  Defining Intersections: The INTERSECTIONS
    Element 405
  Defining Guided-Vehicle Links:
    The LINKS Element 406
  Defining the System Map:
    The NETWORKS Element 407
  Defining The Modified Flow-Line System Map 408
  Creating The Shortest-Distance Matrix 409
  The STATIONS and TRANSPORTERS Elements for
    Guided Transporters 410
  Guided-Vehicle Movement 412
  Controlling Guided Vehicles 417
  Allocating and Moving the Empty Transporter 418
  Transporting the Entity: The TRANSPORT
    Block 420
  The Modified Flow-Line Model and
    Experiment Frame 421
  Staging Area Logic for Guided Transporters 425

SIMAN Guided-Transporter Variables 428
Modeling Changing Vehicle Speeds 431
Modeling Systems with Continuous Control 432
Changing the Shortest-Distance Matrix:
   The REDIRECTS Element 434
Modeling Vehicle Failures and Changing
   Vehicle Size 436
Additional Sample Problems 437
   Sample Problem 9.2: An AS/RS Model 438
   Sample Problem 9.3: A Overhead Crane Model . . . 443
Exercises 447

Chapter 10: Interfacing User-Written Subprograms . . . 455
The Need for User-Written Subprograms 455
An Overview 456
Interfacing with the User Code 457
   User-Written Routines 458
   The Event Routine and User Functions 459
   The EVENT Block 460
   Special User-Written Routines 460
   The Entity Identifier and Record Location 462
Interfacing from User Code to the Block Model 462
   Accessing the SIMAN System Variables 463
   Retrieving and Assigning Entity Attribute Values . . . 464
   Manipulating Entities 466
   Changing Status Variables and System Values 470
   Performing Statistical Functions 471
   Avoiding Common Errors 472
Additional Sample Problems 473
   Sample Problem 10.1: The Single-Machine
   Problem 473
   Sample Problem 10.2: Reading from a Data File and
   User-Menu System 478
   Sample Problem 10-3: A User-Defined
   Decision Rule 486
Exercises 491

Chapter 11: Continuous and Combined Models 495
Introduction 495
Continuous Modeling 495
   Describing Systems in Terms of States and Rates 496
   Converting an Nth-Order Equation to N First-Order
   Equations 498
   Solving Rate Equations by Euler's Method 499
   Solving Rate Equations by Runge-Kutta Methods . . . 499
SIMAN's Continuous Framework 500

Defining State and Rate Equations in Subroutine
   STATE 500
Initializing S, D, and X Variables: The INITIALIZE
   Element 503
Using the Continuous Time-Advance
   Mechanism 504
Specifying Integration and Time-Advance Parameters:
   The CONTINUOUS Element 505
Recording Statistics on Continuous-Change Variables:
   The CSTATS Element 506
Sample Problem 11.1: Cedar Bog Lake 507
Combined Discrete-Continuous Models 511
   Modeling Combined Discrete-Continuous
   Interactions 511
   Detecting State Events: The DETECT Block 512
Combined Discrete-Continuous Examples 516
   Sample Problem 11.2: A Soaking Pit Furnace 516
   Sample Problem 11.3: A Chemical Reaction
   Process 520
Exercises 526
References 528

Chapter 12: Variance Reduction Techniques 531
Introduction 531
Classification of Methods 531
Methods Based on Prior Information 532
   Indirect Measures 532
   Control Variates 535
Induced Correlation 540
   Common Random Numbers 540
   Antithetic Variates 544
Conclusions 549
Exercises 549
References 550

Appendix A: Distributions 555
Beta 557
Continuous 558
Discrete 559
Erlang 560
Exponential 561
Gamma 562
Lognormal 563
Normal 564
Poisson 565
Triangular 566

Uniform 567
Weibull 568

Appendix B: Critical Values 569
B-1: Kolmogorov-Smirnov Critical Values 569
B-2: Chi-Square 570
B-3: Students t Distribution 571

Appendix C: SIMAN Variables, Functions,
and Routines 573
Attributes 573
Conveyor Variables 573
Functions 573
Group Variables 573
Queue Variables 573
Resource Variables 574
Simulation Replication Variables 574
Special Purpose Variables 574
Station Variables 574
Statistics Collection Variables 574
Storage Variable 574
Table Look-Up 574
Transporter Variables 575
User-Assignable Variables 575
Built-In Functions 576
Queue, Resource, and Transporter Selection Rules . . . 576
Subprogram Libraries, Subroutines 577
Subprogram Libraries, Functions 578
User-Written Routines 579

Appendix D: SIMAN Blocks 581
ACCESS 581
ACTIVATE 581
ALLOCATE 581
ALTER 581
ASSIGN 582
BEGIN 582
BRANCH 582
CAPTURE 582
CLOSE 582
COMBINE 583
CONVEY 583
COPY 583
COUNT 583
CREATE 583
DELAY 584
DETECT 584

DROPOFF 584
DUPLICATE 584
EVENT 584
EXIT 585
FINDJ 585
FREE 585
GROUP 585
HALT 585
INCLUDE 585
INSERT 586
MATCH 586
Block Modifiers 586
MOVE 586
PICKQ 587
PICKUP 587
PREEMPT 587
QPICK 588
QUEUE 588
READ 588
RELEASE 588
RELINQUISH 589
REMOVE 589
REQUEST 589
ROUTE 589
SCAN 590
SEARCH 590
SEIZE 590
SELECT 590
SIGNAL 590
SPLIT 591
START 591
STATION 591
STOP 591
SYNONYMS 591
TALLY 591
TRANSPORT 591
WAIT 592
WRITE 592

Appendix E: SIMAN Elements 593
ARRIVALS 593
ATTRIBUTES 593
BEGIN 593
CONTINUOUS 594
CONVEYORS 594
COUNTERS 594
CSTATS 595

DISCRETE 595
DISTANCES 595
DISTRIBUTIONS 596
DSTATS 596
EVENTS 596
FILES 597
INCLUDE 597
INITIALIZE 597
INTERSECTIONS 597
LAYOUTS 598
LINKS 598
NETWORKS 598
OUTPUTS 599
PARAMETERS 599
PROJECT 599
QUEUES 599
RANKINGS 600
REDIRECTS 600
REPLICATE 600
RESOURCES 600
RULES 601
SCHEDULES 601
SEEDS 601
SEGMENTS 601
SEQUENCES 601
STATIONS 602
STORAGES 602
SYNONYMS 602
TABLES 602
TALLIES 603
TRACE 603
TRANSPORTERS 603
VARIABLES 604

Index 607

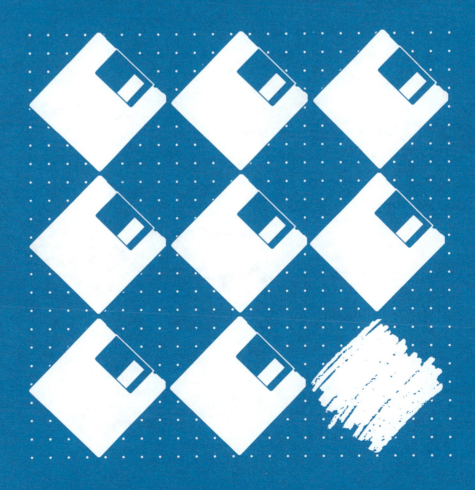

CHAPTER 1
Introduction to Modeling

Simulation is one of the most powerful analysis tools available to those responsible for the design and operation of complex processes or systems. In an increasingly competitive world, simulation has become a very powerful tool for the planning, design, and control of systems. No longer regarded as the approach of "last resort," it is today viewed as an indispensable problem-solving methodology for engineers, designers, and managers.

To simulate, according to Webster's Collegiate Dictionary, is "to feign, to obtain the essence of, without the reality." According to Schriber [1987], "Simulation involves the modeling of a process or system in such a way that the model mimics the response of the actual system to events that take place over time." We will define *simulation* as the process of designing a model of a real system and conducting experiments with this model for the purpose of understanding the behavior of the system and/or evaluating various strategies for the operation of the system. We consider simulation to include both the construction of the model and the experimental use of the model for studying a problem. Thus, you can think of simulation modeling as an experimental and applied methodology that seeks to accomplish the following:

- describe the behavior of systems,
- construct theories or hypotheses that account for the observed behavior, and
- use the model to predict future behavior, i.e., the effects produced by changes in the system or in its method of operation.

The terms "model" and "system" are key components of our definition of simulation. By a *model* we mean a representation of a group of objects or ideas in some form other than that of the entity itself. By a *system* we mean a group or collection of interrelated elements that cooperate to accomplish some stated objective. We can simulate systems that already exist and those that can be brought into existence, i.e., those in the preliminary or planning stage of development.

2. Systems and Models

The conceptualization and development of models have played a vital part in our intellectual activity ever since we began to try to understand and manipulate our environment. People have always used the idea of models to attempt to represent and express ideas and objects. Historically, modeling has taken many forms: from communicating through wall paintings to writing complex systems of mathematical equations for the flight of a rocket through outer space. As a matter of fact, the progress and history of science and engineering are most accurately reflected in the progress of our ability to develop and use models.

One of the major elements required in attacking any problem is the construction and use of a model. We use models because we want to learn something about some real system that we cannot observe or experiment with directly — either because the system does not yet exist, or because it is too difficult to manipulate. A carefully conceived model can strip away the complexity, leaving only that which the analyst finds important. Such a model can take many forms, but one of the most useful — and certainly the most often used — is simulation.

Likewise, the concept of systems plays a critical role in our modern view of the world. The fundamental idea of thinking about the world in terms of systems and trying to take the systems approach to attacking problems has become so ingrained in contemporary practice that we tend to take it for granted. The systems approach tries to consider total system performance rather than simply concentrating on the parts [Weinburg, 1975]; it is based on our recognition that, even if each element or subsystem is optimized from a design or operational viewpoint, overall performance of the system may be suboptimal because of interactions among the parts. The increasing complexity of modern systems and the need to cope with this complexity underscore the need for engineers and managers to adopt a systems approach to thinking.

Although complex systems and their environments are objective, i.e., they exist, they are also subjective, i.e., the particular selection of included (and excluded) elements and their configuration are dictated by the problem solver. Different analyses of the same objective process or phenomenon can conceptualize it into very different systems and environments. For example, an architect may consider a factory and its electrical, heating, and water systems to be one large system. But a mechanical engineer may view the heating system as the system and the factory as its environment. To an industrial engineer, the material-handling equipment and its relationships to the machines may be the system; the relationship between the heating and electrical systems may be irrelevant. Hence, several different conceptualizations of any particular real-world system — and thereby several different models — can simultaneously exist.

System elements are the components, parts, and subsystems that perform a function or process. The relationships among these elements and the manner in which they interact determine how the overall system behaves and how well it fulfills its overall purpose. Therefore, the first step in creating any model is to specify its purpose. There is no such thing as *the* model of a system: we can model any system in numerous ways, depending on what we wish to accomplish. Both the elements and the relationships included must be chosen to achieve a specific purpose. The model developed should be as simple as the stated purpose will allow.

The types of simulations of interest in this book are those used to develop an understanding of the performance of a system over time. We typically use simulation models to help us explain, understand, or improve a system. To be effective, simulation must concentrate on some previously defined problem (otherwise we do not know what elements to include in the model or what information to generate and collect). We typically use models to predict and compare, i.e., to provide a logical way of forecasting the outcomes that follow alternative actions or decisions and (we hope) to indicate a preference among them. Although this use of models is important, it is by no means their only purpose. Model building also provides a systematic, explicit, and efficient way to focus judgment and intuition. Furthermore, by introducing a precise framework, a simulation model can effectively communicate system configuration and assist the thought process.

3. Types of Models

Simulation models can be classified in a number of different ways. These classifications (and the terms used to describe them) refer to differences in the models and not to differences in the real systems they represent.

We can usually simulate a particular system by using several different types of models. For example, a simulation model can be a precise replica of an object (although executed in a different material and to a different scale) or it can be an abstraction of the object's salient properties. Therefore, we can classify simulation models as *iconic* or *symbolic*. Iconic simulation models (usually called simulators) look, in some sense, like the real system. Iconic simulators are used primarily for training purposes; examples include flight simulators (for teaching pilots how to fly and to handle emergencies) and driving simulators (for teaching students how to drive a car). Symbolic simulation models are those in which the properties and characteristics of the real system are captured in mathematical and/or symbolic form. In this book we are concerned only with symbolic simulation models.

Symbolic models are usually run on a computer, and indeed, in most cases, simulation would be of no practical value without computers. Therefore, another way we can classify simulation models is by the type of computer used to execute the model: analog, digital, or hybrid.

The *analog computer* operates by representing the variables and relationships of a problem by physical devices and physical quantities that are easily generated and controlled, such as shaft rotations and electrical voltages. The advantages of the analog computer are its speed and parallel operations, particularly for solving systems of differential equations. The *digital computer*, on the other hand, has much greater precision and dynamic range than the analog computer because it can count, obey logic rules, perform floating point arithmetic, and use long word lengths. *Hybrid computers* represent an attempt to combine the best characteristics of both while avoiding their shortcomings. But, with the advent of supercomputers and parallel processing, much of the interest in simulation on hybrid machines has disappeared. One exception is the use of hybrid computers for simulation models containing real hardware in the loop, i.e., when part of the model consists of physical components from the real system, and the rest of the system is modeled in analog or digital form. In this book we are concerned only with simulation models executed on digital computers.

The next dimension of simulation model classification deals with whether the model explicitly recognizes the presence of random variation in the system being modeled. Very few real-world systems are free from the influence of random or unpredictable variables in the environment or in its own components. *Deterministic* simulation models ignore this randomness, assuming it to be unimportant to the decision to be made. A simulation model that explicitly tries to capture the important random components of the system is called a random or *stochastic* model. In this book we are concerned primarily with stochastic models.

Another manner of classifying simulation models relates to time. A model that describes the behavior of the system through time is called a *dynamic* model. A model that portrays the behavior of a system at a single point in time is called a *static* model. For example, a model that simply tells me the profit at the end of the year is a static one, whereas a model that shows behavior as a function of time throughout the year is dynamic; the difference is analogous to a still photograph versus a movie. Many static simulation models are run by using spreadsheet or financial software. In this book we are concerned primarily with dynamic models.

The final dimension of model classification relates to the manner in which the model represents changes of state within the system modeled. Models can be said to be discrete, continuous, or combined. If a model describes changes in the status of the system as occurring only at isolated points in time, we call it *discrete*. If a model treats change like a continuously occurring phenomenon, we call it *continuous*. Continuous models usually consist of sets of algebraic, differential, or difference equations. And, if a model represents some parts of the system as continuous and other parts as discrete, we call it a *combined* model. This book discusses all three representations.

4. Simulation Applications

Because of its great versatility, flexibility, and power, simulation is favored in every research study on the utility and use of operations research techniques [Shannon et al 1981, Ford et al 1987, or Forgionne 1983]. Almost any type of system has (or can be) simulated, and the broad range of modeling applications almost defies classification. Rather than try to give an exhaustive list, we will simply point out some representative applications.

■ COMPUTER SYSTEMS: hardware components, software systems, networks of hardware, data base structure and management, information processing, reliability of hardware and software.

- MANUFACTURING: material-handling systems, assembly lines, automated production facilities, automated storage facilities, inventory control systems, reliability and maintenance studies, plant layout, machine design.

- BUSINESS: stock and commodity analyses, pricing policy, marketing strategies, acquisition studies, cash flow analyses, forecasting, transportation alternatives, manpower planning.

- GOVERNMENT: military weapons and their use, military tactics, population forecasting, land use, health care delivery, fire protection, police services, criminal justice, roadway design, traffic control, sanitation services.

- ECOLOGY AND ENVIRONMENT: water pollution and purification, waste control, air pollution, pest control, weather prediction, earthquake and storm analysis, mineral exploration and extraction, solar energy systems, crop production.

- SOCIETY AND BEHAVIOR: food/population analysis, educational policies, organizational structure, social systems analysis, welfare systems, university administration.

- BIOSCIENCES: sports performance analysis, disease control, biological life cycles, biomedical studies.

This list does not even begin to cover all of the simulation applications; in fact, we would be hard-pressed to find any arena of human endeavor that has not seen some simulation activity. The list merely suggests simulation's great utility for helping to solve a broad range of significant problems. Simulation is a cost-effective way of pre-testing proposed systems, plans, or policies before incurring the expense of prototypes, field tests, or actual implementations. Management is increasingly viewing simulation as a very inexpensive insurance policy.

5. Simulation in Manufacturing

Because of fierce competition, industry is now being forced into implementing expensive factory automation and is, therefore, carefully reexamining its operating policies and procedures. Unfortunately, even the most careful planning of these highly automated, computer-controlled manufacturing systems sometimes fails to prevent major design blunders — like major mismatches in machine capacities, insufficient buffer space to hold waiting parts, and automatic guided vehicles that pile up in traffic jams as a result of congested paths. Traditional design and analytical methods have simply proved inadequate for studying the complex interactions of integrated manufacturing systems. Organizations are turning increasingly to simulation as a vehicle for dynamic analysis prior to implementation. The stakes are too high and the costs too great to do otherwise.

Simulation predicts the behavior of complex manufacturing systems by calculating the movement and interaction of system components. By evaluating the flow of parts through the machines and work stations and by examining the conflicting demands for limited resources, we can evaluate physical layouts, equipment selections, and operating procedures. Simulation gives us the ability to experiment on the model rather than the real-world system, thereby allowing us to examine contemplated changes or new designs before actual purchase or installation.

In simulating automated manufacturing systems, we are concerned with systems in which performance is principally affected by competition for resources (machines, workers, material-handling devices, etc.). We face several basic problems when trying to model these systems: determining the resources (and their characteristics) that most affect performance, formulating a model or description representing these resources and their relationships, and determining the values of the performance measures of interest under given scenarios.

The planning, design, installation, and operation of a manufacturing system hinge on decisions made in the following three areas.

■ Hard-system configuration decisions, i.e., setting the system's capabilities by selecting the number and types of equipment to be included, the physical layout configuration, and the parts to be processed through the system.

■ Soft-system configuration decisions, i.e., planning, scheduling, and sequencing of the parts, tools, and workers over some specified time period.

■ Real-time control, i.e., control of the flow of jobs within the system and response to contingencies, such as tool failures, equipment breakdowns, etc.

It therefore seems likely that in the future simulation will be used in three distinct manufacturing modes:

■ As a design and analysis aid for factory layouts, equipment decisions, alternative operating policies, problem evaluation, etc. These are the traditional roles currently played by simulation models.

■ As a tool for scheduling, particularly with automated systems. This use allows the decision maker to explore and plan changes to the existing schedule and/or to find the optimal schedule starting with current conditions. For example, current conditions may include the fact that a particular piece of equipment has broken down. The model would then generate an alternative schedule that would be used until the equipment was repaired.

■ As a part of a real-time, on-line control system. Such a system would periodically be activated, read the current conditions from a data base, project the schedule forward, and then, depending on the results, leave well enough alone, modify the schedule, or call for human intervention.

When simulation is used as a design tool, the study is typically motivated by questions such as these:

■ Which will be the throughput of this design? Will it meet our production goals?

■ Where are the bottlenecks? What can we change to increase throughput?

■ What is the best among several design alternatives? How does the system performance change as a function of the number and type of machines, number of workers, types of automation (particularly materials handling), in-process storage, etc.? (The typical evaluation criteria are throughput and cost, with additional concerns about delivery schedules, work in process, and resource utilization.)

■ How reliable is the system? How will breakdowns affect throughput?

6. Advantages and Disadvantages of Simulation

Because its basic concept is easily comprehended, a simulation model is often easier to justify to management or customers than some of the analytical models. In addition, simulation might have more credibility because its behavior has been compared to that of the real system, or because it has required fewer simplifying assumptions and thereby has captured more of the true characteristics of the real system.

Virtually all simulation models are so-called input-output models, i.e., they yield the output of the system for a given input. Simulation models are therefore "run" rather than "solved." They cannot generate an optimal solution on their own as analytical models can; they can only serve as tools for the analysis of system behavior under specified conditions. (The exception is a simulation model used to find the optimum values for a set of control variables under a given set of inputs.)

We have defined simulation as experimentation with a model of the real system. An experimental problem arises when a need develops for specific system information that isn't available from known sources. The following list describes some of the benefits associated with simulation.

■ New policies, operating procedures, decision rules, organizational structures, information flows, etc. can be explored without disrupting ongoing operations.

■ New hardware designs, physical layouts, software programs, transportation systems, etc. can be tested before committing resources to their acquisition and/or implementation.

■ Hypotheses about how or why certain phenomena occur can be tested for feasibility.

■ Time can be controlled: it can be compressed, expanded, etc. allowing us to speed up or slow down a phenomenon for study.

■ Insight can be gained about which variables are most important to performance and how these variables interact.

■ Bottlenecks in material, information, and product flow can be identified.

■ A simulation study can prove invaluable to understanding how the system really operates as opposed to how everyone thinks it operates.

■ New situations, about which we have limited knowledge and experience, can be manipulated in order to prepare for theoretical future events. Simulation's great strength lies in its ability to let us explore "what if" questions.

Even though simulation has many strengths and advantages, it is not without drawbacks:

■ Model building requires specialized training. The quality of the analysis depends on the quality of the model and the skill of the modeler. Model building is an art, and, as such, the skill of practitioners varies widely.

■ Simulation results are sometimes difficult to interpret. Because the model is trying to capture the randomness of the real system, it is often hard to determine whether an observation made during a run is due to a significant relationship in the system or to the randomness built into the model.

■ Simulation analysis can be time-consuming and expensive. An adequate analysis may not be feasible, given available time and/or resources; a "quick and dirty" estimate that uses analytical methods may be preferable.

7. Simulation Example

Before going any farther, perhaps we should look at a very simple example demonstrating the concept of simulation. Suppose we have a single-channel queueing (waiting line) system, such as a checkout counter in a drug store. Assume that the time between customer arrivals is uniformly distributed from 1 to 10 minutes (for simplicity's sake, we will round off all times to the nearest whole minute). Let us assume further, that the time to service a customer is also uniformly distributed between 1 and 6 minutes. We are interested in determining the average total time a customer spends being checked out (both waiting time plus service time) and the percentage of time that the clerk is idle.

To simulate this system, we need a way of generating artificial experience that is characteristic of the situation. Therefore, we need to artificially generate arrival times for each customer and service times for each customer; we also need a good bookkeeping system to keep track of what happens. One way we can generate the times between arrivals of customers is to use a spinner dial (such as those used in some board games) with the dial face divided into 10 equal and numbered parts. We can use a single die (half of a pair of dice) to generate the service times.

We will start our simulated clock at time 00:00 and then spin the dial to see how many minutes until the first customer comes up to the counter. We can then roll the die to find out how long it will take to service this customer. By continuing this process for subsequent customers and setting up a bookkeeping system to keep track of when a customer arrives, begins service, and ends service (as well as when the server is idle), we will get information resembling that in the following table for the first 20 customers.

Customer	Time Between Arrivals	Service Time	Arrival Clock Time	Service Begins	Service Ends	Time in System	Idle Time
1	–	3	00:00	00:00	00:03	3	0
2	6	1	00:06	00:06	00:07	1	3
3	6	6	00:12	00:12	00:18	6	5
4	4	4	00:16	00:18	00:22	6	0
5	7	2	00:23	00:23	00:25	2	1
6	1	4	00:24	00:25	00:29	5	0
7	1	5	00:25	00:29	00:34	9	0
8	9	4	00:34	00:34	00:38	4	0
9	8	3	00:42	00:42	00:45	3	4
10	9	1	00:51	00:51	00:52	1	6
11	6	6	00:57	00:57	01:03	6	5
12	5	4	01:02	01:03	01:07	5	0
13	4	5	01:06	01:07	01:12	6	0
14	8	1	01:14	01:14	01:15	1	2
15	8	4	01:22	01:22	01:26	4	7
16	7	2	01:29	01:29	01:31	2	3
17	4	2	01:33	01:33	01:35	2	2
18	2	6	01:35	01:35	01:41	6	0
19	7	1	01:42	01:42	01:43	1	1
20	9	4	01:51	01:51	01:55	4	8
					TOTALS	77	47

Average Time in System = 77/20 = 3.85 minutes
% Idle Server = 47/115(100) = 41%

Obviously, to obtain statistical significance we would have to obtain a much larger sample. However, the important point is that we have used two devices for generating random variables (a spinner dial and a die) to produce artificial (simulated) experience with a system in order to examine some of its time-dependent behavioral characteristics. Likewise, the system simulated had two random variables (the time between arrivals and the service times). Although we can conduct simulations such as this one by hand, it should be obvious that, once the system to be simulated becomes the least bit complicated or has a large number of component parts, we must use a computer both for generating the random variables and for doing the bookkeeping.

To adequately simulate real-world systems we must also be able to generate behavioral characteristics that are realistic. For example, the time between arrivals and the service times generated must allow for something other than uniform distribution rounded to the nearest whole number. Monte-Carlo sampling is a simulation prerequisite if the model is to represent stochastic or random elements realistically.

8. Monte-Carlo Sampling

At the heart of every stochastic simulation model lies a mechanism for generating values of those random variables influencing the behavior of the system being analyzed. For stochastic or probabilistic models this mechanism is called Monte-Carlo sampling. Monte-Carlo sampling originated with the work of von Neumann and Ulan on the atomic bomb project. The mathematical technique, known for many years, was revived for the secret work at Los Alamos and given the security code name "Monte-Carlo." The term has almost become synonymous with simulation. Although we are primarily interested in the use of the Monte-Carlo sampling technique for simulating probabilistic events, it can also be used in certain completely deterministic problems that cannot be solved analytically (Hammersly and Handscomb 1964).

In the Monte-Carlo technique, artificial data are generated through the use of a random-number generator and the cumulative distribution of interest. An acceptable random-number generator must be able to generate random variables that are uniformly distributed on the interval from 0 to 1. Although a number of methods have been used in the past to generate random numbers, today we use algorithms executed on the digital computer (Marse and Roberts 1983, Thesen 1985). Because the random numbers are generated by using an algorithm, they are in fact not truly random, and so we call them pseudo-random numbers — meaning that the sequence produced is in fact reproducible and hence not random. However, were we to compare a set of numbers derived from a reliable digital random-number generator with numbers that were truly random, the distinction between the two sets of numbers would not be detectable (i.e., the computer-generated data would pass all the statistical tests for randomness).

The probability distribution to be sampled can be a known theoretical distribution, e.g., normal or exponential, or it can be based on empirical data gathered and/or observed from the real system. Chapter 2 includes more information on choosing the correct distribution to represent various types of random processes.

9. The Simulation Process

The essence or purpose of simulation modeling is to help the ultimate decision maker solve a problem. Therefore, to learn to be a good simulation modeler, you must merge good problem-solving techniques with good software-engineering practice. The following steps should be taken in every simulation study.

1. PROBLEM DEFINITION. Clearly defining the goals of the study so that we know the purpose, i.e., why are we studying this problem and what questions do we hope to answer?

2. PROJECT PLANNING. Being sure that we have sufficient personnel, management support, computer hardware, and software resources to do the job.

3. SYSTEM DEFINITION. Determining the boundaries and restrictions to be used in defining the system (or process) and investigating how the system works.

4. CONCEPTUAL MODEL FORMULATION. Developing a preliminary model either graphically (e.g., block diagrams) or in pseudo-code to define the components, descriptive variables, and interactions (logic) that constitute the system.

5. PRELIMINARY EXPERIMENTAL DESIGN. Selecting the measures of effectiveness to be used, the factors to be varied, and the levels of those factors to be investigated, i.e., what data need to be gathered from the model, in what form, and to what extent.

6. INPUT DATA PREPARATION. Identifying and collecting the input data needed by the model.

7. MODEL TRANSLATION. Formulating the model in an appropriate simulation language.

8. VERIFICATION AND VALIDATION. Confirming that the model operates the way the analyst intended (debugging) and that the output of the model is believable and representative of the output of the real system.

9. FINAL EXPERIMENTAL DESIGN. Designing an experiment that will yield the desired information and determining how each of the test runs specified in the experimental design is to be executed.

10. EXPERIMENTATION. Executing the simulation to generate the desired data and to perform a sensitivity analysis.

11. ANALYSIS AND INTERPRETATION. Drawing inferences from the data generated by the simulation.

12. IMPLEMENTATION AND DOCUMENTATION. Putting the results to use, recording the findings, and documenting the model and its use.

It is important for inexperienced modelers to understand that, the longer you wait to start step 7, the faster you will complete the model and the project — assuming, of course, that you spend that time understanding the problem, designing the model, and designing the experiments to be run. Computer scientists have devoted a great deal of effort to "Software Engineering"; and have developed design and management methods aimed at yielding rapid software development while minimizing errors. One of the major ideas that has emerged from this effort is the validity of the "40-20-40 Rule." This rule states that 40 percent of the effort and time in a project should be devoted to steps 1 through 6, 20 percent to step 7, and the remaining 40 percent to steps 8 through 12 (Sheppard 1983, McKay et al 1986).

10. Problem Definition and Project Planning

It should be obvious that before you can solve a problem you must know what the problem is (sometimes easier said than done). Experience indicates that beginning a simulation project properly may well make the difference between success and failure. Simulation studies are initiated because a decision maker or group of decision makers faces a problem and need a solution. Often the project is initiated by someone (a sponsor) who can't necessarily make the final decision, but who is responsible for making recommendations. In such a case, the results of the study may have to serve two purposes simultaneously: helping the sponsor to formulate the recommendations; and justifying, supporting, and helping to sell those recommendations.

We begin our analysis by collecting enough information and data to provide an adequate understanding of both the problem and the system to be studied. A typical project begins with the sponsor's describing the situation to the analyst in a general and imprecise way. The sponsor usually describes the problem in terms characteristic of the sponsor's background and experience, such as profit and loss figures, inventory levels, delays, bottlenecks, or other operational data of concern. We must view the sponsor's problem description as a set of symptoms requiring diagnosis. We begin, therefore, by diagnosing the symptoms; then we define the problem; and, finally, we formulate a model.

To make that diagnosis, we must become thoroughly familiar with all relevant aspects of the sponsoring organization's operations, including influential forces (or factors) outside the organization and the subjective and objective aspects of the problem. Minimally, we should perform the following steps.

1. Identify the primary decision maker(s) and the decision-making process relative to the system being studied.

2. Determine the relevant objectives of each of those responsible for some aspect of the decision.

3. Identify other participants in the final decision (especially those likely to oppose changes in the system) and determine their objectives and vested interests.

4. Determine which aspects of the situation are subject to the control of the decision maker(s) and the range of control that can be exercised.

5. Identify those aspects of the environment or problem context that can affect the outcome of possible solutions but that are beyond the control of the decision maker(s).

An important aspect of the planning phase involves ensuring that we have considered certain factors critical to project success:

■ Clearly defined goals. Do we know the purpose of the study, i.e., why are we doing it and what do we expect to find?

■ Sufficient resource allocation. Are we sure that there are sufficient time, personnel, and computer hardware and software available to do the job?

■ Management support. Has management made its support for the project known to all concerned parties?

■ Project plans and schedules. Are there detailed plans for carrying out the project?

■ Competent project manager and team members. Are we assured of having the necessary skills and knowledge available for successful completion of the project?

- Responsiveness to the clients. Have all potential users of the results been consulted and regularly apprised of project progress?

- Adequate communication channels. Are we continually concerned that sufficient information is available on project objectives, status, changes, user or client needs, etc. to keep everyone (team members, management, and clients) fully informed as the project progresses?

The major thrust of the planning and orientation period is the determination of the explicit goals or purpose of the simulation project. Simulation experiments are conducted for a wide variety of purposes, including the following:

- EVALUATION: determining how well a proposed system design performs in an absolute sense when evaluated against specific criteria.

- COMPARISON: comparing competitive systems designed to carry out a specified function, or comparing several proposed operating policies or procedures.

- PREDICTION: estimating the performance of the system under some projected set of conditions.

- SENSITIVITY ANALYSIS: determining which of many factors affect overall system performance the most.

- OPTIMIZATION: determining exactly which combination of factor levels produces the best overall system response.

- FUNCTIONAL RELATIONS: establishing the nature of the relationships among one or more significant factors and the system's response.

- BOTTLENECK ANALYSIS: discovering the location of bottlenecks restricting entity flow through the system and the options for increasing throughput.

Although not exhaustive, this list identifies the most common simulation goals or purposes. The explicit purpose of the model has significant implications for the entire model-building and experimentation process. For example, if a model's goal is to evaluate a proposed (or existing) system in an absolute sense, then the model must be accurate and there must be a high degree of correspondence between the model and the real system. On the other hand, if a model's goal is the relative comparison of two or more systems or operating procedures, the model can be valid in a relative sense even though the absolute magnitude of responses varies widely from that which would be encountered in the real system. The entire process of designing the model, validating it, designing experiments, and drawing conclusions from the resulting experimentation must be closely tied to the specific purpose of the model. No one should build a model without having an explicit experimental goal in mind. Unfortunately, the analyst does not always understand the real-world problem well enough at first to ask the right questions. Therefore, the model should have an easily modified structure so that additional questions arising from early experimentation can be answered later.

11. System Definition and Model Formulation

The essence of the modeling art is abstraction and simplification. We try to identify that small subset of characteristics or features of the system that is sufficient to serve the specific objectives of the study. So, after we have specified the goal or purpose for which the model is to be constructed, we then begin to identify the pertinent components. This process entails itemizing all system components that contribute to the effectiveness or ineffectiveness of its operation. After we have specified a complete list, we determine whether each component should be included in our model; this determination may be difficult because, at this stage of model development, a component's significance to the overall goal is not always clear. One of the key questions to be answered is whether a particular component should be considered part of the model or part of the outside environment, which is represented as inputs to the model.

In general, we have little difficulty deciding on the output variables. If we have done a good job specifying the goals or purposes of the study, the required output variables become apparent. The real difficulty arises when we try to determine which input and status variables produce the effects observed and which can be manipulated to produce the effects desired.

We also face conflicting objectives. On the one hand, we try to make the model as simple as possible for ease of understanding, ease of formulation, and computational efficiency. On the other hand, we try to make the model as accurate as possible. Consequently, we must simplify reality — but only to the point where there is no significant loss of accuracy of outputs with respect to the study's objectives.

We want to design a model of the real system that neither oversimplifies the system to the point where the model becomes trivial (or worse, misleading) nor carries so much detail that it becomes clumsy and prohibitively expensive. The most significant danger lies in the model's becoming too detailed and including elements that contribute little or nothing to understanding the problem. Frequently, the analyst includes too much detail, rather than too little. The inexperienced tend to try to transfer all the detailed difficulties in the real situation into the model, hoping that the computer will somehow solve the problem.

This approach is unsatisfactory: it increases programming complexity (and the associated costs for longer experimental runs), and it dilutes the truly significant aspects and relationships with trivial details. The definition of the model boundary is usually a tradeoff between accuracy and cost. The greater the degree of detail to be modeled, the more precise and expensive the required input data. Therefore, the model must include only those aspects of the system relevant to the study objectives.

One should always design the model to answer the relevant questions and not to precisely imitate the real system. According to Pareto's law, in every group or collection of entities there exist a vital few and a trivial many. In fact, 80 percent of system behavior can be explained by the action of 20 percent of its components. Nothing really significant happens unless it happens to the significant few. Our problem in designing the simulation model is to ensure that we correctly identify those few vital components and include them in our model.

Once we have tentatively decided which components and variables to include in our model, we must then determine the functional relationships among them. At this point we are trying to show the logic of the model, i.e., what happens. Usually we use graphics or pseudo-code to describe the system as a logical flow diagram. Starting in Chapter 3, we will see how this is done using SIMAN's graphical Blocks. The pseudo-code for the example given in Section 7 can appear as follows:

CREATE arrivals
QUEUE to await service
SEIZE the server when available
DELAY by the service time
RELEASE the server
TALLY the time in system and depart.

12. Experimental Design

We have defined simulation as being experimentation via a model to gain information about a real-world process or system. It then follows that we must concern ourselves with the strategic planning of how to design an experiment (or experiments) that will yield the desired information for the lowest cost. The next step, therefore, is to design an experiment that will yield the information needed to fulfill the study's goal or purpose.

The design of experiments comes into play at two different stages of a simulation study. It first comes into play very early in the study, before the model design has been finalized. As early as possible, we want to select which measures of effectiveness we will use in the study, which factors we will vary, and how many levels of each of those factors we will investigate. By having this fairly detailed idea of the experimental plan at this early stage, we have a better basis for planning the model to generate the desired data efficiently.

Later, after we have developed the model, verified its correctness, and validated its adequacy, we again need to consider the final strategic and tactical plans for the execution of the experiment(s). We must update project constraints on time (schedule) and costs to reflect current conditions, and we must impose these constraints on the design. Even though we have exercised careful planning and budget control from the beginning of the study, we must now take a hard, realistic look at what resources remain and how best to use them. At this point we adjust the experimental design to account for remaining resources and for information gained in the process of designing, building, verifying, and validating the model.

The design of a computer simulation experiment is essentially a plan for purchasing a quantity of information that costs more or less depending on how it was acquired. Design profoundly affects the effective use of experimental resources for two reasons:

■ The design of the experiment largely determines the form of statistical analysis that can be applied to the results.

■ The success of the experiment in answering the questions of the experimenter (without excessive expenditure of time and resources) is largely a function of choosing the right design.

Simulation experiments are expensive both in terms of experimenter time and labor and, in some cases, in terms of computer time. We conduct simulation studies primarily to learn the most about the behavior of the system for the lowest possible cost. We must carefully plan and design not only the model but also its use. Thus, experimental designs are economical because they reduce the number of experimental trials required and provide a structure for the investigator's learning process.

13. Input Data

Stochastic systems contain one or more sources of randomness. The analyst must be concerned about data related to the inputs for the model, such as the arrival rate of entities to the system, the processing times required at various machines, reliability data (e.g., the pattern of breakdowns of machines), the time needed to repair machines, or the rejection rate of parts coming from a certain process. Although data gathering is usually interpreted to mean gathering numbers, this interpretation addresses only one aspect of the problem. The analyst must also decide what data are needed, what data are available, whether the data are pertinent, whether existing data are valid for the required purpose, and how to gather the data.

The design of a stochastic simulation model always involves choosing whether to represent a particular aspect of the system as probabilistic or deterministic. If we opt for probabilistic and if empirical data exist, then we must make yet another decision. Will we sample directly from the empirical data or will we try to fit the data to a theoretical distribution and, if successful, sample from the theoretical distribution? This choice is fundamentally important for several reasons.

First, using raw empirical data implies that we are only simulating the past; by using data from one year, we replicate the performance of that year but not necessarily of future years. When sampling directly from historical data, the only events possible are those that transpired during the period when the data were gathered. It is one thing to assume that the basic form of the distribution will remain unchanged with time; it is quite another to assume that the idiosyncrasies of a particular year will always be repeated.

Second, it is much easier to change certain aspects of the input if theoretical random variate generation is being used, i.e., there is greater flexibility. For example, if we want to determine what happens if inputs increase by 10 percent per week, we need only increase the mean arrival rate of the theoretical distribution by the required 10 percent. On the other hand, if we are sampling directly from the empirical data, it is not clear how we increase the arrival rate by the required amount.

Third, it is highly desirable to test the sensitivity of the system to changes in the parameters. For example, we may want to know how much the arrival rate can increase before system performance deteriorates to an unacceptable degree. Again, sensitivity analysis is easier with theoretical distributions than with sampling directly from empirical data.

The problem is exacerbated when no historical behavioral data exist (either because the system has not yet been built or because the data cannot be gathered). In these cases we must estimate both the distribution and the parameters based on theoretical considerations. The problems of gathering and interpreting data for model inputs are discussed in some detail in Chapter 2.

14. Model Translation

Eventually we face the problem of describing or programming the model in a language acceptable to the computer that will be used. Well over 100 different simulation languages are commercially available, and hundreds of other locally developed languages are being used by companies and universities. We must decide which to use.

It should be noted that any general algorithmic language (FORTRAN, BASIC, PASCAL, C, etc.) is capable of expressing the desired model; however, the specialized simulation languages have very distinct advantages in terms of ease, efficiency, and effectiveness of use. Here are some of these advantages:

- reduced programming task,
- conceptual guidance,
- increased flexibility when changing the model,
- fewer programming errors, and
- automated gathering of statistics.

All programming languages try to close the gap between what users conceptualize as a representation of a model and how they actually express that relationship in some executable form. As pointed out by Nance (1984), simulation software development can be divided into five periods. Until about 1960, all simulations were written in general-purpose languages such as FORTRAN, and many simulations are still written that way. During the second period, 1960-65, there was an unprecedented outburst of creativity as the first special-purpose simulation languages appeared. The third period, 1966-70, saw the introduction of revised and improved versions of the languages introduced during the second period. And the fourth period, 1971-80, saw the introduction of languages allowing combined discrete and continuous modeling. (An excellent history of the development of several currently popular languages can be found in Wexelblat [1981].)

Toward the end of the fourth period, attention began to shift to easier model development and execution. Several authors, such as Heidorn (1974, 1976) and Mathewson (1974), began to discuss potential methods for easier programming.

Zeigler (1976), Kleine (1977), Nance (1977) and others began to take a more formal approach to the modeling process. In a very significant paper, Oren and Zeigler (1979) pointed out several shortcomings in current languages and proposed developing new languages based on two concepts. First, simulation languages should functionally separate the logically distinct stages of modeling, experiment specification, and output analysis into separate activities. Second, simulation environments should be created to take advantage of current computer capabilities for data base management, graphics, and program verification.

Thus, new simulation languages were developed and old ones enhanced. The language developers focused their attention on three objectives: reduced model development time, improved accuracy, and improved communication. There is currently an explosion of creative activity taking place in simulation modeling and language development. This has been fostered by developments in desktop computing, graphics, artificial intelligence, and expert systems.

Simulation software development is now in a transitional period. Emphasis has shifted to providing ease of use and an integrated simulation environment rather than simply providing more powerful languages. This book describes SIMAN, one of today's most advanced and widely used simulation languages.

15. Verification and Validation

After the development of the model is functionally complete, we should ask ourselves a question: Does it work? There are two aspects to this question. First, does it do what the analyst expects it to do? Second, does it do what the user expects it to do? We find the answers to these questions through model verification and validation. Verification seeks to show that the computer program performs as expected and intended, thus providing a correct logical representation of the model. Validation, on the other hand, establishes that model behavior validly represents that of the real-world system being simulated. Both processes involve system testing that demonstrates different aspects of model accuracy.

Verification can be viewed as rigorous debugging with one eye on the model and the other eye on the model requirements. In addition to simply debugging any model development errors, it also examines whether the code reflects the description found in the conceptual model. One of the goals of verification is to show that all parts of the model work, both independently and together, and use the right data at the right time.

The greatest aid to program verification is correct program design, followed by clarity, style, and ease of understanding. Very often, simulation models are poorly documented, especially at the model statement level. Verification becomes much easier if the analyst comments the model liberally. With SIMAN's in-line and end-of-line commenting capabilities, almost every line of the model should have a comment explaining what the analyst intended that model statement to do.

Validation is the process of raising to an acceptable level the user's confidence that any simulation-derived inference about the system is correct. Validation is concerned with three basic questions:

- Does the model adequately represent the real-world system?
- Are the model-generated behavioral data characteristic of the real system's behavioral data?
- Does the simulation model user have confidence in the model's results?

Consequently, we are concerned with tests that fall into three groups: tests of model structure, tests of model behavior, and tests of the policy implications of the model.

Because a model is constructed for a specific purpose, its adequacy or validity can only be evaluated in terms of that purpose. We try to build a model that creates the same problems and behavioral characteristics as the process or system being studied. Validation occurs throughout model development, beginning with the start of the study and continuing as the model builder accumulates confidence that the model behaves plausibly and generates symptoms or modes of behavior seen in the real system. Validation then expands to include persons not directly involved in constructing the model.

Validation is a communication process requiring the model builder to communicate the basis for confidence in a model to a target audience. Unless that confidence can be transferred, the model's usefulness will never be realized. Thus, through verification testing, we develop personal confidence in the model and, through validation measures, transfer that confidence to others.

We must realize that there are degrees of validation; it is not merely an either-or notion. Validation is not a binary decision variable indicating whether the model is valid or invalid. No one or two tests can validate a simulation model. Rather, confidence in the usefulness of a model must gradually accumulate as the model passes more tests and as new points of correspondence between model and reality are found. Validation testing occurs continually in the process of designing, constructing, and using the model.

We should also remember that verification and validation are never really finished. If the model is to be used for any period of time, then the data and the model itself will need periodic review to ensure validity. Verification and validation are intertwined and proceed throughout the study. They are not tacked on toward the end of the study; rather, they are an integral process that starts at the beginning of the study and continues through model building and model use. It should also be pointed out that involving the ultimate user in the entire simulation process makes validation much easier.

16. Experimentation and Analysis

Next we come to the actual running of the experiments and the analysis of the results. Some difficult statistical issues must be addressed so that we can correctly use the computer program to generate model behavioral data through planned experimentation, and so that we can analyze the results. At this stage numerous pitfalls still await the unwary. We now have to deal with issues such as how long to run the model (i.e., sample sizes), what to do about starting conditions, whether the output data are correlated, and what statistical tests are valid on the data.

Because the output of a simulation model is a sample of system behavioral data, all concerns regarding statistical inference from samples apply. We are most concerned that the data be representative of typical system behavior, that the sample size be large enough to provide some stated level of confidence in the performance measure estimates, and that none of the assumptions underlying the statistical calculations be violated.

Before addressing these concerns, we must first ascertain whether the real system is terminating or non-terminating, because this characteristic determines the running and analysis methods used. In a terminating system the simulation ends when a critical event occurs (e.g., in a bank, the simulation ends when the bank closes at the end of the day). In other words, a system is considered to be terminating if the events driving the system naturally cease at some point in time. In a non-terminating system no such critical event occurs, and the system continues indefinitely (e.g., a telephone exchange).

Terminating systems can be physically terminating (e.g., the piece of equipment fails) or arbitrarily terminating in accordance with the goal of the study (e.g., determining the maximum profit for the next year). In the latter example, the critical terminating event is arbitrarily set as the end of the planning period of interest.

Non-terminating systems can be stationary or non-stationary. A system is stationary if the distribution of its response variable (and therefore its mean and variance) does not change over time. With such systems we are generally concerned with finding the steady-state conditions, i.e., the value which is the limit of the response variable if the length of the simulation were to go to infinity without termination.

Whether the system is terminating or non-terminating, we must decide how long to run the simulation model, i.e., we must determine sample size. But first we must precisely define what constitutes a single sample. For example, if we are considering a bank that opens each morning with no customers present and closes each day empty and idle (i.e., a terminating, non-steady-state system), a single sample can be the waiting time of individual customers, or the average waiting time for all customers serviced on a particular day.

If the system is a non-terminating, steady-state system, we must define the starting conditions of the simulation, i.e., the status of the system at the start of the simulation run. If we have an idle and empty system, i.e., no customers present, we may not have typical steady-state conditions. Therefore, we must either wait until the system reaches steady state before we begin collecting data, or we must start with more realistic conditions. This approach requires, of course, that we be able to recognize when steady state has been achieved.

Finally, most statistical tests require that the data points in the sample be independent, i.e., not correlated. As we shall see later, the data from many of our models do not meet this condition, and we must take corrective action before we can draw valid conclusions.

17. Documentation and Implementation

At this point we have completed all the steps for the design, development, and running of the model and for analyzing the results; the final elements in the simulation effort are implementation and documentation. No simulation project can be considered successfully completed until its results have been understood, accepted, and used. Although documentation and implementation are obviously very important, many studies fall short in the reporting and explanation of study results.

Documentation and reporting are closely linked to implementation. Careful and complete documentation of model development and operation can lengthen the model's useful life and greatly increase the chances that recommendations based on the model will be accepted. Good documentation facilitates modification and ensures that the model can be used — even if the services of the original developers are no longer available. In addition, careful documentation can help us to learn from previous mistakes; it may even provide a source of submodels that can be used again in future projects.

Amazingly, modelers often spend a great deal of time trying to find the most elegant and efficient ways to model a system, and then they throw together a report for the sponsor or user at the last minute. If the results are not clearly, concisely, and convincingly presented, they will not be used. If the results are not used, the project is a failure. Presenting results is as critical a part of the study as any other part, and it merits the same careful planning and design.

Several issues should be addressed in model and study documentation: appropriate vocabulary, i.e., suitable for the intended audience and devoid of jargon; concise written reports; and timely delivery. We must also ensure that all reports (both oral and written) are pertinent and address the issues that the sponsor or user considers important.

18. World Views

The term "world view" appears in many publications on simulation languages. The term is used to describe the way the language designer conceptualized the systems to be modeled with that language. Each simulation language has an implicit world view, which is invoked when we use it. The world view implicit in a typical discrete-change language might be expressed in the following way.

■ The world consists of a set of entities or transactions that flow through the system. These entities are described, characterized, and identified by their attributes.

■ These entities interact with resources, facilities, and activities in a manner consistent with certain conditions that determine the sequence of interactions.

■ These interactions are regarded as or create system events that result in changes to the state of the system.

Within this generalized world view there are distinct differences in the approach or method used for implementing the mechanics of this view. Three approaches are currently used: event scheduling, activity scanning, and process interaction. In each of these approaches, when the next event is selected for processing, the corresponding model logic is executed to model appropriate changes in the model state. These events can be conditional or unconditional. An unconditional event is eligible to be executed when its scheduled clock time occurs, i.e., execution depends entirely on time. Execution of a conditional event may depend on additional conditions that typically involve the status of system components, e.g., a resource is busy.

The *event-scheduling* strategy involves a succession of unconditional events over time. The system to be modeled is described in terms of status-disturbing events or changes that occur in the system at discrete points in time. The user constructs a simulation model by defining each event that can occur in the system (e.g., arrival of a job to be processed, breakdown of a machine), specifying the causes and effects of each event, creating mechanisms to execute event change, logically linking events to one another, providing for the update of time and statistics at each status-disturbing event, and collecting statistics of interest. The event-scheduling time control procedure then selects from the event list the event notice having the earliest occurrence time (with ties being resolved by assigned or default priority), updates the simulation clock to that time, and invokes the corresponding event routine. Each event routine in a model specification describes related actions that can all occur in one instant. Any condition testing (other than clock time) must occur within event routines. Events are chosen and processed successively until termination time.

The *activity-scanning* strategy chooses the next event based on both scheduled time and condition testing. In some models events that are known to occur cannot be scheduled strictly on the basis of time; however, it is usually possible to define the event mechanism in terms of those physical influences that trigger the event at an unknown time. Each activity routine in a model specification describes all actions that must occur because the model assumes a particular state, i.e., because a particular condition becomes true. For example, in a manufacturing system, when a job is present in the input buffer and the machine is idle, the start of processing for the job can begin. The procedure by which events of this nature are monitored is called activity scanning. The basic concept is activity, i.e., a system state transition requiring a period of time.

According to the world view of a language or model based on activity scanning, a system consists of components that engage in activities subject to specified conditions. The state of the system is represented by dependent variables that change over time. Each component can have an associated activity routine which, when executed, models active phases of the component. Each component also has an associated component clock, which indicates the time at which the component can next be considered for activation, and a condition routine, which determines whether activation conditions (other than time passage) have been met. The time control procedure scans activities in priority order for time eligibility and other activation conditions, executing the activity routine of the first component whose activation conditions are met. When an activation occurs, the scan starts over again in priority order, and the process continues until termination time.

The *process-interaction* strategy views the world as a set of competing and cooperating entities modeled in terms of interacting, concurrent processes. Each process routine in a model specification describes the action sequence of a particular model object. Processes are viewed as being composed of sequences of events occurring in a definite pattern. The process-interaction strategy resembles both the event-scheduling and activity-scanning strategies. The process-interaction perspective uses statements to define the flow of entities (customers, jobs, transactions, etc.) through the model. Entities progress through a sequence of steps (referred to as a process), each of which can consist of a condition segment and an action segment. Execution of the condition segment determines whether execution of the action segment may occur.

19. SIMAN

Later chapters will demonstrate the concepts of modeling, statistical analysis, experimental design, and implementation with SIMAN. SIMAN is a powerful, general-purpose simulation language for modeling discrete, continuous, and/or combined systems. Discrete-change systems can be modeled by using either a process-interaction or event-scheduling orientation. Continuous-change systems are modeled with algebraic, difference, or differential equations. A combination of these orientations can be used to model combined discrete-continuous models.

SIMAN is designed around a logical modeling framework in which the simulation problem is segmented into a "model" component and an "experiment" component. This framework is based on the theoretical concepts about systems developed by Zeigler (1976). The model describes the physical elements of the system (machines, workers, storage points, transporters, information, parts flow, etc.) and their logical interrelationships. The experiment specifies the experimental conditions under which the model is to run, including elements such as initial conditions, resource availability, type of statistics gathered, and length of run. The experiment frame also includes the analyst's specifications for such things as the schedules for resource availability, the routing of entities, etc. Because experimental conditions are specified external to the model description, they are easily changed without modifying the basic model definition.

Once a model and experiment have been defined, they are linked and executed by SIMAN to generate the simulated response of the system. As the simulation is executed, SIMAN automatically saves the responses specified in the experiment. The SIMAN Output Processor can then be used to generate plots, tables, bar charts, histograms, correlograms, and confidence intervals from the saved data. The data can also be displayed by using commercially available mainframe, minicomputer, or microcomputer presentation-quality graphics packages. The following list describes some of the features of SIMAN.

■ A set of special-purpose constructs to simplify and enhance the modeling of manufacturing systems.

■ Compatibility of mainframe, minicomputer, and microcomputer versions to permit movement between computer systems without modification.

■ Interactive graphics capability for building models, defining experiments, and displaying model outputs.

■ An interactive debugger for interactive monitoring and control of simulation execution.

■ The Cinema system, which generates a real-time, high-resolution, color graphics animation of the modeled system.

■ A modular structure that encourages integration with other analysis technologies (Suri and Tomsicek 1988) and intelligent interfaces (Brazier and Shannon 1987, Murray and Sheppard 1987, Ford and Schroer 1987).

Later in this book we describe the general-purpose and special-purpose manufacturing features of SIMAN. First, however, we discuss some basics: how to get started and how to conduct a simulation study.

References

BRAZIER, M. K. and R. E. SHANNON (1987), "Automatic Programming of AGVS Simulation Models," Proceedings of 1987 Winter Simulation Conference, Atlanta, GA, pp: 703-709.

FORD, D. R. and B. J. SCHROER (1987), "An Expert Manufacturing Simulation System," *Simulation*, Vol. 48, No. 5, pp: 193-200.

FORD, F., D. A. BRADBARD, W. N. LEDBETTER, and J. F. COX (1987), "Use of Operations Research in Production Management," *Production and Inventory Management*, Vol. 28, No. 3, pp: 59-62.

FORGIONNE, G. A. (1983), "Corporate Management Science Activities: an Update," *Interfaces*, Vol. 13, No. 3, pp: 20-23.

HAMMERSLY, J. M. and D. C. HANDSCOMB (1964), Monte-Carlo Methods, Methuen & Co., Ltd., London.

HEIDORN, G. E. (1974), "English as a Very High Level Language for Simulation Programming," *SIGPLAN Notices*, Vol. 9, No. 4, pp: 91-100.

HEIDORN, G. E. (1976), "Automatic Programming Through Natural Language Dialog: A Survey," IBM J. Research and Development, Vol. 20, pp: 302-13.

KLEINE, H. (1977), "A Vehicle for Developing Standards for Simulation Programming," Proceeding of the 1977 Winter Simulation Conference, Gaithersburg, MD, pp: 730-741.

MATHEWSON, S. C. (1974), "Simulation Program Generators," *Simulation*, Vol. 23, No. 6, pp: 181-189.

MARSE, K. and S. D. ROBERTS (1983), "Implementing a Portable FORTRAN Uniform (0,1) Generator," *Simulation*, Vol. 41, No. 4, pp: 135-139.

MCKAY, K. N., J. A. BUZACOTT, and C. J. STRANG (1986), "Software Engineering Applied to Discrete Event Simulation," Proceedings of the 1986 Winter Simulation Conference, Washington, D.C., pp: 485-493.

MURRAY, K. J. and S. V. SHEPPARD (1987), "Automatic Model Synthesis: Using Automatic Programming and Expert Systems Techniques," Proceedings of 1987 Winter Simulation Conference, Atlanta, GA, pp: 534-544.

NANCE, R. E. (1977), "The Feasibility of and Methodology for Developing Federal Documentation Standards for Simulation Models," Final Report to National Bureau of Standards, Department of Computer Science, Virginia Tech.

NANCE, R. E. (1984), "Model Development Revisited," Proceedings of 1984 Winter Simulation Conference, Dallas, TX, pp: 75-80.

OREN, T. I. and B. P. ZEIGLER (1979), "Concepts for Advanced Simulation Methodologies," *Simulation*, Vol. 32, No. 3, pp: 69-82.

SCHRIBER, T. J. (1987), "The Nature and Role of Simulation in the Design of Manufacturing Systems," *Simulation in CIM and Artificial Intelligence Techniques*, (Editors — J. Retti and K. E. Wichmann), Society for Computer Simulation, pp: 5-18.

SCHULTZ, R. L., D. P. SLEVIN, and J. K. PINTO (1987), "Strategy and Tactics in a Process Model of Project Implementation," *Interfaces*, Vol. 17, No. 3, pp: 34-46.

SHANNON, R. E., S. S. LONG, and B. P. BUCKLES (1981), "Operation Research Methodologies in Industrial Engineering: A Survey," *AIIE Transactions*, Vol. 12, No. 4, pp: 364-367.

SHEPPARD, S. (1983), "Applying Software Engineering to Simulation," *Simulation*, Vol. 10, No. 1, pp: 13-19.

SURI, R. and M. TOMSICEK (1988), "Rapid Modeling Tools for Manufacturing Simulation and Analysis," Proceedings of the 1988 Winter Simulation Conference, San Diego, CA, pp: 25-32.

THESEN, A. (1985), "An Efficient Generator of Uniformly Distributed Random Variates Between Zero and One," *Simulation*, Vol. 44, No. 1, pp: 17-22.

WEINBURG, G. M. (1975), An Introduction to General Systems Thinking, John Wiley & Sons, Inc., NY.

WEXELBLAT, R. (1981), History of Programming Languages, Academic Press:

ZEIGLER, B. P. (1976), Theory of Modeling and Simulation, John Wiley & Sons, Inc.

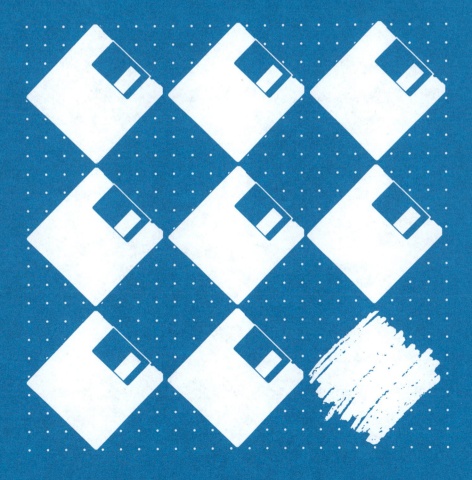

CHAPTER 2

CHAPTER 2

Beginning the Study

1. Definition of the Study Objective

Albert Einstein once stated that the proper formulation of a problem was even more essential than its solution. To find an acceptable or optimal solution to a problem, one must first know what the problem is. And yet, each year, we spend millions of dollars to come up with elegant and sophisticated answers to the wrong questions. Every simulation study should begin by developing a clear statement of the purpose, goals, and objectives of the project. Unfortunately, most studies start with a relatively vague statement describing a general problem or, even worse, a symptom of the problem. As the analyst, you are responsible for converting this vague description into an appropriate problem definition.

There can be many different models of the same system, each of which is valid for its particular goal or purpose. The goal or purpose of the study is the factor that will (or should) drive the design of the model and the experiment(s) to be run with it. A simulation study should never aim merely at building a model just for the sake of the model itself. We develop a model to help us answer certain questions about the system. As with any design, we will have to make design tradeoffs, but the study goal or objective must determine how we make those tradeoffs.

Although a model can be built for many reasons — to describe a current system, explore a hypothetical system, or design an improved system — most simulation models aim at answering questions like these:

■ Will the system work the way we intend it to (evaluation and prediction)?

■ Why doesn't the system work and what can we do to make it work (bottleneck determination and optimization)?

■ Which is our best alternative (comparison and sensitivity analysis)?

Thus, simulation studies are used for designing new systems and/or modifying and improving the operation of existing systems. But the objective must be defined in more detail than a simple question. We must be able to define the kind of decision that must be made in order to answer the question. For manufacturing systems, decision definition translates into goals, purposes, or objectives involving hardware design or operational issues. The following lists identify typical studies in both categories.

- Hardware Design Issues
    Numbers and types of machines
    Number, type, and physical arrangement of material-handling equipment
    Location and size of inventory buffers and storage
    Effect of a new piece of equipment on an existing line

- Operational Issues
    Manpower requirements
    Changes in product mix (the effects of new products)
    Production scheduling policies
    Reliability analysis (the effect of planned versus unplanned maintenance)

After we determine the issue, the next logical step is to determine what kind of data we must have to answer the question(s). For example, if our goal is to compare two or more designs, what basis will we use to decide that design "A" is better than design "B"? What data will we need? How accurate must those data be? Are there multiple measures of performance that are of interest? If so, can we define an objective function to obtain a composite value? The following list identifies measures of performance typically used in manufacturing studies.

- Throughput: the number of jobs of each type produced per time period
- Cycle time: the amount of time it takes to get an order through the system
- Queue time: the amount of time that jobs are delayed
- WIP: the sizes of work-in-process inventories
- Down time: the percentage of time that a machine is down or blocked
- Utilization: the percentage of time that people and machines are busy

One of the major problems you will face as a simulation analyst is the fact that management almost always has multiple, highly inter-related, and often conflicting objectives. For example, in a study to evaluate two different scheduling policies, we might want to consider the following goals:

- minimizing cycle times (order start to order completion),
- maximizing asset utilization (equipment, personnel, tooling, etc.),
- minimizing late shipments, and
- minimizing work-in-process levels.

There is a tendency in management to say that all of these goals are important. However, on closer examination, we can see that any two are potentially conflicting and that all cannot concurrently be achieved in factories. In most cases we must at least assign tentative weights denoting their relative importance.

2. Information Collection

To correctly identify the objective and define the system boundaries, we obviously must gather information about the system. With most systems, we have four potential sources of information and knowledge:

- Documentation
- Interviews

- Observation and Measurement
- Participation.

Unfortunately, all of these potential sources can provide erroneous information. For example, one obvious source of data is design documentation, which describes the system, i.e., drawings, specifications, wiring diagrams, reports, etc. Such documentation is usually available for existing and planned systems, but, because records are seldom kept up-to-date, the existing information is probably incomplete and inaccurate. On the other hand, although documentation may not precisely reflect the current configuration, it is usually reasonably accurate and therefore represents a good starting point.

Interviews also provide excellent sources of information about the system to be modeled. For existing systems interviewees would consist of the system operators and managers; for planned systems they would consist of the system designers. These sources are also prone to error stemming from oversight, forgetfulness, or even deliberate deception. When analyzing existing systems, you must remember that those who operate the system may perceive the study as a direct threat. The very fact that you are doing the study means that someone is displeased with the way the system currently operates and is considering a change. That displeasure and the concept of change constitute threats, and you may find operators and managers of existing systems to be less than forthright and helpful.

Designers may be the only sources of information for planned systems that do not yet exist. Unfortunately, we are probably asking them to provide information that they do not yet have and that is perhaps changing daily. We may, for example, be told something by one member of the design team only to find out later that the information was dated or that it only represented one of many alternatives.

For existing systems, we have at least two more sources of information in addition to documentation and interviews: 1) observation and measurement and 2) direct participation. Both of these forms of personal involvement can lead to understanding and insights that no degree of documentation or interviewing can provide — no matter how accurate.

The act of observing, or, better still, participating in, the operation of the system helps confirm your understanding of the manner in which the system operates. You may also discover quirks and significant but rare events that would otherwise have been overlooked. If at all possible, after you have read the documentation and discussed the operation of the system with the designers or operators, you should observe the system in operation. In the early years of Operations Research, it was considered standard operating procedure to observe or participate in the operation of the system being studied. Such observations should still be considered critical today.

We must remember that each of our potential sources of information on and knowledge about the system under study can leave us with an incomplete — or even erroneous — understanding of how the system operates. It behooves us, therefore, to follow the rule most newspaper reporters try to use: Don't accept any information as fact unless you can confirm it from at least two other independent sources.

The problems of gathering information about the system under study are further discussed in Section 6 of this chapter.

3. Boundary Definition

Having ascertained why we are conducting the study and what our objectives are, we next turn to the problem of deciding what to include in the model and, equally important, what not to include. We previously defined a system as a set of interacting objects. The objects that make up the system can be defined at many levels of detail. We usually describe the objects that make up a system as a set of interacting subsystems. Any subsystem might itself be considered a system consisting of subsystems at a still higher level of detail. One of our first activities, then, is to decide on the level of subsystem detail that will apply in our study.

The inexperienced commonly make the mistake of trying to build a highly detailed model right from the start. When considering simulation modeling, many people automatically assume that, to be useful, a model must be full-scale and detailed, i.e., there must be a one-to-one correspondence between the elements of the model and those of the real system. Take the example of a manufacturing facility that consists of 400 machines and that processes 3,000 different parts during the year. The novice might believe that the model must also have 400 machines and run long enough to process the 3,000 parts. Not only is this supposition untrue, but it also probably represents the single most common source of simulation study failure. We would do better to start with relatively simple models and gradually elaborate until we have the simplest model that will answer our questions.

We can consider the full spectrum of models with their varying degrees of realism and complexity. However, always keep in mind that increasing the complexity of the model does not necessarily increase its realism. Our goal is to construct a model of the real system that is neither oversimplified and hence trivial, nor too detailed and hence clumsy and prohibitively expensive to operate.

Having specified the objectives and goals of the study, we are ready to begin establishing boundary conditions, i.e., defining what is and what is not part of the system to be studied. Two boundaries or interfaces concern us: the boundary that separates the problem from the rest of the universe and the boundary that separates the system of interest from the environment (i.e., what we consider to be an integral part of the system and what we consider to be the environment in which it operates).

Most fields of engineering accept the idea of dealing with partitioned and scaled models, particularly in the early stages of a study. It is not always necessary (or even desirable) to do full-scale complete-system modeling. Even problems that eventually will be subjected to full-scale modeling should usually initially be attacked in sections. There are obvious risks associated with studying a partial model. There are less obvious but none the less real risks associated with over-modeling because the model takes longer to build and run, is usually harder to modify, and is generally harder to understand and analyze.

As an analyst, you often do not know what or where the problem is until you have done some preliminary modeling. As a general rule, you should use the smallest and least detailed model that provides the required information. Again, do not automatically assume that the greater the detail, the better the model. According to Conway et al [1987], the "KISS" principle holds in simulation as it does elsewhere except that it stands for "Keep It Small and Simple."

There are basically two ways to keep a simulation model small. The first way is through *simplification and reduction* [Innis and Rexstad 1983]; this approach is discussed in Section 2.4. The second way is through *partitioning* or modeling only a portion of the full system. In other words, divide the system into sections or modules and initially model these partial sections rather than trying to model the entire system at once.

According to Conway et al [1987], there are both serial and parallel partitioning strategies. Serial partitioning involves studying successive stages in the process separately by looking for natural "fault-lines." These fault lines might lie along geographic (physical location) or organizational (departmental or divisional) lines. We can also sometimes partition a system that appears to be an integrated whole. For example, an integrated system's natural "fault-line" might consist of a large buffer that always contains entities to be processed but is never filled to capacity. Conway et al [1987] suggest that a bottleneck might also provide a useful point of partition. The idea is to model or represent the rest of the system (and Universe) as inputs.

Parallel partitioning simply recognizes that many facilities and systems consist of replications of a basic unit, i.e., there are two or more copies of essentially the same unit operating in parallel to achieve or handle the required volume. Unless these parallel units interact in some significant manner, it may be possible to build a model with only one unit.

4. Simplification and Reduction

The art of modeling involves the representation of a complex system by an approximation. To be of value, the approximation must behave sufficiently similarly to the real system so that meaningful conclusions can be drawn about the real system based on the behavior of the model. The problem we face is deciding what simplifications to make. We must remember that our goal is not to mimic reality precisely but to capture the essence of the real system without including unnecessary detail. We can knowingly exclude many details as long as they do not affect the conclusions drawn from the model.

A complex model has a number of significant disadvantages over a simpler yet adequate model. Not only does it take more time to develop, but it is also more difficult to understand, debug, validate, modify, document, and explain; it requires substantially more data; and it takes longer to run or execute. Why build more detail into a model than available data can support?

The usual argument for a more complex model is the need for precise results. However, the increased run-time for the more complex model may lead to fewer replications, which in turn produce wider confidence intervals on the measures of performance. Hence, the more detailed model may actually produce less precise results. A large and complex model is also more likely to contain undetected bugs that can introduce errors of a much larger magnitude than would be introduced with a simpler model.

The time available to develop the model also influences the level of detail incorporated. If decisions (e.g., which equipment to purchase) must be made by a specific deadline, then the model results must be available by that time; otherwise, they are meaningless. Having timely (even if approximate), pre-deadline results from a simple model is infinitely superior to having post-deadline results from a highly detailed model.

Although experience and good judgement play an important role in many aspects of the modeling project, they are critical in determining the appropriate level of detail. Beginning modelers are unwilling to trust their own judgement as to what can safely be left out and hence tend to leave little out. They persistently cling to the mistaken belief that a good model replicates reality in great detail.

The best piece of advice that we can offer beginners is to approach the problem in an iterative fashion: begin with a very simple model that can later be embellished with more detail. The iterative approach offers a number of important advantages over trying to build the final model in a single step. A simple first-cut model can be developed very quickly and can be used as a point of discussion for further modeling refinements. By successively adding refinements and comparing the results to those of the previous, simpler model, you can estimate the impact of each set of refinements. At some point in this process, the refinements being made will have only minor effects on results, and you will have a basis for determining that additional refinements of the model are unwarranted.

You can simplify a model in a number of ways. The most obvious simplification is the omission of certain details from the model, such as infrequent machine breakdowns, small travel times, etc. A second type of simplification involves aggregating or lumping details into a single, approximately equivalent function. For example, a part-setup activity and a part-machining activity might be aggregated into a single part-processing function. A third type of simplification involves substituting a simpler but approximate process for a complex one. For example, a workstation containing several different lathes with slightly different performance characteristics might be approximated by a set of parallel identical machines. Each of the three model simplification techniques is discussed in the following section.

5. Omission, Aggregation, and Substitution

In simulation studies, we typically model large, complex systems that involve highly detailed processes. The primary vehicle for simplifying these systems is the omission of much of the detail from the model. The premise underlying this approach is that not all factors are equally important to determining system behavior. You must determine which factors are critical, and which are not. In engineering, the few significant effects are called "first-order" effects, and the minor effects are called the "second-order" effects.

Although beginners resist omitting detail and view the general notion of deliberately introducing imperfections as somehow wrong, it is typically only by omitting detail that we can produce a practical and useful model. We often ignore minor factors because retaining them would not significantly alter overall model behavior.

In general we want the level of detail throughout the model to vary in proportion to the impact that the detail has on the results. More specifically, we want the gradient of the simulation response with respect to the addition of new detail to be the same throughout the model. For example, in a system in which it is anticipated that the jobs will spend roughly 10% of their time in queues, 85% of their time in material handling, and 5% of their time in machine processing, we want to include more detail in the material-handling portion of the model than in the machine-processing portion. In short, we want to expend our modeling effort where it influences the results the most.

In aggregation, we do not completely ignore detail in the real system, but rather combine or lump together several detailed processes into an equivalent process. For example, in a manufacturing flow line, an operator may perform several distinct tasks related to each workpiece as it moves past the workstation. Rather than individually modeling each of these tasks, we can model the entire operation as a single process. The rule of thumb is that the more closely two operations or activities are tied together, the safer it is to lump them. Thus, if operation A is always followed by operation B, then we can probably lump them together as if they were a single operation.

The Central Limit Theorem often helps to determine the nature of the resulting probability distribution when combining several random sub-processes together. This theorem states that, whenever we replace the processing times of several independent sub-processes with a single processing time, which is the sum of these times, the resulting overall processing time has a distribution that approaches normalcy as the number of lumped sub-processes increases. Unless the individual processing times are heavily skewed, this approximation is often reasonable for as few as four observations.

We can also simplify a model by replacing a complex process with a different but simpler process, which we hope behaves in an equivalent or nearly equivalent way to the original process. The most obvious substitution of this type involves replacing a stochastic process with a constant, e.g., replacing a probabilistic service time with a deterministic service time. In this approximation we set the service time equal to the mean of the process.

Another example of substitution is the representation of a complex process by a random process. Throughout our models we will make use of random distributions to approximate complex processes that we do not understand, or that we do not want to model in sufficient detail to reduce them to deterministic processes. For example, if we are modeling an Automatic Storage and Retrieval System (AS/RS), the most accurate way to model demands on the system is to actually model in detail the factory that makes requests for parts stored in the AS/RS. An alternative method is simply to create demands for parts randomly by using a distribution that approximates the behavior of the actual factory.

6. Impact of Model Simplification on Results

When considering simplifications in model formulation, we must understand the impact that the simplification is likely to have on model-generated data. In many instances, substantial simplifications in a model may have no real impact on the usefulness of the model for drawing valid conclusions; in other cases, relatively minor simplifications may lead to erroneous conclusions.

To evaluate these impacts, we must judge our simplification in light of the model's purpose. If the purpose of the model is to estimate precise system performance, then we must evaluate each simplification in terms of its direct impact on the performance measure. On the other hand, if the purpose of the study is to compare two or more systems or procedures, we only need to determine whether a proposed simplification affects all systems in approximately the same way. For this reason, estimating the absolute performance of one system typically demands considerably more modeling detail than comparing several systems.

If we are estimating actual system performance (e.g., how many parts are produced in a single shift), each simplification must be evaluated to see how it is likely to bias the performance estimation. Certain simplifications degrade model performance (negative bias), whereas others enhance it (positive bias). For example, ignoring machine breakdowns in a manufacturing system results in a positive bias of performance, i.e., production appears better in the model than it is in the real system. On the other hand, ignoring the capability of the human operator to override the system logic in an automated system, may make the model operate worse than the real system, thereby creating a negative bias in model results. Only those simplifications likely to have a minor impact (positive or negative) on model results can safely be incorporated in the model. Consequently, the objective of estimating the actual system performance typically leads to a highly detailed model.

If our objective is to determine whether the performance measure for the modeled system will exceed a specified level, we can safely incorporate simplifications that create a negative bias without endangering the results. Likewise, if our objective is to demonstrate that the performance of the real system will fall below a specified level, we can safely incorporate simplifications that create a positive bias. In both cases, however, if the specified level is not achieved, we will not know if the shortfall occurred because of the model simplifications or because of the capabilities of the underlying system. In such a case, we would have to refine the model further to distinguish between the two possibilities.

When our objective is to compare the performance of two or more systems or policies, we can typically get by with a far simpler model because we are only concerned with the relative performance of each system. Ignoring a detail in each system is inconsequential as long as the errors are of equal magnitude. For example, when comparing two alternative scheduling rules in a production system, we can ignore coffee breaks in both systems as long as including coffee breaks would have the same impact in both systems. When we compare system A with system B, we examine only the difference between A and B; hence, errors of equal magnitude simply cancel out.

7. Sources of Input Data

We need data to drive our simulation model: interarrival times, demand rates, loading and unloading times, processing times, times to failure for different machines, repair times, travel times, etc. Although all of these examples involve time delays, we also need other types of data, many of which are probabilistic: the percentage of parts expected to fail an inspection, the percentage of arriving items that require different services, the probability of detecting a target, the probability of destroying a target, etc.

Having good data to drive a model is just as important as having sound model logic and structure. The old cliche, "garbage in — garbage out," applies to simulation models as well as to any other computer programs. In most real-world simulation studies (as opposed to classroom exercises), the determination of what data to use is a very difficult and time-consuming task. Again, we have two different situations. With most existing systems we can obtain actual data, either because historical data exist, or because they can be gathered. In other cases we cannot obtain what we need: with non-existing systems the data don't exist and cannot be gathered; with some existing systems, it is just impossible, for one reason or another, to gather any data.

As Bratley, Fox, and Schrage [1983] point out, we sometimes have copious data; other times we have few. The latter situation can stem from several study limitations:

■ a small sample,

■ data restricted to summary statistics (e.g., mean, variance, maximum, minimum, median, mode), and/or

■ data restricted to qualitative guesses by informed people.

Furthermore, even when we have copious data, we can still face a problem: What if the data are not relevant? For example, we may need daily demand but only have monthly demand numbers available, we may have last year's data but need this year's, or we may need demand data but only have sales data, which do not show demand that was not met. Depending on the circumstances, we can try to obtain data about the system from a number of sources:

- Historical Records
- Observational Data
- Similar Systems
- Operator Estimates
- Vendor's Claims
- Designer Estimates
- Theoretical Considerations.

Historical records take the form of production, quality control, past-time studies, and down-time reports. Although these data may appear ideal, we must ensure that the historical data represent the performance of the current system. Most organizations generate voluminous data, many of which are dated, inaccessible, or, as previously discussed, available in the wrong form. In many cases, we have to expend a great deal of effort to write special computer programs to extract the data from the corporate data base and translate them into a useable form.

It may be possible to observe the system in operation and gather our own data by performing time studies or recording the data as the system operates. If at all possible, the data should be gathered personally. Depending on operators to record data seldom yields accurate information because the recording process interferes with their routine. Automatic data collection may also be unreliable because it fails to distinguish between a machine that is not operating because it is broken and one that is waiting for a part (starved) or an operator who hasn't returned from lunch or a coffee break.

It is also sometimes possible to gather and use information from another system. Many designs are in fact variations of other, similar systems (components). In these cases, we can often collect data from similar systems (components). However, when such a surrogate is used, any inferences are risky, and we may not be able to test the validity of the model.

Even with existing systems, we often find that either there are no data available, or there is insufficient time or personnel to gather data. We must often resort to asking the operating personnel to give us their best estimate of operating characteristics. For example, we may ask the operators how often a machine breaks down or how long it takes to do something. Such data are highly suspect for a number of reasons. Research by Tversky and Kahneman [1974] and others has clearly demonstrated that people are very poor at estimating events even when they are highly familiar with them. Numerous research studies show that people tend to forget extreme cases and to overemphasize recent ones.

Vendors usually provide estimates of operating characteristics for new equipment: processing times, mean time between failures, etc. For obvious reasons, vendor performance estimates are invariably highly optimistic. If similar equipment is operating elsewhere in the client's facility or at other non-client facilities, it may be possible to temper the vendor's estimates with these more realistic data.

Designer estimates are often the only source of data available. These data may include vendor claims, in which case the above-discussed caveats apply. Clearly, the designer thinks that the system will work as intended, and therefore great care must be exercised to determine how close (or far off) the claims may be.

Often we can choose a probability distribution based on theoretical considerations, *a priori* knowledge, or past research. We know, for example, that the mean time between failures of electronic equipment generally follows a Weibull distribution, and we know that the interarrival time of customers arriving at random is exponentially distributed.

8. No Existing Data

Let's start with the most difficult problem: modeling systems that do not yet exist or those for which it is not possible to obtain data. If the system does not yet exist, we have no past operating data and no chance of gathering any. Even when the system being studied does exist, we still may not be able to obtain the required data. Data collection and analysis take time, a rare commodity when answers are needed in a hurry. In many studies it takes longer to gather and analyze the data than it does to design and program the model [Markowitz 1981]. When the system does not exist, or the time constraint precludes all but the most cursory inferences from available data, we may have to rely on the following:

- operator or designer estimates,
- vendor claims, and/or
- theoretical considerations.

There are a number of possibilities for quantifying the probabilistic estimates given by people (e.g., operators, designers, vendors, or modeler) depending on what estimated values are available.

8.1 Mean Value Only

If only the mean value can be estimated, then we have several options. First, the mean value may itself be used directly as a constant time delay. However, this option should be used only when there is a very small variability in the actual process. On the other hand, depending on the phenomena being represented, it may be justifiable to use an exponential distribution with the given estimate as the mean value. The exponential distribution has a very large variability. If the times being estimated vary independently and randomly (i.e., they are not influenced by the preceding values), if the estimated mean value is not large, and if the estimate applies to an interarrival time, then the exponential distribution can usually be justified. So, if we have rate data (i.e., arrivals per time period), which can be justified as being Poisson-distributed with a mean of λ, then the time between arrivals can be modeled as exponentially distributed with a mean of $\mu = 1/\lambda$ (i.e., if $\lambda = 0.1$, then $\mu = 10$).

It should be noted that the exponential distribution is typically not a good choice for representing service times. Most service processes do not exhibit the high variability that is associated with the exponential distribution. Although the exponential distribution is used in analytical models to represent service times, this is done to simplify the mathematics, and not because it is a realistic representation of actual service processes.

Another method sometimes used (at least initially) involves introducing variability by taking the estimate of the mean, plus and minus some percentage, and then using either a uniform or symmetric triangular distribution. For example, if the estimate of the mean is 10, and we decide to use a variability of $+/-20\%$, we can use a uniform distribution from 8 to 12, or we can use a symmetric triangular distribution with 8, 10, and 12 as the minimum, mode, and maximum.

As the analyst, you should be aware, however, that the results vary greatly depending on the choice made. For example, the following table shows the results for 10,000 samples drawn by using each of these approaches. Each approach uses a mean of 10 with a range from 8 to 12 for the triangular and uniform distributions. Note that, although the mean values are close, the variance, minimum, and maximum values obtained vary greatly. The differences in the variances are particularly significant because the waiting time of customers in a system is increased as the variance of the distributions for the arrival and service processes increases. As we will see later, the exponential distribution produces much longer customer waiting times than does the triangular and uniform distributions.

Distribution	Mean	Variance	Min.	Max.
Exponential	9.93	9.98	0.0001	93.77
Triangular	10.00	0.81	8.03	11.98
Uniform	10.00	1.15	8.00	12.00

8.2 Range Only (Largest and Smallest Values)

In some cases we have estimated performance in the form of the maximum and minimum values expected (i.e., the feasible range). Although most authors recommend using the uniform distribution in this situation, we don't believe that this is necessarily the best choice. We have yet to see, or even imagine, any real-world situation in which the service time, interarrival time, time to machine breakdown, etc. is uniformly distributed. The use of the uniform distribution in simulation studies is predicated not on any empirical or theoretical justification but rather on convenience, ignorance, and (perhaps) historical accident. The first widely used simulation language, GPSS, originally did not allow the use of any other distribution. Schriber in his classic book on GPSS [Schriber 1976] therefore used the uniform distribution for all of his examples. The widespread use of these examples by other authors has perpetuated the perception that real-world phenomena should be represented with the uniform distribution. The uniform distribution is sometimes called the distribution of maximum ignorance because it is justified by the assertion, "since I have no reason to believe otherwise (i.e., ignorance), I will assume equal probabilities for all possible outcomes."

We believe that it often makes more sense to use a triangular distribution as we did in the preceding section, with the mean at the midpoint, or even a normal distribution if the values are large and it can be justified. If the normal distribution can be justified, the mean should be estimated as being equal to the midpoint with the standard deviation equal to one fourth of the range (i.e., range $= 4\sigma$). The use of four standard deviations instead of six is again based on the work of Tversky and Kahneman [1974], which clearly shows that people underestimate the range of feasible values by forgetting about or ignoring the extremes. One problem with using the normal distribution is its range, which theoretically goes from $+\infty$ to $-\infty$. Because this range does not make sense in most situations, and because we do not want to generate unrealistic values, it is usually good practice to test the variate generated and to truncate it if it is too large or too small. Alternatively, we should not use the normal distribution unless the mean is at least four standard deviations above 0.

Again, we can expect differences but not as pronounced as those in the previous section. The following table gives the results for an estimated range from 80 to 120. As shown, this example gives us a uniform distribution from 80 to 120 or a Triangular distribution with Minimum $= 80$, Mode $= 100$, and Maximum $= 120$. The normal distribution would be derived as:

$$\text{Range} = 120 - 80 = 40 = 4\sigma$$
$$\sigma = 10 \quad \mu = 100$$

Distribution	Mean	Variance	Minimum	Maximum
Normal	99.98	10.05	62.3	137.4
Uniform	99.88	11.88	80.0	120.0
Triangular	100.03	8.10	80.3	119.8

8.3 Range and Most Likely Value

If, in addition to the minimum and maximum values, we can get a reasonable estimate of the most likely or most often occurring value, then a triangular, beta, or normal distribution is probably the best guess. Although other distributions are theoretical possibilities (gamma, Weibull, etc.), we believe that their use is unwarranted when dealing with risky and perhaps even unreliable estimates.

The triangular distribution is the most convenient distribution to use when estimates of the minimum, maximum, and most likely values are available. These values are used directly for specifying the parameters for the triangular distribution. In addition, most simulation languages (including SIMAN) incorporate a very efficient algorithm for sampling from a triangular distribution.

Another possibility is to use the beta distribution, which has been widely used for estimating the time to complete a task in project management (i.e., PERT). However, a disadvantage of the beta distribution is that it is defined over the range 0 to 1. We must therefore rescale and shift the beta samples within our model to accommodate other ranges. We can generate a beta variate, Y, in the range [0,1] and then transform it to the variate, X, defined over the range [a,b] by

$$X = a + (b-a)\,Y.$$

A second disadvantage of the beta distribution is that we must specify the two shape parameters, α_1 and α_2, rather than the minimum, maximum, and most likely values. We can estimate these shape parameters from our estimates of the minimum (a), maximum (b), and most likely (m) values. We do this by first estimating the mean as

$$\mu' = \frac{a + 4m + b}{6}$$

If $\mu' \neq m$, we can then estimate the two parameters of the beta as

$$\alpha_1 = \frac{(\mu'-a)\,(2m-a-b)}{(m-\mu')\,(b-a)}$$

$$\alpha_2 = \frac{(b-\mu')}{(\mu'-a)}\,\alpha_1$$

The requirement to estimate α_1 and α_2, along with the need to rescale and shift the resulting beta samples, makes the beta distribution less convenient to use than the triangular distribution.

9. Existing Data

Assuming that we have copious data from a reliable source, we still face several decisions. There are two ways we can use the data. We can sample directly from the empirical distribution, or, if the data fit a theoretical distribution, we can sample from the theoretical. Simulation experts do not agree on this issue [Brately et al 1983, Fox 1981, Kelton 1984]. If we sample directly from the empirical data, we faithfully replicate the past, but no values other than those experienced in the past can occur. If we fit the data to a theoretical distribution and then sample from it, we get values from the tails, which are either bigger or smaller than the historical data. Thus, one side argues that the empirical distribution may give a poor fit to the underlying parent distribution in one or both tails. The other side argues that the tails of distributions can't be estimated accurately from limited data regardless of whether an empirical or a theoretical approach is used.

The appropriate solution to the above controversy is still not clear. Therefore, most commercially available simulation languages, including SIMAN, allow the use of either approach. If empirical data are to be used, they are input in the form of a cumulative probability distribution. Observed values are put in the form of an empirical cumulative distribution by arranging them in ascending order, grouping identical values, computing their relative frequencies, and then computing their cumulative probability distribution.

To organize raw data — whether for direct sampling, for fitting data to a theoretical distribution, or simply for presenting results in an understandable way — we usually first put it in the form of a histogram. To develop a histogram, we group the data into *classes* or *categories* and determine the number of individuals belonging to each class, called the *class frequency* (number observed). A tabular arrangement of the data by classes, together with the corresponding class frequencies, is called a *frequency distribution* or *frequency table*. The following table shows a frequency distribution for 117 service times recorded to the nearest minute.

Upper Limit of Class	Number Observed	Relative Frequency
∞	4	0.034
115	5	0.043
112	6	0.051
109	7	0.060
106	16	0.137
103	10	0.085
100	22	0.188
97	17	0.145
94	14	0.120
91	13	0.111
88	3	0.026
Totals	117	1.000

As shown, the first class or category contains all observations that exceed 115, whereas the last category contains all observations of 88 or less.

When using continuous data, we still have some issues that are not easily resolved. How many cells (i.e., class intervals or breakpoints) should we use? Since the very act of grouping data destroys much of its original detail, this choice is an important one. There are some general rules that apply to forming frequency distributions:

▪ Determine the largest and smallest numbers in the raw data, thereby finding the range (the difference between the two).

▪ Divide the range into a convenient number of class intervals having the same size. The number of class intervals usually ranges from 5 to 20, varying with the data; most often 8 to 12 intervals are used. Choose the class boundaries such that class membership is unambiguous. You would like to have at least three to five observations in each class.

▪ Determine the number of observations falling in each class interval, i.e., find the class frequencies, by using a tally or score sheet.

The frequency distribution can then be graphically represented as a histogram (for display purposes) or converted to a *relative frequency distribution* (or *percentage distribution*) by dividing each class by the total number of observations. In the

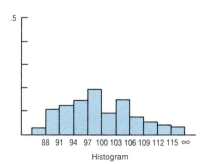

Histogram

sample distribution table just presented, this information appears in the last column. The class mark is the midpoint of the class interval and is called the *class midpoint*. For purposes of further mathematical analysis, all observations belonging to a given class interval are assumed to coincide with the class mark. Thus all service times in the table that fall between 91 and 94 are considered to be 92.5 minutes.

If we want to try to fit the data to a theoretical distribution, then we must perform the following three steps.

1. Select a distributional form to try.

2. Estimate the parameter values to use for the distribution chosen.

3. Determine the relative "goodness of fit" by using an appropriate method.

In the sections that follow we discuss each of these steps. As you will see, the manual analysis and testing of data can be burdensome, and several excellent computer software packages are available to perform these functions. These packages can greatly simplify the task of selecting and evaluating a distribution to model the input data. We have used the programs developed by Phillips [1972] and by Law and Vincent [1988].

10. Distribution Selection

To test the compatibility of a set of observed frequencies with some theoretical frequency, we must first identify the theoretical distribution we wish to try. Usually we cannot reasonably guess or hypothesize about the distribution until we look carefully at the data. First, the collected data are summarized and analyzed. If we are dealing with a discrete variable, we record the frequency with which each individual value occurs. If the variable is continuous, we break the range of values into equal intervals or classes and record the frequency occurring within each interval or class. The relative frequency in each interval is then the observed frequency count in each class divided by the total number of data points. These data are then plotted as a frequency distribution.

After we have obtained a relative frequency distribution, selecting the possible probability distribution from which it may have derived becomes a matter of judgement and experience. We get some help from visually comparing the observed frequency distribution with those of several theoretical ones. Visual comparisons of distributions only suggest which distributions we want to try; they never sufficiently justify accepting a certain hypothesis or theoretical distribution.

We can (and should) also use theoretical considerations to select candidate distributions [Law and Kelton 1982]. In the following sections we consider the characteristics of different distributions that might influence a modeler to select a particular distribution to represent an activity.

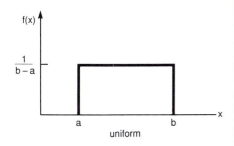

f(x)

$\frac{1}{b-a}$

a   b

x

uniform

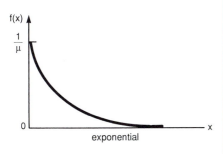

f(x)

a   m   b

x

triangular

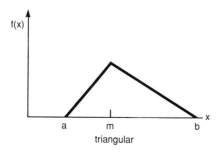

f(x)

$\frac{1}{\mu}$

0

x

exponential

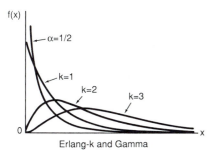

f(x)

$\alpha=1/2$

k=1

k=2

k=3

0

x

Erlang-k and Gamma

10.1 Continuous Distributions

In this section we discuss the following continuous distributions: uniform, triangular, negative exponential, Erlang, gamma, Weibull, normal, lognormal, and beta.

The *uniform* distribution specifies that every value between given minimum and maximum values is equally likely. We use it as a starting point for a variable believed to vary randomly between a and b, but about which little else is known. As discussed earlier, the uniform distribution is known as the distribution of maximum ignorance since by using it we are saying that we have absolutely no idea of the form or shape of the distribution; hence, we say that all values between a and b are equally likely. Also sometimes known as the *rectangular* distribution, the uniform distribution from 0 to 1 is essential in generating random numbers and random variates from other distributions.

Although not easily identified with any physical process, the *triangular* distribution is useful as a first approximation or rough model in the absence of data. We use it when the described random variable is expected to be uni-modal over a defined range. As discussed earlier, the triangular distribution is defined by three values: a minimum, mode, and maximum. The density function consists of two linear segments, one rising from the minimum value to the mode, and the other decreasing from the mode to the maximum value specified. This distribution is most often used when attempting to represent a process for which data are not easily obtained but for which bounds (minimum and maximum) and most likely value (mode) can be established based on knowledge of its characteristics.

The *exponential* function is widely used for times between independent events such as interarrival times, and lifetimes for devices with a constant hazard rate (when describing the time to failure of a system's component). It is related to the Poisson function in that, if the number of arrivals in a given time period is Poisson-distributed with a mean of λ, then the interarrival times (i.e., the times between arrivals) are exponentially distributed with a mean of $\mu = 1/\lambda$. Many phenomena are exponentially distributed such as the lengths of telephone conversations, the expected lives of many electronic components, the times between arrivals of orders to a firm, the times between arrivals of aircraft to an airport, the times between job submissions to a computer facility, etc.

When the exponential random variable represents time, the distribution possesses the unique property of forgetfulness or lack of memory. Given that T is the time period since the occurrence of the last event, the remaining time, t, until the next event is independent of T. Therefore, events for which interarrival times can be represented by the exponential are said to be completely random. The only parameter needed to describe the exponential distribution is the mean (the variance is equal to the square of the mean). The exponential ranges from 0 to infinity.

The *Erlang* distribution closely resembles the exponential distribution. If we have "k" random variables $x_1, x_2, \ldots, x_k$, which are independent, and each is exponentially distributed with a common mean $= 1/k\lambda$, then the sum of the random variables $x_1, x_2, \ldots, x_k$ follows the kth Erlang distribution with parameter λ.

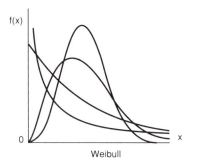

f(x)

0   x

Weibull

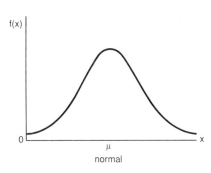

f(x)

0   μ   x

normal

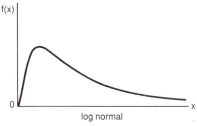

f(x)

0   log normal   x

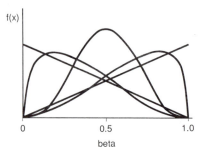

f(x)

0   0.5   1.0

beta

Thus, a servicing station in which an entity sequentially goes through k independent servicing phases, each exponentially distributed with mean = $1/k\lambda$, will have a service time through that station that obeys the kth Erlang distribution. This property is often used to simplify models for it allows us to lump several similar steps together. Another application derives from a situation in which jobs are arriving from a source with exponential interarrival time and mean $\mu = 1/\lambda$, which are then assigned on a rotational basis to k machines. The time between the allocation of jobs at each machine would then be distributed as an Erlang (λ,k).

The *gamma* distribution is used to model the time to complete some task, e.g., customer service or machine repair. The gamma distribution is conceptually a generalization of the Erlang distribution in which the parameter k need not be an integer. Hence the Erlang distribution is a special case of the gamma distribution. In the gamma distribution, the parameter k is denoted by α. The gamma can assume a wide variety of shapes depending on the values of the shape parameter $\alpha > 0$ and the scale parameter $\beta > 0$.

Like the gamma distribution, the *Weibull* distribution is a multi-parameter distribution that can take on various shapes. It is widely used in reliability models for representing lifetimes (time until failure) of devices for which wear or usage affects expected life, such as electronic devices, ball bearings, and springs. The Weibull distribution is also sometimes used for the time to complete some task. This family of distributions whose range is from 0 to ∞, depends on a shape parameter $\alpha > 0$ and a scale parameter $\beta > 0$ for definition.

The familiar bell-shaped curve of the *normal* distribution describes phenomena that have symmetric variations above and below the mean. More importantly, it represents quantities that are sums of a large number of other quantities. The normal distribution is important in simulation because the Central Limit Theorem often has applicability for determining the nature of the resulting probability distribution when combining several random sub-processes. This theorem states that, whenever we replace the processing times of several independent sub-processes by a single processing time, which is the sum of these times, the resulting overall processing time has a distribution that approaches normalcy as the number of lumped sub-processes increases. Unless the individual processing times are heavily skewed, this approximation is often reasonable for as few as four observations.

Another version of this theorem helps us to analyze simulation outputs. This version states that the distribution of a sample average tends toward normalcy regardless of the identity of the distribution describing the population from which the sample is drawn. Thus we can determine confidence intervals as well as conduct hypothesis testing of the output of simulation experiments.

If log X is normally distributed, then X has the *lognormal* distribution. In addition, whenever we combine independent sub-processes by multiplication, the overall process has a distribution that approaches the lognormal distribution as the number of sub-processes increases. Because of this characteristic, the lognormal distribution is being used for special applications in modeling system reliability.

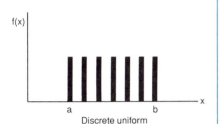

f(x)

a   b   x

Discrete uniform

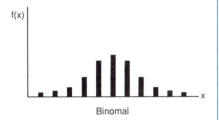

f(x)

x

Binomal

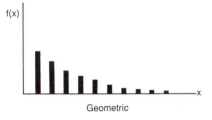

f(x)

x

Geometric

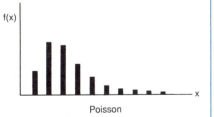

f(x)

x

Poisson

11. Parameter Estimation

As we previously discussed, the *beta* distribution is used as a rough model in the absence of data to represent a random proportion, e.g., the proportion of defective items in a shipment, and time to complete a task, e.g., a PERT network. Its advantage lies in the ease with which estimates can be used to describe a wide range of different distribution shapes. The distributions in this family are defined by α_1 and α_2 and cover the range from 0 to 1. The transformation from the beta to a wide variety of finite-range distributions was discussed in Section 8.3.

10.2 Discrete Distributions

This section describes the following discrete distributions: discrete uniform, binomial, geometric, and Poisson.

A *discrete* uniform distribution is used to represent an event with several possible outcomes, each of which is equally likely. It is used as a "first" model for a quantity that varies among the integers i through j but about which little else is known.

A *binomial* distribution is used to represent situations consisting of repeated trials, in which each trial is independent and has a probability of success equal to p, i.e., the number of successes in t Bernoulli trials with the probability p of success on each trial. Examples include the number of defective items in a batch of size t, or the number of items in a batch of random size. A binomial distribution can also be used to calculate the probability of error or of no error in a message consisting of a specific number of independent bits of digital information.

A *geometric* distribution calculates the number of failures before the first success in a sequence of independent Bernoulli trials with probability p of success on each trial. One example is calculating the number of items inspected before encountering the first defective item.

A *Poisson* distribution is used to describe the number of events that occur in an interval of time when the events occur independently, such as the number of arrivals to a system or the number of entities served per time period. The mean and variance of a Poisson distribution are equal. This property can sometimes be helpful in recognizing whether a set of raw data are compatible with a Poisson distribution.

Once the form of a distribution has been hypothesized, the next step is to estimate the parameters of the distribution using the available data. Although this step is relatively simple for most distributions, for some distributions (e.g., the Weibull) it can be quite difficult. In some cases there are alternative methods for obtaining estimates for the parameters. When this is the case, we have elected to present the easiest method and provide a reference to the alternative method.

In many cases the sample mean, or sample mean and variance, provide the basis for estimating the parameters of the selected distribution. This is the case for the exponential, Poisson, normal, and lognormal distributions. If the observations in a sample of size n are $x_1, x_2, \ldots, x_n$, the sample mean and variance are defined by

$$\overline{x} = \frac{\Sigma x_i}{n}$$

$$s^2 = \frac{\Sigma(x_i - \overline{x})^2}{n-1}$$

In the case of the gamma, Erlang, and beta distributions, we can employ our estimates for the mean and variance of the distribution to construct estimates for the distribution parameters using the method of moments. Estimates based on the maximum likelihood method can also be obtained [Law and Kelton, 1982], but these procedures are considerably more complicated.

The gamma distribution has a shape parameter, α, and a scale parameter, β. These parameters are related to the mean, μ, and variance, σ^2, of the gamma distribution as follows:

$$\alpha = (\mu/\sigma)^2 \text{ and } \beta = \sigma^2/\mu$$

We can use our sample mean and variance in the above equations to estimate α and β.

Recall that the Erlang distribution is a special case of the gamma in which the shape parameter, α (denoted by k), must be an integer. Hence we can employ the same equation given above for the gamma distribution for estimating the shape parameter for the Erlang distribution, except that we must round the result to the nearest integer to obtain an estimate for k. We then estimate the scale parameter from the relationship $\beta = \alpha/k$.

The beta distribution has two shape parameters: α_1 and α_2. These parameters are related to the mean, μ, and variance, σ^2, of the beta distribution as follows:

$$\alpha_1 = \mu\left[(1-\mu)\,\mu/\sigma^2 - 1\right]$$

$$\alpha_2 = \mu\,(1-\mu)\left[(1-\mu)\,\mu\sigma^2 - 1\right]$$

We employ our sample mean and sample variance in the above equations to obtain estimates for the two shape parameters.

The minimum and maximum parameters for the uniform distribution can be estimated using the smallest and largest values in the data set. If the minimum parameter is known to be 0, a better estimate for the maximum parameter in this case is the largest value in the data set times the quantity $(n + 1)/n$. In the case of the triangular distribution, the minimum and maximum parameters can be estimated by using the smallest and largest values in the data set, and the mode can be estimated by multiplying the sample mean by 3 and subtracting the smallest and largest values in the data set.

Unfortunately, there are no simple procedures for estimating the parameters for the Weibull distribution. The easiest approach is to use the method of moments [Brately et al, 1983]. Another approach is to use a numerical method to obtain the maximum likelihood estimate for the parameters [Law and Kelton, 1982]. From a practical standpoint, the use of a computer program such as those mentioned earlier is very useful to fit data to this distribution.

12. Goodness-of-Fit Test

Once we have selected a distribution (based on visual inspection and theoretical grounds) that we believe may adequately represent the data, and we have estimated the parameters for the selected distribution, we then need to assess the quality of our fit [Kelton 1986]. This can be done by using formal statistical tests or by employing a simple graphical method in which an overlay of the theoretical distribution is displayed on a histogram of the data and a visual assessment is made to determine the quality of the fit.

To test statistically the hypothesis that a set of empirical (observed) data does not differ significantly from that which would be expected from some specified theoretical distribution, we use one of the goodness-of-fit tests. A goodness-of-fit test attempts to measure and evaluate the deviation of the sample distribution from the theoretical. In this section we consider both the Chi-Square (χ^2) and the Kolmogorov-Smirnov tests.

It should be noted that goodness-of-fit tests such as these generally have a low probability of rejecting an incorrect fit. As a result, these tests often repeatedly fail to reject a fit when the same set of data is tested against several different distributions. The fact that the test does not reject the fit for a distribution should not be taken as strong evidence that the selected distribution is a good fit. As a result, it is useful to augment the formal statistical tests discussed in this section with a simple graphical assessment of the fit.

12.1 Chi-Square

One of the most widely used measures or tests of the discrepancy between an observed and an expected set of data is the χ^2 statistic. The Chi-Square test was proposed by Karl Pearson in 1903, but was not fully developed until 1924 when Sir Ronald Fisher published the table of critical values that we use today. The Chi-Square statistic is calculated as follows:

$$\chi^2 = \frac{\overset{k}{\Sigma}(f_o - f_e)^2}{f_e}$$

where

$\qquad$ k = number of classes or intervals,

$\qquad$ f_o = observed frequency for each class or interval,

$\qquad$ f_e = expected frequency for each class or interval predicted by the theoretical distribution, and

$\qquad$ $\overset{k}{\Sigma}$ = sum over all k classes or intervals.

If $x^2 = 0$, then the observed and theoretical distributions match exactly. The larger the value of x^2, the greater the discrepancy between the observed and expected. To determine if the calculated value is too big to be attributed solely to chance, we must compare it with the tabulated, critical values recorded in an x^2 table. The critical values of the x^2 statistic are tabulated by degrees of freedom vs. $(1-\alpha)$ or significance level (see Appendix B). The null hypothesis, H_0, being tested is that there is no significant difference between the observed distribution and what we would expect from the specified theoretical distribution with the same parameters.

If the calculated value of x^2 is greater than the tabulated value (at a given level of significance and appropriate degrees of freedom), then we reject the H_0 of no difference, and conclude that the observed frequencies differ significantly from the expected frequencies at that level of significance. The degrees of freedom, ν, used in the test is

$$\nu = k - 1 - p$$

where

$p =$ the number of population parameters used in the calculation of the theoretical frequencies, which were estimated from the observed sample.

Thus, if we have used the estimated mean and standard deviation calculated from the observed data to calculate the expected frequencies for a normal distribution, then $p = 2$ and the degrees of freedom are $\nu = k - 1 - 2$.

For example, let's suppose that a die is tossed 120 times with the results shown in the following table. If the die is fair, we would expect to get about 20 occurrences of each face. Using a significance level of 5%, we can test the hypothesis that the die is fair.

Face	1	2	3	4	5	6
Observed frequency	25	17	15	23	24	16
Expected frequency	20	20	20	20	20	20

$$x^2 = \frac{(25\text{-}20)^2}{20} + \frac{(17\text{-}20)^2}{20} + \frac{(15\text{-}20)^2}{20} + \frac{(23\text{-}20)^2}{20} + \frac{(24\text{-}20)^2}{20} + \frac{(16\text{-}20)^2}{20}$$

$$x^2 = 5.0$$

degrees of freedom $= 6 - 1 = 5$

The critical value of x^2 from the table at $\alpha = 0.05$ and $\nu = 5$ is 11.1. Since $5.00 < 11.1$ we do not reject the H_0 that there is no difference between what we observed and what we would expect to get with a fair die.

Take another example. Suppose we take another look at the data for the 117 service times recorded to the nearest minute, as shown on the next page.

Upper Limit of Class	Number Observed	Relative Frequency
∞	4	0.034
115	5	0.043
112	6	0.051
109	7	0.060
106	16	0.137
103	10	0.085
100	22	0.188
97	17	0.145
94	14	0.120
91	13	0.111
88	3	0.026
Totals	117	1.000

The calculated mean $= 100.265$ with an estimated variance of 62.3. The data look as if they may be normally distributed. This supposition is enforced by the fact that each value is the sum of five separate operations. Using $\alpha = 0.05$, we want to test the following hypothesis:

H_0: there is no significant difference between these data and what would be expected from a normal distribution with a mean of 100.265 and a variance of 62.3.

To do this, we first convert the data to the standard normal scale, i.e., calculate Z values, by using

$$Z = \frac{(x - \bar{x})}{s}$$

where

$s = \sqrt{62.3} = 7.89$, $\bar{x} = 100.265$, and $x =$ upper class limit.

Using these Z values, we then look up the cumulative probability values from a standard normal distribution table. By subtraction, we then obtain the probability of occurrence for each class, and we multiply each probability by 117 to get the expected or theoretical number of occurrences as shown in the following table.

Upper Class Limit	Z	$P(x<z)$	Probability of Occurrence	Expected Number in Class	Observed Number in Class	χ^2 Statistic
∞	—	1.0000	0.0307	3.59 }7.97	4 }9	
115	−1.87	0.9693	0.0374	4.38	5	0.719
112	−1.49	0.9319	0.0654	7.65	6	0.356
109	−1.11	0.8665	0.0992	11.61	7	1.830
106	−0.73	0.7673	0.1305	15.27	16	0.035
103	−0.35	0.6368	0.1488	17.41	10	3.154
100	−0.03	0.4880	0.1471	17.21	22	1.333
97	−0.41	0.3409	0.1261	14.75	17	0.343
94	−0.79	0.2148	0.0938	10.97	14	0.837
91	−1.17	0.1210	0.0942	11.02 }14.16	13 }16	
88	−1.93	0.0268	0.0268	3.14	3	0.239
Totals			1.0000	117.00	117	8.846

Degrees of freedom $= \nu = 9-1-2 = 6$

For $\alpha = 0.05$ and $\nu = 6$ the critical $\chi^2 = 12.6$

Because $8.846 < 12.6$ we do not reject the H_0 of no significant difference between what we observed and what we would expect to observe from a normally distributed variable with a mean of 100.265 and a variance of 62.23.

Notice that, in calculating the degrees of freedom, p = 2 because we used $\bar{x}$ and s from the observed data to calculate the expected number in each class. When using the Chi-Square test, we must be sure that there is a frequency or count of at least 5 in each class. If we do not have an expected class size of 5, then we must group adjacent classes together until we have the desired number. We usually drop below 5 at the tails or ends. In our example, both the top and bottom classes have expected numbers below 5 (i.e., 3.59 and 3.14, respectively), and each is lumped with an adjoining class.

12.2 Kolmogorov-Smirnov

The Kolmogorov-Smirnov test was first suggested by Smirnov in 1939, and the tables of critical values were published nine years later [Smirnov, 1948]. The Kolmogorov-Smirnov test assumes that the probability distribution under test is continuous and that the population mean and variance are known. Like the Chi-Square test, it can be used to test the degree of agreement — or, more accurately, the disagreement — between the distribution of a set of empirical or sample data and some specified theoretical distribution. The test is conducted by developing, specifying, and comparing the cumulative probability distributions for both the observed data and the theoretical distribution. The two distributions are divided into classes, and the absolute deviation between the two cumulative distributions for each class is calculated. The calculated Kolmogorov-Smirnov (K-S) statistic, which is to be compared to the tabulated critical value, is the class deviation with largest absolute value.

For example, suppose that we want to use a K-S test to evaluate the following data for uniform distribution at $\alpha = 0.05$:

12.36	14.15	6.76	14.46	7.47
5.71	16.83	5.17	20.03	19.65
16.79	19.33	17.46	15.45	16.08
18.01	11.99	10.72	11.51	11.99
5.12	20.18	11.53	19.80	9.51
7.69	18.73	20.41	15.10	8.04
19.41	6.31	6.21	9.83	14.66
8.58	15.83	12.52	16.39	6.57
8.42	12.87	8.03	9.60	5.42
15.56	18.04	8.97	17.11	7.79
10.00	12.00	16.00	18.00	14.00
18.00	17.00	15.00	19.00	13.00

We first put the observed data into 10 classes, compute the observed frequency for each class, and then establish the cumulative distribution for the data. Because we are testing to see if these data are consistent with a hypothesis that they are uniformly distributed, then the theoretical frequency for each of the 10 classes equals 0.10. The calculated K-S statistic is the absolute difference between the two cumulative frequencies for that class.

Lower Class Limit	Upper Class Limit	Observed Number in Class	Observed Relative Frequency	Observed Cumulative Frequency	Theoretical Cumulative Frequency	K-S Statistic
5.12	6.65	7	0.1167	0.1167	0.1	0.0167
6.65	8.18	6	0.1000	0.2167	0.2	0.0167
8.18	9.71	5	0.0833	0.3000	0.3	0.0000
9.71	11.24	3	0.0500	0.3500	0.4	0.0500
11.24	12.77	7	0.1167	0.4667	0.5	0.0333
12.77	14.30	4	0.0667	0.5333	0.6	0.0667 *
14.30	15.83	6	0.1000	0.6333	0.7	0.0667
15.83	17.36	8	0.1333	0.7666	0.8	0.0334
17.36	18.89	6	0.1000	0.8666	0.9	0.0334
18.89	20.42	8	0.1334	1.0000	1.0	0.0000

Looking down through the computed K-S statistics, we pick the largest (0.0667) and compare it with the tabulated critical value. Looking up the critical value for a K-S one-sample test, with degrees of freedom = 60 and $\alpha = 0.05$, we get 0.1756. The degrees of freedom are equal to the sample size, not the number of classes used. Because $0.0667 < 0.1756$, we do not reject the H_0 of no difference between what we observed and what we would expect to see from a uniformly distributed variable.

Now let's re-test the data for the 117 observations, which we just tested for being normally distributed using the Chi-Square test. We will use the theoretical expected, cumulative frequency for a normal distribution that we already calculated for the χ^2 test.

Upper Class Limit	Observed Relative Frequency	Observed Cumulative Frequency	Theoretical Cumulative Frequency	K-S Statistic
∞	0.034	1.000	1.0000	0.0000
115	0.043	0.966	0.9693	0.0033
112	0.051	0.923	0.9319	0.0089
109	0.060	0.872	0.8665	0.0055
106	0.137	0.812	0.7673	0.0447
103	0.085	0.675	0.6368	0.0382
100	0.188	0.590	0.4880	0.1020 *
97	0.145	0.402	0.3409	0.0611
94	0.120	0.257	0.2148	0.0422
91	0.111	0.137	0.1210	0.0160
85	0.026	0.026	0.0268	0.0008

The largest K-S Statistic calculated is 0.1020. The critical value for significance at $\alpha = 0.05$ and degrees of freedom = 117 is 0.1257. Therefore, because $0.1020 < 0.1257$ we do not reject the H_0 of no significant difference between our observed data and what we would expect from a normal distribution with the same parameters.

The question of when to use the Chi-Square test and when to use the Kolmogorov-Smirnov test naturally arises. In general we make this decision based on the nature of the distribution and the available sample size. The K-S test is only valid for testing continuous distributions, whereas the Chi-Square test is applicable to both discrete and continuous distributions. Because we need at least five observations in each cell, and because we want a reasonably large degrees of freedom, the Chi-Square test is not applicable to small samples, whereas the K-S test is valid for any sample size. In general, for the Chi-Square test we need a sample size of at least 100, although some authors indicate that they have obtained good results with sample sizes as small as 30.

13. Summary

The system definition and model formulation phases are undoubtedly the most difficult and crucial parts of any simulation study. Gathering information on how a system works and deciding which data to use in driving the model are time-consuming tasks. However, our success or failure at later modeling stages is largely determined by how well we have

■ defined the problem,

- established the goals of the study,
- defined the boundaries of the system,
- determined the relevant components and variables,
- hypothesized and abstracted the relationships among the components and variables, and estimated the values of the pertinent parameters.

If we are skillful and careful in the initial model design phases, we can easily modify the model as we learn more about the system being studied. Unless we make simplifying assumptions about how the real-world system works, we can be overwhelmed by its complexity. It should be obvious that the more mistakes we make in the beginning, the more difficult and costly the modifications we must make at later stages [Balci and Nance 1985]. Authorities in software engineering recommend that we spend 40% of project time on these early stages before we begin to develop the model [McKay et al 1986].

References

BALCI, O. and R. E. NANCE (1985), "Formulated Problem Verification as an Explicit Requirement of Model Credibility," *Simulation*, Vol. 45, No. 2, pp: 76-86, August.

BRATLEY, P., B. L. FOX and L. E. SCHRAGE (1983), *A Guide to Simulation*, Springer-Verlag, New York.

CONWAY, R., W. L. MAXWELL, J. O. McCLAIN, and S. L. WORONA (1987), *User's Guide to XCELL + Factory Modeling System*, 2nd Edition, The Scientific Press, Redwood City, CA.

FOX, B. L. (1981), "Fitting Standard Distributions to Data is Necessarily Good: Dogma or Myth," Proceedings of 1981 Winter Simulation Conference (Oren, Delfosse & Shub — editors), IEEE 81CH1709-5, pp: 305-307, December.

INNIS, G. and E. REXSTAD (1983), "Simulation Model Simplification Techniques," *Simulation*, Vol. 43, No. 1, pp: 7-15, July.

KELTON, W. D. (1984), "Input Data Collection and Analysis," Proceedings of the 1984 Winter Simulation Conference (Sheppard, Pooch & Pegden — editors), IEEE 84CH2098-2, pp: 9195, November.

KELTON, W. D. (1986), "Statistical Analysis Methods Enhance Usefulness, Reliability of Simulation Models," *Industrial Engineering*, Vol. 18, No. 9, pp: 74-84, September.

LAW, A. M. and W. D. KELTON (1982), *Simulation Modeling and Analysis*, Chapter 5, McGraw-Hill, New York.

LAW, A. M. and S. G. VINCENT (1988), "A Tutorial on UNIFIT: An Interactive Computer Package for Fitting Probability Distributions to Observed Data," Proceedings of 1988 Winter Simulation Conference, San Diego, CA, pp: 188-194.

MARKOWITZ, H. M. (1981), "Barriers to the Practical Use of Simulation Analysis," Proceedings of the 1981 Winter Simulation Conference, (Oren, Delfosse & Shub — editors), IEEE 81CH1709-5, pp: 3-9, December.

McKAY, K. N., J. A. BUZACOTT, J. B. MOORE, and C. J. STRANG (1986), "Software Engineering Applied to Discrete Event Simulations," Proceedings of the 1986 Winter Simulation Conference, (Wilson, Henriksen & Roberts — editors), IEEE, pp: 485-493, December.

PHILLIPS, D. T. (1972), *Applied Goodness of Fit Testing*, OR Monograph Series, AIIE-OR-72-1, American Institute of Industrial Engineers, Atlanta, GA.

SCHRIBER, T. J. (1974), *Simulation Using GPSS*, John Wiley & Sons, Inc., NY, NY.

SMIRNOV, N. (1948), "Table for Estimating the Goodness of Fit of Empirical Distributions," *Annuals of Mathematical Statistics*, Vol. 19.

TVERSKY, A. and D. KAHNEMEN (1974), "Judgement Under Uncertainty: Heuristics and Biases," *Science*, September.

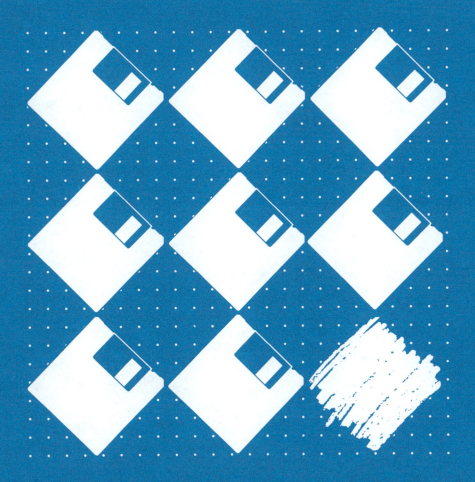

CHAPTER 3

Basic Modeling Concepts

This chapter presents basic concepts for using SIMAN to construct simulation models of discrete systems. Only a small subset of SIMAN's modeling features will be discussed in this chapter; however, this subset will allow us to develop and run complete models of relatively simple systems. In later chapters we will discuss additional modeling features that will greatly expand on the complexity of the systems that we can model.

We have opted to introduce the modeling concepts of SIMAN by means of a specific example, which we will gradually embellish throughout the chapter. Although this example should simplify your initial understanding of the concepts being presented by making them more concrete, there is a danger that you may overlook the generality of the modeling concepts being presented. It is important, therefore, that you attempt to get beyond the specific example by imagining other situations in which the same modeling constructs can be applied.

We begin this chapter with an overview of some general concepts, terms, and conventions employed in SIMAN. We then present a problem, which we use as a vehicle for introducing specific modeling constructs in SIMAN. After presenting the problem, we introduce a small subset of SIMAN features sufficient to model the problem and discuss its solution. We then embellish our problem as a means of introducing some additional SIMAN modeling constructs. We conclude the chapter by presenting two additional examples to underscore the generality of the concepts presented.

Throughout this book we make use of many everyday terms that have specific meaning in the SIMAN modeling framework, such as "entities," "attributes," and "resources." You must first face the task of learning the specific meanings of these terms as they are used in SIMAN. To ease this process, we have chosen different ways of presenting different types of terms. For example, important terms having a specialized meaning in SIMAN appear in italics the first time they occur in the text. Within the model listings, all SIMAN-reserved words appear in uppercase letters, and all user-assigned names appear with initial capitals. Although we have adopted this convention within this book, SIMAN is case-insensitive and you may freely mix upper and lower case letters in both reserved words and user-assigned names.

2. Process Modeling in SIMAN

In this section we present some basic concepts and define some important terms that you must learn before modeling processes in SIMAN.

2.1 The Relationship Between the Model and Experiment

In SIMAN's modeling framework, there is a fundamental distinction between the *Model Frame* and the *Experiment Frame*. The *model* is a functional description of the system's components and their interactions. The *experiment*, on the other hand, defines the experimental conditions (run length, initial conditions, etc.) under which the model is exercised to generate specific output data. A SIMAN simulation program comprises both a model and a corresponding experiment.

In this section we concentrate on developing the Model Frame. In describing SIMAN's Model Frame, we occasionally must refer to information that is separately defined in the Experiment Frame which is discussed later in this chapter.

2.2 Entities, Attributes, Processes

Discrete systems are normally modeled in SIMAN by using a *process orientation*. In a process orientation, we model a particular system by studying the *entities* that move through that system. Our model consists of a description of the processes through which the entities move as they progress through the system.

The word entity is a generic term used in SIMAN to denote any person, object, or thing — whether real or imaginary — whose movement through the system causes changes in the state of the system. Within a given system, there can be many types of entities, and each can have specific, unique characteristics. These characteristics are referred to in SIMAN as *attributes*. In a factory, for example, an entity may correspond to a workpiece and have attributes specifying the part number, due date, and priority of the workpiece. Some additional examples of entities and attributes are shown on the left.

System	Entity	Attributes
Computer	Programs	CPU time
		Priority
		I/O
Bank	Customers	Type
		Account
		Amount
Hospital	Patients	Ailment

In SIMAN, entities are dynamic; their entrance to and exit from the model correspond to their arrival and departure from the system. The number of entities in the model changes each time a new entity enters the model or an existing entity exits the model.

The term *process*, as used in SIMAN, denotes the sequence of operations or activities through which the entities move. Processes are static and are activated by entities. In a factory, for example, a process may consist of a drilling operation, followed by an inspection activity. The process remains dormant unless an entity, such as a workpiece, arrives to activate the process.

2.3 Block Diagrams

Processes are modeled in SIMAN by using a *block diagram*. A block diagram is a linear, top-down flow graph depicting the process through which the entities in the system move. The block diagram is constructed as a sequence of *blocks*, the shapes of which indicate their general function. The sequencing of blocks is shown by arrows, which represent the flow of entities from block to block.

A model is constructed by selecting standard blocks from the available set and combining them into a block diagram in such a way that the block diagram describes the process being modeled. The blocks are selected and arranged within the block diagram based on their functional operation and interaction. Learning to model with SIMAN requires that you master both the set of standard blocks contained within the language and the art of combining and arranging the blocks to model general processes.

You can construct a block diagram in either a graphical flow-chart form or in an equivalent statement form. Although SIMAN requires the statement form of the model for input to the Model Compiler, most users customarily proceed by first constructing the block diagram in graphical flow-chart form and then transcribing that block diagram into an equivalent statement form. Selecting and combining blocks to form the block diagram is the creative and difficult part of modeling; in constructing the block diagram, we conceptualize the process. Once the graphical block diagram has been developed, generating the equivalent statement form is straightforward and mechanical.

You can also interactively develop a block diagram in graphical flow-chart form on a graphics terminal. To accomplish this task, you use a special editor which enables automatic generation of the equivalent statement form of the model from the graphical flow chart. The editor can also read in a model in statement form. Once the model has been read into the editor, it can then be displayed, edited, or printed in graphical flow chart form.

2.4 Basic Block Types

During the initial design of the SIMAN system, over 40 distinct process modeling functions were identified for inclusion in the language. These functions could have been organized by employing a unique symbol for each; however, this approach was discarded because it would result in a large set of symbols that would be both difficult to remember and awkward to use. Instead, when possible, similar process modeling functions were grouped together to share a common symbol. This reduction resulted in the 10 *basic block types* shown in Figure 3-1.

The first three blocks shown in Figure 3-1 are multi-function blocks, i.e., each represents a group of similar yet distinct process-modeling functions. The first of these, the *Hold* block, is used to represent all modeling functions that detain an arriving entity outside of the block based on the current state of the system. For example, the Hold block can be used to model a workpiece waiting for a busy machine, a tote waiting to access a congested conveyor, or a finished part waiting for a robot to move it. The second multi-function block, the *Transfer* block, represents the movement of an entity from one location in the system to another. For example, the Transfer block can be used to model the movement of workpieces between workstations in a factory — whether by conveyor belt, hand truck, or overhead crane. The third multi-function block, the *Operation* block, represents a wide range of modeling functions in which an arriving entity always enters the

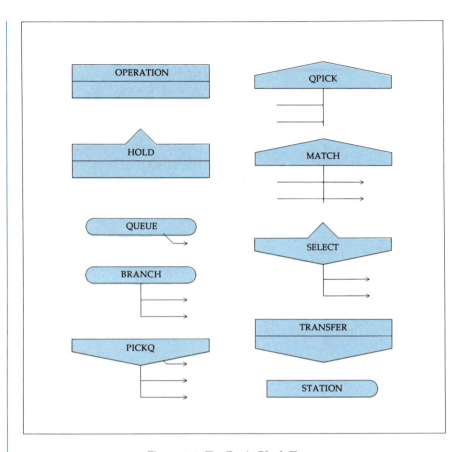

Figure 3-1. Ten Basic Block Types

block, performs some function, and then exits the block. Approximately one-half of the modeling functions in SIMAN are represented by the Operation block.

The remaining seven blocks shown in Figure 3-1 are single-function blocks. These blocks represent seven distinct modeling functions, which are unlike all other functions and therefore are each assigned a unique block symbol.

2.5 Block Function Names

As discussed in the previous section, the Hold, Transfer, and Operation blocks are multi-function blocks each of which represents a group of similar, yet distinct, modeling functions. The exact function represented by the block is established by specifying a *block function name* as an operand of the block. Each block function name corresponds to a specific modeling function in SIMAN and consists of a verb suggestive of the block's function. For example, the Operation block is used to represent a wide range of modeling functions: the creation of entities, the assignment of values to the attributes of entities, the delay of an entity by a specified time, etc. The function of creating entities is specified by the name CREATE, the function of assigning attributes is specified by the name ASSIGN, the function of delaying an entity is specified by the name DELAY, and so forth.

In this book we typically refer to a multi-function block by its function name rather than by its basic block type. For example, we typically refer to the Operation block with the ASSIGN function name as simply the ASSIGN block. In the case of single-function blocks, the block's function name is the same as its basic block type.

2.6 Block Operands

Each block models a general function within a process. You control the exact operation of the block by specifying its *operands*. For example, the DELAY block (described later in this chapter) is an Operation block that models the general function of delaying an entity by a specified amount of time. The duration of the delay is an operand of the block, which you enter as data for the block. A DELAY block with a value of 10.0 entered for the time-delay operand is shown on the left.

DELAY
10.0

The number of operands to be specified for each block, as well as the meaning of each operand, depends on the particular block. Some operands are optional and need to be specified only when you wish to override the pre-established default value for the operand; others are mandatory and have no default value.

The operands for each block are divided into one or more *line segments*. A line segment is a grouping of operands within a horizontal line of the block. The number of line segments differs from block to block. For example, the DELAY block shown earlier has two line segments: the top line segment has the name DELAY entered, and the bottom line segment has the value 10.0 entered to represent the duration of the delay.

When a line segment within a block has more than one operand, you enter the operands on the same line segment but separate them by commas. Optional operands can be defaulted by simply omitting them from the line; however, if you omit an interior operand, you must include its trailing comma to delineate the missing operand. Examples of line segments containing multiple operands are provided later in this chapter.

The valid options for entering a specific block operand vary from operand to operand. In some cases, you must use a symbolic name; in other cases you must use a numerical value. In the following sections we summarize the basic rules for specifying operands.

Constants

Two types of constants are defined within SIMAN. An *integer* constant is a signed whole number (without a decimal point). If unsigned, the number is assumed to be positive. A *real* constant is a real, rational number composed of an optional sign, an integer, a decimal point, and an optional fraction. Real numbers can also be entered with or without an exponent. An exponent follows the letter "E" and equals "times 10 to the exponent." If you omit the "E," the exponent defaults to 0 and has no effect. For example, the number 10 can be entered in any of the following ways: 10.0 or 1.e1 or 100.E-1.

Variables

In SIMAN, the term *variables* refers to the set of changeable values characterizing the components of the system as a whole. The term does not refer to the characteristics of individual entities that move through the system. There are two types of variables: *special-purpose variables*, which have a pre-defined meaning in SIMAN, and *general-purpose variables*, which are assigned meaning based on the process being modeled. There are no restrictions (other than system memory constraints) on the number of general-purpose variables that you can use in a model.

An example of a special-purpose variable is the SIMAN variable TNOW. SIMAN uses this variable to record the current real value of the simulated time, and automatically updates the value as entities move through the model.

General-purpose variables (that is, those variables with no pre-defined meaning in SIMAN) are numbered and can be assigned an optional name. You can interchangeably reference a variable by using either its number or its name. The nth variable can be referenced by using its number as V(n). For example, V(1) denotes the current value of Variable 1, V(2) denotes the value of Variable 2, etc. If the first variable was assigned the name ReorderPoint, this variable could be referenced interchangeably in the model as either V(1) or ReorderPoint.

The names that you assign to the general-purpose variables must follow a simple naming convention. Names can consist of letters, numbers, and the special characters underscore (_), pound (#), at sign (@), percent sign (%), and dollar sign ($). The name can also contain embedded blanks, but the underscore is commonly used in lieu of blanks. The name can start with any of the previous characters, but, if it starts with a number, it must contain at least one letter or special character other then the letter E. For example, #1, Data, and 1_ Job are all valid symbol names; 1E is invalid (because it represents a numerical value). There is no restriction on the number of characters in the name.

Names are case-insensitive — therefore, SIMAN considers "DATA," "Data," and "data" to be the same names. This insensitivity to case also applies to variables, names of blocks, and other keywords. For example, you can reference the first variable by v(1) as well as V(1), and you can enter the block named DELAY as Delay or delay.

It is often desirable to group two or more variables into an array of values referenced by a common name. The *array name* is an alphanumeric name given to the entire array of values. An *array element name* is an array name further qualified by a *subscript*. The subscript is appended to the array name within parentheses to address a specific element within the sequence of data values. For example, we could define an array named Rejects with three elements referenced as Rejects(1), Rejects(2), and Rejects(3). Each element of the array is also given a unique variable number, and you can interchangeably reference the elements of the array by the array element name or V(n), where n is the number assigned to the variable.

SIMAN permits you to define both one- and two-dimensional arrays. A one-dimensional array has a single subscript, which addresses elements in the array; a two-dimensional array has two subscripts separated by a comma. For example, Matrix(3,4) denotes the third-row, fourth-column entry in the two-dimensional array named Matrix. A subscript of an array can be an integer, a constant, or any valid expression, possibly involving other arrays. Because the value of a subscript must be an integer, SIMAN discards any fraction.

The variable's name and properties are defined in a VARIABLES element, which is included in the Experiment Frame. In the case of an array, the properties include upper- and lower-dimension bounds on each subscript. We describe the format for this element later in this chapter.

Attributes

As discussed earlier, entities have associated, characteristic attributes that are attached to, and move with, each entity. Some attributes have a pre-defined meaning within SIMAN; these are referred to as *special-purpose attributes*. (We discuss special-purpose attributes in later chapters). Other attributes have no pre-defined meaning; these are referred to as *general-purpose attributes*. You assign a meaning to general-purpose attributes based on the particular process being modeled; the meaning is never explicitly declared to SIMAN. General-purpose attributes can be used to record any general information related to the entity. For example, in a model of a factory in which entities represent workpieces, we can use general-purpose attributes to store the type of part and due date for the workpiece.

Each general-purpose attribute has a number and an optional user-defined name, which follows the same naming conventions as variables. You reference the attribute by using either its number or its name. The nth attribute can be referenced by using its number as A(n). Hence A(1) denotes an entity's first attribute and A(2) its second. If the first attribute was assigned the name DueDate, it could be referenced within the model as either A(1) or DueDate. Any names assigned to an attribute must be defined in the experiment by using the ATTRIBUTES element. We discuss the format for this element later in this chapter.

Attributes can also be grouped together under a-common array name, which follows the same naming conventions as variables. For example, we can have an attribute array named MarkTime with three elements named MarkTime(1), MarkTime(2), and MarkTime(3). Again, there is no limit to the number of general-purpose attributes you can use in the model; however, you usually need only a small number.

In many cases it is convenient to specify a block's operand as an attribute of an entity passing through the block. For example, in the DELAY block, we can specify the duration of the delay as the attribute ProcessTime. In this way, the delay for each arriving entity is not constant, but is given by the attribute ProcessTime, which is unique to, and carried with, each entity. Hence, by assigning different values to this attribute for each entity in the model, we can easily represent the situation wherein the duration of the delay differs from entity to entity.

Random Variables

Many of the processes that we model contain one or more random components. For example, in modeling a factory, the processing time for a workpiece may randomly vary according to some prescribed distribution. Consequently, we need a facility for specifying operands as *random variables*. In this way, the actual value used for the operand is randomly sampled from the specified probability distribution as each entity passes through the block. SIMAN contains a set of built-in functions for obtaining samples from the commonly used probability distributions. In this section we describe the syntax for specifying a random variable for use within a block's operand.

Each of the distributions included in SIMAN has one or more *parameter values* (mean, standard deviation, etc.) associated with it. You must specify these values to define the distribution completely. The number and meaning of the values depend on the distribution. For example, the exponential distribution has a single parameter value, which is the mean of the distribution. On the other hand, the uniform distribution has two parameter values corresponding to the minimum and maximum of the distribution. Appendix A contains a complete description of the included distributions and the associated parameter values.

Random variables can be specified by using two formats; you can select one format, or you can mix formats within the same model. The random variable's format is determined by the name used to specify the distribution. The primary format is selected by using either the variable's full name or a four-letter abbreviation shown in Figure 3-2. Our current discussion is restricted to using the primary format.

Distribution	Abbreviation	Parameters
Beta	BETA	$(Alpha_1, Alpha_2)$
Continuous	CONT	$(CumP_1, Val_1, CumP_2, Val_2, \ldots)$
Discrete	DISC	$(CumP_1, Val_1, CumP_2, Val_2, \ldots)$
Erlang	ERLA	$(ExpoMean, K)$
Exponential	EXPO	$(Mean)$
Gamma	GAMM	$(Beta, Alpha)$
Lognormal	LOGN	$(Mean, StdDev)$
Normal	NORM	$(Mean, StdDev)$
Poisson	POIS	$(Mean)$
Triangular	TRIA	$(Min, Mode, Max)$
Uniform	UNIF	(Min, Max)
Weibull	WEIB	$(Beta, Alpha)$

Figure 3-2. Random Variable Abbreviations and Parameters

In the primary format, you explicitly enter the parameters of the distribution as arguments of the random variable. Using this format, you specify random variables in SIMAN as D(PVL),

where

> *D* denotes either the random variable's full name or the four-letter abbreviation (from Figure 3-2) defining the probability distribution from which the random samples are to be generated; and

> *PVL* denotes a *Parameter Value List*, which contains the parameter values (separated by commas) associated with the distribution.

Examples of specifying an operand as a random variable are shown on the left. In the first example the Duration operand for the DELAY block is specified as a sample from the exponential distribution. In this case the distribution is specified by using the four-letter abbreviation from Figure 3-2. The mean for this distribution is 3. In the second example the operand is specified as a uniform distribution by using the full name instead of the abbreviation. The minimum and maximum values for the distribution are 10 and 20.

DELAY
EXPO(3)

DELAY
UNIFORM(10,20)

Expressions and Conditions

For most of SIMAN's numerical operands, you can specify an *expression* formed from one or more constants, attributes, variables, or random variables. Expressions can be formed by using the standard arithmetic operators for addition (+), subtraction (−), multiplication (∗), division (/), and exponentiation (∗∗), with parentheses used to indicate order of evaluation. SIMAN also provides built-in functions for a wide range of standard mathematical functions, such as sine, cosine, modulo, etc. (see Appendix C). In forming expressions, no two operators can appear in succession; for example, the expression DueDate/−4 is invalid and must be entered as DueDate/(−4).

Certain operands in SIMAN expect a *condition*. Conditions are formed by combining two expressions that use the relational operators shown in Figure 3-3. For example, TNOW < 40 denotes the condition that the current time TNOW is less than 40. Note that you can enter the same condition as TNOW .LT. 40, by using the FORTRAN-style relational operator. You can combine conditions by using the logical operators .AND. and .OR. to form complex logical statements. In this case, use parentheses to establish the order of evaluation.

Relation Operator	Primary Operator	Alternative
less-than	<	.LT.
greater-than	>	.GT.
equal	==	.EQ.
not-equal	<>	.NE.
greater-than-or-equal	>=	.GE.
less-than-or-equal	<=	.LE.

Figure 3-3. Relational Operators

Unlike some programming languages, such as FORTRAN, SIMAN does not implement conditions as a separate, logical variable. Rather, these conditions have numerical values just like expressions and can actually be used to specify numerical operands. Upon evaluation, conditions are assigned a numerical value of 1 or 0, respectively corresponding to true or false. Likewise, you can enter an expression for an operand that expects a condition. In this case a value of 0 is treated as false, and any non-zero value is treated as true.

Expressions and conditions are evaluated in SIMAN by using the following operator priorities.

1. Evaluation within parentheses (innermost first)
2. Arithmetic Operators
    i. exponentiation ($**$)
    ii. multiplication and division ($*,/$)
    iii. addition and subtraction ($+,-$)
3. Relational Operators
        .LT. , .GT. , .EQ. , .NE. , .GE. , .LE. or
        $<$, $>$, $==$, $<>$, $>=$, $<=$
4. Logical Operators
    i. .AND.
    ii. .OR.

Symbolic Names

In some cases you do not specify a block's operand as a numerical value, but instead enter it as a *symbolic name*. Symbolic names refer to various types of objects (conveyors, resources, queues, etc.) within the model. Each such object is identified by either its symbolic name or its corresponding number. For example, when modeling queues (i.e., waiting lines) in SIMAN, we may assign each queue a symbolic name (e.g., Buffer) and then use this name as a block's operand to reference the queue. The queues within the model are also numbered, and the queue number can be used to reference this same queue.

A symbolic name follows the same conventions as names for variables and attributes, i.e., names can consist of letters, numbers, and the special characters underscore (_), pound (#), at sign (@), percent sign (%), and dollar sign ($). The name can contain embedded blanks, but the underscore symbol is commonly used in lieu of blanks. The name can start with any approved character, but, if it starts with a number, it must contain at least one letter or special character other then the letter E. SIMAN imposes no limit on the length of a symbolic name, and symbolic names are case-insensitive. All symbolic names must be unique, even though they refer to different types of objects. For example, if we assign the name Belt to a conveyor, we cannot assign this same name to another type of object within the model.

Although symbolic names reference objects within the model, they can also be used within expressions. A symbolic name within an expression is replaced by its corresponding object number. For example, if the third conveyor is named Belt, then the symbol Belt is replaced by SIMAN with the number 3 within an expression.

2.7 Block Sequence Numbers

SIMAN automatically assigns each block a *block sequence number*. In flow-chart form, the block sequence numbers appear adjacent to the blocks on the far left side of the diagram. The numbers also appear on the far left side of model listings generated by the SIMAN Model Compiler. You do not enter these numbers yourself; they are automatically added by SIMAN. The first block is numbered 1, and each successive block number is increased by 1 (i.e., they are numbered 2, 3, 4, etc.)

The sequence numbers provide a mechanism for referencing blocks within the model. They facilitate referencing portions of a model for documentation purposes and are also used by the Interactive Debugger (which is discussed in Chapter 4).

2.8 Block Labels

Each block in a SIMAN model can be assigned an optional *block label*. Typically, you only assign a block label when the block must be referenced by one or more other blocks in the model. When used, a block label is appended to the left side of the block. An Operation block with the label Drill appended is shown on the left.

Block labels must follow the same naming conventions as variables, attributes, and symbolic names. Labels can be of arbitrary length and are case-insensitive.

2.9 Block Comments

A special field on each SIMAN block allows you to include one or more *block comments* to describe the block's function within the model. Although using the comment field is optional, we highly recommend your doing so. The comments document the model without affecting the actual functioning of the block. The comment is located to the right of each block symbol.

2.10 Block Modifiers

SIMAN includes a set of special pre-defined symbols that can be appended to the standard block symbol to modify or extend the block's basic function. These spe-

Drill

cial ancillary symbols are call *block modifiers* and, depending on the type of modifier, are appended to either the right or bottom side of the block. We introduce several block modifiers throughout our description of SIMAN. In the next section we describe two specific block modifiers that control the flow of entities between blocks in the model.

2.11 Entity Flow Between Blocks

The block diagram represents the static component of the model. The dynamic component is represented by the entities that move from block to block through the block diagram, thereby activating the function associated with each block.

The entity flow between blocks is controlled by the *sequential flow connector* and the NEXT and DISPOSE block modifiers, which are appended to the bottom (exit) side of the blocks. These symbols are shown attached to an Operation block in Figure 3-4. The first symbol, the sequential flow connector, directs all departing entities to the next block in sequence. The second symbol, the NEXT modifier, causes all departing entities to be redirected to the block specified by the operand Label. The third symbol, the DISPOSE modifier, causes all entities departing the block to depart the model.

Figure 3-5 shows a block diagram illustrating the use of both the sequential flow connector and the NEXT and DISPOSE modifiers to control the flow of entities between the blocks. The operands which would normally be shown on the block diagram have deliberately been omitted to focus attention on the pattern of entity flow.

Notice that this block diagram actually comprises two separate *model segments*. The first model segment starts at Block 1 and terminates at Block 3 with the DISPOSE modifier. An entity entering the model at Block 1 would sequentially proceed from block to block until it departed the model upon exiting at Block 3. The second model segment begins at Block 4 and ends at Block 6. An entity entering the model at Block 4 would proceed from block to block through Block 6. Upon exiting Block 6, the entity would be redirected by the NEXT modifier back up to the block labeled Loop, which would return it back to Block 4. Thus, an entity entering the second segment of the model would indefinitely loop through the segment.

In this particular example, the blocks at sequence numbers 1 and 4 represent *source* points where entities enter the model. The block at sequence number 3 represents a *sink* point where entities depart the model.

Many of our models will make use of separate model segments like those shown here. For example, we may use one model segment to represent the processing of workpieces at a machine, and a second model segment to represent the breakdown and repair process for the machine. There is no restriction on the number of separate model segments included in a model. During execution of the simulation, entities can simultaneously move through several of the model's segments.

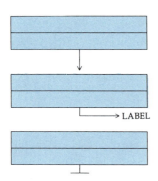

Figure 3-4. Entity Flow Options

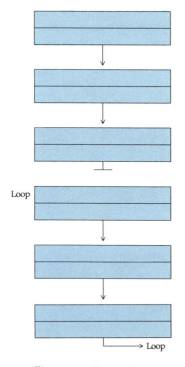

Figure 3-5. Entity Flow Example

Consider the simple workstation depicted in Figure 3-6. It consists of workpieces that enter the system, wait their turn to be processed on a single machine, and then depart the system. The workpieces enter the system one at a time with an exponentially distributed random time between arrivals with a mean of 4.4 minutes. The combined setup and machining time for each workpiece on the machine is a random variable having a triangular distribution with a minimum of 3.2 minutes, a mode of 4.2 minutes, and a maximum of 5.2 minutes.

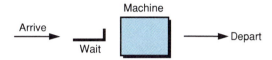

Figure 3-6. Schematic for Sample Problem 3.1

The system operates on a single, eight-hour shift during weekdays and shuts down over the weekend. No arrivals occur during the off-shift or weekend hours. Any work in progress at the end of one day is carried forward to the next day and continued without interruption. However no work is carried forward from one week to the next.

In analyzing the performance of this system, there are a number of measures that may be of interest. The following list identifies some of the possible measures.

■ Average weekly production rate, in terms of the number of completed workpieces per week.

■ Percentage of time the machine is busy, a measurement of the machine's utilization.

■ Average time that a workpiece spends in the system.

■ Maximum time that a workpiece spends waiting to begin being processed.

■ Average number of workpieces waiting to begin being processed.

We are initially interested in obtaining results for only the first measure (the system's average weekly production rate).

We will begin modeling this problem by developing a description for the system's process. Our first task in developing this description is to define the system's entities. Recall that entities are the "things" that move through the system and activate the processes. In this example, the entities are the workpieces; they move through the system and cause its state to change.

Once we have defined the system's entities, our next task is to describe the process through which the entities move. In this system, we can use the following steps to describe the process.

1. Enter the system.

2. Wait in line for the machine to become idle.

3. Take possession of the machine.

4. Keep the machine for the time required to set up and machine the workpiece.

5. Release the machine for the next waiting entity, if any.

6. Increase the count of completed workpieces and depart the system.

Note that the movement of workpieces through the system corresponds to the movement of entities from step to step in this process description. Our next task is to represent the process by a block diagram.

4. An Initial Subset of Blocks

In this section we present an initial subset of SIMAN blocks. These blocks are sufficient to represent the process description that we developed in the previous section.

4.1 Entering Entities into the Model: The CREATE Block

The CREATE block, one of several mechanisms for entering entities into the model, is typically used to model arrival processes in which entities sequentially enter the model according to a specified pattern. Because the CREATE block serves as an entity source point, model segments frequently begin with a CREATE block. There are no restrictions on the number or location of CREATE blocks within the model.

To control the arrival of entities at a CREATE block, you specify any of four operands. The first operand, BatchSize, specifies the number of entities to enter the block at each point in the arrival sequence. BatchSize defaults to one, so, if not specified, only one entity will enter the model through the block at each point of arrival. The second operand, Offset, specifies an offset time between the start of the simulation and arrival at the first point in the sequence. This operand defaults to 0; if not specified, the point of the first arrival will coincide with the beginning of the simulation. The third operand, Interval, specifies the delay between arrival at successive points after the first. If this operand is not specified, it defaults to infinity, which means that the second arrival never occurs. The last operand, MaxBatches, specifies the maximum number of arrival points. When the specified number is reached, no additional entities can enter the model through the block. By default, the value of this operand is infinity.

The time units used to specify the Offset and Interval operands are not predefined. You can use minutes, hours, days, or any other convenient unit. The only restriction is that you consistently use the same unit throughout your model.

The CREATE block is an Operation block containing two line segments. The top line segment contains the block's function name, CREATE, followed by the BatchSize and Offset operands. The bottom line segment contains the Interval and MaxBatches operands. The CREATE block, with its operands, is shown below.

CREATE,BatchSize,Offset:Interval,MaxBatches;

CREATE,BatchSize,Offset
Interval,MaxBatches

```
┌─────────────────────────┐
│        CREATE           │
├─────────────────────────┤
│   EXPONENTIAL(30)       │
└─────────────────────────┘
```

The CREATE block modeling the arrival process in our example is shown on the left. Note that we have defaulted the batch size to 1, the offset time to the first arrival point to 0, and the creation limit to infinity. The time between arrivals is specified as a sample from an exponential distribution having a mean of 30, with a pattern of arrivals consisting of an infinite sequence of arrivals, one entity at a time. The first entity enters the block at the beginning of the simulation. At the time of the first arrival, the second arrival is scheduled to occur at the current simulated time, TNOW, plus a sample from an exponential distribution. When the second arrival occurs, the third arrival is scheduled based on the second arrival, and so forth. In this way, only one future arrival is scheduled for each CREATE block in the model, but an entire sequence of arrivals is generated.

```
┌─────────────────────────┐
│  CREATE,EXPONENTIAL(30) │
├─────────────────────────┤
│   EXPONENTIAL(30)       │
└─────────────────────────┘
```

Two additional examples of the CREATE block are shown on the left. The first block shown generates exactly the same sequence of arrivals as the CREATE block example shown above, except that the time of the first entity arrival has been offset by a sample from the exponential distribution. The second CREATE block shown here creates a single entity, which enters the model at the beginning of the simulation.

```
┌─────────────────────────┐
│        CREATE           │
├─────────────────────────┤
│                         │
└─────────────────────────┘
```

4.2 Providing Waiting Space for Entities: The QUEUE Block

The primary purpose of the QUEUE block is to provide waiting space for entities whose movement through the model has been suspended based on the system's status. This type of delay is referred to in SIMAN as a *status delay*. An example of a status delay is a workpiece waiting its turn to be processed on a busy machine. Note that status delays are typically caused by a limited availability of resources such as machines, people, or raw materials.

The processes that can cause status delays, thereby creating the potential for a queue of waiting entities, are modeled in SIMAN by using the basic block type called the Hold block. Hence a QUEUE block, which models the waiting space, is used in conjunction with a Hold block, which models the status delay. In fact, whenever a Hold block is employed, it *must* be preceded by a QUEUE block — even if no entities are actually delayed at the Hold block. A QUEUE-Hold block combination (with the operands omitted) is shown on the left.

When one or more entities are being held in a QUEUE block, the relative position of each entity within the queue is referred to as the entity's *queue rank*. An entity with a queue rank of 1 is the first entity in the queue. By default, the entity's queue rank is established by using a first-in-first-out discipline. As we will see later in this chapter, you can easily redefine this ranking in the Experiment Frame with the QUEUES element.

The QUEUE block is one of the seven single-function blocks included in SIMAN. The symbol for the QUEUE block, along with its operands, is shown below. The operands include QueueID, Capacity, and BalkLabel.

QUEUE,QueueID,Capacity,BalkLabel;

```
 ⌜⎺⎺⎺⎺⎺⎺⎺⎺⎺⎺⎺⎺⎺⎺⎺⎺⎺⎺⎺⌝
( QUEUE,QueueID,Capacity )
 ⌞_____⌟
            └──→ BalkLabel
```

Each queue in SIMAN is assigned an integer number and an optional, user-defined symbolic name. The QueueID can be interchangeably specified by using either its number or its symbolic name. Numbers are typically assigned consecutively beginning with 1 and increasing by 1 until all the queue blocks have been totalled and numbered. The same QueueID (name or number) may not be assigned to two different QUEUE blocks within the same model. The QueueID has no default value and therefore is a required operand for the block.

The second operand, named Capacity, specifies a limit on the number of entities that can simultaneously reside in the QUEUE block. The default value for the capacity is infinity; this operand can therefore be omitted if no limit is desired on the length of the queue. If a finite capacity is specified, then entities will be denied entrance if they attempt to enter the QUEUE block when the queue is full.

If entrance is denied, then the arriving entity can be redirected to an alternative block specified by the BalkLabel. The BalkLabel need only be specified for queues with a finite capacity and can reference any labeled block within the model. If no BalkLabel is specified, then an entity arriving at a full QUEUE block is destroyed (i.e., the entity departs the model at that point and never re-enters). Note that entity destruction is considered to be a valid operation for the block; you will not, therefore, receive any message warning that the entity was destroyed.

SIMAN provides a special-purpose variable to provide information about the current number of entities residing in a QUEUE block. The variable NQ(QueueID) represents the current length for the queue with identifier QueueID. Specify the QueueID by using either the queue's number or corresponding symbolic name. For example, NQ(1) equal to 3 denotes that there are currently three entities waiting in Queue 1, and NQ(Buffer) equal to 5 denotes that there are currently five entities residing in the queue named Buffer. You do not have the responsibility for updating each NQ variable; SIMAN automatically updates the value whenever an entity enters or departs a QUEUE block.

Some examples of QUEUE blocks are shown on the left. The first QUEUE block, QueueID 1, has an infinite capacity. The second QUEUE block, Buffer, has a capacity specified by the general-purpose variable Length. In this case the current value of Length determines the queue's maximum length, which can be changed during the simulation. Since BalkLabel is not specified for this block, any entities arriving when queue length equals or exceeds the value of Length will be destroyed.

The third QUEUE block, named Line, has a capacity of 5, and a specified balk label, Retry. In this example, an entity arriving when the queue is at capacity will not be destroyed, instead being redirected to the block labeled Retry. The last example, the queue named NoSpace, has a specified capacity of 0. In this example, no arriving entities are permitted to wait in the QUEUE block. Therefore, all arriving entities, except those which do not encounter a delay at the following Hold block, will be redirected to the block labeled Out.

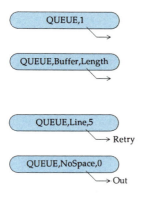

4.3 Allocating Resources to Entities: The SEIZE Block

Although the QUEUE-Hold block combination discussed in the previous section can be used to model several different types of status delays, the one of immediate interest for our example is a delay related to the allocation of resources. The generic term *resources* defines one or more identical "objects," called *resource units*, which can be allocated to an entity. The number of identical resource units corresponding to a specific resource is called the *resource capacity*.

Each individual resource unit has a status: busy or idle. When an entity seizes an idle resource unit, its status automatically changes to busy, thereby making the unit temporarily unavailable for allocation to other entities. Once an entity is finished with a resource unit, it can release the resource unit, returning its status to idle and making it available for allocation to other entities.

In our example, we will model the machine as a resource with a capacity of 1. Whenever the resource unit is seized, its status changes to busy, and arriving entities can form in a queue while waiting for the resource unit to become idle. Once the seizing entity releases the resource unit, SIMAN automatically attempts to re-allocate the now idle resource unit to the first waiting entity, if any. If no entity is currently awaiting a resource unit, then the unit remains in an idle state until a new entity arrives to seize it.

Resources in SIMAN are both named and numbered. The *resource name*, which can be any valid symbolic name, is used for specifying the resource on blocks that seize and release resource units. In our example, we will use the resource name Machine to represent the machine. The resources are also numbered consecutively beginning with 1. The number can be used in place of the name as an index for special-purpose variables that provide current status information on the resource. For example, the variable NR(ResourceID) denotes the current number of busy resource units for resource identifier ResourceID, which can be either the resource's number or symbolic name. Likewise, the variable MR(ResourceID) denotes the number of resource units (idle or busy) in the model. In our example, we will have only one resource, which we will name Machine. It will be Resource 1. SIMAN will automatically change the value of NR(1), or alternatively NR(Machine), from 0 (idle) to 1 (busy), corresponding to changes in the state of the machine. The variable MR(1), or alternatively MR(Machine), will remain at a value of 1.

The number, name, and capacity of each of the model's resources must be defined in the Experiment Frame by using the RESOURCES element, which we describe in detail later in this chapter. Note that you can change the capacity without affecting the block diagram because the capacity is defined in the experiment, rather than in the model.

You can allocate a resource unit to an entity at a SEIZE block. The SEIZE block is a Hold block and therefore must be preceded by a QUEUE block. The SEIZE block and its operands are shown below. The first line segment in the block contains the

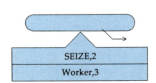

block's function name, SEIZE, followed by its priority, Pr. The second line segment contains the resource name, ResName, followed by the number of units required, Qty.

SEIZE,Pr: ResName,Qty;
    repeats ;

The priority appearing in the first line segment of the block is an integer that establishes a priority for the allocation of entities awaiting the same resource. In this case SIMAN examines the QUEUE-SEIZE blocks for allocation of newly released resource units, based on priority, by using a rule of *low-value-first* (LVF). Any ties are broken in favor of QUEUE-SEIZE blocks at the top of the block diagram. In our example we will have only a single QUEUE-SEIZE block combination for allocating the machine; hence, the priority will play no role.

The resource's name defines which resource is being requested by the entity, and Qty specifies how many units are to be allocated to the entity. If you do not specify Qty, then a default value of 1 is used. In our problem the resource's name is Machine and the required quantity is 1.

When the required quantity exceeds 1, the entity waits until all required resource units are available before seizing any of them. Resource units can only be allocated to the first waiting entity in the QUEUE block. For example, if the first entity in the queue is waiting for two units of Machine and the second entity in the queue is waiting for one unit of Machine, the second entity must wait until the first entity receives both units of Machine and departs the QUEUE block. Only then is the second entity eligible to seize its unit of Machine.

To allocate units of several different resources at the same SEIZE block, simply repeat the second line of operands for each additional type of resource to be allocated. Precede each repetition by a colon to terminate the line segment. There is no limit to the number of different resources that can be included on the same SEIZE block.

Some examples of the SEIZE block are shown on the left. The associated QUEUE block, which must be used in conjunction with the SEIZE block, is shown without operands. The first example models the resource allocation process for our problem. Entities arriving at this QUEUE-SEIZE block combination wait their turn in the QUEUE block to be allocated one unit (the default) of the resource named Machine. If at least one unit of Machine is idle at the time an entity arrives at the preceding QUEUE block, then the number of busy units of Machine is increased by one, and the entity passes through the SEIZE block without waiting in the preceding QUEUE block. On the other hand, if all the units of Machine are busy, the entity is held in the preceding QUEUE block until a unit of Machine becomes available for allocation to the entity.

In the second example arriving entities wait in the preceding QUEUE block to seize three units of the resource named Worker. No units are allocated to the entity until all three units are available. The priority for seizure is 2. Available units are

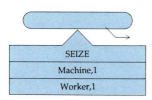

SEIZE
Machine,1
Worker,1

only allocated at this block if they cannot be allocated to the first entity in a Priority 1 block elsewhere in the model.

In the last example arriving entities wait in the preceding QUEUE block to simultaneously seize one unit each of both Machine and Worker. Neither resource is allocated to the entity until both are available.

4.4 Representing Time Delays: The DELAY Block

Once an entity has been allocated the necessary resources, it typically engages in time-consuming activities, such as setup, machining, inspection, etc. In SIMAN, delays such as these can be modeled by using the DELAY block. The DELAY block, an Operation block, is shown below with its operands.

DELAY
Duration,StorID

DELAY: Duration,StorID;

The top line segment contains the block's function name, DELAY, and the second line segment contains the operands Duration and StorID. Duration specifies the amount of simulated time each entity requires to pass through the DELAY block. If an entity arrives at the DELAY block at time T, it will exit the block at time T + Duration.

There is no limit to the number of entities that can simultaneously be delayed. At any given time there can be several different entities passing through the block, each at a different point in its delay within the block. Note that, depending on the delay for each entity, the order in which the entities enter the block need not be the same as the order in which the entities depart the block.

The last operand of the DELAY block is the storage facility (denoted StorID). This optional operand serves two purposes. First, it provides a mechanism for collecting statistics on the number of entities residing in one or more DELAY blocks. The storage facility references an area in which the entities reside during the delay. Each storage facility has an identifier, which can be either a number or a symbolic name. If a storage facility's identifier is specified on a DELAY block, SIMAN automatically increases the variable NSTO(StorID) whenever an entity enters the DELAY block, and decreases this same variable whenever an entity exits the block. If the same storage facility is specified on two or more DELAY blocks, then the value of NSTO(StorID) will equal the current number of entities in all the DELAY blocks that have been assigned to this storage facility.

The storage facility's second purpose is to serve as an interface to the Cinema Animation System by providing a mechanism for animating entities currently passing through a DELAY block. This use of the storage facility in Cinema is discussed in Chapter 7.

DELAY
SetUp + Process

DELAY
10,2

Two specific examples of the DELAY block are shown on the left. In the first example arriving entities are delayed by the sum of the attributes named Setup and Process. The entities passing through this block are not assigned to a storage facility. In the second example arriving entities are delayed by a constant 10 units of time. The delayed entities reside in Storage Facility 2 during the time that they are in the block.

4.5 Releasing Resources: The RELEASE Block

When an activity that requires resources has been completed, the entity possessing the resources typically releases them so that they can be allocated to entities either currently waiting or yet to arrive at QUEUE-SEIZE blocks. In our problem, once a workpiece has been processed, the entity can release Machine so that this resource can be allocated to the next workpiece. The RELEASE block provides the mechanism for this release.

The RELEASE block, an Operation block, is shown with its operands below.

```
RELEASE: ResName, Qty:
          repeats ;
```

The first line segment contains the block's function name, RELEASE. The second line segment contains two operands: the name of the resource to be released, ResName, and the quantity to release, Qty. The default value for Qty is 1. To simultaneously release resource units for several different types of resources at a single RELEASE block, simply repeat this pair of operands, separating each pair with a colon, as you would with the SEIZE block.

When an entity arrives at a RELEASE block, the specified number of units for each resource changes from busy to idle. SIMAN then automatically attempts to allocate the idle units to any entities currently awaiting them at QUEUE-SEIZE blocks. The order in which SIMAN examines these blocks is established by the priority specified on the SEIZE blocks. After all the appropriate SEIZE blocks have been examined for possible allocation of idle resource units, the entity at the RELEASE block then departs the block and continues through the block diagram.

If desired, allocated resource units can be released in stages. For example, an entity that has been allocated three units of the resource named Worker, could release one unit of Worker at the end of one activity, keeping the remaining two units of Worker for a subsequent activity. There are no restrictions on the number or order of resources to be seized and released, other than the requirement that the number of units to be released not exceed the current number of busy units.

In most modeling applications, the same entity seizes a resource and then releases it. Typically, the entity seizes one or more resources, is delayed for some amount of time, and then releases the resources; however, this need not always be the case. In some instances we want to release a resource from an entity that did not originally seize the resource. Although seldom used, this operation is completely valid in SIMAN. In fact, within SIMAN, units for a given resource are treated as identical and interchangeable. SIMAN does not keep a complete record of which entities have been allocated individual units of a resource; it does, however, maintain information about the number of busy and idle units of the resource.

Specific examples of the RELEASE block are shown on the left. In the first example each arriving entity releases one unit of the resource named Machine. In the second example each arriving entity releases two units of the resource Nurse and one unit of the resource Doctor.

4.6 Counting Events: The COUNT Block

In many simulation models it is necessary to count the number of occurrences of some event, e.g., workpieces entering the system, workpieces exiting the system, workpieces sent through rework, etc. In some cases we may also wish to use this count to control the length of the run. We achieve this control by terminating the simulation run when the count reaches some prescribed value. The COUNT block is provided for this purpose.

Each counting operation in SIMAN uses a *counter*, which has an associated value that can be increased or decreased when an entity passes through the COUNT block. Each counter is referenced by CounterID, which can consist of either a number or a symbolic name. A given counter can be referenced by one or more COUNT blocks. Each counter also has an associated limit; if the current value of any counter ever reaches or exceeds the limit, the simulation run is automatically terminated by SIMAN. The counters' numbers, names, and associated limits are externally defined in the COUNTERS element of the experiment (as opposed to being defined in the model). We describe the format for this element later in this chapter.

The COUNT block, an Operation block, is shown with its operands below.

COUNT: CounterID,Increment;

The function name COUNT is entered in the top line segment, and the CounterID and Increment operands are entered in the bottom line segment. If you do not specify a value for Increment, then a default value of 1 is assumed. At each arrival at the COUNT block, the increment is added to the current value for the specified identifier. Because the increment can be positive or negative, the value either increases or decreases as the result of this operation. The new value is then tested against the counter's limit. If the value is greater-than-or-equal-to the limit, the simulation run is terminated; otherwise, the entity exits the COUNT block and continues through the block diagram.

The SIMAN variable NC(CounterID) provides the current value for the Counter specified by CounterID. You may enter the CounterID interchangeably as either the counter's name or number. For example, NC(JobsDone) denotes the current value for the counter named JobsDone, and NC(7) denotes the current value for counter 7.

Some specific examples of the COUNT block are shown on the left. In the first example, each arriving entity causes JobsDone to be increased by 1 and tested against the counter's limit. In the second example, Counter 7 is increased by the attribute NumBatch.

4.7 Constructing the Block Diagram Model

We are now ready to combine constructs from our small subset of SIMAN blocks to model our simple example. The block diagram, shown in Figure 3-7, is patterned

| COUNT |
| CounterID,Increment |

| COUNT |
| JobsDone |

| COUNT |
| 7,NumBatch |

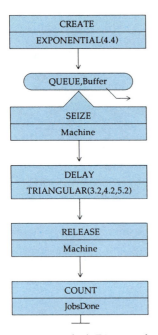

CREATE

EXPONENTIAL(4.4)

QUEUE,Buffer

SEIZE

Machine

DELAY

TRIANGULAR(3.2,4.2,5.2)

RELEASE

Machine

COUNT

JobsDone

Figure 3-7. Block Diagram for Sample Problem 3-1

directly after the description of the process developed earlier. Recall that each individual entity in this case represents a workpiece.

We will describe this model by tracing the movement of an individual entity through the block diagram. An entity enters the model at the CREATE block, where the time between the arrival of successive entities is a random sample from an exponential distribution with a mean time between arrivals of 4.4. After entering the model at the CREATE block, an entity proceeds to the QUEUE-SEIZE block combination, where it attempts to seize one unit of Machine. If there is no idle unit of Machine at that time, the entity is held at the QUEUE block in the queue named Buffer, where it waits its turn until a unit of Machine becomes available. Otherwise, the entity is not held in the QUEUE block, but instead immediately seizes an idle unit of Machine and exits the block. In either case, after seizing a unit of Machine, the entity continues to the DELAY block, where it requires time to traverse the block. The delay, which equals the sum of the setup and processing times, is a sample from a triangular distribution with a minimum value of 3.2, a mode of 4.2, and a maximum of 5.2. At the end of this delay, the entity exits the block and continues to the RELEASE block, where it releases one unit of the resource Machine. At this point, SIMAN automatically looks back at the QUEUE-SEIZE block combination and attempts to allocate idle units of Machine. If there are one or more entities waiting in the QUEUE block at that time, a unit of Machine is allocated to the first waiting entity in the queue Buffer, which then exits the SEIZE block and continues on its way through the block diagram. Otherwise, the unit of Machine remains idle until the next arrival at the QUEUE-SEIZE block combination. After attempting to re-allocate the unit of Machine, SIMAN causes the entity to exit the RELEASE block. The entity then passes through the COUNT block, where the counter JobsDone is increased by 1. After exiting the COUNT block, the entity departs the model as the result of the DISPOSE modifier, which is attached to the output side of the block.

This simple block diagram contains a very basic block sequence comprising the QUEUE — SEIZE — DELAY — RELEASE blocks, which we will repeatedly use throughout many of our models. This block sequence, with minor variations, provides the basis for modeling a wide range of systems in which entities wait their turn to use limited resources.

5. Translation of the Block Diagram into Statement Form

As discussed earlier, a block diagram can be defined in graphical or statement form; however, SIMAN requires the statement form for input to the Model Compiler. If you use the BLOCKS editor, the statement form of the model is automatically generated for you. On the other hand, if you develop the graphical block diagram manually, then you must also manually translate the block symbols into their equivalent statement form.

There is a one-to-one correspondence between block symbols and statements in SIMAN, i.e., for each block symbol in the block diagram there is a corresponding statement that contains exactly the same information. Each block statement is entered into a file in exactly the same order as the block symbols occur in the graphical block diagram. This file of ordered block statements is called the model's source file.

In addition to the individual block statements, the model's source file also contains a BEGIN statement and an END statement. The BEGIN statement, which is mandatory, must always be the first statement in the file. The format for the BEGIN statement is shown below.

BEGIN,Listing;

The operand, Listing, is a YES/NO operand which controls the generation of the model listing during the model processing. If Listing is specified as YES (the default), then the model statements are echoed to the screen as they are processed. If Listing is specified as NO, then the model listing is not generated. The model compiles much faster when Listing is set to NO. We will normally default the Listing operand to YES. In this case the BEGIN statement consists simply of the name BEGIN followed by a semi-colon (;) anywhere on the first input line.

The ordered sequence of block statements follows immediately after the BEGIN statement. The last block statement is followed immediately by the END statement, which is the last statement in the model's source file. The END statement has no operands and consists of the word END followed by a semi-colon (;) entered anywhere on the last input line.

5.1 The Block Statement Format

Each block statement in the model's source file is generated by entering the data from the block symbol into a data statement. If the statement form of the model was not automatically generated by the graphical block editor, you must translate the block symbols into statements. You can enter the statements in a free format, which allows a block statement to be spaced across one or more input lines with blanks freely used to improve the statement's readability. Although a given block statement can be spaced across any number of input lines, each individual input line is limited to 74 characters. To terminate an input line, use the standard line-feed and carriage-return character; the latter is typically generated by pressing the [Return] or [Enter] key.

If using a block label, you enter it as the first field of the block statement. The label can begin in any column of the statement but must be followed by at least one blank character. The next field to enter is the function name. If a block label is specified, the name of the function will be the second field in the statement; otherwise, it will be the first field. Start this field in any column, as long as it follows any block label. The function name is followed by any other operands that occur in the first line segment of the block. Use commas to separate these operands from each other and from the function name. Again, the specific columns in which this information is entered is insignificant; only the relative positions are important.

To delineate the end of the first line segment in the block symbol, enter a colon (:), which is called the *segment terminator*. Follow this colon with operands for the second line segment of the block symbol, again separated by commas. Likewise, delineate the end of each additional line segment, if any, by a colon, and follow the colon with the operands for the next line. An example statement translation for a CREATE block is shown on the left.

```
CREATE:EXPO(30),100;
```

CREATE
EXPO(30),100

Enter any block modifiers following the colon terminating the last line segment in the block. If more than one modifier is attached to a block, separate the modifiers with commas. The two modifiers that we have discussed so far are the DISPOSE modifier and the non-sequential flow modifier. Enter the DISPOSE modifier by specifying the keyword DISPOSE; enter the non-sequential flow modifier by specifying the keyword NEXT followed by the destination block's label in parentheses (( )).

Terminate block statements with a semi-colon (;), which is called the *statement terminator*, and follow the semi-colon with an optional block comment. If one or more modifiers are attached to a block, enter the semi-colon following the last modifier. Otherwise, enter the semi-colon in place of the colon following the operands for the last line segment specified in the block. The semi-colon causes all remaining operands to be assigned their default value.

You can continue a block statement over as many lines as necessary by simply continuing the statement onto the next line. The only restriction is that a numerical value, symbolic name, or operator cannot be split between two lines. The block statement is not terminated until the semi-colon is encountered. The remainder of that input line is assumed to be a comment, and the first field of the next block statement is assumed to start on the next input line.

SIMAN provides a special delimiter that allows embedded comments, called *in-line comments*, within the middle of a statement. To include comments within the block statement, enter an exclamation point (!) in the input line. SIMAN processes this special character as an artificial end-of-line delimiter and considers the remainder of the line to be a comment. When the exclamation point is encountered, the block statement is not terminated; it is merely continued on the next input line.

5.2 The Sample Model's Source File
The source file for our model is shown in Figure 3-8. Note that, although we entered the BEGIN and END statements beginning in the first column, we arbitrarily elected to indent the function names for each block statement. Although no block labels were used in this model, indenting of the function names is typically used to make the block labels more readable.

```
BEGIN;
    CREATE:     EXPONENTIAL(4.4);          Enter the system
    QUEUE,      Buffer;                    Wait for the machine
    SEIZE:      Machine;                   Seize the machine
    DELAY:      TRIANGULAR(3.2,4.2,5.2);   Delay by the
    RELEASE:    Machine;                   Release the machine
    COUNT:      JobsDone:DISPOSE;          Count completed jobs
END;
```

Figure 3-8. Model Source File for Sample Problem 3.1

6. An Initial Subset of Experiment Elements

As discussed earlier, a SIMAN simulation program comprises both a model and an experiment. The block diagram that we developed for our problem represents only the model portion of the program. We have yet to specify the experimental conditions, such as the length of the simulation run, the number of replications of the simulation, the characteristics of resources and queues, etc. As noted earlier, we develop the experiment by using special data records called elements.

The elements comprised in an experiment can be specified in either statement form or tabular form. The statement form, which can be entered by using any standard text editor, is required for input to the Experiment Compiler. The tabular form of input requires the use of a special editor. This editor plays the same role for the experiment as the graphical blocks editor does for the model: it allows you to create the experiment interactively by simply entering the information into forms. The elements editor automatically checks experiments for errors and consistency. If you use the elements editor to enter your experiment, the statement form of the experiment can be generated automatically by the editor.

In this section we focus on the statement form of the experiment. The rules for formatting element statements closely follow those for formatting model statements. The free format allows you to space an element statement across one or more 74-character input lines, with blanks freely used to enhance readability. Begin each element statement with the element's name, followed by one or more operands. Each element can consist of multiple line segments. Separate operands within a line segment with commas (,); separate entire line segments with colons (:). Finally, use a semicolon (;) to terminate the element statement, after which you can add an optional comment. Use the exclamation point (!) to include in-line comments within an element statement. As in the case of model statements, the specific interpretation of each input field is established by its relative position within the statement and not by the specific column or input line in which it is entered.

Experiment elements that consist of multiple line segments have repeating groups of operands, with each group falling within a single line segment. Therefore, you must separate repeating groups of operands with a colon (:). Each repeating group is also assigned an integer as the first operand of the line segment. This number can have a specific meaning or can simply number the repeating groups within the element. In either case, consecutively number the groups of operands, beginning with the number 1.

To allow the Experiment Processor to number the repeating groups of operands automatically during compilation, omit the number and its trailing comma (,) from the operand group. As you will see when you gain experience in using SIMAN, this feature is very useful when line segments are added or deleted from the middle of an element, because you avoid manual renumbering of repeating operand groups. We typically make use of this feature in our examples.

An element's operands can be either required or optional. In the case of optional operands, you can use a pre-established default value by omitting an entry from the operand field.

In the following sections we present an initial subset of elements sufficient for defining the experiment in our small problem. In this and later chapters, we gradually expand this set.

6.1 Describing the Simulation Project: The PROJECT Element

The PROJECT element is used to describe the simulation project used by SIMAN in labeling the SIMAN Summary Report. When the PROJECT element has been included in the experiment, SIMAN automatically generates this report at the end of each replication of the simulation. The report consists of a statistical summary of response variables selected by the modeler. If no PROJECT element is included, the SIMAN Summary Report is not generated.

The PROJECT element, summarized below, consists of a single line segment. The input statement for this element begins with the element's name, PROJECT, and is followed by operands specifying the project title and analyst name as well as the date of the project. Note that the operands are separated by commas and that the element is terminated by a semi-colon.

    PROJECT,Title,Analyst,Date;

The names of the project and analyst can be any valid alphanumeric name, with the restriction that the length of each name not exceed 24 characters. If more than 24 characters are specified, the excess characters are truncated.

Enter the date of the project as three integers separated by commas. The three integers specify the date in either a MONTH/DAY/YEAR format or a DAY/ MONTH/YEAR format. The default is established by the host computer system's clock.

Below is an example of the PROJECT element.

```
PROJECT, Example 3.1, SM;
```

This element causes a SIMAN Summary Report to be generated at the end of each replication of the simulation. The project's name is Example 3.1 and the analyst's name is SM. The date is defaulted to that read from the host computer.

6.2 Limiting the Number of Entities: The DISCRETE Element

During the execution of the simulation, entities are continuously entering and departing the model. The difference between the number of entities that have entered the model and the number of entities that have departed the model is the number of current entities in the model. These entities are waiting in QUEUE Blocks, passing through DELAY blocks, and so forth.

The DISCRETE element is optional and can be included in the experiment to limit the number of current entities in the model. The main purpose for using this element is to force the run to terminate with an error message when an error in the model logic causes the number of entities in the system to grow beyond a reasonable value. Note that this limit has no impact on the number of entities that can pass through the model.

If the DISCRETE element is omitted, then the maximum number of entities in the model is a computer- and model-dependent value determined by available memory allocated to SIMAN on the host computer, by the amount of general memory required by the model, and by the number of attributes allocated to each entity. In general, the larger the number of attributes, the smaller the default limit on the number of entities.

The limit on the number of entities is typically set by making an intelligent guess at the maximum number of entities that could simultaneously be in the system, and then multiplying this number by a safety factor of 2 or 3. The limit cannot be set at a value larger than the default limit. If you attempt to set the limit at a value larger than the default limit, an error message will occur during the link operation to indicate that available memory was exceeded.

The format for the DISCRETE element is shown below.

DISCRETE,Entities;

Although this element contains several additional operands, we restrict our attention to the first operand, Entities, which defines the entity limit for the model. This operand is entered as an integer between 0 and the default entity limit.

An example of the DISCRETE element is shown below.

```
DISCRETE,100;
```

This element limits the number of entities in the system to 100. In this case, if an entity attempts to enter the model at a point in time when 100 entities are already in the model, the simulation terminates with a message that the limit on the number of entities was exceeded.

6.3 Describing Queues: The QUEUES Element

The QUEUES element defines information about the model's queues. This information includes the queues' numbers, names, and ranking rules; the ranking rules determine the order in which arriving entities wait in the queue.

The three operands comprised in each definition are grouped into line segments within the element. Hence, each new queue definition follows a colon, and commas separate the operands defining each queue. The format for the QUEUES element is shown below.

QUEUES:Number,Name,Ranking:
    repeats;

The first two operands in each of the repeated line segments are the queue's number and name. Recall that you can interchangeably use the number and name to specify the identifier for QUEUE blocks within the model. The number and name can also be used interchangeably as an argument to the SIMAN variable NQ, which provides the current number of entities residing in the queue.

If you omit the first operand and its trailing comma in the repeating line segments, the Experiment Processor automatically assigns the queue's number during compilation. The queues must be consecutively numbered, from 1 through the total number of queues in the model.

The third operand in each of the repeating line segments is the ranking rule. (If you omitted the queue's number, the ranking rule will actually appear as the second operand.) This rule defines the mechanism by which SIMAN establishes the relative position of each waiting entity within a queue. By default, SIMAN ranks the entities within queues on a first-in-first-out (FIFO) basis, that is, entities wait in the queue in the order in which they arrive at the queue. Situations occasionally arise that make other ranking rules more desirable. In such cases, you can choose from any of three additional rules for ranking the entities.

The first option is the last-in-first-out (LIFO) rule, which causes the entities to be ranked in reverse order of their entry into the queue, i.e., the last to arrive is the first in line. The second option is the low-value-first rule or LVF(AttributeID), where AttributeID denotes an entity's attribute. This rule causes the queue to be ordered by increasing values of the specified attribute, with ties broken by the FIFO rule. The third option is the high-value-first rule or HVF(AttributeID), where again AttributeID denotes an entity's attribute. This rule causes the queue to be ordered by decreasing values of the specified attribute, with ties broken by the FIFO rule.

In the case of the LVF and HVF rules, the AttributeID included as an argument can be interchangeably specified by either its number or its name. For example LVF(1) denotes low-value-first ranking based on attribute 1, and HVF(Priority) denotes high-value-first ranking based on the attribute named Priority.

To illustrate the QUEUES element, consider the following example:

```
QUEUES:Buffer;
```

This element defines a single queue named Buffer and defaults to the FIFO ranking rule. Because the queue's number has been omitted, it will be assigned by the Experiment Processor during compilation.

6.4 Describing Resources: The RESOURCES Element

Include the RESOURCES element in the experiment when the model uses one or more resources. This element provides descriptive information about the model's resources, including the resource's number, name, and capacity.

The three operands comprised in each resource definition are grouped into separate line segments within the element. Hence, each new resource definition follows a colon, and commas separate the operands defining the resource. The format for the RESOURCES element is summarized below. Note that this description applies only to *standard resources*. In Chapter 8 we discuss *indexed resources*, an extension of this element to accommodate a generalization of the resource concept.

> RESOURCES:Number,Name,Capacity:
> repeats;

The first operand in each of the repeating line segments is the resource's number. This number must be consecutively assigned to the resources in the order of their listing in the element, beginning with the number 1. Thus, you call the first resource listed Resource 1, you call the second resource listed Resource 2, and so forth until all resources in the model are numbered. If you omit the resource's number and trailing comma, the Experiment Processor automatically assigns the next consecutive integer during compilation.

The next operand in each repeating line segment is the name of the resource. If you omitted the resource's number, the resource name appears as the first operand in the line segment. You assign this name, which is later used for specifying operands for the resource related blocks, such as the SEIZE and RELEASE blocks. The resource name cannot be defaulted.

The last operand in each of the repeating line segments is the capacity, which defaults to 1. For now, we specify this capacity as an integer defining the number of identical and interchangeable units that initially exist for the resource. Later, we will talk about a more flexible way of specifying the capacity by associating it with a resource schedule, which causes the capacity to change automatically over time as prescribed by the schedule.

An example of the RESOURCES element is shown below.

```
RESOURCES:Machine,1;
```

This element defines a single resource, Resource 1, which is named Machine. It has an initial capacity of 1.

6.5 Describing Counters: The COUNTERS Element

Include the COUNTERS element in the experiment when the model references one or more counters. (Recall that counters are values that can be increased or decreased from within the model by using the COUNT block.) The purpose of this element is to provide descriptive information about the model's counters: number, name, limit, reinitialization option, and output file name.

The operands for each counter are grouped into separate line segments within the element. Begin each counter's definition with a colon (:) and separate the operands within the definition with commas (,). The format for this element is summarized below.

COUNTERS:Number,Name,Limit,InitOpt,OutFile:
        repeats;

The first operand in each counter line segment is the counter's number. Consecutively number the counters, beginning with 1 and continuing through the total number of specified counters. Or, alternatively, omit the first operand and its trailing comma (,) thereby allowing the Experiment Processor to assign the numbers automatically during compilation.

The second operand in each counter line segment is the symbolic name assigned to the counter. If the automatic numbering feature is being used, this operand appears as the first operand within each operand group. You can interchangeably use the symbolic name or the counter's number to reference the counter within the model. The counter's name is also used to label the output for counters in the SIMAN Summary Report.

The next operand in each counter line segment is the limit. As discussed earlier, if the counter's value ever reaches or exceeds its limit, SIMAN automatically terminates the simulation run at that point. You can, therefore, control the length of the simulation run by specifying a limit for one or more counters. Unspecified limits default to infinity.

The reinitialization option controls the initialization of counters when conducting multiple model replications. By default, this option assumes a value of YES, which causes the counter's value to be reinitialized to 0 at the beginning of each run. This reinitialization allows you to terminate each replication in a set of runs based on the counter's value. If you override the default by entering a NO for the reinitialization operand, the counter's value is initialized to 0 for the first replication, but subsequent replications retain the ending value as the initial value for the next replication. Hence, the counter's value is totalled across all replications.

The last operand in each counter line segment is the optional output file for the counter. If you specify an output file, SIMAN stores a complete time history of the counter's value in this file. As we discuss in Chapter 5, time historical values can be used to construct plots and perform other analyses; however, this detailed history of the counter's value is usually not needed. Therefore, we often do not specify the name of the output file, and SIMAN only retains a record of the current counter value.

You specify the output file as either a FORTRAN unit number or a *file descriptor*. A file descriptor is any file or device specification that is valid for the host computer and that can be opened and written to from FORTRAN. The exact form of the file descriptor varies with the system, but it typically contains a valid file name for the host system and, in some cases, path or node information. Because the file descriptor may require the use of special characters such as the colon (:) or backslash (\), you must enclose the descriptor within double quotes (").

The following is an example of the COUNTERS element.

```
COUNTERS:JobsDone:
        Rejects,20,NO,"c:\Rejects.dat";
```

This element defines two counters: JobsDone, which has no limit or file descriptor, and Rejects, which has a limit of 20, is not reinitialized to 0 between replications, and has a specified output file, c:\Rejects.dat.

6.6 Controlling Replications: The REPLICATE Element

If desired, include the REPLICATE element in the experiment to control the number of simulation replications, as well as the length and initialization options of each replication. This element consists of a single line segment containing operands for specifying the number of replications, the start time of the first replication, the maximum replication length, the system initialization option, the statistics initialization option, and the statistics warm-up period. The format for this element is shown below.

REPLICATE,NumReps,BeginTime,Length,InitSys,InitStats,WarmUp;

The first operand, named NumReps, prescribes how many consecutive replications of the simulation are to be executed. You specify this value as an integer. At the beginning of the first replication, the value of TNOW is initialized to the starting time of the first replication, the element's second operand. The maximum length of the replication, which is the third operand, limits the duration of each simulation replication. If a simulation run is not terminated by some other means (e.g., a counter reaches its limit), it will be terminated automatically when the simulated time, TNOW, reaches this maximum.

The two initialization operands, named InitSys and InitStats, control the initialization that takes place between successive replications of the simulation. To perform initialization, use the default YES; otherwise, enter NO. Entering (or defaulting) YES for both operands causes the replications to be performed with exactly the same initialization of both the system and the statistics. If you initialize the system, its state (including the simulation clock, TNOW) is reinitialized to exactly the same starting state as the first replication, so that each state involves the same starting conditions. However, as we discuss in Chapter 5, each replication typically yields different results because of different random numbers within each replication. If you do not initialize the system, the starting state of the next replication is the ending state of the previous replication, and each replication is simply a continuation of the last replication. If you initialize the statistics, all statistical values recorded for the previous replication are discarded before the beginning of the next replication, and the SIMAN Summary Report generated at the end of each replication reflects only the values recorded for the previous replication. If you do not initialize the statistics, each Summary Report is based on observations recorded from both the current replication and all previous replications.

Use the WarmUp operand to offset or delay the time at which the statistics are initialized. By using this operand you can avoid including biased observations in the results by discarding the initial, transient portion of the simulation replication. If the system initialization option is set to YES, then the warm-up period is applied to each model replication, and the length of each replication is effectively reduced by this amount. If the system initialization option is set to NO, then the warm-up period is applied once before the start of the first replication, and the length of each replication remains unchanged. We further discuss the use of this option for dealing with biased observations in Chapter 5.

The following is an example of the REPLICATE element.

```
REPLICATE,10,0,480;
```

This element specifies the performance of 10 simulation replications. The first simulation will start at time 0 and have a maximum duration of 480 units of time. Each of the remaining nine replications will be initialized back to this same starting point, all statistics will be cleared, and each subsequent replication will have a maximum run length of 480 units. The 10 replications will be identical except for the random numbers generated during each replication.

6.7 Using the Experiment Source File

The elements defining the experiment are entered into a file called the *experiment source file*, which also contains a BEGIN statement and an END statement. The BEGIN statement, which is required, must always be the first statement in the experiment's source file. The format for the BEGIN statement is shown below.

BEGIN,Listing,Debugger;

The first operand, Listing, is a YES/NO field used to control the generation of the experiment listing. If you specify the operand as YES (the default), the experiment statements are echoed to the screen as they are processed. If you specify the operand as NO, a listing is not generated. The experiment compilation executes much faster when you use the NO option.

The second operand, Debugger, controls the interactive debugger. We discuss this operand in Chapter 4.

For now, we will use the defaults for these operands and assume that the BEGIN statement consists of the word BEGIN, followed by a semi-colon (;) entered anywhere on the first input line.

After the BEGIN statement, you enter the elements in any order, with the following exceptions.

■ Any DISCRETE and/or CONTINUOUS elements (discussed later) must precede all elements except the PROJECT element.

■ Elements that define symbolic names (such as QUEUES) must precede the elements that reference those names.

You include only those elements pertaining to the associated model, and you do not enter any element more than once. Follow the last element with the END statement, which consists of the word END followed by a semi-colon (;) entered anywhere on the last line of input.

The experiment's source file for our example is shown in Figure 3-9. The file contains the BEGIN statement, followed by the PROJECT, DISCRETE, QUEUES, RESOURCES, COUNTERS, and REPLICATE elements, followed by the END statement.

```
BEGIN;
PROJECT,        Sample Problem 3.1,SM;
DISCRETE,       100;
QUEUES:         Buffer;
RESOURCES:      Machine;
COUNTERS:       JobsDone;
REPLICATE,      1, 0, 480;
END;
```

Figure 3-9. Experiment Source File for Sample Problem 3.1

7. Simulation Compilation, Linking, and Execution

After we have created model and experiment source files for our problem, we are ready to take the steps necessary to execute our simulation. Unfortunately, the exact commands used to accomplish this task vary with the host computer's operating system. We therefore provide a general outline for executing the simulation and provide a specific example of the necessary commands for an MS-DOS operating system. Although the specific syntax may differ, similar commands can be used for other operating systems.

7.1 Compiling the Model and Experiment Source Files

For the purpose of discussion, we will assume that the model source file is named Example.mod and that the experiment source file is named Example.exp. These files contain the input statements shown in Figures 3-8 and 3-9, respectively. The

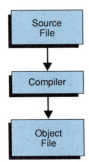

Source File

Compiler

Object File

first step in executing our simulation example is to translate the source statements in these two files into a coded format. In general, this translation step is called *compiling*, and the program that performs this step is called a *compiler*.

As depicted on the left, a compiler reads statements from one file, called the *source file*, and writes the coded equivalent into a second file, called the *object file*. SIMAN has two separate compilers: one for the model, and one for the experiment. The program MODEL compiles the model source file, and the program EXPMT compiles the experiment source file. In each case there are two files associated with the compiler: an input source file from which input statements are read, and an output file to which the object code is written.

In our problem, the source files are named Example.mod and Example.exp. We arbitrarily use the .mod and .exp file extensions to denote model and experiment source files, respectively. In a similar way, we arbitrarily name the corresponding model and experiment object files by using the .m and .e file extensions. Hence, the model object file is written by the program MODEL to the file named Example.m, and the experiment object file is written to the file named Example.e. We could, of course, use any other file name for this purpose.

To compile, you run each of the compiler programs and specify the appropriate source file and object file names for each. For example, with the MS-DOS operating system, you enter the following command.

MODEL Example.mod Example.m

The corresponding MS-DOS command for compiling the experiment is

EXPMT Example.exp Example.e

When compiling either the model or the experiment, SIMAN sends an extended listing of the source file to the screen as each input statement is compiled. Figure 3-10 shows the extended listings for our problem, which are generated by MODEL and EXPMT. The extended listing for the model includes the sequence numbers, which SIMAN automatically appends to each block.

```
BEGIN;
1 CREATE:   EXPONENTIAL(4.4);           Enter the system
2 QUEUE,    Buffer;                     Wait for the machine
3 SEIZE:    Machine;                    Seize the machine
4 DELAY:    TRIANGULAR(3.2,4.2,5.2);    Delay by the proc. time
5 RELEASE:  Machine;                    Release the machine
6 COUNT:    JobsDone:DISPOSE;           Count completed jobs
END;

BEGIN;
1   PROJECT,        Sample Problem 3.1,SM;
2   DISCRETE,       100;
3   QUEUES:         Buffer;
4   RESOURCES:      Machine;
```

```
5    COUNTERS:        JobsDone;
6    REPLICATE,       1, 0, 480;
END;
```

Figure 3-10. Extended Model Listing for Sample Problem 3.1

The extended listings for both the model and experiment also include error messages for any invalid input statements contained in the source files. The error message consists of a pointer to the beginning and end of the offending field within the statement, as well as a descriptive comment about the nature of the error.

Errors detected by MODEL and EXPMT during the compilation step are called *compile-time errors*. You correct these errors in the source files and repeat the compilation step with the corrected source files. Changing the source file without recompiling does not update the corresponding object file.

7.2 Linking the Model and Experiment Object Files

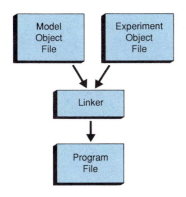

Once the model and experiment source files have been compiled without error into object files, the next step is to link the two resulting object files into a *program file*. The program file contains model- and experiment-related information in a form that can be read and executed by the SIMAN simulation program. The linking of model and experiment object files into a program file is illustrated in the figure to the left.

You link the files by running the SIMAN program named LINKER. LINKER reads the model and experiment object files as input and writes the program file as output. In our example, the model and experiment object files are named Example.m and Example.e, respectively. Because we have arbitrarily adopted the convention of naming all program files with a .p extension, we will call our program file Example.p. Again, you can use any convenient name for your program file, as long as it meets any naming restrictions required by your operating system.

The specific command for executing the LINKER program varies with the operating system. The following command executes the link step for our problem with the MS-DOS operating system:

LINKER Example.m Example.e Example.p

It is possible that errors exist because of incompatibilities between the model and the experiment, even though both source files compile without errors. For example, the model may reference a resource by a name that isn't properly defined in the corresponding experiment. If such incompatibilities between the model and experiment exist, the LINKER program detects them and displays an error message. Errors of this type are called *link-time errors*. When a link-time error occurs, correct the model and/or experiment source file(s), re-compile the modified file(s), and repeat the link step.

7.3 Executing the Program File

When you have successfully linked the files, you are ready to execute the simulation. To accomplish this task, run the program named SIMAN, which is referred to as the *run processor*. This program reads in the program file and executes the simulation. The SIMAN run processor also creates and writes data to any output files specified in the experiment.

As in the case of the compilers and linker, the command to invoke the SIMAN run processor varies with the specific system being used. The MS-DOS command invoking this program for our problem would appear as follows:

SIMAN Example.p

It is possible for an error to occur during execution of the simulation, even though no errors were detected during the compile and link steps. These errors are called *run-time errors*. For example, an attempt to divide by 0 generates a run-time error. When a run-time error occurs, simulation execution terminates, and SIMAN displays an error message.

Run-time errors are much more difficult to isolate and correct than compile-time errors and link-time errors. The *Interactive Debugger* (described in detail in the next chapter) is frequently the simplest and quickest way to debug these errors. The debugger allows you to step through the execution of the program, display and change the values of variables and attributes, and generally monitor and control simulation execution.

If the simulation run executes without error, the SIMAN Summary Report is displayed at the end of each simulation replication. Figure 3-11 shows this report for our problem. The top section of the report consists of the general information entered on the PROJECT element. This section also shows the current replication number and ending time of the replication.

```
Project:   Sample Problem 3.1
Analyst:   SM
Simulation run ended at time : 480.0
                              COUNTERS
          Identifier          Count            Limit
          JobsDone             93            Infinite
```

Figure 3-11. SIMAN Summary Report for Sample Problem 3.1.

The top section of the report is followed by one or more sections that provide summary statistics about the simulation replication. In our problem, there is only one such section; it summarizes the value of the counter included in the model to count completed workpieces. There are other types of summary statistics that can be generated automatically by SIMAN; these are discussed later in this chapter.

As we can see from the SIMAN Summary Report, 93 workpieces were processed through the model during 480 minutes of simulated time. We must, however, use great care when interpreting this number (as discussed in detail in Chapter 5). We cannot simply make one replication of the simulation as we have done here and perceive the values in the SIMAN Summary Report as reliable estimates of the true system's response.

8. Sample Problem 3.2: Two Job Types and a Second Workstation

Now that we have completed our first sample simulation program, we will continue our introduction to SIMAN's modeling concepts by enlarging the problem to include two distinct types of jobs and a second workstation. These embellishments to the problem statement require additional blocks and elements, which we will describe later in this section. The enlarged system is depicted in Figure 3-12.

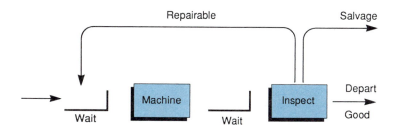

Figure 3-12. Schematic for Sample Problem 3.2

Workpieces enter the system and wait their turn to be processed on a single machine. After completing processing on the machine, they continue to a second workstation where they are inspected. At the inspection station the workpieces are classified as Good, Repairable, or Bad. Good workpieces depart the system; repairable workpieces are recycled back to the machine where they are reworked; and bad workpieces are sent to salvage. The time between job arrivals is exponentially distributed with a mean time of 9 minutes. There are two types of jobs randomly ordered in the arrival stream; 30 percent are Type 1, and 70 percent are Type 2.

The waiting workpieces are ordered at both the machines and the inspection stations. The Type 1 jobs have priority over the Type 2 jobs within the queue. The first portion of the queue contains any Type 1 jobs, ordered according to arrival at the queue. The Type 2 jobs follow the Type 1 jobs, again ordered according to their sequence of arrival. The priority scheme is non-preemptive, that is, if a Type 2 job is being processed when a Type 1 job arrives, processing is not interrupted.

The repairable workpieces returned to the machine's queue have the lowest priority. These jobs must wait behind any regular Type 1 and 2 jobs and are ordered according to the time at which they re-enter the queue. This same priority scheme is used for reinspection of the reworked jobs. Thus, there are three distinct classes of priority at both machine and inspector queues: Type 1, Type 2, and Repairable.

The inspection time for each workpiece, regardless of type or rework status, has a triangular distribution with a minimum time of five minutes, a most likely time of eight minutes, and a maximum time of ten minutes. Of the jobs inspected at this station, 80 percent are classified as Good and depart the system, 10 percent are classified as Bad and are sent to salvage, and 10 percent are classified as Repairable and are returned to the machine queue for rework. The same percentages apply to both types of jobs, regardless of rework status. Note that a reworked job classified as Repairable at the inspection station will be recycled through the machining station.

The combined setup and machining times for regular and rework Type 1 and 2 jobs are normally distributed with the means and standard deviations (given in minutes) provided below.

	Regular		Rework	
	Mean	Standard Deviation	Mean	Standard Deviation
Type 1	5	2	3	1
Type 2	4	1	2	1

Our problem is to simulate this system for 480 minutes and to record the number of workpieces completed by job type and the total number of rejected workpieces sent to salvage.

8.1 Describing the Process

As before, we begin modeling by developing a description of this system's process. Our first task is to define the entities in the system. In this example, the entities that flow through the system are the workpieces. Unlike the previous example, however, the entities in this system are not identical; they must be distinguished as either Type 1 or Type 2 jobs and as either regular or rework jobs. In this example it is convenient to use the entities' attributes to maintain the appropriate descriptive information about each entity. And so we use an attribute named JobType to record the type of job (one or two); an attribute named Status to record the job's status (regular or rework); and an attribute named Priority to record each entity's priority in the queue (1, 2, or 3). Because attributes can only be assigned numerical values, we denote regular jobs with a status of 0 and rework jobs with a status of 1.

In addition to the three attributes described above, we also use two two-dimensional variable arrays named Mean and Std. These arrays assign the means and standard deviations for the normal distribution used on the DELAY block, which represents the processing time on the machine. We address the elements of these arrays based on the current entity's job type and status.

In our previous example entities entered the system at the top of the model, sequentially flowed from step to step, and then departed at the last process step of the model. In this example the entity flow is more complicated. We now have arriving entities merging at the machine queue, with rework jobs being fed back from the inspection station. In addition, the flow of entities from the inspection station is split into three different paths. Finally, the entities depart the system at different points, depending on whether they have been classified as good or rejected.

The following summary describes the process steps and entity flow for this problem.

1. Create arriving jobs.
2. Assign JobType = 1 or 2, Status = 0, and Priority = JobType.
3. Wait according to Priority for the machine to be idle.
4. Seize the machine.
5. Delay by the processing time.
6. Release the machine for the next waiting entity, if any.
7. Wait according to Priority for the inspection station.
8. Seize the inspector.
9. Delay by the inspection time.
10. Release the inspector for the next waiting entity, if any.
11. Branch with the following probabilities:
    0.8 probability go to step 12 (Good)
    0.1 probability go to step 13 (Reject)
    0.1 probability go to step 14 (Bad).
12. Count completed jobs by JobType and depart the system.
13. Count the rejects and depart the system.
14. Assign Status = 1, Priority = 3, and return to Step 3.

In order to model this process in SIMAN, we must expand our initial subset of blocks to provide functionality for attribute and variable assignments and for entity branching. In the following sections we describe two additional elements to define attributes and variables used in the model and two additional blocks that perform the assignments and provide for entity branching.

8.2 Describing General-Purpose Attributes and Variables: The ATTRIBUTES and VARIABLES Elements

In our embellished problem we are using symbolic names for the general-purpose attributes (JobType, Status, and Priority) and variable arrays (Mean, StdDev). Whenever you reference a general-purpose attribute or variable in a model or experiment by its symbolic name, you must define the attribute or variable in an ATTRIBUTES or VARIABLES element included in the corresponding experiment source file. These elements provide general information about the symbolic names and properties of attributes and variables.

The ATTRIBUTES and VARIABLES elements follow a similar format consisting of the element's name followed by a series of attribute or variable definitions, with each definition being entered as a line segment within the statement. Recall that line segments are separated by colons (:) and that the last line segment is terminated by a semi-colon (;). Each definition consists of an optional attribute or variable number, followed by the symbolic name, followed by an optional initial specification of the value. In the case of an array definition, include the array dimensions as an Index appended within parentheses to the Name. The format for the ATTRIBUTES and VARIABLES element is summarized below.

ATTRIBUTES:Number,Name(Index),Value,...:
             repeats;

VARIABLES:Number,Name(Index),Value,...:
             repeats;

Consecutively number attributes or variables, beginning with 1. To activate SIMAN's automatic-numbering feature, omit the number and its trailing comma (,) from the line segment. This omission prompts the Experiment Processor to assign the numbers automatically during compilation. For example, the following element defines the attributes for our problem:

```
ATTRIBUTES:JobType:Status:Priority;
```

This element defines three attributes: JobType, Status, and Priority.

To initialize a variable or attribute to a specific value, specify the value as the third operand of the line segment. If specified, the value must be entered as a constant; the initial value of all unspecified variables and attributes defaults to 0. In the following example a VARIABLES element initializes the variable named StockLevel to 50:

```
VARIABLES:StockLevel,50;
```

When two or more attributes or two or more variables are grouped into an array, the element must include, in addition to the symbolic name assigned to the array, the array's dimensions. Both one- and two-dimensional arrays are permitted in SIMAN, and these can be defined for attributes or variables. Append the dimensions to the name of the array, enclosing them within parentheses. The format consists of an optional lower bound and a required upper bound for each dimension of the array. If you do not specify the lower bound, it defaults to 1. The upper bound must always be greater-than-or-equal-to the lower bound. To specify both bounds, use the following format:

Lower-Dimension-Bound .. Upper-Dimension-Bound

where the double period indicates that all integer subscript values between the lower and upper bounds are permitted. For example, Array(−5 .. 5) denotes a one-dimensional array with permissible subscript values ranging from −5 to +5. To default the lower bound to 1, simply omit the lower bound and the double period. For example, Vector(30) denotes a one-dimensional array with permissible subscript values between 1 and 30.

In the case of two-dimensional arrays, use a comma (,) to separate the lower and upper bounds. For example, Matrix(−3 .. 6 , 10) denotes a two-dimensional array, with the first subscript ranging from −3 to 6, and the second subscript ranging from 1 to 10.

When an ATTRIBUTES or VARIABLES element includes an array specification, each element of the array is assigned a separate number. You must therefore replace the array's single attribute or variable number with a range of numbers. Specify the range in the following format:

LowerNumber — UpperNumber

where LowerNumber is an integer specifying the number of the first element of the array, and UpperNumber is the number of the last element of the array. For example, consider the following element:

```
VARIABLES:1,ReorderPoint:2-11,StockLevel(10);
```

It defines Variable 1, named ReorderPoint, and Variables 2 through 11, elements of the array named StockLevel. The array StockLevel has valid subscript values between 1 and 10. Interchangeably reference the first element of this array as either V(2) because it is Variable 2, or StockLevel(1) because it is the first element of the array named StockLevel.

The range must be consistent with the number of elements in the array. For one-dimensional arrays, the difference between the upper and lower numbers should be the same as the difference between the upper and lower bounds. For two-dimensional arrays, the difference between the upper and lower numbers should be 1 less than the product of the number of rows and columns in the array.

If you do not explicitly enter the range, the Experiment Processor automatically assigns the range during compilation. Hence, our previous example can be equivalently entered as

```
VARIABLES:ReorderPoint:StockLevel(10);
```

We normally use SIMAN's automatic numbering feature to avoid having to explicitly number the variables and attributes.

To initialize the array's elements, include an initial list of values as the last operand of the line segment. The initial list consists of one or more constants separated by commas (,). The first number in the list corresponds to the first element of the array, the second number corresponds to the second element, and so forth. In the case of two-dimensional arrays, enter the values in column-major format, i.e., enter the first-column-first-row entry, then enter the first-column-second-row, and so forth. If the initial list of values contains fewer values than required to define all of the array's elements, SIMAN uses the last value in the list as the initial value for all remaining array elements. For example, the following element defines an array named Data, with all elements of the array initialized to 5:

```
VARIABLES:Data(10),5;
```

In our problem, we have two variable arrays, named Mean and Std, containing the mean and standard deviation of normal distribution used for the processing time on the machine. Each of these variables is a two-dimensional array in which the first index corresponds to the current job type (1 or 2) and the second index corresponds to the rework status (1 or 2). Hence, Mean(JobType,Status) and Std(JobType,Status) respectively denote the mean and standard deviation of the processing time for the current job. The following element defines these arrays and initializes them to their proper values.

```
VARIABLES:   Mean(2,2),    5, 3,
                           4, 2:
             Std(2,2),     2, 1,
                           1, 1:
```

8.3 Assigning Values to General-Purpose Attributes and Variables: The ASSIGN Block

When we employ general-purpose attributes and/or general-purpose variables in a model, we typically need to be able to assign them values during model execution. In our current example, we need to assign values to three attributes: JobType, Status, and Priority. SIMAN provides the ASSIGN block for this purpose.

The ASSIGN block, an Operation block, is shown with its operands below.

ASSIGN: Variable = Value;

ASSIGN
Variable=Value

The top line segment consists of the block's function name, ASSIGN, and the bottom line segment consists of an attribute or variable followed by an equals sign, which is followed by a value. Each time an entity passes through the ASSIGN block, the value on the right side of the equals sign is copied into the variable or attribute on the left side of the equals sign. The value on the right side of the equals sign can be any valid SIMAN expression. The left side of the equals sign can contain any general-purpose attribute or variable or any user-assignable special-purpose attribute or variable. For now, we restrict our attention to using the ASSIGN block with general-purpose attributes and variables.

Recall from our basic definition that a model's variables are global, whereas its attributes are local to a specific entity. When an assignment is made to a variable, its new value can be referenced by any entity throughout the model. On the other hand, when an assignment is made to an attribute, the value of the attribute is updated only for the entity currently passing through the ASSIGN block. This local assignment does not alter this same attribute for any other entities in the model.

ASSIGN
JobType=1

ASSIGN
JobType=1
Status=0
Priority=1

To make multiple assignments at a single ASSIGN block, enter the assignments in the order in which they are listed, and separate assignments with a colon (:). Two examples of the ASSIGN block are shown on the left. In the first example the attribute JobType is assigned the value of 1. In the second example, three attributes are assigned at the same block: JobType is set to 1, Status is set to 0, and Priority is set to 1. These assignments are made sequentially in the order in which they appear.

8.4 Sampling from a User-Defined Discrete Probability Distribution

In our current example, we would like to assign the attribute JobType a randomly selected value of either 1 or 2, with a 30-percent chance of the value being a 1 and a 70-percent chance of the value being a 2. We can accomplish this assignment easily by using the random variable DISCRETE, for sampling from a user-defined discrete probability distribution. This random variable returns one of a set of discrete values, according to probabilities specified in the form of a cumulative probability distribution. You enter the set of possible discrete values and corresponding cumulative probabilities for the DISCRETE random variable.

The cumulative probability for a given value within the set is defined as the sum of the probabilities corresponding to that value (and all preceding values) in the set. In our current example, then, the set of discrete values consists of 1 and 2; and the corresponding cumulative probabilities are 0.3 and 1.0, respectively. Note that we obtained this last value by adding 0.7 (the probability of a 2) to 0.3 (the probability of a 1). We list the cumulative probabilities and associated values in pairs, with the cumulative probability entered first. In our current example, we would enter DISCRETE(.3,1, 1.0,2). This random variable returns a value of 1 with a probability of 0.3, and a value of 2 with a probability of 0.7 (corresponding to a cumulative probability of 1.0).

When first encountered, the use of cumulative probabilities in lieu of actual probabilities may seem cumbersome; however, this approach makes the DISCRETE random variable consistent with the CONTINUOUS random variable, which is used in SIMAN for sampling from a user-defined continuous probability distribution. Note that for a continuous random variable, only the cumulative probability function is defined.

8.5 Directing the Flow of Entities Among Blocks: The BRANCH Block

In modeling systems, we frequently encounter situations in which we must direct the flow of entities among several destination blocks. For example, in our current problem, we must direct entities exiting from the inspection station to one of three sections of our model, based on a classification of Good, Bad, or Rejected. The BRANCH block provides a generalized branching capability for directing the flow of entities in situations such as this.

The BRANCH block, one of the single-function blocks, is shown below.

BRANCH,MaxTake:
    WITH,Probability,Label:
    IF,Condition,Label:
    ELSE,Label:
    ALWAYS,Label;

As with the other blocks that we have discussed, entities enter this block on the top side; however, unlike the previous blocks, the entities do not exit on the bottom side of the BRANCH block. Instead, entities are redirected along the emanating branches pointing to the right of the block. There can be any number of emanating branches associated with a BRANCH block.

Each branch represents a possible exit direction for each arriving entity. The operands for each branch consist of the branch condition and branch destination label. The branch condition specifies the conditions under which an arriving entity selects the branch, and the destination label directs the exiting entity to the appropriate block.

The first operand, MaxTake, defines the maximum number of branches that each arriving entity can select; it is specified as an integer. When an entity arrives at a BRANCH block, each emanating branch's condition is examined in order until either all branches have been examined or MaxTake branches have been selected, whichever occurs first. The default value of MaxTake is the total number of emanating branches, which results in each branch always being examined for possible selection, regardless of how many preceding branches have already been selected for the arriving entity. To restrict any entity to a subset of branches, specify a value for MaxTake. For example, you specify the value of MaxTake as 1, then the arriving entity is sent over the first selected branch, if any. The remaining branches at the block are ignored, regardless of the specified branch conditions.

For each entity arriving at the BRANCH block, the number of selected branches can range from 0 to the maximum of MaxTake. If no branches are selected, SIMAN disposes of the arriving entity, i.e., the arriving entity departs the model at that point. If exactly one branch is selected, the arriving entity is redirected to the selected branch. If more than one branch is selected, the arriving entity is sent along the first selected branch, and clones of the arriving entity are created and sent along the remaining selected branches. These clones, duplicates of the arriving entity, have identical attribute values. We refer to the clones as secondary entities, and the original entity as the *primary entity*. (The distinction between primary and secondary entities becomes important in later chapters.)

You specify the branch condition (which determines whether a branch is selected) in one of three forms. These forms can be combined in any order within the same BRANCH block. The first form provides for a random selection of the branch based on a specified probability. In this form, you enter the branch condition as WITH,P where P is an expression with a value between 0 and 1, which specifies the probability of selection. For example, WITH,.8 denotes that, for each arriving entity, the branch will be selected with a probability of 0.8. We refer to branches of this type as *probabilistic branches*.

When several probabilistic branches emanate from the same BRANCH block, they are considered to be mutually exclusive, i.e., the sum of the probabilities for all the branches at the block cannot exceed 1. For each entity's arrival, there will always be (at most) one branch selected from the set of probabilistic branches, regardless of the value of MaxTake. The probability that one of the probabilistic branches will be selected is equal to the sum of the probabilities.

The second form for the branch condition allows selection to be based on a logical condition involving variables or attributes. To use this form, enter the branch condition as IF,C where C denotes any valid logical expression in SIMAN. For example, the branch condition IF, ArrivalTime < TNOW specifies that a branch is selected if the logical expression ArrivalTime < TNOW is true and the maximum number of preceding branches has not been exceeded. We call branches of this type *conditional branches*.

The third form for the condition is a null condition, which causes the branch to be selected unless the maximum number of preceding branches has already been selected. Branches of this type are referred to as *deterministic branches*. You specify deterministic branches by entering the condition as either ALWAYS or ELSE. The condition is specified as ALWAYS on branches that must be selected at each arrival to the block. The condition is specified as ELSE if the branch is only taken when MaxTake previous branches have not been taken. If MaxTake branches have been selected and SIMAN encounters an ALWAYS branch, a run-time error will result.

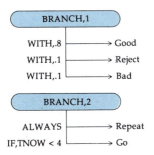

Examples of the BRANCH block are shown to the left. In the first example, each arriving entity is branched to one of the blocks labeled Good, Reject, and Bad with probabilities of 0.8, 0.1, and 0.1, respectively. In the second example, each arriving entity is sent to the block labeled Repeat. In addition, if the current value of TNOW is less than 4, a copy of the arriving entity is also sent to the block labeled Go.

8.6 Solving the Sample Model

We are now ready to combine our new constructs and model our second example. The Block Diagram for this system is shown in Figure 3-13. Entities enter the model at the CREATE block with an interarrival time sampled from an exponential distribution with a mean of nine minutes. At the ASSIGN block, assignments are sequentially made to the attributes JobType, Status, and Priority. Note that, on average, 30 percent of the arriving jobs will be Type 1 and the remaining 70 percent will be Type 2. The Status of all arriving entities is initially set to 1, indicating a regular job, and the Priority is initialized to the JobType.

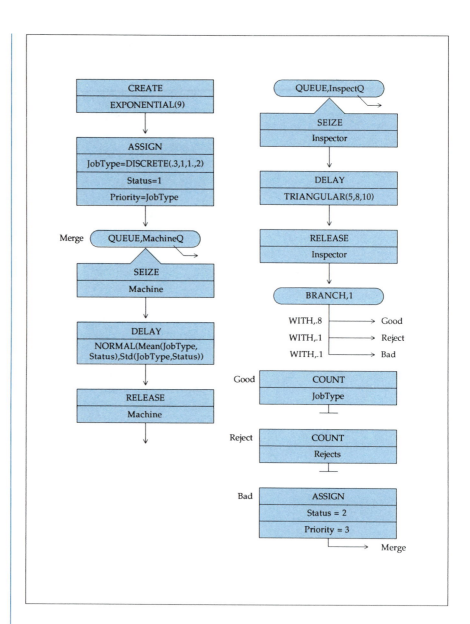

Figure 3-13. Block Diagram for Sample Problem 3-2

Following the attribute assignments, the entities proceed through a QUEUE-
-SEIZE–DELAY–RELEASE sequence representing the processing of the workpieces
on the machine. Note that the mean and standard deviation used for sampling
from the normal distribution at the DELAY block is specified as the two-
dimensional arrays named Mean and Std, respectively. The element in each array
is addressed based on the current value of JobType and Status for the active entity.

Following this block sequence, the entities proceed through a second QUEUE-
-SEIZE–DELAY–RELEASE sequence that represents the inspection process. In this
case, the inspection time specified on the DELAY block is independent of the value
of JobType or Status.

After completing the inspection process, each entity continues to the BRANCH
block where it is sent to the block labeled Good, Reject, or Bad, with probabilities
of 0.8, 0.1, and 0.1, respectively. The entities sent to the branch labeled Good
represent completed jobs; these entities increase either counter number 1 or counter number 2, depending on the value of JobType. The entities sent to the branch
labeled Reject represent rejected parts that cannot be reworked; these entities
increase the counter named Rejects. In both cases the entities are disposed of after
passing through the COUNT blocks. The entities sent to the branch labeled Bad
represent jobs that failed inspection but can be reworked at the machining station.
These entities have their attribute Status reset to 2 and their attribute Priority reset
to 3; they are then sent back to the QUEUE block labeled Merge where they repeat
the same process as a rework job.

The equivalent statement form of this model is shown in Figure 3-14. These
statements follow directly from the Block Diagram shown in Figure 3-13.

```
       BEGIN;
               CREATE:  EXPONENTIAL(9);                    enter the system
               ASSIGN:  JobType=DISCRETE(.3,1,1.,2):       !set job type attribute
                        Status = 1:                        !set status attribute
                        Priority = JobType;                set priority attribute
       Merge   QUEUE,   MachineQ;                          wait for the machine
               SEIZE:   Machine;                           get the machine
               DELAY:   NORMAL(Mean(JobType,Status),       !delay by processing
                        Std(JobType,Status));              time
               RELEASE: Machine;                           release the machine
               QUEUE,   InspectQ;                          wait for the inspector
               SEIZE:   Inspector;                         get the inspector
               DELAY:   TRIANGULAR(5,8,10);                delay by inspection
               RELEASE: Inspector;                         release the inspector
               BRANCH,  1:
                        WITH,.8,Good:                      !good part
                        WITH,.1,Reject:                    !reject part
                        WITH,.1,Bad;                       rework part
       Good    COUNT:   JobType:DISPOSE;                   count good jobs by type
       Reject  COUNT:   Rejects:DISPOSE;                   count the rejects
       Bad     ASSIGN:  Status = 2:                        !reset status attribute
                        Priority = 3:NEXT(Merge);          reset prior. attribute
       END;
```

Figure 3-14. Model Statements for Sample Problem 3-2

The experiment for this model, shown in Figure 3-15, includes elements for
defining the attributes, variables, queues, resources, and counters. The REPLI-
CATE element is included to control the length of the simulation.

```
BEGIN;
PROJECT,         Sample Problem 3.2,SM;
ATTRIBUTES:      JobType:
                 Status:
                 Priority;
VARIABLES:       Mean(2,2),           5, 3,
                                      4, 2:
                 Std(2,2),            2, 1,
                                      1, 1;
QUEUES:          MachineQ,            LVF(Priority):
                 InspectQ,            LVF(Priority);
RESOURCES:       Machine:
                 Inspector;
COUNTERS:        Type 1 Jobs Done:
                 Type 2 Jobs Done:
                 Rejects;
REPLICATE,       1, 0, 480;
END;
```

Figure 3-15. Experiment Statements for Sample Problem 3-2

Note that the priority structure for processing jobs at the machining center and inspection station is enforced by specifying low-value-first queue ranking on the QUEUES element. This ranking convention causes Type 1 regular jobs to be processed first, followed by Type 2 regular jobs, followed by rework jobs.

The simulation is executed by compiling both the model and experiment and then linking them together to form a program file. SIMAN then reads the program and executes the simulation experiment. The results are shown in Figure 3-16.

```
Project:  Sample Problem 3.2
Analyst:  SM
Simulation run ended at time  : 480.0
```

                                 COUNTERS

Identifier	Count	Limit
Type 1 Jobs Done	23	Infinite
Type 2 Jobs Done	24	Infinite
Rejects	7	Infinite

Figure 3-16. SIMAN Summary Report for Sample Problem 3-2

9. Sample Problem 3.3: Statistics on Queues, Resources, and Time in System

In our previous sample problem the only information that we recorded during the simulation was the number of parts processed. We will now embellish our previous problem by adding the requirement the we collect statistics on the length of the queues, utilization of the resources, and the time the workpieces spend in the system. We will also record statistics on the utilization of the inspector by job type.

9.1 Collecting Observational and Time-Dependent Data

In general, we record two types of response data: *observational* data, consisting of a sequence of equally weighted observations, the value of which does not persist over time and the timing of which is insignificant; and *time-dependent* data, consisting of a sequence of values, the value of which does persist over some specified amount of time with that value being weighted by the amount of time that the value persists. Observational data are recorded when triggered by some event, e.g., an entity's departure from the system, whereas time-dependent data must be recorded whenever the value of a time-dependent variable changes.

An example of observational data is the record of the amount of time each workpiece spends in the system. In this case, each time an entity departs the system, we wish to record the amount of time that the entity spent in the system. The recorded value does not persist over time, but is a single observation of this random variable. If we want to compute the mean time that departing customers spent in the system, we can simply compute the unweighted average of all the recorded observations. If x_i denotes the ith observation, and there are a total n observations recorded, then the average observation is given by the following equation:

$$\bar{x} = \Sigma x_i / n$$

For example, the values recorded for the number of entities residing in a queue over time are time-dependent data. In this case, each time the queue length changes, we must record the new length and the time at which the length changed. If we wish to compute the queue's average length, we cannot simply average the recorded values for the length; instead, we must compute a weighted average of these values based on the time that each value persisted. If the ith value is denoted as x_i and it persists for a period of time denoted by t_i, then the following equation gives the variable's average value:

$$\bar{x} = \Sigma t_i x_i / \Sigma t_i$$

9.2 Recording Time-Dependent Data: The DSTATS Element

To record data about time-dependent variables in a SIMAN model, include the DSTATS element in the corresponding experiment. This element causes automatic recording of statistics about one or more time-dependent variables during execution of the simulation.

The format for the DSTATS Statement is shown below. The statement consists of the element's name, DSTATS, followed by repeated line segments containing the dstat's number, expression, name, and output file.

```
DSTATS:Number,Expression,Name,OutFile:
        repeats;
```

The first operand in the repeating line segment is the dstat number. The dstats are consecutively numbered, beginning with 1 and continuing (2, 3, 4, etc.) through the total number of dstats. To enable the Experiment Processor to assign this number automatically during compilation, omit this operand and its trailing comma (,) from the line segment.

The next operand is the dstat's expression, which can be any expression involving one or more variables with values defined over time. The expression may also involve user-defined variables. Two commonly specified SIMAN dstat variables are NQ(QueueID) and NR(ResourceID), which correspond to the number of entities in a queue and the number of busy resource units, respectively.

The next operand is the name, which you can use interchangeably with the number to identify the dstat entry. As we discuss in Chapter 5, this identifier is used as an argument to special-purpose SIMAN variables that return summary statistics about the dstat variable. The name is also used to label summary statistics for dstat variables displayed in the SIMAN Summary Report.

The last operand in each dstat line segment is the output file, to which a complete time history of the dstat variable is written. Enter the output file as a valid FORTRAN file unit number or as a system-specific file descriptor. Recall that a file descriptor typically includes a system-dependent file name and, on some systems, also includes path or node information. Enclose all file descriptors within double quotes (").

In Chapter 5 we discuss both graphical and statistical methods for analyzing the data in the dstat file. Frequently, the detailed history of the dstat variable is not needed, and you can omit the output file. In this case, only summary statistics, including the average, standard deviation, minimum, and maximum values, are maintained.

The following is an example of the DSTATS element:

```
DSTATS:NQ(Buffer),Buffer Size:
       NR(Machine),Machine Util.,"c:\Machine.dat";
```

This element defines two dstat variables: Buffer Size, which records statistics about the length of the queue named Buffer and has no Output File; and Machine Util., which records statistics about the number of busy units of the resource named Machine and saves the raw data in the host system file named c:\Machine.dat.

9.3 Recording Observational Data: The TALLY Block

You can record observational data during simulation execution by using the TALLY block. The TALLY block records one value at each arrival of an entity at the block. In our example, we will use the TALLY block to record the time that each entity spends in the system. The operands for the TALLY block are summarized below.

TALLY
TallyID,Value

TALLY:TallyID,Value;

The TALLY block's operands include the TallyID and Value. TallyID specifies the register to which the observations are added. You specify this operand interchangeably as either the tally's number or name, both of which you define in the TALLIES element of the experiment. The Value operand specifies what value is recorded at each entity's arrival at the block. Specify this operand as any SIMAN or user-defined variable or as an expression involving one or more variables.

The TALLY block is commonly used to record the time required for an entity to move between two points in the model. For our problem, we want to record the time that each entity spends in the system, i.e., the time required to move from the CREATE block (where it enters the model) to the point at which it departs the model. SIMAN provides a simple means of recording the interval of time required for an entity to travel between two points. First, you append a special MARK modifier to any block in the model. This modifier stores the time at which an entity arrives at the block in an attribute of the activating entity. The format for this modifier is MARK(AttributeID), where AttributeID denotes the identifier of the attribute used to record the mark time. After marking the time at which the entity passes through the first point, you then record the time elapsed in reaching a second point. To record the elapsed time, include the TALLY block with the special option INTERVAL(AttributeID) specified for the Value operand, where the argument AttributeID denotes the identifier of the attribute containing the marked time. The keyword INTERVAL is commonly abbreviated as INT. In our example, we will include the TALLY block at the entity's point of departure from the model.

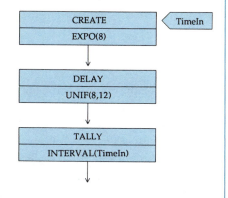

To illustrate the MARK modifier and INTERVAL option on the TALLY block, let's consider the block diagram shown on the left. The time at which each entity enters the CREATE block is recorded by the MARK modifier in the attribute named TimeIn. (Note that this configuration is equivalent to having an ASSIGN block immediately after the CREATE block, with the assignment TimeIn = TNOW. By using the MARK modifier, we save this extra block.) Each entity then passes through the DELAY block with a uniformly distributed delay of between 8 and 12 units and then enters the TALLY block. At the TALLY block, the INTERVAL (TimeIn) causes the time value to be recorded, i.e., the current time, TNOW, minus the time stored in attribute TimeIn. This interval corresponds to the time required for the entity to travel from the CREATE block to the TALLY block.

We should emphasize that you can append the MARK modifier to any block in a model, not just to CREATE blocks. Also, it is important to realize that using the INTERVAL option on the TALLY block assumes that the specified attribute has already been properly marked in the model. Failure to mark the attribute before using it in the INTERVAL specification will not cause a SIMAN execution error, but it will produce erroneous results. This type of logical error can be very difficult to find.

The TALLY block is also commonly used to record the time between successive arrivals at the block. For example, we may want to record statistics on the time between entity departures from the system. SIMAN includes a special provision to record this information by simply specifying the Value operand as BETWEEN (or BET). In this case, the time between successive arrivals to the TALLY block is recorded for each arrival at the block, with the exception of the first arrival. For example, if entities arrive at the block at times 5, 7, and 11, no value would be recorded at the time of the first arrival; the value 2 would be recorded at the time of the second arrival; and the value 4 would be recorded at the time of the third arrival.

Some examples of the TALLY block are shown on the left. In the first block the value of attribute BatchSize is recorded in tally register number 1. In the second example the time between successive arrivals at the block is recorded in the TBDeparts register. In the third example the time interval is computed by using the time marked in the attribute named Time and recorded in the register identified by the number contained in the attribute named PartType. Note that in this case a single TALLY block records statistics across several registers by using an attribute's numerical value instead of a register's symbolic name.

9.4 Describing the Tally Records: The TALLIES Element

Include the TALLIES element in the experiment when you use one or more TALLY blocks. This element provides descriptive information about the model's tally records, including the tally's number, name, and optional output file.

Group the operands for each tally definition into separate line segments within the element, begin each definition with a colon (:), and separate the operands within the definition by commas (,). The format for this element is summarized below.

TALLIES:Number,Name,OutFile:
      repeats;

The first two operands in each tally line segment are the number and name. Recall that the number and name can be used interchangeably for the TallyID, which identifies a specific register. In addition to serving as a TallyId for the register, the tally's name labels the summary statistics for each register's recorded observations, which are displayed in the SIMAN Summary Report. If you omit the tally's number and trailing comma, the Experiment Processor automatically assigns the next number in the sequence. In this case the name will appear as the first operand in the line segment.

The last operand in each line segment is the optional output file, to which SIMAN writes each individual observation recorded for that register. The data set contained in the output file can be subjected to a number of statistical and graphical analyses with the Output Processor, which we discuss in Chapter 5. If you do not specify any output file, then SIMAN maintains only summary statistics (including the mean, coefficient of variation, minimum and maximum values, and number of observations for the tally register); no additional analysis can be performed with the Output Processor.

You can specify the output file as any valid FORTRAN file unit number or as a system-specific file descriptor. A file descriptor typically includes a system-dependent file name and, on some systems, path or node information. All file

TALLY
1,BatchSize

TALLY
TBDeparts,BET

TALLY
PartType,INT(Time)

descriptors must be enclosed within double quotes ("). The following is an example of the TALLIES element.

```
TALLIES:TSysOne:
        TSysTwo,"c:\TSysTwo.dat";
```

This element defines two registers: Tally 1 is named TSysOne and has no output file; Tally 2 is named TSysTwo and has individual observations saved in the host system file c:\TSysTwo.dat.

9.5 Describing Storages: The STORAGES Element

One of the statistics that we would like to record for this model is the individual utilization of the inspector for each of the two job types. Although we can easily record statistics on the variable NR(Inspector) to obtain the overall utilization of the inspector, these do not provide us with the desired individual utilization by job type. To obtain this information, we specify a separate storage for each of the two jobtypes as an operand on the DELAY block representing the inspection delay. We can then record statistics on the number of entities in each of the two storages to obtain the desired values for utilization by job type.

You must include the STORAGES element in the experiment when the model uses one or more storages. This element defines the symbolic names for each of the model's storages. (Recall that storages may be associated with DELAY blocks and provide a count of the number of entities in the delay.)

There are two operands in each storage definition, and they are grouped into separate line segments within the element. Hence, each new storage definition is preceded by a colon, and the two operands defining the storage are separated by a comma. The format for the STORAGES element is shown below.

STORAGES:Number,Name:
        repeats;

The first operand in each of the repeating line segments is the storage's number. This number must be consecutively assigned to the storages in the order of their listing in the element, beginning with the number 1. If you omit the storage's number and trailing comma, the Experiment Processor automatically assigns the next consecutive integer during compilation.

The next operand in each repeating line segment is the name of the storage. If you omit the storage's number, the storage name will appear as the first operand in the line segment. You can interchangeably use the symbolic name or the number to reference the storage within the model.

An example of the STORAGES element is shown below.

```
STORAGES: InspType1:
          InspType2;
```

This element defines two storages named InspType1 and InspType2. Note that we have defaulted the storage numbers to 1 and 2, respectively. The SIMAN variables NSTO(InspType1) and NSTO(InspType2) (or alternatively NSTO(1) and NSTO(2)) define the current number of entities in each of these storages.

9.6 Solving the Model

Figures 3-17 and 3-18 respectively show the modified model and experiment source files to incorporate the embellishments for collecting additional statistics on this model. The only changes made in the model are the addition of the MARK modifier on the CREATE block, the replacement of the COUNT blocks by TALLY blocks, and the incorporation of the storage identifier on the DELAY block representing the inspection delay. All the other necessary changes are made in the experiment, including the addition of the STORAGES element for defining the two storages in the model and the DSTATS element for recording time-dependent statistics on the queue lengths, resource utilizations, and storage utilizations.

Note that the storage identifier on the DELAY block is specified as the attribute named JobType. This attribute has a value of either 1 or 2, depending on the job type. Hence the type 1 jobs are placed in storage number 1 (named InspType1), and the type 2 jobs are placed in storage number 2 (named InspType2).

```
       BEGIN;

              CREATE:    EXPONENTIAL(9):              !create jobs
                         MARK(TimeIn);                 set entry time
              ASSIGN:    JobType = DISCRETE(.3,1,1.,2):  !set job type attribute
                         Status = 1:                   !set status attribute
                         Priority = JobType;           !set priority attribute
       Merge  QUEUE,     MachineQ;                     wait for the machine
              SEIZE:     Machine;                      seize the machine
              DELAY:     NORMAL(Mean(JobType,Status),  !delay by processing
                         Std(JobType,Status));          time
              RELEASE:   Machine;                      release the machine
              QUEUE,     InspectQ;                     wait for the inspector
              SEIZE:     Inspector;                    seize the inspector
              DELAY:     TRIA(5,8,10),JobType;         delay by the inspection
              RELEASE:   Inspector;                    release the inspector
              BRANCH,    1:
                         WITH,.8,Good:                 !good parts
                         WITH,.1,Reject:               !rejected parts
                         WITH,.1,Bad;                  rework parts
       Good   TALLY:     JobType,INT(TimeIn):DISPOSE;  tally time in system
       Reject COUNT:     Rejects:DISPOSE;              count the rejects
       Bad    ASSIGN:    Status = 2:                   !reset status attribute
                         Priority = 3:NEXT(Merge);     reset priority attribute
       END;
```

Figure 3-17. Model Statements for Sample Problem 3.3

```
BEGIN;
PROJECT,        Sample Problem 3.3,SM;
ATTRIBUTES:     TimeIn:
                JobType:
                Status:
                Priority;
VARIABLES:      Mean(2,2),           5,3,
                                     4,2:
                Std(2,2),            2,1,
                                     1,1;
QUEUES:         MachineQ,            LVF(Priority):
                InspectQ,            LVF(Priority);
RESOURCES:      Machine:
                Inspector;
STORAGES:       InspType1:
                InspType2;
COUNTERS:       Rejects;
TALLIES:        Type 1 Time in Sys.:
                Type 2 Time in Sys.;
DSTATS:         NQ(MachineQ),        Machine Queue:
                NQ(InspectQ),        Inspector Queue:
                NR(Machine),         Machine Util.:
                NR(Inspector),       Inspector Util.:
                NSTO(InspType1),     Insp. Type 1 Util.:
                NSTO(InspType2),     Insp. Type 2 Util.;
REPLICATE,      1, 0, 480;
END;
```

Figure 3-18. Experiment Statements for Sample Problem 3.3

The SIMAN Summary Report for this modified example is shown in Figure 3-19. Note that this report contains separate sections summarizing statistics for the observational variables, i.e., time in system, and for the time-dependent variables, i.e., queue lengths and resource utilizations.

```
Project:  Sample Problem 3.3
Analyst:  SM
Replication ended at time  : 480.0
```

TALLY VARIABLES

Identifier	Average	Variation	Minimum	Maximum	Observations
Type 1 Time in Sys.	23.964	.38340	13.830	56.724	23
Type 2 Time in Sys.	50.848	.88666	9.8338	202.43	24

DISCRETE-CHANGE VARIABLES

Identifier	Average	Variation	Minimum	Maximum	Final Value
Machine Queue	.40941	2.2953	.00000	5.0000	.00000
Inspector Queue	2.6506	.87934	.00000	8.0000	3.0000
Machine Util.	.49982	1.0004	.00000	1.0000	1.0000
Inspector Util.	.94047	.25159	.00000	1.0000	1.0000
Insp. Type 1 Util.	.43984	1.1285	.00000	1.0000	.00000
Insp. Type 2 Util.	.50063	.99874	.00000	1.0000	1.0000

COUNTERS

Identifier	Count	Limit
Rejects	7	Infinite

Figure 3-19. SIMAN Summary Report for Sample Problem 3.3.

We have presented the basic modeling concepts of SIMAN by means of a single example, which we have embellished as necessary to present each new set of constructs. Although this approach simplifies the process of learning the constructs, there is the danger of overlooking the full generality of the constructs. Therefore, we conclude this chapter by presenting two additional examples that permit using the same constructs in a different context. The first example involves simulating a restaurant, and the second involves simulating a hospital emergency room.

10.1 Sample Problem 3.4: A Restaurant

Consider a restaurant where the owner is interested in studying the flow of customers for dinner (5:00 P.M. to 9:00 P.M.). Customers arrive in parties of 2, 3, 4, or 5 with respective probabilities of 0.4, 0.3, 0.2, and 0.1, and the time between arrivals is exponentially distributed with a mean of 1.6 minutes. Customers must arrive at the restaurant before 9:00 P.M. to be seated.

The restaurant has 50 tables, each of which can seat two people. These tables are moved together to accommodate parties of more than two persons. Each arriving group gets in line to be seated, but, if there are already five parties in line, the newest customers leave and go to another restaurant. The time it takes to be served is triangularly distributed with minimum, most likely, and maximum times of 15, 18, and 20 minutes, respectively. The time it takes to eat is normally distributed with a mean of 20 minutes and a standard deviation of 2 minutes. When the customers are finished eating, they go to the cashier and pay their bill. The time it takes the cashier to process these customers is normally distributed with a mean of 2.0 minutes and a standard deviation of 0.5 minute.

The objective is to simulate this system for the four-hour dinner period and to record statistics about the number of customers served, the number of busy tables, the number of waiting customers, the number of parties that departs without eating, and the utilization of the cashier.

We begin modeling this system by developing a description for the system's process. The first step is to define the entities that move through the system and that activate the processes. In this model we define an entity as a party of customers. We define an attribute named PartySize to distinguish among entities representing parties of sizes 2, 3, 4, and 5.

The process through which these entities move consists of two main sub-processes. In the first, the entities wait for an available table, seize the table, delay by the service time, and then release the table. However, entities that arrive when the queue for tables has five waiting parties balk the system. In the second sub-process, the entities wait for the cashier to become available, seize the cashier, delay by the service time, and then release the cashier.

Both of these sub-processes can be modeled in SIMAN by using a simple QUEUE-SEIZE-DELAY-RELEASE sequence. In the first sequence we place a capacity on the queue to enforce balking and seize and release resources representing tables. In the second sequence we permit an infinite queue capacity and seize and release a resource representing the cashier.

Entities enter the model at the CREATE block with the operand MaxBatches specified by the variable named Door. This variable is initialized in the experiment to a large value (10,000), and then it is reset to a value of 0 within the model when the first entity arrives after 9:00 P.M. The resetting of MaxBatches to 0 causes the arrival process to terminate after 9:00 P.M.

Entities that enter the model at or before 9:00 P.M. are sent by the BRANCH block to the block labeled Open. These entities represent the parties that arrive before closing. Entities that arrive after 9:00 P.M. are sent to the block labeled Closed. The block labeled Closed is an ASSIGN block that sets the variable Door to 0 in order to shut down the arrival process; it then disposes of the entity. Note, however, that by the time Door is set to 0, the next arrival past 9:00 P.M. is already scheduled by the CREATE block. However, this arrival is also sent to the ASSIGN block labeled Closed where it is disposed of in a similar manner. At this point the arrival sequence is terminated because no additional arrivals are scheduled.

At the ASSIGN block labeled Open, the attribute PartySize is assigned a value from a discrete probability function. The value returned by this function is a 2, 3, 4, or 5 with respective probabilities of 0.4, 0.3, 0.2, and 0.1. Recall that the probabilities in the DISCRETE function must be entered as cumulative probabilities (i.e., as 0.4, 0.7, 0.9, and 1).

At the QUEUE block, entities wait in the queue named TableQ to seize the resource named Table. The queue has a capacity of 5, and arriving entities are balked to the block labeled Leave (a COUNT block) when the queue is at capacity. At the SEIZE block, the number of resource units is specified as the value of Party-Size plus 1, divided by 2. This quantity is the number of two-person tables required to seat the party. For example, a party of size 3 requires $(3+1)/2 = 2$ tables.

After passing through the SEIZE block, the entities are delayed at the DELAY block by a time that is equal to the service time plus the eating time. At the end of this delay, the entities enter the RELEASE block where they release their tables for other waiting parties. Note that this model assumes that there is no delay involved with preparing the tables for the next party.

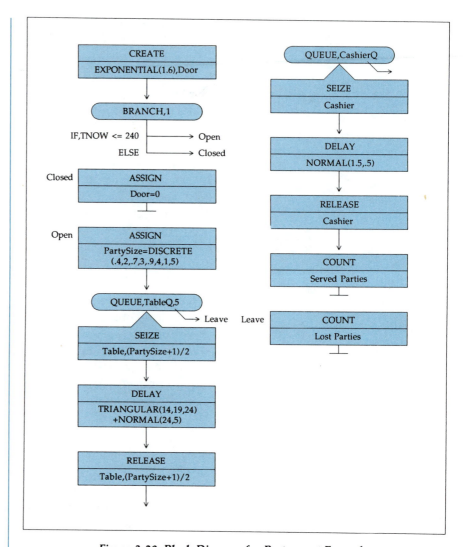

Figure 3-20. Block Diagram for Restaurant Example

The entities next enter the second QUEUE-SEIZE-DELAY-RELEASE sequence representing the processing by the cashier. The entities wait in the queue named CashierQ, seize the resource named Cashier, delay by the time required to pay the bill, and then release the Cashier. At the completion of this sequence the entities enter a COUNT block where the counter named Served Customers is increased by 1, and the entities are disposed of.

The entities that are balked during the arrival process are sent to the last block in the model, which is labeled Leave. This block is a COUNT block, which increases the value of the counter named Lost Parties by 1. The balking entities are then disposed of.

The Model Listing for this example is shown in Figure 3-21. The statements are a direct translation of the Block Diagram.

```
        BEGIN;
                CREATE:     EXPONENTIAL(1.6), Door;        Create parties
                BRANCH,     1:
                            IF, TNOW <= 240, Open:
                            ELSE, Closed;                  Open or Closed ?
        Closed  ASSIGN:     Door = 0: DISPOSE;             Set MaxBatches to 0
        Open    ASSIGN:     PartySize=DISCRETE(.4,2,       !party size 2 (40%)
                                             .7,3,         !party size 3 (30%)
                                             .9,4,         !party size 4 (20%)
                                             1,5);         !party size 5 (10%)

                QUEUE,      TableQ, 5, Leave;              wait for table
                SEIZE:      Table,(PartySize+1)/2;         get tables
                DELAY:      TRIANGULAR(14,19,24)+          !delay by service
                            NORMAL(24,5);                  delay by dining
                RELEASE:    Table,(PartySize+1)/2;         release tables

                QUEUE,      CashierQ;                      wait for cashier
                SEIZE:      Cashier;                       seize cashier
                DELAY:      NORMAL(1.5,.5);                delay to pay bill
                RELEASE:    Cashier;                       release cashier

                COUNT:      Served Parties:DISPOSE;        count served cust.

        Leave   COUNT:      Lost Parties:DISPOSE;          count balked cust.
        END;
```

Figure 3-21. Model Listing for Restaurant Example

The Experiment Listing for this example is shown in Figure 3-22. The experiment defines the attributes, variables, queues, resources, and counters used in the model. In addition, the DSTATS element is included to obtain statistics on the queue lengths and the utilization of the cashier and tables. Note that the value NR(Cashier), which denotes the number of busy Cashiers, is multiplied by 100 in the DSTATS element in order to convert the utilization from a fraction (0-1) to a percentage (0-100). The last element in the experiment is the REPLICATE element, which specifies a single replication with no ending time. In this case the simulation terminates when the arrival process is terminated and the model empties of entities.

```
BEGIN;
PROJECT,                 Sample Problem 3.4,SM;
ATTRIBUTES:              PartySize;
VARIABLES:               Door,10000;
QUEUES:                  TableQ:
                         CashierQ;
RESOURCES:               Table,50:
                         Cashier;
COUNTERS:                Lost Parties:
                         Served Parties;
DSTATS:                  NR(Table),Number of Busy Tables:
                         NQ(TableQ),# of Waiting Parties:
                         NR(Cashier)*100,Cashier Utilization:
                         NQ(CashierQ),# Waiting for Cashier;
REPLICATE,               1;
END;
```

Figure 3-22. Experiment Listing for Restaurant Example

The SIMAN Summary Report for this example is shown in Figure 3-23. As can be seen from the results, 148 parties were served with no customers balking during this one replication of the dinner period. There was an average of 37 tables busy, and the cashier was busy 76% of the time. If we replicate the model more than once, each replication will produce different results. Therefore, it is not really possible to draw any meaningful conclusions from the results obtained from this single replication. In Chapter 5 we return to this problem to interpret the results in detail based on multiple model replications.

```
Project:  Sample Problem 3.4
Analyst:  SM
Replication ended at time  : 288.294
                    DISCRETE-CHANGE VARIABLES
```

Identifier	Average	Variation	Minimum	Maximum	Final Value
Number of Busy Tables	37.342	.35865	.00000	50.000	.00000
# of Waiting Parties	.07187	4.0702	.00000	2.0000	.00000
Cashier Utilization	76.083	.56068	.00000	100.00	.00000
# Waiting for Cashier	2.3952	1.0425	.00000	10.000	.00000

```
                         COUNTERS
```

Identifier	Count	Limit
Lost Parties	0	Infinite
Served Parties	148	Infinite

Figure 3-23. SIMAN Summary Report for the Restaurant Model

10.2 Sample Problem 3.5: A Hospital Emergency Room

Patients arrive at an emergency room where they are treated and then depart. Arrivals are exponentially distributed with a mean time between arrivals of 0.3 hour. Upon arrival, patients are assigned a rating of 1 to 5, depending on the severity of their ailments. Patients in Category 1 are the most severe, and they are immediately sent to a bed where they await medical attention. All other patients must first wait in the receiving room until a basic registration form and medical record are completed. They then proceed to a bed.

The emergency room has three beds, one registration nurse, and two doctors. In all cases the priority for allocating these resources is based on the severity of the ailment. The registration time for patients in Categories 2 through 5 is 0.15 hour. The treatment time for all patients is triangularly distributed with the minimum, most likely, and maximum values differing according to the patient's category. The distribution of patients by category and the corresponding minimum, most likely, and maximum treatment times are summarized below.

Category	1	2	3	4	5
Percent	6	8	18	33	35
Minimum	.8	.7	.4	.2	.1
Most Likely	1.2	.95	.6	.45	.35
Maximum	1.6	1.1	.75	.6	.45

The problem is to simulate this system over a 30-day period and record statistics about the utilization of the resources and the time that the patients spend in the system, categorized by ailment.

We begin model development by identifying the entities in the model. In this case the entities in the model represent the patients in the system. We use two attributes for the entities. The first attribute, named TimeIn, is used to mark the arrival time of patients to the system, so that interval statistics can be recorded on the time in the system. The second attribute, named Category, is used to store the patient category as a number between 1 (Open Wounds) and 5 (Chronic Complaints).

The Block Diagram model for this problem is shown in Figure 3-24, and the correponding Model Listing is shown in Figure 3-25. Entities enter the model at the CREATE block where their arrival time is marked in the attribute TimeIn. The entities then pass through the ASSIGN block where their attribute Category is set to a random value from a discrete probability distribution. The value assigned is 1, 2, 3, 4, or 5 with respective probabilities 0.06, 0.08, 0.18, 0.33, and 0.35. The entities then enter the BRANCH block where the category 1 patients (Open Wounds) are sent to the QUEUE block labeled ToBed, and all other categories are sent to the QUEUE block labeled Records.

The entities that are sent to the QUEUE block labeled Records wait in the queue named NurseQ to seize the resource named Nurse. The entities then delay by the time required to complete the forms and then release the Nurse. These entities then merge with the category 1 patients at the QUEUE block labeled ToBed.

The entities arriving at the QUEUE block labeled ToBed are either category 1 patients who have skipped the registration process or are other category patients who have completed the registration process. These entities wait in the queue named BedQ to seize the first available unit of the resource named Bed. The entities that have received beds then wait in the queue named DoctorQ to seize the first available unit of the resource named Doctor. The entities are then delayed by the DELAY block by a time that is triangularly distributed with parameters determined by the patient's category. At the completion of the delay, the entities release both the Bed and Doctor resources, and they then pass through the two TALLY blocks before exiting the model. The first TALLY block records the time in system by category, and the second TALLY block records the time in system for all patients.

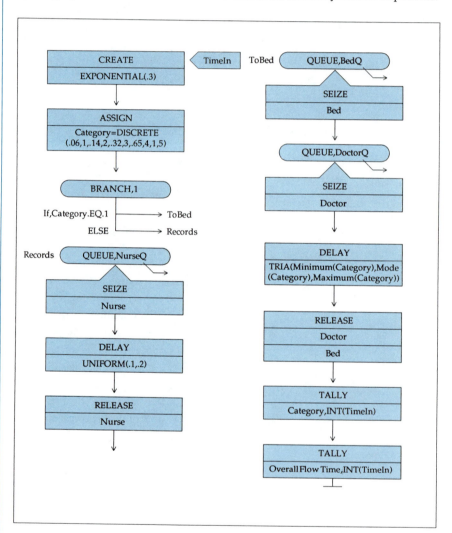

Figure 3-24. Block Diagram for the Hospital Example

```
      BEGIN;
            CREATE:      EXPONENTIAL(.3):           !Patient arrival
                         MARK(TimeIn);               set arrival time
   ;    Set severity of injury
            ASSIGN:      Category=DISCRETE(.06,1,    Open Wounds
                                           .14,2,   !Closed Injuries
                                           .32,3,   !Multiple Trama
                                           .65,4,   !Visceral Complaints
                                           1,5);    !Chronic Complaints

            BRANCH,1:
                         If,Category.EQ.1,ToBed:     !Very severe to bed
                         ELSE,Records;               !Fill out medical records
   ;    Types 2-5 must complete forms and wait for records
   Records QUEUE,        NurseQ;                     !Wait for nurse
           SEIZE:        Nurse;                      !Get nurse
           DELAY:        UNIFORM(.1,.2);             !Delay to complete forms
           RELEASE:      Nurse;                      !Release nurse
   ;    All types wait for bed and then doctor
   ToBed   QUEUE,        BedQ;                       !Wait for bed
           SEIZE:        Bed;                         Get bed
           QUEUE,        DoctorQ;                     Wait for doctor
           SEIZE:        Doctor;                      Get doctor
           DELAY:        TRIA(Minimum(Category),     !Delay for treatment
                         Mode(Category),
                         Maximum(Category));
   ;    Treatment completed—exit the system
            RELEASE:     Doctor:Bed;                 !Release all resources
            TALLY:       Category,INT(TimeIn);       !Severity flow time
            TALLY:       Overall Flow Time,INT       !All flow time
                         (TimeIn):
                         DISPOSE;                    Dispose of patient
      END;
```

Figure 3-25. Model Listing for the Hospital Example

The Experiment Listing for this problem is shown in Figure 3-26. The experiment defines the attributes, variables, queues, resources, tallies, and dstats for the model. Note that the rankings for all of the queues are defined as LVF(Category), which causes the patients to be ordered in the queues according to the severity of their ailments. The REPLICATE element specifies a single replication of the simulation for a 30-day (720-hour) period.

```
BEGIN;

PROJECT,    Sample Problem 3.5,SM;

ATTRIBUTES: Category:
            TimeIn;

VARIABLES:  Minimum(5),      .8, .7,.40,.20,.10:!  minimum treatment
            Mode(5),        1.2,.95,.60,.45,.35:!  mode of treatment
            Maximum(5),     1.6,1.1,.75,.60,.45;!  maximum treatment

QUEUES:     BedQ      ,LVF(Category):
            DoctorQ   ,LVF(Category):
            NurseQ    ,LVF(Category);

RESOURCES:  Bed,3:
            Doctor,2:
            Nurse,1;

TALLIES:    Open Wounds:
            Closed Injuries:
            Multiple Trauma:
            Visceral Complaints:
            Chronic Complaints:
            Overall Flow Time,"Time.dat";

DSTATS:     NR(Bed), Number of Busy Beds:
            NR(Doctor), Number of Busy Doctors:
            NR(Nurse), Number of Busy Nurses:
            NQ(BedQ),Bed Queue Length:
            NQ(DoctorQ),Doctor Queue Length:
            NQ(NurseQ),Nurse Queue Length;

REPLICATE,  1, 0, 720;

END;
```

Figure 3-26. Experiment Listing for the Hospital Example

The SIMAN Summary Report for this example is shown in Figure 3-27. As can be seen from the results, 2,379 patients were processed by the emergency room during this 30-day simulated period. The time spent by the patients in the system (flowtime) ranged from 0.23 hour to 13.8 hours. However, before we draw any conclusions from these results, we must deal with a number of important issues, such as the selection of the starting conditions for the model and the run length. In Chapter 5 we discuss these important topics and then return to this problem to interpret the results from this model in detail.

```
Project:  Sample Problem 3.5
Analyst:  SM
Replication ended at time  : 720.0
```

TALLY VARIABLES

Identifier	Average	Variation	Minimum	Maximum	Observations
Open Wounds	1.4186	.20885	.83392	2.5421	141
Closed Injuries	1.3333	.22874	.88326	3.1810	174
Multiple Trauma	1.0677	.34556	.53932	4.0369	406
Visceral Complaints	1.0421	.66916	.34407	6.3397	825
Chronic Complaints	1.6258	1.1206	.23144	13.772	833
Overall Flow Time	1.2945	.92551	.23144	13.772	2379

DISCRETE-CHANGE VARIABLES

Identifier	Average	Variation	Minimum	Maximum	Final Value
Number of Busy Beds	2.1297	.49040	.00000	3.0000	3.0000
Number of Busy Doctors	1.6103	.41021	.00000	2.0000	2.0000
Number of Busy Nurses	.46372	1.0754	.00000	1.0000	1.0000
Bed Queue Length	1.5029	1.8094	.00000	17.000	3.0000
Doctor Queue Length	.51936	.96199	.00000	1.0000	1.0000
Nurse Queue Length	.19719	2.7058	.00000	5.0000	2.0000

Figure 3-27. SIMAN Summary Report for the Hospital Example

Exercises

Exercise 3.1

A manual car wash has five identical booths for which cars must wait in a single queue. Cars arrive exponentially with a mean interarrival time of five minutes. A person washes his car according to a normal distribution with mean of 20 minutes and a standard deviation of 4 minutes. The car wash is open 16 hours per day. Simulate the system for a 16-hour day and count the number of cars washed.

Exercise 3.2

Modify the model for Sample Problem 3.1 from Chapter 3 to limit the queue named Buffer to a maximum of three waiting jobs by using a variable. In addition to counting the number of jobs completed, also count the number of jobs balked from queue Buffer. Run the simulation for 480 time units.

Exercise 3.3

Modify the model for Sample Problem 3.3 from Chapter 3 to accommodate a change in the procedure for handling rejected jobs. Under the modified system, rejects are still sent back to the machine, but now have their own queue, which is ranked low-value-first by the time the job entered the system. Rejected jobs have priority over regular jobs for gaining access to the machine. Record statistics on the length of the rejected jobs queue. Run the simulation for 480 time units.

Exercise 3.4

Consider a manufacturing system comprising two different machines and a single operator who is shared between the two machines. Parts arrive with an exponentially distributed interarrival time with a mean of three minutes. The arriving parts are one of two types. Sixty percent of the arriving parts are type 1 and are processed on machine 1. These parts require the operator for a one-minute setup operation. The remaining 40 percent are part type 2 and are processed on machine 2. These parts require the operator for a 1.5-minute setup operation. The service times (excluding the setup time) are normally distributed with a mean of 4.5 minutes and a standard deviation of 1 minute for part type 1, and a mean of 7.5 minutes and a standard deviation of 1.5 minutes for part type 2.

Two different priority schemes have been proposed for allocating the operator between the two types of waiting jobs. The first scheme is to assign priority to the type 1 jobs. Under this proposal, a job type 2 setup will only be performed if there are no job type 1 setups waiting to be performed. The second proposed scheme is to alternate the priority between the two job types.

Simulate each of these systems for an 80-hour period, and collect statistics on the machine and operator utilizations, the average number of parts waiting for each machine, and the average flowtime for all parts.

Exercise 3.5

In the preceding two machine problems the operator periodically must do paperwork associated with the parts flowing through the work area. The time required to perform this paperwork has a triangular distribution with minimum, mode, and maximum values of three, five, and eight minutes, respectively. The time between paperwork requests is exponentially distributed with a mean of 25 minutes. The paperwork is prioritized over servicing parts. In addition to the previous statistics, collect statistics on the utilization of the operator for performing the paperwork.

Exercise 3.6

An airline ticket counter has two customer queues, one for regular customers, who are serviced by 4 agents, and one for frequent-flyer-membership customers, who are serviced by one agent. Approximately 2 out of every 10 customers have frequent-flyer memberships. Customers arrive with an exponential interarrival time of two minutes from 8:00 A.M. to 4:00 P.M., and four minutes from 4:00 P.M. to closing at 12:00 midnight. During the second shift (4:00 P.M. to closing) all customers use the first counter with four agents. During first shift, if an arriving frequent-flyer-membership customer observes that the regular customer queue has two or fewer people while the frequent-flyer agent is busy, the customer will enter the regular customer queue. Service time of regular customers is normally distributed with a mean of 10 minutes and a standard deviation of 4 minutes. Service time of frequent-flyer customers is also normally distributed with a mean seven minutes and a standard deviation of two minutes.

Simulate the system for one 16-hour day and collect statistics on the queue size and utilization for all agents, and the flow time by customer type. Also count the number of times a frequent-flyer customer decides to enter the regular customer queue during first shift.

Exercise 3.7

A small warehouse provides work-in-process storages for a manufacturing facility at which four types of parts are produced. Each part has an associated inventory cost. The part type percentages and inventory costs for the four parts are shown in the table below.

Part Type	Percentage	Inventory Cost
1	20%	$ 5.50
2	30%	$ 6.50
3	30%	$ 8.00
4	20%	$10.50

Parts arrive at the warehouse with a triangularly distributed interarrival time with minimum, mean, and maximum values of 1.5, 2.0, and 2.8 minutes, respectively. The part type is assigned upon arrival based on the above percentages. Two cranes store and retrieve parts in the warehouse, with a travel time following a uniform distribution in the range of 1.2 to 3.0 minutes. Requests for removal of parts from the warehouse follow the same distribution as part arrivals, and are processed with priority given to requests for parts with the highest individual inventory cost. If there are no parts of the type requested, the request is not filled.

Model this warehouse for one day (24 hours), starting with four of each part type in the warehouse. Track the inventory cost by part type and the overall inventory value. Also count the number of unfilled requests (shortages) for each part type and report the overall utilization (percentage of time busy) of the cranes.

Exercise 3.8

A three-station serial assembly process is plagued by high rework rates. Rework rates are as follows;

FROM (end of)	TO (beginning of)	Percentage
Station2	Station1	5%
Station3	Station2	5%
Station3	Station3	5%

Rework service times are identical to regular service times.

This system is fed by another system that has times between exits that are normally distributed with a mean of 10 minutes and a standard deviation of 2 minutes. Parameters for triangular service and inspection times (minutes) are combined for each station as follows;

	Minimum	Mode	Maximum
Station1	6	9	12
Station2	5	8	11
Station3	4.5	7	8.5

a. Simulate this system for a 100-hour period and collect statistics on the flowtime through the system, queue sizes, and machine utilizations.

b. In an attempt to keep the flowtime under control, the production manager has proposed a priority-based expediting strategy. Jobs initially enter the system with a priority value of 1. Whenever a job is reworked, its priority is increased by 1. Each queue in front of each machine is ranked according to the priority of the job.

Simulate the system with the proposed expediting strategy and collect additional statistics on the average priority level for jobs exiting the system.

Exercise 3.9

In the preceding serial three-machine problem (Exercise 3.8) the supervisor has been informed that 10 percent of the jobs entering the system are modifications of the original parts, which will be less complex to inspect. The service times of the new part type are on the average 20 percent shorter.

a. Simulate the system with the expediting strategy.

b. A preventive maintenance program has been implemented affecting the uptime of the second machine. Once every 100 parts the machine must undergo a preventive maintenance delay, which is normally distributed with a mean of 15 minutes and a standard deviation of 3 minutes. Simulate this system with the expediting strategy. Also count the number of preventive maintenance events on the second machine.

Exercise 3.10

A professor teaching a simulation class of fifteen students gives a homework assignment every class meeting; the assignments are collected at the beginning of the next class period. The number of students completing the day's assignment follows a discrete probability distribution with probabilities listed in the table (left).

Probability	# Students Completing Assignment
0.2	11
0.2	12
0.3	13
0.1	14
0.2	15

The professor grades the assignments during office hours, which are scheduled for 90 minutes after class each day. The time to review an assignment follows a uniform distribution with a minimum of two minutes and a maximum of three minutes. Students also may make appointments to see the professor during office hours; visits are given higher priority than assignments, but the professor finishes grading the current assignment before helping the student. The professor schedules appointments with three to seven students per day (with equal probability of each number of students in the range) at 15-minute intervals starting at the beginning of office hours. Of the students who schedule appointments, 10 percent typically do not show up. The time that the professor spends with each student is triangularly distributed with minimum, mean, and maximum of 5, 10, and 20 minutes, respectively.

Simulate the operation of a day's office hours, collecting overall statistics on the time required to complete the day's tasks (grading papers, seeing students), the average time spent by students waiting to see the professor, and the percentage of time spent by the professor on each of the two tasks.

Exercise 3.11

In a highway construction project a dump truck service terminal refuels trucks and performs maintenance 24 hours per day. There are 20 trucks in the system. During the first 12 hours of the day, trucks must be refueled once every 2 hours according to a triangular distribution +/− 5%, once every 3 hours during the last 12 hours of the day. The refuelling time is normally distributed with a mean of 15 minutes and a standard deviation of 3 minutes. On the average, there are two maintenance requirements per day, and the time between these is exponentially distributed. The maintenace requirements are distributed randomly and evenly among trucks 1 through 20. If a truck is scheduled for maintenance, it will be incorporated into the next refuelling stop, thereby tripling the duration of the stop.

The number of trucks that can simultaneously be processed at the terminal is limited by the number of workers assigned to the terminal. Trucks that arrive at the terminal when all workers are busy must wait their turn to be processed.

Simulate the system for a 10-day period and assume a staffing level of five workers. Collect statistics on the flow time through the terminal, the length of the truck queue, and the utilization of the workers.

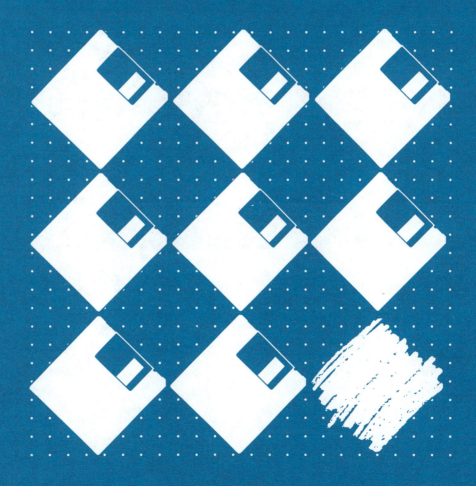

CHAPTER 4

CHAPTER 4
Model Verification and Validation

1. Introduction

In the previous chapter we learned how to construct models and experiments for simple systems by using SIMAN. Although at this point we can build and execute models to obtain output statistics, we face the task of determining whether these results are correct. The fact that a model compiles, executes, and produces numbers does not guarantee that it is correct or that the numbers being generated are representative of the system being modeled. In this chapter we discuss methods for determining whether the simulation model is operating correctly and whether it is actually simulating its real-world counterpart.

In the context of simulation modeling, the process of determining the correctness of model operation typically consists of two separate functions: verification and validation. *Verification* is the process of determining that a model operates as intended. Throughout the verification process, we try to find and remove unintentional errors in the model's logic. This activity is commonly referred to as *debugging* the model. In contrast, *validation* is the process of reaching an acceptable level of confidence that the inferences drawn from the model are correct and applicable to the real-world system being represented. Through validation we try to determine whether the simplifications and omissions of detail, which we have knowingly and deliberately made in our model, have introduced unacceptably large errors in the results. Validation is the process of determining that we have built the right model, whereas verification is designed to see if we have built the model right.

Verification activities are restricted to the model itself; during verification, we make sure that the model contains as few errors as possible. Validation, on the other hand, requires that we convey the basis for our confidence in the model to a target audience. As analysts, we must assume the full responsibility for detailing our assumptions, simplifications, and methodologies and for offering evidence that the rationale behind our approach will produce trustworthy answers that can be used in the real world by the ultimate decision maker. Unless our confidence in the model can be transferred to others, the model's usefulness will never be realized. Thus, through verification testing, we develop personal confidence in the model; through validation, we transfer that confidence to others.

No single test can verify or validate a simulation model. Confidence in the usefulness of a model must gradually accumulate as the model passes many tests and as new points of correspondence between model and empirical reality are examined. Testing goes on continually in the process of constructing and using the model.

Although both of these tasks are challenging, verification, the simpler of the two, is normally performed before validation. We therefore begin this chapter by discussing useful techniques for verification; we then turn our attention to the more difficult problem of validation.

2. Verifying Model Operation

As already noted, the verification process consists of isolating and correcting unintentional errors in the model. Although the general approach to verification is largely a skill developed through experience, the beginner can use a number of techniques to aid in the verification process.

To a large extent, the complexity of the verification process increases with the size of the model. With large models it becomes increasingly difficult to isolate errors, and yet it is much more likely that errors are present. Therefore, the verification process is easier if we use an approach to modeling like that discussed in Chapter 2, whereby we start with a small, simple model and gradually embellish it. In this way we can test and correct errors in stages, adding more detail at each stage. This approach is much easier than trying to debug a large, complex model from scratch.

The most difficult part of the verification process is not the correction of errors—it is the isolation of errors. Although the SIMAN processor can detect certain types of errors in a model's logic, it cannot detect others; these undetected errors produce erroneous results. In some cases an error in a model produces results that are very clearly wrong; unfortunately, many errors produce results that look believable but are still wrong. The latter types of errors are particularly dangerous because they can remain concealed within the model, continuing to produce errors and continuing to mislead the decision maker. Therefore, much of our discussion is devoted to the process of isolating these hidden errors within the model.

2.1 Establishing a Doubting Frame of Mind

Model verification must be approached with a doubting frame of mind. Adopting this outlook can be very difficult; after all, when the model appears to be working properly, we very much want to believe in its correctness. This desire to believe in the model's correctness is often amplified when the modeling team is under pressure and the project falls behind schedule.

Although verification is commonly defined in the literature as showing that a model operates as intended, success actually requires taking the opposite approach. In other words, rather than trying to show that the model works as intended, we should try to show that the model indeed contains errors, which we must find and correct. Because verification activities focus on finding errors in the model rather than on demonstrating its correctness, they are said to be destructive, rather than constructive. Hence, verification may be better defined as the process of examining a simulation model with the intent of finding and correcting all errors.

We must realize that many simulation models execute properly for a given set of input but then fail under a new set of data. The fact that a model operates properly in one scenario does not mean that the model is free of errors. Do not make the mistake of many other modelers by viewing the successful running of a scenario as "verifying the correct execution of the model." If you adopt the proper approach, you will instead view the successful running of a scenario as a failure because it did not expose any errors in the model. Our goal during verification is to find scenarios that cause the model to fail so that we can isolate and correct errors. Progress is made by identifying and removing errors, not by demonstrating situations in which the model works correctly.

2.2 Incorporating Outside Doubters

Whenever possible, the verification process should incorporate outside doubters, that is, persons who were not involved in the actual design and implementation of the model. Because they have no emotional attachment to the model, outside doubters are better able to adopt the necessary critical perspective and accept their destructive role. In contrast, the person involved in the constructive phase of model development and design finds it difficult to form a completely destructive frame of mind toward the same model. Outsiders typically have no such bias toward the model and are often eager to expose its errors.

The outside doubters should know and understand the modeled system and its intended operation; they should not, however, have been directly involved in its construction. Their primary role is to detect and isolate errors. Once errors are exposed, the correction of errors is typically best performed by those individuals involved in the design and construction of the model.

2.3 Conducting Model and Experiment Walkthroughs

A walkthrough is a very simple but effective method for finding errors in simulation models. The walkthrough procedure involves gathering a small group for an informal review of the model's logic. The group typically consists of the person who developed the model's logic and two or three outside individuals who are familiar with the system being modeled and the simulation language being used. Walkthroughs can involve either going through the model block by block or manually simulating the movement of a small number of entities through the block diagram.

The code walkthrough is a well-established software-testing procedure, which achieved popularity in *The Psychology of Computer Programming* [Weinberg 1971]. Experience has shown that simulation models benefit from walkthroughs in the same way that general software programs do. The use of this technique within IBM [Perriens 1977] for general software testing has shown error-detection efficiencies as high as 80 percent.

The walkthrough participant's attitude is crucial to success. The group should focus on analyzing the program for errors, not on evaluating the developer's modeling skills. In other words, errors should not be viewed as black marks against the modeler who made them, but rather as the natural consequence of a difficult modeling task. In general, comments should be directed toward the model and not toward the modeler.

2.4 Performing Test Runs

Theoretically, an important part of model verification involves using test cases that effectively reveal errors of logic in the model. In practice, this activity poses two problems: first, it is very difficult to develop a comprehensive set of test cases that generates the sequence of events necessary to produce most of the errors that can occur in a model over time; second, even if we succeed in designing an appropriate set of test cases, we still face the problem of recognizing that a given test case has indeed produced an error. Recognizing an error becomes very difficult in a complex stochastic simulation model, which produces random output with an unknown true response. The dual problems of generating and observing errors make the effective design and use of test cases very challenging.

The separation of SIMAN programs into Model and Experiment frames greatly simplifies the development of test cases because the test case can usually be defined by modifying only the Experiment frame. Thus, once built, a set of test cases can be saved and reused to evaluate additional changes to the model.

One effective method for designing test cases involves replacing random times with constant times. This approach generally leads to reduced queueing in the model and produces results that are easier to follow and predict. Error detection can be further simplified by incorporating cases that test only one portion of the model at a time. Although both approaches are useful, they are, by themselves, insufficient because they sometimes reduce interactions within the model, thereby suppressing errors that might otherwise occur.

Finally, test cases that explore boundary conditions are more likely to expose modeling errors than test cases that operate the model under typical conditions. Therefore, it is useful to exercise the model under conditions that "stress" its interactions by using extreme parameter settings. The following list suggests some possibilities.

■ Increase the arrival rate and/or reduce the service rate to create congestion within the model.

■ Reduce the buffer sizes on the queues to force more blocking/balking within the system.

■ Modify the job mix to increase the occurrence of infrequent job types.

- Increase the rate of occurrence of infrequent events, such as machine breakdowns.
- Reduce the arrival rate and/or increase the service rate to force "starvation" within the model.

2.5 Tracing the Model's Operation: The TRACE Element

SIMAN executes a simulation model by moving entities block by block through the model. During verification, we search for situations wherein the entity flow is incorrect and/or the function performed at a specific block is incorrect. The trace feature of SIMAN lets us examine in detail the movement of entities through the system. It also gives us a summary of the action taken at each block through which an entity has passed.

Although the model can simultaneously contain many entities, SIMAN actually moves only one entity at a time. We refer to the currently moving entity as the *active* entity. The active entity moves as far as it can through the block diagram until it encounters a status or time delay (e.g., a QUEUE block or DELAY block) or departs the Model. In the case of a status or time delay, the entity becomes active again and resumes moving through the block diagram once the delay is complete.

When the active entity encounters a delay or departs the model, a new entity becomes active and moves through the block diagram until it likewise encounters a delay or departs the system. In order to simulate the simultaneous movement of entities, SIMAN holds the simulated time, TNOW, fixed until all entities to be moved at that point in time have been processed. The simulated time, TNOW, is then moved forward to the time at which the next entity becomes active and begins moving through the block diagram. This process continues until the simulation terminates.

The SIMAN trace consists of a detailed history of all entity movements through the block diagram. Figure 4-1 shows a portion of a trace for the first problem in Chapter 3. Note that the trace is divided into repeating sections of information. As each individual entity becomes active and begins moving through the block diagram, the trace displays a section header containing both the entity identifier and the simulated time at which the movement started. Each section contains a summary of the action that occurred at each block through which the entity passed during this movement. Note that all actions within a section are processed at the same instant of simulated time.

```
                    SIMAN System Trace Beginning at Time: .000
  Seq#        Label          Block              System Status Change
  ─────────────────────────────────────────────────────────────────────
  TIME: 0.0 ENTITY: 1
        1                    CREATE      Next creation scheduled at time 6.01894
        2                    QUEUE       Entity 1 sent to next block
        3                    SEIZE       Seized 1 unit(s) of MACHINE(1)
        4                    DELAY       Delayed by 4.2856 until time 4.2856
                                         NQ(Buffer) = .0000
                                         NR(Machine) = 1.000

  TIME: 4.2856 ENTITY: 1
        5                    RELEASE     MACHINE available incr by 1 to 1
        6                    COUNT       Counter JOBSDONE incremented by 1 to 1
                                         Disposed entity 1
                                         NQ(Buffer) = .0000
                                         NR(Machine) = .0000

  TIME: 6.01894 ENTITY: 2
        1                    CREATE      Next creation scheduled at time 8.12828
        2                    QUEUE       Entity 2 sent to next block
        3                    SEIZE       Seized 1 unit(s) of MACHINE(1)
        4                    DELAY       Delayed by 3.80339 until time 9.82233
                                         NQ(Buffer) = .0000
                                         NR(Machine) = 1.000

  TIME: 8.12828 ENTITY: 1
        1                    CREATE      Next creation scheduled at time 10.5094
        2                    QUEUE       Entity 1 sent to next block
        3                    SEIZE       Could not seize resource MACHINE(1)
                                         Availability is 0 with 1 required
                                         Entity 1 added to queue BUFFER at rank 1
                                         NQ(Buffer) = 1.000
                                         NR(Machine) = 1.000

  TIME: 9.82233 ENTITY: 2
        5                    RELEASE     MACHINE available incr by 1 to 1
                                         Entity 1 removed from queue BUFFER
                                         Resource allocated to entity 1
                                         Seized 1 unit(s) of MACHINE(1)
        6                    COUNT       Counter JOBSDONE incremented by 1 to 2
                                         Disposed entity 2
                                         NQ(Buffer) = .0000
                                         NR(Machine) = 1.000

  TIME: 9.82233 ENTITY: 1
        4                    DELAY       Delayed by 4.62926 until time 14.4516
                                         NQ(Buffer) = .0000
                                         NR(Machine) = 1.000
```

Figure 4-1. Portion of Trace for Sample Problem 3.1

The entity identifier displayed in the header of each trace section can be used to track a specific entity through the model. SIMAN assigns this identifying number to the entity when it first enters the model, and it remains assigned to that entity until it departs the model. Once an entity has departed, its identifier is reused for newly created entities; therefore, the same entity identifier number can reappear later in the trace for a new entity.

To activate the trace option, include the TRACE element in the experiment. The format of the TRACE element is summarized below.

TRACE,BegTime,EndTime,Condition,Expression, ... ;

With large models or long run-times, millions of blocks may be activated by entities moving through the block diagram, and a trace of the entire simulation can produce many boxes of paper. Therefore, two options are available for limiting the trace within the simulation. First, we can specify a trace period by providing a starting (BegTime) and ending (EndTime) time for the trace. In this case, the trace is only generated during the specified period. Second, we can specify a trace condition that limits the generation of trace information to periods when the trace condition is true. For example, we may suspect that an error only occurs when a specific buffer reaches capacity, and we may therefore wish to generate the trace only during periods when we know that the buffer is full.

The Expression operand can be used to display the value of one or more user-specified variables, attributes, or expressions. The values of the listed expressions are displayed at the end of each trace section. In our example, the current queue length and resource status are being displayed.

Two examples of TRACE elements are shown below. The first TRACE element was used to generate the trace shown in Figure 4-1. The second TRACE element has both a trace period and a trace condition.

```
TRACE,,,, NQ(Buffer), NR(Machine);

TRACE, 0, 10, NQ(Buffer) > 5, NQ(Buffer);
```

2.6 Isolating and Correcting Errors with the Interactive Debugger

Although SIMAN's trace facility can effectively detail the movement of entities through the model, its main disadvantage is that it is batch-oriented. The interactive debugger provides similar capability in an interactive mode, thereby permitting you to monitor and control model execution. As such, it works more effectively than the trace facility for isolating and correcting model errors.

The interactive debugger allows you to step through the execution of the model by exercising complete control from the keyboard. You can move an entity through one or more blocks, examine the value of a variable or attribute, examine the entities residing in a queue, etc. by using simple keyboard commands. You can also suspend execution at critical points (called *breakpoints*) or when specified variables (called *watch variables*) reach defined values. The debugger also provides access to a model's source statements, which can be listed during execution.

The interactive debugger was designed as a tool for searching for bugs in the model and for conducting walkthroughs during verification. As we will see, the debugger greatly simplifies the activity of stepping through the execution of the model.

Starting and Stopping a Debug Session

A YES/NO field on the BEGIN element in the experiment is used to specify whether the interactive debugger is invoked at the beginning of each simulation run. The default for the debug operand is NO, which means that SIMAN models run without debugging interruptions.

The format for the BEGIN element is shown below.

BEGIN,Listing,Debugger;

As discussed in Chapter 3, the first operand, Listing, is a YES/NO option to specify whether a listing of the experiment should be generated. This operand defaults to YES, which causes a listing to be generated. The second operand, Debugger, is the YES/NO option for turning the debugger on or off. This operand defaults to NO.

If the debug option has been specified as YES, then the command to run the SIMAN processor will respond with a message, indicating that the model will be executed under control of the debugger. The debugger will then display the following line:

.00000>

The line .00000> is the debugger's prompt, which consists of the current simulated time, TNOW, followed by the greater than symbol (>). The prompt indicates that the debugger is waiting for a command.

On most SIMAN installations, it is also possible to enter the debugger during execution. To enter the debugger, press the appropriate key on the keyboard after entering the command to run the SIMAN processor. This action suspends execution of the simulation, and the debugger prompt appears. For example, on MS-DOS and OS/2 computers, you can enter the debugger at any time during execution by pressing the [ESC] key.

To terminate the debugging session, type either END or QUIT (followed by a carriage return) in response to the debugger prompt. This action terminates the current simulation run and returns you to the operating system. The END command causes the standard end-of-run SIMAN Summary Report to be displayed before termination, whereas the QUIT command does not.

Entering Debugger Commands

Debug commands are interactively entered from the keyboard in response to the prompt TNOW>. The general form of the command is

command [/qualifier] [keyword [,keyword]] [operand [,operand]...]:

where

> command specifies the name of the command,
>
> qualifier specifies an optional qualifier,
>
> keyword specifies the command's type, and
>
> operand specifies the target of the command.

The brackets indicate that the modifying keywords and operands are not always present; they are optional with certain commands and are not used with others. Two-letter abbreviations are sufficient to uniquely specify any command or keyword when entering a command.

Command operands commonly take the form of an identifier, which can be entered either as a block sequence number or as a block label. For example, the command that lets us set a breakpoint on a block (SET BREAK) has an operand specifying the particular block for which the breakpoint is to be set. This command can be entered as SET BREAK 12, meaning "set the breakpoint at block sequence number 12," or as SET BREAK Drill, meaning "set the breakpoint at the block labeled Drill."

With some commands, the operand takes the form of a SIMAN variable or expression. For example, the command to show the value of an expression (SHOW) has another expression as its operand. The command SHOW NQ(DrillQueue) + NQ(LatheQueue) displays the numerical value corresponding to the sum of the lengths of the queues named DrillQueue and LatheQueue.

Many commands accept repeats of an operand, and these are separated by commas. For example, SHOW Duedate,Priority shows the value of Duedate and Priority by using a single command. In many cases the asterisk (*) can be used as a wild card to denote a range of all valid values. For example, SHOW NQ(*) displays the value for NQ for all queues in the model.

Finally, some commands permit an operand to be entered as a range of values. The beginning and ending entries within the range are separated by a double dot (..). For example, SET BREAK 1..10 sets breakpoints on all blocks with sequence numbers between 1 and 10.

With this brief introduction to the command syntax, we will now summarize some of the more commonly used debugger commands.

Controlling Execution: The GO and STEP Commands

Once the debugger issues its prompt, it waits with the simulation suspended until a command is issued. The GO command begins or resumes simulation execution. If you do not specify any operands, then execution resumes at the current time and continues until the simulation run terminates, until the simulation is interrupted from the keyboard, or until the simulation is interrupted by a debug event (for example, an entity arrives at the block for which a breakpoint has been set).

If you enter the keyword UNTIL along with a time-value, the simulation continues (unless otherwise interrupted) until the specified time. At that time the execution is suspended, and the debugger issues its prompt. For example, the command GO UNTIL 30 causes the simulation to continue until time 30. The time value can be entered as any valid expression; for example, the command GO UNTIL TNOW + 480 causes the simulation to continue for an additional 480 units of time.

It is also possible to advance the simulation by moving entities through one or more blocks with the STEP command. This command causes entities to move through a specified number of blocks. The number of blocks to process defaults to 1; therefore, STEP 1 (or simply STEP) causes the current entity to move through the next block in its sequence. This command allows the simulation to execute one block at a time.

If the STEP operand is greater than 1, note that the number of blocks processed may or may not pertain to the same entity. For example, if the specified value is 4, and on its third movement the current entity is placed in a QUEUE block to await a resource, then the remaining movement will be applied to the next entity in the model.

The effect of the STEP command is canceled if the execution is interrupted by another event in the debugger, e.g., an entity arrives at a block that has a set breakpoint.

Setting and Canceling Options: The SET and CANCEL Commands

Many useful options in the debugger are controlled with the SET and CANCEL commands. You turn on (or set) the options with the SET command; you turn off (or cancel) them with the CANCEL command. The SET and CANCEL commands always have an associated keyword specifying which option is to be set or canceled.

You use the SET BREAK command to set a breakpoint on one or more blocks in the model. A breakpoint causes the execution to be suspended and the debugger to issue a prompt each time an entity arrives at the block. We can, for example, set a breakpoint on a CREATE block to examine the new arrivals into the system, or we can set a breakpoint on a RELEASE block for a resource that seems to be the cause of a problem in our model.

The SET BREAK command includes a required operand that specifies the block (or range of blocks) for which to set the breakpoint. For example, the command SET BREAK Drill .. Lathe sets breakpoints on all blocks between the block labeled Drill and the block labeled Lathe; the command SET BREAK 10, 12 .. 15 sets breakpoints on blocks with sequence numbers 10, 12, 13, 14, and 15.

The CANCEL BREAK command cancels previously set breakpoints by specifying their identifiers. For example, the command CANCEL BREAK Drill, 12 .. 15 cancels breakpoints at both the block labeled Drill and at the blocks with sequence numbers 12 through 15.

Although ideal for many debugging activities, the ability to set breakpoints to interrupt the simulation when an entity arrives at a specific block doesn't always meet our needs. In some cases we need the ability to monitor the value of a variable or expression, and we want automatic interruption of the simulation whenever the value changes. In SIMAN, a *watch* provides this capability. To set a watch, use the SET WATCH command, which has an operand specifying the variable or expression to be monitored. For example, the command SET WATCH NQ(DrillQueue) suspends the execution and issues the debugger command prompt immediately following any change in the current length of the queue named DrillQueue. The command SET WATCH NQ(LatheQueue) > 10 monitors the expression NQ(LatheQueue) > 10 and suspends the execution whenever the condition changes from false to true or vice versa.

A watch expression can involve attributes of entities as well as system variables; however, whenever the watch expression contains attributes, they correspond to the entity that was active at the time that the watch was initially set. For example, the command SET WATCH A(1) sets a watch on the first attribute of the currently active entity. The first attribute of this entity continues to be monitored even if this entity is no longer the currently active entity. Hence, the value of A(1) for a new active entity can change without triggering the watch. The VIEW ENTITY command (described in the next section) can be used to examine the currently active entity.

It is also possible to set watches on expressions that do not interrupt the simulation but simply display a message and continue the simulation. To do so, append the /NOSTOP qualifier to the SET WATCH command. For example, the command SET WATCH /NOSTOP NQ(Buffer) monitors the number in the queue named Buffer. Whenever the length of this queue changes, SIMAN displays a message but continues running the simulation. This method is useful for monitoring the status of some model components, such as a queue (by watching variable NQ), without interrupting the simulation when changes occur.

Use the CANCEL WATCH command to cancel one or more watches on an expression. Specify the watch to be canceled by entering the expression exactly as entered when the watch was set or by entering a watch-expression number. (To obtain the watch-expression number, use the VIEW command, which is discussed in the next section). For example, the command CANCEL WATCH NQ(Buffer) cancels the previously set watch on the expression NQ(Buffer); the command CANCEL WATCH ∗ uses the wild-card character (∗) to cancel all currently active watches.

When we suspect that an error is associated with a specific entity, we may want to follow the entity through the model. When the entity enters a QUEUE block or a DELAY block, we want to advance the simulation to the point where the entity exits this block; then we want to *intercept* this entity and enter the debugger so that we can continue to follow the entity's progress. The SET INTERCEPT command provides this capability: it allows us to specify an entity to intercept when it resumes movement through the model. The operand for this command is the entity's number, which is automatically assigned by SIMAN to each entity in the model. For example, SET INTERCEPT 7 establishes an intercept for Entity 7.

An entity's number can be obtained in several ways. Because entity numbers are displayed as part of the SIMAN trace information, you can obtain the number for an active entity by using the VIEW command, which is discussed in the next section. If an entity's number is not specified, an intercept is established for the active entity.

To cancel an entity intercept, use the CANCEL INTERCEPT command, which accepts the entity's number as its operand. For example, CANCEL INTERCEPT 7 cancels the intercept on entity number 7. The command CANCEL INTERCEPT * uses the wild card (*) to cancel all currently set intercepts.

The SET and CANCEL commands can also be used in other ways: selectively turning the trace of the model on and off during simulation, limiting the trace to specific entities or to a specific set of blocks within the model, or customizing the trace to display values of specific variables during execution. (Note that the debugger provides much better control over the trace than does the TRACE element in the experiment.)

The SET TRACE BLOCKS command activates the SIMAN trace by setting *tracepoints* for one or more blocks in the model. Unlike breakpoints, tracepoints do not suspend execution; SIMAN displays the trace information on the screen, and the simulation continues. The operand for this command specifies the block(s) for which tracepoints are to be set. For example, the command SET TRACE BLOCKS * sets tracepoints for all blocks in the model; the command SET TRACE BLOCKS Inspect,Adjust sets tracepoints for only those blocks labeled Inspect and Adjust. You can remove tracepoints by using the CANCEL TRACE BLOCKS command. This command uses as its operand the block(s) for which tracepoints are to be removed. For example, the command CANCEL TRACE BLOCKS * uses the wild-card character (*) to remove tracepoints from all blocks in the model; the command CANCEL TRACE BLOCKS 1..10 cancels tracepoints for those blocks with sequence numbers between 1 and 10.

Trace messages are normally generated for all entities moving through blocks that have been set as tracepoints. To restrict messages to a specific list of entities at these blocks, use the SET TRACE ENTITY command. This command accepts the entity's number as its operand and adds the specified entity or entities to the *Entity Trace List*. For example, the command SET TRACE ENTITY 1,7 adds Entities 1 and 7 to the Entity Trace List. Remove entities from the Entity Trace List with the CANCEL TRACE ENTITY command. For example, the command CANCEL TRACE ENTITY 7 removes Entity 7 from the list of trace entities. When the list of traced entities is empty, SIMAN resumes tracing all entities that pass through tracepoints.

To further restrict the generation of trace messages, set a condition with the SET TRACE CONDITION command. When a condition is set, the trace is generated only when the specified condition is true. For example, the command SET

TRACE CONDITION NQ(Buffer) > 10 restricts the generation of trace messages to situations in which the length of the queue named Buffer is greater than 10. Remove the condition restricting the generation of trace messages by using the CANCEL TRACE CONDITION command, which has no operands.

The SET TRACE EXPRESSION command causes the value of an expression to be displayed as part of the trace message. For example, the command SET TRACE EXPRESSION NQ(Drill) + NQ(Lathe) causes the sum of the Drill and Lathe queue lengths to be displayed in the trace. Remove these values from the trace message by using the CANCEL TRACE EXPRESSION command. For example, the command CANCEL TRACE EXPRESSION NQ(Drill) + NQ(Lathe) removes the previous value from the message.

Showing Current Status: The SHOW and VIEW Commands

During the verification process we want to be able to interactively examine the current status of the system. We also want to see which debug options (such as breakpoints, watches, etc.) are currently set. SIMAN provides this capability through the SHOW and VIEW commands.

The SHOW command displays the value of either an expression involving variables (system- or user-defined) or the attributes of the active entity. The operand for SHOW is an expression (or list of expressions) to display. For example, the command SHOW JOBTYPE displays the current value of the attribute JOBTYPE for the active entity; the command SHOW NQ(Lathe)+NQ(Drill) displays the current value of the specified expression.

To show all the values of a variable or attribute, use the wild-card character (*) as an index. For example, the command SHOW NQ(*) displays the current length of each queue in the model; the command SHOW A(*) displays all of the values of each active entity's attributes. A variable or attribute's indexes can also be specified as a lower-to-upper range using a double dot (..). For example, SHOW NQ(5..8) displays the current queue length for Queues 5 through 8.

Whereas the SHOW command is limited to displaying the value of a specific expression, the VIEW command lets you examine a wide range of information about the system's status. The VIEW SOURCE command lets you examine any portion of the model's source code during the execution. For example, VIEW SOURCE 1..10 displays the model source lines between sequence numbers 1 and 10; the command VIEW SOURCE Inspect displays the source line for the block labeled Inspect. The commands VIEW SUMMARY, VIEW DSTATS, VIEW TALLIES, and VIEW COUNTERS are useful for displaying complete or partial listings of the SIMAN Summary Report. For example, the command VIEW TALLIES generates a partial SIMAN Summary Report containing only the Tally variables. The VIEW ENTITY command displays the entity record number and attribute values for the currently active entity. The VIEW ENTITY command also accepts an entity number as an operand, thereby allowing it to be used to examine the attributes of any entity in the system.

The command VIEW QUEUE can be used to display the current membership of one or more queues in the model. For example, the command VIEW QUEUE Drill displays a list of the current members of the queue named Drill; the command VIEW QUEUE 1 .. 5 displays the same information for Queues 1 through 5. The displayed information includes the entity's number along with the current value of the attributes for all entities in the queue.

When queues are large or attributes many, the displayed information can become lengthy. SIMAN provides two options for limiting displays. The first option involves including an additional operand to specify the rank (or range of ranks) within the queue for which the entities are to be displayed For example, VIEW QUEUE Buffer: 1..3 displays only the first three entities in the queue named Buffer. To specify the last entity in the queue, use the string 'NQ'. For example, VIEW QUEUE Buffer: NQ displays only the last member in the queue named Buffer. The second option involves appending the /BRIEF qualifier to the VIEW QUEUE command, thereby specifying that only the entity's record numbers and attributes be displayed. For example, the command VIEW QUEUE /BRIEF Buffer generates a list of entities currently residing in the queue named Buffer but does not show the current values of each entity's attributes.

Sometimes it is useful to look at the contents of the Event Calendar to see the list of entities ordered according to the time when they will be entering blocks. For example, we may want to know which entity will become active when the currently active entity completes its movement at the current simulated time. The VIEW CALENDAR command displays a summary of the entities currently scheduled on the Event Calendar. This summary includes the scheduled time, the description of the events, and the entity's attributes. The /BRIEF qualifier can be appended to the VIEW CALENDAR command (as with the VIEW QUEUE command) to suppress listing of the entity's attribute values.

The VIEW command also provides a convenient way of examining the options set within the debugger. For example, the VIEW BREAK command displays a summary of current breakpoints; the VIEW TRACE BLOCKS command displays a summary of current tracepoints; and the VIEW WATCH command displays a summary of all currently active watch expressions.

Assigning Values: The ASSIGN Command

When using the debugger to track down an error, you may be able to use the SHOW or VIEW command to isolate the cause of the error to an uninitialized or an incorrect value for a variable or attribute. When a correction is needed, it is useful to be able to set the variable or attribute to its correct value and then continue the run to see if the correct value solves the problem.

Use the ASSIGN command to modify the value of a variable or an attribute during model execution. This command's operand consists of the assignment variable or attribute, followed by an equals sign (=), followed by an expression defining the assignment value. For example, the command ASSIGN

Reorder_Point = 100 sets the current value of the variable Reorder_Point to 100. Any attribute on either side of the equals sign refers to the active entity. For example, the command ASSIGN A(1) = 15 sets the first attribute of the active entity to 15. The operation of the ASSIGN command is identical to that of the ASSIGN block in the model.

Note that assigning a new value to a variable or an attribute during execution may make the model run properly, but it does not change the model itself. The change only alters the value of the variable or attribute during that execution. Any errors detected in variable or attribute assignments must still be corrected in the original model.

Redirecting Entity Flow: The NEXT Command

In some situations you may isolate the cause of a problem to an error in the flow of logic within the model. Perhaps, for example, the conditions are incorrectly entered on a BRANCH block, and an entity is being sent to the wrong destination. When this error is isolated from within the debugger, you want to be able to redirect the entity flow to the correct block and continue the simulation to determine whether this change solves the problem.

The NEXT command redirects the active entity from the current block to a specified destination block. Instead of being processed by the current block, the entity enters the destination block. The destination block can be specified as a sequence number or a label. For example, the command NEXT 10 sends the active entity to the block at Sequence Number 10; the command NEXT Exit sends the current entity to the block labeled Exit. In either case, the entity is not processed through the current block before the redirection.

Saving and Recalling Snapshots: The SAVE and RESTORE Commands

In large, complex models it may take several hours of work with the debugger to reach the point in the simulation where an error is occurring. If, for any reason, you are interrupted and cannot continue the debugging session, you must save the current state of the simulation. Saving the state enables you to return to the same point in the simulation without starting the execution over again from the beginning.

The SAVE and RESTORE commands let you save and recall *snapshots* of the current state of the simulation model. Each saved snapshot is written to a file, and you can save as many snapshots as you wish. By saving snapshots at different points during a simulation, you can easily jump back and forth in time while you examine the model for errors. This capability is particularly useful when you suddenly realize that observed anomalies are probably symptomatic of an error that occurred earlier in the simulation. If you have saved a snapshot earlier in the run, you can backtrack to this point and continue your search for the error without having to restart the simulation from the beginning.

The operand for both the SAVE and RESTORE block is a file descriptor or a valid FORTRAN file unit number. The file descriptor typically consists of a system-dependent file name which, on some systems, includes path or node information. If, for example, you are using MS-DOS, the file identifier can have eight characters followed by a period and a three-character extension. Hence, SAVE Pointa.snp saves a snapshot of the simulation in the file named Pointa.snp. You can return to this same point in the simulation at any time by issuing the command RESTORE Pointa.snp.

Obtaining On-Line Help: The HELP Command

On-line help about the debugger is available via the HELP command. If given the command HELP, SIMAN displays general information about the debugger's commands and operands. If you qualify your request by appending a command name, SIMAN provides specific help for that command. For example, the command HELP VIEW QUEUE displays help for the command VIEW QUEUE.

It should be noted that only a commonly used subset of available debugger commands is discussed in this text. The HELP command provides a good way of learning about the other available commands.

2.7 Using Animation as a Verification Aid

Successful verification often depends on one's ability to comprehend the complex interactions occurring among the many components within a model. As noted earlier, verification can be a very frustrating and mentally taxing process. Of all the techniques available to help in this difficult process, animation is without a doubt the single, most powerful aid available. Only animation can present a dynamically moving picture of the many interactions taking place within the simulation. In contrast to the interactive debugger, which examines the model's individual components one at a time, animation displays the same information for all model components simultaneously. This simultaneous display is easier to comprehend than the interactive debugger's single-component display. Simultaneous display also makes it easier to follow the complex interactions occurring within the model. Such interactions are often the source of errors.

For the purpose of debugging, we do not need a highly detailed animation; an animation with a rough appearance can still be effective for debugging. And, as will be shown in Chapter 7, this type of animation is easily and quickly developed, thereby contributing very little to the overall modeling effort. In general, the modest amount of time needed to construct the animation is repaid many times over in the savings in time required to verify the model's operation.

2.8 Correcting Errors

The methods discussed in the previous sections (i.e., walkthroughs, tracing, animation, and the interactive debugger) are powerful aids for identifying unintentional errors in the simulation model. However, although these techniques often provide the indication that an error occurs in the model, you still face the task of identifying the precise cause of the error and of correcting the model or experiment to resolve the problem.

Once an error is detected, SIMAN's interactive debugger helps tremendously in isolating the problem — but it is no substitute for careful reasoning. Don't take the shotgun approach to debugging as many modelers do; by failing to use reason and logic to isolate the true cause of an error, they treat only its symptom. And don't try to change the model without fully understanding the error, in the blind hope that these changes will somehow "fix" the problem. Even if your changes make the model appear to work correctly, it is most unlikely that this approach will correct the true error. As a result, the error may remain undetected.

Also be careful not to let your joy over having "fixed" a nagging error obscure the need to test the model rigorously after making a correction. The fact that the correction fixes the problem in one case does not mean that the problem is solved. No matter how obvious the fix or simple the change, never assume that the fix is correct without rigorously verifying it. An error can have multiple causes, and correcting one error can introduce additional errors elsewhere in the model.

In closing our discussion about verification aids, we want to emphasize that, although the interactive debugger and animation are extremely valuable verification tools, they should be viewed as adjuncts to — and not substitutes for — thinking. Tools can help you uncover errors within the model, but reasoning is the ultimate weapon. In many cases the cause of an error can be determined without using the computer.

2.9 Avoiding Some Common Errors

Experience shows that certain types of errors are more common than others, particularly for beginners. In this section we summarize these frequent errors.

Data Errors

Almost all models depend on a substantial amount of data for such things as arrival rates, processing times, etc. These data may be directly specified in the model's blocks or indirectly specified through the elements in the experiment. In either case, even if our logic is flawless, our answers can still be incorrect because we have entered one or more values incorrectly.

Incorrectly entered data can be very difficult to detect within a model. A single data entry error, such as a misplaced decimal point or an extra digit in a number, can have a substantial impact on the model's results. This error may be located in a single line of several hundred statements for a model or an experiment. As anyone who has tried to proofread his or her own writing knows, the author (in this case, the modeler) is the least likely person to locate an error by simple inspection. Often the most effective method of detecting such errors is the walkthrough (discussed earlier in this chapter).

Although we typically focus on collecting output data for analysis, we should also collect statistics on input data. For example, we can collect data on the time between arrivals to the system, even though we know what the value should be, based on the parameters specified at the CREATE block. Such statistics can be used to cross-check our input data against the model.

Initialization Errors

By default, SIMAN automatically initializes variables and attributes to 0, which is the most commonly correct starting value for a variable or attribute. If, as in many cases, 0 is not the correct starting value, then we must initialize the variable or attribute. If we don't perform this initialization, the results generated by the model are invalid.

As in the case of data errors, initialization errors are often difficult to detect, but the debugger can help. We can use the debugger's SHOW command to step through the execution of the model for the first entity in the system and examine the contents of its attributes and the system variables.

Errors in Units of Measurement

Many of the operands in both the model and experiment involve units of measurement. For example, the first operand of the DELAY block, Duration, is expressed in units of time. In specifying this operand, you are free to use minutes, hours, or any other convenient unit for measuring time. However, you must use the same unit of time throughout the entire model and experiment. For example, if you specify the Duration operand in hours, then you must also specify the length of the replication in hours.

In later chapters we will encounter operands involving distances and speeds. Like units of time, these also must be used consistently throughout the model and experiment. Once you have selected a unit of measurement for distance and time, the unit of measurement for speed is determined by these units. For example, if you measure distances in feet and time in hours, then you must enter speeds in units of feet per hour.

The units of measurement for time, distance, and speed are not explicitly declared in a SIMAN model. When performing calculations, SIMAN assumes that no conversion of units is required. If this is not the case, the simulation will still execute; however, the results will be corrupted as a result of the inconsistent use of time units.

Errors in units of measurement can be extremely difficult to find. The problem is often even more difficult than that of finding standard data errors, because the values may look reasonable and may conform to the units of measurement for the available data on the system. Often the most effective method of detecting such errors is the model and experiment walkthrough.

Flow Control

When we combine a set of blocks into a model, we control the flow of entities between the blocks by using features such as the BRANCH block and the NEXT modifier. If we err when specifying the flow, then the entities may be processed through the wrong set of blocks.

Although up to this point the flow of entities through the model has been relatively simple, it can become quite complex, as we will see in later chapters. In some cases we have many different types of entities, each taking a separate path through the system. The trace, the interactive debugger, and animation are all effective methods for detecting errors in entity flow.

Blockages and Deadlocks

In most of our models we allocate a resource to an entity, which normally releases that resource once its activity is complete. The released resource can then be reallocated for use by other entities. If we fail to release the resource, a *blockage* is created at the queue corresponding to the resource's allocation point. Because the resource is left in a busy state, entities waiting for the resource will queue indefinitely at this point.

Another situation, a *deadlock*, is illustrated by the following example. An entity currently has possession of Resource A and is going to release it, but only after it seizes Resource B. Another entity has possession of Resource B and is going to release it, but only after it seizes Resource A. In this case, we have a deadlock: neither entity can move forward in the model.

In an open system (i.e., one in which entities arrive and depart) the best indications of a possible blockage or deadlock are uncontrollable growth in one or more queues and increased run-time. In a closed system (i.e., one in which a fixed number of entities remain in the system and repeatedly cycle through it) blockage or deadlock is usually signaled by entities remaining stuck in a queue. These trapped entities no longer contribute to the number of completed cycles.

Blockages and deadlocks are relatively easy errors to find and correct because they trigger queues of unusual length. Animation, trace, and the interactive debugger are effective weapons for isolating the problem within the model. Although this discussion of blockage and deadlock is presented in terms of resources, the concepts also apply to other modeling constructs that appear in later chapters.

Arithmetic Errors

Many of the operands within a SIMAN model can be entered as any valid expression involving variables or attributes. If the expression is entered incorrectly, the value used for the operand will also be incorrect.

Parentheses are a frequent cause of arithmetic errors. For example, you may intend to enter

(A > B .or. A > C) .and. A > D

but instead may enter

A > B .or. A > C .and. A > D

The latter is incorrect because the .and. operator binds more tightly than the .or. operator. Thus, SIMAN evaluates A > C .and. A > D first, when you intended to evaluate A > B .or. A > C first.

Another common arithmetic mistake involves errors in rounding and/or conversion between reals and integers. Within SIMAN, all arithmetic is computed as reals, which are then converted to integers for things such as indexes into arrays. By default, the system truncates the number rather than rounding it to the nearest integer. Hence, if we specify an operand as Duedate(unif(0,3)), the index of the array Duedate will be randomly selected from among 0, 1, and 2 with equal probability.

The normal cautions relating to equality testing with reals apply to SIMAN just as they do to other computer languages. Specifically, if we add 0.1 to itself 10 times, and test the result against 1.0, the test may say that the two are not equal because of numerical rounding on the computer.

Overwriting Variables and Attributes

Sometimes model errors occur when a variable or an attribute containing a correct value is overwritten with another value before the first value is used. For example, we sometimes use the same attribute for several different purposes to conserve memory. Perhaps at one point in the model an attribute stores the time, and at another point it stores some other piece of information. Reusing the attribute works only if the timing statistics are recorded before the attribute is reset to its new value.

A similar situation occurs with the special SIMAN variable, J, which we discuss in Chapter 8. Several different blocks return information by assigning values to this variable; however, as we will see later, it is important that the value of J be examined and used before it is changed elsewhere in the model by another block.

Data Recording Errors

The model may have flawless logic and operate just as intended, and yet we may still have problems because of errors in recording data. These errors result in incorrect statistics — even if the model is operating properly.

One common recording error is the failure to mark an attribute when collecting interval statistics at the TALLY block. When we make this error, SIMAN calculates the time interval by using whatever value happens to be in the specified attribute. This value is often 0, the default initial value for an attribute. If the value is 0, the recorded values at the TALLY block will be much larger than they should be because the value recorded will equal the arrival time to the block.

Another type of recording error involves mislabeling a counter, DSTAT, or TALLY within the experiment. For example, we may mislabel the statistics recorded on the lathe queue to read "drill queue." Unlike errors in the model's logic, mislabeling errors are not effectively detected using animation. The model may operate correctly during animation, but the results in the SIMAN Summary Report may still be erroneous. As effective as animation is, we cannot rely on it exclusively for model verification.

Language Conceptual Errors

Perhaps the most difficult errors to find are those that result not from a language transcription error but from a genuine misconception about the operation of a specific language construct. Ideally, the best way to cope with these errors is to prevent their occurring, rather than trying to deal with them afterwards. If you are using a construct in SIMAN for the first time and you are unsure just how it works, you can easily build a small test model with a simple animation, or you can use the trace option to verify the construct's operation. Building a test model is more efficient than using the construct in the model and hoping that it operates the way you think it does.

Language conceptual errors are best detected using animation and the interactive debugger.

3. Validating the Model

A model is created for a specific purpose, and its adequacy or validity can only be evaluated in terms of that purpose. We develop a model to generate the same problem and/or behavioral characteristics as contained in the referent process or system being studied. As already stated, we validate a model to develop an acceptable level of confidence that the inferences drawn from the performance of the model are correct and apply to the real-world system. We must remember that a simulation model is a theory or approximation of how the referent real-world system operates or will operate. We also know that we have deliberately simplified, abstracted, and combined features of the real system in order to obtain a viable model. Thus, we know ahead of time that the model and real system will not have identical outputs.

The significant question is whether the output or behavior of the model will be close enough to that of the real system for our purposes. Unfortunately, just how to measure or evaluate the validity of a given model is an open question; the answer depends on what real-world system is being modeled, who is asking the questions, and who is interpreting the answers. Basically, validation focuses on three questions:

■ Does the model adequately represent the real-world system (conceptual validity)?

■ Are the model-generated behavioral data characteristic of the real-world system's behavioral data (operational validity)?

■ Does the simulation model's ultimate user have confidence in the model's results (believability)?

In many modeling studies, the ultimate user or decision maker is far removed from the modeling process and needs a basis for deciding whether to accept the model's results. Because it is difficult for a lay person to assess the impact of a model's assumptions, data availability, and other elements of model structure and results, there is often a formal independent evaluation by an intermediary or technical evaluator. This evaluator functions like the outside doubter in the verification process. Hence validation takes place from three different perspectives:

- the model builder (or modeler),
- the technical evaluator, and
- the ultimate user (or decision maker).

Only the model builder can conduct all of the confidence-building tests. The role of the technical evaluator (generally a supervisor, referee, or client) is usually limited to reviewing the information and technical data provided by the modeler. The ultimate user or decision maker is usually an expert in another field and rarely has the background needed to understand the validation tests conducted. Yet, ultimately, all three must be convinced of the model's validity if its results are to be used.

We must also recognize that validation takes place under several distinctly different circumstances. In the first (and easiest) case, the real-world system being modeled exists and is accessible; in this case, validation can proceed through direct experimentation. We can perhaps gather response data from the real system to compare to the data being produced by the model. We can try, using the model, to duplicate the behavior being observed in the real-world system.

In the second case, the real-world system exists and may, in fact, be operational, but it is not available for direct experimentation. For example, we cannot fly a real airplane into the ground or shoot down an incoming ballistic missile. In such cases, validation must be conducted indirectly by extrapolating from the known, observable behavior of the referent system, or by conducting indirect observations or experiments on it by whatever means are available.

In the third (and by far most difficult) case, the referent system does not yet exist. For example, we may be modeling alternative designs for a factory that has yet to be built, or we may be simulating the logistics of building a space station. One can argue philosophically as to whether it is even possible to talk about validating a model of a proposed system; yet we obviously must convince ourselves and others that the observed model behavior is actually giving us indications of how the proposed referent system would behave if implemented.

3.1 Defining Validity

As already stated, a simulation model is our theory describing the structure and interrelationships of a system. The theory (model) can be useful, useless, or outright dangerous, depending on whether it is sound, inadequate, or wrong. Correctness (validity) can only be judged in relationship to the real system. Since all models contain both simplifications and abstractions of the referent, real-world system, no model can ever be absolutely correct, i.e., it can never have a one-to-one correspondence with its real-world counterpart. The problems associated with validating a simulation model are no different from those associated with proving any theory or hypothesis. The questions remain the same: What does it mean to validate a hypothesis (model)? What criteria should be used?

The answers will vary greatly for truth, like beauty, often lies in the eye of the beholder. Take this example, which resembles one provided by Elmaghraby[1968]. Suppose that we come to you and tell you that we have a wonderful new model that will predict the daily closing value of the DOW Jones Industrial Average within two points, 20 days ahead of time. Of course, if this is true, we can become very, very rich in a very short time by playing the Stock Index Futures Market.

Knowing that you will be skeptical of such a claim, we offer to provide unequivocal "proof" by predicting the closing DOW Jones every day for a month starting 20 days from now. Sure enough, we not only predict each day's closing within two points, but we actually hit it exactly — without error. Then, to prove that it was no fluke, we do it again; and again we predict the closings each day for a month — without error.

By now you are quite impressed, and you question the basis of our model. We reluctantly tell you that it is based on correlation with sunspot activity. When you press us for a theoretical or logical explanation, we have to admit that the model is empirically derived and that we do not really know why it works. All we know is that it works, and that we can provide you with as much empirical "proof" as you wish. After all, we argue, the model's usefulness is paramount; the truth of its structure should be irrelevant.

Now here's the question: Would you go out and sell everything you have and give us all your money to invest for you? Many readers would, having been convinced by the "evidence." Others would not, despite the evidence, because there is no known theory or logical explanation. In other words, the proof of validity offered convinces some decision makers but not others, depending on their validation criteria. Historically, we have used three distinct approaches to validation.

■ *Rationalism* assumes that most of the underlying assumptions on which the model is to be based are so obviously true that they need not be proved. Logical deductions are then used to develop a valid model from these assumptions. Therefore, if the assumptions and logic of the model are obviously true, then the model is obviously valid.

■ *Empiricism* requires that every assumption and outcome be empirically tested and validated. No postulate or assumption is admissible unless it can be independently verified, preferably through the testing of descriptive data.

■ *Positive Economics* requires only that the model be able to predict the future and is not concerned with the underlying model assumptions or structure. Therefore, if the model can be shown to work, it is assumed to be valid. Only the usefulness of the model is important; the truth, understandability, and rationality of the assumptions and structure are irrelevant.

We can see that our model for predicting the daily closing value of the DOW Jones Industrial Average would be valid for a "positive economist" but invalid for a rationalist or an empiricist. Most decision makers show a mixture of these three approaches when accepting or rejecting a concept or an idea. We will therefore look at tests and approaches from each of these viewpoints, i.e., tests for reasonableness, structure, and behavior.

When we design and validate simulation models we are torn between the need to be objective and the need to make intelligent and constructive use of our subjective knowledge and beliefs. By subjective knowledge and beliefs we mean those insights, intuitions, opinions, hunches, guesses, or impressions about how a system of interest operates. Objectivity means laying aside or ignoring our subjective beliefs or pre-judgements and considering only the experimental evidence. This apparent conflict can be resolved readily if we recognize that both are legitimate sources of information for validation purposes. In fact, we usually alternate between subjective and objective tests.

3.2 Testing for Reasonableness

For a model to appear credible, it must exhibit behavior that resembles that of the real-world system. Likewise, it cannot exhibit unreasonable or unrealistic behavior. Therefore, the first set of tests run should resemble those suggested by Schlesinger et al. [1974] for reasonableness of behavior, including the following:

■ *Continuity.* Small changes in the input parameters should usually cause consequent small, but appropriate, changes in the output and state-of-the-system variables. For example, a small increase in the arrival rate to a service facility should result in a small (not huge) increase in the average number in the queue. If the changes are disproportionate, the analyst should understand why and be able to justify the behavior.

■ *Consistency.* Essentially similar runs of the model should yield essentially similar results. For example, there should not be widely different results simply because I changed the random-number seed for the random variate generators.

■ *Degeneracy.* When certain features of the model are removed, the output should reflect their removal. For example, if I remove one of the machines from a manufacturing cell, then the model should respond as if it had been removed, i.e., the performance of the system should deteriorate somewhat.

■ *Absurd Conditions.* This test has two aspects. First, if I introduce absurd inputs, I should *not* get equally absurd outputs. For example, if I increase the advertising budget to infinity, sales should not also go to infinity because we know that infinite sales are not possible. Second, absurd conditions should not arise during the simulation. For example, the model should not generate people that have negative weights or material transporters that pass through each other going in different directions. Absurd conditions arising during model execution will often be detectable from watching animated results.

These and similar tests for reasonableness are in fact a part of both the verification and validation processes. Tests for reasonableness can, and usually will, be done by end users or decision makers to build their own confidence in model results. If the model obviously fails to behave in a reasonable and plausible manner at any point in the checkout process, it will be very difficult to regain the end user's confidence. It is therefore imperative that the results or output of the model be examined very carefully and that the model be exercised in all kinds of unreasonable ways to try to detect any problems. Because model output should be plausible even for extreme and unlikely conditions, the model should restrict behavior outside of normal operating ranges.

3.3 Testing Model Structure and Data

The second area of concern in model validation involves testing the structure of the model for adequacy and verification. Every validation process must assess the correspondence between the basic modeling assumptions and the referent system being modeled. We must establish that the theories and assumptions underlying the model are correct and that the representation of the problem is reasonable for the intended use. The following list describes several tests that might be used.

■ *Face Validity.* Face validity is achieved by asking persons familiar with and/or knowledgeable about the referent system whether the model and/or its behavior appear reasonable. This technique can be used to validate the correctness of the logic in the model and the reasonableness of the model's input-output relationships. Face validity is often used in conjunction with animation, whereby the model's operational behavior is displayed graphically as the model moves through time.

■ *Parameters and Relationships.* Tests of the underlying assumptions about parameter values and variable relationships should be run whenever feasible. Typically these are statistical tests: means, variances, regression analyses, goodness-of-fit, etc. We should also run a dimensional analysis to test the consistency of any equations used in the model.

■ *Structural and Boundary Verification.* The goal here is ensuring that the structure of the model does not obviously contradict reality. We must ensure that there is a mapping or homomorphism between the conceptual model and the referent system. We also need to consider whether the model incorporates all of the relevant relationships needed for achieving the model's purpose.

■ *Sensitivity Analysis.* By varying the values of the model's parameters and seeing how these changes affect the behavior of the model, we can get a feel for the impact of uncertainty on the parameter values. If slight changes in parameter values yield different decisions or policy implications, we should be suspicious of our results [Gass 1983].

Ensuring face validity by soliciting the opinions of persons knowledgeable about the referent system can powerfully assist validation and foster model acceptance by the decision maker(s). For example, suppose that we are trying to explore the effect of some proposed change on an existing manufacturing system. Instead of modeling the system as it would be after the change, we first model the system as it currently exists. We then seek the advice and opinions of operators or those in charge of the system regarding the accuracy of our model. Is the model behaving like the existing real system? After everyone concerned agrees that the model is indeed a good representation of the existing system, we can proceed to change the model to reflect the proposed changes.

Because we have already convinced the decision makers that we can reproduce the behavior of the existing system through simulation, the probability of their accepting the final study results has risen considerably. On the other hand, if we cannot convince them that we can reproduce the behavior of the existing system (which they know and understand), then the probability of their accepting the validity of our changed system model is small.

We also need to discuss one of the major problems associated with using statistical tests during study validation. When we perform a statistical test and make a decision about the null hypothesis, we can make two types of errors. We can reject the validity of what is in truth a valid model (a Type I error), or we can fail to reject an invalid model (a Type II error). The probability of making a Type I error is given by alpha and is called the model builder's risk. The probability of making a Type II error is given by beta and is called the model user's risk.

It should be self-evident that the significance of making a Type II error far outweighs that of making a Type I error. If we make a Type I error, we usually spend more time refining the model, probably by adding more detail or refining some of our inputs. On the other hand, if we make a Type II error, we base our decisions on bad information — with potentially disastrous results.

The two types of errors are directly related, and their probabilities vary as a function of sample size. For a fixed sample size, the two types of error are inversely related, i.e., if you decrease one, you increase the other. The only way you can reduce both simultaneously is to increase the sample size; consequently, statisticians always want to increase the sample size. The only way you can eliminate the chance of making such errors is to avoid basing the decision on a statistical test, i.e., base the decision on the entire universe. Because using the entire universe is impossible, we must make tradeoffs among the three (i.e., among alpha, beta, and sample size) by using Operating Characteristic Curves (see, for example, Miller and Freund [1985]).

Further discussion of using statistical hypothesis testing for validation purposes can be found in Balci and Sargent [1981 and 1982] and in Banks and Carson [1984].

3.4 Testing Model Behavior

Probably the most convincing validation tests are based on studying the behavior of the model in relation to the behavior of the referent system. In fact, when most people talk about validation testing, they are referring to comparative tests of behavior. Like the tests for reasonableness and structure, these tests can be subjective or objective.

For the technically naive decision maker, the subjective tests are usually the most convincing. The following list identifies the most widely used tests of model behavior.

■ *Behavior Comparison.* Many statistical tests can be used to compare the output of the model to the output of the referent system. The following list identifies some of these tests.

Chi-Square test [Ringuest 1986]

Kolmogorov-Smirnov test

Regression analysis (X vs. Y: Does slope $= 1$ and intersect $= 0$?) [Cohen and Cyert 1961]

Spectral analysis [Brately et al. 1983]

Theil's Inequality test [Kheir and Holmes 1978]

Turing test [Schruben 1980]

Hotelling's Two Sample T^2 test [Balci and Sargent 1982]

■ *Symptom Generation.* These tests can take several forms and can answer questions like the following:

Does the model re-create the difficulties that show up in the real-world system?

Does the model produce known results under certain inputs, e.g., if unemployment increases, do sales decrease?

If previous changes have been tried in the real-world system, can we make the same changes in the model and see if it reacts the same way that the referent system did?

■ *Behavior Anomaly.* If the behavior of the model conflicts with our expectations of the real-world system, but we can find instances of the real system's actually behaving the same way, we have strong proof of validity. If, on the other hand, we cannot find instances of identical behavior, we must trace the model structure and try to find the cause of such behavior.

■ *Behavior Prediction.* We can sometimes test whether the model can predict system behavior by running field tests. These controlled tests use the model to predict an outcome and then run a field test to see if it was right.

4. Building Confidence

One of the most important tasks in the entire simulation exercise consists of determining a process for developing confidence in our simulation models and of communicating this confidence to non-model developers. The model end user has every right to be skeptical of our claims of accuracy and to be wary of the model's predictions. If the ultimate user of the model and/or its results does not have confidence in the model and is not convinced of its credibility, then the utility and purpose of the entire simulation effort is lost.

The user or decision maker who is supposed to accept model results wants to know that the model will do several things: work as intended under normal conditions, work properly under a wide range of conditions, and make readily apparent any bizarre outputs. Confidence in a model evolves through the joint effort of model developers and decision maker and requires the latter's intimate involvement.

Unlike most computer programs, simulation models are never completely verified or validated. The purpose of simulation is to make you smarter about your world, to help you learn. You create a scenario, try some things, review the results, change a few things, and go again. Because you are continually changing the model, you run the risk of introducing new programming errors or of moving the model outside the range of its validity.

Exercises

Note: For all of the following exercises edit the BEGIN statement of the Experiment to ensure that the SIMAN interactive debugger is invoked at time 0.

Exercise 4.1
For Sample Problem 3.3 from Chapter 3, use the GO UNTIL command to run the simulation until time 100. Then use the SHOW command to determine the number of parts that have been produced by time 100.

Exercise 4.2
Modify Sample Problem 3.3 from Chapter 3 to incorporate a queue limit of 1 for the queue named MachineQ. Use the debugger commands to determine the time at which the first entity is denied access to the queue.

Exercise 4.3
For Sample Problem 3.3 from Chapter 3, use the debugger commands to determine the time at which the last job exited the system prior to time 100.

Exercise 4.4
For Sample Problem 3.3 from Chapter 3, capture the first entity inspected as "bad," and trace this entity to determine the time at which it exits from the model.

Exercise 4.5
For Sample Problem 3.3 from Chapter 3, use the debugger commands to:

a. determine the entity identifier and attribute values for the first entity which must wait for the machine in the queue named MachineQ.

b. intercept this entity after the processing time delay and change the value of attribute Priority so that the entity is placed first in line for the inspector, and

c. trace only this entity out of the system and determine at what time it exits.

Exercise 4.6

For Sample Problem 3.3 from Chapter 3, change the mean interarrival time in the model from 9 to a variable called MTBA. Add this variable to the experiment and initialize it to 9. Use the debugger commands to conduct the following experiment on this model.

a. Run the simulation model for 60 time units and examine the length of the queue named MachineQ.

b. Decrease the mean time between arrivals (MTBA) to 3 and continue the simulation to determine at what time the queue length reaches 60.

c. Increase the MTBA to 20 and determine at what time the queue length first returns to 0.

References

BALCI, O. and R. G. SARGENT (1981), "A Methodology for Cost-Risk Analysis in the Statistical Validation of Simulation Models," *Communications of ACM*, Vol. 24, No. 4, pp: 190-197.

BALCI, O. and R. G. SARGENT (1982), "Validation of Multivariate Response Simulation Models by using Hotelling's Two-Sample T^2 Test," *Simulation*, Vol. 39, No. 6, pp: 185-192.

BALCI, O. and R. G. SARGENT (1984 a), "A Bibliography on the Credibility, Assessment and Validation of Simulation and Mathematical Models," *Simuletter*, Vol. 15, No.3, pp: 15-27.

BALCI, O. and R. G. SARGENT (1984 b), "Validation of Simulation Models via Simultaneous Confidence Intervals," *American Journal of Mathematical and Management Science*, Vol. 4, No. 3 and 4, pp: 375-406.

BANKS, J. and J. S. CARSON, II (1984), Discrete-Event System Simulation, Prentice-Hall, Inc., Englewood Cliffs, NJ.

BRATLEY, P., B. L. FOX and L. E. SCHRAGE (1983), A Guide to Simulation, Springer-Verlag, NY.

COHEN, K. J. and R. M. CYERT (1961), "Computer Models in Dynamic Economics," *Economic Quarterly*, Vol. 75, pp: 112-127.

ELMAGHRABY, S. E. (1968), "The Role of Modeling in I.E. Design," *The Journal of Industrial Engineering*, Vol. XIX, No. 6.

GASS, S. I. and B. W. THOMPSON (1980), "Guidelines for Model Evaluation: An Abridged Version of the U.S. General Accounting Office Exposure Draft," *Operations Research*, Vol. 28, No. 2, pp: 431-479.

GASS, S. I. and L. S. JOEL (1981), "Concepts of Model Confidence," *Computers and Operations Research*, Vol. 8, No. 4, pp: 341-346.

GASS, S. I. (1983), "Decision-Aiding Models: Validation, Assessment, and Related Issues for Policy Analysis," *Operations Research*, Vol. 31, No. 4, pp: 603-631.

KHEIR, N. A. and W. M. HOLMES (1978), "On Validating Simulation Models of Missile Systems," *Simulation*, Vol. 30, No. 4, pp: 117-128.

MILLER, I. and J. E. FREUND (1985), Probability and Statistics for Engineers, Prentice-Hall, Englewood Cliffs, NJ.

OREN, T. (1981), "Concepts and Criteria to Assess Acceptability of Simulation Studies: A Frame of Reference," *Communications of the ACM*, Vol. 24, No. 4, pp: 180-189.

PERRIENS, M. P. (1977), "An Application of Formal Inspections to Top-Down Structured Program Development," RADC-TR-77-212, IBM Federal Systems Division, Gaithersburg, MD.

RINGUEST, J. L. (1986), "A Chi-Square Statistic for Validating Simulation-Generated Responses," *Computers and Operations Research*, Vol. 13, No. 4, 379-385.

ROWLAND, J. R. and W. M. HOLMES (1978), "Simulation Validation with Sparse Random Data," *Computers and Electrical Engineering*, Vol. 5, No. 1, pp: 37-49.

SARGENT, R. G. (1982), "Verification and Validation of Simulation Models," Chapter IX in Progress in Modelling and Simulation, edited by F. E. Cellier, Academic Press (London), pp: 159-169.

SARGENT, R. G. (1984), "Simulation Model Validation," Simulation and Model-Based Methodologies: An Integrative View, edited by T. Oren et al., Springer-Verlag, NY.

SCHLESINGER, S. et al. (1974), "Developing Standard Procedures for Simulation, Validation, and Verification," Proceedings of 1974 Summer Computer Simulation Conference, pp: 927-933.

SCHLESINGER, S. et al. (1979), "Terminology for Model Credibility," *Simulation*, Vol. 32, No. 3, pp: 103-104.

SHANNON, R. E. (1981), "Tests for Verification and Validation of Computer Simulation Models," Proceedings of Winter Simulation Conference, pp: 573-577.

SCHRUBEN, L. W. (1980), "Establishing the Credibility of Simulations," *Simulation*, Vol. 34, No. 3, pp: 101-105.

WEINBERG, G. M. (1971), The Psychology of Computer Programming, Van Nostrand Reinhold, New York, NY.

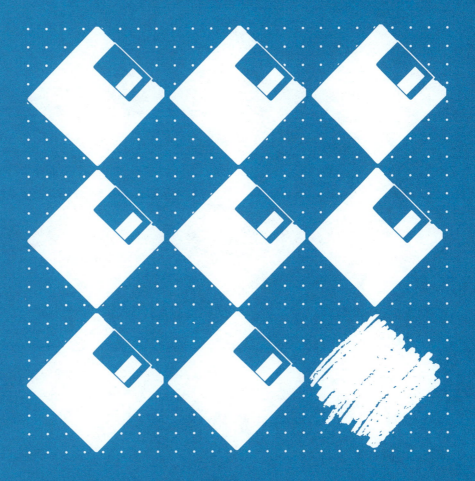

CHAPTER 5
Interpreting Simulation Output

1. Conducting Statistical Analyses

The preceding chapters have discussed the basic concepts and methods for developing, verifying, and validating simulation models. At this point we are able to build and execute computerized models of simple systems to generate data about the system's performance. Our aim is to use the simulation-generated data to make inferences about real-system performance. For example, we may want to use the model to draw conclusions about the expected time a job spends in a system or waits in a queue.

Although a large amount of effort is devoted to modeling, verification, and validation activities, incorrect conclusions are often drawn from model results. Frequently the problem does not lie with a poorly constructed model but rather with poorly and improperly analyzed output and, hence, erroneously interpreted results.

One common cause of poor analysis is the tight time constraints often placed on modelers who have little or no training in statistics. Because the interpretation phase occurs at the end of a study, it often suffers when the project falls behind schedule. However, project success hinges on devoting the same level of attention and commitment to the analysis of results as to the construction of the model.

Some mistakenly believe that graphical animation of a simulation model can serve the same purpose as analysis. Although an extremely powerful tool, animation is generally ineffective as a means of interpreting simulation results. We normally cannot draw credible conclusions regarding system performance from watching an animation of the system.

In this chapter we first discuss simulation output analysis and describe the graphical and statistical procedures for interpreting simulation results. The statistical procedures are presented in detail, including the appropriate equations needed to calculate the relevant statistics for each procedure. We must emphasize, however, that you need not actually use these equations, because all of the discussed procedures are automated within the SIMAN Output Processor. We will discuss the SIMAN Output Processor and illustrate its use later in this chapter. Although the Output Processor allows you to interpret the results of a simulation without fully understanding the details of each procedure, it is important that you understand the purpose and underlying assumptions of each procedure so that you know which data to analyze and which analysis tool to use.

Analysis of simulation results begins by examining the summary statistics displayed in the SIMAN Summary Report, which is displayed at the end of each model replication. Although the Summary Report provides an overview of the simulation model's response, it is not intended to serve as the primary basis for decision making.

One of the common pitfalls involves drawing conclusions based on the results of a single model replication with an arbitrary run length. The analyst mistakenly perceives the information displayed on a single SIMAN Summary Report as the true system's parameter when, in fact, it actually represents only one of many possible outcomes. This approach equates to throwing a die once, getting a 6, and concluding that each face of the die is a 6.

The SIMAN Summary Report includes summary information for the model replication categorized by type. We have seen several examples of these reports in Chapter 3; Figure 5-1 again presents the Summary Report for sample problem 3.3.

```
Project:   Sample Problem 3.3
Analyst:   SM
Replication ended at time  : 480.0
                           TALLY VARIABLES
      Identifier      Average  Variation  Minimum  Maximum  Observations
Type 1 Time in Sys.   23.964    .38340    13.830   56.724        23
Type 2 Time in Sys.   50.848    .88666    9.8338   202.43        24
                     DISCRETE-CHANGE VARIABLES
      Identifier      Average  Variation  Minimum  Maximum   Final Value
Machine Queue          .40941   2.2953    .00000   5.0000       .00000
Inspector Queue       2.6506     .87934   .00000   8.0000      3.0000
Machine Util.          .49982   1.0004    .00000   1.0000      1.0000
Inspector Util.        .94047    .25159   .00000   1.0000      1.0000
Insp.Type 1 Util.      .43984   1.1285    .00000   1.0000       .00000
Insp.Type 2 Util.      .50063    .99874   .00000   1.0000      1.0000
                           COUNTERS
      Identifier         Count        Limit
      Rejects              7         Infinite
```

Figure 5-1. Summary Report for Sample Problem 3.3

The first category in the report summarizes the observations recorded at any TALLY blocks in the model. The sample report contains two tally variables corresponding to the time in system for each of the two job types in the model. The report contains the average, coefficient of variation, minimum observation, maximum observation, and number of observations generated during the replication.

The average displayed on the report is the sum of all observations recorded at the TALLY block divided by the total number of observations. This value, commonly referred to as the arithmetic mean, is used as a measure of the center of the data. The quality of this value as an estimator of the true mean depends on several factors, including the total number of observations. From the Summary Report in Figure 5-1, we see that the Type 1 jobs that completed processing during the replication spent an average of 23.964 minutes in the system.

The coefficient of variation, defined as the standard deviation of the observations divided by the mean, is used as a measure of the spread of the data. Because this value gives the standard deviation as a proportion of the mean, a coefficient of variation of 0 indicates that there is no variation within the data. A large coefficient of variation indicates a large variation within the data relative to the mean. The exponential distribution (which has a very large variation) has a coefficient of variation of 1, because the mean and the standard deviation are equal. From the Summary Report we see that the time in system observations recorded for the Type 1 jobs have a coefficient of variation of 0.38. This value indicates a moderate degree of variation within the samples.

The report displays the coefficient of variation rather than the standard deviation because the former provides a measure of relative variation, whereas the latter provides a measure of absolute variation. One disadvantage of the coefficient of variation is that it becomes very large when the mean is small, and that it is undefined for a mean of 0; the value should be ignored with a small mean.

Another reason why we present the coefficient of variation rather than the standard deviation is that the standard deviation estimate is biased for a small number of observations and is often misused in statistical formulas. Although the standard deviation can be computed from the Summary Report by multiplying the coefficient of variation by the mean, the value should not be used in any statistical procedures that assume (as is the case in most standard procedures) independent observations. In particular, it is not appropriate to use this value in the standard formula for computing a confidence interval on the mean, because this procedure assumes independent observations. As we discuss later in this chapter, rarely are the observations within a replication independent. Use of this standard deviation estimate in formulas that assume independent observations can result in very large errors.

The minimum and maximum (i.e., the largest and smallest) observations also provide a measure of spread within the data. The smallest and largest recorded values of time in system for the Type 1 jobs in the example are 13.83 and 56.724, respectively.

The last value displayed in this category is the number of observations recorded for the variable; this value is commonly referred to as the sample size of the data. We see from the Summary Report that 23 observations of time in system were recorded for job Type 1.

The second category of summary statistics involves discrete-change variables. For our example these values, which are recorded automatically by the DSTATS element in the experiment, include statistics on the length of the queues and utilization of the resources and storages. The statistics consist of the average, coefficient of variation, minimum observation, maximum observation, and final value.

The interpretations for the average, coefficient of variation, minimum, and maximum are similar to those for observations recorded at TALLY blocks. In the case of the average and coefficient of variation, however, each value used in the calculation is weighted by the length of time for which the value persists. For example, if a variable has a value of 2 for one time unit and a value of 6 for three time units, the average over the four time units is computed as $(2*1 + 6*3)/4$, which equals 5. In our sample problem, the average and coefficient of variation for the length of the machine queue are 0.40941 and 2.2953, respectively.

For discrete-change variables, the final value — that is, the value at the time when the Summary Report was generated — is displayed in the last column. In our example, the report shows that there were no entities in the machine queue at the end of the simulation. Note that, if a variable is increasing (e.g., in an overly congested system or a system during startup), the final value typically is close to the maximum value for the variable.

The next category on the report displays Counter summary statistics and includes the current count and the count limit for each Counter in the model. In our example, the report shows that there were a total of seven rejected jobs during this replication.

3. Estimating Unknown Parameters

In most cases a simulation model contains sources of random variation. For example, the models developed in Chapter 3 have random variations in both their arrival and their service processes. Consequently, the summary statistics generated for the simulation (e.g., the average queue length, average time in system, etc.) are a function of the random processes within the model and are therefore random variables. When we execute the simulation, we actually conduct a sampling experiment in which we observe the random variable. These observations can be used to estimate unknown parameters with the aid of statistical analysis.

In simulation, we want to use observations generated by the simulation model to estimate a particular parameter. Because the generated observations are subject to the random fluctuations within the model, the numerical estimates of the parameters based on these observations are subject to error. To account for these errors, we should provide both a *point* estimate and an *interval* estimate of the parameter.

A point estimate is a single value that estimates the parameter of interest but gives no indication of the magnitude of the possible error resulting from fluctuations in the underlying random process. For example, the average queue length for a machine displayed on the SIMAN Summary Report provides a point estimate of the true (but unknown) mean queue length. From this value alone, however, we have no basis for interpreting the reliability of this estimate.

Interval estimates (also called confidence intervals) provide a range of values around the point estimate that have a specified likelihood of containing the parameter's value. For example, we may present the decision maker with a single value, which represents our best estimate of the expected queue length for the machine, but then further qualify this value by saying that we believe that the true value falls between specific lower and upper limits. Note that a range of values is given, and that the conclusion is not asserted with certainty, but rather with high likelihood.

The advantage of interval estimates is that they provide the decision maker with a quantitative estimate of the possible error in the point estimate of the parameter. In other words, the interval estimate defines the reliability of the point estimate. A large confidence interval implies that the point estimate is not very credible and should be given little weight.

The width of a confidence interval is related to both the variability of the system and the amount of data collected to form the estimate. We can make the confidence interval as small as we like by collecting sufficient data. However, we may need many data to make statements that are precise (i.e., have small confidence intervals) for highly variable systems.

To illustrate these concepts, let's assume that we face the problem of estimating the expected number of jobs completed each day in an operating factory. Although the actual number of jobs completed varies from day to day, let's assume that the expected number remains constant and has a value of 20. The expected number of completed jobs is unknown to us, and we want to estimate this unknown system parameter from data collected on the actual production. We'll also assume that we have counted the number of jobs completed on each of 10 successive days and have obtained the results shown below.

Day	Jobs Completed
1	35
2	12
3	26
4	38
5	8
6	16
7	23
8	41
9	13
10	34
Average	24.6

As shown, the number of jobs completed each day fluctuates randomly. The fluctuation may be attributable to variations in processing times, travel times, or equipment failures. Clearly, we cannot reliably use the observation from a single day to estimate the expected number of jobs completed per day. Using the results from a single day's production could produce an estimate as small as 8 or as large as

41. Either value would yield a very poor estimate of our true expected production rate of 20. In fact, the best daily estimate is 23, recorded for day 7.

Computing the average production over the 10 days provides a much better point estimate of the expected daily production, but fails to capture any information about the reliability of our estimate. We want to know how good our estimate of 24.6 is for the true expected production.

If we assume that our data are independent and normally distributed, we can use standard statistical procedures to compute an interval estimate for the expected day's production. (We discuss the procedures for computing this interval and the implications of the underlying assumptions later in this chapter.) Using standard procedures, we determine that a 95% confidence interval for the mean daily production rate is $[16, 33.2]$. We therefore assert that the true expected production rate (in this case, 20) lies in the interval between 16 and 33.2 with confidence 0.95. The wide interval shows that we cannot place much credibility in our point estimate of 24.6 as an estimator of the true mean daily production rate. To improve the reliability of our estimate, we must collect additional data on the system.

If we replace the actual factory by a simulation model in order to generate a table of results, the analytical concepts remain unchanged. Again, we certainly do not want to use the data from a single model replication of a day's production, because a single replication of a day's production equates to examining factory operation for a single day. Although we can improve our answer by averaging across replications, we still need an interval estimate in order to evaluate the reliability of our point estimate. Without this reliability measure, we have no basis for determining the credibility of simulation results — regardless of the quality of the underlying model.

4. Controlling Randomness

When collecting experimental observations from an actual system, we normally have no control over the random behavior of the system. Our activity is limited to recording observations that result from random behavior within the system, but we have no way to modify or repeat a specific sequence of random values. For example, for the production data discussed in the last section, it would normally not be possible to observe the identical results from the system on a second set of 10 days because the random processes within the system would probably yield completely different results.

We do not encounter this limitation when collecting experimental data from a simulation model because we have complete control over the random processes. If we want to, we can use exactly the same set of random values within the model in a second set of 10 replications, or we can base the second set of replications on different random values. The latter case is analogous to collecting real-system observations on a different set of 10 days.

To analyze the random simulation outputs properly, you must control the model's random inputs. With SIMAN, you control the random processes by using the SEEDS element, which specifies the initial seed and sampling method for the SIMAN random-number generators. In this section we describe the procedure that SIMAN uses to generate random samples and the use of the SEEDS element to control the random-number generators.

4.1 Generating Random Samples

Generating a random sample from a specified distribution is usually a two-step process. The first step is to generate a uniform real random number, r, between 0 and 1 by using a SIMAN random-number generator (explained in this section). In the second step, SIMAN uses the appropriate algorithm to convert r into a sample from the desired distribution.

Although we refer to the samples within a simulation as being random, in actuality they are not random at all because the underlying random numbers are generated from a deterministic algebraic equation. This equation generates numbers that appear to be uniform 0-1 random values even though they are not. Specifically, the values are uniformly distributed between 0 and 1, and the numbers behave as though independent when subjected to commonly used statistical tests for independence. Some authors use the term "pseudorandom" to distinguish the deterministic nature of these values from truly random values; however, in simulation these deterministic pseudorandom values are widely referred to simply as "random."

SIMAN's algebraic method for generating the underlying 0-1 values is called the *multiplicative congruential* method. This method generates an *unnormalized* random number between 0 and m (denoted by x), which is then converted to a *normalized* random number between 0 and 1 (denoted by r). Note that the term normalized as used here has nothing to do with the normal distribution. The unnormalized random number is converted by SIMAN to the normalized number by dividing it by m. The sequence shown below summarizes these steps.

Step 1. Initialization.

$x_0 = $ starting seed

Step 2. General Step.

$x_{i+1} = a\, x_i \,(\mathrm{mod}\ m)$
$r_{i+1} = x_{i+1}/m$

Step 3. Loop.

go to step 2.

As you can see, we begin by initializing the starting unnormalized random number, x_0, to a value called the *starting seed*. In general, the next random number is obtained from the previous random number by 1) multiplying the last unnormalized random number, x_i, by the multiplier a; 2) dividing the result by m; 3) assigning the remainder from the division as the value of the ith + 1 unnormalized random number; and 4) normalizing the result by dividing the new unnormalized value by m.

Note that, once we specify the initial seed, x_0, the entire sequence of numbers is determined. We can repeat this same sequence of random numbers over again on a second simulation by specifying the same initial random-number seed, x_0. To generate a different sequence of numbers, select a different starting seed. Hence, unlike the case with truly random numbers, we can control the random values generated in each simulation by specifying the initial seed value. As you will see in Chapter 12, this important advantage over purely random numbers can be exploited when analyzing simulation results.

The sequence of random numbers generated by a given seed is referred to as a *random-number stream*. Eventually, the algorithm generates the initial seed number for the stream and, from that point, regenerates another identical stream of numbers. The number of distinct values generated before the stream repeats is called the stream's *cycle length*. Ideally, the cycle length should be long enough so that values do not repeat within the simulation.

The random-number generator in SIMAN uses a multiplier, a, of 16,807, and a modulo value, m, of 2^{31}-1. This leads to what is referred to as an *almost full-period generator* [Fishman 1978], meaning that for any initial seed between 1 and 2^{31}-2, all unnormalized random numbers between 1 and 2^{31}-2, are generated exactly once before the generator cycles again. The resulting cycle length is about two billion numbers.

Note that you should not specify the values of 0 or 2^{31}-1 as seeds because, once a 0 is obtained, the stream consists of an infinite sequence of 0s. Otherwise, any seed value is acceptable.

A SIMAN model may employ several different random-number streams. Each stream is generated by using the same multiplier, a, and modulo value, m. However, each stream generates a different sequence of random numbers as determined by its starting seed value.

It is useful to visualize each random-number stream in SIMAN as a large circular tape containing about two billion non-repeating random numbers. Each of the circular tapes is consecutively numbered beginning with 1. By specifying a stream number, we are defining from which of the available circular tapes the random number is read.

Each circular tape has a pointer that points to the next number to be read from the tape. When the number at the current pointer location is read, the pointer is advanced one position on the tape. Because the tape is circular, the numbers repeat after all (roughly two billion) numbers on the tape have been read.

Each of the circular tapes representing the different streams contains the exact same numbers in the exact same order. We can, however, initialize the pointer for each tape to a different initial starting position on the tape by specifying the starting seed. The starting seed does not change the sequence of numbers on the tape, but it does change the starting point from which the first number is read.

4.2 Controlling the Initial Seeds: The SEEDS Element

The random-number streams in SIMAN are referenced by stream numbers starting with 1 and continuing up to the number of available streams. When specifying a random distribution, SIMAN uses a default stream and starting seed to generate the random samples. For example, SIMAN generates the value for UNIF(5,10) by taking a sample from the default stream, which is then converted to a sample that is uniformly distributed between 5 and 10. To use a non-default stream, we include the stream's number as the final argument of the distribution. For example, the specification UNIF(5,10,2) specifies that SIMAN use random stream 2 to generate the sample.

As is discussed in Chapter 12, for certain analyses it is sometimes convenient to use separate streams for various sources of randomness in the model. For example, we can use Stream 1 for the arrival process and Stream 2 for the service process. In many cases, however, we do not care which stream is used, and we can simply use the default stream, as we have done thus far.

The analysis methods discussed in this chapter usually require making multiple, independent replications of the model. You can do this in one of two ways: by specifying the number of replications on the REPLICATE element and making a single run, or by making n separate runs of one replication each. When making multiple replications in the same run, you typically want the random numbers in the second replication to simply continue from the stream in the first replication. This continuation, which is the default, yields different random samples in each replication.

You can use the SEEDS element to specify the initial seed value for each stream. You can also specify an option on the SEEDS element to reinitialize the stream at the beginning of each replication. If your model state is being reinitialized between runs, and you elect to reinitialize the streams, the results on each replication will be identical because the random values will be the same. The same duplication occurs when you make separate runs of one replication each, unless you specifically change the seed between simulation runs by modifying the SEEDS element. Repeating a simulation with the same seed value between replications typically does not make sense, unless you are changing parameters within the model between replications.

The format for the SEEDS element is shown below. The element consists of the stream's number, initial seed value, and initialization option, repeated as necessary.

```
SEEDS:Stream,Seed,InitOpt:
       repeats;
```

For example, the following element specifies that Stream 1 is to be initialized to the value 55555 and defaulted to the reinitialization option NO.

```
SEEDS:1,55555;
```

The easiest way to obtain n independent replications of the model is to make a single run of n replications with the reinitialization option for the streams defaulted to NO. With this approach you can omit the SEEDS element and use the default seeds. If, however, you want to make k additional replications on a second run (as required by two-stage statistical procedures), you must use the SEEDS element to specify a new starting seed for this second set of replications. Otherwise, the random values from the first set of replications are repeated.

5. Terminating and Non-Terminating Systems

The approach used to analyze simulation model results depends on whether the system is terminating or non-terminating. A *terminating* system has a fixed starting condition (to which the system returns after each termination) and an event defining the natural end of the simulation. An example of a terminating system is one that empties and closes at regular intervals, such as a post office. The fixed starting condition in this example is "empty and idle," and the termination event is the close of the business day. A *non-terminating* system has neither a fixed starting condition nor a natural ending point. Examples of non-terminating systems are those that do not close, such as a hospital or a telephone exchange.

Although some systems are clearly terminating or non-terminating, many are difficult to classify. Many systems that at first appear to be terminating may not be. For example, systems that close but do not empty are non-terminating, because they do not have a fixed starting condition to which they return following the termination event. A production system that uses the current day's unfinished work as the next day's starting work is a non-terminating system. Although this system has a natural termination event, i.e., the end of the work day, it does not have a fixed starting condition to which it returns. If we compress time by removing the intervals during which the system is closed, it behaves as a continuously operating system with no point at which the system starts anew.

In general, most manufacturing systems tend to be of the non-terminating type because, although they may close, they do not have a fixed starting condition (e.g., empty and idle) to which they return. The in-process inventory from one day is typically carried over to the next day. The system is terminating if the arrivals are turned off, and the system is emptied before closing for the day.

In contrast, most service systems tend to be of the terminating type. Examples include retail stores, restaurants, banks, dentist offices, barber shops, gas stations, food stores, amusement parks, and airline ticket counters. Once these systems close, the customers do not wait in the system for it to reopen the next day. Hence these systems typically have both a termination event (closed for the day) and a natural starting condition (empty and idle) to which they return. As already noted, exceptions include a hospital or a telephone exchange. Although both of these systems service people, they have no terminating event.

As we will see, it is easier to analyze terminating systems than non-terminating systems. Hence, for the purpose of analysis, we sometimes examine non-terminating systems as if they were terminating systems by defining a specific period of study. For example, we may elect to estimate product throughput for a newly constructed, continuously operating assembly line over the next two years. In this case the terminating event is the end of the planning event, and the fixed starting condition is the initial empty and idle state. However, as we discuss later in this chapter, this simplified approach can lead to erroneous results.

We begin by addressing terminating systems, the easier of the two analysis cases; then we will turn our attention to non-terminating systems. The same general analysis procedures discussed for terminating systems apply to non-terminating systems; the primary differences occur in the data collection and preparation phase of the analysis. Next we discuss the SIMAN Output Processor's role in performing both types of analysis, provide a summary of the procedures for analyzing both types of systems, and conclude the chapter with examples.

6. Analyzing Terminating Systems

In a terminating system, both the starting conditions and the terminating condition are defined by the nature of the system. Because you cannot manipulate the starting conditions or the length of each replication, the only decision in controlling sample size is how many replications of the simulation to execute.

When analyzing a terminating system, we have two sources of observations for our analysis. We can use the individual observations within each replication. For example, we can use the individual customer's waiting time in the queue as the observations for estimating the expected waiting time in the queue. The sample size in this case is the total number of individual entities processed in a single simulation replication. Or, alternatively, we can use the summary values displayed in the SIMAN Summary Report for each replication. In this case each replication produces a single observation; hence, the total number of observations is the number of replications of the model.

The second approach greatly simplifies the analysis because, by properly controlling the random-number streams, we can assume that these observations are statistically *independent*. And, because these observations are typically the sum or average of many individual observations within the replication, it is reasonable to assume, based on the Central Limit Theorem, that they have a normal distribution.

Many standard statistical procedures require the independence assumption. Independence implies that the outcome of one observation does not affect the outcome of any other observation. For example, when you flip a coin, the occurrence of heads or tails on the first flip does not affect the result of the second flip; hence, the outcomes are independent. In most simulation models, the observations within a replication are not independent. For example, in our first sample problem in Chapter 3, the time that a job spends waiting for the machine is influenced by the time spent waiting by the previous job. If the previous job spent a long time waiting in the queue, then it is likely that this job will also spend a long time waiting in the queue. In this case the waiting times for the successive jobs are *correlated*. As the observations are set apart, they tend to become less correlated — i.e. the waiting time of a job will typically not greatly influence the waiting time for the one-thousandth later arriving job.

Although the observations within a given run are typically highly correlated, the observations across replications are independent — as long as we use different random-number seeds for each replication. For example, the observations for average waiting time in the queue for each replication of the model are independent, even though the waiting time for individual jobs within the same replication are correlated. Recall that, when we use SIMAN's REPLICATE element to make multiple replications, different random-number seeds are automatically used for each replication, unless we override the default random-number stream initialization. Thus, by default the REPLICATE element produces independent observations across (but not within) each replication of the simulation.

Many standard statistical procedures also require that the observations have a normal distribution. If we use the observations from within a single replication, we will probably violate this requirement. However, if we use a single value (from each run) that is the sum or average of many individual observations within the replication, then we can assume a normal distribution based on the Central Limit Theorem. The Central Limit Theorem states that, when we sum or average many different individual random values, the resulting sum or average is approximately normal, regardless of the distribution of the individual values.

Occasionally, the parameter of interest may be in the form of a maximum or minimum within the replication rather than an average or a sum. For example, we may be interested in using the model to determine the maximum number of jobs in a machine buffer. Because the Central Limit Theorem does not apply in this case (it is not the sum or average of a set of random values), the maximum observations may not have a normal distribution. Fortunately, many statistical procedures (like the confidence interval and comparison procedures discussed later in this chapter) are robust regarding violations in the normality assumption; in other words, the procedure works reasonably well, even if this assumption is violated by the data. The same is not true, however, regarding violations of the independence assumption.

If we want to use the Output Processor for automatically performing our analysis of the results for a terminating system, then we may use the OUTPUTS element to create an output file containing the observation of interest from each replication of the model. This observation may be the average queue length, the maximum queue length, or any similar value from the replication. The OUTPUTS element contained in the experiment records a single summary observation, e.g., the average time in the system, at the end of each replication of the model.

The format for the OUTPUTS element is shown below. The operands of this element consist of the output variable number (typically defaulted), the output expression, the output file specification, and the identifier, which defaults to the expression and is used for labeling by the Output Processor. The operands are repeated as necessary. This element causes the value of the specified expression to be written to the specified output file at the end of each replication of the simulation. Hence, n replications of the simulation generate n values in the output file, with a single value produced from each replication of the simulation.

```
OUTPUTS:Number,Expression,OutFile,OutputID:
         repeats;
```

The output expression is often specified by using one of the statistical summary variables shown below.

Variable	Description
DAVG(DstatID)	Average dstat value for DstatID
DMIN(DstatID)	Minimum dstat value for DstatID
DMAX(DstatID)	Maximum dstat value for DstatID
TAVG(TallyID)	Average tally value for TallyID
TMIN(TallyID)	Minimum tally value for TallyID
TMAX(TallyID)	Maximum tally value for TallyID
NC(CountID)	Counter value for CountID

The argument of the statistical summary variables shown above is the corresponding dstat, tally, or counter identifier. For example, TAVG(TimeInSystem) denotes the average tally value for the tally variable TimeInSystem. Adding the following OUTPUTS element to the experiment for Sample Problem 3.1 causes the number of completed jobs at the end of each model replication to be recorded in the file named Jobs.dat.

```
OUTPUTS:NC(JobsDone),"Jobs.dat",Jobs Completed;
```

6.1 Constructing Confidence Intervals on the Mean

We now consider the problem of constructing a confidence interval estimate for the expected value of a model parameter. For example, consider the problem of developing a confidence interval for the total number of completed jobs for the first sample problem in Chapter 3. A summary of the results of 10 replications of the model is shown below. These results have been obtained by specifying 10 replications on the REPLICATE element of the experiment and by using the default controls for the random-number streams. To facilitate analysis, the OUTPUTS element shown in the previous section has been added to the experiment to record the value of the number of completed jobs for each replication; this file allows us to read the recorded values directly into the Output Processor for analysis.

Replication Number	Jobs Completed
1	93
2	113
3	107
4	103
5	112
6	103
7	112
8	100
9	98
10	105

We construct a confidence interval on the mean in the form

$$\mu = [\bar{x} - h, \bar{x} + h]$$

where $\bar{x}$ is the point estimate of the mean, and h is called the interval's *half-width*. If constructed properly, a random-sample mean $\bar{x}$ will fall within the interval with a probability of $1 - \alpha$. This probability is called the *confidence level* of the interval.

The half-width, which is calculated from the sample observations, is a measure of the precision of our point estimate, $\bar{x}$, of the true but unknown mean, μ. The smaller the half-width, the better our estimate of the mean. The half-width is reduced by increasing the number of observations used to form $\bar{x}$.

Let x_i denote the sample observation recorded on the ith replication of a terminating system's simulation model. Assume that there are a total of n independent replications of the model. We can compute the sample mean, $\bar{x}$, and the sample variance, s^2, of x and $\bar{x}$ from the n observations as follows:

$$\bar{x} = \sum_i \frac{x_i}{n}$$

$$s^2(x) = \sum_i \frac{(x_i - \bar{x})^2}{n-1}$$

$$s^2(\bar{x}) = \frac{s^2(x)}{n}$$

If the x values are normally distributed, then a half-width, h, gives an exact $1 - \alpha$ confidence interval for the true mean, μ, centered at $\bar{x}$. This is computed as follows:

$$h = t_{n-1,\, 1-\alpha/2}\, s(\bar{x})$$

where $t_{n-1\alpha/2}$ is obtained from a table of t-values and is the upper $\alpha/2$ point of the student-t distribution with n-1 degrees of freedom. A table of t-values for various values of n and α is included in Appendix B.

As previously noted, if the x_i values are themselves the average or sum of observations within the run, then the normality assumption is reasonable, based on the Central Limit Theorem. If the x_i values are not normally distributed, then the results hold (approximately) for replications of 10 or more.

Applying the previous equations to calculate an approximate 0.95 confidence interval for the number of jobs completed in our sample problem yields the following result.

$$\bar{x} = 104.6$$

$$s(x) = 6.6$$

$$n = 10$$

$$s(\bar{x}) = 2.1$$

$$t_{9,.975} = 2.262$$

$$h = 4.7$$

Hence, we can state with a high confidence (0.95) that the true expected number of jobs completed per day for this model is between 99.9 and 109.3. In other words, we have high confidence that the true but unknown value for the expected number of jobs completed is within about 5% of our point estimate for this value. The wide interval results from the large underlying variability of the exponential distribution for the arrival process. Fortunately, many real systems have much less variability and therefore produce a much smaller relative half-width.

The confidence limit is commonly mistaken as a method for predicting the outcome of a simulation replication. It is not true that there is a 0.95 likelihood that the jobs completed on any given day will fall in the range of 99.9 to 109.3. The interval makes a statement about the true but unknown value of the population mean, not about the outcome of a specific experiment. The randomness in the experiment is a system property that we cannot change; however, the confidence interval is a statement of reliability for our estimate of the population mean and can be made as small as desired by increasing the sample size.

The previous procedure is referred to as a *fixed sample-size procedure* because the number of observations, n, is fixed in advance. The main disadvantage of this approach is that we have no control over the resulting half-width; in some instances we want to run the number of replications necessary to achieve a specific half-width. To obtain a specific half-width we use a two-stage sampling procedure. Let's assume that we have made n initial replications, computed the half-width as previously outlined, and determined that the half-width is too large. We can estimate the total number of replications, n^*, required to reduce the half-width, h, to a desired value, h_r^* as follows:

$$n^* = \left[n(h/h^*)^2\right]$$

where [ ] denotes the value rounded up to the next integer. We can see from this equation that an increase in the number of replications is inversely proportional to the square of the fractional decrease in the confidence interval width. For example, to cut the confidence interval width in half, we need four times as many model replications.

After computing n^*, we then make $n^* - n$ additional replications of the model to ensure that the starting seed for the second set of independent replications differs from the starting seed of the first set of replications. Next, using all n^* observations, we recalculate our confidence interval.

Returning to our previous example, let's assume that we want to reduce our half-width from 4.64 to 3. We calculate n^* as follows:

$$n^* = \left[10(4.7/3)^2\right] = \left[24.6\right] = 25$$

An estimate of the number of additional replications required to achieve this half-width is $25 - 10$, where 10 is the number of replications already made. To make these additional replications, we specify the number of replications on the REPLICATE element as 15 and use the SEEDS element to initialize the stream to a new seed. Note that this last step is necessary to prevent the second set of replications from being identical to the first set. Making these runs with an arbitrary starting seed of 11111 yields the results shown below.

Replication Number	Jobs Completed
1	94
2	115
3	111
4	102
5	108
6	96
7	111
8	107
9	113
10	103
11	113
12	113
13	103
14	99
15	104

Combining these results with those from the first set of 10 replications, we compute the new confidence interval as follows:

$$\bar{x} = 106.$$
$$s(x) = 6.5$$
$$n = 25$$
$$s(\bar{x}) = 1.3$$
$$t_{24,.975} = 2.064$$
$$h = 2.7$$

Hence we have reduced the width of our confidence interval from 5% of the mean to about 3% of the mean.

This two-stage sampling procedure does not guarantee that the width of the final confidence interval produced will actually meet the target width used in the first-stage calculations; it may be larger or smaller than the target. It should also be noted that the point estimate should be the sample mean from the combined first- and second-stage calculations.

In this example we have manually performed the calculations needed to construct a confidence interval. In general, however, you need not perform these calculations because the INTERVALS command in the Output Processor uses the same procedure to automatically construct a confidence interval on a set of output data. We discuss this command later in this chapter.

6.2 Comparing Two Systems

In many situations we want to compare two candidate systems. For example, we may want to compare two different scheduling rules or two different material-handling systems to determine which yields the best results.

To illustrate the problem of comparing two systems, we again use the first sample problem in Chapter 3. In the original model, the arriving jobs are processed on the machine in the order in which they arrive; this order is referred to as the FIFO (first-in-first-out) system. Assume that a proposal has been made to change the processing order of the jobs so that the jobs having the smallest processing time are processed first; this order is referred to as the SPT (shortest-processing-time) system. Our objective is to use simulation to determine if the SPT system is better than the original FIFO system in terms of the expected time that a job spends in the system.

To perform this analysis, we must modify our model slightly so that we can use the SPT rule to rank the jobs in the queue. First we assign the processing time to an attribute named ProcessTime, and then we use this attribute to specify the duration on the DELAY block. In the experiment we specify the ranking rule for the queue as LVF(ProcessTime), corresponding to the SPT rule. We must also mark the arrival time and record the time in system for each job. We also include an OUTPUTS element in the experiment to record the average time in system at the end of each replication of the model. The modified SIMAN model and QUEUES, ATTRIBUTES, and OUTPUTS elements are shown in Figure 5-2.

```
BEGIN;
        CREATE:    EXPONENTIAL(4.4):        ! enter the system
                   MARK(TimeIn);            set arrival time
        ASSIGN:    ProcessTime{TRIANGULAR   set processing
                   (3.2,4.2,5.2);
        QUEUE,     Buffer;                  wait for the machine
        SEIZE:     Machine;                 seize the machine
        DELAY:     ProcessTime;             delay by processing
        RELEASE:   Machine;                 release the machine
        TALLY:     TimeInSystem,INT(TimeIn); tally time in system
        COUNT:     JobsDone:DISPOSE;        count completed jobs
END;

ATTRIBUTES: ProcessTime;
QUEUES: Buffer, LVF(ProcessTime);
OUTPUTS: TAVG(TimeInSystem),"TsysSPT.dat",SPT Time In System;
```

Figure 5-2. Modified Model and Experiment for Sample Problem 3.1

The table below shows the results for the average time in system for 10 replications of the FIFO and SPT systems. These results have been obtained by making two separate runs: one with the queue rule defaulted to FIFO, another with the queue ranking rule set to LVF(ProcessTime). In both runs the number of replications on the REPLICATE element has been set to 10, and the random-number seed controls have been defaulted.

Replication	FIFO	SPT
1	8.87	9.19
2	31.52	19.18
3	14.14	12.30
4	14.11	13.04
5	16.72	17.79
6	27.78	11.49
7	34.05	21.61
8	22.96	10.50
9	10.98	13.27
10	11.66	8.50

The general procedure used to compare these two systems assumes that we have obtained the same number of observations for each of the two systems. In our procedural description, we refer to the two systems as System A (FIFO) and System B (SPT), and we assume that we have made n replications (10) of each system. Let x_{ai} and x_{bi} denote the observation recorded on the ith replication of Systems A and B, respectively, and let d_i denote the difference between Systems A and B on the ith replication (i.e., $d_i = x_{ai} - x_{bi}$). We can arrange these values as shown in the following table.

Replication	System A	System B	Difference
1	x_{a1}	x_{b1}	d_1
2	x_{a2}	x_{b2}	d_2
.	.	.	.
n	x_{an}	x_{bn}	d_n

We approach the problem of comparing the two systems by developing a confidence interval on the quantity δ, which is the expected value of d_i. In this way the problem of comparing two systems is reduced to estimating a single parameter, namely, δ. The resulting confidence interval is referred to as a *paired-t confidence interval.*

Although several other methods can be used to compare two systems, this technique is particularly appealing for a number of reasons. First, we do not have to assume that the variance of x_a and x_b is equal, as we must if we use some other methods, e.g., the two-sample-t method. Second, we do not have to assume that x_{ai} and x_{bi} are independent; we need only assume that within System A the observations are independent and within System B the observations are independent. Per our table, we require that the observations within a column be independent, but we permit correlation across a row. As we will see in Chapter 12, we can exploit this property to reduce the size of the confidence interval on δ, without increasing the number of replications.

The procedure for computing the confidence interval on δ is exactly the same as for the single-system case. We begin by computing $\bar{d}$, $s(d)$, and $s(\bar{d})$, as follows:

$$\bar{d} = \frac{\Sigma d_i}{n}$$

$$s(d) = \sqrt{\frac{\Sigma(d_i - \bar{d})^2}{n-1}}$$

$$s(\bar{d}) = \frac{s(d)}{\sqrt{n}}$$

The half-width for a $1-\alpha$ confidence interval on δ centered at $\bar{d}$ is then given by

$$h = t_{n-1,\, 1-\alpha/2}\, s(\bar{d})$$

Note that the statistic $\bar{d}$ is an estimate of the difference in the measured performance of the two systems; if the two systems perform identically, then the expected value of $\bar{d}$ is 0. Therefore, if our computed confidence interval contains 0, we cannot reliably state that System A and System B are different. However, if the interval does not contain 0, we assert with the appropriate confidence level that a difference exists between the two systems.

It should be noted that, if the interval on the difference between the systems contains 0, the two systems are not necessarily the same, but additional replications may be required to discern any difference. Hence, no conclusion can be drawn from the results when the interval contains 0. If we want to make additional runs to attempt to discern a difference between the two systems, we can estimate the number of additional replications needed to exclude 0 from the confidence interval by using the same two-stage sampling procedure.

If the confidence interval does not contain 0, we conclude that the systems differ, and we select between the two systems based on the sign of $\bar{d}$.

Returning now to our example, we compute the difference between the FIFO and SPT results for each of the 10 replications as shown in the following table.

Replication	FIFO	SPT	Difference
1	8.87	9.19	−0.32
2	31.52	19.18	12.34
3	14.14	12.30	1.84
4	14.11	13.04	1.07
5	16.72	17.79	−1.07
6	27.78	11.49	16.29
7	34.05	21.61	12.45
8	22.96	10.50	12.45
9	10.98	13.27	−2.30
10	11.66	8.50	3.16

We next compute the 0.95 confidence interval on δ as follows:

$\bar{d} = 5.6$

$s(d) = 6.96$

$n = 10$

$s(\bar{d}) = 2.19$

$t_{9,.975} = 2.262$

$h = 5.0$

$\text{C.I.} = [.6, 10.6]$

Because the confidence interval does not contain 0, we assert with 0.95 confidence that there is a difference between the two systems. Because d is positive, we assert that the SPT system results in a smaller expected time in system than does the FIFO system.

The Output Processor COMPARISONS command can be used to perform these calculations automatically. We discuss the use of the COMPARISONS command later in this chapter.

It is interesting to note that, in this example, comparing these two systems based on the results from the first replication of each system yields the incorrect conclusion that the FIFO system has a smaller average time in system than the SPT system; this conclusion is also supported by replications 5 and 9.

7. Analyzing Non-Terminating Systems

In a non-terminating system, there is no event that causes the system to return to a fixed initial condition. Hence, there is no natural basis for selecting either the starting conditions or the length of the run. In non-terminating systems we are usually interested in understanding the *steady-state* behavior of the system, i.e., its behavior over a very long period of time.

Non-terminating systems generally go through an initial transient phase that varies with the starting conditions. Thereafter, they have an essentially unchanging distribution that is independent of the starting conditions. There is, however, no definite point at which the system's behavior changes from transient to steady-state. The steady-state response is actually a limiting condition not completely realized in a simulation experiment. We nevertheless refer to a simulation as being in steady-state once the initial transient phase has diminished to the point where the impact of the initial conditions on the system's response is negligible.

Because we want to estimate the system's performance during the steady-state phase, any observations recorded during the transient phase will bias our results. For example, if we are modeling a jobshop and we begin the simulation in the empty and idle state, the initial jobs will arrive at an uncongested system with idle machines. Hence, the early arriving jobs will quickly move through the system and our performance measures (time in system, queue length, machine utilization, etc.) will all be biased downward during the early part of the simulation. After the system has had time to "warm-up," queues will form, and the system will begin to exhibit its true long-term behavior. Observations collected after the warm-up period will be representative of steady-state behavior, whereas observations collected during the transient phase will make our system appear to function better than it really does.

When trying to analyze steady-state performance, we must deal with the bias introduced by the starting conditions. (This is not a problem in terminating systems, because we are specifically interested in evaluating the transient response of these systems to their fixed starting conditions.) As we will see, the three most promising approaches to this problem are 1) to reduce the transient phase by selecting the appropriate starting conditions for the run; 2) to discard data during the initial portion of the simulation, thus avoiding biased observations from the transient phase; and 3) to run the simulation long enough so that any data collected during the transient phase will be dominated by data collected during the steady-state phase.

A second problem with non-terminating systems involves estimating the variance of the mean response in order to develop a confidence interval for the mean. In the case of terminating systems the estimation is simple, because the run length is fixed, and we are generating independent replications of the model with a defined starting condition. Each replication gives an unbiased, independent sample of the variable of interest. In the non-terminating case, however, there is no obvious point to define the end of a replication. In addition, we introduce the initial condition bias for each new replication we make. If we avoid this problem by making a single, long run, we must work with highly correlated observations within the run. The absence of independence among observations greatly complicates our analysis.

In the following sections we further discuss the issues of assessing bias and estimating variance in non-terminating systems. We present a number of alternatives for dealing with these issues; however, unlike terminating systems, for which there is one relatively simple and well-developed approach to analyzing simulation results, non-terminating cases rely on several pragmatic ideas that are neither theoretically well-developed nor universally accepted.

7.1 Reducing the Initial Condition Bias

One of the most effective ways to deal with the problem of initial condition bias is to start the simulation in a state representative of steady-state behavior. By making our best guess of a representative starting state and initializing the simulation to this state at the beginning of the run, we can frequently dramatically reduce the length of the transient phase. By default, a simulation model begins in an empty and idle state. Many non-terminating simulations are, for simplicity, started in this state; however, in most systems the empty and idle state is not representative of the steady-state behavior and can produce a very long transient phase.

It is usually easy to come up with a starting condition that is far more representative of steady-state than the empty and idle state. If the purpose of our model is to evaluate modifications to an existing system, then we can use our knowledge of the existing system to estimate the steady-state behavior of the modified system. If we are modeling a proposed system, then we can base our estimate of the starting state on the performance specifications for the system. A pilot run of the simulation may also be useful to help estimate a reasonable starting condition, although we cannot expect to eliminate the bias completely.

Once you determine a reasonable non-empty starting condition for the model, the next step is to initialize the system to that starting state at the beginning of the simulation. In Chapter 8 we discuss the ARRIVALS element, which you can use to load the model with initial entities.

The second method used to deal with the initial bias problem is to discard those observations recorded during the transient phase of the simulation. This approach necessitates selecting a truncation point, t, at which all previous observations are discarded. The results for the simulation are then based only on observations recorded after point t. This poses an obvious question: How do we determine the truncation point?

The problem with selecting a truncation point is that we must attempt to achieve two conflicting objectives. On the one hand, the more data we truncate, the less bias we will have in our estimate of the mean; from this perspective, we may want to truncate all but the last observation. On the other hand, the more we truncate, the more variability we will have in our estimate of the mean. Hence, we must compromise between reducing bias and increasing the variance for our estimate.

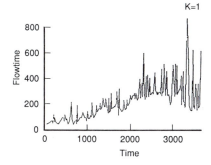

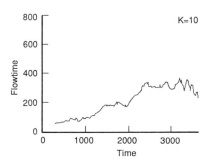

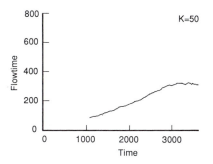

Figure 5-3. Smoothing the Response by using a Moving Average

A number of investigators have proposed simple rules for dealing with the problem of transient data [Wilson and Pritsker 1978, Scruben 1982], but experience suggests that a rule's performance depends largely on the nature of the simulation response. Consequently, these rules are generally not used in simulation applications.

The simplest, most practical, and probably best method for selecting the truncation point is visual determination, i.e., selecting the point from a plot of the simulation response over time. In systems with large fluctuations in the response, you can improve this process by first using a moving-average filter to smooth the response [Welch 1983]. A moving average is constructed by calculating the arithmetic average of the k most recent observations at each data point in the data set. You select the value of k, which is called the moving-average size. As you increase the value of k, you increase the "smoothness" of the response. Figure 5-3 shows the response for an actual simulation model, before and after smoothing, based on moving averages of 10 and 50 observations. This filtering is done by using the Output Processor MOVAVERAGE command, which is discussed later in this chapter.

It is important to note at this point that a number of investigators caution against truncation. Their recommendation is often based on studies with small, well-behaved models [Fishman 1972], for which the steady-state solution is known. These models, however, are not representative of the types of systems that we usually model. Our experience has shown truncation to be a very good way to substantially improve the quality of the results in most non-terminating system models.

A final method for dealing with the initial transient bias problem involves making very long runs in combination with the two aforementioned approaches. With long runs, data recorded during the transient phase are dominated by the data recorded during the steady-state phase. In general, the longer the run, the lower the level of bias attributable to starting conditions; however, longer runs imply fewer replications of the simulation for the same total computing time.

To summarize, the starting condition in the simulation of a non-terminating system creates a potential bias in our estimate of the system's steady-state performance. We can reduce this bias by intelligently guessing at a representative starting condition, by truncating the data from the initial portion of the run, and by making runs as long as possible.

7.2 Estimating the Variance of the Mean

This section discusses three ways to estimate the variance of the mean: by using replication, summing covariances, and batching observations. We prefer using the batching technique; however, we describe the other techniques to show the reason for our preference.

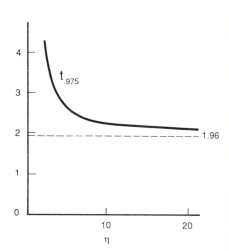

Replication

With terminating systems, we estimate the variance of the mean by generating independent replications of the model; this procedure can also be used for non-terminating systems. The main advantages of replication are its simplicity and the fact that we can make direct use of all of the statistical procedures discussed for the terminating case. Do note, however, that using replication for a non-terminating system introduces the initial condition bias at the beginning of each replication. If the transient phase is substantial, we can waste a good deal of computer time because we must discard data at the beginning of each replication.

We can select the length of the replication and therefore must decide whether it is preferable to make a few long replications or many short replications. As mentioned earlier, long replications are less likely to have initial condition bias, and they waste fewer data; however, if we make too few replications, the degrees of freedom for the t-statistic will be large, resulting in an increased half-width for the confidence interval. A reasonable number of replications to use in most situations is 10, and it probably makes little sense to have more than 20, because improvements in the t-statistic diminish beyond that point. When the starting condition has a noticeable influence, 10 long replications are probably preferable to 20 short runs.

The replication approach is best suited to applications in which the transient phase is minimal. In applications with a significant initial bias, the preferred methods are those based on a single replication, such as the batch-means approach discussed later in this section.

Summing Covariances

Increasing sample size by continuing a single run, rather than by replicating the run, wastes the computer time associated with the transient phase only once. In the discussion that follows, we assume that a single replication has been made and that the data for the transient portion of the replication have been discarded.

The equation used to obtain a confidence interval in the case of a terminating system is derived by assuming independent observations. Each replication of the terminating system gives us a single observation (e.g., the average waiting time), and these observations are independent across runs. In the case of a single run of a non-terminating system, however, the observations are the individual values within the run (e.g., the waiting time of a specific job), and these observations are almost always correlated. For example, in most systems we expect that, if Job j waits for a long time, it is likely that Job $j+1$ will wait for a long time; hence, the waiting times of these two adjacent jobs are correlated.

When correlated observations exist, the direct estimation of the variance of the mean is greatly complicated by the need for estimating covariances. We can simplify our task somewhat by assuming that we have an auto-covariance stationary process, i.e., that the covariance between any two observations that are k observations apart is the same, regardless of where in the sequence the observations fall. The distance k is referred to as the lag between observations.

Assuming that we have n observations remaining after truncating the initial data, we use the following equations to compute the sample mean, variance, and covariances.

$$\bar{x} = \frac{\Sigma\, x_i}{n}$$

$$s^2(x) = \sum_i \frac{(x_i - \bar{x})^2}{n}$$

$$c_j = \sum_{i=1}^{n-j} \frac{(x_i - \bar{x})\,(x_{i+j} - \bar{x})}{n}$$

We then estimate the standard deviation of $\bar{x}$ and the half-width of the approximate confidence interval as follows:

$$csum = 2 \sum_{j=1}^{m} (1 - j/n)\, c_j$$

$$s^2(\bar{x}) = (s^2(x) + csum)\,/\,n$$

$$h = z_{1-\alpha/2}\, s(\bar{x})$$

where z is the $\alpha/2$ point of the standard normal distribution. The use of the standard normal in place of the t-distribution assumes that the sample size is large.

Note that in computing $s(\bar{x})$, we form the statistic csum, which is a weighted sum of covariances of lags through m, where m is small compared to n and is usually less than n/4. The value of m is selected as the largest lag having a sample correlation significantly different from 0. The sample correlation at a lag of j is defined as the sample covariance at a lag of j divided by the sample standard deviation. The most practical way to select m is to examine a correlogram, which is a plot of the sample correlations as a function of the lag.

Figure 5-4 shows a typical correlogram generated from simulation data recorded on the time in system for each job. As can be seen from the correlogram, the correlation in the data is significant for lags up to 50, but is relatively small for a lag of 100 or more. This simply means that the time in system for one job significantly influences the time in system for the jobs that closely follow but has no significant influence on jobs that follow 100 or more jobs later in the sequence.

In most systems the correlations between the observations are positive and typically increase with increased congestion in the system. A positive correlation implies that, if one observation is larger than its expected value, the correlated observation also tends to be larger than its expected value. As we can see from the equations, positive correlations increase the sample variance of the mean, thereby increasing the width of the confidence interval. In other words, positively corre-

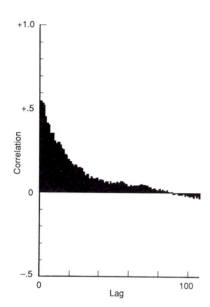

Figure 5-4. Correlogram for Typical Simulation Data

lated observations are less significant than independent observations for reducing the width of the confidence interval.

The Output Processor's CORRELOGRAM command can be used to construct a correlogram automatically for a data set and to compute the statistic, csum, which is the weighted sum of covariances used to form a confidence interval on the mean. We discuss the CORRELOGRAM command later in this chapter.

The main problem with summing covariances is that the sample covariance is a biased estimator of the covariance, and it has a large variance unless the sample size, n, is very large and each lag index, j, is small compared to n. Hence, the method can produce rather poor approximate confidence intervals in some instances. Summing covariances is most likely to succeed when n is very large and the correlation decreases rapidly to 0 as the lag increases. However, in general, the batch-means approach discussed in the next section is a safer and easier approach.

Batching Observations

The easiest and most practical method for interpreting the output for a nonterminating system is the method of batch means. This method parallels the method of independent replications used for terminating systems; however, instead of replicating the simulation with a defined initial starting condition, we divide the sequence of data from a single run into sub-sequences that are approximately independent of each other. We then treat each sub-sequence of data as though it were an independent replication of the system.

We begin by making a single long run and discarding the initial transient phase by examining the moving-average plot. We then divide the remaining observations into n equal, non-overlapping batches, each of size m. Hence, the total number of remaining individual observations equals n times m. We let x_j for $j = 1, \ldots, n$ denote the mean of the observations in the jth batch. Using this notation, we can directly use the results from the terminating case to write confidence intervals or to compare two systems.

If the batches are sufficiently large, the means of the two adjacent batches will be approximately independent, even though the observations at the end of batch j are correlated with the observations at the beginning of batch $j+1$. This statement assumes that the length of each batch is large compared to the time extent of the correlation between the individual observations. The batch size required to achieve this independence is a function of the correlation structure for the system response. A rule of thumb is that the batch size should be at least 10 times as large as the largest lag for which the correlation between observations remains significant. In a typical simulation this rule defines a minimum batch size of several hundred — possibly even several thousand — observations. In general, the more congested the system is, the larger the batches must be because of the higher correlations between the observations.

The key to making the batching method work well is selecting the appropriate batch size. From the standpoint of the independence and normality assumptions, the bigger, the better. On the other hand, if we have too few batches, we have a larger-than-necessary t-statistic, which degrades the half-width. Except for the penalty of a larger t-statistic, there is no problem with having batches containing more observations than necessary to approximately satisfy the independence assumption. The conservative approach is to use fewer but larger batches to decrease the likelihood of correlated data. A reasonable compromise is to divide the observations from the single long run into 10 to 20 batches [Schmeiser 1982].

Although we have discussed a fixed number of discrete observations per batch, the batch-observation method can also be applied to time-persistent quantities (average queue length, utilization of machines, etc.) by defining the batch as a fixed duration of time. We can also define a fixed-duration batch (e.g., an eight-hour shift) for discrete observations, in which case the number of observations per batch is a random variable. We use the same basic analysis procedure in each of these cases.

The Output Processor's FILTER command (discussed later in this chapter) can be used to perform batching on a set of simulation data. This same command is used to truncate the transient data from the run.

As we said at the beginning of this section, the batch-means method parallels the independent-replications method for terminating systems. We can actually perform our batching by using SIMAN's REPLICATE element and by specifying the number of replications as the desired number of batches. The only difference is that we must specify the system initialization option as NO to cause the termination state of one run to remain as the starting state of the next run. Because the terminating state represents steady-state behavior, we avoid the need to truncate the initial portion of each run. Hence, we see that the batch-means method differs from the independent-replications approach only with regard to the initialization of the simulation.

There is both an advantage and a disadvantage to using the REPLICATE element to perform batching. The disadvantage is that we must select the batch size before we make the run. As we will see, the FILTER command allows us to change the batch size without having to run the simulation again. The advantage of using the REPLICATE element is that only the summary value at the end of each replication needs to be written to an output file; we simply include the OUTPUTS element in the experiment. In contrast, the FILTER command requires that each individual observation within the run be saved by specifying an output file on the appropriate TALLIES or DSTATS element. Because fewer data are written to the output file when batching with the REPLICATE element, this approach requires less computer time.

8. Using the SIMAN Output Processor

The SIMAN Output Processor provides the capability of automatically performing many of the data treatments discussed in previous sections. In this section we describe the Output Processor and summarize some of the most commonly used commands for interpreting simulation results. In the next section we provide a step-by-step procedure for analyzing both terminating and non-terminating simulation results with the Output Processor.

The Output Processor, an interactive program, operates in a post-processing mode to help you analyze the data generated from a simulation model. To use the Output Processor, you must save, in one or more output files, the raw data generated during a simulation. To create these files for a non-terminating system, you enter the output file specification on the DSTATS, TALLIES, and COUNTERS elements in the experiment for each variable that you want to analyze. All raw data generated during each replication of the model are then saved in the specified files. Consider, for example, the following DSTATS element added to the experiment for Sample Problem 3.1.

```
DSTATS:NQ(Buffer), Buffer Queue Length, "Queue.dat";
```

This element specifies that time-persistent statistics are to be recorded on the variable NQ(Buffer), and that the value for this variable over time is to be written to the file named Queue.dat.

When you use the REPLICATE element to make multiple replications within a single run, any output files specified on the DSTATS, TALLIES, or COUNTERS elements contain the raw data for all model replications. Using the Output Processor, you can specify the data for a single replication within the data file by appending a slash (/) followed by the replication number to the output file specification. For example, "Queue.dat"/3 refers to the data in the file Queue.dat for Replication 3.

In some cases you do not want to analyze the raw data; instead, you want to analyze a set of n values consisting of a single summary value from each of a set of n replications of the simulation. For example, in a terminating system, for each replication you may want to record the average entity time in system, rather than the time that individual entities spent in the system. To record the average, you include the OUTPUTS element in the experiment for a simulation model.

SIMAN's output files are unformatted to reduce execution time. You cannot directly examine the contents of an unformatted file by simply displaying the file on the screen with a standard operating system command or text editor. However, as we discuss later, you can convert the file to other formats by using commands provided by the Output Processor.

Once an output file has been generated from a simulation, you can subject the data to various treatments by entering commands to the Output Processor. Note that the same data can be subjected to different treatments. For example, we can plot the data in the file Queue.dat and then generate a confidence interval from the same data. Data treatments can also be applied to sets of data files. For example, we can generate a single plot showing the queue length for System A compared to the queue length for System B over time.

Because the Output Processor can always be operated by entering commands via the keyboard, we discuss the functionality of the Output Processor based on command-mode operation. Most systems also provide a menu interface for operating the Output Processor, and this discussion also applies to menu-interface operation.

The command syntax for the Output Processor resembles the syntax of elements in the experiment, except that you enter the commands interactively in response to the Output Processor's prompt. Each Output Processor command specification consists of the command name, followed by one or more operands specific to that command. The operands within a command are separated by commas (,), and sometimes a given set of operands is repeated within a command. Each group is separated by a colon (:), and the end of a command is followed by a semicolon (;). Some operands have qualifiers, which are appended to the operand following a slash (/).

The Output Processor commands are designed so that most operands have default values applicable to most situations. You usually need to specify very few of the available operands, aside from the name of the output file containing the data set to be processed by the command.

In the command mode, you start the Output Processor by entering the command OUTPT in response to the operating system's prompt. The Output Processor then issues its prompt, which is the greater-than sign (>). Enter specific commands to the Output Processor by typing the command after the prompt. The Output Processor executes the command and then prompts for your next command. To terminate a session, enter the QUIT or END command, followed by a semicolon (;).

The Output Processor provides three categories of data treatment. *Graphics commands* are used to generate pictorial representations, which are useful for interpreting simulation results visually. This category includes commands for generating plots, bar charts, histograms, etc. *Statistics commands* are used to perform some of the statistical analyses discussed earlier in this chapter. This category includes commands for generating confidence intervals, truncating the initial bias, batching correlated observations, etc. *Data transfer commands* are useful for converting data for input to other statistics programs or for moving between different operating systems.

Many of the Output Processor commands contain a large number of operands that are typically defaulted. Rather than discuss all of the available operands, we usually present abbreviated forms of the full commands. The abbreviated forms of the commands assume default values for many of the optional operands. The full commands are documented in the *SIMAN Reference Guide* and the on-line help facility within the Output Processor. To use the on-line help facility to see a summary of all available commands, enter the HELP command, followed by a semicolon (;). To receive help on a specific command, enter the HELP command, followed by a comma (,) and the name of the command on which you need help. For example, the command

```
HELP,PLOTS;
```

provides specific information about the use of the PLOTS command.

8.1 Graphics Commands

The Output Processor provides a number of graphics commands that help you visually to interpret the results of a simulation. This visual analysis provides a very important and useful adjunct to a more formal statistical analysis. In this section we summarize some commonly used graphics commands.

Creating Plots: The PLOTS Command

It is often useful to plot one or more output variables over time to visually assess the system's behavior. This can be done with the Output Processor by using the PLOTS command.

The PLOTS command generates a plot of discrete or continuous time-persistent variables, such as queue length, machine utilization, etc.; the independent (X-axis) variable plotted is simulated time. The operands for the PLOTS command are summarized below.

```
PLOTS,Title,LabelX,LabelY:
    DataSet,Legend:
    repeats;
```

The first three operands of the PLOTS command are optional and are used to define labels for the plot. The first operand, Title, defines the title, which is displayed at the top of the plot. This operand defaults to a blank label. The next two operands, LabelX and LabelY, are used to label the independent (X) and dependent (Y) axes of the plot. These operands default to the labels *Time* and *Y-Axis*, respectively.

The next group of two operands is a repeating set that is entered for each variable to be displayed on the plot. Each variable displayed on the plot is drawn with a different color and/or line style. The first operand in this group, DataSet, is the file specification for the data set to be plotted. You must include the file specification within double quotes. You may append a slash and a replication number to reference the data for a specific replication within the data file. For example, the specification "Queue.dat"/3 denotes the data for the third replication in the file named Queue.dat. The second operand in this group, Legend, defines the legend label, which is displayed in the legend next to the line color/style, which is used to draw the plot for this variable. If you omit this operand, the default legend label is assigned by using the identifier associated with the output file, i.e., the identifier specified on the DSTATS, TALLIES, COUNTERS, or OUTPUTS element.

Consider the following example illustrating the use of the PLOTS command.

```
PLOTS: "Queue.dat";
```

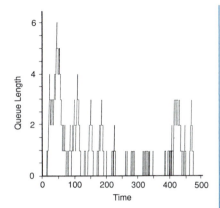

Figure 5-5. Plot of Queue Length for Sample Problem 3.1

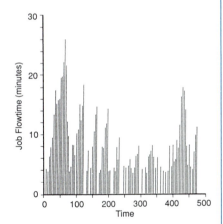

Figure 5-6. Bar Chart of Job Time In System for Sample Problem 3.1

This command generates a plot of the data in the file named Queue.dat by using default labels. Figure 5-5 shows the plot that this command generates for Sample Problem 3.1. As shown, the queue builds and empties many times during the 480 minutes of simulated time.

Creating Bar Charts: The BARCHART Command

The BARCHART command generates a bar chart for a specified variable. The bar chart is useful for depicting the relative magnitude of observations recorded for a tally variable. The bar chart displays each observation as a vertical bar whose length is proportional to the value of the observation. Positive values are drawn above the zero ordinate, and negative values are drawn below the zero ordinate. The independent axis for the bar chart is simulated time. The bar for each tally observation is drawn at the position along the time axis corresponding to the point in time at which the value was recorded.

The format of the BARCHART command is summarized below. The operands resemble those for the PLOT command, except that only one variable can be shown at a time with the BARCHART command.

BARCHART,DataSet,Title,LabelX,LabelY;

Although the first operand, DataSet, is required, the other three operands are optional and override the default labels for the bar chart. The first of these, Title, defaults to blank and defines the title, which is displayed at the top of the bar chart.

The second operand, LabelX, defaults to the label *Time* and defines the label for the X-axis of the bar chart. The third, LabelY, defaults to the identifier assigned to the data file and defines the label for the Y-axis.

An example of the BARCHART command is shown at the left.

```
BARCHART,"Tsys.dat";
```

This command generates a plot of the data contained in the file Tsys.dat and uses default labels. Figure 5-6 shows the command-generated bar chart representing time in system for jobs processed in Sample Problem 3.1. Each bar on the chart corresponds to the time in system for an individual job processed through the model. Comparison of the results shown by the bar chart with those shown by the queue plot shows that time in system follows the same basic pattern as queue length over time.

Interpreting the Distribution of Data: The HISTOGRAM Command

A histogram is useful for discerning data distribution. In a histogram, each observation is assigned to a specific cell, and the number of observations that occur in each cell is displayed as a bar chart. The X-axis of the bar chart represents the cells, and the Y-axis represents the frequency of observations within the cell.

Each cell in the histogram is defined by its lower and upper limits. The observations that are both greater-than-or-equal-to the lower cell limit and less than the upper cell limit are included in the cell. The difference between the upper and lower cell limit is called the *cell width*. For observational data, the number of observations falling into each cell is the *absolute cell frequency*, and this value divided by the total number of observations is the *relative cell frequency*. The absolute and relative cumulative frequencies are obtained by successively adding the absolute and relative cell frequencies. For time-persistent data, the frequency information is calculated by using the time that a variable maintains a specific value.

You define a histogram by specifying the number of interior cells, the lower limit for the first interior cell, and the width of each interior cell. An open cell is appended to each end of the histogram to tabulate observations that do not fall into the interior cells. The first appended cell has a lower cell limit of minus infinity and an upper cell limit equal to the lower limit of the first interior cell; the last appended cell has a lower limit equal to the upper limit of the last interior cell, and an upper limit of infinity.

The HISTOGRAM command generates a histogram for a specified variable. The command displays the histogram in both bar chart and tabular forms. The format for the HISTOGRAM command is shown below.

HISTOGRAM,DataSet,Title,LabelX,NumCells,LowCell,CellWidth;

The first operand, DataSet, is required, but all remaining operands are optional. The second operand, Title, defaults to blank and defines the title, which is displayed at the top of the histogram. The third operand, LabelX, defaults to the identifier for the data set and defines the label for the X-axis. The next operands (NumCells, LowCell, and CellWidth) define the number of interior cells, the lower limit of the first interior cell, and the cell width, respectively. A heuristic is embedded in the Output Processor for automatically selecting from among these three operands, depending on data characteristics. In most cases it is easier to default these values and to let the Output Processor select them for you.

The following example illustrates the HISTOGRAM command.

```
HISTOGRAM,"Tsys.dat";
```

This command generates a histogram of the data contained in the file Tsys.dat by using default cell parameters selected by the Output Processor. Figure 5-7 shows the command-generated histogram representing time in system for jobs processed in Sample Problem 3.1. Note that this same set of data was used to construct the bar chart shown in Figure 5-6. The default cell parameters selected by the Output Processor for this data set are nine interior cells, with a lower limit for the first interior cell of 4, and a cell width of 2. As can be seen from the histogram results, 71 of the 93 jobs processed through the model spent less than 12 hours in the system.

Cell No.	Cell Limits		Absolute Freq.		Relative Freq.	
	From	To	Cell	Cumul.	Cell	Cumul.
0	$-\infty$	4.0	12	12	.1290	.1290
1	4.0	6.0	22	34	.2366	.3656
2	6.0	8.0	18	52	.1935	.5591
3	8.0	10.0	12	64	.1290	.6882
4	10.0	12.0	7	71	.0753	.7634
5	12.0	14.0	4	75	.0430	.8065
6	14.0	16.0	8	83	.0860	.8925
7	16.0	18.0	4	87	.0430	.9355
8	18.0	20.0	3	90	.0323	.9677
9	20.0	22.0	1	91	.0108	.9785
10	22.0	$+\infty$	2	93	.0215	1.000

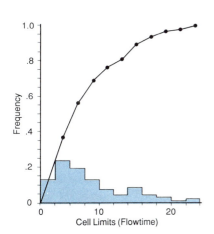

Figure 5-7. Histogram of Job Time In System for Sample Problem 3.1

Interpreting the Correlation Structure: The CORRELOGRAM Command

In a non-terminating system, the observations within an output file typically consist of individual observations within a run. It is often desirable to examine the correlation structure of the observations in an output file as a means of estimating a batch size that will yield approximately independent batch means.

The CORRELOGRAM command generates a correlogram for the observational data in a specified output file. The operands for this command are summarized below.

CORRELOGRAM,DataSet,Title,MaxLags;

The first operand, DataSet, defines the data file containing the observations to be processed by the command. The second operand, Title, defaults to the identifier for the data set and defines the label, which is displayed at the top of the correlogram. The last operand, MaxLags, defines the largest lag for which the correlation between observations is computed.

This command computes the sample auto-covariances and sample auto-correlations for lags between 1 and the maximum number of lags, which is specified as an operand of the command. The auto-covariances and auto-correlations are displayed in tabular form. The auto-correlations are also displayed as vertical bars, with positive correlations indicated by upward bars and negative correlations by downward bars.

The CORRELOGRAM command is illustrated by the following example.

```
CORRELOGRAM,"Tsys.dat",10;
```

This command generates a correlogram for the data set contained in the file Tsys.dat for lags ranging from 1 to 10. The correlogram shown in Figure 5-8 was generated by using this command on the data for time in system generated by the model for Sample Problem 3.1.

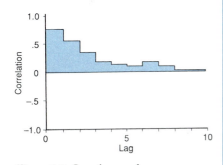

Figure 5-8. Correlogram for Sample Problem 3.1

197 *Interpreting Simulation Output*

The computed auto-covariances are also used to calculate the weighted sum of covariances (csum) discussed in the previous section. This value, along with the sample mean and number of observations, is displayed following the correlogram. These values can be used to construct a confidence interval on the mean for a single replication of a non-terminating system by using the method of summing covariances discussed in the previous section.

8.2 Statistical Commands

In this section we discuss some useful commands for analyzing the data contained in one or more output files. These commands automatically perform many of the statistical tests discussed earlier in this chapter. We begin with commands that are useful for addressing the bias and auto-correlation problem associated with non-terminating systems. Then we turn our attention to specific procedures that assume independent and identically distributed observations.

Smoothing the Response: The MOVAVERAGE Command

One of the most widely used methods for selecting a truncation point for a data set is to plot the response over time and then visually determine the point at which the initial transient phase becomes insignificant. You will find it much easier to identify this point if you first use the MOVAVERAGE command to smooth the data.

The MOVAVERAGE command generates a plot depicting either the moving averages or the accumulating averages of the input data set, as specified by an operand of the command. For cumulative averages, the nth response point is the arithmetic average of the first n observations of the input data set, i.e., of all observations up to that point. For moving averages, the response point is computed as the arithmetic average of the k most recent points, where k is specified as part of this option. As each new point is encountered in the data set, a new moving average is calculated by adding the newest datum and deleting the oldest one.

In general, the cumulative option produces the smoothest response set, but the resulting output can be highly distorted and is insensitive to changes occurring toward the end of the input data set. Any initial bias in the data set usually causes distortions to persist well beyond the end of the bias period. As a result, this option is generally best suited for detecting the presence of bias, rather than for determining the point at which the transient phase has ended.

If our objective is to determine an appropriate truncation point, then we want to smooth out the short-term fluctuations without distorting the underlying long-term trend. This smoothing is usually best accomplished by using the moving-averages option and by selecting the minimum number of observations sufficient to smooth out the short-term fluctuations without distorting the underlying response. This minimally sufficient size is usually determined by experimenting with several increasing values beginning with 10 observations.

The format for the MOVAVERAGE command is summarized below.

MOVAVERAGE,DataSet,Title,TypeAvg,LabelX,LabelY;

The first operand, DataSet, defines the data set to be processed by the command. The next operand, Title, defaults to blank and defines the title, which is displayed at the top of the plot. The next operand, TypeAvg, defines the type of average to be computed (cumulative or moving). You enter the type by specifying this operand as M (moving) or C (cumulative). In the case of a moving average, you also enter a slash followed by the number of observations to be included in the moving average. For example, M/50 denotes a moving average computed by using 50 observations. The next operand, LabelX, defaults to the label *Time* and defines the label for the independent (X) axis. The last operand defaults to the identifier for the data set and defines the label for the dependent (Y) axis.

The following example illustrates the use of the MOVAVERAGE command.

```
MOVAVERAGE,"Time.dat",,M/50;
```

This command generates a moving-average plot for the data set contained in the file named Time.dat. The moving average is computed at each point by using the 50 most recent observations. The plot shown in Figure 5-9 was created by using this command on a data set generated from a SIMAN model. As can be seen from the plot, the initial condition bias ends at around 3000 time units.

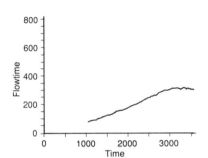

Figure 5-9. Moving-Average Plot (K = 50)

Batching and Truncating: The FILTER Command

Most of the statistical analysis methods used in simulation studies require that the input data set(s) contain observations that are stationary, independent, and normally distributed. In most cases, however, a non-terminating simulation's data sets violate at least one (and usually all three) of these requirements. The FILTERS command provided in the Output Processor allows you to perform truncation and batching on a data set from a non-terminating simulation to generate a new data set whose observations are approximately stationary, independent, and normally distributed. This new data set is then used in place of the original one for performing statistical analyses.

Recall that output files, which are generated by SIMAN and processed by the Output Processor, can contain one of two basic types of data sets. Observational data sets contain a set of n values, each corresponding to an observation recorded at a TALLY block. For these observations, the time at which each value is recorded is of no significance and is not used in computing summary statistics, e.g., the sample mean for the data set. Time-persistent data sets contain values recorded as a function of time by using the DSTATS or COUNTERS element. In this case summary statistics are computed by weighting each value recorded by the length of time that it persists.

The FILTER command accepts any SIMAN output file containing observational or time-persistent values as an input set including, for example, observational data recorded at a TALLY block, time-persistent values recorded by DSTATS or COUNTERS, etc. The newly created output file contains observational values corresponding to the mean of each batch formed from the data set. Hence, the FILTERS command always converts a time-persistent variable into a corresponding observational variable.

Regardless of whether the input data set contains observational or time-persistent values, both the truncation point and the batch size can be independently specified in number of observations or in time. If the truncation point is defined in terms of observations, the specified number of observations is truncated by the FILTER command. If the truncation point is defined in units of time, all observations recorded before the specified time are truncated. If the batch size is defined in terms of observations, each batch contains the specified number of observations. If the batch size is defined in time units, each batch contains all observations recorded during the specified batch time interval. In this case, however, the number of observations per batch varies.

If we are using the MOVAVERAGE command to aid in selecting an appropriate truncation point, we select the truncation point by visually examining a plot of the moving averages for the response over time. In this case the time-unit option is most convenient for defining the truncation point, regardless of the type of data. When defining the batch size, however, we usually specify size in terms of observations or time, depending on whether the input set contains observational or time-persistent data.

In addition to generating the new output file containing the mean of each batch, the FILTER command also displays a summary of the truncation of data and batching calculations. This summary includes the number of batches formed and the number of trailing observations or trailing times, which could not be used as a batch.

The FILTER command automatically tests the independence of the batch means by using a procedure suggested by Fishman [1968]. This procedure tests the null hypothesis that the batch means are independent. If the test rejects the null hypothesis at the 0.05 level, a warning message is displayed. As with any hypothesis test, failure to reject does not imply the truth of the null hypothesis.

The format for the FILTER command is summarized below.

FILTER,DataSet,Title,Truncation,Batching,SaveFile;

The first operand, DataSet, defines the input data set to be processed by the command. This data set is typically created by specifying an output file on the DSTATS or TALLIES element in the experiment. The next operand, Title, defaults to the identifier for the data set and defines the title, which is displayed at the top of the filter summary report. The next operand, Truncation, defines the amount of data, if any, ignored at the beginning of the data set. To specify a time-based truncation point, enter this operand as TIME / TruncAmt, where TruncAmt denotes the truncation time. For example, TIME / 1000 specifies a truncation point at time

1000. To specify an observation-based truncation point, enter this operand as OBS / TruncAmt, where TruncAmt denotes the number of observations to truncate. For example, OBS / 500 specifies that the first 500 observations are to be truncated. The next operand, Batching, defines the batch size to be applied to the remaining data. You enter this operand as TIME / BatchSize or OBS / BatchSize, corresponding to time- or observation-based batching. The last operand is the output file to which the computed mean of each batch is to be written. Like all file specifications in SIMAN, you must enter the output file within double quotes.

The FILTER command is illustrated by the following example.

```
FILTER,"Time.dat",, TIME / 500, OBS / 1000, "Time.fil"
```

This command generates a filtered output file and filter summary report for the data set contained in the file named Time.dat. The observations recorded prior to time 500 are discarded, and the remaining observations are batched by using a batch size of 1000. The batch means are written to the output file named Time.fil.

Generating Confidence Intervals on the Mean: The INTERVALS Command

As we noted in the beginning of this chapter, when we estimate system response based on the simulation results, it is important to use interval estimates rather than simple point estimates. The advantage of the interval estimate is that it provides a measure of the variability in our estimator.

You can use the INTERVALS command to generate a confidence interval for the data set contained in a specified output file. This command uses the procedure outlined in the previous section to compute the confidence interval.

The INTERVALS command assumes that the observations within the data set are stationary, independent, identically distributed, normal samples. This assumption is usually incorrect for output files associated with non-terminating systems; in these cases you first use the FILTER command to truncate the initial transient and to batch the remaining observations. With terminating simulations, however, you can often use the INTERVALS command directly on the observations because they are usually based on independent replications of the simulation.

Although for an exact confidence interval the procedure assumes that the observations are normally distributed, the procedure is very robust to violations of this assumption as long as the number of observations is 10 or greater — again, because of the Central Limit Theorem. The procedure is not robust, however, regarding the assumptions that the observations are independent and stationary.

The format for the INTERVALS command is shown below. The command consists of three optional operands, which you enter once, followed by a repeating set of two operands, which you enter for each confidence interval to be generated. The first operand in the first group, Title, defaults to blank and defines the title, which is displayed at the top of the INTERVALS output. The second operand, Scale, is a YES / NO option that defaults to YES. If you specify this option as YES, the graphical display of multiple confidence intervals is scaled according to the overall minimum and maximum across all the data sets. This feature is useful for visually comparing multiple confidence intervals. The third operand, Alpha, is the confidence coefficient for the interval; it defaults to 0.05 corresponding to a 0.95 confidence interval.

> INTERVALS, Title, Scale, Alpha:
> > DataSet, Label:
> > repeats;

The repeating group of operands specifies the data set to be processed and the label to be displayed for each interval. The first operand, DataSet, is the name of the data file enclosed within double quotes; it is typically generated by either the OUT-PUTS element (corresponding to a terminating system) or the FILTER element (corresponding to a non-terminating system). The second operand, Label, is optional and defaults to the identifier for the data set.

The INTERVALS command displays a summary of the output file data set, which includes the sample mean, sample standard deviation, half-width corresponding to the Alpha confidence interval, minimum and maximum observations, and number of observations. It also displays these values in a horizontal graph, which is particularly useful for visual comparison of results across several different data sets.

An example of the INTERVALS command is shown below.

```
INTERVALS" "TsysFIFO.dat" : "TsysSPT.dat" ;
```

This command generates confidence intervals on the data sets contained in the files named TsysFIFO.dat and TsysSPT.dat. Figure 5-10 shows the command-generated confidence intervals for the data sets containing observations on average time in system recorded by using the OUTPUTS element for the FIFO and SPT model versions developed for Sample Problem 3.1.

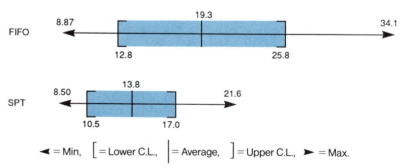

Figure 5-10. *Confidence Intervals on the FIFO and SPT Versions of Sample Problem 3.1*

As can be seen from the graph of the intervals, the SPT version has a lower average time in system. The confidence intervals for the two systems do, however, overlap substantially. In this case it is difficult to draw any conclusions about the relative performance of the two systems based on a visual interpretation of the confidence intervals.

Comparing Two Systems: The COMPARISONS Command

When the purpose of a study is not to estimate the performance of a single system but rather to compare the performance of two systems, the paired t-test procedure is appropriate. Using this procedure we can form a confidence interval on the difference between the observations for each of the two systems.

The COMPARISONS command automatically performs a paired t-test on sets of two separate output files, which are assumed to contain stationary, independent, and normally distributed observations. Again, however, the procedure is robust to violations of the normality assumption. For non-terminating systems, the FILTER command is first used to truncate the transient data and to batch the remaining observations. If the number of observations is not the same in each output file, then the excess observations in the larger file are ignored.

The COMPARISONS command is shown below. This command consists of an optional set of three operands, which you enter once, followed by a repeating group of operands, which you enter for each pair of data sets to be processed. The optional set of three operands is identical to the first three operands in the INTER-VALS command. The first of these operands, Title, defaults to blank and defines the title, which is displayed at the top of the output. The second operand, Scale, is a YES / NO option that can be used to scale the intervals for multiple comparisons. The third operand, Alpha, defaults to 0.05 and specifies the confidence coefficient for the interval.

```
COMPARISONS,Title,Scale,Alpha:
          DataSetA, DataSetB, Label:
          repeats;
```

The repeating group of operands consists of the data sets to be processed and the label to be displayed for each interval on the difference between the data sets. The output files containing the data sets to be processed must be enclosed in double quotes.

An example of the COMPARISONS command is shown below.

```
COMPARISONS: "TsysFIFO.dat" , "TsysSPT.dat" ;
```

This command performs a paired t-test on the data sets contained in the files named TsysFIFO.dat and TsysSPT.dat. Figure 5-11 shows the command-generated confidence interval for the data sets containing observations on average time in system recorded by using the OUTPUTS element for the FIFO and SPT model versions developed for Sample Problem 3.1. Note that these are the same data sets that were used to generate the confidence intervals in Figure 5-10.

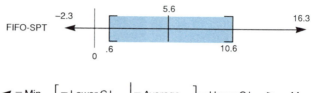

FIFO-SPT

◄ = Min, [= Lower C.L., | = Average,] = Upper C.L., ► = Max.

Figure 5-11. Paired t-test Confidence Interval for FIFO and SPT Versions of Sample Problem 3.1

Because the interval on the difference does not contain 0, the procedure shows a significant difference between the two systems.

Other Useful Statistical Commands

There are a number of other statistical commands in the Output Processor that can be useful in interpreting simulation output. For example, the ONEWAYS command generates a One-Way Analysis of Variance Fixed Effects model to study the relationship between the r levels of the independent and dependent variables. This procedure is useful for testing the hypothesis that the mean response of each of k separate data sets is the same. The ONEWAYS command also allows you to perform multiple comparison tests automatically by using the Bonferroni, Tukey, or Scheffee method.

The ONEWAYS command assumes that the data sets come from populations with equal variances. Two commands are provided for evaluating the validity of this assumption. You can use the SDINTERVALS command to construct a confidence interval on the standard deviation of a specified data set. You can use the VARTESTS command to compare the variance of two specified data sets.

An alternative method developed by Schruben for generating confidence intervals for non-terminating simulations is based on standardized time series [1982]. You can use the STDINTERVALS command to generate a confidence interval with this alternative approach. Unlike the INTERVALS command, the STDINTERVALS command incorporates the truncation and batching of observations, thereby obviating the need for using the FILTER command.

The use of these and other statistical commands is detailed in the *SIMAN Reference Guide.*

8.3 Transferring Data

As previously noted, SIMAN's output files are unformatted to speed the simulation. These unformatted files cannot be examined or edited by using standard ASCII editors, nor can they easily be input to other statistics or graphics packages for additional analysis without conversion. In this section we discuss some useful

Output Processor commands for transforming the output files generated from a simulation into several alternative formats.

Listing Data: The TABLES Command

It is sometimes helpful to be able to examine the contents of one or more output files directly. A simple way to do this is to use the TABLES command, which generates a table of the data values contained within the specified files. The generated table consists of a column of values for the independent variable (observation number or simulated time) and a column of values for each dependent variable. Because all dependent variables share the same independent variable, observational data sets (TALLIES and OUTPUTS) and time-persistent data sets (DSTATS and COUNTERS) cannot be displayed in the same table.

The format for the TABLES command is shown below. The command consists of an optional set of three operands, which you enter once for each table, followed by a repeating group of operands, which you enter for each dependent variable displayed in the table. The first operand, Title, defaults to blank and defines the title, which is displayed at the top of the table. The second operand, LabelX, defaults to blank and is the label displayed for the first column of values corresponding to the independent variable (observation number or simulated time). The next operand, DataSet, is the first operand in the repeating group and specifies the data set to be processed. The last operand, Label, defaults to the identifier for the data set and is the label for the dependent column of values.

```
TABLES,Title,LabelX:
        DataSet,Label:
        repeats;
```

An example of the TABLES command is shown below. This command generates a table of values containing the observations from the files named TsysFIFO.dat and TsysSPT.dat.

```
TABLES: "TsysFIFO.dat" : "TsysSPT.dat" ;
```

Moving Data Between Systems: The IMPORTS/EXPORTS Commands

It is sometimes convenient to make simulation production runs on one computer (e.g., a fast mainframe) and to analyze the results on a second computer (e.g., a PC or workstation). In this situation, the output files generated from the simulation must be moved between the two computers; however, because the output files are unformatted, they cannot normally be copied directly from one computer system to another. The IMPORTS/EXPORTS commands simplify the process of moving output files between computers.

To move an output file from one computer to another, you must first use the EXPORTS command to convert the unformatted file to a standard formatted file. This command reads an unformatted output file and converts it to a formatted file, which can then be moved between computer systems. Once the file has been moved, use the IMPORTS command to reverse the conversion. This command reads a formatted output file generated by the EXPORTS command and produces an unformatted version of that file, which can then be read by the Output Processor.

The formats for the EXPORTS and IMPORTS commands are shown below.

EXPORTS: DataSet, FormFile :
        repeats;

IMPORTS: FormFile, DataSet :
        repeats;

In both commands, the operands correspond to file specifications and therefore must be enclosed within double quotes. Examples of the EXPORTS and IMPORTS commands are shown below.

```
EXPORTS: "Tsys.dat" : "Tsys.frm";
IMPORTS: "Tsys.frm" : "Tsys.dat";
```

The first command formats the data contained in the file named Tsys.dat and writes the formatted data to the file named Tsys.frm. Standard editors can be used to display this file and to move it between systems. The second command reads the formatted data in the file named Tsys.frm and writes the unformatted values to the file named Tsys.dat. The unformatted file can then be read by the other Output Processor commands.

The EXPORTS command is also useful for generating formatted files that can be read by other programs. For example, you can use this command to convert an output file into a formatted file for input to a statistical package or spreadsheet program.

9. Performing an Analysis with the Output Processor: A Step-By-Step Summary

By using the batching technique discussed in the previous section for non-terminating systems, the same statistical analysis procedures can be applied to both terminating and non-terminating systems. The fundamental differences lie in the way data are collected and prepared, not in the analysis procedures themselves. With terminating systems we have unbiased, independent, approximately normal samples generated by the replications of the model. With non-terminating systems, we use truncation and batching to generate observations that approximate these same characteristics. In the end, we use the same procedures to develop a confidence interval or to compare candidate systems.

In this section we summarize the basic steps needed to analyze simulation results. We also note which SIMAN Output Processor commands are used at each step in this process.

9.1 Making Pilot Runs

The first step in the analysis process is to make pilot runs of the model. We use the pilot runs as a basis for making tactical decisions on the starting conditions, run length, number of replications, truncation point, etc. for the production runs that follow.

With a terminating system, we conduct a pilot run primarily to determine the number of replications required for the production runs of the model (see Section 6.1). We recommend making at least five replications of the model on the pilot run. These pilot replications serve as first-stage observations in the two-stage confidence interval procedure. This procedure produces an estimate of the total number of replications needed during the production run to obtain a specified level of precision in the results.

With a non-terminating system, we use a pilot run to establish the starting conditions, the truncation point, the batch size, and the length of the production run. We establish the truncation point visually by using the MOVAVERAGE command in the Output Processor to smooth out the response. We use the CORRELOGRAM command from the Output Processor to examine the correlation structure within the truncated pilot run data set. We usually establish a minimum batch size by visually examining the correlogram and by selecting a size that is an order of magnitude larger than the largest lag for which the correlation remains significant. For example, if the correlation becomes relatively small when observations are 50 units apart, then we select a batch size of 500 or more.

We then use the FILTER command to batch the truncated data set from the pilot run and use the batch means to estimate the minimum number of batches required to achieve a specified level of precision via the previously discussed two-stage procedure. This approach assumes that the initial pilot run is long enough to produce at least five batches; otherwise we need to make a new pilot run of sufficient length to provide at least five batches for our first-stage calculations. We then establish the minimum run length (excluding the warm-up period) by multiplying the minimum batch size by the estimated number of batches. If the minimum number of batches exceeds 20, we compute the run length as outlined above, but then divide the observations within this run into at most 20 batches.

If the initial condition bias is small compared to the total run length for a non-terminating system, the replication approach can be used as an alternative to the batching technique. In this case we make at least five replications of the model in the pilot run and then use the results from the pilot run to compute the required number of simulation replications via the same two-stage sampling procedure used for terminating systems. If, however, the number of required replications exceeds 20, we extend the run length rather than increase the number of replications beyond 20. For example, if the two-stage sampling procedure estimates that 60 replications are required, we make 20 replications and use a run length that is three times as long as the pilot run.

9.2 Making Production Runs

After we have made the necessary tactical decisions based on the pilot runs, we make the production runs for the model.

With a terminating system, we replicate the model based on the desired sample size. We typically use the default seed values and use the OUTPUTS element in the experiment to record the value of the performance measure at the end of each replication. On the production runs, we typically do not need to specify output files on the TALLIES and DSTATS elements because we do not need to examine the individual observations within the run.

With a non-terminating system, we usually make one long replication that uses the length established from the pilot run results. In this case, the OUTPUTS element is not required because we are running a single replication of the model. We must, however, specify output files on the appropriate TALLIES and DSTATS to save the individual observations within the run. We must save the observations so that we can filter them by using the FILTER command.

As previously noted, if the initial condition bias is small, we may also use the replication approach to analyze a non-terminating system. In this case we must truncate the data for the warm-up period from each replication. The easiest approach involves specifying the truncation time for the WarmUp operand on the REPLICATE element in the experiment. Doing so causes the data for the initial portion of each replication to be discarded at the specified time. A single observation is recorded for each replication by using the OUTPUTS element in the experiment. This observation is computed from the truncated data set for the replication.

9.3 Preparing the Data for Analysis

Data preparation need only be conducted if the system under study is non-terminating. In a terminating system the observations recorded by the OUTPUTS element are already unbiased, independent, and approximately normally distributed; hence there is no need for data preparation. In the case of a single replication of a non-terminating system, we use the FILTER command from the Output Processor to truncate the warm-up period and to batch the remaining observations.

If you are using the replication approach for analyzing the results for a non-terminating system, no data preparation is needed as long as you truncate the initial bias for each replication.

9.4 Performing the Analysis

In the final step of the analysis process we assume that we have unbiased, independent, and normally distributed observations. We then use the INTERVALS command to compute a confidence interval on these observations, or we use the COMPARISONS command to compare the means of two systems.

If other analyses are desired (e.g., analysis of variance), you can use other commands provided in the Output Processor, or you can export the observations and analyze them with other statistical packages.

We now return to our two examples presented in Chapter 3 and interpret model output. The first example, a model of a restaurant, illustrates a terminating system; the second example, a model of a hospital emergency room, illustrates a non-terminating system.

10.1 Analyzing the Results of the Restaurant Model

The restaurant model for Sample Problem 3.4 is a typical example of a terminating system. The restaurant opens at 5:00 P.M. in an empty and idle state. Customers continue to enter the system until 9:00 P.M. The system terminates for that evening when the last customer departs the restaurant.

In systems like this one we are not interested in steady-state behavior, and so we do not truncate the initial warm-up period from the data. The initial conditions and termination event are established by the nature of the problem.

As discussed in this chapter, the proper analysis approach to terminating systems makes n independent replications of the model, and uses a single summary value from each replication as an observation for analysis. These n observations are independent and identically distributed, and often are also normally distributed. These observations are then used to construct a confidence interval on the mean or to compare systems through the paired t-test.

In our analysis of the restaurant problem, we assume that the parameter of interest is the number of parties served. We could just as easily select any other measure of performance, such as the utilization of the cashier, the average or maximum number of busy tables, etc. Because we need a summary value from each replication of the model to use as an observation in the analysis, we include the following OUTPUTS element in the experiment to record the number of served parties at the end of each replication.

```
OUTPUTS: NC(Served Parties),"NumParty.dat";
```

We then make 10 model replications, yielding 10 independent observations of the number of served parties. The following table summarizes the results of these 10 replications.

Replication	Parties Served
1	148
2	155
3	154
4	125
5	146
6	145
7	152
8	150
9	150
10	148

We then activate the Output Processor and enter the following command.

```
INTERVALS: "NumParty.dat";
```

This command generates a confidence interval for the data set contained in the file NumParty.dat. The results generated by this command are shown in Figure 5-12.

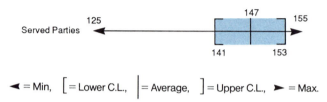

Figure 5-12. Confidence Interval on the Number of Served Parties

The correct interpretation of this interval is that we assert with high (0.95) confidence that the value for the expected number of served parties falls in the range of 141 to 153. Our best point estimate of this value is 147. Based on the width of the confidence interval, we have high confidence that our point estimate is within 4% of the true but unknown value.

We can use these results to estimate the number of replications required to refine our point estimate to within 1% of the true expected number of served parties. We compute the estimate of the total number of replications required, n^* as follows:

$$n^* = \left\{ 10 \, (6.06/1.47)^2 \right\} = 170$$

Next we examine the question of how to modify this system to reduce the number of lost parties, thereby increasing the number of served parties. Possibilities include reducing the service time and increasing the number of tables. We investigate the option of increasing the number of tables from 50 to 60 to see if this change increases the expected number of served parties.

To determine if there is a statistically significant difference between 50 and 60 tables, we make 10 replications of each system and use the OUTPUTS element to save the results in the files named Num50.dat (50-table system) and Num60.dat (60-table system). The following table summarizes the results for these 10 replications of the model with both 50 and 60 tables.

| Replication | Number of Served Customers | |
	50 Tables	60 Tables
1	148	165
2	155	155
3	154	132
4	125	152
5	146	133
6	145	145
7	152	151
8	150	145
9	150	144
10	148	143

We then use the following COMPARISONS element to perform a paired t-test on the results.

```
COMPARISONS: "Num50.dat" ; "Num60.dat"
```

The confidence interval on the difference between the two systems, which is generated by this command, is shown in Figure 5-13. As shown, the interval does contain 0. Hence, based on the results for these 10 replications, we cannot conclude with 0.95 confidence that there is a difference between the two systems. This does not mean that we can conclude that the two systems are the same. The difference between the two systems (which does exists) can be detected by making additional replications of the model.

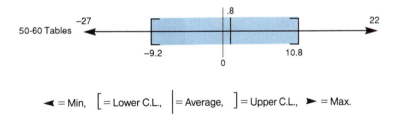

Figure 5-13. Confidence Interval on the Difference Between 50 and 60 Tables

10.2 Analyzing the Results of the Hospital Emergency Room Model

The hospital emergency room model for Sample Problem 3.5 is an example of a non-terminating system. The emergency room does not close, and hence there is no natural terminating event for the simulation. In systems like this one we are typically interested in the long-term behavior of the system, and therefore we need to eliminate any bias introduced into the data as a result of the starting conditions for the simulation.

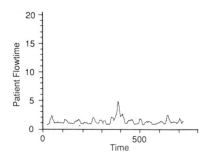

Figure 5-14. Moving-Average Plot with K = 50 (Pilot Run)

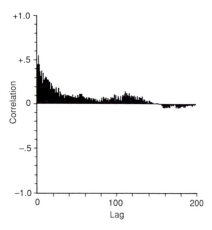

Figure 5-15. Correlogram Computed from Pilot Run

Although there are several possible performance measures for this system, we assume that we want to estimate the expected flowtime across all patient types by using the results from the simulation. Our objective is to develop a 0.95 confidence interval for this value.

We begin analyzing this system by first making a pilot run to examine the initial condition bias and the correlation structure within the data. The 30-day simulation from Chapter 3 serves as the pilot run. Before making the pilot run, we specify an output file named FlowTime.dat on the TALLIES element in the experiment to record the observations of the time in system for each patient processed through the model.

The first purpose of the pilot run is to provide an indication of the initial bias in the data resulting from the starting conditions. We use the pilot run to tell us how much data, if any, must be truncated from the output file. Figure 5-14 shows a moving-average plot with k = 50 for the patient flowtime for this model during the 720-hour simulation. This plot was generated by using the MOVAVERAGE command in the Output Processor. As can be seen from this plot, the initial condition bias is very small for this problem. By the end of the second day of operation, the emergency room appears to have reached a congested state reflective of its steady-state behavior. This suggests that, by truncating the data at time 50, we can eliminate most of the bias attributable to the starting conditions.

Because the initial bias is relatively small in this case, the replication method is a reasonable approach for analyzing the results. Although the replication method wastes 50 simulated hours of data from each independent replication, the actual wasted computer time corresponding to the 50 simulated hours is small. We do, however, use the batching method to perform our analysis of this problem. Although the batching technique is slightly more complicated, it is more efficient for problems with a substantial initial bias.

The second purpose of our pilot run is to provide an indication of an appropriate minimum batch size based on the correlation structure within the data. Figure 5-15 shows a correlogram for the flowtime data. This correlogram was generated from the data file by using the CORRELOGRAM command in the Output Processor with a maximum lag specified as 200. As can be seen from the correlogram, the correlation is relatively small for lags of 120 or greater. Therefore, a reasonable minimum batch size is 10 times this amount or 1,200 observations per batch.

We then make a production run long enough to generate 10 batches, each with 1,200 observations. Because the 720-hour pilot run generated nearly 2,400 observations (two batches of 1,200), a run length five times as long should produce about 10 batches of data. We therefore make a single replication with a run length of 3,600 hours.

Before batching our production data, we can re-examine our choice of truncation point and batch size by constructing a moving average and correlogram on our production data. The moving-average plot supports our earlier conclusion

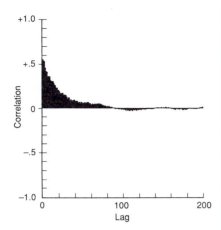

+1.0

+.5

Correlation

0

−.5

−1.0

0   100   200
Lag

Figure 5-16. Correlogram Computed from Production Run

that the initial bias is minimal in this case. However, the new correlogram, which is shown in Figure 5-16, indicates that the correlation is small for lags of 100 or more. Hence, based on this larger data set, we see that a minimum batch size of 1,000 is probably adequate.

We then truncate and batch our production data by using the following FILTER command.

```
FILTER,"FlowTime.dat",,TIME / 50, OBS / 1000, "FlowTime.fil";
```

This command truncates the data at time 50 and groups the remaining observations into batches of size 1,000. The means of these batches are then written by the Output Processor to the file named FlowTime.fil. Note that, whereas the file FlowTime.dat contains many thousands of observations, the filtered file FlowTime.dat contains only the observations corresponding to the means of the batches.

Once we have filtered the data, we then generate the desired confidence interval by using the filtered data set as input to the INTERVALS command as shown below.

```
INTERVALS,"FlowTime.fil";
```

Assuming that the batch means contained in the filtered data set are approximately independent and normally distributed, the INTERVALS command computes a valid confidence interval for the mean.

The confidence interval generated for this data set is shown in Figure 5-17. From the results, we can assert with 0.95 confidence that the expected flowtime for patients arriving to this system is a value between 1.25 and 1.58 hours. Our point estimate for the expected flowtime is 1.42 hours. By using our point estimate for the expected flowtime, we have a 0.95 confidence level of being within about 12% of the true expected value. This error range could be reduced by making a longer production run of the system.

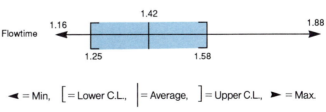

◄ = Min, [= Lower C.L., | = Average,] = Upper C.L., ► = Max.

Figure 5-17. Confidence Interval for Patient Flowtime

Exercise 5.1

Construct a 0.95 confidence interval on the following data. The mean and standard deviation are 10.2 and 0.873, respectively.

Observation	Time in system
1	9.96
2	10.21
3	9.79
4	11.84
5	9.19
6	9.66
7	10.21
8	11.89
9	9.28
10	11.15
11	9.29
12	9.25
13	10.82
14	11.14
15	9.10
16	10.09
17	9.39
18	10.25
19	10.37
20	11.08

Exercise 5.2

Modify Sample Problem 3.3 in Chapter 3 to incorporate random-number stream 1 in all distributions. Initialize the seed for stream 1 to a value of 34,512 by adding the SEEDS element to the experiment. Make one replication of the model and then change the seed value for stream 1 to 24,751 and repeat the simulation. Compare the results of these two runs.

Exercise 5.3

Modify Sample Problem 3.3 from Chapter 3 to incorporate stream 1 for the arrival process and stream 2 for the service process. Make one replication of the model and then switch the stream numbers between the arrival and service processes and repeat the simulation. Compare the results of these two runs.

Exercise 5.4

Repeat Exercise 5.2 by using a run length of 10,000 instead of 480. Comment on the differences in the results.

Exercise 5.5

Build a model that will simulate the processing of 20,000 jobs through a single-server queueing system and collect flowtime statistics. The mean time between arrivals is 10 minutes, and the mean service time is 9 minutes.

a. What is the average flowtime if the interarrival and service times are constant?

b. Repeat the simulation and assume that the interarrival distribution is exponentially distributed with the same mean. Compare the flowtime with that obtained in part a and discuss the difference.

c. Repeat the simulation. This time assume that the interarrival distribution is exponentially distributed with the same mean and that the service time distribution is uniform with the same mean and a range of 4. Compare the results with the previous cases.

d. Repeat the simulation and assume that both the interarrival and service times are exponentially distributed. Compare the results with the previous cases.

Exercise 5.6

Make 10 independent replications of the car wash model for Exercise 3.1 in Chapter 3. Use the results to develop a confidence interval on the number of cars washed per day.

Exercise 5.7

Modify Sample Problem 3.1 in Chapter 3 to record the flowtime through the system and make one replication of the model using a run length of 10,000. Save the observations for flowtime in an output file and examine the response by using the PLOTS command. In addition, construct a correlogram for the data set by using the CORRELOGRAM command.

Modify the model to incorporate a maximum buffer size of 3 and repeat the above. Discuss any observed differences in the correlation structure.

Exercise 5.8

Modify Sample Problem 3.2 in Chapter 3 to record statistics on the overall flowtime through the system. Perform an analysis of the results to obtain a 0.95 confidence interval on the flowtime. The half-width of the confidence interval should be no more than 15% of the mean.

Exercise 5.9

Perform an analysis using the model for Exercise 3.4 in Chapter 3 to determine the difference, if any, between the two proposed priority schemes.

Exercise 5.10

Use the model developed for Exercise 3.6 in Chapter 3 to construct a 0.95 confidence interval on the flowtime by customer type. The resulting half-width for each interval should be no more than 20% of the mean.

Exercise 5.11

Use the models developed for Exercise 3.8 in Chapter 3 to evaluate the benefit, if any, of the proposed expediting strategy for improving the flowtime through the system.

Exercise 5.12

Use the model developed for Exercise 3.10 in Chapter 3 to construct a 0.95 confidence interval on the time required for the professor to complete the day's tasks. The half-width of the interval should be no more than 15% of the mean. Estimate the number of replications required to reduce the half-width to within 1% of the mean.

Exercise 5.13

Use the model developed for Exercise 3.11 in Chapter 3 to evaluate a proposal to increase the staffing at the terminal from five to six workers. Assume that the cost of providing an additional worker is $20 per hour and that the cost associated with a waiting truck and driver is $120 per hour.

References

FISHMAN, G. S. (1968), "Digital Computer Simulation: The Allocation of Computer Time in Comparing Simulation Experiments," *Operations Research*, Vol. 16, pp: 280-295.

FISHMAN, G. S. (1972), "A Study of Bias Considerations in Simulation Experiments," *Operations Research*, Vol. 20, pp: 785-790.

FISHMAN, G. S. (1978), *Principles of Discrete Event Simulation*, John Wiley.

SCHMEISER, B. (1982), "Batch Size Effects in the Analysis of Simulation Output," *Operations Research*, Vol. 30, pp: 556-568.

SCHRUBEN, L. W. (1982), "Detecting Initialization Bias in Simulation Output," *Operations Research*, Vol. 30, pp: 569-590.

WELCH, P. D. (1983), "The Statistical Analysis of Simulation Results," in *Computer Performance Modeling Handbook*, edited by S. S. Lavenberg, Academic Press.

WILSON, J. R. and A. A. B. PRITSKER (1978), "A Survey of Research on the Simulation Startup Problem," Simulation, Vol. 31, pp: 55-58.

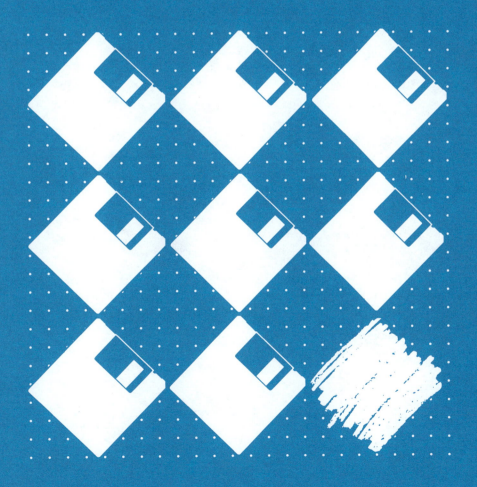

CHAPTER 6
Station Submodels and Entity Transfers

In the examples we have modeled thus far, the systems have been relatively small; however, most practical applications of simulation involve very large and complex systems. Although we can approach these problems directly by using the modeling concepts discussed in previous chapters, it is more convenient to approach the modeling of large systems by dividing them into several subsystems. Using special features of SIMAN, we can then separately model these subsystems. We refer to these individual component models as *submodels*.

Large systems typically have natural boundaries that suggest a systematic segmentation approach. For example, a large manufacturing system usually comprises a set of distinct workstations or workcells. A natural approach to modeling this type of system is to develop submodels of each individual workstation and workcell; these submodels can then be combined to represent the overall system.

There are a number of important reasons for taking this segmentation approach. First, it makes the modeling effort more manageable by replacing a large modeling task with a series of smaller modeling tasks. Second, it provides a logical framework for controlling the flow of entities. For example, a submodel may represent a workcenter, which can be directly related to the product routing. Third, as we discuss in Chapter 8, the functional similarity among submodels that frequently occurs in models of large systems can be exploited to create generalized submodels, which may drastically reduce the size of many models. We will present the basic concepts of submodels and entity transfers in the context of the following example.

Consider the simple three-workstation flow line depicted in Figure 6-1. Parts entering the system are placed at a staging area for transfer to the first workstation. After the parts have completed processing at the first workstation, they are transferred to a paint station manned by a second worker, and then to a packaging station where they are packed by a third worker, and then to a second staging area where they exit the system.

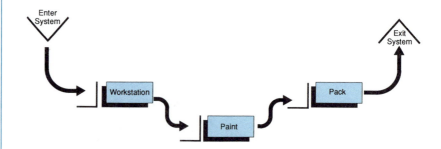

Figure 6-1. Flow-Line Layout: Sample Problem 6.1

The time between the parts' arrivals at the system is exponentially distributed with a mean of 28 minutes. The processing time at the first workstation is uniformly distributed between 21 and 25 minutes. The paint time is normally distributed with a mean of 22 minutes and a standard deviation of 4. The packing time follows a triangular distribution with a minimum of 20, mode of 22, and maximum of 26. The transfers are unconstrained, in that they do not require a vehicle or resource, but all transfer times are exponential with a mean of two or three minutes. Transfer times from the staging to workstation and from pack to exit are 3 minutes. Transfer times from workstation to paint and from paint to pack are two minutes. The performance measures of interest are the utilization and Work-In-Process (WIP) at the workstation, Paint, and packaging operations. We also want to collect statistics on the part flowtime, i.e., the total time a part spends in the system.

Although this problem could be modeled easily with the SIMAN constructs already presented, the submodel concept allows a modular modeling approach and facilitates extension of the model.

3. The Station Concept

A submodel in SIMAN is often referred to as a *station submodel*. The point at which entities enter a station submodel is defined by using a STATION block. Each station is assigned a unique number and an optional name. The station's number and name can be used interchangeably to identify the station. A station can represent a workcell or staging area, as in our example, or an entire department of a larger facility.

The single operand for the STATION block is the station's identifier, which is summarized below. You can specify the station identifier as a number or name. If identifying the station by a number, enter a constant.

STATION, StaID;

STATION,StaID

STATION,1

STATION,Paint

Sample STATION blocks are shown at the left. The first example is a STATION block defining the entry point to Station 1. The second example is a STATION block defining the entry point to the station named Paint.

When an entity is sent to a STATION block, it enters the block and then continues to the next block in sequence. Hence, the STATION block simply defines the entry point into the station submodel; the blocks following the STATION block model the function of the station submodel. There are no restrictions on the number of blocks that can be used within the submodel.

For the flow-line example, we will use three submodels representing the system's different operations. We will model each of these with a QUEUE-SEIZE-DELAY-RELEASE block combination. We will use a fourth submodel for the staging area where finished parts exit the system.

3.1 Moving between Stations: The Transfer Block

The Transfer block provides a mechanism for transferring entities between stations. When an entity enters a Transfer block, it leaves its current station and is sent to a specified destination. The blocks through which the entities pass between their entrance at a STATION block and their exit at a Transfer block represent the particular station submodel's functional logic.

The Transfer block, a multi-function block, models all movement between stations. The shape of this basic block type is shown at the left. We will discuss three specific transfer functions in this chapter: the ROUTE, TRANSPORT, and CONVEY blocks. Because the ROUTE block is the simplest of the three, we begin our discussion with this block.

3.2 Transferring Entities: The ROUTE Block

The ROUTE block, a type of Transfer block, models the unconstrained movement of entities from one station to another. The ROUTE block assumes that time may be required to move the entity between stations, but it operates on the assumption that no additional delay will be incurred because of unavailable resources, e.g., carts, people, conveyors, etc.

The symbol and statement for the ROUTE block are shown below. The top line segment contains the block's function name, ROUTE, and the bottom line segment contains the operands specifying the duration of the delay, Duration, and the destination station, Dest. The Duration operand specifies the time required for the entity to travel from its current station to its destination station; you enter this time as any valid expression in SIMAN. The destination station defines the station to which the entity should be transferred; you identify the station by its number, its name, or a SIMAN expression.

ROUTE: Duration, Dest;

In our first example (shown at the left), each entity arriving at the block is sent from its current station to the station named Paint. The time required to travel to Paint is exponentially distributed with a mean of three units of time. In the second example each entity arriving at the block is sent to station 20. The travel time from the current station to station 20 is a constant 10 units.

3.3 The Station Attribute M

Each SIMAN entity has an integer attribute, M, that denotes the entity's current station number. The default value of M for a newly created entity is 0. You can assign a value to this attribute; in special cases, it will be assigned by SIMAN. The attribute M is updated automatically to the destination station's value whenever an entity is transferred with a Transfer block. For example, assume that an entity arrives at a ROUTE block with its value of M equal to 5. The ROUTE block specifies that the entity be transferred to Station 3 with a transfer time of 20.0 units. In this case, SIMAN schedules the entity to arrive 20.0 units of time later at Station 3 and assigns M the value of 3. Therefore, if you use Transfer blocks to send an entity from one station to another, you can view the value of M at any time during the simulation and determine the entity's current station location (or its destination station if en route).

An alternative way of setting the value of M to the current station's value is to use the ASSIGN block. If you send an entity to a STATION block by using the Sequential Flow Connector or the NEXT modifier, then the value of M is also set to that STATION block's value. You can also use the attribute M in expressions, as an index for SIMAN variables, or in a branching condition on a BRANCH block. This concept becomes particularly useful when the station submodels are generalized (see Chapter 8). Although M is a user-assignable attribute, it cannot be assigned an identifier name with the ATTRIBUTES element.

3.4 The Sample Flow-line Model Frame

The block diagram for our sample problem is shown in Figure 6-2. This diagram consists of five separate sections: Entry, WorkStation, Paint, Pack, and ExitSystem. The last four sections have been modeled as station submodels, with transfers between sections being accomplished by using the ROUTE block. The WorkStation, Paint, and Pack submodels are essentially identical in function but require different resources and delay (or operation) times. The ExitSystem section was developed as a submodel to allow the transfer (ROUTE) of parts from the Pack station to the ExitSystem station of the system.

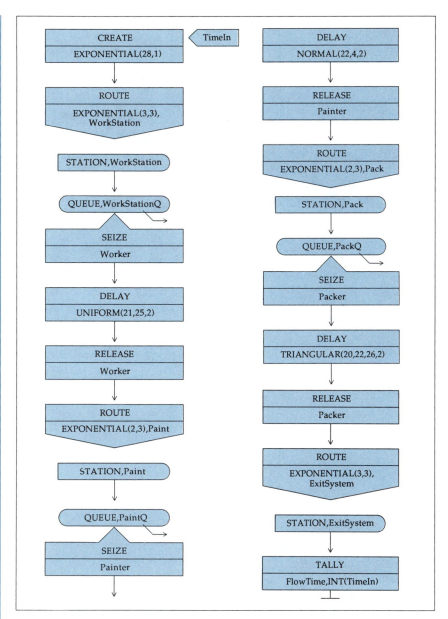

Figure 6-2. Block Diagram For Sample Problem 6.1

Part transfers throughout the system have been modeled by using the ROUTE block with specified transfer times. The time that a part enters the system has been recorded (or marked) in the attribute TimeIn for later use by the TALLY block, which totals the system flowtime observations. Because each part has been routed directly to the next operation, the attribute M has never been used; however, the SIMAN Processor still updates the station value of M during the routing of each entity. Also note that all of the queues and stations have not been referenced by number; instead, they have been identified by names that will be defined in the Experiment Frame. Figure 6-3 gives the Model Frame listing corresponding to our solution for the flow-line problem.

```
BEGIN;

;    THREE-WORKSTATION FLOW-LINE: SAMPLE PROBLEM 6.1

;    Parts enter and transfer to workstation

        CREATE:    EXPONENTIAL(28,1):         !Create jobs
                   MARK(TimeIn);               Set entry time
        ROUTE:     EXPONENTIAL(3,3),          !Route duration
                   WorkStation;                Transfer to workstation

;    Workstation submodel

        STATION,   WorkStation;              Workstation submodel
        QUEUE,     WorkStationQ;             WIP at workstation
        SEIZE:     Worker;                   Get worker
        DELAY:     UNIFORM(21,25,2);         Delay for processing
        RELEASE:   Worker;                   Release worker
        ROUTE:     EXPONENTIAL(2,3),Paint;   Transfer to paint

;    Paint submodel

        STATION,   Paint;                    Paint submodel
        QUEUE,     PaintQ;                   WIP at paint
        SEIZE:     Painter;                  Get painter
        DELAY:     NORMAL(22,4,2);           Delay for painting
        RELEASE:   Painter;                  Release painter
        ROUTE:     EXPONENTIAL(2,3),Pack;    Transfer to pack

;    Pack submodel

        STATION,   Pack;                      Pack submodel
        QUEUE,     PackQ ;                    WIP at packing
        SEIZE:     Packer;                    Get packer
        DELAY:     TRIANGULAR(20,22,26,2);    Delay for packing
        RELEASE:   Packer;                    Release packer
        ROUTE:     EXPONENTIAL(3,3),         !Route duration
                     ExitSystem;              Transfer to exit

;    Exit submodel

        STATION,   ExitSystem;               Exit station
        TALLY:     FlowTime,INT(TimeIn):     !Tally flowtime
                   DISPOSE;                   Dispose of entity
END;
```

Figure 6-3. Model Listing for Sample Problem 6.1

3.5 Defining Information about Stations: The STATIONS Element

The STATIONS element defines information about the stations used in the Model Frame. This information includes the station's number and name. In the Model Frame, use these two operands interchangeably to specify the station. Each station name included in the model must be identified in the STATIONS element.

Separate the two operands by a comma (,) and group them together into line segments separated by colons (:). If you omit the station's number and trailing comma in a line segment, the Experiment Processor automatically assigns the station number during compilation. These default station numbers are assigned consecutively, beginning with 1 and increasing by 1 for each new station. Station numbers can be skipped, but no station number can appear twice, whether specified or defaulted. The syntax for the STATIONS element and two examples are shown below.

```
STATIONS: Number, Name :
          repeats;

STATIONS:    WorkStation:
             Paint:
             Pack:
             ExitSystem;
STATIONS:    Assembly:
             3,Fab:
             Repair;
```

The first example illustrates the STATIONS element for the sample problem. In this example the station's numbers have been defaulted and would be assigned 1 through 4 by the Experiment Processor. In the second example, the station named Assembly is automatically assigned the number 1. Station 2 is not defined: perhaps it is not used in the model, or perhaps it is specified as a number in the model and not named. If station 2 is used in the model, it could have been assigned an optional name. The number 3 is assigned to the station named Fab, and the number 4 is automatically assigned by SIMAN to the station named Repair.

3.6 The Sample Flow-line Experiment Frame and Summary Report

The complete Experiment Frame for our sample problem is shown in Figure 6-4.

```
BEGIN;
;                 THREE-WORKSTATION FLOW-LINE: SAMPLE PROBLEM 6.1
PROJECT,          Sample Problem 6.1,SM;
ATTRIBUTES:       TimeIn;
STATIONS:         WorkStation:
                  Paint:
                  Pack:
                  ExitSystem;
QUEUES:           WorkStationQ:
                  PaintQ:
                  PackQ;
RESOURCES:        Worker:
                  Painter:
                  Packer;
TALLIES:          FlowTime;
DSTATS:           NQ(WorkStationQ),WorkStation WIP:
                  NR(Worker)*100,Worker Utilization:
                  NQ(PaintQ),Paint WIP:
                  NR(Painter)*100,Painter Utilization:
                  NQ(PackQ),Pack WIP:
                  NR(Packer)*100,Packer Utilization;
```

```
REPLICATE,        1,0,985000,,,35000;
END;
```

Figure 6-4. Experiment Frame for Sample Problem 6.1

This Experiment Frame contains all of the elements required for the sample flow-line model. The entries for the ATTRIBUTES, STATIONS, QUEUES, TALLIES and DSTATS elements are all assigned specific identifier names. The numbers will be assigned by the Experiment Processor. For this example, all elements can be assigned identifier numbers or defaulted. Note that the DSTATS element includes several expressions so that the resulting utilization values take the form of percentages rather than fractions.

The REPLICATE element provides for one replication starting at time 0 and ending at time 985,000. The SIMAN statistics — TALLIES and DSTATS — are therefore cleared at time 35,000, as shown in the SIMAN Summary Report in Figure 6-5. Thus, the statistics are accumulated for 950,000 units of time. These values were determined by making an initial run without clearing statistics and by saving the individual observations from the FlowTime tally. A moving-average plot created with the Output Processor was used to determine the approximate steady-state time of the system at time 35,000. The values for this initial period were filtered out and a correlogram of the remaining values developed. The point where the correlogram plot crossed the zero axis was used to determine the number of lags required for zero correlation. This value was then multiplied by 10 to determine the batch size, and the total run-time was adjusted so that approximately 10 of these batches would be obtained. The replicate times for the remaining sample problems in this chapter were determined in the same fashion.

```
Project:  Sample Problem 6.1
Analyst:  SM
Simulation run ended at time  : 985000.
Statistics were cleared at time  : 35000.0
Statistics accumulated for time  : 950000.
```

TALLY VARIABLES

Identifier	Average	Variation	Minimum	Maximum	Observations
FlowTime	138.56	.46021	58.852	613.38	33810

DISCRETE-CHANGE VARIABLES

Identifier	Average	Variation	Minimum	Maximum	Final Value
WorkStation WIP	1.8513	1.3499	.00000	22.000	1.0000
Worker Utilization	81.862	.47071	.00000	100.00	100.00
Paint WIP	.14197	2.5383	.00000	3.0000	.00000
Painter Utilization	78.429	.52444	.00000	100.00	100.00
Pack WIP	.17315	2.2438	.00000	3.0000	.00000
Packer Utilization	80.653	.48977	.00000	100.00	100.00

Figure 6-5. Summary Report for Sample Problem 6.1

The above summary report provides the statistics requested in the Experiment Frame. The average part flowtime was approximately 138 minutes with a fairly wide range of values collected, from 58 to 613. The resource utilizations are approximately 80 percent. Also note that the Work-In-Process values are relatively small with only the WorkStation having any significant number of parts in the queue.

Now we will modify the sample flow line shown in Figure 6-1 to allow the production of a second part, which will be painted a different color. Because this new part replaces a portion of the sales of the first part, the arrival process remains the same, but 30 percent of the arriving parts are randomly designated as the new type of part. The remaining parts (70 percent of the total) are produced in the same manner as in the original flow-line example.

4.1 The Modified Flow Line

The operation for both parts at the first WorkStation requires the same amount of time as before the introduction of the new part. The Paint and Pack times remain the same for the first part; however, the new part requires the addition of a different station with a painting time that is normally distributed with a mean of 49 minutes and a standard deviation of 7 minutes. The existing station paints only the old type of part, and the new station paints only the new parts. After the painting operation, the new part is transferred to the existing packing station and requires a packing time that follows a triangular distribution with a minimum value of 21, a mode of 23, and a maximum value of 26. This modified flow line is depicted in Figure 6-6.

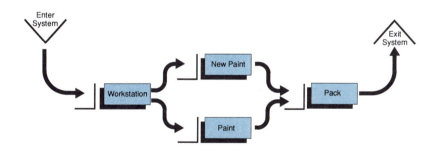

Figure 6-6. The Modified Flow Line: Sample Problem 6.2

This modified example requires that each part follow a different path through a portion of the system. The transfer of parts from the WorkStation to the Paint and NewPaint operations can easily be controlled with a BRANCH block to direct the parts to a different ROUTE block, depending on the part type. However, for a large system with many parts, all having different paths through the system, the number of BRANCH blocks and conditions becomes large. The branching conditions can also become complex if parts visit stations more than once. SIMAN simplifies this task by providing a mechanism to permit easy control of entity transfer between stations.

4.2 The Concept of Visitation Sequences

In many systems each entity moving through the system is processed through a unique sequence of stations. For example, in a jobshop each job processed through the facility typically has its own processing plan defining the sequence of operations required to produce the part.

Although we can easily send an entity to any desired workcenter by specifying the station's name or number as the destination on the Transfer block, this task is not so simple when each entity arriving at the Transfer block has a different destination. To determine a particular entity's destination, we must know its processing plan or visitation sequence (i.e., the sequence of stations that the entity must visit), and we must know its current position or index within the visitation sequence (e.g., first operation, second operation, etc.).

One approach to maintaining the required information about an entity is to define the possible visitation sequences in a two-dimensional array, in which each row stores the numbers of stations to be visited in accordance with a specific processing plan. We can then use the entity's general-purpose attributes to store the visitation-sequence number (corresponding to the row number) and the current position or index (corresponding to the column number) in that sequence for the entity. At the completion of processing at one station, we can increase the index by 1 and retrieve the number of the next station from the appropriate row and column of the visitation-sequence array. The retrieved station number is then used to specify the entity's destination on the Transfer block.

Although this procedure is conceptually simple, it complicates our model by requiring us to include additional logic to keep track of the flow of entities between stations. A much better approach is to use a special feature in SIMAN called a *station-visitation sequence*, which allows the visitation sequence for each entity to be defined in the Experiment Frame and to be used automatically by the Transfer block. Using the station-visitation sequence feature does not require the addition of extra blocks in the station submodel to determine the entity's destination.

4.3 Station-Visitation Sequences: The SEQUENCES Element

The SEQUENCES element defines one or more station-visitation sequences. A station-visitation sequence consists of a list of destination stations and an optional set of attribute assignments to be made at each station. Each entity, following a specific station-visitation sequence, visits each station submodel in the order in which the stations are listed in the SEQUENCES element. In addition, any optional attribute assignments are made for the entity when it is transferred to the destination STATION block.

When using the SEQUENCES element to control the flow of entities between stations, specify (or default) the destination station's identifier on the Transfer block as SEQ (e.g., ROUTE:10,SEQ;). In this way the destination station will be retrieved from the appropriate station-visitation sequence for this entity. SIMAN automatically does all of the bookkeeping necessary to keep track of the next station in the sequence.

The format for the SEQUENCES element is summarized below. You enter each station-visitation sequence within the SEQUENCES element into a separate line segment. The first operand in the line segment is the sequence's number, which is assigned to each station-visitation sequence. These numbers must be consecutively assigned, beginning with 1; they cannot be defaulted. Follow the sequence's number with a series of one or more station-visitation definitions, consisting of the destination station's identifier (name or number) and an optional list of attribute assignments separated by commas (,). Use an ampersand (&) to separate station-visitation definitions included in a sequence.

SEQUENCES: Number, BegStatID ,Assignments ...&
NextStaID ,Assignments ...&
repeats ..... :
repeats;

An optional list of attribute assignments can be included with each station listed in the station-visitation sequence. Attribute assignments are typically used to specify station-specific data for an entity. The assignments are made when the entry arrives at the Transfer block and before execution of the block; the attributes have their new values when they enter the destination STATION block. Attribute assignments can be used in many ways. For example, consider a jobshop in which the setup time and processing time for a workpiece are different for each part at each station. By assigning these attributes in the station-visitation sequence, their values will be reset automatically by SIMAN when the entity is transferred to its next destination station and will be used in that station's submodel.

There are two alternative formats for specifying attribute assignments within a station-visitation sequence. In one case, you explicitly define the attribute to which the assignment is being made on the left side of an equals sign and enter the corresponding assignment value on the right side of the sign, e.g., SetUp = 10.0. In the other case, you enter only the value, omitting both the attribute's identifier and the equals sign. The successive values entered with this method are assigned to the entity's attributes beginning with Attribute 1 and continuing through the number of attribute assignments defined. You can skip assignments by entering the comma (,) for the attribute without entering a value, thereby leaving the corresponding attribute unchanged.

4.4 Sequence Control: The NS and IS Attributes

An entity references a station-visitation sequence through two special SIMAN attributes: NS and IS. NS specifies the number of the entity's current station-visitation sequence as defined in the SEQUENCES element. IS specifies the entity's position or index within its station-visitation sequence. For example, an entity following Sequence 3 (NS=3) with an IS value of 2 is in the second station visitation within the sequence. Note that the entity is not located at Station 2, but rather it is at (or on its way to) the second station defined by the sequence.

The default values for both NS and IS are 0 for newly created entities. We must explicitly assign a value to NS if the entity is to follow one of the station-visitation sequences defined in the experiment; however, we typically default the value of IS to 0. Like the attribute M, NS and IS cannot be assigned identifiers with the ATTRI-BUTES element.

When an entity arrives at a Transfer block that has the destination station specified as SEQ, the actual destination station is determined by the following procedure. First, the attribute IS is increased by 1. Then, the destination station's number is retrieved from the experiment SEQUENCES element based on the current value of NS and the new value of IS. Next, any attribute assignments are made. Finally, the value of M is set to the destination station, and the entity is transferred to the destination station at the time specified on the Transfer block.

In order to use either of the two sequences shown below, the desired sequence must be specified by assigning NS a value of 1 or 2 for each entity that is to follow a sequence. On the first transfer of an entity with an NS value of 1, the sequence element assigns values to attributes SetUp and OpTime and then sends the entity to Station 6 and assigns the attribute M a value of 6. The second time that this entity is transferred, a value of 4 is assigned to attribute OpTime, and the entity is sent to the station identified as Fab with M set to the station number specified for Fab on the STATIONS element. With the next transfer the sequence element assigns a value of 5.5 to Attribute 2, leaves all other attribute values unchanged, sends the entity to the station identified as Assembly, and assigns the new value of M. Subsequent transfers cause assignments to the first two attributes and transfer to Station 23, followed by transfer to the station identified as Exitsystem with no attribute assignments.

```
SEQUENCES:    1,    6, SetUp=10, OpTime=NORMAL(20,3,1) &
                    Fab, OpTime=4 &
                    Assembly, , 5.5 &
                    23, UNIFORM(3,9,1), 14 &
                    Exitsystem:
              2,    Entry & Fab & Exitsystem;
```

The second sequence, followed by entities with attribute NS equal to 2, sends entities to the stations identified as Entry, Fab, and Exitsystem with no attribute assignments.

Although an entity typically follows a specific station-visitation sequence to completion, doing so isn't required. The attribute IS is increased only when the entity is transferred with the SEQ destination option. You can temporarily exit the sequence, transfer the entity directly to a station not included in the sequence, and then re-enter the sequence by using the SEQ destination option on a subsequent transfer. At this point, the entity's attribute IS is increased by 1, and the entity is transferred to the next station in the sequence.

The actual sequence an entity follows can also be changed at any time by assigning a new value to attribute NS. Both the sequence number, NS, and sequence index, IS, can be reset at an ASSIGN block to reflect changes in the job's processing plan. For example, you can simulate an inspection failure by resetting NS and IS to a sequence of operations corresponding to the reworking of the part; however, you should remember to reset the value of IS so that the entity enters the new sequence at the correct point. If the new sequence is to be entered at its start, then set the value of IS to 0 before the first transfer because SIMAN increases its value before referencing the destination station in the SEQUENCES element.

The last station listed in any station-visitation sequence is typically a station that processes the entity's exit from the system. A common mistake when using the SEQUENCES element is allowing an entity to return to a Transfer block with SEQ specified after the entire station-visitation sequence has been exhausted. If an entity activates a Transfer block and the value of NS or IS is inconsistent with the SEQUENCES element, the simulation run terminates with an error.

4.5 The Modified Flow-line Model

Figure 6-7 shows the model listing for the modified flow-line. Several changes to the original flow-line model have been made to accommodate the new requirements. We have altered the entry section of the model to include an ASSIGN block, which determines the part's type and assigns the value 1 or 2 to the sequence attribute NS, which specifies the sequence-visitation number for all transfers. In addition, a fifth station submodel has been added to represent the new painting operation, NewPaint. The destination stations on the ROUTE blocks have been changed to SEQ so that all transfers are determined by the SEQUENCE element.

```
BEGIN;
;    MODIFIED FLOW-LINE: SAMPLE PROBLEM 6.2
;    Parts enter, part type determined, and transfer to workstation
        CREATE:    EXPONENTIAL(28,1):              !Create jobs at staging area
                        MARK(TimeIn);              Mark arrival time
        ASSIGN:    M=Enter;                        Set entry station
        ASSIGN:    NS=DISCRETE(.7,1,1,2,10);       Determine part type
        ROUTE:     EXPONENTIAL(3,3),SEQ;           Transfer to workstation
;    Workstation submodel

        STATION,   WorkStation;                    Workstation submodel
        QUEUE,     WorkStationQ;                    WIP for worker resource
        SEIZE:     Worker;                          Get worker
        DELAY:     UNIFORM(21,25,2);               Delay for processing
        RELEASE:   Worker;                          Release worker resource
        ROUTE:     EXPONENTIAL(2,3),SEQ;           Transfer to next operation
;    Paint submodel

        STATION,   Paint;                          Paint submodel
        QUEUE,     PaintQ;                          WIP at paint resource
        SEIZE:     Painter;                         Get painter
        DELAY:     Optime;                          Delay for painting
        RELEASE:   Painter;                         Release painter resource
        ROUTE:     EXPONENTIAL(2,3),SEQ;           Transfer to pack
;    Pack submodel

        STATION,   Pack;                           Pack submodel
        QUEUE,     PackQ;                           WIP at packing
        SEIZE:     Packer;                          Get packer
        DELAY:     Optime;                          Delay for packing
        RELEASE:   Packer;                          Release packer resource
        ROUTE:     EXPONENTIAL(3,3),SEQ;           Transfer to exit
;    Exit submodel

        STATION,   ExitSystem;                     Exit submodel
        TALLY:     FlowTime,INT(TimeIn):           !Tally flowtime
                        DISPOSE;                   Dispose of job
;    Newpaint submodel

        STATION,   NewPaint;                       Newpaint submodel
        QUEUE,     NewPaintQ;                       WIP at newpaint
        SEIZE:     NewPainter;                      Get newpainter
        DELAY:     Optime;                          Delay for painting
        RELEASE:   NewPainter;                      Release newpainter resource
        ROUTE:     EXPONENTIAL(2,3),SEQ;           Transfer to pack
END;
```

Figure 6-7. Model Listing for Sample Problem 6.2

The experiment listing is shown in Figure 6-8. A new attribute, OpTime, has been added to the ATTRIBUTES element. Note that the process times at the Paint, NewPaint, and Pack stations are taken from the second attribute, OpTime, which is assigned in the SEQUENCES element. Because the operation time at the Work-Station is identical for both types of parts, it is not included in the SEQUENCES element. Also note that the new identifiers for the NewPaint station are added to the RESOURCES, STATIONS, and QUEUES elements and that the new WIP and utilization performance measures are added to the DSTATS element.

```
BEGIN;
;                   MODIFIED FLOW-LINE: SAMPLE PROBLEM 6.2
PROJECT,            Sample Problem 6.2,SM;
ATTRIBUTES:         TimeIn:
                    OpTime;
STATIONS:           WorkStation:
                    Paint:
                    Pack:
                    ExitSystem:
                    NewPaint:
                    Enter;
QUEUES:             WorkStationQ:
                    PaintQ:
                    PackQ:
                    NewPaintQ;
RESOURCES:          Worker:
                    Painter:
                    Packer:
                    NewPainter;
SEQUENCES:          1,WorkStation & Paint,OpTime=NORMAL(22,4,2) &
                    Pack,OpTime=TRIANGULAR(20,22,26,2) &
                    ExitSystem:
                    2,WorkStation & NewPaint,OpTime=NORMAL(49,7,2) &
                    Pack,OpTime=TRIANGULAR(21,23,26,2) &
                    ExitSystem;
TALLIES:            FlowTime;
DSTATS:             NQ(WorkStationQ),WorkStation WIP:
                    NR(Worker)*100,Worker Utilization:
                    NQ(PaintQ),Paint WIP:
                    NR(Painter)*100,Painter Utilization:
                    NQ(PackQ),Pack WIP:
                    NR(Packer)*100,Packer Utilization:
                    NQ(NewPaintQ),NewPaint WIP:
                    NR(NewPainter)*100,NewPainter Utilization;
REPLICATE,1,0,565000,,,35000;
END;
```

Figure 6-8. Experiment Frame for Sample Problem 6.2

The SEQUENCES element specifies the part's route through the system by defining the sequence of stations that the part visits. The original part, NS=1, follows the sequence "WorkStation-Paint-Pack-ExitSystem," and the new part, NS=2, follows the sequence "WorkStation-NewPaint-Pack-ExitSystem." The SEQUENCES element assigns operation times to entity attributes for the painting and packing operations of both parts. Figure 6-9 presents the Summary Report for this model.

```
Project:  Sample Problem 6.2
Analyst:  SM
Simulation run ended at time    : 565000.
Statistics were cleared at time : 35000.0
Statistics accumulated for time : 530000.

                         TALLY VARIABLES

Identifier              Average  Variation  Minimum  Maximum  Observations

FlowTime                157.13    .45078    61.406   620.97     18689

                   DISCRETE-CHANGE VARIABLES

Identifier              Average  Variation  Minimum  Maximum  Final Value

WorkStation WIP          1.7348   1.3951    .00000   21.000     7.0000
Worker Utilization      81.064     .48332   .00000  100.00    100.00
Paint WIP                 .03682  5.1173    .00000    2.0000     .00000
Painter Utilization     54.453     .91457   .00000  100.00    100.00
Pack WIP                  .56226  1.3350    .00000    5.0000    1.0000
Packer Utilization      80.702     .48900   .00000  100.00    100.00
NewPaint WIP              .17751  2.6512    .00000    5.0000     .00000
NewPainter Utilization  51.699     .96659   .00000  100.00    100.00
```

Figure 6-9. Summary Report for Sample Problem 6.2

The above summary report shows that the introduction of the new part has increased system congestion. The average part flowtime has increased from approximately 138 to 157. The resource utilizations for the WorkStation and Pack operations are approximately the same. However, there is a decrease in the Paint utilization, which should be expected because 30 percent of the parts are now being painted in the NewPaint station.

5. Transfers Between Stations: Using Transporters

The transportation of materials or parts within a system, frequently an integral element of the system design, is often accomplished with limited resources, e.g., carts, tote pans, fork trucks, or conveyors. Such transfer mechanisms not only deliver material in a timely fashion, but also can provide temporary storage capacity. These limited resources require a capital investment, which increases production costs. Excess transportation capability represents expenditures that are not accompanied by increased value. Insufficient capability, on the other hand, can adversely affect production by delaying the delivery of material and reducing the total value produced by the system. Simulation provides an excellent tool for evaluating the amount and type of transfer resources required to achieve a desired production level.

5.1 The Modified Flow-Line with Transporters

Let's consider the use of limited transfer resources for our modified flow-line example. Assume that all parts are transferred by using two fork trucks that travel at an average speed of 150 feet per minute. The distances (in feet) between the stations are provided in Figure 6-10. Both the drop-off and pickup points at a station are at the same physical location. Once the truck reaches the pickup/drop-off station, it requires a constant load/unload time of two minutes.

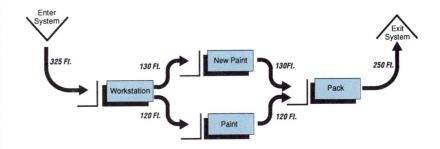

Figure 6-10. Modified Flow-Line with Transporters: Sample Problem 6.3

Let's assume that all requests for transfer are handled on a first-come-first-served basis. This assumption seems realistic for the system being considered because all materials move in a forward direction with no looping or backtracking. Later, in Section 5.3, we discuss more complex types of vehicle dispatching.

5.2 The Concept of a Transporter

The unconstrained transfer of entities between stations modeled by the ROUTE block assumes that the transfer device is always available at the point of transfer and that, during the transfer, the device does not encounter any obstructions. In reality, the movement of parts within systems that use vehicles (such as fork trucks) starts with a request for an available vehicle. If more than one vehicle is currently idle, one must be selected to perform the transfer task. After an idle vehicle is chosen, it must travel from its current position to the part pickup point (if it is not already at that position). Only then can the part be loaded onto the vehicle and the actual transfer take place.

The simplest vehicle transportation system employs a *free-path transporter*. Let's assume that the transporter can freely move about the system without encountering any obstructions that would delay its progress. For these free-path transporters, the time to travel between stations depends on the fixed distance traveled and the speed of the transporter, e.g., hand carts versus fork trucks.

A more complex transportation system uses a *guided transporter*, the movement of which is restricted to a pre-defined network of intersections and connecting links. The travel time for a guided transporter varies with the vehicle's speed characteristics (velocity, acceleration, deceleration), the network's configuration, the path that the vehicle follows, and the congestion caused by other vehicles in the system. The most common example of this type of guided transporter is the class of vehicles referred to as Automated Guided Vehicles, AGVs. Only free-path transporters are discussed in this chapter; guided transporters are discussed in Chapter 9.

In SIMAN, the generic term "transporter" refers to one or more identical transfer devices that can be allocated to an entity for the purpose of transferring entities between stations. The number of transfer devices corresponds to the number of transporter units available. If the number of units is greater than 1, SIMAN automatically distinguishes between the different transporter units. You can reference a specific transporter unit by appending a number within parentheses to the name of the transporter. If you omit this number, it either defaults to 1 or to the unit controlled by the entity. Each individual transporter has several status variables that contain its present status. These variables define its current station or its destination station, its travel velocity, its operational status (active or inactive), and its allocation status (idle or busy).

The previous capabilities are provided by the SIMAN transporter constructs. For free-path transporters, you define the transporter characteristics and the fixed distances between stations in the Experiment Frame. Several SIMAN blocks also facilitate easy modeling of transporter control for free-path transporters. We present the Model Frame constructs first; then we describe the elements required in the Experiment Frame.

5.3 Allocation and Movement of Empty Transporters: The REQUEST Block

The REQUEST block, a type of Hold block, holds an entity in the preceding QUEUE until a transporter becomes available. Based on the REQUEST block's operands, an arriving entity may either request a specific transporter unit or any one of a specified type of transporter. If an entity arrives at a REQUEST block and requests a specific transporter unit, the status of the specified transporter unit is checked to determine if it is both active and idle (available).

If the transporter unit is available, SIMAN changes its allocation status from idle to busy, calculates the travel time from its present station to the station of the requesting entity, changes the location of the transporter to the requesting entity's station number, and imposes a delay equal to the travel time of the transporter to the new station. These changes equate to moving the empty transporter unit to the part pickup point. During the delay, the entity resides at the REQUEST block. Following this delay, the entity departs the REQUEST block. If the specified transporter unit is not available (busy or inactive), the entity is placed in the QUEUE preceding the REQUEST block where it waits for the transporter unit to become available.

An arriving entity may not require a specific transporter unit, but rather can use any available unit of a specified type. If more than one unit of that type is available, then the transporter selection rule specified on the REQUEST block determines which transporter unit is allocated to the entity. The specific transporter unit may be recorded in an attribute of the entity. The subsequent activity is identical to that just described for specific transporter requests.

The first line segment of the REQUEST block contains the block's function name, REQUEST, followed by the priority of the request and the storage identifier.

The second line segment contains the name and unit of the requested transporter, an operand defining the velocity at which the allocated transporter moves (from its current location to the entity's location), and an operand defining the location of the requesting entity.

> REQUEST, Pr, StorID: TrnName(Unit), Vel, EntLoc;

The request priority number, Pr, is an integer used to set an allocation priority if multiple entities waiting at more than one QUEUE-Hold block combination are requesting allocation of the same transporter unit. When available, the transporter unit is allocated based on a low-value-first priority. Ties are resolved by allocating the available transporter unit to the closest waiting entity, based on the distances in the Experiment Frame.

The storage ID, StorID, provides a reference to the animation and can be used to determine the number of entities currently at the REQUEST block.

The transporter name, TrnName, identifies the transporter set from which a transporter unit is requested. The actual transporter unit requested may be specified either as a particular unit or as a transporter selection rule and attribute identifier for storing the specific unit allocated. If you use the first format, then the transporter's number defines which unit is requested by arriving entities. For example, if there are three transporter units in the transporter set named Truck and the second unit is to be requested, then the transporter operand is Truck(2). If you specify the operand as Truck, with no number, SIMAN assumes that the requested unit number has been defaulted to 1 or Truck(1).

If you use the second format, then you must define a transporter selection rule and an optional attribute identifier. The transporter selection rules available are listed in Figure 6-11.

> CYC : Cyclic priority
> LDS : Largest distance to station
> POR : Preferred order rule
> RAN : Random priority
> SDS : Smallest distance to station
> ER(Index) : Experimental rule
> UR(Index) : User rule

Figure 6-11. Transporter Selection Rules

When an entity arrives at a REQUEST block that uses a transporter selection rule, SIMAN applies the rule to all available transporter units of the set defined by the transporter name, chooses one unit, and allocates that unit to the requesting entity. The unit number of the allocated transporter is assigned to the entity's optional attribute, which can be entered as an attribute index or name. For example, if you specify the transporter as Truck(SDS, Truck#), then

SIMAN allocates the closest available unit of transporter set Truck to the entity (following the SDS transporter selection rule) and assigns the number of the selected transporter unit to the attribute Truck#. If you default on the optional attribute, the transporter is specified as Truck(SDS). SIMAN keeps track of which transporter the entity has been allocated. The use of the optional attribute is only recommended if there is a need to distinguish among transporters in a model.

The transporter's velocity, Vel, is the actual velocity used to compute the delay for the empty transporter's travel. The default velocity is that given in the Experiment Frame on the TRANSPORTERS element (described in Section 5.7) or the current value (if the default has been changed). You can express velocity as a constant or as an expression; the latter is based on the default velocity or on some other system condition(s). The entity's location, EntLoc, defines the station value where the requested transporter is to be sent. This value defaults to the current station value, M, of the requesting entity. The operand only needs to be specified if the value differs from the entity's station value.

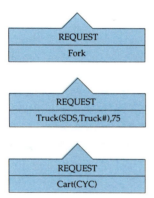

The following examples show three different REQUEST blocks. In the first example, each arriving entity requests the specific transporter unit called Fork. Default of the unit number assumes that there is only one unit of Fork or that the specific unit requested is Fork(1). The priority of the request, the transporter's velocity, and the location of the entity have likewise been defaulted.

The second example requests an available unit of the transporter named Truck. If there is more than one unit available when an entity arrives at the REQUEST block, the transporter selection rule of smallest-distance-to-station (SDS) determines which unit is allocated. The number of the allocated transporter Truck is stored in the requesting entity attribute named Truck#. The transporter's velocity, which is used to calculate the delay for the empty transporter's travel, is 75. The third example requests an available unit of the transporter named Cart and uses cyclic priority if more than one unit is available.

5.4 Transfer to the Destination: The TRANSPORT Block

When an entity departs a REQUEST block, it possesses the requested transporter unit, but no action has been taken to actually transport the entity to another location in the system. In other words, from a modeling standpoint, an empty transporter arrives at the pickup station. In our example we must impose a delay equal to the amount of time required to load the part onto the transporter. We impose this delay by directing the entity, which now controls the transporter, to a DELAY block representing this amount of time. After the part has been loaded onto the transporter, it may be sent to its destination station by using the TRANSPORT block.

The TRANSPORT block, a type of Transfer block, models the movement of an entity and transporter unit from one station to another. The entity executing a TRANSPORT block must already have possession of a transporter unit.

The symbol and statement for the TRANSPORT block are shown below. The top line segment contains the block's function name, TRANSPORT; the bottom line segment contains the operands specifying the transporter unit (TrnName), the destination station (TrnDest), and the velocity at which the transporter travels (Vel).

TRANSPORT: TrnName, TrnDest, Vel;

The Unit operand must reference the specific transporter allocated to the entity. If a transporter selection rule is used to choose a transporter unit, then you may default on the unit number, or, if the optional attribute is used, you may reference that value. For example, if the transporter type selected is Truck and the unit number is stored in Attribute 3 (named Index) of the requesting entity, then you specify the unit number as Truck(A(3)) or Truck(Index) or simply Truck. The Unit operand can be defaulted if the entity performing the transport has ownership of the specific transporter unit (i.e., the entity has been allocated the transporter unit).

The destination station, TrnDest, can be identified by its number or name, by a valid SIMAN expression, or by a reference to the SEQUENCES element (SEQ). The default for the destination is the SEQ entry. The transporter's velocity, Vel, can be defaulted to the current velocity, or it can be entered as a constant or an expression.

When an entity arrives at a TRANSPORT block, the destination is evaluated: If SEQ is defined, the value of IS is increased, the destination is set, and any attribute values in the SEQUENCES element are assigned. If the SEQ option is not used, the destination is directly set. The delay for transportation is then calculated based on the transporter's velocity and the distance between the transporter's current station and its destination. The M attribute of the entity is then set to the destination, and the entity is scheduled to arrive at the destination STATION block after the transportation delay expires.

The following examples illustrate the TRANSPORT block. In the first example, an entity is transferred with transporter unit Fork(2) to a destination specified in the SEQUENCES element. The travel time calculation uses transporter Fork(2)'s velocity and the distance from its current station to its destination.

In the second example, an entity and the unit Truck# of transporter set Truck are transferred to station Paint at a velocity of 150. The third example has the same result if the entity has control of the transporter Truck. The last example illustrates defaulting the transporter unit. If the entity has been allocated transporter unit Fork(2), then this TRANSPORT block equates to the first example.

5.5 The Freeing of Transporters: The FREE Block
The arrival of an entity and transporter unit at their destination equates, in our example, to the arrival of the fork truck at the drop-off point of the next station.

Before the transporter can be released to perform another task, it must first unload the part at the new station (this is modeled as a DELAY).

Once the part has been unloaded, the transporter must be freed, so that it can be allocated to other entities requiring transport. The freeing of the transporter is accomplished with the FREE block.

The symbol and statement for the FREE block are shown below. The first line segment contains the block's function name, FREE, and the second line segment contains the name of the specific transporter unit to be freed, TrnName. You must specify the transporter unit in the same way as previously described for the TRANS-PORT block. As with the TRANSPORT block, the transporter unit can be defaulted if the entity passing through the FREE block has possession of the specified transporter unit.

FREE
TrnName

FREE: TrnName;

If multiple transporter sets are used in a model (e.g., Fork, Cart, and Tote), a single FREE block with a defaulted transporter unit operand can be used to free all transporter units from all sets; however, the entities that pass through this single FREE block must be the same entities that were allocated the transporter units.

The transporter unit that has been freed can then be allocated to another entity. If multiple entities are waiting at different REQUEST blocks for the transporter, SIMAN allocates the transporter to the entity at the REQUEST block with the lowest request priority. In the case of a tie, SIMAN allocates the transporter to the closest entity. If no entity awaits the freed transporter unit, SIMAN sets the transporter's status to available and idle, and the transporter remains at its current station until another request is made.

The following examples illustrate the FREE block. The first example depicts the freeing of transporter unit Fork(2). The second example depicts the freeing of transporter unit Fork with the unit number defaulted.

FREE
Fork(2)

FREE
Fork

FREE

The third example defaults the transporter unit to be freed to the transporter unit possessed by the entity. If the entity passing through the FREE block has been allocated transporter Fork(2), all three examples produce the same result.

5.6 Model Frame for the Transporter Example

Figure 6-12 gives the Block Diagram for the first part of our model for the modified flow line with transporters. The remaining portion of the model is very similar to the WorkStation submodel and is given with the complete model listing in Figure 6-13. The model closely resembles that developed with the ROUTE form of transfer. Because transporters require that the requesting entity have its present station identified, the entry point in the system has been defined as the Station named Enter. Therefore, as soon as an entity arrives at the system via the CREATE block, its station attribute, M, is assigned to the station named Enter. After the part's type has been identified, the entity is sent to GetTruck, which handles all requests for transport.

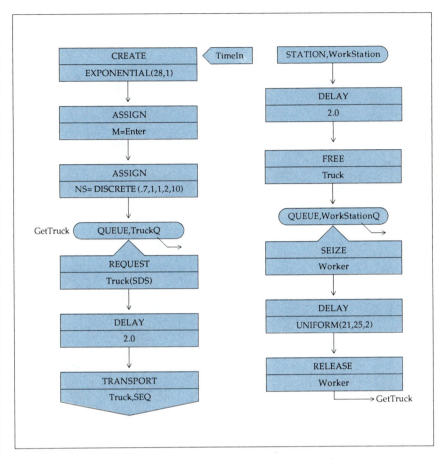

Figure 6-12. Partial Block Diagram for Sample Problem 6.3

Because all transfer requests are to be handled on a first-come-first-served basis, the four blocks starting at the label GetTruck are used for all transporter requests. Each arriving entity has its station identified as its current physical location in the system by attribute M. For example, if an entity is directed to the label GetTruck by the NEXT modifier after having released the resource Worker at station WorkStation, that entity still retains WorkStation (or Station1) as its station identifier. When the entity enters the queue named TruckQ and attempts to request an available transporter, the SIMAN processor recognizes that the entity is located at Station 1. If both transporters, Truck(1) and Truck(2), are available, SIMAN identifies which unit is closest to Station 1, holds the entity in the REQUEST block, and imposes a delay equal to the time that it takes to travel from the selected transporter's current station to Station 1. If only one transporter is available, then SIMAN allocates that unit, regardless of its present location. If the transporter allocated by the REQUEST block is currently at the same location as the requesting entity (Station 1), then the travel time equals 0.

```
BEGIN;
;   MODIFIED FLOW-LINE WITH TRANSPORTERS: SAMPLE PROBLEM 6.3
;   Parts enter, part type determined, and transfer to workstation
            CREATE:      EXPONENTIAL(28,1):        !Create jobs at staging area
                         MARK(TimeIn);             Mark arrival time
            ASSIGN:      M=Enter;                  Set entry station
            ASSIGN:      NS=DISCRETE(.7,1,1,2,10); Set part type
GetTruck    QUEUE,       TruckQ;                   Wait for truck
            REQUEST:     Truck(SDS);               Get truck
            DELAY:       2.0;                      Delay to load part
            TRANSPORT:   Truck,SEQ;                Move to next station in
;                                                  sequence
;   Workstation submodel
            STATION,     WorkStation;             Workstation submodel
            DELAY:       2.0;                      Delay to unload part
            FREE:        Truck;                    Free truck
            QUEUE,       WorkStationQ;             WIP for worker resource
            SEIZE:       Worker;                   Get worker
            DELAY:       UNIFORM(21,25,2);         Delay for
                                                   processing
            RELEASE:     Worker:NEXT(GetTruck);    Release worker resource
;   Paint submodel
            STATION,     Paint;                    Paint submodel
            DELAY:       2.0;                      Delay to unload part
            FREE:        Truck;                    Free truck
            QUEUE,       PaintQ;                   WIP at paint resource
            SEIZE:       Painter;                  Get painter
            DELAY:       Optime;                   Delay for painting
            RELEASE:     Painter:NEXT(GetTruck);   Release painter resource
;   Pack submodel
            STATION,     Pack;                     Pack submodel
            DELAY:       2.0;                      Delay to unload part
            FREE:        Truck;                    Free truck
            QUEUE,       PackQ;                    WIP at packing
            SEIZE:       Packer;                   Get packer
            DELAY:       Optime;                   Delay for packing
            RELEASE:     Packer:NEXT(GetTruck);    Release packer resource
;   Exit submodel
            STATION,     ExitSystem;               Exit submodel
            DELAY:       2.0;                      Delay to unload part
            FREE:        Truck;                    Free truck
            TALLY:       FlowTime,INT(TimeIn):     !Tally flowtime
                         DISPOSE;                  Dispose of job
;   Newpaint submodel
            STATION,     NewPaint;                 Newpaint submodel
            DELAY:       2.0;                      Delay to unload part
            FREE:        Truck;                    Free truck
            QUEUE,       NewPaintQ;                WIP at newpaint
            SEIZE:       NewPainter;               Get newpainter
            DELAY:       Optime;                   Delay for painting
            RELEASE:     NewPainter:NEXT(GetTruck); Release newpainter res.
END;
```

Figure 6-13. Model Listing for Sample Problem 6.3

The transporter unit (1 or 2) allocated by the REQUEST block is stored as part of the entity information by SIMAN. When the allocated unit of transporter arrives at the station of the requesting entity, the entity passes to the subsequent DELAY block where it is delayed by two time units, which represent the load operation;

the entity then passes to the TRANSPORT block where it and its accompanying transporter are transferred to the next station by referencing the SEQUENCES element.

If no transporters are available when the requesting entity arrives at label GetTruck, the entity remains in the queue until a transporter is freed. If other entities are already waiting when an entity arrives at the queue named TruckQ, the arriving entity simply waits in line until it progresses to the front of the queue and its request is granted.

When an entity transferred with the TRANSPORT block arrives at its destination station, it enters the STATION block with its attribute value, M, updated to the current station's identifier. It then enters a DELAY block, which delays the entity by two time units for the unloading operation; during this time the entity retains ownership and control of the transporter unit. After the delay, the entity enters the FREE block and frees its transporter unit, which is then allocated to the next requesting entity. If, when the transporter is freed, there are no other requesting entities, the transporter unit remains at the current station until such a request is made.

The actual travel times are computed automatically by the SIMAN processor based on information supplied in the Experiment Frame.

5.7 Definition of Transporter Characteristics: The TRANSPORTERS Element

The TRANSPORTERS element describes the operating characteristics of the transporters used in the model.

> TRANSPORTERS: Number, Name, NumUnits, Map, Vel,
> Position — Status, repeats :
> repeats;

The transporter's number and name provide the reference to the Model Frame. The name must be identical to the name used in the model. The number can be defaulted, to be assigned by the Experiment Processor in a manner similar to the way numbers are assigned in the STATIONS or QUEUES element. As with these other elements, the numbers must always be assigned in an increasing order. The number of units, NumUnits, defines the maximum number of transporter units that can be active at any time during the simulation run. If the number of transporters is to vary during the simulation, then you must enter the number of units as the maximum number, although some or all units can initially be set to an inactive status at the start of the simulation.

The next number, Map, identifies the location of the system's map or configuration (in this case, a distance set). The transporter velocity, Vel, gives the speed of the transporters; Vel must be specified in terms of a distance per time unit that is consistent with the units used in the rest of the model. The last field allows you to specify where each transporter unit should initially be positioned within the system map and what its initial status should be. This last field can be repeated so that the position and status can be given for each individual transporter unit.

You express the initial transporter position in terms of a station identifier (number or name) and enter a status of Active or Inactive. If you default both operands in this field, all transporters are active, and all are positioned at the first station defined in the distance set. If the position and status are only defined for the first unit, then any remaining units are assumed to have the same starting conditions. You can specify the initial position for each transporter unit and default the status, you can default the initial position and specify the status, or you can use any combination of these options.

The following example defines the transporters for our sample problem as well as two other transporters. The first transporter type is named Truck and has two units, Truck(1) and Truck(2). The system Map is referenced to the first distance set, which can be found in the DISTANCES element (which is discussed in the next section). An initial velocity of 150 feet per minute is specified, with the first transporter unit starting at Station 1 in an active state. Because the position and status of the second unit have been defaulted, Truck(2) will also start at Station 1 in an active state.

```
TRANSPORTERS: 1, Truck, 2, 1, 150, 1-Active:
              2, Fork, 3, 2, 200, 5-I,2-A,3-A:
              3, Cart, 1, 2, 50;
```

The second transporter type has three units named Fork. The system map is defined in Distance Set 2, and the initial velocity is 200 feet per minute. Transporter 1 is to be positioned at Station 5 in an inactive state. The remaining transporters are to start at Stations 2 and 3, both in active states. The third transporter type is named Cart and has one unit. It follows the system map defined by the second distance set, which is also used by the transporters named Fork. The initial velocity of Cart has been set to 50 feet per minute, its position has been defaulted to the first station defined in Distance Set 2, and it is active at the start of the simulation.

The TRANSPORTERS element described in this section is an abbreviated form. Several additional fields and options are available; however, they are not required for this example and involve concepts not presented. The TRANSPORTERS element is completely discussed in Chapter 9, which includes coverage of guided transporters.

5.8 Definition of Travel Distances: The DISTANCES Element

The DISTANCES element allows you to define the transporter's system map by specifying travel distances between all stations that free-path transporters can visit. The syntax for the DISTANCES element is given below. You can use either of two formats to express distances.

DISTANCES: Number, BegStaID — EndStaID, Distance Matrix:
     repeats;

or

DISTANCES: Number, BegStaID — EndStaID — Distance, repeats:
     repeats;

The distance set Number is referenced by the TRANSPORTERS element and indicates which system map a transporter set follows. The first format for specifying the actual distances requires a station range and an associated Distance Matrix. The station range is defined by a beginning station identifier, BegStaID, or the lowest numbered station in the station set, and an ending station identifier, EndStaID, or the highest station number in the set, separated by a dash (-). This station range must include all stations that a transporter can visit.

A Distance Matrix contains the travel distances between all combinations of stations in the distance set. You enter the values as the upper half of an ordinary from-to matrix (excluding the diagonal), with the distance entries separated by commas (,) and the matrix rows separated by slashes (/).

If there were N stations in the station range, the first row would contain N-1 entries, the second row N-2 entries, etc. with a total of N-1 rows. Because the upper half of the matrix provides only one-way distances, the distance between any two stations is the same, regardless of the direction of travel; in other words, the distance from Station J to Station K is the same as the distance from K to J.

The second format allows you to enter individual pairs of stations and the associated distances between just those stations. This format is useful if the upper half of the distance matrix contains many entries that are never used. Only the pairs of stations and associated distances that a transporter actually uses must be included in the second format. This format is also useful if the distance between two stations varies with the direction of travel. If a specific pair of stations, say J and K, appears only once, we assume that the distance between the stations is the same — regardless of the travel direction. If the pair appears twice, say as J-K-50 and K-J-75, then the travel time varies with direction.

This second format is also useful if the actual number of stations that a transporter may visit is small (e.g., five) but, because a station was added to a completed model, the station numbers are not consecutive (e.g., 1, 2, 3, 4, and 20). If the first method is used, this situation would require 190 entries, or (20-1)*20/2, most of which can be entered as 0 because they will never be used. The second method, however, requires only 10 station pairs with associated distances, assuming that the distance between stations does not vary with travel direction and that all combinations of transfer between stations require an entry.

If you use the from-to matrix for entering distances, you should design the simulation model so that all stations to be visited by a transporter can be numbered consecutively. If there is a chance that you will add additional stations to the distance set, you should use the name conventions for all other stations so that they can easily be renumbered; or you should leave several numbered stations unused to allow for easy future expansion. If the model attempts a transport between stations that have not been assigned a distance, an error occurs when SIMAN attempts to compute a travel time.

The first example provides Distance Set 1 for our sample problem. The range of stations is from Station 1, named WorkStation, to Station 6, named Enter. The distances have been computed from the information given in Figure 6-10. For example, the entry of 815 is the distance from Station 4, named ExitSystem, to Station 6, named Enter. This figure represents the sum of the distances from Enter to WorkStation, 325; to Paint, 120; to Pack, 120; and finally to ExitSystem, 250. The total distance is 815 feet. In this example, all distances are greater than 0 because movement from any station to any other station by the transporter is possible. Also, it is assumed that the distance between any two stations is the same regardless of the direction of travel.

```
;                              to Paint
;                              |    to Pack
;                              |    |    to ExitSystem
;                              |    |    |    to NewPaint
;                              |    |    |    |    to Enter
;                              |    |    |    |    |
DISTANCES:        1, 1-6,120,240,490,130,325/   !from WorkStation
                           120,370,250,445/     !from Paint
                               250,130,565/     !from Pack
                                   380,815/     !from ExitSystem
                                       455;     !from NewPaint


DISTANCES: 1,  Enter-WorkStation-325,        WorkStation-Paint-120,
                                             WorkStation-NewPaint-130,
                         Paint-Pack-120, NewPaint-Pack-130,
                         Pack-ExitSystem-250, ExitSystem-Pack-300$
```

The second example is for the same system, but it assumes that the transporter only travels between adjacent stations in the system; therefore, only the adjacent pairs and distances have been given. The second example also assumes that the travel path between the ExitSystem and Pack stations varies with direction; the difference is shown by separate entries for the two directions. This example also uses station names, rather than numbers, throughout.

5.9 SIMAN Transporter Variables

You can use several SIMAN variables to aid in statistical data collection and to provide current information on transporter status. A list of the SIMAN transporter variables is given in Figure 6-14. These variables can be used in the Model or Experiment Frame — as part of an expression or as a means of checking system conditions before selecting a course of action. For example, an entity about to exit an operation can check to see if a transporter is available. If one is available, the entity can request that transporter; if one is not available, the entity can enter a temporary buffer area where it can request a transporter with a lower priority than would be requested by an entity exiting directly from an operation.

VARIABLE	DEFINITION
NT(TrnID)	: Number of busy transporter units
MT(TrnID)	: Number of active transporter units
IT(TrnID,Unit)	: Status of specific transporter unit
LT(TrnID,Unit)	: Current station location or destination of specific transporter unit
VT(TrnID)	: Velocity of transporter set
VTU(TrnID,Unit)	: Velocity of specific transporter unit

Figure 6-14. SIMAN Transporter Variables

These variables also can be used to collect statistics about transporters as part of a DSTATS element: NT, MT, and VT provide information on the transporter set; the remaining variables provide information on individual units of a set. The variable MT returns the active number of transporter units; this value can be less than the number of units specified in the TRANSPORTERS element because it only includes active transporters. The variable NT returns the number of currently busy units in a set. The variable IT returns a transporter unit's current status (0 if idle and active, 1 if busy, and 2 if inactive). The variable LT returns the current station location of a specific transporter unit or its destination station if it is currently being transferred.

The variable VTU allows you to determine or change the velocity of an individual transporter unit within a set. At the beginning of a replication, all transporter units in a set have the same velocity, VT, as defined in the TRANSPORTERS element. Take the following example: three transporters of transporter Set 1, named Fork, were given an initial velocity of 150 in the TRANSPORTERS element; however, you want to change the velocity of individual transporter units during the simulation run. The expressions VTU(Fork,2)=100 and VTU(Fork,3)=200 given in ASSIGN blocks within the model allow all three transporter units to have different velocities; however, an assignment to the variable VT(Fork) specifies the new velocity for all transporters of the set.

5.10 Experiment Frame and Summary Report for the Transporter Example
The Experiment Frame for our sample transporter problem closely resembles that of our most recent sample problem (found in Figure 6-8). Therefore, Figure 6-15 gives only the new or modified elements. As shown, the QUEUES element has been expanded to include the Queue named TruckQ, which was added to the Model Frame to hold entities awaiting allocation of a transporter.

```
QUEUES:          WorkStationQ:
                 PaintQ:
                 PackQ:
                 NewPaintQ:
                 TruckQ;

DSTATS:          NQ(WorkStationQ),WorkStation WIP:
                 NR(Worker)*100.0,Worker Utilization:
                 NQ(PaintQ),Paint WIP:
                 NR(Painter)*100.0,Painter Utilization:
                 NQ(PackQ),Pack WIP:
                 NR(Packer)*100.0,Packer Utilization:
                 NQ(NewPaintQ),NewPaint WIP:
                 NR(NewPainter)*100.0,NewPainter Utilization:
                 NQ(TruckQ),Waiting For Trucks:
                 NT(Truck),Busy Trucks;

TRANSPORTERS:  1, Truck,2,1,150;
;                      to Paint
;                        |   to Pack
;                        |     |   to ExitSystem
;                        |     |     |   to NewPaint
;                        |     |     |     |   to Enter
;                        |     |     |     |     |
DISTANCES:     1, 1-6,120 ,240,490 ,130,325/  !from WorkStation
                        120,370 ,250,445/  !from Paint
                             250 ,130,565/  !from Pack
                                  380,815/  !from ExitSystem
                                       455;  !from NewPaint
```

Figure 6-15. Experiment Frame Listing for Sample Problem 6.3

Two new DSTATS have been added. The first, NQ(TruckQ), is a statistic representing the average number of entities waiting for allocation of a transporter. The DSTAT on NT(Truck) is a statistic representing the number of busy transporters during the simulation. The two new elements, TRANSPORTERS and DISTANCES, were discussed in previous sections. Figure 6-16 presents the SIMAN Summary Report for this sample problem.

```
Project:   Sample Problem 6.3
Analyst:   SM
Simulation run ended at time       : 705000.
Statistics were cleared at time    : 35000.0
Statistics accumulated for time    : 670000.
```

TALLY VARIABLES

Identifier	Average	Variation	Minimum	Maximum	Observations
FlowTime	181.46	.40277	79.500	735.44	23779

DISCRETE-CHANGE VARIABLES

Identifier	Average	Variation	Minimum	Maximum	Final Value
WorkStation WIP	1.7873	1.3617	.00000	20.000	.00000
Worker Utilization	81.623	.47450	.00000	100.00	.00000
Paint WIP	.03659	5.1415	.00000	2.0000	.00000
Painter Utilization	54.575	.91233	.00000	100.00	100.00
Pack WIP	.60247	1.3595	.00000	7.0000	1.0000
Packer Utilization	81.191	.48130	.00000	100.00	100.00
NewPaint WIP	.18823	2.5731	.00000	5.0000	.00000
NewPainter Utilization	52.223	.95649	.00000	100.00	.00000
Waiting For Trucks	.11600	3.4349	.00000	5.0000	.00000
Busy Trucks	1.0131	.76732	.00000	2.0000	.00000

Figure 6-16. Summary Report for Sample Problem 6.3

The introduction of transporters has caused the part flowtime to increase, but the remaining values for WIP and utilization are essentially the same as before. The increased flowtime is most likely due to the increase in travel time between stations caused by the transporters. Note that the transporters are only being used about one-half of the time.

5.11 The Enhanced Example: A Narrow Aisle and Failures

In the example of the modified flow line with transporters, the transporters were allowed to move in an unconstrained fashion anywhere within the system's map. Consider the situation where the only connection between the input staging area, named Enter, and the rest of the stations is through a narrow aisle that only has room for one truck at any given time. Any transfer from or to the Enter station must check a stoplight located at each end of the narrow aisle to see if the aisle is currently being used. A red stoplight indicates that another truck is in the aisle, and the arriving truck waits until the light turns green, indicating that the aisle is vacant.

To keep the existing distances the same, let's confine all truck travel to the aisle patterns shown in Figure 6-10, with the narrow aisle being defined as a 250-foot strip beginning at the input staging area and terminating 75 feet before the WorkStation; the 75 feet before the WorkStation contain a normal two-way aisle. Let's also assume that each fork truck breaks down with exponentially distributed failure and repair times. The mean time between failures is 600 minutes, and the mean time to repair is 10 minutes.

Both the narrow aisle and the failure modifications to our example require additional modeling capabilities. To model the narrow aisle we must be able to allocate an idle transporter and to control its movement to the request point if the vehicle must travel through the narrow aisle. To model vehicle failures we must be able to halt and activate transporter units on the basis of failure characteristics. The following sections present the new model constructs required to represent these modifications.

5.12 The Allocation of Transporters: The ALLOCATE Block

The ALLOCATE block is a Hold block which, like the REQUEST block, holds an entity in the previous queue until a transporter becomes available. Unlike the REQUEST block, however, the ALLOCATE block does not move the newly allocated transporter to the entity's location; it only changes the transporter's status from idle to busy. The entity that has been allocated the transporter then proceeds to the next block. By using the ALLOCATE block instead of the REQUEST block, you can perform other operations before or during the time the empty transporter is moved to the entity's location; however, the ALLOCATE block does not actually move the transporter. The symbol and statement for the ALLOCATE block are shown below.

ALLOCATE, Pr: TrnName(Unit), EntLoc;

ALLOCATE,Pr
TrnName(Unit),EntLoc

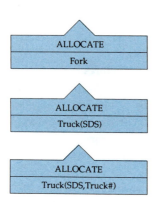

The syntax for the ALLOCATE block greatly resembles that of the REQUEST block. The priority of allocation, Pr, corresponds directly to the priority of request; therefore, if you use multiple ALLOCATE and REQUEST blocks in a model, a newly available transporter unit is allocated on a low-value-first priority across all ALLOCATE and REQUEST blocks. The remaining fields are identical to those described for the REQUEST block in Section 5.3, except for the transporter velocity option, which is excluded because the ALLOCATE block does not cause the transporter to move. Examples of the ALLOCATE block are shown at the left.

The default on the transporter's unit number in the first example assumes that there is only one unit of the transporter named Fork or that Unit 1 is to be allocated. The second and third examples allocate an available unit of the transporter named Truck and use the SDS rule if more than one transporter is available. The number of the allocated transporter is stored in the optional attribute named Truck# on the last example.

5.13 Transporter Movement: The MOVE Block

When an entity departs an ALLOCATE block, it controls the allocated transporter unit, but the unit has not actually been moved to the entity's location. The MOVE block (an Operation block) allows you to move the allocated transporter to any destination station in the defined transporter's station set. You do not have to move the transporter directly to the entity's location. An ALLOCATE block directly followed by a MOVE block, that moves the transporter to the entity's location, performs the same function as a REQUEST block. The symbol and statement for the MOVE block are shown below.

MOVE, StorID: TrnName, TrnDest, Vel;

The syntax for the MOVE block resembles that of the TRANSPORT block described in Section 5.4; however, the blocks yield somewhat different results. With the TRANSPORT block, both the entity and transporter unit are transported to the destination station, TrnDest. When they arrive, the entity appears at the destination STATION block in the model. The MOVE block, on the other hand, only moves the transporter to the destination station. The entity is delayed at the MOVE block until the transporter arrives at its destination station; then the entity enters the next block in the model.

The MOVE block does not change the station identifier, M, of the controlling entity that caused the move; however, the current station location, LT(TrnID,Unit), of the moved transporter is updated. For an entity to move a transporter, the transporter unit must previously have been allocated with an ALLOCATE or REQUEST block. The transporter unit, TrnName, operand can be defaulted if the entity requesting the move has control of the transporter unit.

When an entity arrives at a MOVE block, the duration of its travel is calculated by using the distance (between the transporter's current location and its destina-

MOVE
Fork(2),20,50

MOVE
Truck,Paint

MOVE
Truck(Truck#),Paint

tion) and the specified velocity (or defaulted velocity) for the move. The entity then resides in the MOVE block until the transporter arrives at its destination station. In effect, the entity is delayed until the move has been completed, at which time it is sent to the next block. You can use any number of MOVE blocks or moves to control the position of a transporter. Examples of the MOVE block are shown on the left.

In the first example the transporter unit Fork(2) is moved to Station 20 at a velocity of 50. In the last two examples the transporter type Truck is moved to station Paint. The optional attribute named Truck# has been included in the last example.

You can also use the MOVE block without an associated ALLOCATE block, provided that the transporter unit was allocated at a REQUEST block. For example, an entity can REQUEST a transporter, TRANSPORT the entity to its final destination, MOVE the transporter to a staging area, and then FREE the transporter. As a result, the controlling entity is delayed in the MOVE block until the transporter arrives at the staging area.

5.14 The Enhanced Example: The Narrow-Aisle Logic

Consider the logic required to ensure that there is never more than one transporter in the narrow section of the aisle. First, we include the narrow aisle in the model as a resource that an entity must seize before a transporter can travel through the aisle. We also add a new station named StopLight, which is physically placed 250 feet from station Enter and 75 feet from station WorkStation. As shown in Figure 6-17, the distance between stations Enter and StopLight define the narrow aisle.

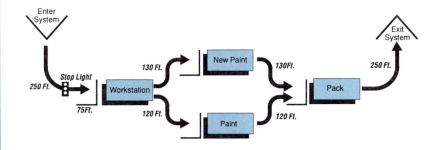

Figure 6-17. The Narrow-Aisle Layout: Sample Problem 6.4

The actions that must be performed by the model vary with the location of the entity and the available transporter unit. Whenever a transporter unit must travel between the Enter and WorkStation stations, special logic is employed to prevent more than one unit from being in the narrow aisle at one time. By using the ALLO-

CATE block in place of the REQUEST block, we can check the location of the allocated transporter unit and compare it to the location of the requesting entity, thereby determining whether the empty transporter must travel through the narrow aisle. This check is performed before the transporter is moved to the requesting entity.

If the requesting entity is at the Enter station and the allocated transporter unit is at any other station, the transporter moves to the StopLight station; the requesting entity waits to seize the narrow-aisle resource, moves the transporter to station Enter, and then releases the resource. If the transporter unit is at the Enter station and the entity is at any other station, the entity waits to seize the narrow-aisle resource, moves the transporter to the StopLight station, releases the narrow-aisle resource, and then moves the transporter to the station of the requesting entity. If the loaded transporter is at the Enter station, the entity seizes the narrow-aisle resource, transports to the StopLight station, releases the resource, and then completes the transport to the final destination. Because parts always flow from the Enter station to the Workstation, and never in the reverse order, a loaded transporter never travels from the StopLight station to the Enter station.

Figure 6-18 shows the listing of the blocks required to implement this logic. (Figure 6-18 also includes the replaced SIMAN block statements from the previous model given in Figure 6-13.) All entities requiring transport are sent to label GetTruck where they are placed in the QUEUE named TruckQ, which provides a place for the entities to reside until an available transporter is allocated at the subsequent ALLOCATE block. Note that we have added the optional attribute name Truck# on the ALLOCATE block because we will need to know which transporter has been allocated when we check transporter location. There are four possible sets of actions at this point, depending on the location of each transporter and each entity. These conditions are defined in the BRANCH block, which follows the ALLOCATE block.

Replace

```
GetTruck QUEUE,      TruckQ;                  wait for truck
         REQUEST:    Truck(SDS);              get truck
         DELAY:      1.5;                     delay to load part
         TRANSPORT:  Truck,SEQ;               move to next station
```

With

```
GetTruck QUEUE,      TruckQ;                  wait for truck
         ALLOCATE:   Truck(SDS,3);            get truck
ChkPos   BRANCH,     1:
                     IF,M.eq.Enter.and.
                     LT(Truck,Truck#).eq.Enter,Load:
                     IF,M.eq.Enter.and.
                     LT(Truck,Truck#).ne.Enter,ToEnter:
                     IF,M.ne.Enter.and.
                     LT(Truck,Truck#).eq.Enter,OutEnter:
                     IF,M.ne.Enter.and.
                     LT(Truck,Truck#).ne.Enter,NoAisle;
;        send truck to stop light station and then to enter station
ToEnter  MOVE:       Truck(Truck#),StopLight; move to stoplight station

         QUEUE,      AisleQ1;                 wait for aisle resource
         SEIZE:      Aisle;                   get aisle resource
         MOVE:       Truck(Truck#),Enter;     move to enter station
         RELEASE:    Aisle:NEXT(Load);        release aisle resource

;        send truck from enter station to stop light station
OutEnter QUEUE,      AisleQ2;                 wait for aisle resource
         SEIZE:      Aisle;                   get aisle resource
         MOVE:       Truck(Truck#),StopLight; move to stoplight station
         RELEASE:    Aisle;                   release aisle resource
         MOVE:       Truck(Truck#),M:         !move to station M
                     NEXT(Load);

NoAisle  MOVE:       Truck(Truck#),M;         move to station M
Load     DELAY:      2.0;                     delay to load part
         BRANCH,     1:                       !check if at enter station
                     IF,M.eq.Enter,GetAisle:  !at enter station
                     ELSE,Dest;               not at enter station
GetAisle QUEUE,      AisleQ3;                 wait for aisle resource
         SEIZE:      Aisle;                   get aisle resource
         TRANSPORT:  Truck(Truck#),StopLight; move to stoplight station
         STATION,    StopLight;               stoplight station
         RELEASE:    Aisle;                   release aisle resource
Dest     TRANSPORT:  Truck(Truck#),SEQ;       move to next station in
```

Figure 6-18. Model Listing for Narrow-Aisle Logic: Sample Problem 6.4

If the first branch condition at block label ChkPos is true, then both the transporter unit and the entity are located at station Enter. If they are, the part can immediately be loaded onto the transporter, and so the entity is sent to label Load where it encounters a delay. After the delay, if the entity and transporter are at station Enter, the entity is sent to block label GetAisle where it enters the queue named AisleQ3 to seize the Aisle resource. When the entity seizes the Aisle resource, it is transported to station 7, named StopLight. After the appropriate travel time has passed, the entity and transporter enter station StopLight, the entity releases the Aisle resource, and the entity transports to its final destination, according to its sequence.

If the second branch condition at block label ChkPos is true, then the entity is at station Enter, and the transporter unit is at some other station in the model. This condition requires that the allocated transporter unit be moved from its current station to station StopLight and then through the narrow Aisle. The initial move is performed at label ToEnter, which transfers the transporter unit to station StopLight. The controlling entity then enters the queue named AisleQ1 to seize the Aisle resource, after which the transporter unit is moved to station Enter. When the transporter arrives, the entity releases the Aisle resource. The entity and the transporter are now both located at station Enter, just as they were in the first condition. The entity is sent to label Load, where the previously described operations are performed.

If the third branch condition at block label ChkPos is true, then the controlling entity is at some station other than Enter, and the transporter unit is at station Enter. In this case, the controlling entity is directed to label OutEnter, where it enters the queue named AisleQ2 to seize the Aisle resource. The entity then moves the transporter unit from station Enter to station StopLight, where it releases the Aisle resource. The transporter is then moved to station M, which is the current location of the controlling entity. The entity is sent to label Load, is delayed for the loading operation, and is passed to the branch block, which determines that the entity is not at station Enter. The entity is then sent to label Dest, which transports the entity to its final destination. This logic assumes that an entity is never transported to station Enter, because all parts in the system only travel from station Enter and go directly to station WorkStation. If this premise were not always true, then the model logic would have to be extended to allow for the seizing of the narrow-Aisle resource.

If the fourth and last branch condition at block label ChkPos is true, then the entity and transporter unit are both at stations other than station Enter. In this case the narrow Aisle is not used. Instead, the controlling entity is sent to label NoAisle, which moves the transporter to the current station location, M, of the entity. The loading operation is performed, and the entity is branched to label Dest, which transports the entity to its final destination, according to its sequence.

These are the only changes required in the Model Frame to include the narrow aisle in our sample problem. Note that the only time that the first and third branch conditions (in which transporters are located at Enter) can occur is at the start of the simulation. Until allocated to another entity, an available transporter unit always stays at the station where it unloaded its last part, and parts are never unloaded at station Enter. Thus, if the transporters are positioned at stations other than station Enter at the start of the simulation, the blocks required for these conditions can be deleted. It is good practice, however, to include all possibilities in the model, in case system conditions change in the future.

The previous changes to the model require several changes to the Experiment Frame; Figure 6-19 gives the modified elements. We have added the attribute Truck# to the ATTRIBUTES element, have added the resource Aisle to the RESOURCES element, have added the station StopLight to the STATIONS element, and have updated the number of queues in the QUEUES element. We have also added a statistic to the DSTATS element to keep track of the fraction of time that a transporter is in the narrow aisle.

```
ATTRIBUTES:      TimeIn:
                 OpTime:
                 Truck#;
RESOURCES:       Worker:
                 Painter:
                 Packer:
                 NewPainter:
                 Aisle;
STATIONS:        WorkStation:
                 Paint:
                 Pack:
                 ExitSystem:
                 NewPaint:
                 Enter:
                 StopLight;
QUEUES:          WorkStationQ:
                 PaintQ:
                 PackQ:
                 NewPaintQ:
                 TruckQ:
                 AisleQ1:
                 AisleQ2:
                 AisleQ3;
DSTATS:          NQ(WorkStationQ),WorkStation WIP:
                 NR(Worker)*100.0,Worker Utilization:
                 NQ(PaintQ),Paint WIP:
                 NR(Painter)*100.0,Painter Utilization:
                 NQ(PackQ),Pack WIP:
                 NR(Packer)*100.0,Packer Utilization:
                 NQ(NewPaintQ),NewPaint WIP:
                 NR(NewPainter)*100.0,NewPainter Utilization:
                 NQ(TruckQ),Waiting Trucks:
                 NT(Truck),Busy Trucks:
                 NR(Aisle),Busy Aisle;
;                        to Paint
;                        |   to Pack
;                        |    |   to ExitSystem
;                        |    |    |   to NewPaint
;                        |    |    |    |  to Enter
;                        |    |    |    |   |  to StopLight
;                        |    |    |    |   |   |
DISTANCES:    1, 1-7,120,240,490,130,325, 75/    !from WorkStation
                      120,370,250,445,195/       !from Paint
                          250,130,565,315/       !from Pack
                              380,815,565/       !from ExitSystem
                                  455,205/       !from NewPaint
                                      250;       !from Enter
```

Figure 6-19. The Modified Elements for Sample Problem 6.4

We have modified the DISTANCES element to include the new station Stop-Light, Station 7. Except for the last column, the entries in the distance matrix remain the same. The last column represents the distances from all the other stations, i.e., 1 through 6, to Station 7.

5.15 Modeling Failures: The HALT and ACTIVATE Blocks

The HALT and ACTIVATE blocks (types of Operation blocks) allow you to change the status of specific transporter units. The HALT block changes the status of an active transporter unit to inactive, and the ACTIVATE block changes the status from inactive to active. The symbols and statements for these blocks are given below. The entity used to HALT or ACTIVATE a transporter unit need not have control of that unit.

```
HALT
TrnName
```

HALT: TrnName;

```
ACTIVATE
TrnName
```

ACTIVATE: TrnName;

If an entity enters a HALT block and the specified transporter unit is idle, the status of that unit is immediately set to inactive. If the transporter unit is currently busy, the entity that entered the HALT block proceeds to the next block, but the transporter unit is not set to inactive until it is freed by its controlling entity. Other entities trying to allocate the transporter unit are held in their associated queues until another unit becomes available or until the inactive unit's status is changed to active by an entity's passing through an ACTIVATE block. An entity's passing through a HALT block that references an already inactive transporter unit has no effect.

An entity's entering an ACTIVATE block immediately changes the specified transporter unit to active. If the unit is already active, no action is taken, and the already active transporter unit is available for allocation to requesting entities.

In the first of the following examples, the HALT block sets the status of Unit 1 of transporter type Truck to inactive as soon as the transporter is freed, or immediately if the transporter is idle. In the second example, the ACTIVATE block changes the status of the transporter to active.

```
HALT
Truck(1)
```

```
ACTIVATE
Truck(1)
```

These two blocks allow you to change the status of individual transporter units. We can use these blocks to include transporter failures in our sample problem. When modeling a failure, we often add an independent submodel to the Model Frame, which essentially provides a failure loop. Figure 6-20 shows a block diagram for a failure loop for our sample problem; Figure 6-21 shows the corresponding model listing. The single CREATE block creates two entities at time 0. The first entity proceeds to the ASSIGN block where the integer system variable, J, is increased by 1 and the resulting value is then assigned to the entity's attribute Truck#. Because SIMAN initializes the value of J to 0 at the start of each run, the first entity has a value of 1 assigned to its attribute named Truck#, and the second a value of 2. The Truck# is used to identify which transporter is to fail. Both entities are then sent directly into the failure loop.

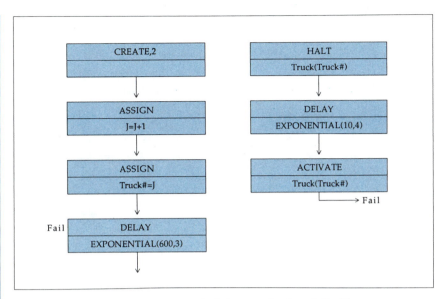

Figure 6-20. Failure Loop Block Diagram for Sample Problem 6.4

Each entity in the failure loop operates independently. An entity is first delayed by an amount of time generated from an exponential distribution; this time period represents the time between failures. The entity then passes to the HALT block, which attempts to set the status of the specified transporter unit to inactive. If the specified transporter unit is currently busy, its status is set to inactive as soon as it is freed. The entity passes through the HALT block without delay and enters the next DELAY block, where it is delayed by an amount of time that represents the repair time. After this delay, the entity enters the ACTIVATE block, where the specified transporter unit is set to active. The entity is then sent back to the start of the failure loop by a NEXT modifier. There are no changes required in the Experiment Frame to implement this logic.

```
;      failure submodel
       CREATE,    2;                             create two failure entities
       ASSIGN:    J=J+1;                          offset for truck number
       ASSIGN:    Truck#=J;                       assign truck number (1-2)
Fail  DELAY:     EXPONENTIAL(600,3);              delay until truck failure
       HALT:      Truck(Truck#);                  fail truck
       DELAY:     EXPONENTIAL(10,4);              delay until repaired
       ACTIVATE:  Truck(Truck#):NEXT(Fail);       truck is repaired
```

Figure 6-21. Failure Loop Modeling Listing for Sample Problem 6.4

The previous logic offers a simple method for modeling failures in transporters; however, it falls short of being entirely accurate because the inactivation of a busy transporter unit is postponed until the unit is freed. Therefore, if the repair times are small and the transport times large, the failure loop entity may be delayed for the repair and sent to the ACTIVATE block before the unit is freed. Thus, the request for status change is cancelled, and the transporter's status is not set to inactive. If this sequence occurs frequently in the simulation, the amount of failure time can be much lower then expected.

An alternative approach involves incorporating a QUEUE-ALLOCATE block sequence just before the HALT block, thereby ensuring that the transporter unit is available for failure. A FREE block is then inserted directly after the HALT block. The resulting logic allocates the specified transporter unit, halts the unit, and frees the unit so that the status can be changed to inactive. If the entities spend a large amount of time in the queue waiting for the specified transporter unit, this method can also distort the results, because it lengthens the expected time between failures; however, the effect is normally less severe than with the previous method. In most modeling situations, the differences would be minor — no cause for concern.

5.16 Summary Report for the Enhanced Transporter Example

Figure 6-22 presents the SIMAN Summary Report for our enhanced transporter example with the narrow-aisle and failure conditions.

```
Project:  Sample Problem 6.4
Analyst:  SM
Replication ended at time       : 705000.
Statistics were cleared at time  : 35000.0
Statistics accumulated for time  : 670000.
```

TALLY VARIABLES

Identifier	Average	Variation	Minimum	Maximum	Observations
FlowTime	182.32	.40243	80.313	740.94	23779

DISCRETE-CHANGE VARIABLES

Identifier	Average	Variation	Minimum	Maximum	Final Value
WorkStation WIP	1.7809	1.3606	.00000	20.000	.00000
Worker Utilization	81.624	.47447	.00000	100.00	.00000
Paint WIP	.03826	5.0288	.00000	2.0000	.00000
Painter Utilization	54.591	.91203	.00000	100.00	100.00
Pack WIP	.61007	1.3595	.00000	8.0000	1.0000
Packer Utilization	81.197	.48122	.00000	100.00	100.00
NewPaint WIP	.18881	2.5651	.00000	5.0000	.00000
NewPainter Utilization	52.184	.95724	.00000	100.00	.00000
Waiting For Trucks	.13939	3.2236	.00000	7.0000	.00000
Busy Trucks	1.0167	.76073	.00000	2.0000	.00000
Busy Aisle	.11847	2.7279	.00000	1.0000	.00000

Figure 6-22. Summary Report Sample Problem 6.4

The above summary report provides results that are very similar to the summary of the system before the narrow aisle and transporters were introduced. The last DSTAT indicates that there is a truck in the narrow aisle about 12 percent of the time. With this small a congestion factor, one would not expect a significant effect. Also, because the trucks are only busy about one-half of the time, the occasional failure has no impact on system performance.

6. Transfers Between Stations: Using Conveyors

The part flow in our modified flow line is essentially the same for both types of parts. The only deviation occurs at the second operation when the different types visit different painting areas; otherwise, the sequences are the same. This type of system represents an ideal application for the use of conveyors to transfer parts. Modifying the flow-line system to use conveyors also eliminates the one-way traffic problem in our previous example because we no longer need to have the transfer device travel in the opposite direction in that area of the system.

6.1 The Modified Flow Line with Conveyors

Let's assume that we replace the fork trucks with belt conveyors to accomplish all part transfers, as shown in Figure 6-23. One continuous belt conveyor is now used to transfer Type 1 parts through the entire system (Enter-WorkStation-Paint-Pack-ExitSystem). As a part arrives at its destination station, it is automatically diverted off the belt conveyor into an infinite buffer at the station. A second continuous belt conveyor will be used to transfer Type 2 parts from the WorkStation to the NewPaint operation and then to Pack. This part will use the first conveyor for the rest of its transfers.

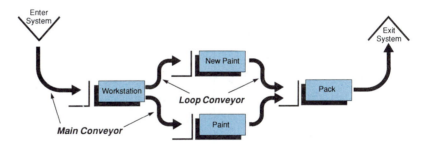

Figure 6-23. Modified Flow Line With Conveyors: Sample Problem 6.5

Both belt conveyors run continuously at a speed of 50 feet/minute. Assume that a Type 1 part requires two linear feet of space on a conveyor for transfer, and that a Type 2 part requires three linear feet.

6.2 The Concept of a Conveyor

A conveyor is a material-handling device for transferring or moving objects along a predetermined path having fixed pre-defined loading and discharge points. Examples include belt, bucket, chain, overhead, power-and-free, pusher, and roller conveyors.

The concept is simple: Each object to be conveyed must wait for sufficient space on the conveyor before it can gain entry and begin its transfer. To implement this concept, we must identify what portions of a conveyor are occupied at any given point in time. So we divide a conveyor into cells of equal length; in a sense, you can think of these moving cells, occupied or not, as the conveyor. We assume that the conveyor does not loop back onto itself; whenever a cell reaches the end, a new cell is placed at the beginning. Each entity that desires to get onto the conveyor at any given point need only wait until a pre-defined number of unoccupied consecutive cells is available at that point.

The SIMAN Conveyor construct requires that you specify the size of the conveyor cell. For a bucket or overhead conveyor with fixed loading points, the size of the cell, i.e., its length, is specified as the center-to-center distance between buckets or the distance between loading points. Each entity desiring access to the conveyor must wait for one unoccupied cell. For a belt or roller conveyor, the cell size must be based on the width of the entities that will use the conveyor.

From an efficiency standpoint, we want to make the cells as large as possible in order to reduce the amount of internal bookkeeping; reduced bookkeeping, in turn, requires less memory and results in a faster running model. Unfortunately, cells that are too large can result in an inaccurate representation of the conveyor. For example, if the size of the cell and the entity are both specified as one foot, an entity is only allowed on the conveyor at one-foot increments. An entity arriving at a loading point just after the one-foot increment has passed, must wait for the next increment before gaining entry to the conveyor — even though the conveyor may be empty. If the cell width is specified as one inch and the entity size as twelve inches, the entity can enter the conveyor and start its transfer much sooner.

In developing a simulation you must also consider the impact of the cell's size on the overall performance of the simulation. Unless the conveyor is highly utilized or the slight delay in gaining access to the conveyor has a significant impact, it is generally advisable to use larger cell widths. For our sample problem, we will specify a cell width of one foot.

The SIMAN Conveyor constructs can be used to model two types or classes of conveyors with different operating characteristics. The first type is referred to as *non-accumulating* and the second as *accumulating*. Both types of conveyors are unidirectional, i.e., they cannot be reversed. Because the non-accumulating capabilities are simpler to understand, we will use them first in our example.

6.3 Non-accumulating Conveyors

Non-accumulating conveyors are best described by comparing them to a bucket conveyor or a belt conveyor that has no accumulating capability. These conveyors travel in a single direction, and the spacing between two entities on the conveyor remains the same unless one entity is removed and then put back. The operating characteristics of a non-accumulating conveyor are unique: When an entity is placed on the conveyor, the entire conveyor is actually disengaged or stopped until instructions are given to transfer the entity to its destination; when the entity reaches its destination, the entire conveyor is again disengaged until instructions are given to remove the entity from the conveyor, at which time it is engaged or started. Here is an example: When a part arrives at the end of a the conveyor, a light sensor activates, stopping the conveyor until a material handler arrives to remove the part from the conveyor; the conveyor is then automatically restarted by the same light sensor that stopped it.

The same constructs can be used to model continuously moving conveyors by assigning a value of 0 to represent the elapsed time between an entity's placement on the conveyor and the giving of an instruction for its transfer on the conveyor. Or you can specify a zero time lapse between the part's arrival at its destination and its removal from the conveyor. The three basic operations that you must perform when modeling conveyors are 1) placing the part or entity on an unoccupied section of the conveyor at its load point (ACCESS block), 2) giving instructions for the transfer of the entity to its destination (CONVEY block), and 3) removing the entity from the conveyor when it reaches it destination (EXIT block). The rest of the operations are taken care of by the SIMAN processor.

6.4 Allocation of Conveyor Cells: The ACCESS Block

The ACCESS block, a type of Hold block, holds an entity in a queue until sufficient space is available on the conveyor for the entity. The ACCESS block must always be preceded by a QUEUE block to provide a place for the entity to reside until space becomes available. For the ACCESS block to "recognize" the entry point on the named conveyor, the arriving entity must have its current station attribute, M, defined as the number of the station where it will enter the conveyor. The ACCESS block then holds the entity until it can allocate the requested number of consecutive conveyor cells. The symbol and statement for the ACCESS block are shown below.

    ACCESS: CnvName, Qty;

The first line segment contains the block's function name, ACCESS. The second line segment contains the name of the conveyor, CnvName, followed by the number of consecutive cells required, Qty. The cell length for each conveyor is defined in the Experiment Frame. Therefore, the number of requested cells must be consistent with the units used in the Experiment Frame. If the number of requested cells is defaulted, SIMAN assumes that only one cell is required.

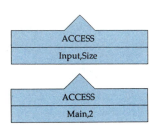

In the first example at the left, the arriving entity requests space on a conveyor named Input. The number of cells required is given by the entity attribute named Size. In the second example, the entity is requesting two consecutive cells on the conveyor named Main.

The ACCESS block holds the arriving entity in the preceding QUEUE block only until space becomes available on the conveyor. You can think of this block as "watching" the conveyor until space is available and then "placing" the entity on the conveyor. Because you have not told SIMAN where the entity is to be conveyed, use of the ACCESS block does not actually cause the entity to start moving on the conveyor. In reality it causes the conveyor to disengage or stop until this information is provided by the CONVEY block. You can, therefore, consider other actions on or by the entity before it is actually conveyed. For example, you might specify a delay equal to the time required to load the entity onto the disengaged conveyor.

6.5 Transfer to the Destination: The CONVEY Block

The CONVEY block, a type of Transfer block, provides a means of transferring the entity to another point on the conveyor. The format for the CONVEY block is shown below.

CONVEY: CnvName, Dest;

The first line segment contains the block's function name, CONVEY. The second line segment contains the name of the conveyor, followed by the destination station, Dest, to which the entity is to be conveyed. You can specify the destination in a SEQUENCES element, in which case the operand would be given as SEQ.

We assume that an entity arriving at a CONVEY block has already accessed the required space on the conveyor, that the station attribute M has the same value as when it arrived at the ACCESS block, and that the conveyor's name is the same. The CONVEY block sets the entity's station attribute equal to the destination station, engages or starts the conveyor, and initiates the transfer of the entity along the conveyor at the velocity stated in the Experiment Frame. The time at which the entity arrives at its destination station depends on the distance to be traveled, as given in the Experiment Frame, and on the status of the conveyor during its transfer, i.e., engaged or disengaged.

In the first of the following examples of the CONVEY block, the entity is to be conveyed to Station 9 on the conveyor named Input. In the second example, the entity is conveyed to Station 9 on the conveyor that it previously accessed because the conveyor name is defaulted. If the most recently accessed conveyor is named Input, this example is identical to the first example. In the last example, the entity is conveyed to the station specified in the SEQUENCE element by the conveyor named Main.

From a modeling viewpoint, we think in terms of an entity's placement on the conveyor and in terms of its arriving at its destination point on that same conveyor. However, as with the transporter construct, the entity actually arrives at the specified destination STATION block, and we must take into account the fact that it has arrived there on a conveyor.

6.6 Exit from the Conveyor Cells: The EXIT Block

When the conveyed entity arrives at its destination, the named conveyor is disengaged until the entity is removed from the conveyor or conveyed to another station. Disengaging the conveyor gives us an opportunity to account for other processes that may occur before the entity is removed from the conveyor — such as an unloading delay. The EXIT block, a type of Operation block, allows us to release accessed cells and to engage the conveyor. The format of the EXIT block is shown below.

EXIT: CnvName, Qty;

The first line segment contains the block's function name, and the second line segment contains the conveyor's name followed by the number of consecutive cells to be released. This number must be less-than-or-equal-to the number of cells that were accessed by the entity. Note that not all the cells need to be released at the same time. For example, an entity may access three consecutive cells, be conveyed to a station, exit one of the cells, and then be conveyed to another station with two cells still in its possession. Thus, we can reduce the occupied conveyor space at a station while allowing the entity to retain the remaining space. You could use this approach if you wanted to load an entire batch of parts onto a conveyor at the same time and then unload them one at a time at different points along the conveyor. If all cells accessed by the conveyor are not released at an EXIT block, the conveyor remains disengaged until the entity is conveyed to another station or until the cells are released. The default case releases all cells currently possessed by the entity.

In the first example of the EXIT block shown at the left, the entity releases the number of cells defined in the attribute Size from the conveyor named Input and engages the conveyor. In the second example, the entity releases two cells from the conveyor named Main and engages the conveyor, provided that the entity only occupies two cells. The last three examples show the different default cases for the second example.

When using the three blocks discussed (ACCESS, CONVEY, and EXIT), you must be careful to refer to the same conveyor name and to exit the same number of cells as were originally accessed. The alternative is to default both the name and quantity whenever possible.

6.7 Model for the Non-accumulating Conveyor Example

The resulting model listing for the modified flow line is shown in Figure 6-24. This conveyor model closely resembles the transporter model except that the REQUEST, TRANSPORT, and FREE blocks have been replaced with the ACCESS, CONVEY, and EXIT blocks. Because of the spur loop used to transfer parts to and from the NewPaint operation, we have included additional logic to ensure that the correct conveyor is accessed and exited. We assign the amount of space required by each part to the entity attribute Size just before assigning the sequence number; the attribute Size is then used whenever the entity accesses or exits a conveyor.

```
BEGIN;
;    MODIFIED FLOW-LINE WITH NON-ACCUMULATING CONVEYORS:
;                  SAMPLE PROBLEM 6.5
;    Parts enter, part type determined, and transfer to workstation
       CREATE:   EXPONENTIAL(28,1):         !Create jobs at staging area
```

```
                         MARK(TimeIn);                    Mark arrival time
            ASSIGN:      M=Enter;                         Set entry station
            ASSIGN:      NS=DISCRETE(.7,1,1,2,10);        Set part type
            ASSIGN:      Size=NS+1;                        Set part size + 2 or 3
Conv        QUEUE,       MainQ;                           Wait for space on conveyor
            ACCESS:      Main,Size;                        Get space on conveyor
            CONVEY:      Main,SEQ;                         Convey to next station
;    Workstation model

            STATION,     WorkStation;                     Workstation submodel
            EXIT:        Main,Size;                        Get off conveyor
            QUEUE,       WorkStationQ;                     WIP at workstation
            SEIZE:       Worker;                           Get worker
            DELAY:       UNIFORM(21,25,2);                 Delay for processing
            RELEASE:     Worker;                           Release worker
            BRANCH,      1:                                !Which conveyor?
                         IF,NS.eq.1,MainQ2:                Main conveyor
                         ELSE,OffLoopQ;                    Off loop conveyor

MainQ2      QUEUE,       MainQ2;                           Wait for space on conveyor
            ACCESS:      Main,Size;                        Get space on conveyor
            CONVEY:      Main,SEQ;                         Convey to next station

OffLoopQ    QUEUE,       OffLoopQ;                         Wait for space on conveyor
            ACCESS:      OffLoop,Size;                     Get space on conveyor
            CONVEY:      OffLoop,SEQ;                       Convey to next station
;    Paint submodel

            STATION,     Paint;                            Paint submodel
            EXIT:        Main,Size;                        Get off conveyor
            QUEUE,       PaintQ;                           WIP at paint
            SEIZE:       Painter;                          Get painter
            DELAY:       OpTime;                           Delay for painting
            RELEASE:     Painter;                          Release painter
;
            QUEUE,       MainQ3;                           Wait for space on conveyor
            ACCESS:      Main,Size;                        Get space on conveyor
            CONVEY:      Main,SEQ;                         Convey to next station
;    Pack submodel

            STATION,     Pack;                             Pack submodel
            BRANCH,      1:                                !Get off which conveyor?
                         IF,NS.eq.1,OffMain1:              !Get off main conveyor
                         ELSE,OffLoop2;                    Get off loop conveyor
OffMain1    EXIT:        Main,Size:NEXT(PackerQ);          Get off main conveyor
OffLoop2    EXIT:        OffLoop,Size:                     !Get off loop conveyor
                         NEXT(PackerQ);

PackerQ     QUEUE,       PackQ;                            WIP at packing
            SEIZE:       Packer;                           Get packer
            DELAY:       OpTime;                           Delay for packing
            RELEASE:     Packer;                           Release packer
            QUEUE,       MainQ4;                           Wait for space on conveyor
            ACCESS:      Main,Size;                        Get space on conveyor
            CONVEY:      Main,SEQ;                         Convey to next station
;    Exit submodel

            STATION,     ExitSystem;                       Exit station
            EXIT:        Main,Size;                        Get off conveyor
            TALLY:       FlowTime,INT(TimeIn):             !Tally flowtime
                         DISPOSE;                          Dispose of job
;    Newpaint submodel

            STATION,     NewPaint;                         Newpaint submodel
            EXIT:        OffLoop,Size;                     Get off conveyor
            QUEUE,       NewPaintQ;                        WIP at newpaint
            SEIZE:       NewPainter;                       Get newpainter
            DELAY:       OpTime;                           Delay for painting
            RELEASE:     NewPainter;                       Release newpainter
            QUEUE,       OffLoopQ2;                         Wait for space on conveyor
            ACCESS:      OffLoop,Size;                     Get space on conveyor
            CONVEY:      OffLoop,SEQ;                       Convey to next station

END;
```

Figure 6-24. Model Listing for Sample Problem 6.5

In this example the conveyors are disengaged whenever a part is placed on a conveyor or arrives at its destination. Because we assume that space is always available for storage at each operation, the conveyor is always engaged as soon as it reaches its destination without any delay. From a practical perspective, the conveyors run continuously.

If the route times equal the convey times, the results from this model would closely resemble the model developed with the ROUTE block (see Section 4.5). The only potential difference occurs when a part has to wait for space on a conveyor before it can start its transfer to the next operation. This event is unlikely, however, because, except for when they enter the system, parts only attempt to access the conveyor after finishing an operation, and the operation times are greater than the time required for the previous part to clear the required space.

To modify the Experiment Frame to include the conveyor information, we use two new elements, CONVEYORS and SEGMENTS.

6.8 Definition of Conveyor Characteristics: The CONVEYORS Element
The CONVEYORS element defines the characteristics of the conveyors used in the Model Frame. The syntax for the CONVEYORS element is shown below.

CONVEYORS: Number, Name, SegmentSet, Vel, CellSize,
          repeats;
       Status, MaxPerEnt, Type, EntSize:

The conveyor's number and name provide the reference to Model Frame. You must use the same name that was used in the Model Frame. You can default the number, in which case it will automatically be assigned by the Experiment Processor in a manner similar to the way numbers are assigned in the STATIONS or QUEUES elements. As with these other elements, you must always assign numbers in an increasing order. You can use the conveyor number as an argument to reference SIMAN variables in either the Model or the Experiment Frame.

The Segment Set Number operand provides a reference to the SEGMENTS element, which defines the path of the conveyor. The Conveyor Velocity operand, Vel, defines the initial speed of the conveyor in length per time units. Length and time units must be consistent throughout the system. A conveyor cell is the smallest unit of a conveyor that an entity can occupy, and CellSize defines the length of a single cell on the conveyor. The total number of cells is obtained by dividing the value of CellSize into the total conveyor length as defined in the SEGMENTS element.

You assign an initial Status of either Active or Inactive, indicating the state of the conveyor at the start of the simulation. The maximum number of cells per entity operand, MaxPerEnt, defines the number of cells for the largest entity that you will place on the conveyor. This value automatically adjusts the length of point-to-point conveyors to ensure that sufficient space is reserved at the end of each conveyor to hold the entity before it exits the conveyor. You specify the conveyor Type operand as Non-accumulating or Accumulating. You use the last operand (EntSize) only if the Accumulating option is specified.

The first conveyor example shown below describes two conveyors. Conveyor 1, named Belt, has its path defined in Segment Set 2. It has a velocity of 10, and the cell size is three units. It starts in an active state and is a non-accumulating conveyor with the largest entity requiring five cells (15 units of length). The units for the velocity, cell size, and largest entity are not stated, but they are assumed to be consistent (e.g., 10 feet per minute, 3 feet per cell, with the largest entity requiring 15 feet of conveyor). Conveyor 2, named Roller, has its path defined in the first segment set and operates at five feet per minute with a cell size of one foot. It starts in an active state and is an accumulating conveyor with the largest entity requiring four cells.

```
CONVEYORS:       1,Belt,2,10,3,A,5,N:
                 2,Roller,1,5,1,A,4,A;

CONVEYORS:       1,Main,1,50,1,A,3,N:
                 2,OffLoop,2,50,1,A,3,N;
```

The second example describes the element for our modified flow line with non-accumulating conveyors. The main conveyor, Conveyor 1, references the first segment set, whereas the Offloop conveyor references the second. Both operate at 50 feet per minute with a cell size of 1 foot, and both are active at the start of the simulation. The largest entity, part Type 2, requires three feet, or three cells, and, because it uses both conveyors, we have set the maximum number of cells per entity at three for both conveyors. Both conveyors are non-accumulating.

6.9 Definition of Conveyor Segments: The SEGMENTS Element

The SEGMENTS element defines the conveyor's actual path in terms of a series of connecting segments between stations that the conveyor serves. The syntax for the SEGMENTS element is given below.

SEGMENTS: Number, BegStaID, NextStaID — Length, repeats:
            repeats;

The segment set Number is referenced in the CONVEYORS element. The conveyor path is defined by the beginning station identifier operand, BegStaID, followed by pairs of next station identifiers, NextStaID, and Length distance operands. These form a serially connected network of directed links. The use of the SEGMENTS element is best described by referring to the examples provided below.

```
SEGMENTS:        1, Fab, Repair-50, Assembly-40:
                 2, 4, 5-120, 6-55, 4-30;

SEGMENTS:        1, Enter, WorkStation-325, Paint-120, Pack-120,
                 ExitSystem-250:
                 2, WorkStation, NewPaint-130, Pack-130;
```

The first example has two segment sets: a straight line conveyor and a circular conveyor. The straight line conveyor defined in the first segment set starts at the station named Fab and goes to station Repair, with a distance between these two stations of 50 feet (we assume that all distances are specified as feet). It then continues from station Repair to station Assembly, a distance of 40 feet. Thus, the straight line conveyor starts at station Fab and ends at station Assembly and is 90 feet in total length.

The circular conveyor goes from Station 4 to Station 5, a distance of 120 feet; then to Station 6, a distance of 55 feet; and then back to Station 4, a distance of 30 feet. The total length of this conveyor is 205 feet. From an operational standpoint, it is possible to convey an entity from Station 6 directly to Station 5. The entity would start at Station 6, pass through Station 4 without stopping, and continue on to Station 5, a total distance of 150 feet. It is also possible to convey an entity from a station, around the loop, and back to the same station. The loop is useful if you are sending an entity to a station that has a limited buffer. If an entity arrives at the station and its buffer is full, you can convey the entity around the entire loop and check the buffer a second time. With this type of control, the entity continues to be conveyed around the loop until room becomes available at the destination, at which time it exits the conveyor.

The second example provides the segment sets for our sample flow-line problem. The first segment set defines the path for the conveyor named Main. It starts at station Enter and proceeds to station WorkStation (325 feet), to station Paint (120 feet), to station Pack (120 feet), and to station ExitSystem (250 feet) where it ends. The total length of this conveyor is 815 feet. The path for the OffLoop conveyor is defined in the second segment set. It starts at station WorkStation, goes to station NewPaint (130 feet), and ends at station Pack (130 feet) for a total length of 260 feet. Both of these lengths will be increased by three cells, MaxPerEnt, by SIMAN to allow for exit space at the last station on each conveyor.

It should be noted that the number of cells in any conveyor must be represented by an integer. The exact number of cells per conveyor can be calculated by dividing the total length of any conveyor, as defined in the SEGMENTS element, by the size of its cells, as defined in the CONVEYORS element, and rounding that value up to an integer. The resulting length of the conveyor may be greater than desired. For example, if the cell's size was specified as 5 feet and the total length was calculated to be 46 feet, the result would be 10 cells, or a conveyor which is 50 feet in length. Such a discrepancy may or may not be significant, but you should be aware of the possibility.

6.10 SIMAN Conveyor Variables

Several SIMAN variables can help you with statistical collection and provide you with current information about the status of conveyors. A list of these variables is provided in Figure 6-25.

VARIABLE	DEFINITION
NEC(CnvID) : Number of entities currently being conveyed	
NEA(CnvID) : Number of accumulated entities	
LEC(CnvID) : Total length of entities currently being conveyed	
CLA(CnvID) : Total length of entities currently accumulated	
MLC(CnvID) : Total conveyor length	
ICS(CnvID) : Conveyor status	
VC(CnvID) : Conveyor velocity	

Figure 6-25. SIMAN Conveyor Variables

These variables can be used in the Model Frame and in the Experiment Frame. For example, an entity about to access a conveyor may want to check to see whether the conveyor is currently moving, ICS(CnvID)=1. If a value of 0 is returned, the conveyor is idle; if 2 is returned, it is blocked; and, if 3 is returned, it is inactive. If the conveyor is not moving, an alternative form of transfer can be considered. You can also check to determine the number of entities currently on a conveyor or the amount of space currently occupied as part of a control mechanism that determines when to release more parts to the system.

These same variables can be used to collect statistics. They can be used directly in the DSTATS element to obtain statistics about the average time the conveyor is active or the average amount of occupied space on the conveyor. Examples of using these variables are provided in the next section, which describes the Experiment Frame for our current non-accumulating conveyor model.

6.11 Experiment Frame and Summary for the Non-accumulating Conveyor Example

Figure 6-26 gives the Experiment Frame for our example. This Experiment Frame has several changes from previous examples. The attribute Truck# is no longer needed; attribute Size has replaced it as attribute 3 in the ATTRIBUTES element. Attribute Size will be used to store the number of conveyor cells that each entity requires. The QUEUES element has been modified to include the queues that were added for the conveyor ACCESS blocks. Two additional DSTATS were added to collect statistics on the number of entities on the conveyors. Finally, the CONVEY-ORS and SEGMENTS elements, discussed previously, have been added.

```
BEGIN;
;   MODIFIED FLOW-LINE WITH NON-ACCUMULATING CONVEYORS:
;                           SAMPLE PROBLEM 6.5
PROJECT,        Sample Problem 6.5,SM;
ATTRIBUTES:     TimeIn:
                OpTime:
                Size;
STATIONS:       WorkStation:
                Paint:
                Pack:
                ExitSystem:
                NewPaint:
                Enter;
QUEUES:         WorkStationQ:
                PaintQ:
                PackQ:
                NewPaintQ:
                ConvQ:
                MainQ:
                MainQ2:
                OffLoopQ:
                MainQ3:
                OffLoopQ2:
                MainQ4;
RESOURCES:      Worker:
                Painter:
                Packer:
                NewPainter;
CONVEYORS:      1,Main,1,50,1,A,3,N:
                2,OffLoop,2,50,1,A,3,N;
SEGMENTS:       1,Enter,WorkStation-325,Paint-120,Pack-120,
                    ExitSystem-250:
                2,WorkStation,NewPaint-130,Pack-130;
SEQUENCES:      1,WorkStation & Paint,OpTime=NORMAL(22,4,2) &
                    Pack,OpTime=TRIANGULAR(20,22,26,2) &
                    ExitSystem:
                2,WorkStation & NewPaint,OpTime=NORMAL(49,7,2) &
                    Pack,OpTime=TRIANGULAR(21,23,26,2) &
                    ExitSystem;
TALLIES:        FlowTime;
DSTATS:         NQ(WorkStationQ),WorkStation WIP:
                NR(Worker)*100,Worker Utilization:
                NQ(PaintQ),Paint WIP:
                NR(Painter)*100,Painter Utilization:
                NQ(PackQ),Pack WIP:
                NR(Packer)*100,Packer Utilization:
                NQ(NewPaintQ),NewPaint WIP:
                NR(NewPainter)*100,NewPainter Utilization:
                NEC(Main),Main Conveyor:
                NEC(OffLoop),OffLoop Conveyor;
REPLICATE,1,0,230000,,,35000;
END;
```

Figure 6-26. Experiment Frame for Sample Problem 6.5

Figure 6-27 contains the SIMAN Summary Report for this sample problem. The resulting values are very close to the results obtained from the model by using routes (see sample Problem 6.2, Figure 6-9). The additional information on the conveyors indicates that on the average there is less than one entity on each conveyor. Note that there was a maximum of six entities on the Main conveyor and two on the OffLoop conveyor.

```
Project:   Sample Problem 6.5
Analyst:   SM
Replication ended at time       : 230000.
Statistics were cleared at time : 35000.0
Statistics accumulated for time : 195000.
```

TALLY VARIABLES

Identifier	Average	Variation	Minimum	Maximum	Observations
FlowTime	164.65	.41165	70.094	547.67	6917

DISCRETE-CHANGE VARIABLES

Identifier	Average	Variation	Minimum	Maximum	Final Value
WorkStation WIP	1.8047	1.3208	.00000	18.000	.00000
Worker Utilization	81.446	.47729	.00000	100.00	100.00
Paint WIP	.03437	5.3018	.00000	2.0000	.00000
Painter Utilization	55.654	.89264	.00000	100.00	.00000
Pack WIP	.57388	1.2870	.00000	4.0000	1.0000
Packer Utilization	81.119	.48245	.00000	100.00	100.00
NewPaint WIP	.15766	2.6527	.00000	3.0000	.00000
NewPainter Utilization	50.386	.99232	.00000	100.00	.00000
Main Conveyor	.52870	1.3355	.00000	6.0000	.00000
OffLoop Conveyor	.05354	4.2581	.00000	2.0000	.00000

Figure 6-27. Summary Report for Sample Problem 6.5

6.12 The Modified Flow Line with Finite Buffers and Conveyor Failures

The previous example allows the conveyors to run continuously because we included infinite buffers at each station and did not include conveyor failures. Consider a modification that only allows room for two parts in front of each operation. If a buffer is full (that is, it already contains two parts) and a third part arrives at the station, the conveyor stops until room is available in the buffer so that the part can be removed from the conveyor. Also assume that each conveyor fails, with an exponentially distributed time between failures with a mean of 55 minutes. The time to repair is represented by a normal distribution with a mean of five minutes and standard deviation of one minute.

6.13 The Stopping and Starting of Conveyors: The STOP and START Blocks

The START and STOP blocks, types of Operation blocks, are similar to the HALT and ACTIVATE blocks for transporters. They allow you to STOP or START a conveyor from the Model Frame. The STOP block is slightly different from the HALT block: When an entity passes through the STOP block, it immediately stops the named conveyor, rather than waiting for all entities to clear the conveyor. The syntax for both blocks is given below.

```
START
CnvName,Vel
```

```
STOP
CnvName
```

START: CnvName, Vel;

STOP: CnvName;

In both cases the first operand on the second line segment is the name of the conveyor to be started or stopped. The START block also allows the entry of a new velocity, Vel. An entity arriving at a START block starts the named conveyor and changes its operational status, variable ICS(CnvID), from 0 (inactive) to 1 (active). An entity's passing through a START block with a named conveyor that is already active has no effect. Note that, if a conveyor has been disengaged by a delay after an ACCESS block or by a delay between an entity's arrival at the station and passage through an EXIT block, the START block will not engage the conveyor, but rather will activate the conveyor so that it will move when re-engaged.

An entity's passing through a STOP block causes the operational status of the conveyor to be changed from active to inactive. The only way to activate an inactive conveyor is with a START block. If a conveyor is already inactive, an entity's passing through a STOP block has no effect.

The examples at the left illustrate how we deactivate and activate the conveyor named Main in order to model failures. You should be aware that there is a distinction between engaging-disengaging a conveyor and activating-deactivating a conveyor. The former, which occurs whenever an entity is placed on or removed from the conveyor, is effected by the ACCESS, CONVEY, EXIT, and STATION blocks. The latter occurs when the conveyor is turned on or off with the START and STOP blocks.

6.14 The Model and Experiment Frames for Finite Buffers and Conveyor Failures

The Model Frame listing for our revised problem is shown in Figure 6-28. The conveyor failures are modeled by two separate failure loops at the end of the model. Each loop creates a single entity, which delays for the time between failures, stops the conveyor, and delays for the repair; it is then sent back to repeat the process.

```
BEGIN;
;     MODIFIED FLOW-LINE WITH NON-ACCUMULATING CONVEYORS,
;     FINITE BUFFERS, AND FAILURES: SAMPLE PROBLEM 6.6

;     Parts enter, part type determined, and transfer to workstation

          CREATE:   EXPONENTIAL(28,1):         !Create jobs at staging area
                    MARK(TimeIn);               Mark arrival time
          ASSIGN:   M=Enter;                    Set entry station
          ASSIGN:   NS=DISCRETE(.7,1,1,2,10);   Set part type
          ASSIGN:   Size=NS+1;                  Set part size = 2 or 3

;     get on main conveyor and move to next station in job sequence

Conv      QUEUE,    MainQ;                      Wait for space on conveyor
          ACCESS:   Main,Size;                  Get space on conveyor
          CONVEY:   Main,SEQ;                   Convey to next station

;     Workstation model

          STATION, WorkStation;                 Workstation submodel
          QUEUE,   Buffer1Q;                    Wait for space in buffer 1
          SEIZE:   Buffer1;                     Get space in buffer 1
          EXIT:    Main,Size;                   Get off conveyor
          QUEUE,   WorkStationQ;                WIP at workstation
          SEIZE:   Worker;                      Get worker
          RELEASE: Buffer1;                     Release space in buffer 1
          DELAY:   UNIFORM(21,25,2);            Delay for processing
          RELEASE: Worker;                      Release worker
          BRANCH,  1:                           !Which conveyor?
                   IF,NS.eq.1,MainQ2:           !Main conveyor
                   ELSE,OffLoopQ;               Offloop conveyor

MainQ2    QUEUE,   MainQ2;                      Wait for space on conveyor
          ACCESS:  Main,Size;                   Get space on conveyor
          CONVEY:  Main,SEQ;                    Convey to next station

OffLoopQ  QUEUE,   OffLoopQ;                    Wait for space on conveyor
          ACCESS:  OffLoop,Size;                Get space on conveyor
          CONVEY:  OffLoop,SEQ;                 Convey to next station

;     Paint submodel

          STATION, Paint;                       Paint submodel
          QUEUE,   Buffer2Q;                    Wait for space in buffer 2
          SEIZE:   Buffer2;                     Get space in buffer 2
          EXIT:    Main,Size;                   Get off conveyor
          QUEUE,   PaintQ;                      WIP at paint
          SEIZE:   Painter;                     Get painter
          RELEASE: Buffer2;                     Release space in buffer 2
          DELAY:   OpTime;                      Delay for painting
          RELEASE: Painter;                     Release painter
          QUEUE,   MainQ3;                      Wait for space on conveyor
          ACCESS:  Main,Size;                   Get space on conveyor
          CONVEY:  Main,SEQ;                    Convey to next station

;     Pack submodel

          STATION, Pack;                        Pack submodel
          QUEUE,   Buffer3Q;                    Wait for space in buffer 3
          SEIZE:   Buffer3;                     Get space in buffer 3
          BRANCH,  1:                           !Get off which conveyor?
                   IF,NS.eq.1,OffMain1:         !Get off main conveyor
                   ELSE,OffLoop2;               Get off loop conveyor
OffMain1  EXIT:    Main,Size:NEXT(PackerQ);     Get off main conveyor
OffLoop2  EXIT:    OffLoop,Size:                !Get off loop conveyor
                   NEXT(PackerQ);

PackerQ   QUEUE,   PackQ;                       WIP at packing
          SEIZE:   Packer;                      Get packer
          RELEASE: Buffer3;                     Release space in buffer 3
          DELAY:   OpTime;                      Delay for packing
          RELEASE: Packer;                      Release packer
          QUEUE,   MainQ4;                      Wait for space on conveyor
          ACCESS:  Main,Size;                   Get space on conveyor
          CONVEY:  Main,SEQ;                    Convey to next station
```

```
;    Exit submodel

        STATION, ExitSystem;                     Exit station
        EXIT:    Main,Size;                       Get off conveyor
        TALLY:   FlowTime,INT(TimeIn):            !Tally flowtime
                 DISPOSE;                          Dispose of job

;    Newpaint submodel

        STATION, NewPaint;                        Newpaint submodel
        QUEUE,   Buffer4Q;                        Wait for space in buffer 4
        SEIZE:   Buffer4;                         Get space in buffer 4
        EXIT:    OffLoop,Size;                    Get off conveyor
        QUEUE,   NewPaintQ;                       Wip at newpaint
        SEIZE:   NewPainter;                      Get newpainter
        RELEASE: Buffer4;                         Release space in buffer 4
        DELAY:   OpTime;                          Delay for painting
        RELEASE: NewPainter;                      Release newpainter
        QUEUE,   OffLoopQ2;                       Wait for space on conveyor
        ACCESS:  OffLoop,Size;                    Get space on conveyor
        CONVEY:  OffLoop,SEQ;                     Convey to next station

;    Conveyor failure loops

        CREATE;                                   Create break down entity
FailMain DELAY:  EXPONENTIAL(55,3);               Delay until failure
        STOP:    Main;                            Fail main conveyor
        DELAY:   NORMAL(5,1,4);                   Delay until repaired
        START:   Main:NEXT(FailMain);             Conveyor is repaired
        CREATE;                                   Create break down entity
FailLoop DELAY:  EXPONENTIAL(55,3);               Delay until failure
        STOP:    OffLoop;                         Fail offloop conveyor
        DELAY:   NORMAL(5,1,4);                   Delay until repaired
        START:   OffLoop:NEXT(FailLoop);          Conveyor is repaired
END;
```

Figure 6-28. Model Listing for Sample Problem 6.6

The finite buffers in front of each operation are modeled by representing the buffer space as a resource that must be seized before the entity arriving at that station can be removed or exited from the conveyor. Only after the entity seizes the resource (which means that it is no longer in the finite buffer) is the buffer resource released for another arriving entity. This process effectively blocks the entity from entering the buffer area; the presence of the entity on the conveyor, in turn, disengages the conveyor until the entity can gain entry to the buffer, at which time the conveyor is reengaged. Note that, if the buffer at the WorkStation is full when a new entity arrives, the entire conveyor named Main is disengaged, thereby preventing other entities from accessing this conveyor and preventing the transfer of any parts on other segments of the conveyor.

Only three elements have been changed in the Experiment Frame, and these are shown in Figure 6-29. The resources representing the four additional buffers, each with a capacity of 2, have been added to the RESOURCES element.

```
QUEUES:      WorkStationQ:
             PaintQ:
             PackQ:
             NewPaintQ:
             ConvQ:
             MainQ:
             MainQ2:
             OffLoopQ:
             MainQ3:
             OffLoopQ2:
             MainQ4:
             Buffer1Q:
             Buffer2Q:
             Buffer3Q:
             Buffer4Q;

RESOURCES:   Worker:
             Painter:
             Packer:
             NewPainter:
             Buffer1,2:
             Buffer2,2:
             Buffer3,2:
             Buffer4,2;

DSTATS:      NQ(WorkStationQ),WorkStation WIP:
             NR(Worker)*100.0,Worker Utilization:
             NQ(PaintQ),Paint WIP:
             NR(Painter)*100.0,Painter Utilization:
             NQ(PackQ),Pack WIP:
             NR(Packer)*100.0,Packer Utilization:
             NQ(NewPaintQ),NewPaint WIP:
             NR(NewPainter)*100.0,NewPainter Utilization:
             NEC(Main),Main Conveyor:
             NEC(OffLoop),OffLoop Conveyor:
             ICS(Main).eq.2,Blocked Main:
             ICS(Main).eq.3,Failed Main:
             ICS(OffLoop).eq.2,Blocked OffLoop:
             ICS(OffLoop).eq.3,Failed OffLoop:
             NQ(Buffer1Q),Blocked At WS:
             NQ(Buffer2Q),Blocked At Paint:
             NQ(Buffer3Q),Blocked At Pack:
             NQ(Buffer4Q),Blocked At NewPaint;
```

Figure 6-29. The Changed Elements for Sample Problem 6.6

The QUEUES element has been modified to include the four additional queues used to seize the finite buffer resources. The DSTATS element has been changed to include both the fraction of time that the conveyors are blocked because there is no room for an arriving entity in the finite buffer and the fraction of time that they are inactive because of failures. The last four statistics are based on the time an entity is waiting in the queue preceding the SEIZE block for the buffer resources.

The logic for these statistics can be described as follows: If an entity enters a queue and space is available, it immediately seizes the buffer space and exits the conveyor. If a buffer resource is not currently available, the entity remains in the queue, causing the entire conveyor to become disengaged; disengaging the conveyor, in turn, prevents any other entity from arriving at that STATION-

QUEUE combination or at any other STATION-QUEUE combination served by the same conveyor.

Thus, the statistics provide a way of measuring the fraction of time that the conveyors are disengaged because of a full buffer. The effects are illustrated in the Summary Report shown in Figure 6-30.

```
Project:   Sample Problem 6.6
Analyst:   SM
Simulation run ended at time    :  230000.
Statistics were cleared at time :  35000.0
Statistics accumulated for time:  195000.
```

                          TALLY VARIABLES

Identifier	Average	Variation	Minimum	Maximum	Observations
Flowtime	246.52	.99994	75.031	1988.8	6917

                    DISCRETE-CHANGE VARIABLES

Identifier	Average	Variation	Minimum	Maximum	Final Value
WorkStation WIP	.99932	.89926	.00000	2.0000	.00000
Worker Utilization	81.517	.47617	.00000	100.00	100.00
Paint WIP	.16496	2.8139	.00000	2.0000	.00000
Painter Utilization	55.495	.89552	.00000	100.00	.00000
Pack WIP	.70995	1.1423	.00000	2.0000	1.0000
Packer Utilization	81.070	.48322	.00000	100.00	100.00
NewPaint WIP	.15455	2.6413	.00000	2.0000	.00000
NewPainter Utilization	50.443	.9911.9	.00000	100.00	.00000
Main Conveyor	3.8538	2.2068	.00000	69.000	.00000
OffLoop Conveyor	.10183	3.1389	.00000	2.0000	.00000
Blocked Main	.29327	1.5524	.00000	1.0000	.00000
Failed Main	.08326	3.3183	.00000	1.0000	.00000
Blocked OffLoop	.03280	5.4305	.00000	1.0000	.00000
Failed OffLoop	.08168	3.3531	.00000	1.0000	.00000
Blocked At WS	.22615	1.8498	.00000	1.0000	.00000
Blocked At Paint	.01312	8.6732	.00000	1.0000	.00000
Blocked At Pack	.11410	3.2061	.00000	2.0000	.00000
Blocked At NewPaint	.00131	27.644	.00000	1.0000	.00000

Figure 6-30. Summary Report for Sample Problem 6.6

Comparing the results from this run with that of the run for sample problem 6.5 indicates several differences. First, the flowtime has increased from 164 to 246. This increase is due to the blocking and failures introduced into the system. Note that the resource utilizations have remained the same. Both conveyors are in a failed state about 8 percent of the time. The Main conveyor is blocked about 29 percent of the time, and the maximum number on the Main conveyor has increased from 6 to 69. The last four DSTATS indicate that most of this blockage (over 22 percent) occurs at the WorkStation. The OffLoop conveyor is only blocked about 3 percent of the time. Even though these blockages are rather large, there is no real effect on system output because the system is not highly utilized.

6.15 Accumulating Conveyors
Accumulating conveyors differ from non-accumulating conveyors in that they run continuously regardless of the parts that are placed on or removed from them. If a part is stopped on a powered roller conveyor, slippage occurs, thereby allowing the part to remain stationary. In either case, the part can remain stationary without stopping the conveyor — although it does block any other parts from entering or passing that portion of the conveyor. In effect, if a part is stopped, all other parts

arriving at that point on the conveyor accumulate behind it until the stopped part is removed or transferred to its destination.

When being loaded onto a conveyor, parts are rarely placed directly next to each other. Typically there is a small space left between parts to prevent damage during the loading operation. When the parts accumulate, however, these spaces disappear as each new part is stopped by the part in front of it. In our sample problem, part Type 2 requires three feet of space to load onto the conveyor, but only two feet of space under accumulation conditions. In this case, we have allowed a minimum of one foot of space between parts during the actual transfer. As parts accumulate, they physically reside right next to each other. When the blockage is removed, however, the first part begins its transfer and subsequent accumulated parts behind it wait until space becomes available before they begin their transfer.

The example shown below illustrates this activity. A blockage exists with the first Type 2 part stopped at point A on the accumulating conveyor section, as shown in the first diagram. The parts behind the blockage continue to move until they reach this blocked part. The second diagram shows the first Type 1 part arriving at the blockage and accumulating behind the stopped part, requiring only one foot of space. The third diagram shows all of the parts stopped behind the blockage. At this stage the parts physically reside right next to each other, requiring only one foot for each Type 1 part and two feet for each Type 2 part. When the blockage is removed, the first Type 2 part begins to move, but the next part waits until the required extra foot of space is available, as shown in the fourth diagram. As soon as the preceding parts move on and the extra foot becomes available, the next part begins to move as shown in the fifth diagram. The last diagram illustrates the final spacing as all parts are again moving.

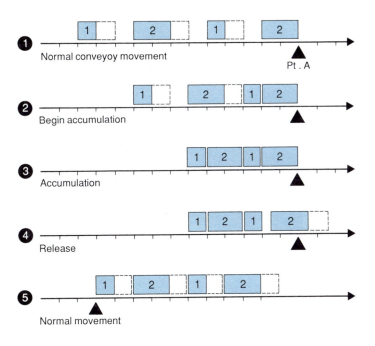

6.16 The Modified Flow Line with Accumulating Conveyors

With the previous non-accumulating conveyor system it was necessary to provide a buffer at each operation to allow the parts to exit the conveyor. Otherwise, the conveyor would disengage, and other entities on the conveyor would not be transferred. As an alternative form of transfer, we can use accumulating conveyors, which provide a buffer on the conveyor at each operation. Let's assume, then, that we replace our belt conveyor system with a powered roller conveyor, which allows accumulation. Because this conveyor provides a buffer, we can eliminate the current buffer in front of each operation and use the conveyor itself as the buffer. Thus, when a part arrives at its destination, it remains on the conveyor until the operation becomes available. When a part stays on the conveyor waiting for the operation, it creates a local blockage (blocking all other parts attempting to reach the station).

Let's further assume that we replace both conveyors, and that the new roller conveyors operate at the same speed as the previous belt conveyors, i.e., 50 feet per minute. The amount of space required to place a part on the conveyor remains the same as before, i.e., two feet of conveyor for each Type 1 part and three feet for each Type 2 part. When the parts accumulate, however, they require one foot less space: one foot for a Type 1 part and two feet for a Type 2 part. The placement of parts on the conveyor requires the additional space for clearance. The rest of the modified flow line remains the same.

6.17 Accumulating Conveyor Constructs

The same constructs for modeling non-accumulating conveyors apply to modeling accumulating conveyors; however, the entities on the conveyor are treated differently because of the accumulation effect. The ACCESS block allocates the required number of cells in the same way as before, except that it does not disengage the conveyor. Instead, if the entity that has just accessed the conveyor is not immediately conveyed, it blocks other entities from passing the accessing entity's station location and initiates an accumulation of entities behind it. The CONVEY block works in the same fashion as before, except that it does not engage the conveyor because the conveyor was never disengaged. If the entity being conveyed had established an accumulation point, conveying the entity removes that blockage.

When an entity arrives at its destination station, it does not disengage the conveyor but provides a blocking point for other arriving entities — unless it is removed with an EXIT block. Subsequent arrivals accumulate behind the entity on the conveyor and occupy the amount of space specified in the Entity Size, EntSize, operand on the CONVEYORS element described in Section 6.8. A blockage, which causes accumulation, only occurs at a station where entities are placed on or removed from the conveyor.

Remember that there are two different values related to entities on accumulating conveyors: the number of cells required (operand Qty on the ACCESS block) and the entity size (operand EntSize on the CONVEYORS element). The number of cells required determines how much conveyor space must be available before the entity can access and be placed on the conveyor. For our Type 2 part, this is three feet. However, if this entity arrives at a point on the conveyor where it is accumulated, it only requires two feet of conveyor (the entity size). Thus, if the entity size is smaller, then whenever accumulation occurs, the amount of conveyor length required will be less than the required space when the entity is moving. For example, five Type 2 parts require 15 feet of conveyor space when moving but only 10 feet when the conveyor is blocked and accumulation occurs.

If the blocking entity is removed or conveyed, the accumulated entities only start to move when the required number of cells becomes available (e.g., three feet for a Type 2 part). If the number of consecutive cells required operand, Qty, specified on the ACCESS block equals the EntSize operand specified on the CONVEYORS element, then all of the accumulated entities start their transfer (or start to move forward) at the same time. Like non-accumulating conveyors, accumulating conveyors can only transfer in a forward direction, i.e., the conveyor can not be reversed.

6.18 Model Frame for the Accumulating Conveyor Example

The Model Frame listing for our new example with accumulating conveyors is shown in Figure 6-31. This model is similar to the Model Frame developed for the non-accumulating example with infinite buffers. The failure loops, which were added to the second non-accumulating model, have been included at the end of the model. The accumulating load size has been assigned to attribute ASize at the same time that the number of required cells is assigned to attribute Size.

```
BEGIN;
;     MODIFIED FLOW LINE WITH ACCUMULATING CONVEYORS
;     AND FAILURES: SAMPLE PROBLEM 6.7
;     Parts enter, part type determined, and transfer to workstation
            CREATE:   EXPONENTIAL(28,1):           !Create jobs at staging area
                      MARK(TimeIn);                 Mark arrival time
            ASSIGN:   M=Enter;                      Set entry station
            ASSIGN:   NS=DISCRETE(.7,1,1,2,10);     Set part type
            ASSIGN:   Size=NS+1;                    Set part size + 2 or 3
            ASSIGN:   ASize=NS;                     Set accumulation size 1 or 2
;     get on main conveyor and move to next station in job sequence
Conv        QUEUE,    MainQ;                        Wait for space on conveyor
            ACCESS:   Main,Size;                    Get space on conveyor
            CONVEY:   Main,SEQ;                      Convey to next station
;     Workstation submodel
            STATION, WorkStation;                   Workstation submodel
            QUEUE,    WorkStationQ;                 WIP at workstation
            SEIZE:    Worker;                       Get worker
            DELAY:    UNIFORM(21,25,2);             Delay for processing
            RELEASE:  Worker;                       Release worker
            BRANCH,   1:                            !Which conveyor?
                      IF,NS.eq.1,Main2:             !Main conveyor
                      ELSE,OffLoopQ;                Offloop conveyor
Main2       CONVEY:   Main,SEQ;                      Convey to next station
OffLoopQ EXIT:        Main,Size;                    Exit main conveyor
            QUEUE,    OffLoopQ;                      Wait for space on conveyor
            ACCESS:   OffLoop,Size;                 Get space on conveyor
            CONVEY:   OffLoop,SEQ;                  Convey to next station
;     Paint submodel
            STATION, Paint;                         Paint submodel
            QUEUE,    PaintQ;                        WIP at paint
            SEIZE:    Painter;                      Get painter
            DELAY:    OpTime;                        Delay for painting
            RELEASE:  Painter;                      Release painter
            CONVEY:   Main,SEQ;                      Convey to next station
;     Pack submodel
            STATION, Pack;                          Pack submodel
            BRANCH,   1:                            !Get off which conveyor?
                      IF,NS.eq.1,Main1:             !Get off main conveyor
                      ELSE,OffLoop2;                Get off loop conveyor
OffLoop2 QUEUE,       MainQ2;                        Wait for space on main conv
            ACCESS:   Main,Size;                    Get space on main
            EXIT:     OffLoop,Size;                 Exit off loop conveyor
Main1       QUEUE,    PackQ;                         WIP at packer
            SEIZE:    Packer;                       Get packer
            DELAY:    OpTime;                        Delay for packing
            RELEASE:  Packer;                       Release packer
            CONVEY:   Main,SEQ;                      Convey to next station
;
            STATION, ExitSystem;                    Exit station
            EXIT:     Main,Size;                    Get off conveyor
            TALLY:    FlowTime,INT(TimeIn):         !Tally flowtime
                      DISPOSE;                      Dispose of job
;     Newpaint submodel
```

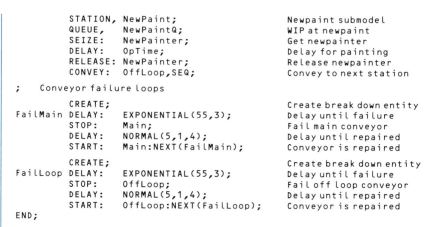

```
              STATION,  NewPaint;                  Newpaint submodel
              QUEUE,    NewPaintQ;                  WIP at newpaint
              SEIZE:    NewPainter;                 Get newpainter
              DELAY:    OpTime;                     Delay for painting
              RELEASE:  NewPainter;                 Release newpainter
              CONVEY:   OffLoop,SEQ;                Convey to next station
;      Conveyor failure loops
              CREATE;                               Create break down entity
   FailMain  DELAY:    EXPONENTIAL(55,3);           Delay until failure
              STOP:     Main;                       Fail main conveyor
              DELAY:    NORMAL(5,1,4);              Delay until repaired
              START:    Main:NEXT(FailMain);        Conveyor is repaired

              CREATE;                               Create break down entity
   FailLoop  DELAY:    EXPONENTIAL(55,3);           Delay until failure
              STOP:     OffLoop;                    Fail off loop conveyor
              DELAY:    NORMAL(5,1,4);              Delay until repaired
              START:    OffLoop:NEXT(FailLoop);     Conveyor is repaired
   END;
```

Figure 6-31. Model Listing Sample Problem 6.7

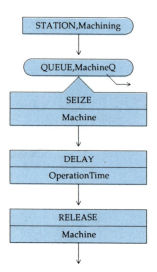

In the original non-accumulating model, the entities arriving at an operation passed through an EXIT block, which removed them from the conveyor; they then entered the queue to wait for the resource at that operation. In our accumulating model, the entities arriving at a station appear to enter the queue directly to wait for the resource. However, if there are other entities already waiting for the resource, the arriving entity will remain on the conveyor until all of the other entities have their operations completed. Note that an entity seizing the operation resource still maintains control of its space on the accumulating conveyor. Only after the resource has been released is the entity conveyed to its next station, or exited from its current conveyor and placed on the other conveyor. This modeling approach is illustrated at the left.

The above logic is required because of the way that accumulating conveyors work. Consider a Type 1 part being conveyed to the WorkStation. Further assume that the WorkStation is currently idle. If the entity, which represents the part, is exited from the conveyor while the WorkStation operation is performed, then another part can arrive at the Workstation and occupy the same space that the departing entity requires in order to get back onto the conveyor and be conveyed to its next operation. There are three ways to avoid this type of deadlock. The first method is employed by our sample problem. The part arriving at the WorkStation is not exited from the conveyor, in effect reserving the conveyor so that, when its operation is completed, the space is not occupied by another part. You can think of this as a part on a pallet arriving at the WorkStation; the part is then removed for the operation, but the pallet remains on the conveyor. This method creates a blocking point on the conveyor at the station. The next entity conveyed to that station does not enter the station because it is blocked by the previous entity, and accumulation starts. During this time, the accumulating conveyor continues to run.

The first method is difficult to employ if an operation has multiple servers because several parts can be accommodated at the same time. A second method requires two stations at each operation: one station for arriving parts and one

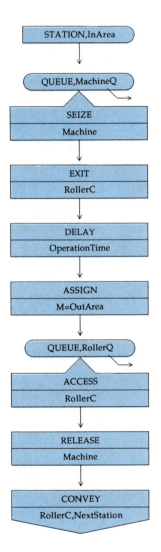

station for departing parts. These two stations must be separated by at least the size of the largest entity that is to use that conveyor. In this case the arriving entity is exited from the conveyor as soon as it has seized the required resource. This approach allows the next entity to arrive at the queue to await the next available resource. An entity that has completed its operation joins a queue where it attempts to access space on the conveyor. Because the arriving parts are stopped upstream of this point, no deadlock occurs. This modeling approach is illustrated on the left. Note that, because the entity departs at a different station, the attribute M must be reset before the RollerC conveyor is accessed.

The last method requires that each link of the conveyor system be modeled as a separate conveyor. Although this method prevents deadlocking, it is rather cumbersome for large conveyor systems with many off and on points.

The method employed for the solution of our sample problem requires including operation rules whenever two different conveyors converge or diverge. For example, when a Type 2 part arrives at the WorkStation, it maintains space on the Main conveyor. When the operation is completed the resource is released, and the entity is directed to label OffLoopQ where it is immediately exited from the Main conveyor. Only then is the OffLoop conveyor accessed, and the entity conveyed to the NewPaint operation. If the NewPaint operation is blocked and the OffLoop conveyor between the WorkStation and NewPaint stations is full, then entities reside in the queue with identifier OffLoopQ until they can access the OffLoop conveyor. This logic assumes an infinite buffer at this location. If this is not the case, then the model should be structured so that the OffLoop conveyor is accessed before the Main conveyor is exited.

Similar assumptions are required when parts arrive at the Pack station. The current model assumes that parts arriving from the Paint operation on the Main conveyor have priority over parts arriving from the NewPaint operation on the OffLoop conveyor. Note that parts arriving from the NewPaint operation (Type 2 parts) must first access the Main conveyor before they are allowed to exit the OffLoop conveyor. The logic of this model only allows the Type 2 parts to access the Main conveyor when the Packer resource is idle because, if the Packer is busy, the part type in that operation has control over the conveyor space required by the entering part.

No additional changes to the Model Frame are needed to convert it from non-accumulating to accumulating conveyors; however, several minor changes are necessary in the Experiment Frame.

6.19 Experiment Frame and Summary Report for the Accumulating Conveyor Example

The Experiment Frame elements requiring changes for this model are shown in Figure 6-32. The ATTRIBUTES element has been modified to include an attribute, named ASize, that defines the entity size for accumulation. The QUEUES element has been expanded to include the additional queues used in the model, and the

RESOURCES element has been modified to remove the Buffer resources, which are not used in this model. The DSTATS element has also been modified. The previous statistics on number in queue prior to each operation have been deleted. These statistics represent the WIP at each station; however, in this model the WIP is maintained on the accumulating conveyors. Thus, several dstats have been added to provide additional statistics on the conveyor's status (ICS), on the number of accumulating entities (NEA), and on the length of the accumulating entities (CLA).

```
ATTRIBUTES:    TimeIn:
               OpTime:
               Size:
               ASize;
QUEUES:        WorkStationQ:
               PaintQ:
               PackQ:
               NewPaintQ:
               MainQ:
               MainQ2:
               OffLoopQ;
RESOURCES:     Worker:
               Painter:
               Packer:
               NewPainter;
CONVEYORS:     1,Main,1,50,1,A,3,A,ASize:
               2,OffLoop,2,50,1,A,3,A,ASize;
DSTATS:        NR(Worker)*100.0,Worker Utilization:
               NR(Painter)*100.0,Painter Utilization:
               NR(Packer)*100.0,Packer Utilization:
               NR(NewPainter)*100.0,NewPainter Utilization:
               NEC(Main),Main Conveyor:
               NEC(OffLoop),OffLoop Conveyor:
               ICS(Main).le.1,Main On:
               ICS(OffLoop).le.1,OffLoop On:
               NEA(Main),Main Accumulated:
               NEA(OffLoop),OffLoop Accumulated:
               CLA(Main),Main A Length:
               CLA(OffLoop),OffLoop A Length;
```

Figure 6-32. The Changed Elements for Sample Problem 6.7

Finally, the CONVEYORS element has been changed. The conveyor has been changed from "N" (for non-accumulating) to "A" (for accumulating), and the attribute ASize has been added as the last operand to define where the accumulating load size can be found. Otherwise, the Experiment Frame remains the same as it was for the original non-accumulating example.

The SIMAN Summary Report is shown in Figure 6-33. As would be expected, the resource utilizations are similar to those from the previous conveyor sample problem. The first two conveyor statistics are the average number of entities being conveyed, not accumulated. These numbers are both relatively small.

```
Project:  Sample Problem 6.7
Analyst:  SM
Replication ended at time     :  980000.
Statistics were cleared at time :  35000.0
Statistics accumulated for time:  945000.
                         TALLY VARIABLES
Identifier           Average  Variation  Minimum  Maximum  Observations
Flowtime             174.96    .49616    71.781   892.81      33641
                    DISCRETE-CHANGE VARIABLES
Identifier           Average  Variation  Minimum  Maximum  Final Value
Worker Utilization    81.902    .47008    .00000   100.00   100.00
Painter Utilization   55.050    .90363    .00000   100.00    .00000
Packer Utilization    81.393    .47814    .00000   100.00   100.00
NewPainter Utilization 51.968   .96139    .00000   100.00   100.00
Main Conveyor          .58207  1.3050     .00000   8.0000    .00000
OffLoop Conveyor       .06040  4.0398     .00000   5.0000    .00000
Main On                .91695   .30095    .00000   1.0000   1.0000
OffLoop On             .91602   .30279    .00000   1.0000   1.0000
Main Accumulated      4.4958    .70978    .00000   28.000   3.0000
OffLoop Accumulated   1.0817    .91927    .00000   7.0000   1.0000
Main A Length         5.5881    .74057    .00000   34.000   4.0000
OffLoop A Length      2.1635    .91927    .00000   14.000   2.0000
```

Figure 6-33. Summary Report for Sample Problem 6.7

The accumulated number and accumulated length statistics indicate that the average accumulation is small. However, the maximum values recorded indicate that there are times when large numbers of parts accumulate.

7. Additional Sample Problems

This chapter first presented the concepts of submodels and stations. Then it introduced the constructs that allow the transfer of entities between stations, initially with unconstrained transfers and sequences. Finally, the material-handling constructs for transporters and conveyors were covered. The following two sample problems provide additional insight as to how many of these constructs can be applied.

The first sample problem illustrates a system in which several different types of material-handling devices are included in the same system. The second problem provides a modeling approach for power-and-free conveyors and illustrates the manipulation of the sequences construct.

7.1 Sample Problem 6.8: A Circuit Board Assembly System

Consider the two-workstation assembly process shown in Figure 6-34. Two different assemblies are produced by this facility. The time between the arrivals of the totes containing the parts for both assemblies is exponentially distributed with a mean of 4.5 minutes. Forty percent of these totes only require a final assembly. The remaining 60 percent require a sub-assembly, followed by the same final assembly as the first part type.

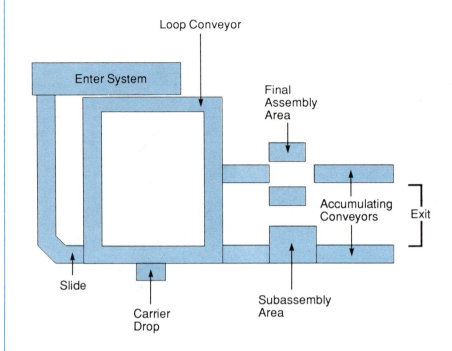

Figure 6-34. Layout of Circuit Board Assembly System

The arriving totes enter a buffer area, or queue, where they wait for access to a gravity slide, which feeds the loop conveyor containing the totes waiting for assembly. Only two totes are allowed on the slide at any time to avoid damage to the circuit boards. The time to traverse the slide follows a normal distribution with a mean of three minutes and a standard deviation of one minute. Once a tote reaches the end of the slide, it waits for space on the non-accumulating loop conveyor, which has space for 30 totes. The loop conveyor has a length of 60 feet and is divided into two-foot spaces, each of which can hold one tote. It travels at a speed of 30 feet per minute. When an open space becomes available at the end of the slide, the loop conveyor is stopped, and the arriving tote is loaded onto the conveyor. This loading process is automatic but requires an operation time that follows a triangular distribution (minimum of 0.1, mode of 0.3, and maximum of 0.5 minute). When the loading operation is completed, the space on the slide is released for any waiting totes, and the loop conveyor is activated.

The totes then travel on the loop conveyor until they reach their required assembly station: final assembly for Type 1 parts and sub-assembly for Type 2 parts. The queue in front of each assembly operations has room for two totes. If the queue is full, the tote continues around the loop conveyor until it can enter the queue. If space is available in the queue, the tote is automatically diverted off the loop conveyor into the queue. The diverting of a tote from the loop conveyor does not cause the conveyor to stop and requires no time.

The final assembly operation has two identical assemblers, and the sub-assembly operation has one assembler. The final assembly operation time is normally distributed with a mean of 8 minutes and a standard deviation of 1.5 minutes for both part types. The sub-assembly operation time is normally distributed with a mean of six minutes and a standard deviation of one minute. Once a part, tote, has finished an operation, it exits the assembly operation and enters an accumulating roller conveyor. Each roller conveyor is 10 feet long, and parts travel at a speed of 25 feet per minute. This arrangement allows 10 totes or parts to await transportation. If the accumulating roller conveyor is full, the assembled parts are not permitted to leave the assembly operation, thereby blocking the operation.

Finished parts or totes at the end of the roller conveyors request transportation from one of two available carriers. The carrier moves to the end of the roller conveyor, picks up the tote, and proceeds to its destination. Carriers are selected according to the shortest-distance rule. Finished parts exiting from the roller conveyor after the final assembly operation are taken to a packing area where their flowtimes are tallied, and they exit the system. Totes exiting from the roller conveyor after the sub-assembly operation (Type 2 parts) are transported back to the loop conveyor where they are placed in a queue to wait until conveyor space is available. The carrier is released as soon as it places the tote in the queue. When space becomes available, the loop conveyor is stopped, and the tote is loaded onto the conveyor (triangular distribution with a minimum of 0.2, a mode of 0.3, and a maximum of 0.6 minute).

The movement of a Type 2 part through the system is as follows: It enters the buffer and then enters the slide to the loop conveyor; it then travels on the loop conveyor to the sub-assembly area; after sub-assembly it is transported by the carrier back to the loop conveyor where it travels to the final assembly area; after final assembly it is transported to the packing area where it exits the system. A Type 1 part enters the system and loop conveyor just like a Type 2 part, but it proceeds directly to the final assembly area and then exits the system.

The exact travel distances for the carrier and the positions of the various stations on the loop conveyor are provided in the Experiment Frame. The model listing for the circuit board assembly system is shown in Figure 6-35.

Entering totes are created by the CREATE block, and the attribute EntryTime is marked for the flowtime tally. The first ASSIGN block determines the part type and sets the sequence type. The arriving tote is then placed in the buffer queue, SlideQ, to seize space on the slide. Having space, it is routed to the end of the slide where it enters STATION LoopInput and waits in QUEUE LoopQueue1 for space on the Loop conveyor. Having accessed the Loop conveyor and delayed for loading, the tote is conveyed, according to its sequence, to the proper assembly area, STATION AssemblyArea or SubAssemArea. When it arrives at the proper station, the number in the queue preceding the operation is checked at the BRANCH block labeled Check. If the queue is full, the tote is conveyed around the Loop back to the same station. If space is available, the tote exits the Loop conveyor and is directed to the proper queue, AssemQueue or SubAssemQueue. At both assembly operations, the entity seizes the Assembler or SubAssembler, delays for the operation, accesses the following accumulating conveyor, releases the assembler, and moves along the conveyor.

At the end of the accumulating conveyors, an entity requests one of the carriers. When a carrier arrives, the entity exits the accumulating conveyor and is transported to station SystemExit or CarrierToLoop, depending on the part type and position in sequence. Totes transported back to the Loop conveyor (Type 2 parts) free the carrier upon arrival, wait for space on the Loop conveyor, are loaded onto the Loop conveyor, and are conveyed to the final assembly area. Finished parts arriving at the SystemExit station delay for unloading, free the carrier, and are tallied and disposed of.

```
BEGIN;

          CREATE:     EXPONENTIAL(4.5,1):
                      MARK(EntryTime);              create the parts
          ASSIGN:     NS=DISC(.40,1,1.0,2):         !assign sequence set #
                      PartType=NS:                  !assign part type
                      M=PartArrivals;               set current station
          QUEUE,      SlideQ;
          SEIZE:      Slide;
          ROUTE:      NORMAL(3,1),SEQ;              carry parts to loop

          STATION,    LoopInput;                    loop input for loader
          QUEUE,      LoopQueue1;                   wait for access to loop
          ACCESS:     Loop,1;                       access 1 cell of loop
          DELAY:      TRIANGULAR(.1,.3,.5),2;       load time
          RELEASE:    Slide;
          CONVEY:     Loop,SEQ;                     convey to process

          STATION,    AssemblyArea:NEXT(Check);     assembly process

          STATION,    SubAssemArea:NEXT(Check);     sub-assembly process
Check     BRANCH,     1:
                        IF,NQ(PartType+2).GT.QueueCapacity(PartType),
                        GoAround:
                        ELSE,Process;
GoAround  CONVEY:     Loop,M;                       convey around on loop
Process   EXIT:       Loop,1;
          BRANCH,     1:
                        IF,IS.eq.2.and.NS.eq.2,GoSubasm:
                        ELSE,GoAsm;

GoAsm     QUEUE,      AssemQueue;
          SEIZE:      Assembler;
          DELAY:      Optime;                       process time
          QUEUE,      AccessAccum1;
          ACCESS:     Accum1,1;                     access 1 cell of accum1
          RELEASE:    Assembler;
          CONVEY:     Accum1,SEQ;                   convey to end of accum1

GoSubasm  QUEUE,      SubassemQueue;
          SEIZE:      Subassembler;
          DELAY:      Optime;                       process time
          QUEUE,      AccessAccum2;
          ACCESS:     Accum2,1;                     access 1 cell of accum2
          RELEASE:    Subassembler;
          CONVEY:     Accum2,SEQ;                   convey to end of accum2
```

```
          STATION,     EndAccum1;                             end of accum1 conveyor
          QUEUE,       Accum1Carrier;                         wait for carrier
          REQUEST,     1,7:Carrier(SDS);
          EXIT:        Accum1,1;
          TRANSPORT:Carrier,SEQ;                              transport to exit

          STATION,     EndAccum2;                             end of accum2 conveyor
          QUEUE,       Accum2Carrier;                         wait for carrier
          REQUEST,     1,8:Carrier(SDS);
          EXIT:        Accum2,1;
          TRANSPORT:Carrier,SEQ;                              transport to loop

          STATION,     CarrierToLoop;                         carrier dropoff at loop
          FREE:        Carrier;
          QUEUE,       LoopQueue2;                            wait for access to loop
          ACCESS:      Loop,1;                                access one cell of loop
          DELAY:       TRIANGULAR(.2,.3,.6),10;               load time
          CONVEY:      Loop,SEQ;                              convey to assembly

          STATION,     SystemExit;
          DELAY:       TRIANGULAR(.2,.3,.6),9;                unload carrier
          FREE:        Carrier;
          TALLY:       3,INT(EntryTime);                      overall flowtime
          TALLY:       PartType,INT(EntryTime):
                       DISPOSE;                               flowtime/part type
END;
```

Figure 6-35. Model Listing for Sample Problem 6.8

The Experiment Frame for this model is shown in Figure 6-36. The ATTRI-BUTES, STATIONS, and QUEUES elements define the corresponding items used in the Model Frame. The RESOURCES element defines the three resources used in the model. Note that the Slide and Assembler resources each have a capacity of 2. The VARIABLES element has been used to define two variables, which are initialized to the number of available positions in front of the assembly operations. This approach allows these capacities to be changed from the Experiment Frame or with the interactive debugger during execution.

```
      BEGIN;

      PROJECT,        Sample Problem 6-8, SM;

      ATTRIBUTES:     Optime:
                      EntryTime:
                      PartType;

      VARIABLES:      QueueCapacity(2),2;

      STATIONS:       PartArrivals:
                      LoopInput:
                      AssemblyArea:
                      SubAssemArea:
                      EndAccum1:
                      EndAccum2:
                      SystemExit:
                      CarrierToLoop;
```

```
QUEUES:           SlideQ:
                  LoopQueue1:
                  AssemQueue:
                  SubassemQueue:
                  AccessAccum1:
                  AccessAccum2:
                  Accum1Carrier:
                  Accum2Carrier:
                  LoopQueue2;

RESOURCES:        Slide,2:
                  Assembler,2:
                  SubAssembler,1;

TRANSPORTERS: 1,Carrier,2,1,60,7-A,7-A;
;                   to EndAccum2
;                     | to SystemExit
;                     |  | to CarrierToLoop
;                     |  |  |

DISTANCES:    1,5-8,  40,  80,160/  !from EndAccum1
                           80,120/  !from EndAccum2
                              200;  !from SystemExit

CONVEYORS:    1,Loop   ,1,30,2,A,1,N:
              2,Accum1,2,25,2,A,1,A,1:
              3,Accum2,3,25,2,A,1,A,1;

SEGMENTS:       1,2,3-30,4-20,8-5,2-5:   !loop
                2,3,5-10:                !accum1
                3,4,6-10;                 accum2

SEQUENCES:1,    LoopInput           &
                AssemblyArea        ,Optime=NORMAL(8,1.5,2) &
                EndAccum1           &
                SystemExit:
          2,    LoopInput           &
                SubAssemArea        ,Optime=NORMAL(6,1,2) &
                EndAccum2           &
                CarrierToLoop       &
                AssemblyArea        ,Optime=NORMAL(8,1.5,2) &
                EndAccum1           &
                SystemExit;

TALLIES:        Type 1 Flowtime:
                Type 2 Flowtime:
                Overall Flowtime;

DSTATS:         NR(Slide)*100/MR(Slide),Slide Util%:
                NR(Assembler)*100/MR(Assembler),Assemble
                  Util%:
                NR(SubAssembler)*100,Subassem Util%:
                NT(Carrier)*100/MR(Carrier),Carrier Util%:
                LC(Loop),Jobs On Loop:
                LC(Accum1),Jobs On Acc1:
                LC(Accum2),Jobs On Acc2:
                NQ(SlideQ),Jobs Wait Enter:
                NQ(LoopQueue1),Slide To Loop:
                NQ(LoopQueue2),Carrier Dropoff;

REPLICATE,      1,0,50000;

END;
```

Figure 6-36. Experiment Listing for Sample Problem 6.8

The CONVEYORS, SEGMENTS, TRANSPORTERS, and DISTANCES elements provide the information on the conveyors and transporters used in the model. Finally, the DSTATS and TALLIES elements provide the requested statistics. A summary of the results is given in Figure 6-37.

```
Project:  Circuit board assembly
Analyst:  SM
Simulation run ended at time:  50000.0
                         TALLY VARIABLES
Identifier          Average  Variation  Minimum  Maximum  Observations
Type 1 Flowtime     43.050    1.2411    10.707   711.48      4381
Type 2 Flowtime     55.028     .51182   22.801   316.05      6634
Overall Flowtime    50.264     .80746   10.707   711.48     11015
                    DISCRETE-CHANGE VARIABLES
Identifier          Average  Variation  Minimum  Maximum  Final Value
Slide Util%         37.422    1.0213     .00000  100.00      100.00
Assemble Util%      88.567     .29223    .00000  100.00      100.00
Subassem Util%      79.828     .50268    .00000  100.00      100.00
Carrier Util%       62.857     .56844    .00000  100.00      100.00
Jobs On Loop         3.2955   1.5008     .00000   30.000       1.0000
Jobs On Acc1          .08816  3.2927     .00000    2.0000      .00000
Jobs On Acc2          .05308  4.2236     .00000    1.0000      .00000
Jobs Wait Enter       .07132  4.7518     .00000    6.0000      .00000
Slide To Loop         .01849  7.8654     .00000    2.0000      .00000
Carrier Dropoff       .00962 10.145      .00000    1.0000      .00000
```

Figure 6-37. Summary Report for Sample Problem 6.8

No attempt will be made to draw conclusions from this model, but several observations will be noted. First, on examining the moving-average plot of the overall flowtime, it is observed that the system entered a steady state almost immediately, even though the time between arrivals is exponential. This observation can be explained by the fact that the loop conveyor serves as a buffer area that absorbs the variability caused by the exponential arrivals. The difference between the two flowtimes, for Type 1 and Type 2 parts, is almost equal to the additional travel and operation time required by Type 2 parts. However, there is an extremely wide range of flowtime values for the Type 1 parts. Note that the loop conveyor reaches its maximum of 30 parts, full capacity. When this occurs, the Type 2 parts trying to access the conveyor after the sub-assembly operation have priority over any other parts because this access is in front of the gravity slide. The large maximum time is probably due to the long wait to access the loop conveyor and to multiple trips on the loop conveyor until space becomes available at the correct time at the final assembly station.

7.2 Sample Problem 6.9: A Power-and-Free Conveyor System

The power-and-free overhead conveyor system illustrated in Figure 6-38 is used for final assembly and inspection of transmissions. The conveyor system has dogs, located every four feet, to catch a carrier. However, a loaded carrier requires five feet, so there must be at least eight feet (two dogs) separating moving carriers. When carriers accumulate because of a blockage, they only require five feet of space. Every carrier in the system always has a transmission. When a carrier arrives at the load/unload station, it is assumed to have an assembled transmission. This transmission is unloaded, and a shell for the next transmission is loaded onto the freed carrier. The time for these load/unload operations follows a triangular distribution with a minimum value of one minute, a mode of two minutes, and a maximum of three minutes.

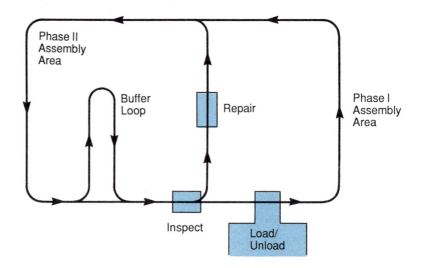

Figure 6-38. Layout for Sample Problem 6.9

The carrier with the loaded shell is then conveyed into the phase I area where the first part of the assembly is performed. It then continues into the phase II area where the assembly is completed. We will assume that there are always workers available and that there is sufficient time as the carrier passes through the assembly area to complete the necessary operations. The carriers never stop in these areas unless a blockage occurs downstream.

After these operations have been completed, the carriers with assembled transmissions arrive at the point where the buffer loop merges with the main conveyor loop. At this point the system checks to see if sufficient space exists for the carrier in the conveyor section between the buffer loop merge point and the inspection area. If room exists, the carrier is sent directly to the inspection area. Otherwise, the carrier is sent into the buffer loop. If a carrier enters the buffer loop, it travels around the loop and attempts to re-access space on the main loop. If there is still no space on the main loop, the carriers accumulate at the merge point until they can re-enter the main conveyor loop. Carriers from the assembly area always have priority over carriers in the buffer loop.

Carriers arriving at the inspection area require the attention of the single inspector. The inspection time is exponentially distributed with a mean of 1.5 minutes. If the transmission passes inspection, it is conveyed to the load/unload operation where the process starts over again. If it fails (30% of the time), the carrier is conveyed to the repair area via the repair loop conveyor. The repair time follows a normal distribution with a mean of 3 minutes and a standard deviation of 0.5 minute. The repaired transmissions are then conveyed along the repair loop to re-enter the main conveyor at the merge point between the phase I and phase II assembly areas. These repaired transmissions receive the operations performed in phase II and then are reinspected.

The conveyor system has a fixed number of carriers, 20, which never changes, and it is assumed that there is an unlimited supply of transmission shells. All conveyors travel at a speed of 60 feet per minute; no failures are assumed. (The conveyor lengths are given when the experiment frame is discussed.)

The approach to be used in developing a model for this problem recognizes that there is a fixed number of carriers in the system and that, whenever an assembled transmission reaches the load/unload area, it is removed and replaced with an empty shell. Thus, the entities in this model represent transmissions in varying stages of assembly, each on a carrier. At the start of the simulation we create 20 carriers and arbitrarily access the conveyor system at the load/unload station. These entities are placed in the system at the start and continue to circulate through the system for the duration of the simulation run.

The system is represented with three SIMAN accumulating conveyors: the Main conveyor (primary conveyor), which starts and ends at the load/unload area; the OverFlow conveyor, which provides the buffer loop before the inspection area; and the RepConv conveyor, which contains the repair area. The specifics of these conveyors can be found in the Experiment Frame listing given in Figure 6-39.

```
BEGIN;
;    POWER-AND-FREE CONVEYOR SYSTEM: SAMPLE PROBLEM 6.9
PROJECT,      POWER AND FREE CONV.,SM;
VARIABLES:    Ncarriers,20:
              InspBuf:
              InspBufMax,08:
              Fail%,.30:
              MaxBuf,15:
              JobsDone;
STATIONS:     Unload:
              Buffer:
              Inspect:
              Repair:
              Merge:
              ReEnter;
ATTRIBUTES:   AccumSize;
RESOURCES:    Inspector:
              RepOp:
              UnlOp;
```

```
QUEUES:      MainQ:
             OverFlowQ:
             InspectQ:
             RepConvQ:
             MainQ2:
             MainQ3:
             RepOpQ:
             UnlOpQ;

SEQUENCES:   1, Buffer & Inspect & Unload;

CONVEYORS:   Main,     1, 60, 4, A, 2, A, 5:
             OverFlow, 2, 60, 4, A, 2, A, 5:
             RepConv,  3, 60, 4, A, 2, A, 5$

SEGMENTS:    1,UnLoad, Merge-170,Buffer-160,ReEnter-8,
                       Inspect-40,Unload-30:
             2,Buffer, ReEnter-85:
             3,Inspect,Repair-40,Merge-40;

TALLIES:     JobsPerHour;

DSTATS:      NEA(OverFlow)+NEC(OverFlow),No. in
               Overflow Area:
             InspBuf,No. in Inspection area:
             NEA(RepConv)+NEC(RepConv),No. in Repair Area:
             NR(Inspector)*100.0,Inspector Utilization:
             NR(RepOp)*100.0,Repair Operator Utilization:
             NR(UnlOp)*100.0,Unload Operator Utilization;

REPLICATE,   1,0,15000,,,100;
END;
```

Figure 6-39. Experiment Listing for Sample Problem 6-9

The Model Listing is given in Figure 6-40. At the start of a run, the first CRE-ATE block in the model creates the 20 carriers and assigns the station and sequence attributes. The carriers then access the Main conveyor and are conveyed to the Buffer station where a decision exists to determine if there is room in front of the inspection station. As these carriers are conveyed, it is assumed that all assembly work is performed in the phase I and II areas between the Unload station and the Buffer station. When a carrier reaches the Buffer station, the BRANCH block determines if the carrier is to be conveyed directly to the Inspection station or to the buffer loop. This decision is based on the current number of carriers in the inspection and buffer areas. A carrier is only directed to the buffer loop if there are 8 carriers in the inspection area and less than 15 carriers in the buffer loop. Other-wise, it is directed to to the inspection area. The number of carriers on the conveyor between the Buffer station and the Inspection station is stored in a user-defined global variable, InspBuf. The inspection buffer size is also stored in a variable, InspBufMax. The value of InspBuf is increased or decreased each time a carrier enters or leaves these sections of the conveyor. The number of carriers in the buffer loop is calculated by using the conveyor variables NEA and NEC.

```
        BEGIN;
;       POWER-AND-FREE CONVEYOR SYSTEM: SAMPLE PROBLEM 6.9
                CREATE,  Ncarriers;                 Create carriers
                ASSIGN:  M=Unload:                  !Set beginning station
                         NS=1;                      !Set sequence set to 1
                QUEUE,   MainQ;                     Wait for space on main
                ACCESS:  Main,2;                    Get space on main
MainConv CONVEY:  Main,SEQ;                          Convey to next station
;       Check if there is room in the inspector buffer

                STATION, Buffer;
                BRANCH,  1:
                         IF, InspBuf.GE.InspBufMax.and.
                           NEA(OverFlow)+NEC(Overflow).LT.
                           MaxBuf,BufRoom:
                         Else,InspArea;             Room in Buffer

InspArea ASSIGN:  InspBuf=InspBuf+1;
                  NEXT(MainConv);

;       Enter overflow area

BufRoom  QUEUE,   OverFlowQ;                        Wait for space on overflow
                  ACCESS:  OverFlow,2;              Get space on overflow
                  EXIT:    Main;                    Exit main conveyor
                  CONVEY:  Overflow,ReEnter;        Convey to reenter station
;       Inspection area

                STATION, Inspect;                   Inspector station
                ASSIGN:  InspBuf=InspBuf-1;
                QUEUE,   InspectQ;                  Wait for inspector
                SEIZE:   Inspector;                 Get inspector
                DELAY:   EXPO(1.5);                 Delay for inspection
                RELEASE: Inspector;                 Release inspector
                BRANCH,  1:
                         WITH,Fail%,Failed:         !Part failed inspection
                         ELSE,MainConv;             !Part passed inspection

;       Move part to repair area

Failed   QUEUE,   RepConvQ;                         Wait for space on repair
                  ACCESS:  RepConv,2;               Get space on repair conv.
                  EXIT:    Main;                     Exit main conveyor
                  CONVEY:  RepConv,Repair;          Convey to Repair station

;       Unload area for completed parts

                STATION, Unload;                    Unload station
                QUEUE,   UnlOpQ;                    Wait for unload operator
                Seize:   UnlOp;                     Get unload operator
                DELAY:   TRIA(1,2,3);               Delay to unload/load
                RELEASE: UnlOp;                     Release unload operator
                ASSIGN:  JobsDone=JobsDone+1;       Count completed jobs
                ASSIGN:  IS=0:NEXT(MainConv);       Reset carrier sequence

;       Repair area

                STATION, Repair;                    Repair station
                QUEUE,   RepOpQ;                    Wait for repair operator
                SEIZE:   RepOp;                     Seize repair operator
                DELAY:   NORM(3,.5);                Delay until repaired
                RELEASE: RepOp;                     Release repair operator
                CONVEY:  RepConv,Merge;             Convey to merge point

;       Merge area. Carriers from repair reenter main carrier flow

                STATION, Merge;                     Merge station
                QUEUE,   MainQ2;                    Wait for space on main
                ACCESS:  Main,2;                    Get space on main
                EXIT:    RepConv;                   Exit repair conveyor
                ASSIGN:  IS=0:NEXT(MainConv);       Reset sequence index
```

```
;      ReEnter area. Carriers enter main flow from overflow buffer
            STATION,  ReEnter;                      ReEnter station
            QUEUE,    MainQ3;                        Wait for space on Main
            ACCESS:   Main,2;                        Get space on main
            ASSIGN:   InspBuf=InspBuf+1;
            EXIT:     OverFlow:
                        NEXT (MainConv);             Exit overflow conveyor
;                                                      move to inspection area
            CREATE;
Del60       DELAY:    60;
            TALLY:    JobsPerHour,JobsDone;
            ASSIGN:   JobsDone=0:
                        NEXT(Del60);
END;
```

Figure 6-40. Model Listing for Sample Problem 6.9

If there is no space available, i.e., InspBuf equals InspBufMax, and space exists on the OverFlow conveyor, the entity is sent to label BufRoom where it is placed on the Overflow conveyor and exited from the Main conveyor. If the Overflow conveyor is full, the entity waits until space is available in the inspection area before being conveyed directly to the Inspection station.

An entity arriving at the Inspection station seizes the inspector and delays by the inspection time. The following BRANCH block determines if the transmission has failed, label Failed, or passed, label MainConv. A failed transmission accesses conveyor RepConv, exits the Main conveyor, and is conveyed to the Repair station. After a transmission is repaired, it is conveyed to the Merge station where the IS attribute is set to 0 so that the CONVEY block at label MainConv can use the SEQ option. It then accesses the Main conveyor, exits the RepConv conveyor, and is conveyed through the phase II assembly area and back to the inspection station. A passed transmission is conveyed directly to the Unload station.

At the Unload station, the carrier seizes resource UnlOp and is delayed for the unload/load operation. The attribute IS is then set to 0, and the carrier is conveyed back through the assembly area. The Unload station also increases the JobsDone variable. This variable is then tallied every hour in a separate entity loop at the end of the model, thereby providing a measure of the throughput per hour.

The carriers are not exited from their respective conveyors during the load/ unload, inspection, or repair operations. Also note that, when a carrier attempts to re-enter the Main conveyor from the buffer loop or repair area, the priority for conveyor space is always given to any carriers already on the Main conveyor.

DSTATS are kept on the number of carriers in the inspection area, in the repair area, and in the overflow loop. Utilization statistics on the inspector, unloader, and repairer are also provided. The resulting Summary Report is given in Figure 6-41.

```
Project:  POWER AND FREE CONV.
Analyst:  SM
Replication ended at time      :  15000.0
Statistics were cleared at time :  100.0
Statistics accumulated for time:  14900.0
```

```
                              TALLY VARIABLES
Identifier               Average   Variation  Minimum  Maximum  Observations
JobsPerHour               24.863    .11746     17.000   29.000      249

                         DISCRETE-CHANGE VARIABLES
Identifier               Average   Variation  Minimum  Maximum  Final Value
No.in Overflow Area       4.8561    .45635      .00000   11.000   8.0000
No.in Inspection area     7.4531    .81885E-01  3.0000   8.0000   7.0000
No.in Repair Area          .99655  1.0546       .00000   9.0000   1.0000
Inspector Utilization    86.379    .39710       .00000  100.00   100.00
Repair Operator Utiliz   49.895   1.0021        .00000  100.00   100.00
Unload Operator Utiliz   82.877    .45454       .00000  100.00    .00000
```

Figure 6-41. Summary Report for Sample Problem 6.9

The results indicate an average throughput of 24.863 transmissions per hour, with the maximum being 29 per hour. Because the unload/load time has an average of two minutes and because a small amount of time is required to advance the carrier in position, the maximum of 29 per hour is to be expected. Interestingly, the utilization of the inspector (mean operation time of 1.5 minutes) is greater than the unload/load operation. This result is due to the high percentage of transmissions that fail the inspection and must then be repaired and reinspected before there can be counted as completed jobs. The bottleneck in this system is not completely obvious. Further experimentation would show that additional carriers do not increase the throughput. The actual bottleneck is caused by carriers backing up behind the unload/load position and preventing the carriers from leaving the inspection area. The throughput could be increased by extending the length of the main conveyor between the inspection area and the unload/load operation.

Exercise 6.1

Parts arrive to a three-station serial assembly system according to a uniform distribution with a minimum of 5 and a maximum of 15 minutes. The parts are processed at each of the three stations and are inspected at the last two stations. The combined time follows a triangular distribution with values in minutes shown below.

	Minimum	Mode	Maximum
Station1	6	9	12
Station2	5	8	11
Station3	5	7	10

If a part fails inspection, it is sent backwards to repeat at least the present operation. The percentage of parts that backtrack and the station that they repeat are given in the following table.

From (end of)	To (beginning of)	Percentage
Station2	Station2	5%
Station3	Station3	5%
Station2	Station1	5%
Station3	Station1	5%

Parts that backtrack have their rework times taken from the same triangular distributions. Use SEQUENCES to model this system. Report on the flowtime, queue sizes, and machine utilizations for a simulation run of 30,000 time units.

Exercise 6.2

A three-machine shop processes heated metal parts. Three different parts are produced by this operation with the following routes.

Type	Percentage	Machine	Mean	Standard Deviation
1	30%	1	6	1
		2	10	2
		3	10	2
2	45%	2	9	2
		3	5	1
		1	4	1
3	25%	1	12	2
		3	7	1
		2	5	2
		3	4	1

Parts arrive according to an exponential distribution with a mean of seven minutes, and all operation times follow a normal distribution. All transfer times are exponentially distributed with a mean of two minutes. Because parts must remain heated during the entire production process, the buffer space in front of each machine is limited to three parts. If a part arrives to a full buffer, it is placed in an oven located right next to each buffer. Each oven can hold five parts and, if the oven is full, parts are balked to an overload area where they are counted by machine center number and exited from the system. If a part is placed in an oven, it remains there for one hour and then tries again to enter the buffer. There is no limit to the number of times that a part can be placed in an oven.

a. Run the simulation for 5,000 time units and keep statistics on the number in each buffer and oven and on the utilization at each machine. Also record the part flowtime and the number of parts balked from each oven.

b. Use the OUTPUT processrer to determine the approiate truncation point and batch size for developing a confidence interval on flowtime.

c. Develop a .95 confidence interval on flowtime using ten batches.

Exercise 6.3

Engine blocks arrive at the end of a finishing system according to a normal distribution with a mean of five minutes and a standard deviation of two minutes. A forklift truck is requested to take the engine block to storage. However, the forklift truck needs to get a pallet before it can pick up the engine block. The storage area also serves as a staging area for the forklift trucks. Upon receiving a request, an available forklift travels to the pallet area. If there is an available pallet, the forklift loads the pallet (one minute) and travels to the requesting block. The engine block is loaded onto the pallet (three minutes) and moved to the storage area where the forklift is freed. If no pallets are available, the forklift travels to the pallet storage and loads 10 pallets (two minutes) and travels back to the pallet area. It then unloads nine pallets (two minutes) and continues to the requesting block.

Assume that there are 15 pallets in the pallet area at the start and simulate this system for 10,000 minutes. Keep statistics on the flowtime of the engine blocks from arrival to storage, on the waiting blocks, on forklift utilization, and on the number of pallets in the pallet area. Forklifts travel at a speed of 75 feet per minute, and the travel distances are as follows:

From	To	Distance (feet)
Finish Area	Pallet Area	200
Finish Area	Block Storage	250
Pallet Area	Pallet Storage	1500
Pallet Area	Block Storage	150

a. Simulate the system with five forklift trucks.

b. Increase the number of forklift trucks to six and evaluate the results to determine if there is a significant change in the number of waiting blocks.

c. Decrease the number of forklift trucks to four and evaluate the results to determine if there is a significant change in the number of waiting blocks.

Exercise 6.4

A three-department serial transformer assembly process runs 24 hours per day and uses battery-driven forklift trucks for material handling. Forklifts must have their batteries recharged once every 24 hours; the charging time is four hours. Battery charging is evenly staggered throughout the day. Departments 1 and 2 have 9 operators, and department 3 has 10 operators, each capable of working on a single transformer. The forklift trucks transport the transformers from receiving to the first station, from the first department to the input buffer of the second department, from the second department to the input buffer of the third department, and then to the system exit.

Transformers arrive to the system input according to a triangular distribution with a minimum of 0.6, a mode of 1.0, and a maximum of 1.5 minutes. Cycle times (in minutes) for the serial stations are normally distributed with the values given below:

	Mean	Standad Deviation
station1	8.9	2
station2	9	2.7
station3	10	3

Distances for this system are as follows:

From	To	Distance (feet)
receiving	dept1	75
dept1	dept2	40
dept2	dept3	40
dept3	shipping	75

Assume that the distance from receiving to shipping is in a straight line.

a. Simulate the system with four forklift trucks for a three-day period. The forklift trucks travel at 175 feet per minute. Report on forklift utilization, buffer levels, total inventory in the system, transformer flowtime, and the number of transformers awaiting transport.

b. Concerned about the level of inventory and the amount of floor space the transformers are taking up, the plant superintendent suggests imposing limits on the buffers between the departments. To maintain control of this inventory, he will replace forklift trucks with accumulating conveyors. The conveyors connecting departments 1 and 2 and departments 2 and 3 are 30 feet long and travel at 40 feet per minute. The receiving and shipping conveyors are 60 feet long and travel at 40 feet per minute. A transformer needs five feet of conveyor space, but when accumulated it takes up four feet of space. If an operator is not available in the department following the conveyor, the transformer must remain on the conveyor. Simulate this system reporting the same statistics as above. Also track the number entities conveyed and accumulated on the first three conveyors.

Exercise 6.5

Modify the restaurant problem (Sample Problem 3.5 from Chapter 3) to include waiters. After a table for the appropriate party size becomes available, a waiter picks up the customers from the waiting area and escorts them to the dining area of the restaurant. Upon arriving at the dining area, the waiter takes the food order (20 percent of the service time). The waiter then delivers the food order to the kitchen and returns to the waiting area. When the order is ready (80 percent of the service time), the same waiter is requested to take the food to the dining area. After delivering the food to the customers, the waiter remains in the dining area until another request is made. When the customers finish their meals, they make their way to the cashier and pay on their way out.

Assume that the cashier and the waiting area are in the same location. Travel distances between the areas are as follows:

From	To	Distance (feet)
waiting area	dining area	100
waiting area	kitchen	100
dining area	kitchen	150

The waiter travels at 100 feet per minute.

a. Simulate the system once with three waiters and compare the results with those from Sample Problem 3.5.

b. Simulate the system to determine the maximum number of waiters that this restaurant would ever require.

Exercise 6.6

(Modified from Gordon, 1975) Ten barges are to be used to form a canal transportation system. The barges are to be loaded by one of two cranes at the lower end of the canal and unloaded by one of two cranes at the upper end. Travel on the canal is divided lower and upper legs, which are separated by a lock that can only raise or lower one barge at a time. Loaded barges have priority over empty barges. The barges move in a circuit on the system.

What is the average number of loads per day that this system is capable of delivering? Run the simulation for 1,100 hours, clearing statistics after 100 hours. Assume that all processing times are triangularly distributed with the following parameters.

Canal Transportation System
Process times in hours

	Minimum	Mode	Maximum
Loading time	2.00	2.25	3.00
Unloading time	1.50	2.25	2.50
Lock time	0.40	0.50	0.6
Lower leg trip time			
Up	2.00	2.50	3.00
Down	1.50	1.75	2.00
Upper leg trip time			
Up	1.00	1.25	1.50
Down	0.50	0.75	1.00

Exercise 6.7

A circular conveyor system consists of two non-accumulating conveyor sections. Unassembled parts arrive at the start of the first section according to an exponential distribution with a mean of 14 minutes. These parts are conveyed 10 feet to the first assembly operation and are removed from the conveyor. There is a single assembler at this station, and the operation time is normally distributed with a mean of 13 and a standard deviation of 3 minutes. Parts are then placed back on the conveyor (5 feet ahead of the point where they were removed) and are conveyed 15 feet to the second operation. The second operation is similar to the first but requires a constant time of 13 minutes. The completed part is then placed back on the conveyor (5 feet from the point where it was removed) and is conveyed 10 feet to the end of the first conveyor section.

When parts reach the end of this section, they are transferred to the second conveyor, conveyed 10 feet, and removed from the conveyor for an inspection operation. Inspection time is normally distributed with a mean of eight minutes and a standard deviation of 1 minute. Parts passing inspection (95%) are removed from the system. Parts failing inspection (5%) are torn down by the inspector, placed back on the conveyor (5 feet from the point where they were removed), and conveyed 10 feet to where the end of the second conveyor meets the beginning of the first conveyor. The parts are then sent back through the system. The teardown time is normally distributed with a mean of 25 minutes and a standard deviation of 4 minutes. Parts that have been torn down have preference over new arrivals in accessing the first conveyor.

Both conveyors run at a speed of 10 feet per minute, and an assembly requires 2 feet of conveyor space. How long will it take to produce 500 completed assemblies? Report on the time worked for each operation and the fraction of time that each operation was blocked. Keep statistics on the number of arrivals waiting for access to the conveyor, the number in the system, and the part flowtime from when it enters the system until it exits the system. Also count the number of assemblies that failed inspection.

Exercise 6.8

Take the system described in Exercise 7. Allow for accumulation on the conveyor.

Exercise 6.9

Take the system described in Exercise 8 and require that each arriving assembly be placed on a carrier. There are 10 permanent carriers on the conveyor loop. Assume that the carriers continuously circulate along the conveyor and that, if a carrier is empty, it will have a zero operation time. (Hints: Model the pallets as entities and use an attribute to indicate the status of the pallet (full/empty). Model the number of parts waiting to enter the system as a global variable that is decreased when an empty carrier arrives at the load point.)

Exercise 6.10

An aggregate level capacity analysis is to be performed on a new warehouse. The warehouse is serviced by one crane. Arriving parts are placed on a conveyor system (40 feet in length, 30 feet per minute, 3 feet per part) and must gain access to the crane before they can exit the conveyor. Only the last 10 feet of this conveyor system is accumulating. The crane must also service shipping orders, which have priority over arriving transformers. For a shipping order, the crane retrieves a part from the warehouse and places it onto a second non-accumulating conveyor (50 feet in length, 30 feet per minute, 3 feet per part). At the end of the non-accumulating conveyor three operators are available to package the parts; after being packaged, the parts exit the system.

Incoming parts arrive 24 hours per day according to a uniform distribution (minimum of 9 and maximum of 15 minutes). The average time that a crane takes to store or retrieve a part from the warehouse follows a triangular distribution (minimum of two, mode of three, and maximum of five minutes.) Shipping orders are released only during seven hours of each day at a constant rate of once every four minutes. The packing time for an operator is normally distributed with a mean of 6 minutes and standard deviation of 1.5 minutes. Operators are only present during the first shift, but they stay until all shipping orders are processed.

Simulate the system for five days. Preload the warehouse with 75 parts at the start of the simulation. Report on the average inventory in the entire system and the warehouse. Also report on the length of occupied space for each conveyor and on crane utilization. The packaging operators are there only for the first eight hours in a day; report their utilization based on these eight hours.

(Hints: Keep track of the parts in the warehouse through a global variable, not through entities. Model the shipping orders as parts in need of the crane.)

GORDON, GEOFFREY (1975), The Application of GPSS V to Discrete Systems Simulation, Prentice-Hall, Englewood Cliffs, NJ.

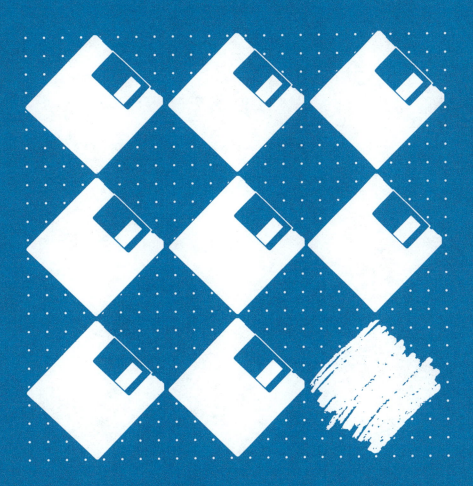

CHAPTER 7

CHAPTER 7

Animating the Simulation by Using Cinema

Computer animation is becoming an increasingly important tool in the application of simulation modeling to real-world systems. Animation brings a simulation model to life by generating a moving picture of model operation. With animation you see the model execute; you see the entities as they wait in queues, occupy resources, travel between stations, etc. This dynamic portrayal of model execution can provide valuable insights into model behavior, insights not easily obtained by examining statistical outputs.

SIMAN's Cinema animation system provides integrated real-time animation capability, allowing you to construct a detailed graphical representation of the system being modeled. This representation changes during execution to reflect the movement of entities through the model and the corresponding changes in the state of the system.

As with simulation itself, it is easy to abuse the animation tool by trying to draw conclusions about the system that overstate those warranted by the animation. Animation should not be viewed as an alternative to the analysis methods discussed in Chapter 5, but rather as an adjunct to those methods.

We begin this chapter with brief discussions of the primary benefits of simulation animation: verifying and validating the model, providing insights into dynamic interactions within the model, and presenting the model result.

1.1 Model Verification

As discussed in Chapter 4, model verification is the process of determining that the simulation program executes as intended. This process does not ensure that the model appropriately represents the real system; it only ensures that the model is free of errors.

As noted in our discussion of model verification, many different types of logical errors can mistakenly be introduced during model development. Some of the more common mistakes include forgetting to initialize or overwriting variables and failing to release resources after completing an operation. These errors can take substantial time to isolate and fix; worse yet, they can remain undetected in the model and lead to incorrect conclusions about system performance. In the latter case the simulation may lead to our making poor — and very costly — decisions.

Without a doubt, animation is the single most effective way to attack the problem of verifying a model's operation. An animation can immediately expose most errors in logic. For example, while watching an animation, you may observe that an entity retains control of a resource long after it has departed the station. Such direct observation of errors in model execution speeds the debugging process and, even more important, it decreases the likelihood of undetected errors.

1.2 Model Validation

Model validation is the process of determining that a model is a sufficiently adequate approximation of the real system so that it can effectively answer a specific set of questions about that system's operation. As discussed in Chapter 4, it is important to remember that validation is always tied to the objectives of the simulation study. A model that works reasonably well for comparing systems may work very poorly for predicting a specific quantity, e.g., the production rate.

Because animation allows us to view model operation, we can see the impact and the interaction of the simplifications made in the modeling phase. Often a simplification that seems reasonable during the abstraction and modeling phase becomes inappropriate when seen in a graphical animation.

Animation also allows us to communicate model operation to individuals (e.g., clients) who know the system, but who know little about modeling. In this way we — who are usually not authorities on the real system's operation — can benefit from the expert's understanding of the system without having to spend a great deal of time describing the details about how processes have been modeled. Any system experts, who may have provided information about how the system operates, can later validate that their information was modeled correctly and interpreted correctly.

Because animation tends to push us in the direction of trying to mimic reality, it can sometimes lead to overly complex models. Such "over-modeling" not only increases the time required to develop a simulation model but also introduces superfluous detail, which increases the likelihood of errors in critical logic. It is easy to get caught up in making the animation look real and to forget that much of the imposed realism may not affect the decisions made from the model — especially when we are comparing systems and can often achieve valid results with relatively simple models.

1.3 Dynamic Interactions

In the previous chapter we discussed statistical and graphical methods for interpreting the simulation results. We stressed the importance of statistics in prop- erly interpreting results and the danger of drawing conclusions based on a single run. Although animation cannot replace statistical analysis, it can augment a formal statistical analysis and provide additional insights into the system as we analyze the simulation.

Animation's main contribution to our understanding of the system's operation is the insight that it provides about interactions among system components. Whereas the statistical methods discussed in the last chapter are limited to estimating or comparing performance, animation can often show which processes are interacting to limit that performance. Thus animation often leads to proposed improvements, which are then tested in the model before being made in the real system. These improvements are frequently not obvious from statistical analyses or graphical plots of variables; they only become obvious when "seen" through animation.

1.4 Presentation of Model Results

Ultimately a simulation project's success is measured by its impact on the design or operation of the real system. Those making decisions about the real system must therefore understand and use model results if the simulation study is to have its desired effect. Hence, an important part of any simulation project is the presentation of the model and its results to decision makers.

As noted by Johnson and Poorte [1988]: "Since the overall objective of any modeling effort is to provide information to the decision maker, it is critical that the information be credible. The decision maker must decide to accept or reject the modeler's claims concerning information derived from the model. This acceptance is often based on the modeler's presentation. Obviously, effective communication is directly linked to credibility. Animation provides effective communication often necessary to sell the proposed solution." Animation not only helps to sell the usefulness of a particular modeling project, but it also helps to sell the simulation approach in general.

Those of us initially attracted to animation because of its presentation advantages are surprised to learn of the additional benefits it offers in verification, in validation, and in understanding dynamic system interactions. Although animation is indeed a convincing tool for presentation of model results, it would be tragic to limit it to this use.

2. Animation's Limitations in Interpreting Model Results

The problems with animation arise when it is used as the primary method for interpreting the results of a simulation, rather than as an adjunct to statistical analysis.

2.1 The Small-Sample Problem

When a simulation model is animated, the execution speed for the simulation is usually slowed by several orders of magnitude in order to make the dynamic action on the viewing screen comprehensible to the viewer. As a result, a simulation run that normally requires only two minutes to process a thousand jobs through the system may last for a full day when animated. Because an animation is typically viewed for a far shorter time, the system's response during the animation corresponds to a relatively small sample size.

As discussed in Chapter 4, it is dangerous to attempt to draw conclusions about a random process based on a small sample. Because the fluctuations in the real system's response occur over time, the simulated operation viewed during a three- or four-hour animation session may not typify real-system behavior. In the case of non-terminating system models, the system's response may be in the transient phase during the entire animation.

2.2 Trends Over Time

Although an animation is very effective at showing the simultaneous interaction of many processes, it is less effective at showing a specific variable's trend over time. For example, if we want to understand how the length of a specific queue varies over time, watching a lengthy animation of the system is not the best option. A simple plot of the variable over time would convey this information much better.

During animation we are seeing a system snapshot involving many variables viewed at the same instant in time. We need this snapshot to study the interactions among the variables. But, to understand trends over time, we must compare the current state of a variable being displayed against our recollection of the variable's state over time. We have trouble doing this without a graphical portrayal of the system's state over time as provided by traditional graphics, e.g., plots and bar charts.

When trends over time are important, it is useful to include conventional graphics as part of the animation display for important variables. Together these two media allow the viewer to discern the interactions between variables and the behavior of specific variables over time.

3. Overview of Cinema

A Cinema animation is a dynamic display of graphical objects that change position, shape, or color on a static background. The changes correspond to alterations in state of a concurrently executing SIMAN model. The graphical objects may represent the state of the system's various physical components, or they may communicate the value of a system variable or statistical measure.

Cinema is designed to make animation an optional part of the simulation project. The Cinema animation can be developed concurrently with the SIMAN model, or it can be developed after the model is completed. Because the definition of the system's graphical representation is separate from its logical representation, a SIMAN model generally does not have to be modified to run with or without the animation. The same model that generates the results for a detailed statistical analysis by making long replications on a mainframe computer can be used on a personal computer or workstation to drive a Cinema animation. There are no special animation blocks included in SIMAN.

We can animate any portion of the entire model. For example, we can separately animate a facility's shipping/receiving, assembly, and inspection areas, and all can be driven by a single model of the entire facility. Or, for debugging purposes, we can animate one small portion of a large model to observe only that part of the system. We can also have several different animations of the same system, each showing various levels of detail or alternative presentations of the same information. For example, we may begin with a very simple animation for debugging purposes and then later replace it with a highly detailed animation for presentation to management.

A Cinema animation can be added to an existing SIMAN model with minimal effort. Developing the Cinema animation is essentially a drawing task requiring no programming or modeling skills. You must, however, be familiar with the model and know which identifiers were assigned to the queues, resources, etc. to be animated by Cinema. You interact with Cinema by using a mouse to make selections from menus. The system incorporates on-line help.

3.1 The Animation Layout and its Relationship to the Model

You need two files to run a Cinema-animated simulation: a SIMAN program file and a Cinema *layout* file. The program file is a regular SIMAN program that describes the real system's process flow, logic, and parameters. The layout file contains the graphical images that will be viewed during the simulation execution. You typically construct the layout file by using the menu-driven Cinema program; no programming is needed. Because there are no animation-specific blocks, there are no modeling changes required to add animation to an existing model.

To execute a Cinema animation, run the CSIMAN program in place of the normal SIMAN program. The CSIMAN program reads a SIMAN program file and a Cinema layout file, links these two files together, and executes the simulation under the control of the user. CSIMAN, an enhanced version of SIMAN, contains the extra logic necessary to animate the simulation during its execution.

The layout file contains two types of graphical objects: *static* objects and *dynamic* objects. The static objects of the layout do not change during simulation execution; they are typically used to represent the physical structure or background environment in which the simulated system exists. For example, in an animation of a factory the static objects may consist of lines, boxes, circles, etc. depicting the facility's walls, aisle markings, storage bins, and general fixtures. Hence, static objects include anything that helps to represent the scene pictorially but that does not need to change during the simulation. In contrast, the dynamic objects change shape, color, or position during simulation. For example, work-pieces, workers, machines, and transporters are represented as dynamic objects within a layout. Dynamic objects also include the changing digital and graphical representation of the values of system variables and summary statistics.

An example of a Cinema animation layout is shown in Figure 7-1 for Sample Problem 6.8 involving a circuit board assembly system, which we presented at the end of Chapter 6. The layout depicts the flow of two different assemblies through two separate workstations. The static objects in this layout include the background sketch of the facility, the part type legend, and the text used to label the objects within the layout. The dynamic objects include the entities, transporters, conveyors, system clocks, bar charts, and numerical values displayed on the layout.

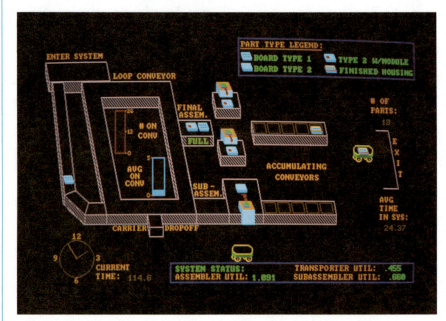

Figure 7-1. Cinema Layout for the Circuit Board Assembly System

We refer to this sample animation layout throughout this chapter as a device for illustrating the Cinema animation concepts presented. At the end of this chapter we include several additional layouts to illustrate the generality of these constructs.

3.2 The Static Component

The static component of the layout is constructed by using a set of elementary, computer-aided drawing functions such as line, box, bar, circle, and arc. You use the mouse to choose functions from the Cinema menus and to set the drawing function's current attributes, e.g., color, width, style, and line orientation. The basic functions are drawn in *rubberband* mode, which allows you to view an object's size and orientation before actually adding it to the layout. For example, a box is drawn by using the mouse to position the cursor on a screen location that represents one corner of the box before pressing a button on the mouse. You then see the box expand and contract as the cursor is moved to locate the opposite corner of the box. After positioning the opposite corner, you press the mouse button again to fix box size and to add the box to the layout.

You can add text to the static background in various fonts, sizes, colors, and orientations — all of which you select from menus. Closed objects such as polygons and circles can be filled with solids or patterns. Static objects on the screen can be moved or copied to other areas within a layout by using the *move* and *copy* functions. These same objects can be moved between layouts by using the *cut* and *paste* functions.

A flexible snap grid coordinate system allows accurate positioning of objects in the layout. You can easily adjust the horizontal and vertical spacing of the snap grid to accommodate positioning requirements.

Cinema also provides a CAD import facility, which allows you to read-in a static background that was drawn with a CAD system such as AutoCAD. This capability is particularly useful when a CAD drawing of the facility already exists.

In our sample layout, the facility background was drawn by using the line and box drawing functions in Cinema. The legend and component labeling were added by using the text functions.

3.3 The Dynamic Component

The dynamic component of the animation layout comprises objects that change position, shape, or color during model execution. Dynamic objects are used to depict the movement of entities across the screen, to display the changing value of a variable, and so forth.

Symbol Libraries

The primary means of representing change of position or shape in Cinema is the use of symbols that you draw and then store in libraries for later use. Symbols are drawn to look like the real-system objects that they are intended to represent. The Libraries section of Cinema contains all of the functions needed to build and maintain your symbol libraries. These include functions for adding, editing, and deleting symbols.

Symbols are used for a variety of purposes in Cinema. For example, during animation the entities that move through the system and the resources that change state are represented by symbols: the entity symbol moves across the screen to represent the movement of the entity in the model; the resource symbol changes shape in the layout to represent its changing state.

Many of the dynamic objects included in a layout are *passive*, i.e., they do not directly change position, shape, or color. Their purpose is to define points called *display points*, which are used for locating symbols. During the execution of the model, symbols move onto and off of these display points, thereby creating the dynamic behavior associated with these objects. For example, later in this chapter we discuss a Cinema object called a queue, which is a passive object used to represent a queue in the SIMAN model. This object defines display points where the symbols for the entities residing in the queue are displayed on the screen. When the first entity symbol in the queue is removed, the remaining symbols move forward.

Passive objects are generally only visible in the layout when they are being added or edited, and are invisible during the execution of the animation.

Some symbols may themselves have display points, which are used to display other symbols. For example, the symbol representing a busy machine may have a display point defining the location at which the entity symbol, to which the machine is currently allocated, is to be displayed. Using this feature, you can display the symbol representing the workpiece on the symbol representing the processing machine.

Each symbol has an associated *reference point*, which defines its alignment with invisible display points on the layout, such as queues and routes. The reference point is always placed exactly on top of the destination display point on the screen.

Entity Symbols

Entity symbols graphically represent the entities that move through the system. Entities are depicted as symbols that can travel along paths, wait in queues, seize resources, etc. The entity symbol can be a sketch of a workpiece or a partially assembled car. During the execution of the simulation, Cinema automatically moves the entity symbol across the screen.

Cinema requires that you specify an animation attribute, which is an expression involving one or more attributes of the entity. This value controls which symbol, if any, is displayed on the screen during the animation to represent the entity. To change the animation attribute's value, use the ASSIGN block in the model. Consider, for example, a simulation of an automotive assembly plant in which the animation attribute is specified as an attribute of the entities representing the cars. The animation attribute for an entity arriving at an assembly station may have a value of 1, denoting Symbol 1, which corresponds to an entity symbol of a car without doors. After leaving the workstation, the animation attribute can be reset at an ASSIGN block in the model to a value of 2, which corresponds to an entity symbol of a car with doors.

Any association between the animation attribute's assigned values and its corresponding symbol is made by constructing an *entity symbol list* for the layout. Each layout has only one entity symbol list, which you construct and maintain by using the mouse and menus to move entity symbols from one or more entity libraries into the entity symbol list. The entity symbol list is a two-column table with values for the animation attribute in the left column, and the corresponding symbol in the right column.

When you assign an animation attribute during the execution of the model, SIMAN checks to determine whether the new value for the attribute has a corresponding symbol in the entity symbol list for the layout. If it does, then the symbol in the entity symbol list is assigned to the entity and is used to display the entity on the screen. If the new attribute value is not in the entity symbol list, then the entity is not displayed.

Even if the entity does have an associated symbol, it may not be displayed in the animation layout. An entity symbol is only displayed on the screen when it is residing in a dynamic object included in the layout, which includes a display point for the entity symbol. For example, if the entity is currently in a QUEUE block in the SIMAN model and a corresponding queue object is not included to define the entity display point for the queue, then the entity will not be visible on the screen as a member of the queue.

In the most basic SIMAN block sequence, consisting of QUEUE-SEIZE-DELAY-RELEASE, entities wait in a queue, seize a resource, delay by a processing time, and then release the resource. To animate this basic sequence, we need to include display points in the layout to define the screen location of the entity symbol while it is waiting in the queue and again while it is occupying the resource. In the sections that follow we discuss the methods for defining these entity display points.

Queues

When an entity is held in a Hold block, it waits in the preceding QUEUE block until it is released from the Hold block. The entities residing in a QUEUE block can be animated by using a Cinema *queue* object. The Cinema queue object is a passive object used to define display points for symbols assigned to entities residing in the QUEUE block. You add a Cinema queue object to the layout by first specifying the queue's identifier, which is associated with the symbol. The identifier is the symbolic name or number assigned to the queue in the SIMAN model.

There are two types of queue objects available in Cinema, and these are illustrated in Figure 7-2. The first type, a *straight* queue, is depicted on the left and is defined by digitizing two points corresponding to the head (starting point) and tail (ending point) of the queue. The line that joins these two points is called the *queue line* and defines the location, length, and orientation of the queue. When an entity enters the corresponding QUEUE block in the SIMAN model, its symbols are displayed along the queue line at the proper location relative to the other members of the queue. When an entity departs the QUEUE block, its symbols are removed from the queue line, and all following entity symbols move forward to fill the gap.

The second type of queue object, a *ragged* queue, is defined by digitizing each entity display point where an entity can sit while residing in the queue. These points, called *queue points*, need not be in a straight line. When an entity enters the corresponding QUEUE block in the SIMAN model, its entity symbols are displayed at the first free queue point. When an entity departs the QUEUE block, its symbols are removed from the queue point, and all following entity symbols shift forward one queue point. To override this forward shift, specify the "noshift" option for the queue object. This option causes all entities to remain on their current display points, even though forward display points are available. Because these forward display points may be allocated to future arrivals to the queue, the display

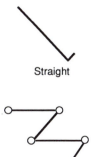

Straight

Ragged

Figure 7-2. Straight and Ragged Queues

order will not necessarily match the physical order of entities in the QUEUE block when the "noshift" option is specified.

Under certain circumstances a QUEUE block in the model may contain more entities than can be shown in the corresponding queue object in the layout. This will occur in a straight queue if the sum of the entity symbol sizes in the queue exceeds the length of the queue line, and it will occur in a ragged queue if the number of displayed entities in the queue exceeds the number of queue points. In either case, the animation only displays as many entity symbols (beginning with the first) as there is room for in the queue object. Those entities not displayed eventually become visible as they move forward when preceding entities exit the queue.

Queues were employed in several different locations in the circuit board assembly layout. For example, the totes waiting in front of the two workcenters are represented by entities waiting in queues. These queues are straight queues having a queue line length sufficient to simultaneously display two tote symbols.

Resource Symbols

Resources are used in SIMAN to model limited items in a system, such as machines and workers. Entities compete for the limited resources and must wait in a queue when shortages occur. In a SIMAN model, a resource can assume one of four possible states: busy, idle, inactive, or preempted. In our modeling constructs thus far, we have only dealt with two of these states: busy and idle. The resource is in a busy state when it has been allocated to an entity at a SEIZE block. The resource remains busy until it is released by the entity at a RELEASE block, at which time its status resets to idle. Units can be removed from service with the ALTER block (see Chapter 8), which changes the resource's status to inactive until it is returned to service (again with the ALTER block). When a resource is allocated to an entity at a PREEMPT block (also discussed in Chapter 8), its state is preempted until it is released by the entity at a RELEASE block.

A resource object can be placed in a Cinema layout to depict the resource's status over time. A resource object consists of a resource symbol set, which is associated with a resource in the model. Each resource symbol set contains four distinct symbols: the *idle* symbol, the *busy* symbol, the *inactive* symbol, and the *preempted* symbol. A resource symbol library is constructed and maintained just like an entity symbol library, except that each row of the library table has four symbols — corresponding to the resource's four possible states — instead of just one.

The resource symbol library for our example is shown in Figure 7-3. In this case, resource symbols are used to represent the machines at the sub-assembly and final assembly stations. As shown, you do not have to use all four symbols for each resource; you need to draw and include only those states that must appear in the animation.

Resource Library

Index	Idle	Busy	Inactive	Preempt
1		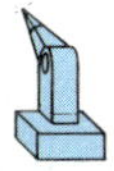		
2				
3				

Figure 7-3. Resource Symbol Library for the Circuit Board Assembly System

Once the resource symbol library is drawn, you add a resource object to the Cinema layout by selecting the idle symbol from the resource library and by using the mouse to position it on the layout. The SIMAN resource identifier is used to associate the resource object with a specific resource within the SIMAN model.

During model execution the symbol appearing at the position where the resource object was added to the layout changes as the status of the resource changes. All symbols appear on the screen relative to their reference points. The symbol also has an optional *seize point*, which is an entity display point associated with the busy (and preempted) symbol. When the entity seizes (preempts) the resource, the seizing (preempting) entity symbol is displayed on the seize point. The entity symbol remains on the seize point until either the resource is released or the entity is displayed at another entity display point (e.g., a storage point).

In our example, a seize point is used to specify the location of a tote being processed at one of the two workstations. The tote symbol is displayed on the seize point until the processing is completed, at which time the resource is released.

For resources with a capacity greater than 1, use the *resource copy* function to create multiple copies of the first unit placed. For example, to animate the resource named Assembler having a capacity of 2, first retrieve the idle symbol for the Assembler from the resource library and place this symbol on the layout. Then select the copy function and point to the resource unit to be copied, thereby creating the second unit of the resource. Use the mouse to place the copy on the layout. This procedure was used to place the two assemblers in the sample layout.

Storages

When an entity encounters a time delay (e.g., at a DELAY block), it can be placed in a storage facility by specifying the facility's identifier as an operand of the block. Entities residing in SIMAN storages can be animated in Cinema by using a Cinema *storage* object. This is a passive object, the purpose of which is to define display points for entities residing in the storage. You add a Cinema storage object to the layout by first specifying the SIMAN storage facility's identifier, which is the symbolic name or number assigned to the storage in the SIMAN model.

There are two types of storage objects in Cinema: a *straight* storage and a *ragged* storage. Storage objects resemble queue objects in appearance and function. A straight storage is added to the layout by digitizing the head and tail of the storage line — similar to adding a straight queue object. A ragged storage is added to the layout by digitizing each storage point where an entity can reside in the storage.

In our typical QUEUE-SEIZE-DELAY-RELEASE block sequence, a storage object can be used to display the entity symbol for each entity passing through the DELAY block; however, this same entity can also be displayed on the seize point of the resource object associated with the SEIZE block. Cinema never simultaneously displays the same entity symbol on two different display points. When an entity symbol is simultaneously associated with two or more display points, it is only displayed on the display point associated with the most recently entered object. For example, if both a seize point and a storage display point are defined, during the delay the entity symbol is displayed only on the storage display point.

In our sample layout, a storage is used at the exit station to display the departing totes during the delay time required to unload the totes from the carrier. Storages are also used to display the totes during the loading time required to place the totes on the circulating conveyor.

Variables

Sometimes it is convenient to display a numerical value describing the system's status in the form of a continuously updated digital display. For example, we can use a queue object to show the entity symbols for the first few entities in the queue, and then display the current length of the queue in digital format adjacent to the queue object. It is also convenient to be able to display performance values (such as number of workpieces completed, average time in the system, etc.) in a digital format.

A digital display of the current value of an expression involving one or more SIMAN variables can be added to a layout by using a Cinema feature called *variables*. Using the menus, you enter the expression to be displayed and then select the format (number of significant digits and places to the right of the decimal), size, and color of the display. Using the mouse, you then position the variable display anywhere on the screen. When the expression changes value during the simulation run, the new value will be output to the screen at that location with the defined size, color, and format.

In our example, we use variables to display several different model status values. The utilization of the assembler, transporter, and sub-assembler is displayed in the box on the layout labeled System Status. In addition, the number of completed parts and the average flowtime are displayed in the exit area of the layout.

Levels

In some cases it is convenient to be able to display a numerical value from the SIMAN model in the form of an analog display rather than a digital readout. For example, we may want to depict the current length of a queue as a bar that varies in length as the queue length changes in the model.

An analog display of the current value of an expression involving one or more SIMAN variables or attributes can be added to a layout by using a Cinema feature called *levels*, which provides three different analog indicators for displaying a numerical value. These three types of levels are illustrated in Figure 7-4. Two of the indicators, one rectangular and the other circular, fill and empty in response to changes in the associated expression's numerical value; the third, called a *dial*, is a circular level with a sweep hand that rotates either clockwise or counter-clockwise in response to changes in the numerical value of the associated expression. The dial's level is frequently used to represent a clock displaying the current value of simulated time, TNOW.

The shape, fill and empty colors, fill direction, size, and location of a level are specified by using the mouse and menus, as are the minimum and maximum values used for scaling the output on the screen. For the rectangular and circular levels, which fill and empty, the minimum and maximum values are used to establish the filled portion of the level. For the dial indicator, the minimum and maximum values are used to establish the position of the sweep hand on the dial. If the numerical value exceeds the maximum value for the fill-type levels, the level remains completely filled until the value drops below the maximum value. If the numerical value exceeds the maximum for the dial-type level, the dial wraps around and continues.

In our sample problem, we use rectangular levels to depict the current number and the average number of parts on the loop conveyor. We also use dial levels to depict the current value of simulated time. The two separate sweep hands for hours and minutes are created by employing two separate dial levels which are co-located on the layout. The hour hand is displayed by specifying the expression as TNOW/60, with a circular scale between 0 and 12. The minute hand is displayed by specifying the expression as TNOW, with a circular scale between 0 and 60.

Global Symbols

Consider a situation in which we have an expression whose value falls into a set of pre-defined, non-overlapping sub-ranges. For example, the status of a queue containing parts to be used in an assembly operation can be categorized into three sub-ranges based on the current length of the queue. The sub-ranges Low, Satisfactory, and High can correspond to ranges in length of 0 to 5, 6 to 15, and greater than 15, respectively.

Variables and levels allow us to display the current value of the length of the queue in either digital or analog format. Although these formats are convenient for displaying the current magnitude of the length, they are not effective in drawing

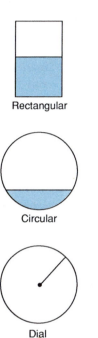

Rectangular

Circular

Dial

Figure 7-4. Rectangular, Circular, and Dial Levels

·attention to the sub-range within which the value falls. A SIMAN feature called *global symbols* provides this capability.

Global symbols associate a user-defined symbol on the layout with a sub-range of values for an expression. A separate symbol is associated with each sub-range of interest. During an animation the symbol changes as the value of the expression moves among its various sub-ranges. A given sub-range may have no symbol associated with it.

Like other symbols, global symbols are maintained in libraries and can be shared among layouts. To add a global symbol to a layout: 1) enter the expression associated with the symbol, 2) build a *global symbol list* for the expression, and 3) place the first symbol in the list at the appropriate location on the layout. The global symbol list is a two-column table in which the left column contains numerical values called *trigger values*, and the right column contains associated symbols. These symbols are moved from one or more global symbol libraries and are placed in the global symbol list for the layout. The first trigger value corresponds to the low value of the sub-range for the associated symbol, and the second trigger value corresponds to the high value of the sub-range. The symbol will be displayed on the layout whenever the value of the expression is greater-than-or-equal-to the first trigger value, but less than the second trigger value.

In our sample problem, global symbols are used to display the sign "Full" above the two accumulating conveyors whenever the accumulators are at their capacities of 5. The global expressions are specified as LC(Accum1) and LC(Accum2), and the trigger value for each symbol is 5.

Frequencies and Plots

In some cases it is desirable to display on the layout information summarizing the value of a response variable over time, rather than its current status. The *frequency* and *plot* features of Cinema provide this capability.

A frequency object may be added to a layout to display a dynamic histogram of a response variable over time. The histogram consists of a series of adjacent vertical bars that move up and down during model execution. The current height of each bar is proportional to the frequency of observations recorded in the histogram cell defined for that bar. An optional cumulative plot line can be displayed above the bars.

A plot object may be added to a layout to display a dynamic plot of the system response over time. The plot is continuously drawn on the layout as the model executes. Multiple plots may be placed and sized at any location in the layout. Plots can also be superimposed at the same location in the layout.

Dynamic Colors

Colors are formed in Cinema by combining different amounts of the colors red, green, and blue. Any of the colors in Cinema may be defined as a *dynamic color*, which can change its red, green, and blue content according to the value of a specified expression. As the value of the expression changes during the animation, any objects drawn with this color — whether symbols, levels, or static background objects — will undergo chromatic change.

Although dynamic colors are not used as commonly as variables, levels, and global symbols to display an expression's status, in some cases they can add an extra degree of realism to the animation. For example, when simulating a steel-making facility, a dynamic color can be used to represent the temperature of an ingot in a furnace. As its temperature increases, the ingot's color will gradually change from gray, through red and yellow to white (hot).

To define dynamic colors, you enter the relevant SIMAN expression and define the trigger values for the colors; then you assign the corresponding hues (red, green, and blue content) to be displayed at the trigger levels. The trigger values and corresponding hues are maintained in a *dynamic color table*, which you can edit with the functions provided. During the animation, the colors continually change with the value of the expression as defined by the entries in the table. To effect this change, Cinema linearly interpolates red, green, and blue intensities between trigger values of the SIMAN expression. When the expression is below the lowest trigger value or above the highest trigger value, the color remains at the nearest specified color.

(No dynamic colors were used in our sample problem.)

Transfers

We model a system's workcenters in SIMAN by using the submodel construct discussed in Chapter 6. Each workcenter has a STATION block, which defines the entrance to the workcenter, and a Transfer block (ROUTE, TRANSPORT, CONVEY), which defines the point of exit from the workcenter. Entities move from block to block within a submodel and then transfer to another submodel via a Transfer block. The first of these Transfer blocks, called the ROUTE block, represents basic transfers involving only a simple delay with no limiting resources constraining the transfer. The second, called the TRANSPORT block, models movements that are constrained by a limited number of transporter devices, such as hand carts or fork trucks. The last, called the CONVEY block, models both accumulating and non-accumulating conveyor movements between submodels.

To animate transfers between submodels in Cinema, use the Transfer menus to define the paths for the entities and associated material-handling devices on the layout. First, you add Cinema *station symbols* to the layout; these symbols correspond to the STATION blocks in the model. Associate the Cinema station symbol and the SIMAN STATION block by entering the corresponding station identifier for each Cinema station symbol placed on the layout. Next, connect the Cinema station symbols via *route paths*, *distance paths*, or *segment paths*, corresponding to the three basic types of transfers modeled in SIMAN. Each path is entered by moving the cursor to the path's starting station symbol and then digitizing a sequence of points terminating at the destination station symbol. The digitized points define the vertices of a polyline connecting the path's beginning and ending station symbols. Figure 7-5 depicts two Cinema station symbols with a connecting path.

Route paths animate inter-station movements that correspond to the transfer of entities between stations via the ROUTE block. When a route path is placed on the layout, an entity moving between the route's starting and ending stations via a ROUTE block is represented by its current symbol (if any) moving along the route path. The speed of movement is governed by the duration of travel specified on the ROUTE block in the model. To animate the movement along the path, Cinema re-positions the symbol's reference point on the route path drawn on the layout. The symbol's position is continually updated as time advances, so that it arrives at the end of the route path at the same time that the entity enters its destination STATION block in the model. At that point the entity's symbol disappears from the route path; it typically reappears on the screen at a display point within the destination-station submodel.

Figure 7-5. Two Stations and a Connecting Path

When the ROUTE block is used in a model that is not being animated, the entity's station origin (as defined by its current value of M) is unimportant because the ROUTE block only needs the destination to perform its function within SIMAN. If the route is to be animated in Cinema, however, both the origin and destination stations are important. Therefore, if the model is to be animated, it is sometimes necessary to include in the SIMAN model an assignment to the station attribute, M, corresponding to the entity's origin station. This assignment is not necessary, however, if the origin station is entered by using another Transfer block, in which case the station attribute, M, is automatically set to the current station by the previous Transfer block.

Distance paths resemble route paths in function, except that they animate the inter-station movements of entities and transporters that are transferring between stations by using the TRANSPORT, REQUEST, and MOVE blocks. Distance paths are placed on a layout by digitizing the path between the path's origin and destination stations in the same way as is done for the route paths. Each distance path placed on the layout is associated with a specific distance set. The distance set defines the length of each path between pairs of stations in the distance set; it is specified in the DISTANCES element of the experiment. This length, along with the current transporter's speed, controls the symbol's speed of movement along the path.

The symbols that are moved across distance paths can be entity symbols, transporter symbols, or both. Transporter symbols represent physical devices, such as fork trucks or hand carts, that move the entities from one station to another. Each transporter used in the model can be represented by one of three separate symbols corresponding to the transporter's idle, busy, or inactive status. If a transporter's status is idle, it is available but not being used; if its status is busy, it is allocated; if its status is inactive, it is unavailable for use (e.g., broken down).

Like other symbols, transporter symbols are drawn and maintained in one or more symbol libraries, which are independent of any specific layout. The transporter symbol library for our sample problem is shown in Figure 7-6. Transporter symbols are associated with a specific layout by moving the symbol sets from a library to the transporter symbol list for the layout. Each layout has only one transporter symbol list, which contains the transporter's identifier (name or number) from the SIMAN model and the corresponding symbol set that is used during animation to depict the transporter.

Transporter Library

Index	Idle	Busy	Inactive
1	Idle 	Busy 	
2			
3			

Figure 7-6. Transporter Symbol Library for the Circuit Board Assembly System

When transporters are not moving along a path, they can be displayed on the screen at a *staging area* attached to a station. Each station symbol in the layout can have an optional staging area assigned to it. A staging area defines one or more display points on the screen where the symbols for non-moving transporters can sit at a station. These transporters can be idle (waiting for work), busy (waiting for their entities to complete a process), or inactive (out of service).

There are two types of staging areas available in Cinema. A *straight* staging area is defined by digitizing two points corresponding to the head (starting point) and tail (ending point) of the staging area. The line that joins these two points is called the staging line and defines the location, length, and orientation of the staging area. Transporter symbols are displayed along this line in the same way that entity symbols are displayed along a queue line. The second type of staging area, a *ragged* staging area, is defined by digitizing each separate point where a transporter symbol can sit when residing in the staging area. Transporter symbols are displayed in ragged staging areas in the same way that entities are displayed in a ragged queue. If the staging area is too small to accommodate all of the transporter symbols waiting at a station, then as many symbols as possible are displayed.

During the animation, Cinema displays idle and inactive transporter symbols as sitting in the staging area attached to their current station locations. If a staging area is not included in the layout, then the idle and inactive transporter symbols do not appear on the screen. Busy transporters are shown in one of two ways: moving along a path or waiting in a staging area. In either case, any attached entity symbol is placed at a user-defined location on the transporter symbol, called the *ride point*.

The movement of transporter symbols in and out of staging areas is controlled by entity activation of ALLOCATE, REQUEST, MOVE, TRANSPORT, FREE, HALT, and ACTIVATE blocks in the SIMAN model. The ALLOCATE block changes the allocated transporter's symbol from idle to busy but does not move the symbol from its current staging area. The REQUEST block causes the allocated transporter symbol to be changed from idle to busy and to be moved from its current staging area, along the distance path, and into the staging area at the requesting entity's station. The MOVE block moves an allocated busy transporter symbol from its staging area, along the connecting distance path, to its destination staging area, where it remains busy. The TRANSPORT block removes an allocated busy transporter symbol from its staging area, places the entity symbol on the ride point of the transporter symbol, and moves the two symbols together along the connecting distance path to their destination staging area. The transporter symbol, along with its attached entity symbol, then enters the staging area. The entity symbol is removed from the transporter symbol when the entity frees the transporter or is displayed at a display point (queue, resource, etc.) within the submodel.

Note that you must use the TRANSPORT block in your SIMAN model whenever you want the entity symbol to appear on the ride point of the transporter symbol. The MOVE block only moves the transporter symbol; it does not change the station location of the associated entity.

In Chapter 9 we revisit the use of transporters in SIMAN for modeling entity movements between station submodels. The extensions discussed in that chapter relate to the use of transporters for modeling fixed-path devices, such as automatic guided vehicles, which are constrained to move over a specific network of paths. More specifically, Cinema provides constructs called *intersections* and *links*, which define the animation paths for these transporters.

Segment paths in a layout animate inter-station movements corresponding to the transfer of entities between stations via the CONVEY block. When a segment path is placed on a layout, an entity moving between the path's starting and ending stations via a CONVEY block in the model is represented by its current symbol (if any) moving along the path. The speed of movement is governed by the conveyor's speed, starts and stops, and accumulations (for accumulating-type conveyors).

To represent the movement of entities on conveyors in Cinema, segment paths are placed on the layout in a manner similar to placing route and distance paths. A segment path is associated with a specific segment set defined in the SEGMENTS element of the SIMAN experiment. When an entity is conveyed by a CONVEY block to a destination station, the entity symbol's reference point is moved along the defined path from its current station to the next station on its way to its final destination. If the conveyor stops during the simulation or if the entity encounters an accumulation point, the entity remains at its current position on the screen until it starts moving again in the model.

Note that, unlike transporters, conveyors have no symbols. To visualize the presence of the invisible segment paths, a conveyor is typically also represented by depicting it as part of the static background; the only change on the animation is the movement of entity symbols along conveyor paths.

It is not necessary to include paths for all segments of a segment set. If a path for a given segment is not included in the layout, then the entities moving along that segment on the conveyor are not animated. The entity symbols will reappear, however, if they enter a segment on the conveyor for which a segment path has been included in the layout.

In our sample problem, the totes containing parts enter the system along a route path, and then enter the loop conveyor. The animation of the parts entering the system and then moving along the loop conveyor was incorporated into the layout by drawing the route and segment paths. Note that these paths only define the movement of entities on the layout, and not the appearance of the route or conveyor mechanisms. The static drawing functions were used to depict the route and conveyor devices on the screen.

The completed assemblies are moved in their totes from each workstation to an accumulating conveyor where they are stored while they wait to be picked up by a carrier. The carrier then moves them to the exit station. The accumulating conveyor for each workstation is animated by drawing its segment path on the layout.

The animation of the parts moving via the carrier between the accumulating conveyors and the exit station was incorporated into the layout by drawing the distance paths and placing the staging areas for the carriers at the pick-up and drop-off stations. In addition, the transporter symbol representing the carrier was drawn and then placed in the transporter symbol list for the layout.

3.4 Execution of the SIMAN Model with Animation

As discussed previously, the Cinema system consists of two software components. So far we have primarily been discussing the layout drawing program, CINEMA, which is used to define the static and dynamic graphical objects to be included in the animation. We now turn our attention to the second component, CSIMAN. This special version of SIMAN includes the ability to read in a Cinema layout and update the dynamic components of the layout during the execution of the simulation model.

Preparing the Model for Animation: The LAYOUTS Element

Before a SIMAN model can be animated with CSIMAN, the LAYOUTS element must be included in the experiment to define the information which is needed for the animation. The experiment containing the LAYOUTS element is compiled and linked to the model file in the normal way to generate a program file for CSIMAN.

The LAYOUTS element is used to associate one or more Cinema animation layouts with the SIMAN model. Each animation layout has five operands, which are specified in the LAYOUTS element. These five operands are repeated for each animation layout associated with the model. The format for the LAYOUTS element is shown below.

LAYOUTS: FileDesc, AnimAttrib, Scale, Frame, Key:
        repeats;

The first operand, FileDesc, is the system-dependent file descriptor for the Cinema layout file, and it must be enclosed in double quotes. This file is created and saved by using the CINEMA layout program.

The second operand, AnimAttrib, is the animation attribute, which is used to determine which symbol, if any, is to be displayed on the screen for each entity in the model. The animation attribute is entered as any valid SIMAN expression. In most cases, the animation attribute is specified as one of the attributes of the entity.

The third and fourth operands (Scale and Frame) specify the initial values for the two time-advance parameters used by CSIMAN to control the speed of an animation. We discuss the meaning of these parameters later in this section.

The last operand, Key, is used to define a key-binding for the layout. When you press the keyboard character defined by Key during the simulation run, the current layout, if any, is replaced by the layout file associated with this key. In this way, you can easily switch among several different layouts for the model during the execution of the simulation.

An example of the LAYOUTS element for our sample problem is shown below. This element specifies a single layout file with the file descriptor C:\Sample.lay and animation attribute named PartType. The time-advance parameters assume default values, and the key-binding is specified as the character 1.

```
LAYOUTS: "C:\Sample.lay", PartType,,,1;
```

When a LAYOUTS element is included in the experiment, CSIMAN automatically loads and animates the first layout file entered in the LAYOUTS element. The menus or key-bindings can be used to switch to a different layout file.

The information contained in the LAYOUTS element is only used by CSIMAN. The information specified in this element is ignored when executing the model with SIMAN.

Running the Simulation with CSIMAN

The CSIMAN program can be used to execute a SIMAN simulation model with or without a Cinema animation layout. If the model is executed without a Cinema layout file, then the simulation runs without animation and produces results identical to using the standard SIMAN program. If a Cinema layout file is specified, the layout is displayed on the screen and is updated by CSIMAN as the simulation executes.

The user interface for CSIMAN resembles the user interface for Cinema, except that you use the functions on the menus to control the simulation/animation, rather than to construct the layout. These functions include the ability to read and discard Cinema layout files, load SIMAN program files, activate SIMAN's trace or debugger facilities, and control other aspects of simulation execution.

SIMAN's debugger facility can be coupled to the animation. The debugger commands discussed in Chapter 4 can be used in CSIMAN to change model parameters, to examine system status, to break down machines, etc. When these changes are made with the debugger, they are instantly reflected in the animation. For example, using the debugger to decrease a resource's capacity immediately causes its excess idle symbols to change to inactive symbols.

You can associate any number of different layouts with the same SIMAN model, and you can switch from one layout to another in the middle of a simulation. For example, you may have one layout for the shipping and receiving area, and a second layout for the assembly area. Both of these layouts can be driven by a single model of the factory, and you can freely switch back and forth between these layouts as the simulation executes.

Another CSIMAN feature, called *snapshot*, lets you save a picture of a layout and the values of all system variables at any point in the simulation. The snapshot can later be retrieved to return the simulation/animation to that exact point. Hence, with snapshots you can jump back and forth in time. This feature is particularly useful for demonstrating critical situations that occur late in the simulation run.

Controlling the Time Advance

To control an animated model's speed of execution, you specify two parameters that define the relationship between the simulated/animated time and the real time. By changing these parameters you can slow down or speed up the animated execution of the model.

Two types of screen updates occur during an animation. The first type, called *event updates*, is triggered by specific events within the model, such as an entity's entering a queue, freeing a transporter, etc. These updates are always performed on the screen simultaneously with their occurrence in the model. The second type, called *time-advance updates*, occurs between events. The speed at which these updates occur is controlled by the current values of the time-advance parameters. Time-advance updates display the symbol's movements along paths connecting station submodels. By changing the time-advance parameters you can speed up or slow down the symbol's movement along these paths.

During an animation, each time advance in the SIMAN simulation model is broken down into a series of smaller steps called *frames*. A frame in Cinema is analogous to a frame of a movie. At each frame advance, CSIMAN moves the symbols one position farther along their paths. Differences in speed of movement are obtained by enlarging the distance moved between adjacent frames for faster moving symbols.

The first time-advance parameter, called the *scale factor*, specifies the amount of simulated time represented by each animation frame. By increasing the value of the scale factor you speed up the animation, because fewer frame updates are required to animate the simulation. The second time-advance parameter, called the *frame delay*, specifies the amount of time that each frame of the animation is displayed. A stop-action moving picture appearance can be obtained by specifying this parameter. The frame delay parameter is normally defaulted.

In general, an animated model executes much more slowly than a non-animated model — regardless of how the time-advance parameters are set. If you want to observe only the later part of a simulation, you can use a feature called *skip-ahead* to skip forward in time without animation. This function turns off the animation so that the simulation can run forward at full speed without updating the animation layout. At the end of the skipped time period, the animation automatically resumes. You can also use the *clear* function to discard the current layout and continue the remainder of the simulation without animation.

4. Sample Animations

In this section we show several sample Cinema layouts to illustrate the use of the animation concepts discussed in this chapter. These animation layouts are based on actual applications of SIMAN/Cinema. Although the SIMAN model used to drive the animation is not shown or discussed, a brief summary of the modeling results is presented.

4.1 Westinghouse Just-In-Time Metal Fabrication Shop

This application involves the modeling of the operation of a proposed sheet metal fabrication line. The purpose of the study is to evaluate certain operating characteristics such as throughput, cycle time, machine utilization, and work in process. The study incorporates the impact of machine breakdowns and scheduled breaks on these performance measures.

The Cinema layout for this model is shown in Figure 7-7. A turret press initially punches full-sized metal sheets. The sheets are conveyed to an opti-shear where they are cut into parts for bending. A conveyor then delivers the individual parts to press brakes where the metal sheets are prepared for welding, painting, and assembly.

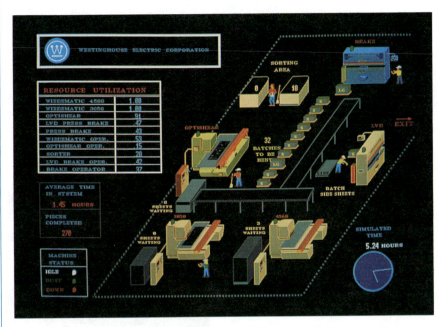

Figure 7-7. Layout for the Westinghouse Just-In-Time Metal Fabrication Shop Model

The model showed that the Just-In-Time (JIT) material flow would result in a 62% decrease in both the cycle time and work in process. Material also would flow more steadily from the system, which in turn would result in better utilization of downstream resources.

Animation was used in this project in several different ways. First, it served as a means of communicating engineering recommendations to all areas of the manufacturing process. Westinghouse used the animation to prepare shop supervisors and workers, to demonstrate the analysis to middle-level managers, to present and explain the layout to upper-level management as part of the project approval process, and to introduce new manufacturing methods to workers during implementation of the sheet metal fabrication shop.

The animation also played an important role in model verification and validation. Suggested changes were immediately evaluated through the use of the interactive debugger. As a result, significant issues, which may not have been considered, were raised and examined. Consequently, management had high confidence in the model.

4.2 General Motors Truck Assembly (Body and Chassis)

A SIMAN/Cinema model was used by General Motors to study the "marriage area" in the assembly of large GMC trucks (Sierras and Cheyennes). Simulation was used to improve the operation by balancing the workload within the facility, evaluating possible changes in the facility, and evaluating alternative decision rules for operating the facility.

The Cinema layout for the model is shown in Figure 7-8. Automatic guided vehicles (AGVs) carry the truck components to various locations within the facility for assembly. An AGV carrying a truck cab and box is matched or "married" with an AGV carrying a truck body. After the components are matched, they are delivered to specific assembly areas, where the cab and box are fastened to the chassis. The married trucks are then taken on a flat-top conveyor to an area for additional assembly.

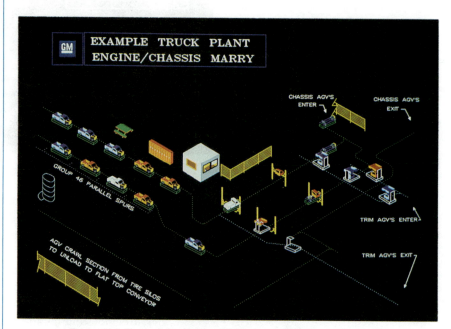

Figure 7-8. Layout for General Motors Truck Assembly Model

The animation was important in this study because it allowed General Motors to capture the complex control logic of the AGVs in a graphical presentation. The graphical perspective was extremely important for model verification. In addition, new methods could be evaluated, and the impact of proposed changes could be understood more easily through the animation.

The animation also played a significant role in communicating engineering recommendations to production managers. Because of the animation, credibility was more readily established, and suggestions were better received.

4.3 United Parcel Service Hub Shifter Simulation

This application involves the simulation and animation of the dispatching of United Parcel Service's drivers (shifters) at a hub location. The animation layout for the hub in Dallas, Texas, is shown in Figure 7-9. Dispatch managers and industrial engineers use the model to perform analyses on past operations. The model employs user-specified parameters that allow easy modification of schedules and vehicle assignments. Its design makes the model a convenient tool for evaluating different operating plans. The model can handle up to a maximum of 100 drivers.

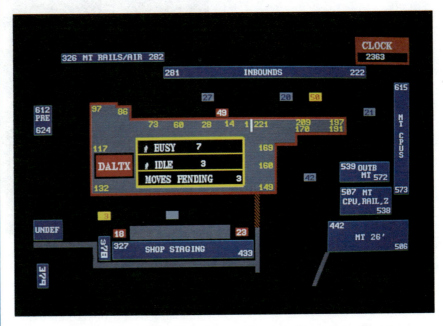

Figure 7-9. Layout for United Parcel Service's Dispatching Model

Initial testing of the simulation at several sites helped United Parcel Service to reduce the number of scheduled hours for drivers. It also helped to establish reasonable levels of expected hub performance.

Animation played a very important role in model verification and validation, which were performed during system design and subsequent implementation.

Animation proved to be a powerful communication tool. Layouts constructed with Cinema highlighted problem areas, such as bottlenecks and underutilized drivers, which were not easily identified in standard operation reports.

4.4 LTV Flexible Machining Cell

This application involves the simulation and animation of LTV's Vought Aero Products Flexible Machining Cell (FMC). The animation layout for this facility is shown in Figure 7-10. The system consists of eight machines, one wash module, two inspection stations, 40 rinsers (pallets), and four automatic guided vehicles. The two carrousels are dynamic queues for the operators and the cutting machines. Parts are fixtured to a riser on a stand, machined, and then washed. Thirty percent of the completed parts are inspected before returning to a carrousel.

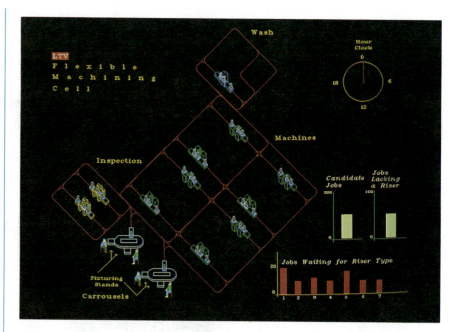

Figure 7-10. Layout for the LTV Flexible Machining Cell

Scheduling of parts occurs every 24 hours. The levels in the bottom right-hand corner of the layout show the number of jobs currently scheduled. These include candidate jobs and jobs lacking a riser. Candidate jobs are jobs not yet introduced into the system. Jobs lacking a riser are jobs that have been introduced but are waiting for a riser.

The simulation model was used as to assess queue requirements, tool quantity requirements, job introduction policies, scheduling, and the impact of inspection sampling frequencies.

The Cinema animation for this model played an important role in verifying and validating the model. Model logic flaws were more easily detected through the use of the animation. The animation was also valuable as a tool for communicating with company management and with customers.

4.5 Department of Energy Nuclear Waste Handling Facility

Two types of nuclear waste are handled by the Department of Energy (Westinghouse) Waste Isolation Plant near Carlsbad, New Mexico: Remote-Handled Transuranic and Contact-Handled Transuranic (CH-TRU). This application involved the simulation and animation of the nuclear waste disposal of CH-TRU waste, which is the more complex of the two types.

Trailers of nuclear waste are initially delivered to the site on trucks. Preliminary inspection tests for contamination. If the trailer passes inspection, it is delivered on a truck to the contact handling area. At this point, additional tests on specific drums of waste verify that no radioactive waste is leaking. If the waste delivery passes this series of testing, it is delivered on a pallet to a below-ground salt mine for permanent storage.

A front-end menu was incorporated into this model to make it easy for the user to modify system parameters. For example, pass probabilities at contamination test locations can be easily altered using this menu.

Through modeling, it was determined that the facility could not handle the forecasted rate of incoming nuclear waste. The parking lot, which was sized to accommodate 12 trailers, would constantly be full. It was shown that the bottleneck occurred in the contact handling area where capacity was less than expected. It was also shown that fewer pallets than expected were required to transport waste to the salt mine.

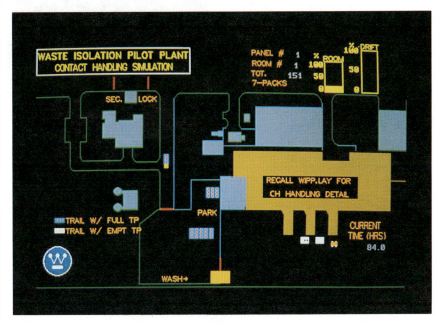

Figure 7-11. Layout 1 for the DOE Waste-Handling Facility

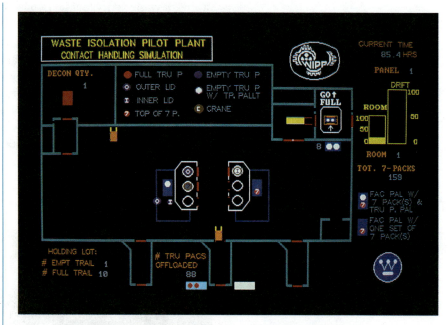

Figure 7-12. Layout 2 for the DOE Waste-Handling Facility

Two separate animation layouts were developed for this model. The first (Figure 7-11) animates the operations involving the arrival of the trailers and the inspection of the waste. The second (Figure 7-12) animates the processing of the waste within the contact handling area. Both of these layouts were driven by the same SIMAN model. It should also be noted that many operations (particularly in the salt mine) were modeled in detail but were not included on either layout. As can be seen on the layouts, important statistics, such as below-ground inventory levels, are displayed as real-time levels.

The animation was important for verifying the model and for communicating its operation. It was particularly useful for verifying the complex decision logic for vehicle movements.

References

JOHNSON, M. ERIC AND JACOB P. POORTE (1988), "A Hierarchical Approach to Computer Animation in Simulation Modeling," *Simulation*, Vol. 50, No. 1, pp: 30-36.

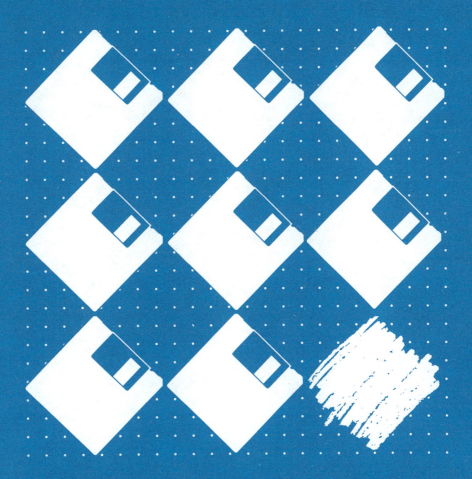

CHAPTER 8
Additional Discrete Modeling Concepts

1. Introduction

At this point we have discussed the basic concepts needed for building, verifying/validating, interpreting, and animating SIMAN simulation models. Thus far we have limited our discussion to a small subset of SIMAN modeling constructs so that we could focus on these critical simulation issues. With these topics presented, we can now turn our attention to SIMAN's other modeling features.

Pareto's 80-20 rule also applies to modeling, i.e., 80 percent of the modeling can be accomplished with 20 percent of the modeling constructs. The modeling constructs discussed in previous chapters represent the 20 percent of SIMAN that is sufficient for 80 percent of the modeling. The constructs that we discuss in this chapter are used far less often than those previously discussed, but they are often essential for accurately modeling the unique operating characteristics of many complex systems.

2. Generic Station Submodels

In Chapter 6 we discussed the concept of segmenting a large complex model into submodels based on stations. We also discussed a station's role and the use of the Transfer block to control the flow of entities through the system. In this section we discuss extensions of these concepts, which can dramatically reduce the size of some of our models. In many instances, these extensions allow us to use a single station submodel to represent several different but functionally equivalent station submodels. We refer to this type of station submodel as a *generic station submodel*.

2.1 The Need for Generic Station Submodels: The Modified Flow Line

Consider Sample Problem 6.2, the modified flow line, presented in Section 4 of Chapter 6. As each part moves through the facility, it is processed at each operation in its visitation sequence before departing the system. At each operation, the part waits in the queue, seizes the resource, delays by the operation time, releases the resource, and then continues to its next operation, if any.

The model for this example, which was shown in Figure 6-7, uses SIMAN's sequence feature. The sequence feature controls the flow of parts and makes assignments to the attribute named OpTime, which defines the delay time at each operation. Observe that the four station submodels used to model the operations are identical, except for the names assigned to the stations, queues, and resources.

With only four operations, the redundancy of blocks is barely noticeable. Imagine, however, a situation in which we have 100 different operations. We have to repeat each submodel 100 different times, with the only differences being the names assigned to the stations, queues, and resources. Fortunately, by using a generic station submodel, we can avoid this repetition.

2.2 The Use of Numbers in Place of Names

In the models presented so far, we have always used names to refer to attributes, variables, and objects such as queues and stations. Using names generally makes our models more readable and understandable; however, to fully exploit the advantages offered by generic station submodels, we must reference some objects by number rather than by name. For example, we must refer to Stations 1, 2, 3, and 4 as opposed to WorkStation, Paint, NewPaint, and Pack. Although the numerical convention makes our models somewhat less readable, it often dramatically reduces the modeling effort.

When symbolic names are no longer used to reference attributes, variables, and objects in the model, we can sometimes omit the definitions of these names from the experiment. We must, however, still declare within the experiment the number of attributes, variables, queues, and stations used by the model. We define the elements (i.e., ATTRIBUTES, VARIABLES, QUEUES, and STATIONS) by entering only the number of the last attribute, variable, or object of that type used in the model. For example, the set of elements shown below defines three attributes (referenced by A(1), A(2), and A(3)), two variables (referenced by V(1) and V(2)), five queues (numbered 1 through 5), and four stations (numbered 1 through 4).

```
ATTRIBUTES:3;
VARIABLES:2;
QUEUES:5;
STATIONS:4;
```

2.3 Station Ranges and the Station Attribute M

The key to developing generic station submodels is the ability to specify ranges on a STATION block. This feature allows us to replace the single station number (which we have used up to this point) by a range of station numbers associated with the block. You enter this range as the first station, followed by a dash (-), followed by the last station, as shown on the left.

STATION,1-4

This STATION block defines the entrance point for entities arriving at any station numbered between 1 and 4. An entity transferred to any station within this range will be sent to this STATION block.

For each entity transferred to a STATION block from a Transfer block, SIMAN automatically sets the special attribute M to the destination station's number. Hence, when the entity finally enters the destination STATION block, its M attribute is set to the station number that it just entered. In our sample STATION block, an entity sent to Station 4 enters this block with an M value of 4. We can use this value of M within the submodel as we use any other attribute or variable, i.e., as a basis for branching, for specifying the number of a queue, etc.

2.4 Indexed Resources

The last feature required to exploit the idea of a generic station submodel is an *indexed resource*. An indexed resource is identical to a normal resource, except that its identifier consists of two parts: a symbolic name and an index. The symbolic component follows the normal naming conventions for resources. The index component is an integer appended within parentheses to the resource's name. Enter this index as any valid expression; if necessary, SIMAN will truncate it to an integer. Each integer index value associated with the name defines a unique resource which, although it shares a common name with other resources, has its own capacity and functions independently. For example, the resources Operator(1) and Operator(2) are completely independent in the same sense that the resources Worker and Painter are independent. The resource Operator(1) may have a capacity of 5, representing five identical Workers; the resource Operator(2) may have a capacity of 3, representing three identical Painters. Thus, an indexed resource provides a method of sharing a single name among distinct resources.

Indexed resources are important in defining generic station submodels because they may incorporate the attribute M within the expression defining the index. Therefore, we can reference different resources within a submodel based on the current station number assigned to M. For example, the identifier Operator(M) can refer to either Workers or Painters, depending on the current value of M.

When using an indexed resource in the model, you must appropriately define it in the RESOURCES element of the corresponding experiment. There are two ways to do so. With the first and simplest method you include the number of indices associated with the resource's name in parentheses. For example, Operator(4) defines four resources with identifiers Operator(1), Operator(2), Operator(3), and Operator(4). With the second method you explicitly assign numbers to the resources rather than employing SIMAN's automatic numbering feature. In this case you can enter a given resource's number as a range in the form LowNumber — HighNumber. When you do so, the associated name is indexed, beginning with 1 and continuing up to the number of identifiers in the range. For example, the range of numbers 6-10 assigned to Tool defines five distinct resources with identifiers Tool(1) through Tool(5).

Do not confuse the resource numbers with the index values. The first is an absolute numbering of all resource identifiers in the model. The second is a relative numbering within a specific indexed resource.

To index a resource, replace the single capacity value normally entered for each resource name with a list of capacities. Use commas (,) to separate the listed values, each of which can be an integer or the keyword SCHED(N), where N denotes number of a schedule. If the number of entries in the list is less than the number of indexed resources, SIMAN uses the last capacity in the list as a default for the remaining entries.

An example of the RESOURCES element for defining indexed resources is shown below.

```
RESOURCES: Worker, 3:
           Machine(6), 4, 2;
```

In this example, we have a standard resource named Worker and an indexed resource named Machine with indices 1 through 6. The capacity of Worker is 3. The capacity of Machine(1) is 4, and the capacities of Machine(2) through Machine(6) are 2.

2.5 Sample Problem 8.1: The Modified Flow-Line Revisited

We now revisit our sample modified flow line and develop a smaller model of this system by using a generic station submodel to represent all four operations, as shown in Figure 8-1 and Figure 8-2. Note that the stations, queues, and index for the resource all use numbers between 1 and 4, each number corresponding to one of the four operations. The STATION block has a specified range of 1-4, meaning that all entities transferred to stations 1 through 4 enter the submodel at this block. The entities then wait in the QUEUE block, where the queue's number is specified as the current value of M. Hence, an arrival at Station 1 waits in Queue 1, an arrival at Station 2 waits in Queue 2, and so forth.

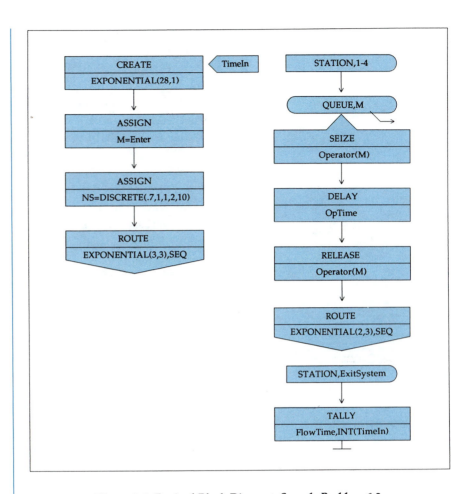

Figure 8-1. Revised Block Diagram: Sample Problem 6.2

```
BEGIN;
;     MODIFIED FLOW-LINE: SAMPLE PROBLEM 6.2
;     Parts enter, part type determined, and transfer
          CREATE:    EXPONENTIAL(28,1):           !Create jobs at staging area
                     MARK(TimeIn);                  Mark arrival time
          ASSIGN:    M=Enter;                      Set entry station
          ASSIGN:    NS=DISCRETE(.7,1,1,2,10);     Determine part type
          ROUTE:     EXPONENTIAL(3,3),SEQ;         Transfer to operation
;     Generic submodel
          STATION,  1-4;                           Operation submodel
          QUEUE,    M;                             WIP for Operator resource
          SEIZE:    Operator(M);                   Get Operator
          DELAY:    OpTime;                         Delay for processing
          RELEASE:  Operator(M);                   Release Operator resource
          ROUTE:    EXPONENTIAL(2,3),SEQ;          Transfer to next operation
;     Exit submodel
          STATION,  ExitSystem;                    Exit submodel
          TALLY:    FlowTime,INT(TimeIn):          !Tally flowtime
                    DISPOSE;                        Dispose of job
END;
```

Figure 8-2. Revised Model Frame: Sample Problem 6.2

The resource to be seized at the SEIZE block is specified as Operator(M), where M again contains the number of the current station. Operator(1) corresponds to the Worker in the WorkStation, Operator(2) corresponds to the Painter in Paint, and so forth. The entities then delay at the DELAY block by the processing time contained in the attribute OpTime. This attribute is set in the SEQUENCES element. Finally, the entities release the appropriate resource and transfer to the next station at the ROUTE block. This process continues until the entity arrives at the station named ExitSystem, where it is tallied and departs the system.

The experiment for this version of the model remains essentially the same (see Figure 8-3), except that numbers are used in place of symbolic names, and the RESOURCES element is modified to define the indexed resource named Operator, which replaces the separately named resources in the previous version. Note that the stations ExitSystem and NewPaint have been switched to facilitate the required indexing.

```
BEGIN;

;                 MODIFIED FLOW-LINE: SAMPLE PROBLEM 6.2
PROJECT,          Sample Problem 6.2,SM;
ATTRIBUTES:       TimeIn:
                  OpTime;
STATIONS:         WorkStation:
                  Paint:
                  Pack:
                  NewPaint:
                  ExitSystem:
                  Enter;
QUEUES:           4;
RESOURCES:        Operator(4);
SEQUENCES:        1,WorkStation, Optime=UNIFORM(21,25,2) &
                  Paint,OpTime=NORMAL(22,4,2) &
                  Pack,OpTime=TRIANGULAR(20,22,26,2) &
                  ExitSystem:
                  2,WorkStation, Optime=UNIFORM(21,25,2) &
                  NewPaint,OpTime=NORMAL(49,7,2) &
                  Pack,OpTime=TRIANGULAR(21,23,26,2) &
                  ExitSystem;
TALLIES:          FlowTime;
DSTATS:           NQ(1),WorkStation WIP:
                  NR(1)*100,Worker Utilization:
                  NQ(2),Paint WIP:
                  NR(2)*100,Painter Utilization:
                  NQ(3),Pack WIP:
                  NR(3)*100,Packer Utilization:
                  NQ(4),NewPaint WIP:
                  NR(4)*100,NewPainter Utilization;
REPLICATE,        1,0,565000,,,35000;
END;
```

Figure 8-3. Revised Experiment Frame: Sample Problem 6.2

When comparing the two approaches to this problem, recognize that, with the second approach, the number of blocks is independent of the number of stations in the system. We can modify the model to accommodate 100 stations by simply changing the station range on the STATION block from 1-4 to 1-100.

In most of our models we make use of one or more resources, which are seized and released by entities as they move through the system. In this section we expand our initial set of resource constructs and introduce additional flexibility for modeling with resources. Let's begin by addressing the problem of representing the allocation of one of several alternative sets of resources based on some decision rule. Then we will examine the problem of representing changes in a resource's capacity over time. We complete this section with a discussion of the concept of resource preemption.

3.1 Selecting among Parallel Resources: The SELECT Block

In some situations an entity may use one of several different sets of resources based on a specific rule for choosing among them. For example, an arriving part may be assigned to Machine A, with additional instructions to use Machine B if it is free and Machine A is unavailable. If Machines A and B are identical, we can conveniently use a single resource with a capacity of 2 to model this situation, thereby ignoring the complication of the selection process. In this case the simulation does not maintain the explicit identity of Machines A and B; however, if Machines A and B have different operating characteristics (e.g., Machine A is faster or has greater output than Machine B), then we must define separate resources and model the selection process explicitly.

To model the process of selecting among non-identical parallel resources, you use the SELECT block, which is shown below. Note that the very top of the block is identical in shape to the Hold block. In both cases this shape indicates that the block must be preceded by a QUEUE block, because entities can be held outside the block, awaiting available resource units. The body of the block has a triangular shape, denoting a decision process, and the triangle points in the direction of this process. The block shape shown on the left has the triangle pointing downward, indicating that the decision process involves blocks on the output side of the SELECT block. The bottom side of the block contains two or more branches defining alternative output flows from the block.

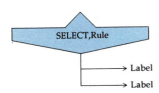

```
SELECT, Rule:
        Label:
        repeats;
```

One of the SELECT block's operands, Resource Selection Rule, specifies the decision rule for selecting among sets of resources. A summary of some of the more commonly used rules appears in Figure 8-4. Experience shows that these rules are effective for modeling most situations; however, as we discuss in Chapter

10, it is also easy to define your own more complicated selection rules (called *user rules*) by programming the selection process in a FORTRAN or C routine.

Rule	Description
CYC	CYClic priority
RAN	RANdom priority
POR	Preferred Order Rule
LNB	Largest Number Busy
SNB	Smallest Number Busy
LRC	Largest Remaining Capacity
SRC	Smallest Remaining Capacity

Figure 8-4. Resource Selection Rules

The CYClic rule selects the first available resource beginning with the successor of the last resource seized; it essentially cycles through the resources. The RANdom rule gives equal probability to the selection of each resource. The Preferred Order Rule prioritizes the resources in the order that they are listed on the output side of the SELECT block. The Largest Number Busy and Smallest Number Busy rules use the current number of busy resources for the selection process. The Largest Remaining Capacity and Smallest Remaining Capacity use the difference between the variables MR and NR for the selection process. The last four rules use the POR rule to break ties.

Each of the branches emanating from the bottom of the SELECT block contains the label of a SEIZE block defining a possible allocation of resources. Although each of these SEIZE blocks may be physically located anywhere in the model, they follow the SELECT block in terms of the logical entity flow. These SEIZE blocks are not preceded by their own individual QUEUE blocks, but instead share the QUEUE block preceding the SELECT block.

When an entity arrives at an empty QUEUE block preceding the SELECT block, SIMAN examines the resources defined at the SEIZE blocks specified on the output side of the associated SELECT block; SIMAN then selects one block from among all those that currently have enough available units to allocate to the entity. This choice is based on the resource selection rule. The arriving entity is then sent to the selected SEIZE block, where the resources are allocated to the entity. If none of the SEIZE blocks specified on the output side of the SELECT block has sufficient resources available, the arriving entity waits in turn in the QUEUE block preceding the SELECT block until the resources become available. When resources are freed elsewhere in the model, SIMAN automatically attempts to allocate available resources to the waiting entities in each of the QUEUE blocks.

An example illustrating the use of the SELECT block for choosing between the resources named MachineA and MachineB is shown on the left. Entities arriving at the QUEUE block attempt to seize either MachineA or MachineB. If one resource is busy and the other is available, the arriving entity is sent to the SEIZE

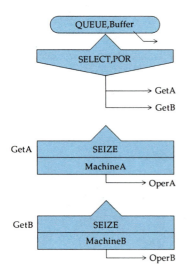

block with the available resource. If both resources are available, the selection is based on the Preferred Order Rule (POR), meaning that the SEIZE block associated with MachineA is selected. If both resources are busy, the arriving entity joins the queue named Buffer, where it waits for the first available resource.

3.2 Changing Resource Capacities: The ALTER Block and SCHEDULES Element

In the models presented so far, the capacity of each resource has remained constant throughout the simulation. In many systems, however, the capacity of the resources may vary over time. For example, the number of available machine repairmen in a manufacturing system may vary over time as the result of lunch (or other scheduled breaks) and differences in scheduled shifts.

There are two ways to represent changes in resource capacity in SIMAN: from within the model by using the ALTER block, or from within the experiment by using the SCHEDULES element. The first method is typically used when an event in the model triggers a change in capacity, whereas the second method is typically used when the capacity follows a specific schedule over time.

The ALTER block, a type of Operation block, is summarized below. The operands of the block are the resource's name, ResName, and capacity change, Qty. The ALTER block changes the capacity by a positive or negative amount, as specified by the capacity change operand. Note that a change in capacity on the ALTER block is a relative change applied to the current resource's capacity each time an entity arrives at the block.

ALTER
ResName,Qty

ALTER: ResName, Qty;

If the change in capacity is positive, the additional units are added to the current number of idle resource units, and an attempt is made to allocate available idle units to any waiting entities. Following the increase in capacity, the value of variable MR for the resource is the old capacity plus the amount of change.

If the change in capacity is negative, idle units of the resource are taken away. If there are enough idle units to satisfy the decrease in capacity, they are immediately removed from the system. If, on the other hand, the magnitude of the change in capacity is larger than the number of available idle units, all of the currently available idle units are removed, and the remaining units required to satisfy the change in capacity are removed as they become idle. In all cases the value of variable MR is changed immediately by the full amount of the change in capacity.

If the ALTER block attempts to reduce a resource's capacity below 0, it is prevented from doing so. For example, if a resource's current capacity is 2, and a change in capacity of −4 is specified, only the two existing units of the resource are removed, and the new value of variable MR is 0.

Because the change in capacity is applied only to idle units of the resource, a negative change followed by a positive change of equal magnitude can result in the changes being canceled out without ever changing the actual capacity of the resource. For this to happen, the resource units must not be released during the time period between the changes in capacity. The value of variable MR changes, however, even though the units of the resource remain busy and cannot be removed from the system.

The second method for controlling the resource's capacity over time is the use of the SCHEDULES element, which is included in the experiment. The SCHEDULES element, summarized below, defines a time-dependent schedule of the resource's capacity. You specify the schedule as an ordered list of pairs of values denoting resource Capacity and Duration. Separate the pairs by a comma, express the capacity as an integer constant, and express the duration as any valid expression. For example, the capacity schedule 1*4,2*4 denotes a capacity of 1 during the first 4 units of time, and a capacity of 2 during the next 4 units of time. Note that you specify the capacity as an absolute capacity, as opposed to the relative change in capacity specified on the ALTER block.

SCHEDULES: Number, Capacity * Duration, ... :
        repeats;

To associate the capacity schedules with resources, use the Capacity field on the RESOURCES element. Enter time-independent capacities as integer constants, in which case the resource's capacity remains at the same value throughout the simulation — unless it is changed by an ALTER block. If, however, you enter the capacity in this field as SCHED(N), the capacity of the resource is time-dependent, with the pattern defined by schedule number N of the SCHEDULES element. Any number of resources can refer to the same schedule.

The resource schedule is implemented as a sequence of events that successively alter a resource's capacity. As with the ALTER block, the capacity decreases do not remove busy resource units. The decrease is only applied to idle units, and the remaining capacity change (if any) is applied as units of the resource are released.

If the sum of the schedule's capacity durations is less than the length of the simulation run, the schedule is regenerated from the beginning with the first resource Capacity and Duration pair. For example, we can enter a schedule for a one-week period and then let the weekly schedule be automatically repeated over a one-year replication of the simulation. If we omit the Duration value from the last pair, then an infinite duration is assumed, using the last specified resource Capacity.

The following example illustrates the use of the SCHEDULES element.

```
RESOURCES: Worker, SCHED(1):
           Machine, SCHED(2);
SCHEDULES: 1, 3*8, 1*16, 2:
           2, 2*40, 1*16;
```

In this example, the capacity of the resource Worker follows Schedule 1, which specifies a capacity of 3 for the first 8 units of time, drops to 1 for the next 16 units, and then remains at 2 for the rest of the simulation replication. The capacity of the resource Machine follows Schedule 2. In this schedule the capacity is 2 during the first 40 units of time and then drops to 1 for the next 16 units. This schedule automatically repeats itself; hence, the capacity returns to 2 at time 56.

Although the ALTER block and SCHEDULES element are often used to model changes in resource capacity resulting from scheduled breaks and shift changes, they can also be used to model unplanned equipment breakdowns. For example, we can represent the breakdown of the resource Machine by decreasing its capacity to 0 at the point in time when it breaks. We then restore its capacity to 1 when the machine is repaired. An example using the SCHEDULES element appears below, and the same example using the ALTER block is shown on the left. The mean time between failures is expressed as exponential with a mean of 600 time units; the repair time is expressed as normal with a mean of 15 time units and a standard deviation of 3 time units.

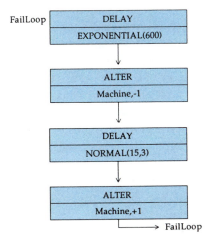

```
SCHEDULES: 1, 1*EXPONENTIAL(600), 0*NORMAL(15,3);
RESOURCES: 1, Machine, SCHED(1);
```

The primary limitation to this approach is a restriction on the ALTER block and the SCHEDULES element; this restriction states that decreases in capacity can only be applied to idle units of a resource. Hence, if the resource Machine is busy when it breaks down, it finishes the current workpiece before being taken out of the system.

Our experience has shown that modeling breakdowns and repairs is often critical to simulating manufacturing systems because they usually have a substantial impact on simulation results. Our experience has also shown that data on repair time is often the most critical element of this model component. However, the error introduced by allowing the machine to finish its current workpiece before breaking down is often insignificant — especially if the processing time on the machine is small compared to the repair time.

In the next section we discuss the PREEMPT block, which provides a more accurate, but more complex, method for modeling breakdowns. Unless the accuracy of this component of the model is critical, we favor the simpler approaches, which use the ALTER block or the SCHEDULES element.

3.3 Preempting a Resource: The PREEMPT Block

When a resource is allocated to an entity at a SEIZE block, it normally remains with that entity until it is explicitly released at a RELEASE block. In some cases, however, it is useful to allow one entity (the preempting entity) to forcibly take away a resource unit from a second entity (the preempted entity) before that entity has completed its use of the resource (by releasing it at a RELEASE block). This process of taking away a resource that is currently allocated to another entity is called *preemption* and can be modeled in SIMAN by using the PREEMPT block.

The PREEMPT block, a type of Hold block, is shown below. Like all Hold blocks, it must be preceded by a QUEUE block, which provides space for waiting entities. When resource units are available, the PREEMPT block essentially operates like a SEIZE block, except that only one unit of a single resource can be allocated. If, however, the resource units are all busy, the PREEMPT block attempts to take away a busy unit of the resource from another entity that is currently using the resource — unlike the SEIZE block, which places the entity in the preceding queue to await the release of the resource.

```
PREEMPT,Pr
ResName,AttributeID,Dest
```

PREEMPT, Pr: ResName, AttributeID, Dest;

This attempt to preempt the resource from another entity may or may not succeed. If it does succeed, the preempting entity departs with the resource unit at the PREEMPT block, and the preempted entity no longer has possession of the resource. If the preemption does not succeed, the arriving entity waits in the preceding QUEUE block until a resource unit becomes available for preemption.

Although the PREEMPT block can only allocate a single unit of a resource to an entity, this block can be used with resources having capacities greater than 1. For example, we may have a resource named Machine that has a capacity of 3, but we can only preempt a single unit of this resource. SIMAN uses the most recently allocated resource rule to select the resource unit to consider for preemption. In other words, only the last allocated unit of the resource, i.e., the one with the shortest busy time, is eligible for preempting.

To determine whether an entity may be preempted, SIMAN examines both the entity's current location and its priority for the resource. To be eligible for preemption, the entity must either be located in a QUEUE block or be undergoing a delay within a DELAY, REQUEST, ROUTE, or TRANSPORT block. Note that these blocks cover almost all entities in the model, the main exceptions being entities on a conveyor or those that are members of a group (the latter are discussed in Section 5.1 of this chapter).

If the entity with the last allocated unit of the resource is eligible for preemption based on its location in the model, SIMAN compares its priority with the arriving entity's priority to determine whether to preempt the resource. For entities whose resources were allocated at a PREEMPT block, the priority is specified as an operand of the block, with lower values representing more important priorities for the resource. Hence, an entity at a PREEMPT block with a priority of 1 preempts an entity whose resource was allocated at a PREEMPT block having a priority of 2. In addition, entities at PREEMPT blocks always have preemptive priority over all entities whose resources were allocated at a SEIZE block, regardless of the latter's priority.

When preemption occurs, SIMAN takes the resource away from the preempted entity and gives it to the preempting entity. The preempting entity then exits the PREEMPT block and continues its flow through the model. The preempted entity, however, no longer has its resource, and its progress through the model is interrupted.

The preempted entity can be processed in one of two ways. By default, it is removed from its current block and waits in a special internal *preempted entity queue* associated with each resource in the model until the resource unit becomes available. Once its resource returns, the entity is removed from the internal queue and is returned to the block from which it was removed at the time of preemption. If this is a QUEUE block, the entity simply rejoins the queue according to that queue's ranking rule. If, however, the entity returns to a DELAY, REQUEST, ROUTE, or TRANSPORT block, the entity re-enters the block, but stays there only for the delay time remaining at the time of preemption. For example, if an entity enters a DELAY block with a duration of 10 and is preempted after 7 units of time, after returning to the DELAY block it will exit the block after only 3 units of time. When using this default mode, you can specify an optional Storage on the PREEMPT block by using operand Dest, which places the entity in the specified Storage during its preempted state. This operand is useful for collecting statistics about the time that the entity spends in the preempted state or for animating the preempted entity within Cinema.

Although this default process applies in most situations, SIMAN provides an alternative entity-processing method. To select this option, specify a destination label, operand Dest, which causes the preempted entity to be redirected to a specified block at the time of preemption, instead of returning to the special internal preempted entity queue. The entity is then placed at the front of the event calendar to be processed from this block in the normal fashion, and it no longer waits for the return of its resource. This method allows you to build your own decision about how the preempted entity is processed. To assist in this task, SIMAN provides a tool for saving the time remaining at the point of preemption in an attribute of the entity. Simply specify the attribute's identifier, AttributeID, as an operand of the PREEMPT block.

Preemption can occur on an infinite number of levels. For example, Entity A may initially seize a resource, but, before being done with the resource, it may be preempted by Entity B. Entity B may then be preempted by Entity C, and so forth. This multi-level preemption is useful in the modeling of multi-tasking computer systems in which jobs of various priorities arrive at the system. When multiple levels of preemption occur, the LIFO (last-in-first-out) rule is used to allocate the freed resources to the waiting preempted entities. Note that this LIFO rule corresponds to the priority of preemption.

In modeling manufacturing systems, the PREEMPT block provides a more exact method for modeling breakdowns, because the workpiece is interrupted from using the resource for the duration of the preemption. A sample model illustrating the use of the PREEMPT block for this purpose is shown in Figure 8-5. In the first part of the model, entities representing the workpieces enter the model, wait for a machine, delay by the processing time, release the machine, and then exit the system. In the second part of the model, a single entity is created that delays by the time between breakdowns, preempts the machine, delays by the time to repair, releases the machine, and then repeats the process. Note that in this example the default mode is being used to process the preempted entity (workpiece) and return it to the DELAY block.

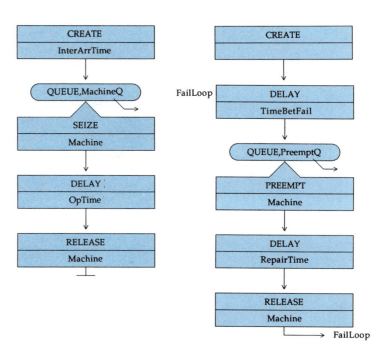

Figure 8-5. Example of PREEMPT Block

To illustrate the alternative mode for processing the preempted entities, let's consider a situation in which the workpiece that is loaded on the machine when the breakdown occurs is ruined and must be scrapped. In this case the preempted entity is directed to a Count block labeled Scrap, where it is counted and disposed of. Only two changes to the model shown in Figure 8-5 are required to model this situation. The revised PREEMPT block and the added COUNT block are shown on the left.

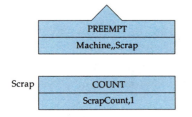

4. Queues Revisited

Now that we have used resources to expand our flexibility in modeling, we next turn our attention to expanding flexibility with queues. We begin by discussing the situation in which we have two or more parallel queues and want to model the selection process among these queues. We then examine the problem of searching the queue members and removing an entity from the queue. Finally, we discuss the concept of entity matching in queues, which is useful for modeling assembly operations and just-in-time (JIT) part flow.

4.1 Selecting Among Parallel Queues: The PICKQ and QPICK Blocks

When a system has multiple, parallel queues, we need a method for conveniently modeling the process for selecting among the queues. There are actually two cases to consider, as illustrated in Figure 8-6. In the first case, we have an entity arriving at a set of parallel queues, and we must decide which queue the arriving entity will join. This process of selecting among downstream queues for entity insertion into the queue is modeled with the PICKQ block. Note that the letter Q follows the verb PICK to emphasize that the selection is from downstream queues. In the second case, we have a Hold block (i.e., a SEIZE block) that pulls entities out of a set of upstream parallel queues. The QPICK block is used to model this process of selecting among upstream queues for entity removal. The letter Q precedes the verb PICK to denote that the selection is upstream of the block.

Figure 8-6. Selecting Among Parallel Queues

We begin by discussing the first case, in which we have an arriving entity and must select between two parallel downstream queues. The PICKQ block used to model this decision process is summarized below. The body of the block has a triangular shape very similar to that of the Transfer block. This triangular shape denotes a decision process. Generally, the triangle points in the direction of this process; hence, in the PICKQ block the triangle points down to indicate that the decision involves blocks on the output side of the PICKQ block. The output side of the block contains two or more output branches with QUEUE block labels, QueueLabel, defining the set of parallel queues from which a selection is to be made.

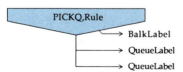

PICKQ, Rule, BalkLabel:
                    QueueLabel:
                    repeats;

Upon arrival at the PICKQ block, the entity is sent to one of the set of output QUEUE block labels, based on the PICKQ block's queue selection rule, Rule. Figure 8-7 summarizes some of the commonly used rules. These rules are almost identical to the Resource Selection Rules presented in Figure 8-4. As with resource selection rules, you can define and incorporate new and different queue selection rules in the simulation by programming the decision process in a FORTRAN or C routine; however, we postpone our discussion of these user-defined queue selection rules until Chapter 10.

Rule	Description
CYC	CYClic priority
RAN	RANdom priority
POR	Preferred Order Rule
LNQ	Largest Number in Queue
SNQ	Smallest Number in Queue
LRC	Largest Remaining Capacity
SRC	Smallest Remaining Capacity

Figure 8-7. Queue Selection Rules

When making a selection from a set of parallel QUEUE blocks, the PICKQ block considers only those QUEUE blocks with space available to accommodate the arriving entity. If a QUEUE block has a finite capacity specified and is full, it will not be selected by the PICKQ block. If all of the QUEUE blocks referenced by the PICKQ block have finite capacities, and if all are full when a new entity arrives, there is no space available for the arriving entity. In this case the arriving entity goes to a balk label, BalkLabel. If no balk label is specified, the entity is automatically disposed of (with no error). The balk label causes entities arriving when all queues are full to be redirected from the PICKQ block to the block with the specified label.

Note that the downstream association of the QUEUE blocks with the PICKQ block is purely logical and has nothing to do with the physical location of the blocks within the block diagram. For example, the PICKQ block can be near the bottom of the block diagram, and the associated QUEUE blocks can be near the top of the block diagram, as long as the logical flow of entities is from the PICKQ block to the QUEUE blocks.

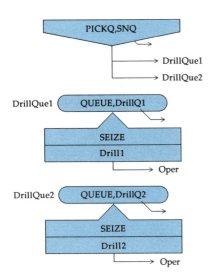

When the PICKQ block is used in conjunction with QUEUE-SEIZE blocks, it provides the capability for modeling parallel servers, with each server having its own queue of customers in front of it. This situation is common in modeling many service systems, such as a supermarket, a gas station, an airline ticketing counter, a fast food restaurant, etc. In contrast, the SELECT block discussed earlier is useful for modeling situations in which we have parallel servers supplied by a single queue.

An example of the use of the PICKQ block is shown on the left. In this example arriving parts are sent to one of two drilling stations, depending on which drill has the smallest number of waiting parts. Although in this example the QUEUE-SEIZE block combinations are located immediately following the PICKQ block, they do not have to be. Note that in this example no balk label is specified on the PICKQ block because both drill queues have an infinite capacity.

The second case that we must consider involves pulling entities from a parallel set of upstream queues. The QPICK block used to model this situation is shown below. Again, the body of the block has a triangular shape, denoting that the block represents a decision process. In this case, however, the triangle points upward to indicate that the decision process involves QUEUE blocks on the input side of the QPICK block. The input side (left) of the block contains two or more input branches that specify the labels of the associated QUEUE block from which a selection is to be made.

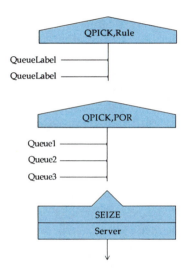

> QPICK, Rule: QueueLabel:
>   repeats;

The QPICK block logically sits between the Hold block, which is pulling the entities from the queues, and the associated QUEUE blocks, from which the entities are being pulled. Although the QUEUE blocks associated with the QPICK block can be located anywhere in the model, the QPICK block must be physically attached to its associated Hold block. In other words, the QPICK block replaces the single QUEUE block, which is normally physically attached to the Hold block. A typical QPICK-Hold block combination appears on the left.

Because the QUEUE blocks listed on the input side of the QPICK block are logically attached to the Hold block that follows the QPICK block, these same QUEUE blocks cannot be attached to any other Hold blocks. SIMAN normally attempts to attach each QUEUE block in the model to the next block in sequence, expecting it to be a Hold block. To override this action, you must include a special modifier on those QUEUE blocks associated with a QPICK block. This modifier, called the DETACH modifier, prevents the QUEUE block from being automatically attached to the next block in sequence. A QUEUE block with a DETACH modifier is not associated in any way with the next block in sequence, and this next block can be any block type. As discussed later in this chapter, detached QUEUE blocks can be used in other ways.

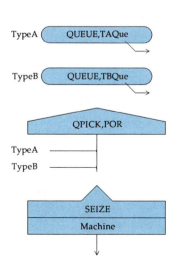

An example of the use of the QPICK block appears on the left. In this example, parts arrive at two separate detached QUEUE blocks, which are associated with a QPICK block. The QPICK block is attached to a SEIZE block, which allocates units of the resource Machine to waiting entities. When the resource becomes available, SIMAN selects the QUEUE block, from which the next entity is removed, and allocates the resource at the SEIZE block. The Preferred Order Rule (POR) is used to make this selection; the POR causes a priority to be assigned to the QUEUE blocks based on the order in which they are listed on the QPICK block. In this example, the QPICK block always pulls from the QUEUE block labeled TypeA unless that QUEUE block is empty. Only when the TypeA QUEUE block is empty can entities be pulled from the TypeB QUEUE block. In other words, preference is always given to the TypeA entities.

Note that on both the PICKQ and QPICK blocks the reference or tie to the associated queues is by block labels and not by QUEUE names.

4.2 Manipulating Entities in Queues: The SEARCH and REMOVE Blocks

Once an entity enters a QUEUE block, it normally waits in the queue until it is removed by the associated Hold block. For example, an entity arriving at a QUEUE-SEIZE block combination typically waits until it is removed from the QUEUE block by the SEIZE block and is allocated a resource. In some cases, however, an entity may depart the queue before being processed in the normal way. This is particularly true for systems in which the entities represent people awaiting a service. This action of giving up the wait and prematurely departing a queue is commonly referred to as *reneging*. To model this situation, we must be able to arbitrarily remove any entity from a queue.

Another type of non-standard queueing action, called *jockeying*, occurs when one of two or more parallel queues becomes shorter than the other(s). When this occurs, the last entity in the longer queue may switch to the shorter queue. This type of queueing behavior is common at check-out lines in a supermarket. To be able to model this situation, we must be able to remove the last entity from the longer queue so that it can be sent to join the shorter queue.

A third type of non-standard queueing action involves situations in which the next entity to be processed is not necessarily the first entity in the queue. This situation arises when the selection process for the next entity cannot easily be translated into one of the standard queue ranking rules. As a result, the members of the queue must be examined to determine which entity should be the next one processed. To model this situation we must be able to search the queue to locate an entity satisfying some condition and then remove the selected entity from the queue and send it to the appropriate block for processing.

Two SIMAN blocks allow easy manipulation of the entities residing in queues to represent these and other types of non-standard queueing processes. These two blocks, both Operation blocks, are called the SEARCH block and the REMOVE block. You use the SEARCH block to search the entities within a queue to find an entity whose rank meets some condition; you use the REMOVE block to remove that entity from the queue.

The SEARCH block is shown below. This block's operands include the target queue's identifier, Set, the starting and ending rank for the search, BegJ and EndJ, and the Condition for which we search. The starting rank can be smaller or larger than the ending rank, resulting in a search in the forward or backward direction, respectively. The search condition can be expressed as a logical condition, as the operator MIN(Expression), or as the operator MAX(Expression). In the first form (e.g., ArrivalTime < 10) the search returns the rank of the first entity in the range that satisfies the logical condition. In the second form (e.g., MIN(JobPriority/ SlackTime)), SIMAN searches all entities in the specified range, and the search returns the rank of the entity, in the special-purpose attribute J, that has the smallest value for the expression. The third form returns the rank of the entity having the largest value for the expression. In all three forms, the condition or expression should involve at least one entity attribute. Note that any attributes specified as part of a search condition reference attributes of entities in the queue to be searched, not attributes of the arriving entity causing the search.

> SEARCH, Set, BegJ, EndJ: Condition;

By default, the range of the search is the entire queue; however, you may limit the range to a subset of the queue by specifying the starting and ending search rank. Use the special keyword NQ to denote the rank of the last entity in the queue. The starting and ending search ranks can be given as constants or as expressions. If attributes are used to specify the ranks, they reference the attributes of the entity causing the search.

The queue search is performed when each entity arrives at the SEARCH block, and the result of the search is returned in the special-purpose variable, J. In other words, the SEARCH block always resets the variable J. In some cases the search may fail to select an entity, e.g., the QUEUE block may be empty. In the case of a logical condition, it is also possible that no entity within the search's range satisfies the condition. When a search fails, a value of 0 is assigned to J. If the search is successful, the variable J is set to the rank of the selected entity.

Some examples of the SEARCH block are shown on the left. In the first example, the queue named Jobqueue is searched to find the first entity with attribute PartType equal to 1. This search is made from the first to the last entity in the queue. In the second example, a backward search from the last to the first entity is made to find the entity with the minimum value of the attribute SlackTime.

The second function for manipulating entities within a queue block is the REMOVE block, shown below. This block removes an entity with a specified rank from a queue. The REMOVE block has three operands: the Rank of the entity to be removed; the queue identifier, QueueID; and the block Label to which the removed entity is to be sent. You may use the special keyword NQ to specify the rank of the last entity in the queue.

> REMOVE: Rank, QueueID, Label;

When an entity arrives at the REMOVE block, it first causes the specified entity to be removed from the QUEUE block where it is currently waiting and then to be sent to the specified block label. At this point there are two entities simultaneously trying to move through the block diagram: the entity arriving at the REMOVE block (the removing entity) and the entity removed from the QUEUE block (the removed entity). SIMAN gives priority to the entity currently moving through the model; in this case the removing entity exits the REMOVE block and continues its movement through the block diagram as far as possible until it encounters a delay or is disposed of. At this point the removed entity

---

SEARCH,Set,BegJ,EndJ

Condition

SEARCH,Jobqueue

PartType.EQ.1

SEARCH,JobQueue,NQ,1

MIN(SlackTime)

REMOVE

Rank,QueueID,Label

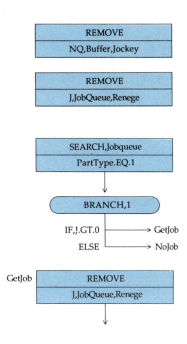

enters the block with the specified block label and continues its movement through the block diagram.

Some examples of the REMOVE block appear on the left. In the first example, each arrival at the block removes the last entity from the queue named Buffer and sends it to the block labeled Jockey. In the second example, the entity with rank J is removed from the queue named JobQueue and sent to the block labeled Renege.

The SEARCH and REMOVE blocks are typically used in combination, with the SEARCH block locating the entity to be removed, and the REMOVE block actually removing the entity from the queue. When using the SEARCH and REMOVE blocks in combination, you must always deal with the possibility of a failed search. If the search is unsuccessful, and J is returned as 0, then using J to specify the rank of the entity to remove in the REMOVE block results in an execution error. To avoid this problem, you can usually use a BRANCH block between the SEARCH and the REMOVE blocks; thus, removals are skipped for unsuccessful searches, i.e., when J is 0, the entity branches around the REMOVE block. This combination of blocks is illustrated on the left.

4.3 Matching Queued Entities: The MATCH Block

Consider a manufacturing system in which there is a set of parallel queues, each containing parts to be assembled. One part is removed from each queue and placed into a kit for assembly; however, each part has a specific identifier that must be matched with the other parts that are assembled together to form the kit. Hence, for a kit to be formed, there must be a part having the same identifier in each of the parallel queues. Only then can the matching parts be removed from the queues and placed in the kit.

To model this type of system, we must be able to monitor a set of parallel queues and to detect when a match occurs between entities within the queues. When the match occurs, we want to be able to specify the processing for the matched entities. SIMAN provides the MATCH block for this purpose.

The MATCH block is shown below. Its triangular shape indicates that it is used to model a decision process. The triangle points upward to denote that the decision involves upstream queues. A varying number of input-output branch pairs appear on the bottom side of the block. The left branches (the input branches) define the labels of the QUEUE blocks that compose the set of matching queues. The right branches (the output branches) specify the destinations for the entities removed from the QUEUE blocks when a match occurs.

MATCH, AttributeID: QueueLabel, DestLabel:
repeats;

The MATCH block has an optional operand, called the *matching attribute*, AttributeID, specified within the triangular body. When this operand is specified, a match occurs if each of the associated QUEUE blocks contains an entity having the same value for this attribute. If this operand is omitted, then a match occurs when there is at least one entity in each of the associated queues. In either case, when a match does occur, the matching entities are removed from their queues and sent to the destination labels specified on the output side of the MATCH block.

Each of the QUEUE blocks specified on the input side of the block must have a DETACH modifier and cannot be specified on the input side of other QPICK or MATCH blocks (or other Hold blocks). Although the QUEUE blocks logically precede the MATCH block in terms of the flow of entities, they can be physically located anywhere in the model.

When an entity arrives at a QUEUE block that is associated with a MATCH block, SIMAN examines the companion QUEUE blocks listed on the input side of the MATCH block. If a match occurs, SIMAN removes the arriving entity and one matching entity from each of the associated QUEUE blocks, and sends them to their respective destinations as specified on the output branches. If a destination's label is omitted, then SIMAN disposes of the entity removed from the QUEUE block associated with that output branch.

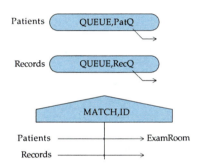

An example of the MATCH block is shown on the left. In this example, entities representing patients and health records are queued in the detached QUEUE blocks labeled Patients and Records. The MATCH block monitors these queues for a match on the attribute named ID. When a match occurs on this attribute, the matching entity in the QUEUE block labeled Patients is removed and sent to the block labeled ExamRoom, and the corresponding matching entity in the queue labeled Records is removed and disposed of.

Although the MATCH block is most commonly used for modeling assembly operations, it applies to any situation in which we need to synchronize a set of randomly arriving entities before further processing. For example, in a JIT (Just-in-Time) manufacturing system both the availability of the raw material to produce a part and an indication of a downstream demand for the part trigger processing. Indication of demand can come by means of a kanban, empty tote, computer signal, etc. We can model this demand-driven flow logic by placing the raw material in one queue and the indication of demand in a second queue and then matching entities within these two queues. In this way processing only takes place at the workcenter when both the material and demand for the part are present.

5. Entity Sets

In some situations, the entities within the system are either temporarily or permanently brought together into *entity sets* before further processing through the system. For example, we may have a manufacturing situation in which we place several different workpieces (each with different attributes) on a pallet before moving the parts to the next workstation. We want to move the entire pallet as a unit represented by a single entity, but we must be able to get back to the original entities representing the workpieces after the pallet has arrived at its destination station. We refer to the temporary grouping of entities in this fashion as the formation of a *temporary entity set*.

As a second example of entity sets, consider entities representing six-packs brought together at a casing machine into a single entity representing cases of four six-packs. If the boundaries of the system are such that we do not model the splitting of each case back into individual six-packs (or if all the six-packs have identical attribute values), then the original entities representing the six-packs can be destroyed. In other words, each set of four entities representing arriving six-packs can be permanently replaced by a single entity representing the departing case. We refer to the permanent combining of entities in this fashion as the formation of a *permanent entity set*.

In the next section we discuss the concept of entity sets and the SIMAN blocks used to form them. We begin our discussion with temporary entity sets and then proceed to permanent entity sets.

5.1 Temporary Entity Sets: The GROUP, SPLIT, PICKUP, and DROPOFF Blocks

A temporary entity set is a grouping of entities that is attached to another entity called the *representative entity*. A temporary entity set is also sometimes referred to as a *group*. The representative entity moves through the model seizing resources, riding on conveyors, making assignments to its attributes, etc. as though it were a single entity. Although the attributes of the representative may change during this process, the attributes of the member entities within the entity set do not. At some later point in the model, the original member entities may be removed from the set.

To form a temporary entity set, use the GROUP block. This block's operands are summarized below. The GROUP block, a type of Hold block, holds arriving entities in the preceding QUEUE block until a sufficient number of entities are present to form the entity set. When the entities are present, a new representative entity is created, and the entities in the QUEUE block are removed from the queue and linked to the representative. The representative entity then departs the GROUP block, carrying with it the member entities; however, the representative functions as an individual entity.

GROUP: Qty, SaveCrit;

Each time a new entity set is formed, the first operand for the GROUP block, the size of the set (Qty), defines the number of entities attached to the newly created representative entity. Whenever an entity arrives at the QUEUE block preceding the GROUP block, the new length of the queue is compared to the required set size. If the length equals or exceeds the size of the set, SIMAN removes the first Qty entities in the QUEUE block and uses them in their current order within the queue to form the entity set, where Qty corresponds to the current size of the set.

When the representative entity is created for a new entity set, the initial values of the attributes for this entity are assigned as some combination of the attributes of the set's members. To control this assignment, specify the SaveCrit operand as

FIRST or LAST to denote that the attributes of the first or last member in the entity set are assigned to the representative entity. This operand can also be specified as SUM or PRODUCT to denote that each general-purpose attribute of the representative entity is assigned the sum or product of the corresponding attribute values for all members in the entity set. The attributes M, NS, and IS of the representative entity are set to the values of the first entity in the set if SaveCrit is FIRST, SUM, or PRODUCT or to the last entity in the set if SaveCrit is LAST.

As the representative entity moves from block to block, it engages in the function associated with each block; however, the members of the entity set do *not* engage in these functions. Hence, these entities are completely hidden from any activity within the model during their membership within the entity set. Note, however, that there is one restriction on a representative entity: it cannot be disposed of without first freeing the member entities at a SPLIT or DROPOFF block (described below).

If the group's size is specified as a variable, and if this variable falls below the current length of the queue, then multiple sets may be formed at the same point in time; however, set formation only occurs when there is an arrival at the QUEUE block. In the case of a decreased set-size requirement, set formation is delayed until the next arrival — even if there are enough waiting entities to form a set with the new set size.

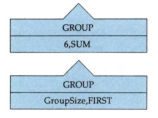

Some examples of the GROUP block appear at the left. In the first example, entities wait in the preceding QUEUE block until there are at least six entities in the queue. Where there are six entities, a new representative entity is created, and the first six entities are removed from the QUEUE block and attached to this entity. The attributes of the representative entity are set to the sum of the corresponding general-purpose attributes of the six member entities. (M, NS and IS from the first entity), and the representative entity departs the block. In the second example, entities wait in the preceding QUEUE block until the length of the queue reaches the value specified by the variable GroupSize. When the required length is reached, the first GroupSize entities are removed from the queue and are linked as members of a set attached to a newly created representative entity. The attributes of this entity are set to the attributes of the first member in the set.

The members of an entity set can themselves be representatives that carry other entities in an entity set. For example, we can form a group of entities representing individual workpieces into a representative entity corresponding to a pallet. These pallet entities can then be grouped into a new representative entity corresponding to a rack, and so forth. There is no limit to the number of levels that can be formed.

At any point in the model, the original member entities of a temporary entity set can be returned to the model by sending the representative entity to a SPLIT block, a type of Operation block, which is summarized below. When the representative entity arrives at this block, the member entities are unlinked from the representative and depart the block as individual entities. The representative entity is then disposed of at the SPLIT block; only the member entities depart the block. By default, the departing entities have the same attribute values that they originally had at the time that the entity set was formed — including special-purpose attributes M, NS, and IS. You may, however, cause the departing members to inherit one or more of the current values for the representative by listing the attributes to be inherited in the bottom line segment of the block.

SPLIT: Attributes;

In the case of hierarchical groupings, the SPLIT block only splits one level at a time. In our earlier example with racks and pallets, the first SPLIT block would split the rack back into pallets, and a second SPLIT block would split the pallets back into individual workpieces. At each execution of the SPLIT block, the representative entity (rack or pallet) is disposed of. The members of the group depart the SPLIT block one at a time, in the order that they waited in the original queue to form the group.

Some examples of the SPLIT block are shown on the left. In the first example, each arriving representative entity is disposed of, and the members of the attached set depart the block as individual entities having their original attribute values. In the second example, the same basic events occur, except that, each time a member entity departs, the attribute value MarkTime is reset to the executing entity's current value of this attribute.

Although the GROUP and SPLIT blocks are useful for grouping and splitting entire entity sets, we sometimes want to add entities to, or remove entities from, a temporary entity set. For example, if we are using a temporary entity set to represent a pallet containing several different workpieces, we may want to add a new workpiece to the pallet or remove a workpiece from the pallet. The PICKUP and DROPOFF blocks allow you to add and remove entities, respectively. When a representative entity arrives at the PICKUP block, it removes one or more entities from a specified queue and adds them as new members to its attached entity set. When the representative entity arrives at a DROPOFF block, it removes one or more entities from its current entity set and sends them to a specified block. As their names imply, these blocks are commonly used to model situations in which several entities are simultaneously moved as a unit load for which individual entities are picked up and dropped off along the way.

The PICKUP block, a type of Operation block, is summarized below. The operands for this block include the identifier for the queue from which entities are to be removed, QueueID; the beginning Rank of the entities to be removed; and the number of entities to be picked up, Qty. When an entity arrives at the PICKUP block, it removes the specified number of entities from the designated queue. The removed entities are added to the end of the entity set carried by the entity that executes the PICKUP block.

PICKUP: QueueID, Rank, Qty;

The GROUP and PICKUP blocks perform similar functions in slightly different ways. The GROUP block, a type of Hold block, always creates a new representative entity whose set members are removed from the preceding QUEUE block when the required number has arrived. The PICKUP block, a type of Operation block, also removes entities from a queue and places them in a set; however, the queue can be any queue in the model, and the representative entity is the one that executes the PICKUP block, not a new entity created at the time of the set's formation. The PICKUP block can be used to form a new set or to add entities to an existing set; the GROUP block always forms new sets.

A run-time error results if the PICKUP block attempts to remove entities from undefined queues or if an entity's rank exceeds the number of entities currently residing in a queue. It is good practice to use a SEARCH block or BRANCH block that examines NQ to verify that the required number of entities reside in the queue before attempting to remove them with the PICKUP block.

Some examples of the PICKUP block are shown on the left. In the first example, the first entity in the queue named BusQueue is removed and added as the last entity to the set attached to the entity executing the block. In the second example, the queue named WorkQueue is searched for the entity with the minimum value of the attribute SlackTime. This entity is then removed from the queue and added as the last entity of the set attached to the entity executing the block. In the last example, all entities currently residing in the queue named WaitQ are removed and added to the set of the currently executing entity.

The DROPOFF block, the complement of the PICKUP block, removes member entities from the set of the executing entity and then sends the removed entities to a specified block. The DROPOFF block, a type of Operation block, is summarized below. The operands for this block include the Rank of the first entity to be removed from the set, the number of entities to be removed (Qty), and the Label of the block to which the removed entities are to be sent. You can also enter the executing-entity's Attributes, the values of which will be inherited by each departing set member.

DROPOFF, Rank, Qty: Label, Attributes;

When an entity arrives at the DROPOFF block, the block removes the specified number of entities from the set of the executing entity and sends them to the specified block Label. If you enter an attribute list for the DROPOFF block, the values for these attributes are now copied to entities departing from the set. The executing entity then departs the block and continues its movement through the model. The removed entities begin moving through the model at the labeled block to which they have been sent.

To specify which entities are dropped off, you enter the rank of the first entity to be removed from the set and the number of entities to be dropped off. Only consecutive entities can be dropped off at each execution of the block. A FIFO (first-in-first-out) rule establishes the rank of members within an entity set. Hence, the entity with a rank of 1 is the entity that has been a member of the set the longest.

The number of entities that are currently members of an entity set is maintained by the SIMAN attribute NG (denoting number in group). If the rank of an entity to be removed exceeds this value, a run-time error results. In some instances we may want to search the members of a set to determine which entity to drop. To do so, use the SEARCH block with the queue's identifier defaulted or with an entry of GROUP. The SEARCH block then searches the members of the set attached to the executing entity and returns the rank of the selected entity within the set in the variable J.

The SPLIT and DROPOFF blocks, both Operation blocks, perform similar functions, yet they differ in several significant ways. First, the SPLIT block always releases all members of the set attached to the representative entity, whereas the DROPOFF block can selectively remove one or more entities without disturbing the other members of the set. Second, the SPLIT block always destroys the arriving representative entity, whereas the DROPOFF block does not. Finally, in the SPLIT block the released members from the set depart directly from the SPLIT block, whereas in the DROPOFF block the released members go to a designated labeled block elsewhere in the model, and the arriving representative entity departs the DROPOFF block.

Some examples of the DROPOFF block are shown on the left. In the first example, the first entity belonging to the executing entity's set is removed and sent to the block labeled InBuffer. In the second example, the first three entities in the executing entity's set are removed and sent to this same block; however, each departing entity's MarkTime attribute is assigned to the executing entity's current value for this attribute. In the last example, a search determines the rank of the entity in the attached set with the largest value of the attribute named Weight; the rank of the selected entity is returned by the SEARCH block in the variable J, and this entity is removed from the executing entity's set and is sent to the block labeled DropPoint.

5.2 Permanent Entity Sets: The COMBINE and DUPLICATE Blocks

With temporary entity sets, entities are grouped together and attached to a representative entity; this attachment can be accomplished by using a GROUP or PICKUP block. These member entities, which are attached to the representative, are not lost and can be returned to the model at any point by using a SPLIT or DROPOFF block. In some cases, however, we may not need to return the member entities to the model because they will remain in the set permanently. In this situation it is more efficient to use a permanent entity set.

Permanent entity sets are conceptually similar to temporary entity sets, but there is no corresponding SPLIT block for splitting a permanent entity set back into its member entities. In a permanent entity set the member entities are not attached to the representative entity; instead, they are destroyed when the representative entity is created. Hence, all information about the original entities is completely lost. This information loss poses no problem as long as we have no need to recover the attribute information.

The advantage of permanent entity sets over temporary entity sets lies in a considerable saving in memory requirements, because the member entities are not stored once the set is formed. In addition, a representative entity for a permanent entity set can be destroyed without having to split the set.

A permanent entity set is formed by using a COMBINE block, which is shown below. The COMBINE block, a type of Hold block, has operands identical to the GROUP block, i.e., the size of the set and the criterion for saving. The COMBINE block holds arriving entities in the preceding QUEUE block until a sufficient number of entities is present to form the entity set, operand Qty. When this occurs, a new representative entity is created, and the entities in the QUEUE block are removed from the queue; however, rather than being linked to the representative (as with the GROUP block), these removed entities are destroyed. The representative then departs the GROUP block and functions like a regular entity.

COMBINE: Qty, SaveCrit;

When SIMAN creates the representative entity for a new entity set, the initial values of the attributes for this entity are assigned as some combination of the attributes of the members of the entity set. This assignment is accomplished by using the SaveCrit operand in the same way as the GROUP block, that is, by using the FIRST, LAST, SUM, or PRODUCT option.

Some examples of the COMBINE block are shown on the left. In the first example, the COMBINE block holds the entities in the preceding QUEUE block until there are at least six entities in the queue. At this point, a new representative entity is created, and the first six entities are removed from the queue and destroyed. The values assigned to the attributes of the newly created representative entity are those of the first entity that was removed from the queue in forming the set. The representative entity then departs the block. In the second example, the size of the set is specified as 10, and the SaveCrit operand is specified as PRODUCT. In this case the values assigned to the attributes of the representative entity are formed as the product of the corresponding attributes of the 10 member entities comprised in the set.

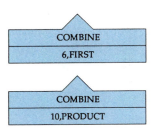

Although you cannot split a permanent set formed at a COMBINE block into its original members, you can duplicate the representative entity a specified number of times by using the DUPLICATE block. This block performs the partial equivalent of the SPLIT block by duplicating the representative entity Qty times, where Qty is 1 less than the size of the permanent set. In this case, each arriving entity, plus Qty additional exact copies of the executing entity, depart the block. Hence, the DUPLICATE block can be used to restore the correct number of member entities; however, the attributes of all entities will be identical to the current values of the attributes for the representative entity.

The DUPLICATE block's operands, shown below, include the number of duplicates to create, Qty, and the Label of the block to which the duplicates are to be sent. When activated by an arriving entity, the operand specifying the number of duplicates to create is evaluated and truncated to an integer. If the result is less-than-or-equal-to 0, no duplicates are created, and the arriving entity departs the block. Otherwise, the prescribed number of entities is created, and the attributes for these newly created entities are set to the attributes of the executing entity. Any objects — Resources, Transporters, Conveyors, etc. — or temporary entity sets linked to the entity are not assigned to the duplicates. If a destination block's label is specified, the duplicates are sent to the specified block, and the executing entity exits on the output side of the DUPLICATE block. Otherwise, all the duplicates depart with the executing entity on the output side of the block.

DUPLICATE
Qty,Label

> DUPLICATE: Qty, Label:
>   repeats;

Although the DUPLICATE block is commonly used to clone representative entities associated with permanent entity sets, it can also be used for many other purposes. The block does not have to be associated with a COMBINE block, nor does the arriving entity have to represent a permanent set. In essence, we can use the DUPLICATE block any time we want to clone one entity into many.

Some examples of the DUPLICATE block are shown on the left. In the first example, five duplicates are made of each arriving entity. Hence, there will be six departing entities (the executing entity plus five duplicates) exiting the output side of the block for each arrival to the block. In the second example, a single duplicate is created and redirected to the block labeled SubAssemA, and three duplicate entities are sent to the block labeled SubAssemB. The arriving entity then departs the DUPLICATE block by itself.

DUPLICATE
5

DUPLICATE
1,SubAssemA
3,SubAssemB

6. Input/Output

In our previous simulations, all associated data were contained directly within either the Model or Experiment Frames. In some situations, however, we have data in an external source that we want to access from within the model. For example, when simulating a production schedule for a manufacturing system, we often have an external data file containing the scheduled arrival times and process plans for a set of jobs. Although we can transcribe these data into the appropriate ARRIVALS (presented in Section 9.1) and SEQUENCES elements, it is much more convenient to be able to read the data directly from within the model, thereby eliminating the need for reformatting.

To address these types of situations, SIMAN provides a READ block, which enables us to read data into the model from an external source. The external source can be a formatted file, an unformatted file, or a WKS spreadsheet file. (WKS, the spreadsheet file format used by Lotus 1-2-3, is widely supported by other spreadsheet programs.) The READ block also supports both free- and fixed-format reads and direct- and sequential-access files.

In addition to reading external data, it is also useful to write data from the model to an external source. In some cases we may desire special reports from the model in addition to SIMAN's standard reports. For example, we may want to display a special historical trace for one or more workcenters within a manufacturing facility. Although we can use the built-in SIMAN trace facility for this purpose, the standard trace option gives us no control over the specific format of the report.

Here's another example. Consider a situation in which we want to break a large model of a facility into two smaller component models (e.g., fabrication and inspection), which we can inspect separately. In this case the two component models are related: the departures from the first model are the arrivals at the second model. To model this interconnection, we can write information about the departures from the first component model (fabrication) into a file, which can then be read by the second component model (inspection) and used to generate arrivals to this second process.

To accommodate these situations, SIMAN provides a WRITE block, which writes data to an external file. The external file can be formatted or unformatted, or it can be a WKS spreadsheet file. The WRITE block supports free- and fixed-format writes as well as direct- and sequential-access files.

6.1 Defining an Input/Output File: The FILES Element

When using READ and WRITE blocks within a model, you use the FILES element to define the characteristics of the associated file in the experiment. The operands for this element are summarized below. For each file in the model, this element specifies the symbolic name that references the file from within the model, the system-dependent file descriptor that references the file within the host operating system, the access method for the file (direct or sequential), the type of formatting (unformatted, formatted, WKS binary), and the file's operational characteristics.

```
FILES: Number, Name, FileDesc, Access, Structure, EndOpt,
       Comment, InitOpt, Unit:
       repeats;
```

As with other elements, you have the option of assigning a Number (the first operand) to each file defined in the FILES element. Typically, this Number is omitted, and SIMAN assigns the default number to the file specification (beginning with 1 and increasing by 1). Do not confuse this file number with the unit numbers associated with file input/output (I/O) in FORTRAN and other languages.

The second operand is the symbolic Name of the file. You can think of this Name as an abbreviation or substitute for the actual system-dependent file descriptor. As we soon discuss, within the READ and WRITE blocks, you reference the associated file with an identifier, which you interchangeably specify as either the file's Number or symbolic Name. For example, if the first file defined in the FILES element is assigned the symbolic name Data, this file can be referenced either as file 1 or as Data.

The next operand is the file descriptor, FileDesc, a system-dependent specification of an operating system file name or device name to which the I/O is to be directed. The file descriptor may contain network node or path information in addition to the actual system file name. In some operating systems the file descriptor may contain characters, such as slashes and colons, normally used by SIMAN; therefore, the entire file descriptor must always be enclosed in double quotes ("). For example on an MS-DOS system, the file descriptor "c:\testcase\job.dat" defines a file named job.dat, located on the C drive in a subdirectory named testcase.

The next operand defines the method of Access for the file: sequential or direct. In a sequential-access file, selected by entering SEQ, the records in the file must be written or read in sequential order. When writing to a sequential file, record 1 must be written first, followed by record 2, and so forth. Likewise, when reading a sequential file, record 1 must be read first, followed by record 2, and so forth. A sequential file can be opened for reading or for writing, but not for both at the same time. In other words, if you write to a sequential file, you must close it and reopen it before reading from the same file. In contrast, with a direct-access file, specified as DIR, the records can be read or written in any order, and you can alternately read and write to the same file without first closing and reopening the file. Records are numbered sequentially beginning with 1, and this number references the record within the file to which you read or write.

Although the direct-access file is more flexible because you can access any record by its number, there are advantages to using a sequential-access file when the data can conveniently be read or written in sequential order. In general, sequential-access files are faster and smaller, and the records can be of varying length, thereby making efficient use of file space. In contrast, all records in a direct-access file must be of the same length, which is set (in bytes) to the length of the largest data record. Hence, if the data records written to the file vary greatly in size, direct-access files waste substantial space. This option is selected by entering DIR(Length), where the operand Length is the number of bytes in each data record.

The format structure of a file is also important. The formatting of the file defines exactly how the data are represented within the file records. The Structure operand in the FILES element defines the format used by the file.

An unformatted file, selected by entering UNF, permits the fastest access to data and produces the smallest files. Its efficiency makes this file's structure an ideal vehicle for passing data from one component model to another. However, these files cannot conveniently be moved between operating systems, nor can you read these files as a standard text file, so they are not suitable for preparation or review with a standard text editor.

Although slower, the use of a formatted file solves both of these problems. This option is selected by entering "(Format)." Note that this option requires that the operand Format be enclosed in double quotes and parentheses. You can easily move formatted files across operating systems and create or view them by using standard text editors. Formatted files can be one of two basic types. With free-formatted (also known as list-directed) files, the data values are separated by either a comma (,) or one or more blanks. To select this file format, enter the keyword FREe as the structure's operand. In the second type, fixed-format files, the data values are spaced with a fixed user-defined pattern within each record. Using fixed-format records, you can control the appearance of each record by specifying the exact type and location of each field within the record.

When using a fixed-format record, enter the default format for all file access as the Structure operand of the FILES element. SIMAN uses these formats if a format is not directly specified on the READ or WRITE block. If all data for a file share a single format, however, it is convenient to specify the format on the FILES element, thereby avoiding repeated specifications on the READ and WRITE blocks. If a format is specified on the READ or WRITE block, it overrides the format entered on the FILES element.

To enter a format, use FORTRAN syntax enclosed by double quotes (") and parentheses (()). Only real data formats are supported—hence, only the Fw.d, Ew.d, and Gw.d Fortran edit descriptors are allowed. Edit descriptors for data types other than real (e.g., Aw, Iw, and Dw) are not allowed. However, the use of character strings, repeat factors, and characters indicating a new page, skipped line, skipped space, tab, etc. are fully supported. For example, the format specification "(//5x,'value = ',F3.2)" causes two lines and five spaces to be skipped and causes the string 'value = ' to be displayed followed by the data value in the F3.2 format. For details about FORTRAN format syntax, see any FORTRAN reference manual.

Another option for the file structure is the WKS worksheet format, which is used by spreadsheet programs such as Lotus 1-2-3. The WKS worksheet format is a special binary, sequential-access data file that can be written or read by many commonly used spreadsheet programs. The support within SIMAN for this optional file structure makes it easy to interface SIMAN simulation models to spreadsheet programs. The spreadsheet program can then be used to enter data for the simulation or to analyze data generated by the simulation. For example, cost data can conveniently be incorporated into the output analysis by using a spreadsheet.

The remaining operands specify the file's operational characteristics and an optional designation of what output unit to associate with the file. The operational characteristics include specifications for what to do when an end-of-file indicator is encountered, EndOpt (rewind, terminate with an error, ignore and continue, dispose of the entity and continue); what character, if any, is to be used in Column 1 to indicate a Comment record, which is ignored during reads; and what is to be done with the file between replications of the model, InitOpt (rewind or not). Although the operand for specifying the file's output unit, Unit, is typically not used, it allows you to override the automatic assignment of unit numbers and to force a specific FORTRAN output unit to be associated with the file.

An example of the FILES element is shown below.

```
FILES" In,"c"\testcase\job.dat",SEQ,UNF:
      Out,"d"\testcase\results.dat",SEQ,WKS;
```

This element defines two files, named In and Out; the file numbers 1 and 2 have been defaulted. The first file (named In) has the file descriptor "c:\ testcase\job.dat" and is a sequential, unformatted file. You can use the identifier In or 1 to reference this file in a READ or WRITE block. The second file (named Out) has the file descriptor "d:\testcase\results.dat" and is a sequential WKS file. You can use the identifier Out or 2 to reference this file in a READ or WRITE block.

6.2 Reading Data from a File: The READ Block

Once you use the FILES element to define a file in the experiment, you can use the READ block to read the file's data from within the model. This block, a type of Operation block, is summarized below.

READ, FileID, Format, Rec: Variables;

READ,FileID,Format,Rec
Variables

The READ block reads one record of data each time an entity arrives at the block, and it assigns the input values to the specified variables. If the file is not open when the entity arrives, SIMAN automatically opens it to allow reading from the file. SIMAN then assigns the values contained in the data record to the list of assignable attributes or variables listed in the block's second line segment.

You specify which file to read by entering the file's identifier (Name or Number) on the top line segment, FileID. The identifier defaults to the standard input unit (normally the keyboard). Otherwise, SIMAN reads the file identified by the system-dependent file descriptor in the FILES element. For example, in the FILES element shown earlier, the identifier In causes SIMAN to read c:\testcase\job.dat.

If the file is formatted, you use the Format operand to directly specify the format used during the read (fixed or free) on the READ block. By omitting this operand, you use the default format specified on the FILES element. If the file is unformatted or is a WKS file, then SIMAN ignores this operand.

If the file is a direct-access file, you specify the record to be read as an operand of the block, Rec. This record's number must be greater than 0 and less-than-or-equal-to the current number of records in the file. If no number is specified for a direct-access file, the number defaults to 1 greater than the last record accessed. For sequential-access files the number accessed always corresponds to the next record in the file, and the Record Number operand is ignored.

In the case of sequential WKS files, each arrival at the READ block accesses the next row in the worksheet. If there are n attributes or variables listed for input, the values in the first n cells of this next row of the worksheet are assigned in order to these inputs. On the next read from the WKS file, the remaining cells in that row (if any) are skipped, and the read retrieves the first n cells in the next row of the worksheet.

```
┌─────────────────────────┐
│     READ,Shift1         │
├─────────────────────────┤
│   PartType,DueDate      │
└─────────────────────────┘

┌─────────────────────────┐
│ READ,InventData,,NumRecord │
├─────────────────────────┤
│   PartNum,Quantity      │
└─────────────────────────┘


┌─────────────────────────┐
│        CREATE           │
├─────────────────────────┤
│                         │
└─────────────────────────┘
              ↓
┌─────────────────────────┐
│      READ,AbsData       │   NextRead
├─────────────────────────┤
│     Time,PartType       │
└─────────────────────────┘
              ↓
┌─────────────────────────┐
│         DELAY           │
├─────────────────────────┤
│      Time-TNOW          │
└─────────────────────────┘
              ↓
┌─────────────────────────┐
│       DUPLICATE         │
├─────────────────────────┤
│      1,NextRead         │
└─────────────────────────┘


┌─────────────────────────┐
│        CREATE           │
├─────────────────────────┤
│                         │
└─────────────────────────┘
              ↓
┌─────────────────────────┐
│      READ,RelData       │   NextRead
├─────────────────────────┤
│ TimeBetArrivals,PartType│
└─────────────────────────┘
              ↓
┌─────────────────────────┐
│         DELAY           │
├─────────────────────────┤
│    TimeBetArrivals      │
└─────────────────────────┘
              ↓
┌─────────────────────────┐
│       DUPLICATE         │
├─────────────────────────┤
│      1,NextRead         │
└─────────────────────────┘


┌─────────────────────────┐
│ WRITE,FileID,Format,Rec │
├─────────────────────────┤
│      Variables          │
└─────────────────────────┘
```

Some examples of the READ block are shown on the left. In the first example, data are read from the formatted file named Shift1 and assigned to the attributes PartType and DueDate. In the second example, the attributes PartNum and Quantity are read from record number NumRecord in the direct-access file named InventData. In both examples, the READ block uses the format specified in the FILES element.

One common use of the READ block is to generate arrivals for input to a model from data contained in an external file. This external file may have been generated from another model or may be a "print" file of a data base. The file normally contains the arrival times for the entities and initial attribute values. In some cases it may contain the entities' absolute arrival times, and in other cases it may contain their relative arrival times (i.e., the times between arrivals).

A sample sequence of blocks for generating arrivals based on absolute times is shown on the left. A single entity is created at the CREATE block; this entity executes the READ block to read in the value of the variable Time and the attribute PartType. The entity is then delayed at the DELAY block; the duration of the delay is the difference between the entity's scheduled arrival time (Time) and the current time (TNOW). At the end of this delay, the entity passes through the DUPLICATE block and continues through the remainder of the model (not shown). At the DUPLICATE block, however, a clone of the entity is created and sent back to the block labeled Read, where the process is repeated.

Note that this block sequence only works properly when the run terminates before the end of the file is encountered, or when the end-of-file option on the FILES element is specified as DISPOSE. In the latter case the arrival stream from this block sequence is terminated once the end of the file is reached.

A similar block sequence for generating arrivals based on relative times is shown on the left. The only difference between this and the previous example is the DELAY block. In this case the duration of the delay is specified as the inter-arrival time, which is read into the variable TimeBetArrivals.

6.3 Writing Data to a File: The WRITE Block

The WRITE block provides the ability to output data to an external file. Like the READ block, the WRITE block requires that the characteristics of the associated file be defined in the FILES element of the experiment. The WRITE block, a type of Operation block, is summarized below.

WRITE, FileID, Format, Rec: Variables;

When an entity arrives at the WRITE block, SIMAN evaluates the expressions listed in the bottom line segment, Variables, and writes these values to the file referenced by the identifier. If the file is not open, SIMAN automatically opens it before attempting to write. If you omit the identifier from the block, then the values are written to the standard output unit (normally the screen), in which case no FILES element is required.

Either formatted or unformatted writes can be performed. If the file is formatted, you can use both free and fixed formats. You define a fixed format by entering the exact FORTRAN equivalent format within double quotes (") and parentheses (()) for the Format operand. When, however, the exact spacing of the values in the output record is not critical, you specify the word FREE for the Format operand to select the free-formatted output option. Finally, if a default format was assigned in the FILES element, you can select this format by defaulting the format operand on the WRITE block.

For direct-access files, specify the record number to be written as an operand of the block (this operand is ignored for sequential files). The default value for the record number with a direct-access file is 1 greater than the last record accessed. In the case of sequential WKS files, each arrival at the WRITE block writes the next row in the worksheet. The cells within the row are sequentially updated in the order in which the expressions are listed.

Examples of the WRITE block are shown on the left. The first example writes to the default file (assume the screen) the time that each new part exits the system. The second writes to the file Setup the current values of TNOW and M and uses the format specified in the FILES element.

6.4 Closing Files: The CLOSE Block

SIMAN automatically opens a file on the first attempt to read or write to the file. Likewise, all files are automatically closed by SIMAN at the end of the simulation run. Therefore, you usually need not be concerned with the opening and closing of files. In some situations, however, the ability to close a file is useful. For example, some operating systems limit the number of simultaneously open files. In this case, closing a file allows you to open another file. Also, closing a sequential file and then reopening it with a READ or WRITE block has the effect of rewinding it. Hence, the next READ or WRITE block applies to the first record. Note that you can repeat this process indefinitely with a READ block, thereby reprocessing the same information again and again. On the other hand, each time you open a sequential file with the WRITE block, you destroy any previously written information.

The CLOSE block, an operation block, is summarized below. This block has a single operand, which is the identifier of the file to be closed.

CLOSE, FileID;

An example of the use of the CLOSE block appears on the left. An entity passing through this CLOSE block causes the file identified as Shift1 to be closed.

7. Conditional Holds

The Hold blocks that we have used so far have been related to very specific types of processes within the model. For example, the SEIZE block holds entities when the appropriate resources are not available, the ACCESS block holds entities when there is no space on a conveyor, etc. Although these more specific types of Hold blocks are very powerful and useful, we sometimes need to model processes of a more general nature. In this section we discuss two Hold blocks provided for modeling these more general types of processes. The first, the WAIT block, represents situations in which an entity waits in a queue until an event signals the entity to continue its movement through the model; the SIGNAL block is used to signal the entity. The second HOLD block, SCAN, represents situations in which an entity waits in a queue until some condition becomes true; when condition becomes true, the entity passes through the block.

7.1 Waiting for an Event to Occur: The WAIT and SIGNAL Blocks

The WAIT block, shown below, holds an entity in a queue until a specific signal is received. Because it is a type of Hold block, the WAIT block must be preceded by a QUEUE block. The operands for this block include the signal Code and the release limit, WaitLimit.

> WAIT: Code, WaitLimit;

When an entity arrives at a QUEUE-WAIT block combination, the expression entered for the Code signal operand of the block is evaluated and truncated to an integer. The entity, with its assigned integer signal value, is then placed in the queue where it awaits a signal. When a SIGNAL block elsewhere in the model issues a specific integer signal, the entities with identical signal numbers are eligible to be released from the QUEUE-WAIT block combination.

By default, all entities eligible for release are removed from the QUEUE block and exit on the output side of the WAIT block. For each signal received, however, it is possible to restrict the number of entities released from the QUEUE block at each WAIT block by entering a value for the WaitLimit operand. This value defines the maximum local number of entities that can be released at this block each time a signal is received.

The SIGNAL block shown below is used to send a signal to the waiting entities at the QUEUE-WAIT block combinations throughout the model. The first operand on this block, Code, is the signal number to be sent. At each entity's arrival, the expression entered for the signal number is evaluated and truncated to an integer. This integer signal is then sent to each WAIT block throughout the entire model. The second operand specifies the maximum total number of entities to be released.

> SIGNAL: Code, TotalLimit;

Three factors determine the total number of entities released from WAIT blocks in the model: the WaitLimit operand on the WAIT blocks, the TotalLimit operand on the SIGNAL block, and the number of entities currently waiting for a given signal Code. When an entity enters a SIGNAL block, the specified signal is sent, and SIMAN checks the WAIT blocks in the model in the order that they are listed. Any entities waiting for the signal Code are released up to the WaitLimit on individual WAIT blocks, until the TotalLimit is reached, or until there are no more entities to release.

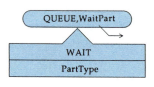

An example of a QUEUE-WAIT block combination and SIGNAL block are shown on the left. Entities arriving at the QUEUE-WAIT block combination wait in the QUEUE block for a signal specified by the attribute named PartType. Note that the entities waiting in this queue can be waiting for different signals, depending on their value for this attribute. Entities arriving at the SIGNAL block send a signal to all WAIT blocks. In this case, an arriving entity to the SIGNAL block sends a signal of 3, and all entities in queue WaitPart with attribute PartType equal to 3 are released and processed after the signalling entity has been processed.

7.2 Waiting for System Status to Change: The SCAN Block

SIMAN also provides a generic mechanism for holding an entity until some specified condition is true. For example, we can hold an entity until the total processing time in the input buffer at a downstream workcenter is less than some critical value. This feature is very powerful and flexible because you can specify the condition as any arbitrary expression involving any SIMAN variables or attributes.

The QUEUE-SCAN block combination provides this holding mechanism. Because the SCAN block (shown below) is a type of Hold block, the preceding QUEUE block is mandatory. The SCAN block's operand represents the Condition that must be true before entities can pass through the block.

SCAN: Condition;

When an entity arrives at the QUEUE-SCAN block combination, the scan condition is evaluated. If the condition is true, the arriving entity is permitted to depart the SCAN block without delay. Otherwise, the entity is placed in the preceding QUEUE block, where it awaits a status change, i.e., for the condition to become true. When there are entities waiting in the QUEUE block, SIMAN scans the condition to detect the point at which it becomes true. To scan, SIMAN evaluates the condition for each SCAN block as the last function before each discrete advance in simulated time. If the condition is true, SIMAN removes the first waiting entity in the preceding QUEUE block and releases it from the SCAN block. This entity then moves through the model until it is either delayed (e.g., at a QUEUE block or DELAY block) or is disposed of. At this point the scan condition is checked again, and, if it is still true, the new first entity is removed from the queue and released from the SCAN block. This one-at-a-time release process is continued until either the queue is empty or the condition becomes false.

Because the process associated with a SCAN block involves evaluating the condition every time the simulated time advances, including this block can increase the run-time in some models. However, in most cases the increase in run-time is not significant. We recommend modeling the system initially in the most direct

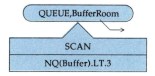

way possible and using the SCAN block only where appropriate. If the resulting run-times are too slow, consider replacing the SCAN blocks with some alternative representation.

Consider a situation in which a downstream workcenter has space for only three waiting parts; parts are blocked from departing the upstream station until there is space available. If we assume that the parts at the downstream station wait in a queue named Buffer, then the QUEUE-SCAN block combination shown on the left represents this blocking process. Entities arriving at this block combination at the upstream station are held until the downstream queue named Buffer has a length of less than 3.

Rather than use the SCAN block in this example, we could incorporate a resource named BufferSpace with a capacity of 3 to represent the waiting spaces at the downstream station. We would require that each entity seize a unit of BufferSpace before departing the upstream workcenter and then release this unit only after departing the Buffer queue at the downstream workcenter. The limited capacity of BufferSpace forces the blocking of entities at the upstream station whenever there are three entities in the downstream Buffer queue, because each of these is allocated one of the three available units of BufferSpace. Although this approach is less direct and slightly more complicated than using the SCAN block, it does provide an alternative approach, which executes more quickly. Other approaches could also be used to avoid the SCAN block when modeling blocking between workcenters.

8. Evaluating System Status: The FINDJ Block

When modeling systems, we frequently need to make a selection based on the current status of the system. The QPICK, PICKQ, and SELECT blocks provide the capability of selecting among queues and resources; however, you cannot use these blocks to model a general selection process. SIMAN's FINDJ block provides this more general feature.

The FINDJ block searches for an expression's value over a specified range of an index whose value must meet some prescribed condition. For example, we can search the value of the expression NQ(J) for J equal to 1 to 10 in order to find the value of J corresponding to the smallest queue. When the search is complete, the variable J is set at the FINDJ block to the first index that satisfies the condition. Hence, in this example, J is set at the FINDJ block to the shortest queue numbered between 1 and 10. Although we can use this block in place of the PICKQ block to implement the SNQ rule, Smallest Number in Queue, for selecting between parallel queues, the real advantage of this block is that the selection process can be based on an expression involving any status variables within the model.

The operands for the FINDJ block, which are summarized below, include the beginning and ending index for the search and the Condition that the search must meet. The beginning index can be smaller or larger than the ending index, corresponding to a forward or backward search. The Condition operand can be specified as a logical expression or as the operator MIN(expression) or MAX (expression), where the expression must involve the index J. In the first form (e.g., NQ(J) > 10), J is returned as the first index value in the range that satisfies the logical condition. In the second and third forms (e.g., MIN(NQ(J))), J is returned as the index value within the search range that minimizes or maximizes the expression. In case of a tie, the first tested index value is selected.

FINDJ, BegJ, EndJ: Condition;

Each time an entity arrives at the FINDJ block, SIMAN makes an assignment to the variable J. Therefor J, should not contain any other value important to the model, because the value is overwritten by an entity's executing this block. If the search is successful, J contains the selected index value. If the search fails (e.g., the logical condition is not satisfied by any J within the range), then J is assigned a value of 0.

Some examples of the FINDJ block are shown on the left. In the first example, a search is made over queues numbered 1 through 10 for the queue having the shortest queue length. In the second example, a backward search is made from Stations 5 to 1 for the first station that does not currently have any entities en route.

At first glance the FINDJ block seems to function very much like the SEARCH block. Although some of the operands are similar, the function is actually quite different. Recall that you use the SEARCH block to locate entities residing in a specified QUEUE block or in an entity set, as a means of selecting an entity to remove from the queue via a REMOVE block. The SEARCH block easily locates an entity within a queue or in the set, but it is limited to this specific function. In contrast, the FINDJ block does not examine the members of a queue; rather, it examines the value of some expression involving system-wide variables. Hence, the FINDJ block is useful for searching the system's status, typically for the purpose of modeling decision making based on status.

FINDJ,BegJ,EndJ
Condition

FINDJ,1,10
MIN(NQ(J))

FINDJ,5,1
NE(J)==0

9. Some Additional Experimental Controls

In this section we discuss some additional elements that you can use in specifying the experiment for a SIMAN simulation model. These elements provide greater control and flexibility in establishing the conditions for which the model is exercised. Specifically, they allow you to create external arrivals to the model, define the value for a block operand from within the experiment, define the decision rule for a decision block from within the experiment, and define table functions, which can be referenced from within the model.

9.1 Creating External Arrivals: The ARRIVALS Element

In our previous examples, entities have entered the model at CREATE blocks included within the model. It is sometimes convenient, however, to be able to define entity arrivals to the model from within the experiment, without having to explicitly include CREATE blocks in the model for this purpose. This approach makes it possible to modify the arrivals to the model from within the experiment, thereby leaving the model unchanged.

Entity arrivals can be created from within the experiment by using the ARRIVALS element. This element causes entities to enter the model at a specified destination block. The element contains a repeating group of operands for defining the optional arrival number, destination block, batch size, arrival time, and optional attribute assignments. These operands are summarized below.

ARRIVALS: Number, Type, Time, BatchSize, Assignments:
            repeats;

The destination block, operand Type, can be specified in one of four ways. The first method applies when the destination block is a QUEUE block and is specified as QUEUE(QueueID), where QueueID is the identifier of the queue associated with the block. For example, QUEUE(Buffer) causes the entities to arrive at the QUEUE block in the model with the queue named Buffer. In the second method, STATION(StationID) can be used to define the destination of the arriving entities as the STATION block identified by StationID. For example, STATION(Drills) defines the destination block as the STATION block named Drills. The third, and most general method, involves specifying the destination block as BLOCK (BlockID), where BlockID is the sequence number or block label assigned to the block. For example, BLOCK(1) defines the destination block as the first block in the model, and BLOCK(Start) defines the destination block as the model block labeled Start. The last method, EVENT(EventNumber), allows the arriving entity to call a SIMAN event, which will be discussed in Chapter 10.

The value specified for the Time operand defines the time — from the start of the replication — at which the arrival set enters the model. The BatchSize operand is used to define the number of entities that enter the model for this arrival set. All entities within an arrival set are scheduled to enter the model at the same time. All entities defined in the ARRIVALS element are created at the beginning of the simulation run and are placed onto the calendar.

Optional attribute Assignments can be made for each arrival set to initialize one or more entity attributes. Default attribute values are taken from the INITIALIZE element or are set to 0. You make attribute assignments by listing assignments in the form AttributeID = Value or by entering a list of values in order with no AttributeID or equals sign. In the latter case the values are assigned to the attributes in the order in which they are listed, i.e., the first value is assigned to attribute number 1, the second is assigned to attribute number 2, and so forth.

An example of the ARRIVALS element is shown below. This element defines two arrival sets. The first arrival set has five entities that enter the QUEUE block associated with the queue named Buffer at time 10.0. The attribute ProcessTime is initialized to 30.0 for all five entities in the arrival set. The second arrival set contains a single entity that enters the block labeled Startup at time 20.0. The first three attributes of this entity are initialized to 3., 5., and 1.

```
ARRIVALS: QUEUE(Buffer), 10.0, 5, ProcessTime = 30:
         BLOCK(Startup), 20.0, 1, 3., 5., 1.;
```

Note that in both cases above, the arrival Number has been defaulted. The SIMAN Experiment processor will expect this default or a sequential numbering by the modeler.

9.2 Experimentally Defining Block Operands: The DISTRIBUTIONS Element

Many of the block operands define model data that we may wish to change from one experiment to another. For example, we may wish to change the form of the distribution (e.g., exponential, normal, etc.) as well as the associated parameter values (e.g., mean, standard deviation, etc.) for the TimeBetween operand on a CREATE block. If you enter the distribution and associated parameter values directly on the CREATE block, then you must modify the model to change the operand.

The DISTRIBUTIONS element, shown below, makes it easy to experimentally define the expression or distribution associated with an operand for a block in the model. To use this feature, you specify the block operand that you wish to experimentally define as ED(N), where N is an integer assigned to the corresponding expression in the DISTRIBUTIONS element. The block then uses for this operand the current value of the Nth expression defined in the DISTRIBUTIONS element for the active experiment. Note that you can change the expression associated with this operand by simply modifying the DISTRIBUTIONS element in the experiment. The DISTRIBUTIONS element contains repeating groups of the expression Number and the associated Expression. The element is summarized below.

DISTRIBUTIONS: Number, Expression:
                   repeats;

An example of the CREATE block with the TimeBetween operand specified as ED(1) is shown on the left. An example of the DISTRIBUTIONS element, which defines the distributions corresponding to ED(1) and ED(2), is shown below.

CREATE
ED(1)

```
DISTRIBUTIONS" 1, EXPONENTIAL(15):
               2, UNIFORM(10,20) + NORMAL(15,4);
```

Note that this element causes the time between creations for the CREATE block shown earlier to be exponentially distributed with a mean of 15.

9.3 Experimentally Defining Decision Rules: The RULES Element

SIMAN offers a wide range of decision rules, which are used to determine how queues, resources, and transporters are selected. The purpose of some simulation studies is to compare different decision rules within the system. For example, we may want to compare the difference in system performance when we use a cyclic rule rather than a random rule for selecting queues in a model. To perform this comparison without having to modify the model, we must have a way of experi-

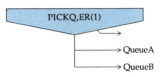

PICKQ,ER(1)

→ QueueA
→ QueueB

mentally defining the decision rule used for a block in the model. This capability is provided by the RULES element included in the experiment.

To use this feature, you specify the decision rule operand in the model as ER(N), where N is an integer assigned to the corresponding decision rule defined in the RULES element of the experiment. The model block then uses for this operand the Nth decision rule listed in the RULES element of the active experiment. For example, the PICKQ block shown on the left uses the first rule defined in the RULES element.

The RULES element contains repeating groups of the rule Number and associated decision Rule. The rule number can be a single integer or a range of numbers entered in the form LowNumber — HighNumber. In this case the rule is defined for all rule numbers between LowNumber and HighNumber. The associated rule can be any valid SIMAN decision rule such as SNQ, SDS, LRC, RAN, etc. The RULES element is summarized below.

```
RULES: Number, Rule:
        repeats;
```

An example of the RULES element which defines rules 1 through 3 as the SNQ rule and rule 4 as the LRC rule is shown below.

```
RULES: 1—3, SNQ:
        4, LRC;
```

Note that this element would cause the PICKQ block shown earlier to employ the SNQ decision rule.

9.4 Defining Table Functions: The TABLES Element

When modeling certain types of systems the processing time is commonly a function of some variable in the model; for example, a worker may work faster when there is a larger number of parts waiting in the input buffer to a workstation. In some systems learning plays an important role, i.e., the processing time varies with the number of times that the same process has been performed before.

Consider a situation in which the time required to process a job is a function of the input queue length as defined below. In this example the processing time decreases as the queue length increases. When the queue length is 1 or less, the processing time is 10; with a queue length of 2 the processing time is 9, etc.

Processing Time	10	9	7	5	3
Queue Length	1	2	3	4	5+

This type of functional relationship can be incorporated into a SIMAN model as a table function. A table function consists of a list of dependent values that correspond to a fixed-increment independent variable. The table is completely defined by specifying the low value of the independent variable, the fixed increment between successive values of the independent variable, and the list of dependent values.

In our example, the dependent variable is the job processing time and the independent variable is the queue length. The low value of the independent variable is 1, and the fixed increment is 1.

Table functions are defined in the TABLES element of the experiment. The format of this element is summarized below. Each table definition includes the table Number and Name, the low value of the independent variable, the fixed increment, and the list of dependent values.

TABLES: Number, Name, XLow, XInc, $Y_1, \ldots, Y_n$:
    repeats;

For example, the TABLES element corresponding to the function for processing time, given queue length, is shown below. We have arbitrarily assigned the name JobTime to this table and defaulted the table number to 1.

```
TABLES: JobTime, 1, 1, 10, 9, 7, 5, 3;
```

You use the TableID to reference a table within the model; you can specify the TableID interchangeably as the table number or name. To obtain a value from a table corresponding to a specific value of the independent variable, you use the SIMAN table function TF(TableID, Value), where Value denotes the value of the independent variable. You can specify Value as any valid SIMAN expression. The function TF returns the corresponding value of the dependent variable. For example, in the DELAY block shown on the left, the delay time is specified as a value from the table named JobTime, where the independent variable is the current length of the queue named Buffer. In this case the delay time for an arriving entity to the block is determined from the JobTime table based on the current length of the queue named Buffer.

DELAY
TF(JobTime,NQ(Buffer))

When the value of the independent variable falls between two defined values in the table, SIMAN uses linear interpolation to establish the value returned by TF. For example, the TABLES element shown below returns the inspection time based on the number of parts to be inspected. Hence TF(InspectTime, 12) returns a value of 24. If the value of the independent variable is outside the table range, the appropriate endpoint is assigned to TF. Hence TF(InspectTime, 50) returns a value of 45.

```
TABLES: InspectTime, 5, 5, 15, 20, 30, 45;
```

9.5 Experimentally Defining Parameters: The PARAMETERS Element

In our previous models we have completely defined the parameters for distributions in the Model Frame, or used the DISTRIBUTIONS element to define these values in the Experiment Frame. An alternative format is to specify the distribution type in the Model Frame and the parameters in the Experiment Frame.

The PARAMETERS element, shown below, provides this capability. The first two operands allow a Number or Name to be assigned to the parameter set. At least one of these two operands is required. The values for P_i are the parameters required by a distribution.

PARAMETERS: Number, Name, $P_1, \ldots P_n$:
        repeats;

The number of parameters depends on the distribution being used. In referencing the distribution in the Model Frame, a different identifier must be used so that SIMAN interprets the first operand as a parameter number or name, rather than the actual parameter value. Figure 3-2 provided a complete listing of the available distributions with the four-letter abbreviations. This listing is given in Figure 8-8 with the two-letter abbreviations added.

Distribution	Abbreviations		Parameters
Beta	BE	BETA	$(Alpha_1, Alpha_2)$
Continuous	CP	CONT	$(CumP_1, Val_1, CumP_2, Val_2, \ldots)$
Discrete	DP	DISC	$(CumP_1, Val_1, CumP_2, Val_2, \ldots)$
Erlang	ER	ERLA	$(ExpoMean, K)$
Exponential	EX	EXPO	$(Mean)$
Gamma	GA	GAMM	$(Beta, Alpha)$
Lognormal	RL	LOGN	$(Mean, StdDev)$
Normal	RN	NORM	$(Mean, StdDev)$
Poisson	PO	POIS	$(Mean)$
Triangular	TR	TRIA	$(Min, Mode, Max)$
Uniform	UN	UNIF	(Min, Max)
Weibull	WE	WEIB	$(Beta, Alpha)$

Figure 8-8. Random Variable Abbreviations and Parameters

Examples of a CREATE and DELAY block referencing the PARAMETERS element are shown on the left. The PARAMETERS element referenced by these blocks is shown below. The CREATE block uses an exponential distribution for the offset time of the first arrival, with a mean of 15 given in the PARAMETERS element. The Mean Time Between Arrivals, MTBA, is normal with a mean of 40 and a standard deviation of 4.

```
PARAMETERS: 1, OffSet, 15:
            2, MTBA, 40, 4:
            3, 45, 50, 55:
            4, 52, 60, 65;
```

The Delay block references a triangular distribution based on attribute PartType. When an entity with PartType of 1 passes through this block, the parameters for the triangular delay will come from parameter set 3; for an entity with PartType of 2, it will come from parameter set 4.

The PARAMETERS element can also be used to initialize and store values used during the simulation. When used in this fashion they are similar to variables. A specific parameter is referenced from the Model Frame by using the notation P(SetID,NumValue). The SetID references the parameter set number or name,

CREATE,,EX(Offset)
RN(MTBA)

DELAY
TR(PartType+2)

and the NumValue references the specific value requested. For example, P(3,2) for the above PARAMETERS element yields a value of 50. Note that you can also use the P variable on the left side of an expression; thus you can change parameter values during a simulation run.

This chapter has presented a large number of new and somewhat unrelated constructs. No attempt will be made to illustrate the use of all of these constructs in the following sample problems. However, these problems should provide some insight into the use of many of these new constructs.

10.1 Sample Problem 8.1: The Jobshop Problem

Consider the problem of modeling a simple jobshop facility. We use an example taken from Scriber [1974] who presents a GPSS model for this same system. The job shop consists of a number of identical machines, as summarized in the following table.

Group	Machine Type	Number
1	Casting Units	14
2	Lathes	5
3	Planers	4
4	Drill Presses	8
5	Shapers	16
6	Polishing Machines	4

Jobs arrive at this facility according to a Poisson process with a mean inter-arrival time of 9.6 minutes. There are three types of jobs, each having a different machine visitation sequence and a different machine operation time. The travel time between groups of machines is assumed to be negligible. All operation times are exponentially distributed. The data for the three types of jobs are summarized below.

Job Operation Type	Percent of Jobs	Sequence Number	Machine Type	Mean
1	24	1	Casting Unit (1)	125
		2	Planer (3)	35
		3	Lathe (2)	20
		4	Polishing Unit (6)	60
2	44	1	Shaper (5)	105
		2	Drill Press (4)	90
		3	Lathe (2)	65
3	32	1	Casting Unit (1)	235
		2	Shaper (5)	250
		3	Drill Press (4)	50
		4	Planer (3)	30
		5	Polishing Unit (6)	25

As each job moves through the facility, it is processed at each group of machines in its visitation sequence before departing the system. At each group, the job waits in the queue, seizes the first available machine, delays by the processing time, releases the machine, and then continues to its next group, if any.

The block diagram for this example (Figure 8-9) and the Model listing (Figure 8-10) use SIMAN's sequence feature. The sequence feature controls the flow of parts and makes assignments to the attribute named ProcessTime. This attribute defines the delay time at each group of machines. Observe that the six station submodels used to model the groups of machines are identical, except for the names assigned to the stations, queues, and resources.

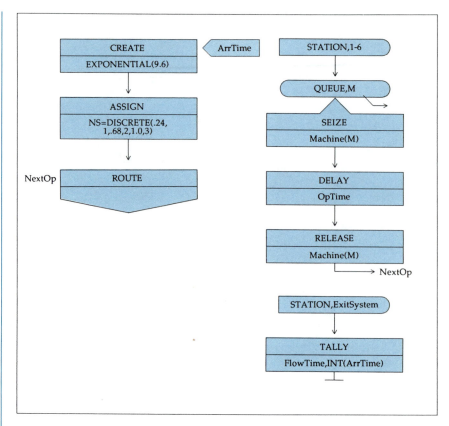

Figure 8-9. Block Diagram for Sample Problem 8.1

```
BEGIN;

;    JOBSHOP: SAMPLE PROBLEM 8.1

        CREATE:    EXPONENTIAL(9.6):
                   MARK(ArrTime);                Create arrivals

        ASSIGN:
          NS=DISCRETE(.24,1,.68,2,1.0,3);        Set job type
NextOp  ROUTE;                                   Send to next operation
        STATION,   1-6;                          Station macro
        QUEUE,     M;                            Queues 1-6
        SEIZE:     Machine(M);                   Get machine
        DELAY:     OpTime;                       Delay for operation
        RELEASE:   Machine(M):NEXT(NextOp);      Release machine
        STATION,   ExitSystem;                   Exit submodel
        TALLY:     FlowTime,INT(ArrTime):        !Tally and dispose
                     DISPOSE;

END;
```

Figure 8-10. Model Listing for Sample Problem 8.1

The experiment list for this jobshop model is given in Figure 8-11. Note that expressions have been used in the DSTATS element to provide percentage utilizations for each group of machines.

```
BEGIN;
PROJECT,        Sample Problem 8.1, SM;
ATTRIBUTES:     OpTime:
                ArrTime;
STATIONS:       1,Casting:
                2,Lathes:
                3,Planers:
                4,Drills:
                5,Shapers:
                6,Polishers:
                7,ExitSystem;
QUEUES:         6;
RESOURCES:      Machine(6), 14, 5, 4, 8, 16, 4;
SEQUENCES:      1, 1,EXPO(125) & 3,EXPO(35) & 2,EXPO(20) &
                   6,EXPO(60) & ExitSystem:
                2, 5,EXPO(105) & 4,EXPO(90) & 2,EXPO(65) &
                   ExitSystem:
                3, 1,EXPO(235) & 5,EXPO(250) & 4,EXPO(50) &
                   3,EXPO(30) & 6,EXPO(25) & ExitSystem;
TALLIES:        FlowTime;
DSTATS:         NQ(1), Casters Queue:
                NQ(2), Lathes Queue:
                NQ(3), Planers Queue:
                NQ(4), Drills Queue:
                NQ(5), Shapers Queue:
                NQ(6), Polishers Queue:
                (NR(1)/14)*100, Casters Utilization:
                (NR(2)/5)*100, Lathes Utilization:
                (NR(3)/4)*100, Planers Utilization:
                (NR(4)/8)*100, Drills Utilization:
                (NR(5)/16)*100, Shapers Utilization:
                (NR(6)/4)*100, Polishers Utilization;
REPLICATE,      1,0,26000,,,1000;
END;
```

Figure 8-11. Experiment listing for Sample Problem 8.1

The resulting Summary Report is shown in Figure 8-12. The casters and shapers have the highest utilization. Note that there are always at least two casters and three shapers in use over the time period during which statistics have been collected. This observation is based on the minimum value recorded for each set of machines.

```
Project:  Sample Problem 8.1
Analyst:  SM
Replication ended at time:  26000.0
Statistics were cleared at time:  1000.0
Statistics accumulated for time:  25000.0
                      TALLY VARIABLES

Identifier          Average Variation Minimum Maximum Observations

FlowTime            411.64   .71898   19.025  4231.7      2560

                 DISCRETE-CHANGE VARIABLES

Identifier          Average Variation Minimum Maximum  Final Value

Caster Queue         1.1459   2.0524   .00000  13.000     .00000
Lathes Queue          .79519  2.5402   .00000  14.000     .00000
Planers Queue         .18249  4.8661   .00000  10.000    1.0000
Drill Queue          1.8234   2.3088   .00000  28.000     .00000
Shapers Queue         .96244  2.3255   .00000  18.000     .00000
Polishing Queue       .67836  3.4104   .00000  19.000     .00000
Caster Utilization   78.493    .26206  14.286  100.00    71.429
Lathes Utilization   66.388    .45292   .00000  100.00   100.00
Planers Utilization  44.550    .70480   .00000  100.00   100.00
Drill Utilization    72.411    .36538   .00000  100.00    50.000
Shapers Utilization  78.329    .26115  18.750  100.00    100.00
Polishing Utilization 58.496   .56107   .00000  100.00   100.00
```

Figure 8-12. Summary Report for Sample Problem 8.1

10.2 Sample Problem 8.2: Highway Toll Booth

Assume that we have cars arriving at six toll booths, with the arrival times exponentially distributed with a mean of two seconds. Booths 4, 5, and 6 are exact-change-only booths; the others are not. Forty percent of the arriving cars can only go to booths 1, 2, or 3. We can assume that the cars go to the toll booth with the shortest line. In the case of ties, exact-change customers prefer high-numbered booths, and regular customers prefer low-numbered booths. The time that it takes to pay at an exact-change booth is uniform from 5 to 7 seconds, and the time that it takes to pay the toll at the other booths is uniform from 10 to 13 seconds.

The Block model for the toll-booth problem is shown in Figure 8-13, and the Model Frame listing is given in Figure 8-14. The first two blocks CREATE the arriving customers and ASSIGN the customer type. The FINDJ block then determines which toll booth the customer will use. The range operands on the FINDJ block are taken from parameter sets 1 or 2, depending on customer type. The FINDJ block finds the lane, from 1 to 3, with the minimum number for regular customers, CusType 1. Exact-change customers check lanes 6 to 1. The resulting lane is then assigned to M in the next ASSIGN block, and the customer joins QUEUE M. Note that no STATION block has been included because the assignment of J to M defines the station value. After the booth is seized, the pay time is taken from a uniform distribution, with the parameters given in the Experiment Frame. Note that the reference to the parameter set is offset by a value of 2 so that parameter sets 3 and 4 are referenced. The entities are then tallied for SysTime and disposed of.

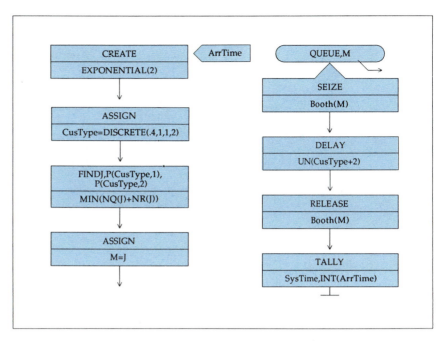

Figure 8-13. Block Model for Sample Problem 8.2

```
BEGIN;
     ;     TOLL BOOTH: SAMPLE PROBLEM 8.2
          CREATE:      EXPONENTIAL(2):
                       MARK(ArrTime);            Create arriving cars
          ASSIGN:
            CusType=DISCRETE(.4,1,1,2);          Set customer type
          FINDJ,P(CusType,1),P(CusType,2):
                       MIN(NQ(J)+NR(J));          Find short lane
          ASSIGN:      M=J;                       Set lane number
          QUEUE,M;                                Queue for toll
          SEIZE:       Booth(M);                  Get toll booth
          DELAY:       UN(CusType+2);             Pay toll
          RELEASE:     Booth(M);                  Release booth
          TALLY:       SysTime,INT(ArrTime):
                       DISPOSE;                   Tally system time
     END;
```

Figure 8-14. Model Listing for Sample Problem 8.2

The corresponding Experiment Frame is shown in Figure 8-15. The STATIONS and QUEUES elements have been included to declare the six stations and queues required by the model. The RESOURCES element identifies six Booth resources, each with a default capacity of 1. The PARAMETERS element contains four parameter sets. The first two sets provide the search range for the FINDJ block, and the last two sets provide the parameters for the uniform distribution for the pay time. The remaining elements are similar to other experiments that we have shown.

```
BEGIN;
;                TOLL BOOTH: SAMPLE PROBLEM 8.2
PROJECT,         Sample Problem 8.2,SM;
ATTRIBUTES:      ArrTime:
                 CusType;
QUEUES:          6;
RESOURCES:       Booth(6);
PARAMETERS:      RegRange, 1,3:
                 ExcRange, 6,1:
                 RegPay, 10,13:
                 ExcPay, 5,7;
TALLIES:         SysTime;
DSTATS:          NR(1)*100.0,Booth 1 Busy:
                 NR(2)*100.0,Booth 2 Busy:
                 NR(3)*100.0,Booth 3 Busy:
                 NR(4)*100.0,Booth 4 Busy:
                 NR(5)*100.0,Booth 5 Busy:
                 NR(6)*100.0,Booth 6 Busy;
REPLICATE,1,0,20000;
END;
```

Figure 8-15. Experiment Listing for Sample Problem 8.2

The Summary Report for this model is given in Figure 8-16. As expected, booth 1 has the highest utilization and booth 4 the lowest because of the way in which the model determines the lane that a customer enters.

```
Project:  Sample Problem 8.2
Analyst:  SM
Replication ended at time:  20000.0
```

TALLY VARIABLES

Identifier	Average	Variation	Minimum	Maximum	Observations
SysTime	10.884	.64789	5.0000	60.824	9918

DISCRETE-CHANGE VARIABLES

Identifier	Average	Variation	Minimum	Maximum	Final Value
Booth 1 Busy	89.546	.34167	.00000	100.00	100.00
Booth 2 Busy	79.965	.50055	.00000	100.00	100.00
Booth 3 Busy	70.361	.64903	.00000	100.00	100.00
Booth 4 Busy	38.686	1.2589	.00000	100.00	.00000
Booth 5 Busy	55.716	.89152	.00000	100.00	.00000
Booth 6 Busy	71.274	.63486	.00000	100.00	100.00

Figure 8-16. Summary Report for Sample Problem 8.2

10.3 Sample Problem 8.3: The Bank Teller Problem

Customers arrive at the walk-in portion of a bank according to an exponential distribution with a mean of one minute. Upon arriving, the customer joins a single queue to wait for service by one of two different tellers. The first teller serves only walk-in customers, with the service time being exponential with a mean of 1.3 minutes. The second teller is primarily responsible for servicing drive-in customers (exponential arrivals with a mean of six minutes). The service time for drive-in customers is exponential with a mean of three minutes. When not busy with drive-in customers, the second teller also serves walk-in customers. Because of occasional long waits, walk-in customers renege, i.e., they leave the line before they are serviced. The renege time is different for each customer and follows a uniform distribution with a minimum value of 5 minutes and a maximum value of 15 minutes. We are interested in the time in system, the number of customers that renege, and the statistics on teller utilization and waiting line times.

The resulting model listing for this problem is shown in Figure 8-17. The first part of the model deals with walk-in customers. An arriving customer has an arrival time marked and is assigned a renege time. This renege time is then compared to the current minimum renege time stored in variable TimeOut. The minimum of the two times is then stored in Timeout. The new arrival joins the single queue to wait for an available teller to be selected by the SELECT block. When a teller has been seized, a duplicate entity is created and sent to label Reset. The blocks starting at label Reset check to see if the variable TimeOut needs to be reset. Resetting is necessary if the entity that just departed the queue had the minimum renege time. This duplicate entity first checks the TellerQ at the block labeled FindMin; if the queue is empty, the variable Timeout is set to a large time. Otherwise, the renege times for all entities in the TellerQ are searched to find the current minimum, this value is assigned to variable TimeOut, and the entity is disposed of. The customer that previously seized a teller is serviced, its system time is tallied, and it is disposed of.

```
       BEGIN;
       ;         BANK TELLER: SAMPLE PROBLEM 8.3
       ;            Walk-in customers
                 CREATE:     EXPONENTIAL(1.0):      !Create walk-in
                             MARK(ArrTime);          Customers
                 ASSIGN:     RenegeT=TNOW+UNIFORM   !Set renege time
                             (5,15):
                             TimeOut=MIN(TimeOut,
                             RenegeT);               Set time out
                 QUEUE,      TellerQ;                Wait for teller
                 SELECT,POR:                        !Select teller
                             MainTell:              !Walk-in teller
                             BackUpT;                Drive-in teller
       MainTell  SEIZE:      Teller(1);              Get walk-in teller
                 DUPLICATE:  1,Reset;               Send entity to reset
                 DELAY:      EXPONENTIAL(1.3);       Delay for service time
                 RELEASE:    Teller(1):
                             NEXT(TimeIn);           Release teller
       BackUpT   SEIZE,2:    Teller(2);             Get drive-in teller
                 DUPLICATE:  1,Reset;               Send entity to reset
                 DELAY:      EXPONENTIAL(1.3);       Delay for service
                 RELEASE:    Teller(2);             Release teller
       TimeIn    TALLY: SysTime, INT(ArrTime):      !Tally system time
                             DISPOSE;
       RenegSys  TALLY:      CusRenege, INT(ArrTime):
                             DISPOSE;                Tally renege customer

       ;          Drive-in customers

                 CREATE:     EXPONENTIAL(6):        !Create drive-in customer
                             MARK(ArrTime);
                 QUEUE, DriveIn;                     Wait for teller
```

```
              SEIZE,1:    Teller(2);              Get drive-in teller
              DELAY:      EXPONENTIAL(3);         Delay for service
              RELEASE:    Teller(2);              Release teller
              TALLY:      DriveTime,
                            INT(ArrTime);         !Tally system time
                          DISPOSE;
;          Check for TimeOut reset
Reset      BRANCH,1:   IF,NQ(TellerQ).GT.0,
                           FindMin:               !Check for empty queue
                        ELSE,SetMax;              Queue empty
FindMin    SEARCH,TellerQ,1,NQ:                   !Find minimum renege
                        MIN(RenegeT);             time in teller queue
           ASSIGN:      TimeOut=AQUE(Teller
                          Q,J,2):                 !Reset time out
                        DISPOSE;
SetMax     ASSIGN:      TimeOut=2000000.0:        !Rest time out to max
                        DISPOSE;
;          Scan and renege customer
           CREATE;                                Create scan entity
ScanQ      QUEUE,CheckQ;                          Wait for condition
           SCAN:        TimeOut.LE.TNOW;          Scan condition
           SEARCH,TellerQ,1,NQ:                   !find entity with
                        MIN(RenegeT);             Minimum renege time
           REMOVE:      J,TellerQ,RenegSys;       Remove renege entity
           DUPLICATE:  1,ScanQ:                   !send back to scan queue
                        NEXT(Reset);              Create reset entity
END;
```

Figure 8-17. Model Listing for Sample Problem 8.3

The second portion of the model creates the drive-in customers. Note that these customers enter a separate queue and have priority for service over the walk-in customers by the second teller. The last part of the model contains the logic for a reneging customer. A single control entity is created and placed in the queue preceding a SCAN block. This SCAN block checks whether the current value of TimeOut is less than the current simulation time, TNOW. If this condition is true, there is an entity in the TellerQ that wants to renege. The control entity is then released by the SCAN block; the TellerQ is searched to find the rank of the reneging entity; the entity is removed from the TellerQ, is sent to be tallied, and is disposed of. A duplicate of the controlling entity is created and is sent back to the queue preceding the SCAN block. The controlling entity is sent to label Reset, which computes the new TimeOut value.

The sequence of events at this DUPLICATE block is critical to model logic. Remember that there are two types of events that can trigger a SCAN block condition check: an advancement of the simulation time and the arrival of an entity to the queue connected to the SCAN block. If the duplicate entity is sent to label Reset, and the primary entity sent to the scan queue, the primary entity will arrive at the SCAN block before the new value of TimeOut is computed, and the condition will still be true. Thus, the next entity with the minimum RenegeT will be removed, and the process will repeat until the TellerQ is empty. SIMAN will terminate with an error because the model is attempting to remove an entity from an empty queue.

The corresponding Experiment Frame for our bank teller model is given in Figure 8-18. Note that the variable TimeOut is initialized to a large value to avoid the problem of having the control entity released at time 0.

```
BEGIN;
;
;              BANK TELLER: SAMPLE PROBLEM 8.3
PROJECT,       Sample Problem 8.3, SM;
ATTRIBUTES:    ArrTime:
               RenegeT;
VARIABLES:     TimeOut,2000000.0;
QUEUES:        TellerQ:
               DriveIn:
               CheckQ;
RESOURCES:     Teller(2);
TALLIES:       SysTime:
               DriveTime:
               CusRenege;
DSTATS:        NR(1)*100.0, Teller 1 Utilization:
               NR(2)*100.0, Teller 2 Utilization:
               NQ(TellerQ), Walk In Line:
               NQ(DriveIn), Drive In Line;
REPLICATE,     1,0,25000;
END;
```

Figure 8-18. Experiment Listing for Sample Problem 8.3

The Summary Report for this model is given in Figure 8-19. There are 1,559 customers who reneged, with an average time spent waiting in line of approximately 7.5 minutes.

```
Project:  Sample Problem 8.3
Analyst:  SM
Replication ended at time:  25000.0
```

TALLY VARIABLES

Identifier	Average	Variation	Minimum	Maximum	Observations
SysTime	4.0653	.76592	.00000	20.717	23511
DriveTime	6.6956	.84078	.15625E-01	39.361	4063
CusRenege	7.5276	.24749	5.0271	14.934	1559

DISCRETE-CHANGE VARIABLES

Identifier	Average	Variation	Minimum	Maximum	Final Value
Teller 1 Utilization	84.536	.42770	.00000	100.00	100.00
Teller 2 Utilization	85.829	.40632	.00000	100.00	100.00
Walk In Line	3.0774	1.1159	.00000	21.000	6.0000
Drive In Line	.60205	1.8571	.00000	11.000	1.0000

Figure 8-19. Summary Report for Sample Problem 8.3

Although this model uses several of the new constructs illustrated in this chapter and appears to model the problem accurately, there is a potential flaw in the model logic. Remember that the condition on the SCAN block is only checked when an entity arrives at the preceding queue or when the simulation time is to be advanced. A problem can arise under the following conditions. Suppose that an entity resides in the TellerQ with a renege time of 100 and that the current simulation time is 99.999. Assume that the activities in the model result in an advancement of the simulation clock to time 105. The advance at time 99.999 will check the scan condition, but it will not release the controlling entity because the condition is not yet true. Only after the activities scheduled to occur at time 105 will the condition be rechecked. Thus, the entity with a renege time of 100 will not be reneged from the system until time 105, five minutes after it was scheduled.

It is even possible that this customer will be served after its renege time, if at time 105 the entity to be reneged is first in line in the TellerQ and if the activities scheduled at time 105 release the teller selected for that entity. In this case the customer will not be reneged. There are several ways to prevent this from happening. The existing model can be modified with a delay loop that ensures that the time advance of the simulation occurs in small increments. The added blocks are shown on the left. This added logic results in the simulation time being advanced in increments no greater than the delay on the loop entity, i.e., 0.1 minute. This method does not totally prevent the problem, but it does decrease the likelihood of its happening. It will, however, result in a slower running model.

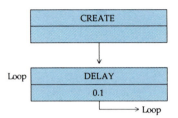

A better alternative is to reformulate the model to remove the problem. The resulting model listing is given in Figure 8-20. The two models differ only in the manner by which the reneging is detected. The revised model creates a duplicate entity of each arriving walk-in customer and sends it to label REntity. This new set of blocks delays the duplicate entity by the renege time, plus a very small time increment. After this delay, the duplicate entity checks to see if the original entity is still in the TellerQ. If so, the original entity is removed from that queue and is reneged. This new set of code replaces the reset and scan portion of code that the first model presented. Although the model is shorter, there will be more entities on the event calendar because of the duplicate entities. This approach could result in a slower running model. In this case, the time to run both simulation models is essentially the same.

```
BEGIN;
;          REVISED BANK TELLER: SAMPLE PROBLEM 8.3
;          Walk-in customers
           CREATE:     EXPONENTIAL(1.0):        !Create walk in
                       MARK(ArrTime);            Customers
           ASSIGN:     RenegeT=
                       TNOW+UNIFORM(5,15);       Set renege time
           DUPLICATE: 1,REntity;                 Create renege entity
           QUEUE,      TellerQ;                  Wait for teller
           SELECT,POR:                           !Select teller
                       MainTell:                 !Walk in teller
                       BackUpT;                  Drive in teller
  MainTell SEIZE:      Teller(1);                Get walk in teller
           DELAY:      EXPONENTIAL(1.3);         Delay for service time
           RELEASE:    Teller(1):NEXT(TimeIn);   Release teller
  BackUpT  SEIZE,2:    Teller(2);                Get drive in teller
           DELAY:      EXPONENTIAL(1.3);         Delay for service
           RELEASE:    Teller(2);                Release teller
```

```
TimeIn    TALLY: SysTime, INT(ArrTime):        !Tally system time
                   DISPOSE;
RenegSys TALLY:   CusRenege,   INT(arrTime):
                   DISPOSE;                    Count renege customer

;         Drive-in customers

          CREATE:    EXPONENTIAL(6):          !Create drive in customer
                     MARK(ArrTime);
          QUEUE, DriveIn;                      Wait for teller
          SEIZE,1:   Teller(2);                Get drive in teller
          DELAY:     EXPONENTIAL(3);           Delay for service
          RELEASE:   Teller(2);                Release teller
          TALLY:     DriveTime, INT(ArrTime): !Tally system time
                     DISPOSE;

;         Renege logic

REntity   DELAY:     RenegeT-Tnow+0.0001;      Delay until renege time
          BRANCH,1:                            !Check for empty queue

                     IF,NQ(TellerQ).GT.0,
                     CheckR;                   Dispose if queue empty
CheckR    ASSIGN:    TimeOut=RenegeT;          Set time out
          SEARCH, TellerQ, 1, NQ:             !find entity with
                     RenegeT.EQ.TimeOut;        renege time
          BRANCH,1:  IF,J.GT.0,GetReneg;       Check if entity is there
GetReneg REMOVE:     J, TellerQ,RenegSys:     !Remove renege entity
                     DISPOSE;
END;
```

Figure 8-20. Revised Model Listing for Sample Problem 8.3

The same Experiment Frame has been used with this new revised model. The resulting Summary Report is shown in Figure 8-21. As might be expected, the results are very similar to the first model. The number of reneges increases from 1,559 to 1,827. There is also an expected corresponding decrease of waiting time from 7.5 to 7.0 minutes for these customers because of the more accurate renege logic.

```
Project:  Sample Problem 8.3
Analyst:  SM
Replication ended at time:  25000.0
```

TALLY VARIABLES

Identifier	Average	Variation	Minimum	Maximum	Observations
SysTime	4.0033	.76383	.00000	19.246	23191
DriveTime	6.6043	.85339	.48828 E-02	43.506	4117
CusRenege	7.0931	.24932	5.0000	14.524	1827

DISCRETE-CHANGE VARIABLES

Identifier	Average	Variation	Minimum	Maximum	Final Value
Teller 1 Utilization	84.474	.42871	.00000	100.00	100.00
Teller 2 Utilization	86.112	.40160	.00000	100.00	100.00
Walk In Line	3.0211	1.1158	.00000	21.000	2.0000
Drive In Line	.59306	1.8410	.00000	9.0000	2.0000

Figure 8-21. Revised Summary Report for Sample Problem 8.3

10.4 Sample Problem 8.4: A Production Scheduling System

Consider the use of a simulation to predict the short-term performance of a small jobshop that receives its orders from a Material Requirements Planning (MRP) system. The objective is to use the simulation model to develop and evaluate short-term schedules. For a real system the simulation may have to attach several data files for information. In addition to the release schedule, information may be required for the routings, operation times, fixtures, setup times, etc. For this sample problem we will assume that the production release schedule contains information on the part number, part type, release time, and due date. We will also assume a simple three-machine shop, which produces three part types, and an empty starting condition.

For this sample problem we first need to develop a production schedule. We will take advantage of the SIMAN WRITE block and develop a simple model to generate an acceptable release schedule. The resulting model and experiment list are given in Figure 8-22. The model creates arrivals by using an exponential distribution with a mean of 9.5. These arriving entities are then assigned a part number, a part type, an arrival time, and a due date. These values are then written to an output file name MRPFile by using a free-field, formatted, sequential-access file.

```
BEGIN;
;
;     PRODUCTION SCHEDULING SYSTEM: SAMPLE PROBLEM 8.4
;       JOB CREATION MODEL
                CREATE,   1,EXPO(9.5):EXPO(9.5);
                ASSIGN:   J=J+1:
                          PartNo=J:
                          PartType=DISC(0.3,1,0.6,2,1.0,3):
                          ArrTime=TNOW:
                          DueDate=TNOW+UNIF(75,250);
                WRITE,MRPFile,FREE:
                          PartNo,PartType,ArrTime,DueDate:DISPOSE;

END;

BEGIN;

PROJECT,        SAMPLE PROBLEM 8.4,SM;

ATTRIBUTES:   PartNo:
              PartType:
              ArrTime:
              DueDate:
              OpTime;

FILES:  1,MRPFile,"MRPIN.001",SEQ,FRE;

REPLICATE,    1, 0, 5025;

END;
```

Figure 8-22. Model and Experiment Listing for Job Data File Creation

The accompanying Experiment Frame contains only the ATTRIBUTES, FILES, and REPLICATE elements. Figure 8-23 shows the first 20 jobs created by this model; the actual file is much longer. Each line represents a new part release with the numbers being part number, part type, release time, and due date.

1.000000	3.000000	12.995430	119.852800
2.000000	3.000000	18.138660	197.541700
3.000000	3.000000	23.279740	139.119400
4.000000	1.000000	24.673270	179.742000
5.000000	2.000000	38.227270	252.490500
6.000000	2.000000	40.304290	190.238800
7.000000	3.000000	41.901900	143.186300
8.000000	3.000000	45.126190	127.088200

```
          9.000000        1.000000        54.962730       174.314500
         10.000000        1.000000        59.385620       184.824100
         11.000000        3.000000        65.255680       185.397500
         12.000000        1.000000        85.950590       317.716700
         13.000000        2.000000        94.099230       220.488300
         14.000000        1.000000        96.040750       303.365100
         15.000000        1.000000       104.507600       325.667900
         16.000000        3.000000       112.479200       295.763800
         17.000000        3.000000       126.214500       201.735000
         18.000000        1.000000       130.379100       325.446900
         19.000000        3.000000       130.463100       248.737600
         20.000000        2.000000       141.535300       371.998200
```

Figure 8-23. Sample Job Data File: Sample Problem 8.4

The model that will use this data file is shown in Figure 8-24. The initial CRE-
ATE block creates a single entity, which reads the four data values for the first part
from the previously created data file. These values are read directly into the attribute values for later use in the model. The part sequence number is then assigned,
and the entity is delayed until the scheduled release time of the part to the system.
After this delay, a duplicate entity is created and sent back to the READ block,
which will generate the next part release. The original entity is routed to the first
machine station in its sequence.

```
BEGIN;
;
;     PRODUCTION SCHEDULING SYSTEM: SAMPLE PROBLEM 8.4
;
          CREATE;                                    create reading entity
ReadNext  READ,        MRPFile,FREE:               !read next part release
                       PartNo,PartType,ArrTime,DueDate;
          ASSIGN:      NS=PartType;                  assign sequence number
          DELAY":      ArrTime-TNOW;                 delay until arrival time
          DUPLICATE: 1,ReadNext;                     duplicate next read entity
SendOn    ROUTE:       EXPO(2),SEQ;                  route to next operation

          STATION,     1-3;                          machine stations
          QUEUE,       M;                            wait for machine M
          SEIZE:       Machine(M);                   seize machine M
          WRITE,,"(17X,'---PART #"',3X,F5.0,3X,'TYPE:',F6.0,
                      3X,'START:',F7.1)":
                      PartNo,PartType,TNOW;
          WRITE,,"(20X,'OPERATION #:',F3.0,3X,'MACHINE:',F3.0,
                      5X,'END:',F7.1)":
                      IS,M,TNOW=OpTime;
          DELAY:       OpTime;                        operation delay
          RELEASE:     Machine(M):NEXT(SendOn);  release machine

          STATION,    ExitSystem;                     exit station
          WRITE,,"(' ******** PART NUMBER"',F5.0,3X',TYPE:',F3.0)":
                      PartNo,PartType;
          WRITE,,"(12X,'TIME IN:',F7.1,3X,'TIME OUT:',F7.1)":
                      ArrTime,TNOW;
          WRITE,,"(30X,'DUE DATE:',F7.1)":
                      DueDate;
          TALLY:       FlowTime,Int(ArrTime):DISPOSE;
END;
```

Figure 8-24. Model Listing for Sample Problem 8.4

This logic for releasing parts to the system works because the input data are
sorted in increasing order of arrival time. If this is not the case, the entire set of
arrivals must be created at the start of the simulation. This can be accomplished

by moving the DUPLICATE block so that the next arrival will be read in before the delay until the arrival occurs. This configuration, however, will result in a large number of entities on the event calendar and a slower running simulation. Thus it is advisable to obtain sorted data for this type of model.

When an entity arrives at a machine station, it waits for the machine in QUEUE 1, 2, or 3, depending on the station number M. After seizing the Machine resource, the entity passes through two WRITE blocks, which write to the screen (the default file) information on the operation about to be performed. After the operation is completed, the part is routed to the next operation in its sequence. The ExitSystem station is the last station in each part sequence. At this station information on the completed job is displayed, the job flowtime is tallied, and the entity is disposed of.

The experiment listing for this model is shown in Figure 8-25. The times for each operation are assigned in the SEQUENCES element. If there are a large number of different parts, the operation times can be stored in an external direct-access file containing data sorted by part type. At each operation, the correct operation time can then be read from this file. Note that there is no REPLICATE element because the simulation is terminated automatically when all jobs have been read in and processed. There is, however, a DISpose option on the FILES element, which cause the reading entity to be disposed of when the end of the data file is reached.

```
BEGIN;

PROJECT,         SAMPLE PROBLEM 8.4,SM;
ATTRIBUTES:      PartType:
                 PartNo:
                 ArrTime:
                 DueDate:
                 OpTime;
QUEUES:          3;
RESOURCES:       Machine(3);
STATIONS:        3:
                 ExitSystem;
TALLIES:         FlowTime;
DSTATS:          NR(1)*100,Machine 1 Utilization:
                 NR(2)*100,Machine 2 Utilization:
                 NR(3)*100,Machine 3 Utilization:
                 NQ(1),Buffer 1:
                 NQ(2),Buffer 2:
                 NQ(3),Buffer 3;
SEQUENCES:    1, 1,OpTime=TRIA(4,6,8) & 2,OpTime=TRIA(5,7,8) &
                 3,OpTime=TRIA(7,9,11) & ExitSystem:
              2, 1,OpTime=TRIA(7,9,10) & 3,OpTime=TRIA(3,6,9) &
                 2,OpTime=TRIA(4,6,7) & 3,OpTime=TRIA(2,6,8) &
                 ExitSystem:
              3, 2,OpTime=TRIA(4,7,10) & 1,OpTime=TRIA(6,9,12) &
                 2,OpTime=TRIA(5,6,7) & 3,OpTime=TRIA(4,7,9) &
                 ExitSystem;
FILES: 1,MRPFile,"MRPIN.001",SEQ,FRE,DIS;
END;
```

Figure 8-25. Experiment Listing for Sample Problem 8.4

An example of the screen output from this model is given in Figure 8-26. Because of the manner in which the WRITE blocks are used in the model, the sequence of events are displayed as they occur, rather than by part number. For example, we can easily follow the progress of part number 1 as it passes through the system. It is released to the system at time 13 (see the entry on the completed part). It reaches its first operation, machine 2, and starts at time 14.1 and ends at time 20.2. Its second operation, machine 1, occurs from time 20.6 to 29.8. It then proceeds back to machine 2 (36.2 to 42.2) and then to machine 3 (43.1 to 47.9) for the last operation. It exits the system at time 50.4, well ahead of the 156.7 due date time.

```
              ---PART #:        1.   TYPE:     3.   START:   14.1
                 OPERATION #" 1.   MACHINE" 2.    END:     20.2
              ---PART #:        1.   TYPE:     3.   START:   20.6
                 OPERATION #: 2.   MACHINE: 1.    END:     29.8
              ---PART #:        2.   TYPE:     3.   START:   21.5
                 OPERATION #: 1.   MACHINE: 2.    END:     28.9
              ---PART #:        3.   TYPE:     3.   START:   28.9
                 OPERATION #: 1.   MACHINE: 2.    END:     36.2
              ---PART #:        4.   TYPE:     1.   START:   29.8
                 OPERATION #: 1.   MACHINE: 1.    END:     37.0
              ---PART #:        1.   TYPE:     3.   START:   36.2
                 OPERATION #: 3.   MACHINE: 2.    END:     42.2
              ---PART #:        2.   TYPE:     3.   START:   37.0
                 OPERATION #: 2.   MACHINE: 1.    END:     45.1
              ---PART #:        4.   TYPE:     1.   START:   42.2
                 OPERATION #: 2.   MACHINE: 2.    END:     49.5
              ---PART #:        1.   TYPE:     3.   START:   43.1
                 OPERATION #: 4.   MACHINE: 3.    END:     47.9
              ---PART #:        3.   TYPE:     3.   START:   45.1
                 OPERATION #: 2.   MACHINE: 1.    END:     53.7
              ---PART #:        7.   TYPE:     3.   START:   49.5
                 OPERATION #: 1.   MACHINE: 2.    END:     56.0
              ---PART #:        4.   TYPE:     1.   START:   49.7
                 OPERATION #: 3.   MACHINE: 3.    END:     57.7
  ******** PART NUMBER:  1.    TYPE: 3.
           TIME IN:  13.0    TIME OUT:    50.4
                             DUE DATE:   156.7
              ---PART #:        5.   TYPE:     2.   START:   53.7
                 OPERATION #: 1.   MACHINE: 1.    END:     62.3
              ---PART #:        2.   TYPE:     3.   START:   56.0
                 OPERATION #: 3.   MACHINE: 2.    END:     61.4
  ******** PART NUMBER:  4.    TYPE: 1.
           TIME IN:  24.7    TIME OUT:    60.1
                             DUE DATE:   204.2
              ---PART #:        8.   TYPE:     3.   START:   61.4
                 OPERATION #: 1.   MACHINE: 2.    END:     68.5
```

Figure 8-26. Example Output: Sample Problem 8.4

Although the output from a long run will be quite large, this information can easily be written to an unformatted file and post-processed to formats that production management is accustomed to seeing. The resulting Summary Report is also given in Figure 8-27.

```
Project: SAMPLE PROBLEM 8.4
Analyst: SM
Replication ended at time: 5081.19
                          TALLY VARIABLES
Identifier                Average Variation Minimum Maximum Observations
FlowTime                  120.73  .56763    27.295  318.28   540
                       DISCRETE-CHANGE VARIABLES
Identifier                Average Variation Minimum Maximum Final Value
Machine 1 Utilization     85.941  .40447    .00000  100.00  .00000
Machine 2 Utilization     94.604  .23882    .00000  100.00  .00000
Machine 3 Utilization     92.334  .28813    .00000  100.00  .00000
Buffer 1                  1.9112  1.2362    .00000  10.000  .00000
Buffer 2                  4.2836  .91766    .00000  15.000  .00000
Buffer 3                  2.8825  1.1985    .00000  15.000  .00000
```

Figure 8-27. Summary Report for Sample Problem 8.4

Exercises

Exercise 8-1

A production line consists of 10 serial workstations, each of which adds a part to a mainframe assembly entering the line at station 1. An inspection is performed prior to the assembly operation at each workstation. If the component is rejected, it is routed back to the previous station where it enters the queue of waiting assemblies with its job priority based on arrival time to the system. Multiple rejections are possible, and therefore an assembly may be sent back several stations. If an assembly is judged unacceptable at station 1, it leaves the system for rework.

The mainframe assemblies enter the system at a constant rate of one every two minutes. The inspection time at each station is uniformly distributed from 0.2 to 0.4 minute. The assembly operations are normally distributed with a mean of 1.5 minutes and a standard deviation of 0.3 minutes. Both the inspection and assembly are performed by the same operator. The transfer time between workstations is two minutes. The probability of rejection at each station is given in the following table.

Station	Rejection Probability
1	0.05
2	0.01
3	0.05
4	0.03
5	0.06
6	0.05
7	0.04
8	0.02
9	0.07
10	0.001

a) Model this system using the generic station submodel feature of SIMAN. Simulate the system for 480 time units, and record statistics on the number of mainframe assemblies sent to rework, on the flowtime for completed assemblies, and on the utilization of each workstation.

b) Use the model to develop a 0.95 confidence interval on the flowtime for a completed assembly.

Exercise 8-2

Parts arrive to a workstation and are processed on one of two machines in parallel. The time between arrivals is exponentially distributed with a mean of eight minutes. The processing time on the first machine is normally distributed with a mean of 10 minutes and a standard deviation of 2 minutes. The processing time for the same parts on the second machine is also normally distributed, but with a mean of 16 minutes and a standard deviation of 4 minutes. Because of the difference in processing speeds, preference is given to machine 1 when both machines are idle. Simulate this system for a 5,000-minute period, and record statistics on the utilization of the two machines and on the number of parts waiting in the queue.

Exercise 8-3

Two different part types arrive to a workstation consisting of a single machine. The time between part arrivals is exponentially distributed with a mean of five minutes. The distribution of arriving parts is 80% Type 1 and 20% Type 2. The part types are maintained in separate queues in front of the machine. Type 1 parts have priority over Type 2 parts, and hence the machine only processes a Type 2 part if no Type 1 parts are available. However, once processing of a Type 2 part begins, it is not interrupted by an arriving Type 1 part. The processing time for each part type is normally distributed with a mean of four minutes and a standard deviation of two minutes. Simulate this system for 480 minutes; record statistics on the lengths of each part queue and on the flowtime by part type.

Exercise 8-4

Modify the model for Exercise 8-3 to permit an arriving Type 1 part to interrupt the processing of a Type 2 part on the machine. Simulate this system for 480 minutes; record additional statistics on the number of Type 2 parts preempted from the machine.

Exercise 8-5

Sub-assemblies A and B arrive to a workcenter where one of each part is assembled into a sub-assembly. The interarrival time for Sub-assembly A is normally distributed with a mean of 10 minutes and a standard deviation of 2 minutes. The interarrival time for Sub-assembly B is normally distributed with a mean of 10 minutes and a standard deviation of 3 minutes. The time required to complete an assembly has a triangular distribution with a minimum of 6, a mode of 9, and a maximum of 12 minutes. Simulate this system for a 1,000-hour period;

record statistics on the utilization of the assembly station and on the number of waiting sub-assemblies by type.

Exercise 8-6

Metal sheets arrive to a stamping station with an exponential interarrival time with a mean of 1 minute. At the stamping station, each metal sheet is stamped and cut into six workpieces. The time required to load a sheet onto the stamping machine is normally distributed with a mean of 0.8 minute and a standard deviation of 0.2 minute. The workpieces are then placed on a pallet. Once the pallet is filled to its capacity of 36, it is moved to a finishing station where the workpieces are removed from the pallet and are individually trimmed and polished. The pallet travel time between the stamping and finishing stations is negligible. The time required to trim and polish each workpiece at the finishing station is normally distributed with a mean of eight seconds and a standard deviation of two seconds. Simulate this system for 480 minutes; record statistics on the flowtime through the system and on the length of the queues at the stamping and finishing stations.

Exercise 8-7

Batches of 40 lbs. of candy arrive to a final coating process according to a normal distribution with a mean of 17.0 minutes and a standard deviation of 2.5 minutes. The batches are held in a single queue feeding two identical coating hoppers; coating time is uniformly distributed with a minimum of 27.0 minutes and a maximum of 34.0 minutes. When a batch has completed coating, it is divided into equal one-pound batches for bagging. These one-pound batches of candy are then routed to one of four baggers; each batch "selects" the bagger having the fewest batches in its input queue. The baggers run at a constant rate of 1.0, 0.9, 0.8, 0.7 minutes for baggers 1 through 4 respectively. Two packaging machines place groups of 16 bags in a box; the bags from the first two baggers use the first packager, and the other two baggers feed the second packager. Packaging time is normally distributed with a mean of 7.0 minutes and a standard deviation of 0.8 minute and all 16 bags must be available before the packing operation can begin.

a. Model this candy production line for 120 hours. Collect statistics on the time to complete bagging; on the queue lengths at final coat, at bagging, and at packaging; on the time spent in the bagging queue; and on the number of boxes of candy produced.

b. Add an inspector to the system. Once each half hour, the inspector removes from each of the bagger queues any 1-pound candy batches that have been waiting (since completion of final coat) for more than 8 minutes. It takes the inspector two minutes to dump each batch into a nearby reject hopper. Re-run the simulation for 120 hours; add a count of how many pounds of candy are rejected.

Exercise 8-8

A drive-in bank has two adjacent service lanes for processing arriving customers. Each lane has room for the car being served plus three additional waiting cars. When a car arrives to the system, it enters the shortest lane, with ties broken randomly between the two lanes. If both lanes are full, the arriving car leaves and does not return. Once a car enters a lane, it cannot leave the system until it is processed. However, a car will change lanes whenever the other lane is shorter by two cars.

We are interested in studying the operation of this drive-in bank during its open hours on Saturday when it is open from 9 A.M. until 1 P.M. The time between arrivals to the system during this period is exponentially distributed with a mean of 35 seconds. The service time is normally distributed with a mean of 1 minute and a standard deviation of 0.2 minute. When the bank closes at 1 P.M., any customers waiting in the lane are denied service.

Develop a model of this system. Record statistics on the number of lane changes, the utilization of the two tellers, the number of lost customers, and the customer flowtime through the system. Construct a 0.95 confidence interval on the number of lost customers based on 20 replications of the model.

Exercise 8-9

Modify the model in Exercise 8-8 such that the customers who arrive to the bank and find both lanes full have a 0.5^n probability of driving around the block and returning to the bank, where n denotes the number of attempts to enter the bank. The time around the block is normally distributed with a mean of 3 minutes and a standard deviation of 0.8 minutes. In addition to the previous statistics, also record the total time spent by each customer in traveling around the block.

Exercise 8-10

Electronic components arrive in "kits" to a kit prep area where they receive one or both of two kit preparations prior to being sent to an assembly operation. The two prepping operations are called Prep 1 and Prep 2. One alternative that has been suggested for operating the kit prep area is to dedicate each of the two preppers to one of the two preparations (i.e., prepper 1 performs only the Prep 1 operation). Arriving kits are placed in the in-buffer where they wait for a prepper. When a prepper completes processing on a kit, the kit is returned to the in-buffer if an additional prep remains. Otherwise, the kit is sent to the assembly operation. In either case the prepper examines the in-buffer for another kit that requires a prep at that prep station. If there is none, the prepper waits for either a new kit arrival or a returned kit from the other prepper.

The time between kit arrivals is exponentially distributed with a mean of 0.6 minute. The following table summarizes the distribution of kit arrivals by type and the kit processing time at each prep station. Zero indicates that no prep is required.

Kit Type	% of Total	Prep 1 Time	Prep 2 Time
1	20	0.70	0.8
2	45	0.75	0.6
3	35	0	0.6

a. Simulate this system for 1,000 time units, and record statistics on the utilization of the preppers, on the flowtime through the kit prep area, and on the size of the in-buffer.

b. Develop a 0.95 confidence interval on the size of the in-buffer.

Exercise 8-11

Compare the flowtime in the proposed system in Exercise 8-10 to a modified system in which each prepper can perform either prep, but the mean prep time is increased by 10% for all operations.

Exercise 8-12

This problem involves modeling the SI^x rule for jobshop scheduling [Eilon, Chowdhury, and Serghiou, 1975]. The jobshop consists of six different machines. The job interarrival time is exponentially distributed with a mean of 15 minutes. There are four different job types processed through the facility. Each job is processed on a series of machines as defined by the visitation sequence for the job. The distribution of job types and the job lead-time (minutes), visitation sequence, and mean processing time (minutes) at each machine within the sequence are summarized in the following table.

Job Type	Percent	Lead-Time	Machine (Mean Processing Time)
1	28	110	2 (14), 5 (22), 1 (17)
2	30	125	6 (24), 4 (17), 3 (14), 1 (7)
3	29	150	3 (12), 2 (28), 6 (15), 5 (19), 4 (16)
4	13	145	1 (27), 6 (13), 5 (6), 2 (25)

The processing times are normally distributed with a standard deviation that is equal to 0.3 times the mean processing time.

When a job arrives, its due date is assigned as the arrival time plus the lead-time. The scheduling rule at each machine divides the jobs into two classes: regular jobs and high-priority jobs. High-priority jobs are those with negative float. Float is the job due date minus the current time, minus the remaining processing time, minus a safety factor of 50 minutes. Regular jobs are those not designated high-priority jobs. The SI^x scheduling rule processes all high-priority jobs before regular jobs, and within each job class processes jobs in the order of shortest mean processing time.

a. Simulate this system for 4,800 minutes. Record statistics on the job flowtime, the machine queue lengths, and the number of tardy jobs.

b. Develop a 0.95 confidence interval on the job flowtime.

Exercise 8-13

Modify the model in Exercise 8-12 to incorporate the shortest-processing-time (SPT) rule with preemption. Specifically, an arriving job may preempt the job in process on a machine if its processing time is five or more minutes less than the remaining processing time of the job being served. When an arriving job preempts the job in process, the preempted job rejoins the queue with its new SPT priority based on its remaining processing time. Evaluate this rule versus the SI^x rule based on the number of tardy jobs.

Exercise 8-14

A Just-In-Time (JIT) assembly operation consists of two serial workstations. Components arrive to the first workstation in a tote. At the first workstation they are assembled into sub-assemblies, which are placed back into the tote and then sent to the second workstation for final assembly. The system operates under a "pull" rather than "push" production strategy whereby work is only performed at a workstation when there is a downstream request for the work. Hence work is initiated at the second workstation by the arrival of an external request for a completed assembly. When such a request arrives, the second workstation issues a request to the first workstation. When the first workstation receives the request, it issues a request to the supplier for an additional tote containing components to be assembled.

Each workcenter has both a work-request queue and an incoming-tote queue. For work to begin at either workstation, there must be both a work request and an incoming tote containing the needed materials (components or sub-assemblies) at the workstation. A small buffer of totes containing work (components or sub-assemblies) is initially stocked at each workcenter as a means of reducing production delays from starvation for needed material.

External requests for completed assemblies arrive at the second workstation with an exponentially distributed interarrival time with a mean of five minutes. The time required to perform the assembly operation at this workcenter is normally distributed with a mean of four minutes and a standard deviation of one minute. The time required to make the sub-assemblies at the first workcenter is normally distributed with a mean of three minutes and a standard deviation of one minute. The time required for the external supplier to supply a tote containing components is normally distributed with a mean of 4.2 minutes and a standard deviation of 1.3 minutes.

Simulate this system for an 80-hour period, and record statistics on the number of totes in each input queue and on the time required for the second workstation to meet external requests for completed assemblies. Assume that the system begins with three totes in the input buffer at each workstation.

Exercise 8-15

Modify the model/experiment for Exercise 8-14 to incorporate four initial totes at each workstation instead of just three. Compare the results obtained to determine if the additional tote at each workstation produces a statistically significant improvement in the time required to satisfy external requests at workstation 2.

References

SCHRIBER, T. J. (1974), *Simulation Using GPSS*, John Wiley & Sons, Inc., NY, NY.

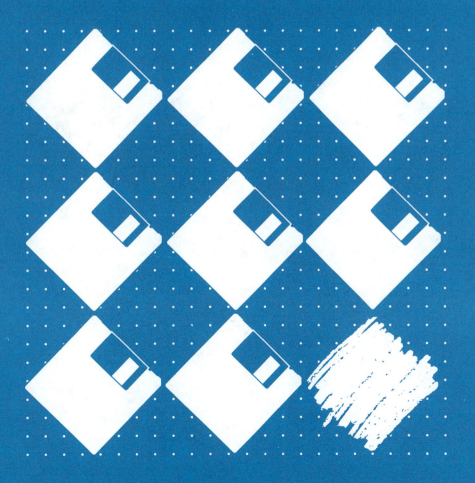

CHAPTER 9
Advanced Manufacturing Features

1. Introduction

Chapter 6, Section 5.2, introduced the concept of transporters and presented the constructs for modeling with free-path transporters. Free-path transporters have unconstrained movement, i.e., they can move freely about a system without consideration for delays imposed by other vehicles obstructing their paths. This chapter presents the concepts of guided transporters. These transporters must follow a pre-defined path, which can be blocked by other guided vehicles.

2. Guided Transporters

The movement of guided transporters is restricted to a network composed of links and intersections that completely define the paths that a vehicle may take in traveling from one point in a system to another. The intersections correspond to network nodes, which are used to define the endpoints of each link. The combination of specific links, with intersections as endpoints, defines the network over which a guided transporter can move and is referred to as the system map.

The most frequently encountered type of guided transporter is the Automated Guided Vehicle (AGV). The term AGV defines a class of vehicles that typically are driverless, are battery-powered, and follow a guide wire embedded in the floor. A controlling computer system usually directs the AGV from one point in the system to another. The links that compose the AGV paths are usually divided into zones that can be occupied by only one vehicle at a time, thereby preventing vehicle collisions. Because the vehicles must follow guided paths, the controlling system must plan vehicle travel to avoid deadlock.

The same SIMAN constructs used to model free-path transporters are used to model guided transporters, except that the DISTANCES element is replaced by several new elements that allow you to define the system map. First we present the SIMAN elements required to define the system map; then we discuss the transporter blocks used in the Model Frame. These new concepts are presented in the context of the following example.

2.1 The Modified Flow-Line with Guided Transporters

Consider the modified flow-line problem presented in Chapter 6, Section 5.1, for free-path transporters and depicted with a guided-vehicle system map in Figure 9-1. The part flow and production times remain the same; the only difference is that in this version AGVs transport the parts within the system. Assume that three AGVs are used, each having a travel velocity of 100 feet per minute.

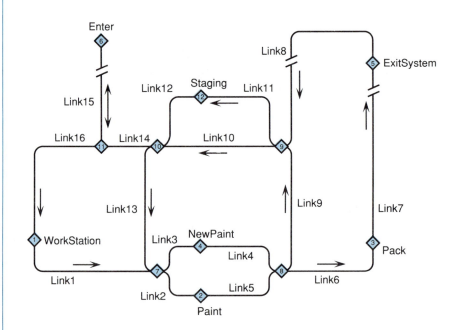

Figure 9-1. The Guided-Vehicle Network: Sample Problem 9.1

The numbers on the network identify intersections, and the lowercase letters identify links to be included in the system map. Intersection 12 lies on an off-loop, which is used as a vehicle staging area. When a vehicle has completed its task and there are no other requests for transport, the vehicle is sent to the staging area at intersection 12 to await the next request. If more than one vehicle arrives at the staging area, they automatically accumulate along link k, behind the vehicles already there. This simple method of control prevents an idle vehicle from blocking another vehicle that is attempting to carry out a transport. Also note that the system map only allows one-way travel, thus preventing vehicle deadlock. The one exception to one-way travel is the spur link for reaching the Enter area at intersection 6. Temporary blocking can occur if a vehicle is loading or unloading a part at an operation and another vehicle needs to pass that operation. In this case, the second vehicle waits until the first vehicle has completed its task and has moved out of the way. More details about the AGV example will be provided as the different blocks and elements are discussed.

2.2 Defining Intersections: The INTERSECTIONS Element

The INTERSECTIONS element describes the characteristics of all intersections in a guided-transporter system. The syntax for this element is given below.

> INTERSECTIONS: Number, Name, Length, Rule, VelChange:
>   repeats;

The intersection number and name provide a reference to the Model Frame and to the LINKS element. If you default the number, it is assigned by the Experiment Processor in a manner similar to the way numbers are assigned for other elements. The name can also be defaulted; however, all references to an unnamed intersection are then made in terms of its number — either explicitly stated or defaulted and assigned by the Experiment Processor. If information for an intersection is to be defined, the number and/or name must be entered. The intersection length defines the distance that a guided vehicle must travel in passing through the intersection. If defaulted, this distance is assumed to be 0. The link-selection rule allows you to define a rule to determine which vehicle is given priority if more than one link enters this intersection. The available link-selection rules are listed in Figure 9-2; the default is first-come-first-served (FCFS). The velocity-change factor, VelChange, allows for adjusting vehicle velocity during its travel through the intersection. If the intersection length is not specified as 0, and a velocity-change factor is given, the velocity of the vehicle during its travel through the intersection is determined by multiplying the vehicle's current velocity by the stated factor. After the vehicle has passed through the intersection, its velocity reverts back to the original value. The default velocity-change factor is 1.0.

Rule	Definition
FCFS	First-come, first-served
LCFS	Last-come, first-served
LVF(K)	Lowest Value of attribute K of controlling entity
HVF(K)	Highest Value of attribute K of controlling entity
CLOSEST	Closest to destination
FARTHEST	Farthest from destination

Figure 9-2. Link-Selection Rules

An intersection must be defined for every network point at which multiple links come together and at all points from which multiple links depart. If we view the system map as a network of arcs and nodes, then the minimum number of intersections that must be defined is equal to the number of nodes in the network. Intersections may also be defined for points in the system where the guided vehicles interact with the SIMAN model, e.g., a load/unload station or vehicle staging area. Intersections must also be defined for any point in the network where the zone length changes (discussed in Section 2.3). Other intersections can also be defined to help clarify the network.

Examples of the INTERSECTIONS element are provided below. The first line segment defines intersection number 1, named Input, with an intersection length of 5 units. The link-selection rule and velocity-change factor have been defaulted to FCFS and 1.0, respectively. The second example defines intersection number 2, not named, with an intersection length of 10 units, a default link-selection rule of FCFS, and a velocity-change factor of 0.8. The third example defaults the intersection number to 3, named ExitSystem, and defaults the intersection length to 0. The link-selection rule is specified to select the vehicle that is closest to its destination, and the velocity-change factor is defaulted to 1.0.

```
INTERSECTIONS: 1,Input,5:
               2,,10,,0.8:
               ExitSystem,,CLOSEST;
```

2.3 Defining Guided-Vehicle Links: The LINKS Element

The LINKS element defines the characteristics of the links that compose the guided-vehicle network. The syntax for the LINKS element is shown below. The link number and link name, which provide the reference to the NETWORKS element, are defined in the same way as for the INTERSECTIONS element. The beginning intersection, BegIntxID, and ending intersection, EndIntxID, define the two endpoints of the link in terms of intersections. You can specify these endpoints by referencing the intersection number or the intersection name as entered in the INTERSECTIONS element. All intersections included in the LINKS element must be listed in the INTERSECTIONS element.

```
LINKS: Number, Name, BegIntxID — BegDir, EndIntxID — EndDir, Zones,
       Length, Type, VelChange:
    repeats;
```

The number of zones and the length of each zone together define the travel distance for a link. SIMAN uses the number of zones to determine how to move guided transporters through the links. When a vehicle reaches the end of an intersection or a zone on a link, SIMAN checks the status of the next zone or intersection to determine if the vehicle can continue on its travel. A complete discussion of the logic used to move a vehicle through a network is presented in Section 2.8 of this chapter.

The travel direction, Type, is specified as Unidirectional, Bidirectional, or Spur. The default is Unidirectional, the most commonly used direction. With unidirectional travel, a vehicle always enters at the defined beginning intersection, BegIntxID, and exits at the defined ending intersection, EndIntxID. Bidirectional travel implies two-way travel, i.e., a vehicle can enter the link at either intersection; however, if more than one vehicle is in a link at the same time, they must both travel in the same direction. Spur travel defines a special case in which the ending intersection of the link is at a dead end, i.e., no other links are connected to this intersection in the specified network. The Spur designation allows the vehicle to enter the spur link and travel to the ending intersection, while at the same time preventing another vehicle from entering the same spur. After the vehicle completes its activity at the ending intersection, it backs out along the spur link to the beginning intersection where it enters the normal network.

The velocity-change factor, VelChange, functions just as it did for the INTER-SECTIONS element. If specified, the vehicle's current velocity is multiplied by the factor to determine its velocity through the link. The beginning and ending direction, BegDir and EndDir, are discussed in Section 2.15 of this chapter.

Examples of the LINKS element are shown below. The first link segment defines link 1, named Aisle, which starts at intersection 1 and ends at intersection 2. Link 1 has five zones of length 6 for a total length of 30 units. The direction is specified as Unidirectional, meaning that all travel begins at intersection 1 and ends at intersection 2.

```
LINKS: 1,Aisle,1,2,5,6,U:
       2,,ExitSystem,Enter,10,4,B,0.8:
       3,,10,ExitSystem,1,20,S;
```

The second line segment defines unnamed link 2, which starts at intersection ExitSystem and ends at intersection Enter. There are 10 zones of length 4, for a total length of 40 units. The travel direction is specified as Bidirectional, and the velocity-change factor is specified as 0.8. The last line segment defines link 3 as starting at intersection Enter and ending at intersection ExitSystem. There is one zone of 20 units, and it is a spur link.

2.4 Defining the System Map: The NETWORKS Element

The NETWORKS element defines the LINKS that compose each guided-transporter system map. The syntax for the NETWORKS element is shown below. The network number and name provide identifiers that are referenced by other elements. The list of beginning and ending link identifiers, BegLinkID—EndLinkID, identifies all links included in the system map or network. These links can be listed by their link number or name as found in the LINKS element. They can be listed individually or in clusters (by using a dash to separate the first and last link in a sequence). Note that, if clusters are used to identify numbered links, the first link must have a lower link number than the second link. All links referenced by the NETWORKS element must be defined in the LINKS element. Multiple networks can be defined, and different networks can have common links.

```
NETWORKS: Number, Name, BegLinkID — EndLinkID, repeats:
          repeats;
```

Examples of the NETWORKS element are shown below. The first network, named AGVSys, includes links 1 through 5, the link named Aisle, and links 11 through 14. The second network, named Tow, contains the link named Aisle, links 12 and 14, links 15 through 17, and the link named ExitSystem. Note that the links 12, 14, and Aisle are shared by the first two networks.

```
NETWORKS: 1,AGVSys, 1-5, Aisle, 11-14:
          2,Tow, Aisle, 12, 14, 15-17, ExitSystem
          3,, Enter-ExitSystem;
```

The third network, unnamed, includes all links from Enter through Exit-System as listed in the LINKS element.

2.5 Defining The Modified Flow-Line System Map

Defining the system map for our modified flow-line example requires listing the intersections and links with the INTERSECTIONS and LINKS elements and then defining the actual network by using the NETWORKS element. The three elements for our sample problem are given in Figure 9-3. The INTERSECTIONS element explicitly defines intersections 1 through 6 and 12, and it provides a name for each. These intersections are assigned names because they represent the nodes in the system map where guided vehicles interact with the SIMAN Model. The remaining intersections, 7 through 11, are included because of the intersection length, but they are unnamed.

```
INTERSECTIONS:     1,IntWorkStation,1:
                   2,IntPaint,1:
                   3,IntPack,1:
                   4,IntNewPaint,1:
                   5,IntExitSystem,1:
                   6,IntEnter,1:
                   7,,1:
                   8,,1:
                   9,,1:
                   10,,1:
                   11,,1:
                   12,IntStaging,1;
LINKS:     1,Link1,    1,7,    8,10:
           2,Link2,    7,2,    4,10:
           3,Link3,    7,4,    4,10:
           4,Link4,    4,8,    8,10:
           5,Link5,    2,8,    6,10:
           6,Link6,    8,3,    7,10:
           7,Link7,    3,5,    25,10:
           8,Link8,    5,9,    22,10:
           9,Link9,    8,9,    10,10:
           10,Link10,  9,10,   11,10:
           11,Link11,  9,12,   10,10:
           12,Link12,  12,10,  3,10:
           13,Link13,  10,7,   8,10:
           14,Link14,  10,11,  4,10:
           15,Link15,  11,6,   23,10,Spur:
```

```
                    16,Link16,  11,1,    9,10;
    NETWORKS:    1,AGVPath,1-16;
```

Figure 9-3. Sample Guided-Transporter Elements

The LINKS element defines all the links in the network. Each link is divided into equal zones of length 10. For example, Link5 starts at intersection 2 and ends at intersection 8. It has six zones of 10 feet each, for a total length of 60 feet. Note that, except for Link15, the Travel direction has been defaulted to Unidirectional, which means that the AGVs always travel from the beginning toward the ending intersection. Link15 has been designated a spur link.

The NETWORKS element defines a single network, named AGVPath, which includes all the links, 1 through 16, listed in the LINKS element.

2.6 Creating The Shortest-Distance Matrix

Although the information provided in the previous three elements completely defines the components of the guided system, it does not define the path that a vehicle takes when traveling from one point in the system to another. In simple networks there may be only one path available. For example, in our modified flow-line example there is only one way to travel from intersection 6 to intersection 7, i.e., links 15-16-1. In complicated networks multiple paths are possible. For example, there are four paths that a vehicle can travel from intersection 9 to intersection 7: links 10-13, 10-14-16-1, 11-12-13, and 11-12-14-16-1. Because of the potential for multiple paths, some mechanism must guide the vehicle to its destination. The same type of problem is encountered if the selection of idle vehicles for allocation to waiting entities is based on travel distance.

The LINKER Processor resolves these path-selection issues by automatically computing and storing the shortest-distance matrix from all intersections in the network to all destinations; corresponding paths are also generated. Figure 9-4 gives the shortest-distance matrix for our sample problem.

```
                              To Intersection
                 1    2    3    4    5    6    7    8    9   10   11   12
              1    0  122  254  122  505  667   81  183  284  395  436  385
              2  405    0  132  395  383  545  354   61  162  273  314  263
              3  715  705    0  705  251  855  664  766  472  583  624  573
              4  425  415  152    0  403  565  374   81  182  293  334  283
              5  464  454  586  454    0  604  413  515  221  332  373  322
From          6  322  444  576  444  827    0  403  505  606  717  231  707
Intersection  7  446   41  173   41  424  586    0  102  203  314  355  304
              8  344  334   71  334  322  484  293    0  101  212  253  202
              9  243  233  365  233  616  383  192  294    0  111  152  101
             10  132  122  254  122  505  272   81  183  284    0   41  385
             11   91  213  345  213  596  231  172  274  375  486    0  476
             12  163  153  285  153  536  303  112  214  315   31   72    0
```

Figure 9-4. Shortest-Distance Matrix for Network AGVPath

This matrix provides the distance for the shortest path between any two intersections in the system map; however, it does not identify the actual paths to be taken. This information is provided by the next-intersection matrix shown in Figure 9-5. This matrix indicates the next intersection to be taken on the shortest path based on the current location and destination. For example, the shortest path from intersection 9 to intersection 7 starts at 9. The entry in row 9 (current intersection), column 7 (destination intersection) tells the guided vehicle to go next to intersection 10. Once at intersection 10, the entry in row 10, column 7 tells the vehicle to go next to intersection 7, which is the destination intersection. The total distance traveled from 9 to 7 can be retrieved from the entry in row 9, column 7, of the shortest-distance matrix. This value, 192 feet, is the sum of the length of link 10 connecting intersections 9 and 10 (111 feet) and link 13 connecting intersections 10 and 7 (81 feet).

		To Intersection											
		1	2	3	4	5	6	7	8	9	10	11	12
	1	1	7	7	7	7	7	7	7	7	7	7	7
	2	8	2	8	8	8	8	8	8	8	8	8	8
	3	5	5	3	5	5	5	5	5	5	5	5	5
	4	8	8	8	4	8	8	8	8	8	8	8	8
	5	9	9	9	9	5	9	9	9	9	9	9	9
From	6	11	11	11	11	11	6	11	11	11	11	11	11
Intersection	7	2	2	2	2	4	2	7	2	2	2	2	2
	8	9	9	3	9	3	9	9	8	9	9	9	9
	9	10	10	10	10	10	10	10	10	9	10	10	12
	10	11	7	7	7	7	11	7	7	7	10	11	7
	11	1	1	1	1	1	6	1	1	1	1	11	1
	12	10	10	10	10	10	10	10	10	10	10	10	12

Figure 9-5. Next-Intersection Matrix for Network AGVPath

These two matrices are used by the SIMAN processor every time a vehicle is moved and every time a decision is made based on distance. For example, assume that there are available vehicles at intersections 6 and 12, and that a request for a vehicle (based on shortest distance) is made at intersection 3. From the shortest-distance matrix we can see that the distance from 6 to 3 is 576 feet, whereas the distance from 12 to 3 is 285 feet. The vehicle at intersection 12 is therefore allocated, and it follows the path designated in the next-intersection matrix, i.e., intersections 12-10-7-2-8-3. Procedures for altering these matrices to direct vehicles on paths other than the shortest distance are shown in Section 2.17.

2.7 The STATIONS and TRANSPORTERS Elements for Guided Transporters

The STATIONS element allows intersections to be associated with specific Stations. The syntax for this element is shown below. The first two operands, Number and Name, remain the same; the third operand, IntxID, provides the capability of associating an intersection with a specific station. Defaulting this last field implies that no intersection is to be associated with the station.

STATIONS: Number, Name, IntxID:
      repeats;

The new STATIONS element for our flow-line example is shown below. Stations 1 through 6 retain the same numbers and names as before. We have also associated Intersections 1 through 6 with each of the Stations. Station 7 has been renamed to Staging and has been associated with intersection 12.

```
STATIONS: WorkStation,1:
         Paint,2:
         Pack,3:
         NewPaint,4:
         ExitSystem,5:
         Enter,6:
         Staging,12;
```

The TRANSPORTERS element defines the guided vehicles and is identical to that used to define free-path transporters, except that several new fields or options need to be described. The revised syntax for the TRANSPORTERS element is shown below. The first three entries — transporter Number, transporter Name, and Capacity — are identical to those used for free-path transporters. Note that the network identifier, Map, is followed by an entry describing the type of control, whereas for free-path transporters only the distance set identifier has been entered. You can enter the map as NETWORK(NetworkID), where the NetworkID is the network number or name. You enter the type of control as S to indicate release-at-start, as E to indicate release-at-end, or as an integer to indicate length. The default entry is S. The differences in these three types of control are discussed in the next section.

TRANSPORTERS: Number, Name, Capacity, Map — Control,
                Vel — Accel — Decel — TurnVel,
                Position — Status — Size, repeats:
      repeats;

Three new optional operands, separated by dashes, follow the transporter velocity, Vel. The first two, acceleration and deceleration, Accel and Decel, describe the additional time required to start or stop the vehicles. These values are given in units of distance per time squared. An entry of 0, the default value, implies that the vehicle reaches full velocity immediately and/or stops immediately. The third operand, TurnVel, allows a turning-velocity factor to be applied when the vehicle makes a turn. The mechanism used to detect if a vehicle is making a turn is discussed in Section 2.15.

    The initial position and status have the same meaning as for free-path transporters. However, there are several different ways to specify where each vehicle is placed in the network. If you enter an integer value or a STATION(Number), the vehicle is placed in the trailing zones of the first link incoming to the intersection associated with that station number. An entry of INTX(Number) has the same effect, except that it directly references the intersection. If you enter LINK(Number), the vehicle is placed on the next available zone on the specified link. If you enter LINK(Number, Zone), the vehicle is placed on a specified zone. In positioning vehicles in a system, you must be sure that room exists; otherwise, SIMAN will terminate with an error when it attempts to initially position the vehicles.

The next operand, Size, defines vehicle size in terms of the number of zones or units of length that it can occupy in the network. You can enter Size as ZONE (Number) or LENGTH(Number) with the default being ZONE(1) or one zone. If you specify a vehicle length, then the actual space it occupies equals the minimum number of zones required to accommodate its total length. Thus, if zones are 3 feet in length, four zones (12 feet) are required to contain a 10-foot-long vehicle.

An example of the TRANSPORTERS element for our flow-line problem is given below. We have only one vehicle type, number 1, named AGV, with a total of three vehicles. For our example, the network identifier is AGVPath, which was defined in the NETWORKS element. Each AGV follows a release-at-start, S, type of control, and each has a travel velocity of 100 feet/min. The three AGVs are initially positioned at link 11 (intersection 12 — the staging area) in an active state with each vehicle requiring one zone. Because there are three vehicles, they are positioned on link 11 on the three zones nearest intersection 12.

```
TRANSPORTERS: 1, AGV, 3, NETWORK(AGVPath) -S, 100,
LINK(11)-A-ZONE(1);
```

We have provided the capability of defining the complete system map: associating specific stations with intersections and defining the transporter characteristics. We now discuss the manner in which the guided vehicles move through the described network.

2.8 Guided-Vehicle Movement

The movement of a guided vehicle within the system map depends on the type of vehicle control, the vehicle's size, the vehicle's velocity characteristics, the link travel direction, the number of zones and their length on the current link or the intersection size, and the degree of vehicle congestion. Each zone of a link and each intersection can only be controlled by a single vehicle at any point in time; however, a single vehicle can control several zones and/or intersections at the same time.

The form of control specified on the TRANSPORTERS element determines when zones are released, thereby allowing other vehicles to gain access. With the release-at-start form of control, the transporter releases its trailing zone as soon as it gains control of the next required zone. Thus the vehicle always has control of the same number of zones. With the release-at-end form of control, the transporter waits to release the trailing zone until it reaches the end of the next zone. Thus the vehicle has control of one more zone during travel than when stopped. When an integer indicating distance is given on the TRANSPORTERS element, the vehicle releases the trailing zone after traveling the specified distance into the next zone.

Consider the simplest case in which the transporter size is one zone, the form of control is release-at-start, and all links in the network are unidirectional. Let's assume that all zones and intersections are the same size. Figure 9-6-a shows a sample section of the defined network with a guided vehicle traveling from left to right. This network section consists of four intersections (1 through 4) and three links (a, b, and c). Link a has three zones, link b has five zones, and link c has two zones.

Assume that the AGV is traveling to intersection 4, is currently in zone a2, and is about to enter zone a3, as shown in Figure 9-6-a. If a3 is unoccupied, the AGV will seize control of a3 and immediately release control of zone a2. Figure 9-6-b shows the AGV part of the way into zone a3; at this point it only controls zone a3, even though part of the AGV may physically remain in zone a2. When the AGV reaches the end of zone a3, it will seize control of intersection 2 and release zone a3. Figure 9-6-c shows the AGV at intersection 2. The AGV will continue traveling in this way until it reaches its destination at intersection 4 where it will stop, controlling only intersection 4 as shown in Figure 9-6-d.

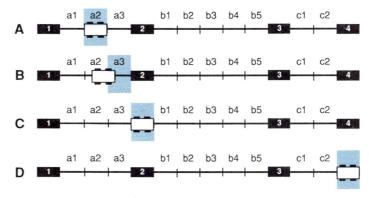

Figure 9-6. Example of Release-at-Start Control

Now consider the same example with the second form of control, release-at-end. Figure 9-7-a shows the AGV at intersection 1. As it begins its travel to intersection 4, it first gains control of zone a1 while retaining control of intersection 1; it then enters zone a1, as shown in Figure 9-7-b. It retains control of the previous zone or intersection until it reaches the end of its next zone, in this case, zone a1. Once it releases intersection 1, it only controls zone a1; however, it will then seize control of zone a2 and continue its travel.

Therefore, when traveling through the system, the AGV controls two zones, except when it reaches the end of its current zone. If it stops because it has reached its destination or because it is blocked from seizing control of the next zone on its path, it only has control of the zone in which it currently resides, as shown in Figure 9-7-c (in this case, the AGV has reached its final destination).

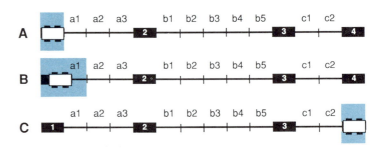

Figure 9-7. Example of Release-at-End Control

If the size of the AGV is two zones, rather than one, the same concepts apply. If release-at-start control is used, the AGV will always control two zones. If release-at-end control is used, the AGV will always control at least two zones, and, when moving, it will control three zones. In either case, when the AGV reaches its final destination at intersection 4, it controls both the zone at intersection 4 and the last zone on the link leading to the intersection, zone c2.

With relatively few exceptions, these two forms of control function identically in terms of zone control — regardless of the zone sizes — as long as the transporter size is specified in number of zones. Even if the zone sizes vary from link to link or from link to intersection, these forms of control are always linked to zone number and not to zone size. The one major exception occurs when zone length, for either a link or an intersection, is defined as 0.

Consider the case of an intersection, say intersection 2, with zero length, release-at-end control, and an AGV size of one zone. When the AGV arrives at the end of zone a3, as in the previous example, it releases control of zone a2, at which time it controls only zone a3. The AGV then seizes control of intersection 2; however, because the intersection has zero length, it does not count as one of the controlled zones. Before the AGV can continue its travel, it must seize zone b1. It then travels to the end of zone b1 with control of zone a3, intersection 2, and zone b1. When it reaches the end of zone b1, it releases control of zone a3 and intersection 2. If intersection 4 has zero length, the AGV arrives at the end of zone c2, releases control of zone c1, seizes control of intersection 4, and stops at its destination with control of zone c2 and intersection 4.

If the system map contains links of zero length, the same logic applies. The AGV must seize control of the zero-length zones before it can continue its travel, but these zero-length zones do not count as part of the controlled zones. For an extreme example, consider the last example with link c also having zones of zero length. In this case the AGV, arriving at the end of intersection 3, releases control of zone b5, seizes zones c1 and c2 (both of zero length), seizes intersection 4 (also of zero length), and stops at its destination, intersection 4. At this point it has control of intersection 3, zones c1 and c2, and intersection 4. It retains control until sent to its next destination.

If the vehicle length is specified in length units, then the number of zones the vehicle controls depends on the size of the zones the vehicle travels over as it moves through the network. Consider the case in which transporter Size has been specified as six feet, with release-at-start control, and all links in the network are unidirectional. Figure 9-8-a shows a sample section of the defined network with a guided vehicle traveling from left to right. This network section consists of four intersections (1 through 4) and three links (a, b, and c). Intersections 1 and 2 are of length 2, intersection 3 is of length 5, and intersection 4 is of zero length. Link a has three zones of size 4, link b has five zones of size 3, and link c has two zones of size 5. All units are expressed in feet.

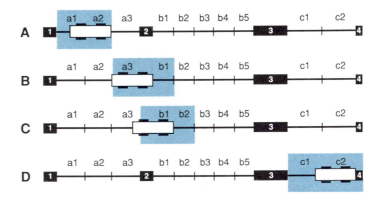

Figure 9-8. Example Using Vehicle Length

Assume that the AGV traveling to intersection 4 is currently at the end of zone a2, about to enter zone a3. It currently controls zones a1 and a2, as shown in Figure 9-8-a. If a3 is unoccupied, the AGV seizes control of a3 and checks to see if it can release any controlled zones. It retains control of enough forward zones to contain its length of six feet and releases all trailing zones not needed. In this case it immediately releases zone a1 — even though it is still physically in that zone — because zones a2 and a3 have sufficient space for it. When it reaches the end of a3, it seizes intersection 2 and releases a2.

Figure 9-8-b shows the AGV at the point where it seizes control of b1. It now controls eight feet of the path: a3, b1, and intersection 2. It does not release a3 because doing so would leave it with control of only four feet, and it requires six feet. It releases a3 when it has control of b2, as shown in Figure 9-8-c. Traveling along link b, it releases a trailing zone each time it seizes a forward zone, retaining three zones of size 2 at all times. When it reaches its destination at intersection 4, as shown in Figure 9-8-d, it controls zones c1, c2, and intersection 4. Remember that intersection 4 has zero length, and that zones c1 and c2 each have lengths of five feet. Therefore, the AGV controls of a total of 10 feet of path.

With release-at-start control and a vehicle size expressed in length units, zones are seized and released at the start of each link. Only the minimum number of forward zones required to contain the vehicle size is retained. All trailing zones are released before the vehicle initiates its travel into the most recently seized zone. The same logic is used with release-at-end control and vehicle size expressed in length units, except that the trailing zones are not released until the vehicle arrives at the end of the most recently seized zone.

The last form of control is release after traveling a specified length. This form of control allows the trailing zones to be released somewhere between the start and the end of the most recently seized zone. Basically, the guided vehicle travels the specified length into the next zone and then releases any trailing zones. However, the length it travels before releasing the trailing zones never exceeds the length of the next zone. The only exception occurs when the zone length is specified as 0, which is equivalent to release-at-start control. If the specified length exceeds or equals the largest zone in the network, it is equivalent to release-at-end control. If we specify this length as three feet for our example, the vehicle will use release-at-end control when it enters zones b1 through b5 and intersections 1 and 2, because their lengths are each less than the length specified. When it enters zones on links a and c and on intersection 3, it will travel the specified three feet and then release any trailing zones.

The spur link is a special case because it has only one connection to the system map. Thus, a vehicle entering a spur link must exit from the same point. In effect, the vehicle backs out along the designated link. To prevent a deadlock, different logic applies to the spur link. When a vehicle enters a spur link, it must control the single intersection that provides access to the system map. If the spur link is long enough to contain the entire vehicle, the intersection will be released, but any vehicle having the spur link as its final destination is not allowed to gain control of the entering intersection until all zones on the spur link are available, i.e., until the first vehicle has moved off the spur. Thus, any other vehicle having the spur link as its destination is not permitted to gain control of the entering intersection, thereby preventing both vehicles from reaching their final destination. Because control of the entering intersection can be released if the entire vehicle fits on the spur, other vehicles are not prevented from passing through the entering intersection on their way to a destination other than the spur link.

When a vehicle on a spur link is ready to leave that link, one of two scenarios will occur, depending on which zones and intersections the vehicle controls. If the entire length of the vehicle can be contained on the spur link (including the entering intersection), then as soon as the vehicle has control of the entering intersection it simply leaves the spur traveling in reverse. In effect, the head and tail of the vehicle are switched. If the entire length of the vehicle cannot be contained on the spur link, then the vehicle must back up along the link on which it arrived until its head is again at the entering intersection. Then it proceeds forward, traveling in the same direction as when it entered the spur. The latter scenario creates a possible source of deadlock. If a second vehicle were to arrive behind the first, the first vehicle would be prevented from backing out, and the second vehicle from going forward. If this occurs during a simulation run, SIMAN will terminate with an error message about the deadlock condition.

Bidirectional links operate in much the same fashion as unidirectional links. However, the direction of travel on a bidirectional link can change during a simulation run, depending on conditions in the system. When a vehicle attempts to enter a bidirectional link, it must gain control of both the entering zones on that link and the travel direction. If the entire link is unoccupied, the travel direction is set to that of the entering vehicle. If the link is occupied and the travel direction is the same as for the entering vehicle, the vehicle is allowed to enter as soon as it can gain control of the required zones. If the link is occupied and the travel direction is different, the vehicle will wait until the link becomes unoccupied or the travel direction is changed by the occupied vehicle. Although several vehicles can occupy a bidirectional link at the same time, the travel direction must be the same for all vehicles.

Caution is recommended in the use of bidirectional links, as deadlocks can easily occur. For example, if a vehicle arrives and gains control of an intersection at the end of a bidirectional link and a second vehicle already occupies the link, and is traveling to the ending intersection, a deadlock will occur. The first vehicle will be unable to gain control of the travel direction and the second vehicle will be unable to gain control of the ending intersection. At this point, SIMAN will detect the deadlock and terminate with an error message.

These concepts describe the way a guided vehicle moves through the system map. All of the above-described logic assumes that no congestion or blockages exist along the path of the traveling vehicle. If another vehicle controls a zone or an intersection required by the traveling AGV, the latter travels along the path until it arrives at the start of the occupied zone. It then stops and waits until the other vehicle releases control of the required zone, at which time it seizes control and continues its travel. (It is assumed that all links are unidirectional.) The travel time is affected if an acceleration and/or deceleration is specified on the TRANSPORTERS element (for discussion of this topic, see Section 2.15).

2.9 Controlling Guided Vehicles

In most situations the control of guided vehicles in SIMAN is fairly straightforward. SIMAN automatically determines the correct path for a vehicle to use in traveling through the network, concurrently allowing only one vehicle at a time to control any zone in the system. It is possible, however, to imagine practical situations that result in a deadlock involving two or more vehicles. A deadlock occurs when vehicle A requires control of a zone controlled by vehicle B, and vehicle B requires control of a zone controlled by vehicle A; neither can release control of its currently held zone until it gains control of the required zone. For example, two AGVs traveling in opposite directions meet at an ending intersection of a bidirectional link. The model must contain control logic to prevent such deadlocks. If a deadlock does occur, SIMAN reports the deadlock and terminates the simulation run.

It is possible to create a set of circumstances that prevents a group of vehicles from moving at all (in effect causing the system to cease operation) but that does not prompt a deadlock message from SIMAN. For example, a vehicle is traveling from intersection A through intersection B on its way to intersection C, and an idle vehicle is at intersection B. If the traveling vehicle must reach its destination, intersection C, before a request is made to move the idle vehicle at intersection B, then the traveling vehicle waits at intersection B, trying to gain control. If the system contains only these two vehicles, and if no request causes the idle vehicle at intersection B to move, then no further movement occurs. The system is not, however, deadlocked because the idle vehicle does not require a zone currently held by the first vehicle. Thus, faulty control logic can prevent the guided-vehicle system from functioning as intended.

2.10 Allocating and Moving the Empty Transporter

The ALLOCATE, MOVE, and REQUEST blocks discussed in Chapter 6 for free-path transporters apply in a very similar way to guided transporters. Recall that the REQUEST block both allocates the transporter and moves the empty transporter to the location of the requesting entity. The ALLOCATE and MOVE blocks together perform the same function as the REQUEST block, although they provide more control over the sequence of events occurring after allocation. The following discussion of these three blocks concentrates on the new operands and options specific to guided transporters and assumes an understanding of the basic concepts presented in Chapter 6.

The revised syntax for the ALLOCATE block is shown below. The request priority number, Pr, and the transporter name, TrnName(Unit), retain the same meaning and are specified just as they are for free-path transporters. The network entity location, EntLoc, which specifies the current location of the entity on the system network, has several new options. If this operand is defaulted, it is assumed that the entity is currently located at the intersection associated with the current station value, M, of the requesting entity. The entity location can also be stated as a specific station within the model.

ALLOCATE,Pr,AltPath
TrnName(Unit),EntLoc

ALLOCATE, Pr, AltPath:
        TrnName(Unit), EntLoc;

You can also specify the network entity location, the transporter destination, and the alternative path, AltPath, by directly referencing an intersection or a zone on a specified link. This syntax is given below. Note that the syntax includes the ability to specify a certain station, which is assumed if the other forms are not used.

INTX(IntersectionID)
LINK(LinkID, Zone)
STATION(StationID)

The entity location, EntLoc, is only required for the ALLOCATE block if the transporter-selection rule used requires that SIMAN know the present location of the requesting entity, i.e., the SDS or LDS rule. If one of these rules is used and the entity location is stated as a station, the specified or defaulted station entered must be associated, in the STATIONS element, with an intersection on the network. If the station value of the requesting entity is not associated with an intersection on the network, then SIMAN will terminate with an error report.

The optional alternative path operand, AltPath, is used only for the ALLOCATE block if the transporter-selection rule is SDS or LDS. Normally, when SIMAN moves a transporter through the network, it follows the path determined by the next-intersection matrix as described in Section 2.6. If the alternative path option is used, it follows the shortest-distance path that takes the transporter through the station, intersection, or link specified by the AltPath operand. The syntax used to designate the AltPath is VIA(Intermediate Network Location), where the intermediate network location is specified by using the syntax shown above for the entity and destination location. For example, the expression VIA (INTX(4)) calculates the distance from the transporter to the entity location, assuming that it would travel through intersection 4. This operand also allows you to deviate from the next-intersection matrix when moving a transporter.

Similar new operands have been added to the MOVE block; the revised syntax is shown below. Recall that the MOVE block allows the previously allocated transporter to be moved through the system map independent of the location of the entity currently controlling it.

MOVE, StorID, AltPath:
        TrnName, TrnDest, Vel;

The storage identifier, StorID, provides a reference to a Cinema layout and indicates where the entity symbol will reside during the actual move operation. The optional AltPath operand allows you to override the next-intersection matrix and is specified in the same manner as described for the ALLOCATE block. The transporter name, TrnName, must correspond exactly to the specific transporter previously allocated. The velocity, Vel, remains unchanged. As previously discussed, the transporter destination, TrnDest, can be expressed in several different ways, which remain essentially the same as those used for the AltPath operand, although the VIA notation is not used. For example, a transporter destination of LINK(6,2) sends the transporter to zone 2 of link 6. Remember that the MOVE block does not cause the entity to be sent to the destination of the transporter; it remains at its current location.

MOVE,StorID,AltPath
TrnName,TrnDest,Vel

The REQUEST block combines the operations of the ALLOCATE and MOVE blocks. It first allocates a transporter and then moves the empty transporter to the location of the entity. The revised syntax for the REQUEST block for guided vehicles is shown below. The operands for the REQUEST block are identical to those discussed for the ALLOCATE and MOVE blocks.

```
REQUEST, Pr, StorID, AltPath:
         TrnName(Unit), Vel, EntLoc;
```

The AltPath operand still allows you to alter the next-intersection and shortest-distance matrices in the same way as before. During the time that the allocated transporter is being moved from its idle position in the network to the location of the requesting entity, EntLoc, the entity remains at its current location. However, this location must be on the system map on which the transporter is currently traveling.

In summary, the ALLOCATE block allocates a transporter to an entity. The MOVE block moves the allocated transporter without moving the entity. The MOVE block is most often used to transport the allocated vehicle to the position of the entity, or to move the vehicle to another position in the system after it has dropped off the entity. The REQUEST block performs both vehicle allocation and vehicle movement.

You control the vehicles in the system by using the same set of modeling constructs or blocks used for controlling free-path transporters. Because of the additional capabilities provided for guided vehicles, each of the blocks allows several new operands to move the vehicles through the system.

2.11 Transporting the Entity: The TRNASPORT Block

The TRANSPORT block is used to transport both the entity and the previously allocated vehicle. The revised syntax for the TRANSPORT block is given below. The AltPath, TrnName, and Vel operands function as they did for the three previously described blocks.

```
TRANSPORT, AltPath:
          TrnName, EntDest, Vel, TrnDest;
```

The major difference with the new syntax is that two different destinations can be specified. The first destination, TrnName, denotes the destination of the allocated transporter and must be on the current network or system map. You can express this destination as a station, an intersection, a link, or a zone on a link. You must specify the entity destination, EntDest, as a station in order to indicate where the entity re-enters the model after completing the transport. By separating these two destinations, you can send the transporter to any location on the system map while directing the entity to any station in the model. Note that the entity will arrive at its destination station at the same time that the transporter arrives at its destination. Also note that the station designated for the entity destination does not have to be associated with the network.

2.12 The Modified Flow-Line Model and Experiment Frame

The Model Frame for our sample problem with guided transporters is given in Figure 9-9. It follows the same form as the solution of the flow-line problem for free-path transporters presented in Section 5.6 of Chapter 6. However, several changes have been made to take advantage of the station and resource index concepts presented in Chapter 8 and to send idle AGVs to the staging area. The model section, which starts with the creation of jobs and ends with the jobs being sent to their first operation, is almost identical to the previous model. The only changes are in the names, which are now expressed in terms of AGVs. Note that the operand for the transporter destination has been defaulted on the TRANSPORT block. Thus, the destination of the transporter is always the intersection associated with the station expressed in the SEQUENCES element (to be presented after the discussion of the Model Frame).

```
BEGIN;
;     MODIFIED FLOW-LINE WITH GUIDED TRANSPORTERS: SAMPLE PROBLEM 9.1

            CREATE:     EXPONENTIAL(28):
                        MARK(TimeIn);                    put TNOW in attrib(TimeIn)

            ASSIGN:     M=Enter:                         !get initial position
                        NS=DISC(.7,1,1,2);               get sequence set
ToStart     QUEUE,      AGVQue;                          wait for AGV
            REQUEST:    AGV(SDS);                        get AGV
            DELAY:      2;                               delay by load time
            TRANSPORT:  AGV,SEQ;                         send AGV to next station
;                                                          according to sequence set
;     -Generic WorkStation submodels-

            STATION,    WorkStation-NewPaint;            workstation submodel
            DELAY:      2;                               delay by unload time
            BRANCH,     1:
               IF,NQ(AGVQue)>0,FreeAGV:   !request waiting, free AGV
               ESLE,SendStage;

                                                         send AGV to staging area

FreeAGV     FREE:       AGV;
WorkQue     QUEUE,      M;                               WIP at workstation
            SEIZE:      Worker(M);                       get worker
            DELAY:      OpTime;                          delay for processing
            RELEASE:    Worker(M):                       !release worker
                        NEXT(ToStart);                   get AGV

SendStage   BRANCH,     2:
               ALWAYS,SendBack:          !entity moves AGV to stage
               ALWAYS,WorkQue;             entity process at station

SendBack    MOVE:       AGV,Staging:
                        NEXT(FreeAGV2);

;     -Exit Submodel-

            STATION,    ExitSystem;
            DELAY:      2;                               delay for unloading
            TALLY:      FlowTime,INT(TimeIn);            take time in system stat
            BRANCH,     1:
               IF,NQ(AGVQue)>0,FreeAGV2:  !request waiting, free AGV
               ELSE,SendBack;

                                                         send AGV to staging area
```

```
FreeAGV2    FREE:       AGV:
                        DISPOSE;
END;
```

Figure 9-9. Model Listing for Sample Problem 9.1

The section of model labeled generic WorkStation submodel contains the major changes in the model. We have taken advantage of the macro concept in combination with resource indexing and have used the attribute M to allow all of the operations (WorkStation, Paint, NewPaint and Pack) to be represented in the same submodel. The station numbers have been changed to allow the M value for this submodel to range from 1 to 4. After the entity controlling a transporter enters the station submodel, it delays for two time units, which represent the unloading time.

The set of blocks following this delay represents the logic for determining what action should be taken with respect to the AGV that has just delivered a part to a station. The guided vehicles for this new system follow a fixed path, and therefore the logic requires that an idle unit be sent to the added staging area to await the next request. However, if there is currently a request for an idle unit, the AGV should be freed so that it can grant that request.

The first BRANCH block after the delay determines whether any requests are currently in QUEUE AGVque. Because all requests wait in this queue until a guided vehicle is allocated, the entity need only check to see if there are one or more requesting entities. If there are requesting entities, i.e., NQ(AGVque) is greater than 0, the entity is sent to label FreeAGV where the vehicle is freed. The entity then enters the queue at the current workstation, designated by M, to await an available resource. The vehicle is immediately allocated at the previous REQUEST block to the first requesting entity in QUEUE AGVque, and it is moved to the position of that entity by the REQUEST block. Once the requesting entity has been allocated an AGV, it is removed from QUEUE AGVque and waits at the REQUEST block for the empty AGV to arrive. Because the entity allocated the freed AGV is not in QUEUE AGVque, other AGVs checking the status of this queue will follow the correct logic.

If there are no requesting entities, i.e., NQ(AGVque) equals 0, the entity is sent to label SendStage. The BRANCH block at this label sends the original entity, the entity that controls the AGV, to label SendBack, a MOVE block that transports the empty AGV to intersection 12, Staging, the staging area. Intersection 12 is associated with station 12, called Staging, in the Experiment Frame. When the transporter arrives at station Staging, the entity is sent to label FreeAGV2 where the AGV is freed, and the entity is disposed of. The BRANCH block at label SendStage also makes a copy of the original entity and sends that entity to label WorkQue, where it enters the queue for its next station to await an available worker resource. Note that this is the same QUEUE that the entity would have entered if the AGV had been freed at label FreeAGV.

The transported entity that enters QUEUE M waits for an available worker with the same index, M, as the entity and then enters the DELAY block for the operation at that workstation. The operation or delay time, Optime, is set in the SEQUENCES element in the Experiment Frame. When the delay is completed, the entity releases the resource and is sent to label ToStart, where it re-enters the request queue for transportation to its next station.

An entity that has completed all of its operations is transported to station ExitSystem, where it delays for the unloading time and tallies the flowtime. The entity then enters a BRANCH block that performs the same status check of QUEUE AGVque as was performed in the generic workstation submodel. If there is a requesting entity, the AGV is freed at label FreeAGV2, and the entity is disposed of. Otherwise, the entity is sent to label SendBack where it moves the AGV to the staging area and is then disposed of.

Except for the station macro submodel and the added logic to return the AGV to its staging area, the resulting guided-vehicle model for the modified flow-line problem is very similar to the model solution for free-path transporters. All of the detail regarding the guided path, or the system map, is included in the Experiment Frame. The logic required for the guided-vehicle model is essentially the same as that for free-path transporters — once the system map has been defined. However, we must ensure that the resulting model functions as planned. For example, if the staging area had not been included in our sample problem layout, idle vehicles would have remained at the pickup/drop-off points until requested by other entities. Other AGVs might not have been able to complete their tasks because they could not pass through the section of path occupied by the idle vehicle and had to wait until the idle vehicle was allocated and moved.

The Experiment Frame for our sample problem is given in Figure 9-10. As shown, several changes have been made to the free-path transporter experiment presented in Chapter 6; only these changes to the experiment are discussed. The resources have been indexed and are now referenced as Worker 1 through 4. Stations 4 and 5, Exit and NewPaint, have been switched to allow for easy use of the submodel concept. Queues have been changed to reflect the station change, and Queue AGVque has been added. The dstats have been altered to reflect the changes in the stations, queues, and resources. The assignment of the uniform time to attribute Optime has been added to the first station in the SEQUENCES element. This distribution was included in the Model Frame in the previous example, but the conversion to the index submodel requires that all operation times be assigned in the SEQUENCES element.

```
BEGIN;
PROJECT,         SAMPLE PROBLEM 9.1,SM;
ATTRIBUTES:      TimeIn:
                 OpTime;
STATIONS:        WorkStation,1:
                 Paint,2:
                 Pack,3:
                 NewPaint,4:
                 ExitSystem,5:
                 Enter,6:
                 Staging,12;
QUEUES:          WorkStationQ:
                 PaintQ:
                 PackQ:
                 NewPaintQ:
                 6,AGVQue;
RESOURCES:       1-4,Worker;
INTERSECTIONS:   1,IntWorkStation,1:
                 2,IntPaint,1:
                 3,IntPack,1:
                 4,IntNewPaint,1:
                 5,IntExitSystem,1:
                 6,IntEnter,1:
                 7,,1:
                 8,,1:
                 9,,1:
                 10,,1:
                 11,,1:
                 12,IntStaging,1;
LINKS:           1,Link1,    1,7,    8,10:
                 2,Link2,    7,2,    4,10:
                 3,Link3,    7,4,    4,10:
                 4,Link4,    4,8,    8,10:
                 5,Link5,    2,8,    6,10:
                 6,Link6,    8,3,    7,10:
                 7,Link7,    3,5,    25,10:
                 8,Link8,    5,9,    22,10:
                 9,Link9,    8,9,    10,10:
                 10,Link10,  9,10,   11,10:
                 11,Link11,  9,12,   10,10:
                 12,Link12,  12,10,  3,10:
                 13,Link13,  10,7,   8,10:
                 14,Link14,  10,11,  4,10:
                 15,Link15,  11,6,   23,10,Spur:
                 16,Link16,  11,1,   9,10;
NETWORKS:        1,AGVPath,1-16;
TRANSPORTERS:    1,AGV,3,NETWORK(AGVPath)-S,
                  100,LINK(11)-A-ZONE(1);
SEQUENCES:       1, WorkStation,OpTime=UNIFORM(21,25,2) &
                  Paint,OpTime=NORMAL(22,4,2) &
                  Pack,OpTime=TRIANGULAR(20,22,26,2) &
                  ExitSystem:
                 2, WorkStation,OpTime=UNIFORM(21,25,2) &
                  NewPaint,OpTime=NORMAL(49,7,2) &
                  Pack,OpTime=TRIANGULAR(21,23,26,2) &
                  ExitSystem;
```

Chapter 9

```
TALLIES:          FlowTime;
DSTATS:           NQ(WorkStationQ),WorkStation WIP:
                  NR(1)*100,Worker Busy:
                  NQ(PaintQ),Paint WIP:
                  NR(2)*100,Painter Busy:
                  NQ(PackQ),Pack WIP:
                  NR(3)*100,Packer Busy:
                  NQ(NewPaintQ),NewPaint WIP:
                  NR(4)*100,NewPainter Busy:
                  NQ(AGVQue),AGV Queue:
                  NT(1)*100/3,Busy AGVs;
REPLICATE,        1,0,115000;
END;
```

Figure 9-10. Experiment Listing for Sample Problem 9.1

The remaining elements, INTERSECTIONS, LINKS, NETWORKS and TRANSPORTERS, were discussed earlier in this chapter. The resulting SIMAN Summary Report is given in Figure 9-11.

```
Project:   SAMPLE PROBLEM 9.1
Analyst:   SM
Replication ended at time:   115000.
                         TALLY VARIABLES
```

Identifier	Average	Variation	Minimum	Maximum	Observations
FlowTime	183.33	.45866	89.219	646.70	4036

```
                    DISCRETE-CHANGE VARIABLES
```

Identifier	Average	Variation	Minimum	Maximum	Final Value
WorkStation WIP	1.7619	1.6733	.00000	21.000	1.0000
Worker Busy	80.769	.48796	.00000	100.00	100.00
Paint WIP	.03497	5.2551	.00000	2.0000	.00000
Painter Busy	54.554	.91271	.00000	100.00	100.00
Pack WIP	.51381	1.3411	.00000	4.0000	.00000
Packer Busy	80.103	.49839	.00000	100.00	100.00
NewPaint WIP	.16122	2.6515	.00000	3.0000	.00000
NewPainter Busy	50.857	.98299	.00000	100.00	.00000
AGV Queue	.06063	4.6680	.00000	5.0000	.00000
Busy AGVs	75.353	.19497	.00000	100.00	66.667

Figure 9-11. Summary Report for Sample Problem 9.1

The results given in the Summary Report are very similar to those obtained for the free-path transporter model (Figure 6-16). Previous simulations have shown that sufficient capacity exists for the required production. The only possible problem would come from the AGV system. The statistic on AGV utilization indicates that the vehicles are only busy about 75 percent of the time. Thus the similarity in the results should be expected.

2.13 Staging Area Logic for Guided Transporters

Because an idle vehicle occupies space on the network and blocks other vehicles from traveling through the section of the network, many AGV systems employ a staging area to house idle vehicles. The logic for developing a guided-vehicle system with a staging area is relatively straightforward as illustrated in the previous example. However, it does require that you consider several additional aspects of the model.

The model must include both the logic to determine when an idle vehicle is sent to the staging area and what the constructs to transport the vehicle are. Our example includes logic that checks each time a vehicle completes a task, to see if there is an entity in the single request queue. This approach allows the vehicle to respond directly to the next request without returning to the staging area. A simpler approach is to always send the vehicle to the staging area, where it is then freed and becomes available for the next request. Although both approaches are valid, the logic used should reflect that of the real-world system. A third approach is to keep the vehicles in motion at all times. In this type of system, an unrequested vehicle that completes a task is directed or moved to some other point in the system. When it arrives at its next destination, the system status is rechecked and, if there are still no requests, it is moved to yet another location. This process is continued until the vehicle is finally allocated to its next task. By keeping all vehicles constantly moving, this type of control logic prevents an idle vehicle from blocking a section of the network.

If a staging area is used, you must be aware of the impact on the resulting transporter-utilization statistics. When a vehicle is allocated in SIMAN, it is assumed to be busy, as reflected in the NT variable. Thus all activities by a vehicle are assumed to be the same, whether the vehicle is traveling to a task, transporting an entity, moving back to the staging area, or waiting on a blocked portion of the network. You can create special variables to separate the various activities by increasing and decreasing these variables at the correct point in the model when the activity of the transporter changes. To do so, you must add a set of ASSIGN blocks to change the status of these variables, and you must include the correct logic to determine which variables to change.

Even with this type of logic, the results can still be misleading. It is difficult to determine when an active vehicle is blocked or prevented from moving because another vehicle controls the next zone it requires. Often this block information is simply included in the other statistics. A second problem pertains to the exact time that vehicles are freed at the staging area.

In our example, an unrequested vehicle is moved to the staging area, and the controlling entity is sent to station Staging, which is associated with intersection 12. When the vehicle arrives at Staging, it is freed and becomes available to respond to other requests. However, if there is an idle vehicle already waiting at intersection 12, the newly arrived vehicle is blocked from reaching its final destination, intersection 12, and must remain allocated until the idle vehicle is requested and yields control of intersection 12. Thus, the second vehicle is not yet at the staging area and is still considered to be allocated. The resulting busy statistics collected by using variable NT may be much higher than reality warrants. For example, if we add five more vehicles to our previous system, they will wait in the staging area most of the time; however, because they are allocated, the transporter utilizations increase, even though the transporters are not, in fact, being used.

There are two relatively simple ways to obtain accurate vehicle-utilization statistics. The first method requires that you establish variables to track vehicle status and collect statistics on these variables, as discussed earlier. With the second method you use an expression for the dstat. The following expression gives fairly accurate results.

MAX(NT(TrnID)-NL(LinkID), 0)

or

MAX(NT(1)-NL(Link11),0)*100/3

The second expression is for our sample problem. This approach subtracts the number of vehicles on the staging link that have not been freed, NL(Link11), from the number of vehicles busy, NT(1). Note that, if there is only one vehicle on the staging link, it is assumed to be idle because otherwise it would be able to reach intersection 12 and be freed. The statistic is slightly inaccurate because, as soon as a vehicle enters Link11, it is assumed to be at the staging area. The method also assumes that Link11, which is identified as the staging link, is long enough to contain all idle vehicles, which happens to be the case for our example.

If we add the above dstat expression to our previous sample problem, we find that the utilization of the AGVs is actually 53.5 percent, which is approximately 22 percent less than with the first method. This implies that there is a fairly large proportion of time when there is more than one AGV at the staging area. This new utilization value implies that we might be able to reduce the number of AGVs in the system from three to two. With only two AGVs the flowtime increases to 197, and the actual AGV utilization is 76 percent.

Although the above discussion on staging areas may point to some minor problems in collecting statistics, this method of modeling prevents the following potentially more serious problem. If a vehicle is freed as soon as it comes to a stop at the staging area, and if a transporter-selection rule (other than shortest distance) is used, SIMAN may allocate the second or third vehicle in line. Because an idle vehicle then blocks the allocated vehicle, system operation can be altered drastically. The same sequence can occur at the start of the simulation because all three vehicles are positioned at the staging area in an idle state. For example, if a random-priority rule is specified, a vehicle other than the first in line may be allocated. Although the event is possible, the effect is short-lived and, if the statistics are cleared after reaching steady-state, the results are not included in the final summary.

Under any circumstances it is important that the resulting simulation model capture the logic of the real-world system as closely as possible, even if this logic results in a non-workable control scheme.

2.14 SIMAN Guided-Transporter Variables

Several SIMAN variables are available to help you collect statistics and to provide you with information on the current status of the guided-vehicle system. All of these variables can be used in either the Model or the Experiment Frame. The two types of variables, status variables and information variables, apply to either transporters or networks. A list of the guided-transporter information variables is given in Figure 9-12.

VARIABLE	DEFINITION
ACC(TrnID) :	Transporter acceleration
DEC(TrnID) :	Transporter deceleration
TVF(TrnID) :	Transporter turning velocity factor
ISZT(TrnID,Unit) :	Transporter size type 1 if zone, 2 if length
VT(TrnID) :	Transporter set velocity
VTU(TrnID,Unit) :	Transporter unit velocity
NSZT(TrnID,Unit) :	Transporter length

Figure 9-12. SIMAN Guided-Transporter Information Variables

The first four variables return the values entered in the TRANSPORTERS element. Although you cannot assign these variables and they do not change during a simulation run, they can be used in the Model Frame. The next two variables (VT and VTU) relate to the velocity of the transporter set or of the individual units and function the same as those for free-path transporters. Recall that these variables can be reset in the Model Frame. The last variable (NSZT) returns the current length of a specific transporter unit. Again, you cannot assign this variable, but it can change during the course of a simulation if the CAPTURE or RELINQUISH blocks are used. These two blocks are discussed in Section 2.18. These variables are rarely used for statistics collecting, but they are frequently used in the Model Frame for decision making.

The variables listed in Figure 9-13 provide the capability of determining the current status of transporters. The first three variables are the same as those used for free-path transporters, and they provide identical information. The next three variables (LT, LTL, and LTZ) return the current location of a transporter. Variable LT returns an intersection for a guided transporter. Note that variable LT is also used for free-path transporters; however, when applied to free-path transporters it returns a station. Selective use of these three variables allows you to determine the exact current location of any transporter. The next three variables (LDX, LDL, and LDZ) allow you to determine the current destination of any transporter. They follow the same format as the three variables used for determining current location.

VARIABLE	DEFINITION
NT(TrnID) :	Number of busy transporters
MT(TrnID) :	Number of active transporters
IT(TrnID,Unit) :	Transporter status 0 if idle, 1 if busy, 2 if inactive
LT(TrnID,Unit) :	Transporter intersection location or ending intersection of current link
LTL(TrnID,Unit) :	Transporter Link location 0 if in intersection
LTZ(TrnID,Unit) :	Transporter Zone number location 0 if in intersection
LDX(TrnID,Unit) :	Transporter destination intersection 0 if destination is on Link
LDL(TrnID,Unit) :	Transporter destination Link 0 if destination is intersection
LDZ(TrnID,Unit) :	Transporter destination Zone 0 if destination is intersection
TAZ(TrnID,Unit) :	Time transporter arrived at current location
TWZ(TrnID,Unit) :	Accumulated waiting time to access required zones transporter

Figure 9-13. SIMAN Guided-Transporter Status Variables

The last two variables (TAZ and TWZ) provide time-related information. Variable TAZ returns the time that the transporter arrived at its current location. This time can be used to determine which vehicle has been idle the longest, or it can be used in any logic statement requiring a wait time. Variable TWZ returns the total amount of time that the transporter has waited to access a required zone. In effect, it provides the total time that a transporter has been blocked during the time that statistics are collected. This variable can be used in conjunction with the OUTPUT element to obtain a fraction or percentage value of blocked time.

Figure 9-14 lists the SIMAN variables that can be used to determine information about a guided-transporter network. They resemble the variables that provide information on transporters in that they return the values entered in the elements in the Experiment Frame. The first two variables, LX and VX, respectively return the length and velocity factor for an intersection. The next four variables (MZ, LENZ, LTYP, and VL) return information on specific links in the network.

VARIABLE	DEFINITION
LX(IntxID)	: Intersection length
VX(IntxID)	: Intersection velocity factor
MZ(LinkID)	: Number of Zones in Link
LENZ(LinkID)	: Length of Zones in Link
LTYP(LinkID)	: Link Type 1 if unidirectional, 2 if bidirectional, 3 if spur
VL(LinkID)	: Link velocity factor.
LNKNUM(IntxID1,IntxID2)	: Link number connecting intersections, 0 if not connected
NEXTX(NetID,IntxID1,IntxID2)	: Next intersection of travel from Intx1 to Intx2 [note: entry from next-intersection matrix]
IDSNET(NetID,IntxID1,IntxID2)	: Distance from intersection Intx1 to Intx2 [note: entry from shortest-distance matrix]
NXB(LinkID)	: Beginning intersection of Link
NXE(LinkID)	: Ending intersection of Link

Figure 9-14. SIMAN Guided-Transporter Network Information Variables

The next variable (LNKNUM) allows you to determine whether there is a link directly connecting two intersections in the network. The next two variables (NEXTX and IDSNET) allow you to access the values stored in the next-intersection matrix and the shortest-distance matrix discussed in Section 2.6. The last two variables (NXB and NXE) return the beginning and ending intersections of a link. All of these variables remain constant during any simulation run; however, you may require this information for decision-making logic during the course of a run. You can also combine a single Model Frame with many different Experiment Frames containing different values.

The last set of variables, given in Figure 9-15, provides information on network status. Variable NX, which returns the status of an intersection, can be used for collecting statistics on the fraction of time a specific intersection is occupied. Variable NL, which returns the number of occupied zones on a link, can be used directly in a dstat to determine the average number of zones occupied, or it can be used as part of the expression

NL(LinkID) / MZ(LinkID)

to yield a value that reflects a utilization of the link. The variable NZ returns the status of a single zone on a link. Again, this variable can be used as part of control logic in the Model Frame or as part of a statistic in the Experiment Frame.

VARIABLE	DEFINITION
NX(IntxID) :	Status of intersection Intx 1 if occupied, 0 otherwise
NL(LinkID) :	Number of occupied Zones in Link
NZ(LinkID,Zone) :	Status of Zone 1 if busy, 0 if idle, -1 if captured
NDX(LinkID) :	Destination intersection of Link, indicates travel direction

Figure 9-15. SIMAN Guided-Transporter Network Status Variables

The last variable (NDX) allows you to determine the current direction of a specific link by returning the destination intersection of any vehicle on the link. This type of information is most useful in models having bidirectional links.

Most simulation models of guided-vehicle systems do not require the above-described variables, except for collecting statistical information. However, for systems having complex control logic or requiring detailed statistics, they do provide the ability to obtain the necessary information and status values.

2.15 Modeling Changing Vehicle Speeds

In most guided-vehicle systems the time required to start, stop, and turn is not a critical element of overall system performance. However, if the vehicle or network characteristics are such that these maneuvers can affect performance, they should be included in the model. For example, when making a turn, some AGVs must come to a complete stop, rotate, and then start up again. Any turns made in highly congested areas can drastically affect system performance or the number of total AGVs required. Stacker cranes often have acceleration and deceleration values that can significantly affect travel time between positions.

These factors can be included in the simulation in several different ways. The simplest technique involves specifying a value for the velocity-change factor, VelChange, on the INTERSECTIONS or LINKS element. Thus, whenever a vehicle travels through an intersection or a link with a velocity-change factor, the vehicle's speed is multiplied by the stated factor before the travel time is computed. This method equates to specifying a longer length for an intersection or link, in order to increase travel time. Although this method provides a degree of control, every vehicle traveling through the link has an increased travel time — even if it is not making a turn.

An alternative — and more detailed — method involves using the beginning- and ending-direction fields, BegDir and EndDir, on the LINKS element and including an entry for the turning-velocity factor, TurnVel, on the TRANSPORTERS element. In this way SIMAN can automatically determine when a vehicle is required to make a turn and can reduce the vehicle's speed by the given turning-velocity factor. The beginning and ending directions for each link are stated in degrees, between 0 and 360, and are defaulted to 0.

Whenever a vehicle exits or enters a link, these directions are compared. When a vehicle enters a link, its beginning and ending directions are compared. If they are different, the turning velocity given on the TRANSPORTERS element is applied to the current velocity of the vehicle during travel through the middle zone of the link. When a vehicle exits a link and enters an intersection, the ending direction of the current link is compared to the beginning direction of the link that the vehicle will take out of the intersection. If they are different, the turning velocity is applied. If the vehicle's destination is the intersection, the comparison is not made. Note that the turning-velocity factor is only applied for a single link, and that the entire factor is always applied, regardless of the magnitude of the difference in the directions.

The acceleration and deceleration properties of a guided vehicle are specified on the TRANSPORTERS element in time units per distance squared. SIMAN will automatically detect when to apply these values. Acceleration is always applied whenever a stopped or slowed vehicle is returning to a higher speed. For example, a vehicle moving through a link where a turning velocity is to be applied will also have the deceleration and acceleration factors applied during the slow down and speed up time. Deceleration is applied whenever a vehicle anticipates a stop. In general, whenever a vehicle enters a zone it checks forward to see if there is space to continue at its current velocity. If a blockage occurs along its path, it will anticipate that blockage and apply the proper deceleration.

The combination of the turning-velocity factor for changing directions and the acceleration/deceleration values allows for very detailed modeling of vehicle speeds.

2.16 Modeling Systems with Continuous Control

The control logic for some guided-vehicle systems continually monitors the status of the system and, under some circumstances, alters the destination of a vehicle before it completes its travel. This monitoring can occur on a continuous basis, or the vehicle can communicate with the control system at pre-defined points along the path. In these types of systems the simulation logic must be capable of changing the final destination of any vehicle. Normally, when a vehicle is moved or transported, it is directed to its final destination, and the controlling entity does not re-enter the model until the vehicle completes its travel.

The ability to check the system status periodically and to change the final destination of a vehicle is accomplished with a new entry for the transporter destination operand on either the MOVE or the TRANSPORT block. The syntax for this operand is FIRSTX(TrnDest), where the transporter destination, TrnDest, is specified as a station, a link, or an intersection by using the syntax given in Section 2.10. When you use this option, SIMAN sends the transporter to the next intersection encountered on its way to its final destination. When you use the MOVE block, the entity exits from the block to the next block in the model. If the TRANSPORT block is used, the entity is sent to the entity destination specified.

If the entity destination is stated as SEQ or defaulted, the entity is sent to the next station in the sequence.

This concept implies that the transporter may stop at several intersections on its way to its final destination. Thus, you must include logic in the model to determine whether the destination of the vehicle should be changed and whether the vehicle has reached its destination. For example, in our modified flow-line problem, a vehicle that has completed its task checks for a current request. If there is a requesting entity, the vehicle is freed. Otherwise, the vehicle returns to the staging area, intersection 12, to await the next request. Let's assume that we change this logic so that the vehicle stops at each intersection on its way to the staging area to see if there is a new request. If there is, the vehicle is freed and is allowed to respond directly to the new request.

Several changes to our previous Model Frame are required. Because we need to be able to check the current location of an AGV, we need to know which AGV the entity controls. To obtain this information we must add a third attribute, AGV#, and alter the single REQUEST block in the model to record the number of the AGV allocated, as shown on the left.

The second change, also shown on the left, involves the transporter destination on the MOVE block at label SendBack, which sends the idle AGV back to the staging area. We have modified this block to send the vehicle to the first intersection on the route to the staging area. When the AGV arrives at that intersection, the entity leaves the MOVE block and enters the new BRANCH block, which has been added to handle the new logic. This BRANCH block checks for two possible conditions: if the AGV has arrived at the staging area intersection and if a new request has been made. If either of these conditions is true, the controlling entity is directed to label FreeAGV2, where the AGV is freed and the cloned entity is disposed of. If neither condition is true, the controlling entity is sent to label SendBack where the move of the AGV to the next intersection on its way to the staging area is performed.

If two or more AGVs are currently being sent to the staging area, and a requesting entity arrives at the request queue, the next AGV performing the above-described check grants the request.

This type of logic can also easily be incorporated into a model to allow a vehicle transporting an entity to check system conditions for a possible change of action. For example, the entity can stop at each intersection to check the current status of the WorkStation and buffer area at its destination. If the WorkStation is failed or the buffer area full, the entity can be redirected to a temporary storage area.

If you enter the transporter destination specification for the FIRSTX option as a zone on a link, the transporter will only be moved to the beginning intersection of that link. You must detect that it has arrived at the beginning intersection of that link and then transport or move the vehicle directly to that zone. The beginning intersection can be obtained by using SIMAN variable NXB. You can direct the vehicle to this intersection by using the FIRSTX option and then transport it directly to the zone representing its final destination.

When you use the FIRSTX option you must ensure that the model checks at each intersection to see if the vehicle is at its final destination. You must also remember that the entity simply advances to the next block after each move, if a MOVE block is used, or the entity is directed to the entity destination as specified on the TRANSPORT block. Finally, remember that the transporter is always sent to the next intersection on the way to its destination.

2.17 Changing the Shortest-Distance Matrix: The REDIRECTS Element

Earlier in this chapter we discussed the VIA option for the MOVE and TRANSPORT blocks; this option allows you to override the next-intersection matrix in traveling from one point in the system to another. The FIRSTX option discussed in the previous section provides the capability of assessing the system at each intersection along the move and of changing the destination of the vehicle. Both options allow you to alter temporarily or to override the next-intersection matrix from the Model Frame. However, sometimes a system condition requires a more permanent change to the next-intersection matrix and the corresponding change to the shortest-distance matrix.

Consider the portion of a system map shown below. Two paths allow a vehicle to travel from intersection A to intersection C. The shortest-distance path is A-B-C with a distance of 10. The alternative path is A-C with a distance of 14. If we assume that intersection B is a load/unload point where the vehicle remains on the path, blocking other traffic, the alternative route can be viewed as a bypass around this intersection. Although the bypass is longer, it may be preferable to send all vehicles not going to intersection B by this route, thus preventing any possible waiting because of blocking at B.

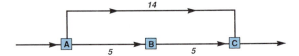

The REDIRECT element shown below provides this capability. The Number and Name provide references, as they have with previously discussed elements. The NetworkID references the network to which the redirect is applied. The beginning, ending, and next-intersection IDs (BegIntxID, EndIntxID, and NextIntxID) specify the actual redirect. The entry in the next-intersection matrix is overwritten, and the shortest-distance matrix is changed to be consistent with the redirect. The IDs for the intersections can be given as numbers or as names. When specifying redirects, remember that you must directly connect the next intersection and the beginning intersection with a link.

```
REDIRECTS: Number, Name, NetworkID,
           BegIntxID—EndIntxID—NextIntxID, repeats:
           repeats;
```

Consider our bypass example with a redirect of A-C-C, which indicates that any vehicle traveling from A to C proceeds directly to C. Only vehicles with a specified destination of B do not take the bypass path. The partial original and revised next-intersection matrices are provided below.

Original				Revised			
from/to	A	B	C	from/to	A	B	C
A	—	B	B	A	—	B	C
B	?	—	C	B	?	—	C

The only change in the next-intersection matrix involves the entry that directs any vehicle from A to C rather than from A to B. However, the shortest-distance matrix may need numerous changes because the distance of any path that includes travel from A to C increases by 4 (the additional travel distance on the bypass).

The REDIRECTS element permits any number of redirects. Be aware that a redirect simply changes a value in the next-intersection matrix and that all paths using this value are then redirected. The impact of several redirects imposed on a single network isn't always immediately obvious. For example, consider the enlarged portion of our system map shown below. If we apply redirect A-E-C, then all travel from A to E takes the bypass. However, a vehicle traveling from A to F follows the shortest-distance path, i.e., A-B-C-F, for a total distance of 14. If we apply only the redirect A-F-C, then all travel from A through F takes the bypass, but travel from A to C or A to E is routed through B.

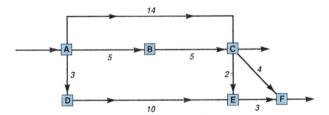

If our intent is to avoid intersection B but still use the shortest path not including B, then the following redirects should be applied: A-C-C, A-E-D, and A-F-D. With these redirects a vehicle takes the bypass only when traveling from A through C; it takes the lower path through D for all other travel. The actual REDIRECTS element for this solution is shown below.

```
REDIRECTS: 1,, example, A-C-C:
           2,, example, A-E-D:
           3,, example, A-F-D:
```

You should also be aware that travel from A to intersections beyond C and F is determined after the redirects have been applied and are based on the shortest distance.

2.18 Modeling Vehicle Failures and Changing Vehicle Size

Guided-transporter failures are modeled by using the same blocks and concepts as used for free-path transporters (discussed in Chapter 6, Section 5.16). The HALT block changes the status of a transporter to inactive, and the ACTIVATE block changes the status to active. As before, a transporter must be idle before the HALT block can set it to inactive. However, unlike free-path transporters, guided transporters occupy space on the network and, if a vehicle is halted, it still controls this space.

In an actual system, a failed vehicle remains on the path for at least a short period of time. If the repair is lengthy, the vehicle is often physically removed from the path so that it does not block other vehicle travel. When the vehicle is repaired, it is placed back on the path. The ability to model this activity is provided with the RELINQUISH and CAPTURE blocks. The syntax for these new blocks is given below. Note that neither block requires the transporter name because each assumes that the entity passing through the block has control of the transporter whose size is to increase or decrease.

RELINQUISH: Qty;

CAPTURE: Qty, Dest;

The RELINQUISH block has only one operand, the quantity, Qty. This quantity must be expressed in terms of consecutive zones or length units controlled or occupied by the transporter. SIMAN interprets the units of the quantity, zones, or length based on the vehicle size entered in the TRANSPORTERS element. The value entered must be less-than-or-equal-to the number currently controlled by the transporter. If the quantity is defaulted, all zones occupied by the transporter are freed. If only a portion of the occupied zones is relinquished, the zones at the back end of the transporter are freed.

The CAPTURE block, a type of hold block, must have a preceding QUEUE block. It has two operands: quantity and destination. Quantity is interpreted just as it is for the RELINQUISH block. The destination operand, which can be expressed as a station, an intersection, or a link, determines the travel direction of the vehicle; the capture path is at the front of the vehicle in the direction of travel. If the vehicle is located at an intersection, the destination operand is used to determine from which outgoing link the path is to be captured.

Using these blocks to remove failed vehicles from the system map can become complicated. Let's first consider only the failure activities. Before we can fail or halt the transporter, we must allocate it to an entity, relinquish the path space, halt the vehicle, and free the transporter so that it can become inactive. The following sequence of blocks is required: QUEUE — ALLOCATE — RELINQUISH — HALT — FREE.

After the transporter is repaired, a similar reverse sequence puts the vehicle back on the path and changes its status to active. The following sequence of blocks is required: ACTIVATE — QUEUE — ALLOCATE — CAPTURE — FREE. In this case, there is one additional problem: The path space cannot be captured until the vehicle has been allocated, and the transporter cannot be allocated until it is activated. However, if a single entity is performing the sequence and if there is a current request elsewhere for the transporter, that request is granted before the transporter is allocated and the required space is captured. It may be necessary, therefore, to use two entities. The first entity is placed in the allocate queue connected to the allocate block having the highest priority of all hold blocks requesting the transporter. When this entity has control of the failed transporter, it performs the remaining logic. The second entity activates the failed transporter, after the first entity is placed in the queue. Because the only function of this second entity is to activate the transporter, it is immediately disposed of.

Although seemingly complicated, this approach allows you to model this type of failure, which requires a similar type of action in the real system. As an alternative you can halt the vehicle and allow it to block the path until it is repaired, or you can move the vehicle to an out-of-the-way place, such as a spur, before allowing it to fail.

Note that it is possible to move and transport a guided vehicle that has relinquished all of its path. In this case it is free to move about the network very much like a free-path transporter. It follows the system map, but it does not require control of any zones. Hence, it can move freely and can essentially pass directly over another stopped vehicle.

The CAPTURE and RELINQUISH blocks can also be used to model guided vehicles that have changing lengths, such as guided trains. These systems may use the PICKUP and DROPOFF blocks described in Chapter 8 to add and delete cars and the CAPTURE and RELINQUISH blocks to adjust vehicle length. These block constructs are designed with these types of systems in mind. Additional space is always captured in the zones at the front end of the vehicle to prevent the possibility of a deadlock, in which a second vehicle is directly behind the vehicle trying to capture additional space. When a vehicle relinquishes zones, it always relinquishes the zones trailing the vehicle.

3. Additional Sample Problems

The new constructs and modeling concepts presented in this chapter are used primarily for modeling the types of systems typically described as AGV systems. However, these constructs can also be used to model any system that requires a constrained set of objects to move about a network that has constrained space. Many material-handling systems require these types of constructs. The two examples that follow, AS/RS and Crane, are typical of these types of systems. Towline conveyors can also be modeled in a similar fashion.

Although we associate these modeling concepts with material-handling systems, they can easily be used to model various transportation systems. In this case the transporters can become trucks, buses, trains, or boats, and the network can become roads, tracks, or waterways. In all cases, we must carefully examine the system and select the most appropriate set of constructs for the situation at hand.

3.1 Sample Problem 9.2: An AS/RS Model

Consider a model of the Automatic Storage and Retrieval System (AS/RS) shown in Figure 9-16. The storage system consists of two bays, which are serviced by a single vehicle. Each bay has a rack on both sides, with each rack having 250 individual storage bins (50 bins long and 5 bins high). This results in a total storage capacity of 1,000 bins. Pallets enter and exit at the right side of the system. The left side of the system is reserved for the vehicle when it needs to change bays. The numbers on the vehicle path represent the intersections to be used in the simulation model.

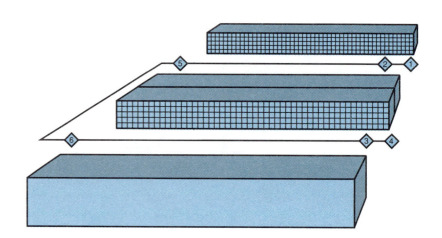

Figure 9-16. AS/RS Layout: Sample Problem 9.2

A "place" operation requires the vehicle to load a part at the input to the AS/RS and place it in the warehouse. In this case, the vehicle moves to the pickup point (at the right side of the bay in which it is to be placed), loads the pallet, moves horizontally to the proper bin location, moves vertically to the proper height, places the pallet in the bin, and moves vertically back down to the floor. It is then freed for the next request.

A "pick" operation requires the vehicle to remove a part from its location in the warehouse and move it to the output of the AS/RS. In this case, the vehicle moves horizontally to the proper location, moves vertically to the proper height, picks up the pallet, moves vertically down to the floor level, moves horizontally to the output location (at the right side of the bay), and unloads the pallet. It is then freed for the next operation.

The control logic for this system is intentionally kept fairly simple. The basic goal is to avoid movement between bays by responding to all requests in one bay before moving to the other bay. Thus, all incoming pick or place requests are separated by bay and are responded to on a first-come-first-served basis in each bay. However, in an attempt to minimize vehicle travel, it is desirable to follow a pick operation with a place, and vice versa.

For this simple system, no attempt is made to keep track of what is in the system, or where the parts are. All requests and place locations are generated randomly. All time units are in seconds, and all length units are in feet.

The Experiment listing for this problem is given in Figure 9-17. The AS/RS vehicle path is defined by the INTERSECTIONS, LINKS, and NETWORKS elements, which correspond to the path shown in Figure 9-16. All links are defined as bidirectional. Note that stations 1 and 4 (Place1 and Place4) are associated with intersections 1 and 4, which represent the input/output of the system. Stations 2 and 3 (Pick1 and Pick2) are associated with intersections 2 and 3, which represent the order picking locations. Separate locations for the pick and place stations are established to allow alternating between the two operations. The attributes contain all of the information regarding the exact location, the type of operation, and the arrival time of the parts. In addition, an attribute named Orders is included to identify the station or intersection where each request is initiated.

```
BEGIN;

PROJECT,       Sample Problem 9.2, SM;

ATTRIBUTES:    Link#:             !link 2 or 4
               Zone#:             !1-50
               Shelf#:            !1-5
               MovType:           !pick=1, place=2
               ArrivalTime:
               Orders;

VARIABLES:     ShelfDelay,2:      !time delay for ASRS to index one shelf
               EndIntx;            calc dist from vehicle to Ending Intx

QUEUES:        4;

INTERSECTIONS: 6;

STATIONS:      Place1,1:
               Pick1,2:
               Pick2,3:
               Place2,4:
               PickLogic:
               PlaceLogic:
               OutBasket;

LINKS:         1,,1,2,   2,5,B:
               2,,5,2,50, 3,B:
               3,,5,6,  1,20,B:
               4,,6,3,50, 3,B:
               5,,3,4,   2,5,B;

NETWORKS:      1,ASRS,1-5;

TRANSPORTERS:  1,AsRsVehicle,1,NETWORK(ASRS),10-2-2,LINK(3,1);

TALLIES:       Pick Flowtime:
               Place Flowtime;

DSTATS:        NT(AsRsVehicle)*100,Vehicle Utilization:
               NQ(2),Orders Waiting Pick1:
               NQ(3),Orders Waiting Pick2:
               NQ(1),Orders Waiting Place1:
               NQ(4),Orders Waiting Place2;

REPLICATE,     1,0,20000;

END;
```

Figure 9-17. Experiment Listing for Sample Problem 9.2

The Model listing for our sample problem is given in Figure 9-18. Arriving orders are generated by the single CREATE block. The following ASSIGN block determines the exact location of the arriving request. The assignment to attribute Link# defines whether the request is for bay 1 or bay 2 (links 2 and 4, respectively), and the attribute Zone# defines the exact location on that link. Zone 1 is adjacent to intersection 5 or 6 and zone 50 is adjacent to intersection 2 or 3. The Shelf defines the vertical position of the request. An attribute to define the side of the aisle could be added, if detailed locations were being tracked. The last line of the ASSIGN block determines if the operation is a pick or a place and assigns a value of 1 or 2 to attribute MovType. The second ASSIGN block determines the source intersection of the request and assigns that value to attribute Orders. A value of 1 implies an input to bay 1, 2 an output from bay 1, 3 an output from bay 2, and 4 an input to bay 2. Note that the logical portions of the expressions return a value of 0 if false or of 1 if true; thus, a value of 1 is evaluated for the expression if the quantity Link#*MovType equals 4 and MoveType equals 2.

```
BEGIN;
;    Clock == seconds;
;    Distance == feet;
        CREATE:      NORM(58.,3.5):              !random requests for
                       MARK(ArrivalTime);            pick/place into as/rs

        ASSIGN:      Link#=DISC(.5,2,1.,4):       !link 2 or 4
                     Zone#=ANINT((RA(1)*50)+.5):  !zone 1-50
                     Shelf#=DISC(.2,1,.4,2,.6,3,
                               .8,4,1.,5¥:        !shelf 1-5
                     MovType=DISC(.5,1,1.,2);       pick/place 1,2

        ASSIGN:      Orders=1*(Link#*MovType==4
                               .AND.MovType==2)+   !place type
                            2*(Link#*MovType==2)+  !pick type
                            3*(Link#*MovType==4
                               .AND.MovType==1)+   !place type
                            4*(Link#*MovType==8);    pick type

        QUEUE,       Orders;                      wait for transporter
        ALLOCATE:    AsRsVehicle,
                       INTX(Orders);              get transporter

        BRANCH,      1:                           !branch to pick or place
                     IF,(MovType==1),PickO:       !order logic
                     ELSE,PlaceO;

PickO   MOVE:        AsRsVehicle,                 !pick order logic: move
                       LINK(Link#,Zone#);           vehicle directly to pick bin
        ROUTE:       0,PickLogic;                 move to logic for removing
;                                                   product from the bins

PlaceO  MOVE:        AsRsVehicle,                 !place order logic: move
                       STATION(Orders);             vehicle to order station
        DELAY:       10;                          load time
        TRANSPORT:   AsRsVehicle,                 !transport vehicle to
                       PlaceLogic,,               !receiving bin
                       LINK(Link#,Zone#);

;    Logical Station defining the picking process

        STATION,     PickLogic;
        DELAY:       2*(Shelf#*ShelfDelay)+10;    delay vert movement time
;                                                 and load time

        ASSIGN:      EndIntx=2*(Link#==2)+        !set ending intx for Picks
                            3*(Link#==4);
        TRANSPORT:   AsRsVehicle,                 !send entity to logical
                       OutBasket,,                !out-basket and transporter
                       INTX(EndIntx);             to physical out-basket

;    Logical Station defining the place process

        STATION,     PlaceLogic;
        DELAY:       2*(Shelf#*ShelfDelay)+10;    delay vert movement time
;                                                 and unload time
        FREE:        AsRsVehicle:                 !free trans for next request
                       NEXT(AsrsOut);

;    Physical Station for out-baskets

        STATION,     OutBasket;
        DELAY:       10;                          unload time
        FREE:        AsRsVehicle:                 !free trans for next request
                       NEXT(AsrsOut);

AsrsOut TALLY:       MovType,INT(ArrivalTime):    !track time in system
                       DISPOSE;                     by movement type pick/place

END;
```

Figure 9-18. Model Listing for Sample Problem 9.2

The entity representing the arriving request for a pick or a place then enters the following QUEUE block, which defines the unnamed queues 1 through 4 based on the attribute Orders. The ALLOCATE block attached to these queues determines the priorities of the requests based on the current position of the AS/RS vehicle. The first entity in each queue attempts to allocate the AS/RS vehicle with its location defined by the intersection in its attribute Orders. If there are multiple entities attempting to allocate the AS/RS vehicle, SIMAN uses the SDS (shortest-distance-to-station) rule to determine which entity is allocated the AS/RS vehicle. The SDS rule is applied because the ALLOCATE priority is identical (default value of 1) for all four queues.

Thus, if the AS/RS vehicle has just completed a pick operation from bay 1, it will be freed at intersection 1, and a place request for bay 1 will be the closest. The next closest request will be a pick operation from bay 1, which will be requesting from intersection 2. If the AS/RS vehicle has just completed a place operation in bay 1, it will be freed at link 2. The closest request will be the next pick operation at intersection 2, followed by another place operation for bay 1 at intersection 1. In either case, if there are no further requests from bay one, the closest task will be a pick operation from bay 2 (intersection 3), followed by a place operation for bay 2 (intersection 4). A similar set of logic applies if the AS/RS vehicle is freed in bay 2. This results in the AS/RS vehicle remaining in a single bay until all requests are exhausted; within the bay, the vehicle alternates between pick and place operations.

The entity allocated the AS/RS vehicle enters the BRANCH block following the ALLOCATE block, which directs the entity to the pick or place logic. If the operation is a pick, the AS/RS vehicle is first moved to the requesting link and zone (at label PickO). With the AS/RS vehicle at the pickup location, the entity is sent by a ROUTE block to station PickLogic where a delay for the vertical move up, the pickup, and the move down occurs. The exiting intersection (1 or 4) is then assigned, and the AS/RS vehicle is transported to that intersection, while the entity is sent to station OutBasket. At station OutBasket, the part is unloaded, the AS/RS vehicle is freed, the system time is tallied, and the entity is disposed of.

If the operation is a place, the AS/RS vehicle is moved to the input intersection 1 or 4 by the MOVE block at label PlaceO. The entity is delayed for the loading operation, and the AS/RS vehicle is transported to the destination link and zone of the place. The entity is directed to station PlaceLogic, which imposes a delay for the vertical movement and unload operation, and then frees the AS/RS vehicle. The entity is then directed to label AsrsOut where the system time is tallied at the entity is disposed of.

The resulting Summary Report for this model is shown in Figure 9-19. This summary shows that the vehicle utilization is almost 100 percent, suggesting a system close to capacity. However, because the queues for the pick and place operations have relatively small values, the vehicle is traveling frequently between the two bays. Increasing the demand would result in large queues and long flowtimes, but additional capacity does exits.

```
Project:  Sample Problem 9.2
Analyst:  SM
Replication ended at time:  20000.0
```

TALLY VARIABLES

Identifier	Average	Variation	Minimum	Maximum	Observations
Pick Flowtime	125.95	.48984	46.361	356.53	172
Place Flowtime	151.56	.55549	36.184	493.62	170

DISCRETE-CHANGE VARIABLES

Identifier	Average	Variation	Minimum	Maximum	Final Value
Vehicle Utilization	99.852	.38452E-01	.00000	100.00	100.00
Orders Waiting Pick1	.27979	1.7576	.00000	2.0000	.00000
Orders Waiting Pick2	.29847	1.8541	.00000	3.0000	.00000
Orders Waiting Place1	.44101	1.3765	.00000	2.0000	2.0000
Orders Waiting Place2	.37083	1.5642	.00000	3.0000	1.0000

Figure 9-19. Summary Report for Sample Problem 9.2

3.2 Sample Problem 9.3: A Overhead Crane Model

Our second sample problem involves modeling a simple crane system as illustrated in Figure 9-20. The system has two cranes servicing a single bay with limited contention. Crane 1 is responsible for pickup requests from bay positions 1 through 5. Crane 2 is responsible for requests from bay positions 8 through 11. All pickup requests, for both cranes, are moved to positions 6 or 7 and are removed from the system. Requests are serviced on a first-come-first-served basis. Contention between the two cranes can occur if crane 1 attempts to drop off a part at bay 7, while crane 2 concurrently attempts to drop off a part at bay 6. The resulting model must incorporate logic to prevent system deadlock between the cranes.

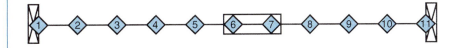

Figure 9-20. Crane Layout: Sample Problem 9.3

The logic need only consider the case in which the two cranes attempt to cross. If both cranes require the same drop zone or if both require the drop zone closest to their pickup areas, the SIMAN Guided Transporter logic can be used to control crane movement. Bay positions 4 and 9 have been established as the respective points where cranes 1 and 2 check for possible contention. If crane 1 receives a request from bays 1 through 3, it picks up its load and moves to bay 4 where it checks for contention. If the request is made at bay 4 or bay 5, the crane checks for contention before it moves.

The Experiment listing for this model is shown in Figure 9-21. The crane system is defined by using 11 unnamed intersections (each of length 10) and 10 unnamed bidirectional links (each with one zone of length 10) connecting the intersections. The two cranes have initially been positioned at intersections 1 and 11. The acceleration and deceleration values have been specified such that the cranes can accelerate to full speed or come to a complete stop in one zone (link or intersection). Note that none of the stations are associated with intersections of the network. The stations are logical only; they are not physical stations on the network.

```
BEGIN;
PROJECT,        Sample Problem 9.3,SM;
ATTRIBUTES:     Crane#:
                CreateTime;
VARIABLES:      DropPt(2):
                DcsnIntx(2),4,9:
                TrvlIntx(2),5,8:
                Interfere;
STATIONS:       1,MoveType:
                2,UnloadLogic:
                3,FreeCrane:
                4,CfltWait;
QUEUES:         3,ScanWait:
                4;
INTERSECTIONS:  1,,10:
                2,,10:
                3,,10:
                4,,10:
                5,,10:
                6,,10:
                7,,10:
                8,,10:
                9,,10:
                10,,10:
                11,,10;
LINKS:          1,,1,2,1,10,b:
                2,,2,3,1,10,b:
                3,,3,4,1,10,b:
                4,,4,5,1,10,b:
                5,,5,6,1,10,b:
                6,,6,7,1,10,b:
                7,,7,8,1,10,b:
                8,,8,9,1,10,b:
                9,,9,10,1,10,b:
                10,,10,11,1,10,b;
NETWORKS:       1,North Cranes,1-10;
TRANSPORTERS:   1,Crane,2,NETWORK(North Cranes),7.5-1.5-1.5,
                INTX(1)-A-ZONE(1),
                INTX(11)-A-ZONE(1);
PARAMETERS:     1,PickZone,.1,1,.2,2,.3,3,.4,4,
                .5,5,.6,8,.75,9,.9,10,1.0,11:
                2,DropZone,.5,6,1.0,7;
TALLIES:        TimeInSys;
```

```
        DSTATS:             NQ(1),Waiting Crane 1:
                            NQ(2);,Waiting Crane 2:
                            NQ(3)*100,Crane 1 Blocked:
                            NQ(4)*100,Crane 2 Blocked:
                            (NX(6)+NZ(6,1)+NX(7))>0,Drop Zone Occupied:
                            IT(Crane,1),Crane 1:
                            IT(Crane,2),Crane 2;
        REPLICATE,          1,0.0,32500;
        END;
```

Figure 9-21. Experiment Listing for Sample Problem 9.3

The corresponding Model listing is given in Figure 9-22. Crane requests are created and then are assigned a pickup position (set to M); a logical expression is then used to determine which crane will respond to the request. Remember that crane 1 services bay positions 1 through 5 and that crane 2 services positions 8 through 11. The requesting entity is then placed in a queue, numbered 1 or 2, to request its crane. All requests are placed in these two queues, thus maintaining the FIFO service by each crane. Note that each request is made from the intersection associated with the pickup position (attribute M). When the crane arrives at the pickup position, a delay occurs to represent the load time, and a drop-off position (6 or 7) is assigned. Note that the drop-off position is assigned to an indexed global variable, DropPt, rather than to an attribute because it will be used for logic checks by both cranes. The entity is then sent to station MoveType to check for possible contention.

```
BEGIN;
        CREATE:     NORM(45.0,3.0):                 !generate crane requests
                    MARK(CreateTime);
        ASSIGN:     M=DP(PickZone):                 !set the pickup point
                    Crane#=1*(M<=5)+2*(M>=8);       !set crane 1 or 2
        QUEUE,      Crane#;                          wait for Crane
        REQUEST:    Crane(Crane#;,,Intx(M);         get Crane
        DELAY:      NORM(15.0,2.0);                 wait load time
        ASSIGN:     DropPt(Crane#)=DP(DropZone);    set drop-off point
        ROUTE:      0,MoveType;                     send to station MoveType
;    Decide type of move required$ move to next intx or evaluate drop zone.

        STATION,    MoveType;
        BRANCH,     1:
                    IF,LT(Crane,Crane#)==           !compare current intx with
                    DcsnIntx(Crane#).OR.            !decision intx
                    LT(Crane,Crane#).==             !or travel intx
                    TrvlIntx(Crane#),TstIntfr:
                    ELSE,NextIntx;                  send to next intx

TstIntfr BRANCH,   1:
                    IF,Interfere==1,Conflict:       !contention is detected
                    ELSE,ContTest;

ContTest BRANCH,   1:
                    IF,DropPt(1)*DropPt(2)<>0 .AND. !this crane will pass to
                       DropPt(1)>DropPt(2),FutrCflt:!the drop zone but the
                                                    !other must hold
                    ELSE,NoConflt;                  send to destination station

FutrCflt ASSIGN:   Interfere=1;                      set Interference flag=1
         TRANSPORT: Crane(Crane#),                  !send crane to DropPt
                    UnloadLogic,,
                    INTX(DropPt(Crane#));

Conflict TRANSPORT: Crane(Crane#),                  !send crane to TrvlIntx
                    CfltWait,,
                    INTX(TrvlIntx(Crane#));
         STATION,   CfltWait;
         QUEUE,     ScanWait+Crane#-1;              wait for other crane to
```

445 *Advanced Manufacturing Features*

```
;                                                   arrive at destination
          SCAN:        Interfere==0;               test on interfere flag
NoConflt  ASSIGN:      Interfere=
                       (Crane#==1.AND.DropPt(1)==7)    !set interfere if the
                       .OR.                            !cranes could cross
                       (Crane#==2.AND.DropPt(2)==6);
          TRANSPORT:   Crane(Crane#),UnloadLogic,,     !send to destination
                       INTX(DropPt(Crane#));              station
NextIntx  TRANSPORT:   Crane(Crane#),MoveType,,         !send to next intx
                       FIRSTX(INTX(DcsnIntx(Crane#)));    and test again
;    Model crane in Drop Zone$ unload, clear varb & choose method for exiting
          STATION,     UnloadLogic;
          ASSIGN:      DropPt(Crane#)=0:               !set dest varb to zero
                       Interfere=0;                      set Interference flag = 0
          DELAY:       NORM(15.0,2.0);                   unload the crane
          BRANCH,      2:                              !decide if the crane needs
                       IF,NQ(Crane#)>=1,FreeCrn:       !to be moved, or if there
                       IF,NQ(Crane#)==0,OutDrop:       !are other jobs waiting
                       ELSE,SysTime;                     entity for tally
OutDrop   TRANSPORT:   Crane(Crane#),FreeCrane,,       !move the crane out of the
                       INTX(TrvlIntx(Crane#));           drop zone
          STATION,     FreeCrane;
FreeCrn   FREE:        Crane(Crane#):                  !free the crane
                       DISPOSE;
SysTime   TALLY:       TimeInSys,INT(CreateTime):      !collect TimeInSystem
                                                         stats
                       DISPOSE;
END;
```

Figure 9-22. Model Listing for Sample Problem 9.3

The first BRANCH block determines if the crane is currently at a decision position: intersection 4 or 5 for crane 1, and intersection 8 or 9 for crane 2. If the crane is not at a decision position, it is sent to the TRANSPORT block at label NextIntx where it is transported to the first intersection on its way to the final drop-off position. Note that the entity will be sent back to station MoveType when the crane reaches its next intersection. This process is repeated until the crane reaches intersection 4 or 9. At this point it must make a decision as to whether it can move into the drop-off area. Because the FIRSTX option is used on the TRANSPORT block, the deceleration is not applied during this travel to intersection 4 or 9. Upon reaching a decision intersection (4 or 9) or a pickup at intersections 5 or 8, the entity is sent to the BRANCH labeled TstIntfr where the interference flag variable, Interfere, is checked. A flag value of 1 indicates potential conflict; in this case the entity is sent to label Conflict where it is transported to intersection 5 or 8. Upon arrival at this intersection, the entity enters station CfltWait where it enters a QUEUE-SCAN combination. The entity remains in this QUEUE until the interference flag is set back to 0.

If the transporter reaches a decision intersection and the flag is equal to 0, it is directed to label ContTest where possible contention is checked. If the current crane destinations can result in a deadlock, the entity is directed to label FutrCflt where the interference flag is set to 1 and the transporter is sent to its drop-off point. The flag is set to 1 to prevent the second crane from entering the drop-off zones and causing a deadlock.

If there appears to be no current conflict, the entity is sent to label NoConflt where a final check is made. If crane 1 is directed to dropoff 7, or if crane 2 is directed to dropoff 6, the interference flag is set to 1 again to prevent the other vehicle from entering the drop-off zones and creating a deadlock. The crane is then transported to its drop-off point at which time the entity enters the UnLoadLogic station, its DropPt is set to 0, and it delays for unloading. After unloading, the corresponding request queue is checked. If a current request exists, the entity is sent to label FreeCrn, where the crane is freed to respond to that request, and the entity disposed of. If there are no requests, the crane is sent to the first intersection out of the drop-off area, 5 or 8. The entity then enters station FreeCrane where the crane is freed and the entity is disposed of. A second entity is always sent to the TALLY block at label SysTime where the flowtime is tallied and the entity is disposed of.

The Summary Report for this sample problem is shown in Figure 9-23. These results indicate that the system can easily handle the current load even though the drop zone is occupied almost 50 percent of the time and both cranes are blocked from entering this area about 8 percent of the time.

```
Project:   Sample Problem 9.3
Analyst:   SM
Replication ended at time:   32500.0
```

TALLY VARIABLES

Identifier	Average	Variation	Minimum	Maximum	Observations
TimeInSys	89.895	.45654	42.186	279.88	724

DISCRETE-CHANGE VARIABLES

Identifier	Average	Variation	Minimum	Maximum	Final Value
Waiting Crane 1	.41649	1.6551	.00000	4.0000	.00000
Waiting Crane 2	.20104	2.3342	.00000	3.0000	1.0000
Crane 1 Blocked	.08012	35.315	.00000	100.00	.00000
Crane 2 Blocked	.08628	34.030	.00000	100.00	.00000
Drop Zone Occupied	.48420	1.0321	.00000	1.0000	1.0000
Crane 1	.79115	.51379	.00000	1.0000	.00000
Crane 2	.67683	.69100	.00000	1.0000	1.0000

Figure 9-23. Summary Report for Sample Problem 9.3

Exercises

Exercise 9.1

Consider a simple AGV system that operates on a rectangular loop with an input/output station at each corner. The distance from corner to corner is 75 feet, and there is only one vehicle that travels at a speed of 125 feet per minute. Parts arrive according to an exponential distribution with a mean of five minutes. The parts have an equal probability of entering each of the four stations and an equal probability of exiting at each of the four stations. (Hint: Generate enter and exit stations and, if they are the same, generate new pairs until the stations are not the same.) Assume the shortest-distance rule to determine the priority for pickup; assume load and unload times of one minute. Simulate the system for 2,000 minutes, and keep statistics on system time per part and on the number of requests at each station.

a. Assume an unidirectional AGV track.

b. Assume a bidirectional AGV track.

c. Compare the results from a and b.

Exercise 9.2

The AGV system map shown below has four AGVs that pick up parts at intersections 1 and 7 and that drop them off at intersections 2 and 10. The part interarrival times are exponentially distributed with a mean of eight minutes at intersection 1 and a mean of seven minutes at intersection 7. The probability of a part being dropped off at intersection 2 is 0.55, and the probability of a part being dropped off at intersection 10 is 0.45. Probabilities are independent of the pickup point. The time to load or unload a part is normally distributed with a mean of 3 minutes and a standard deviation of 0.5 minute.

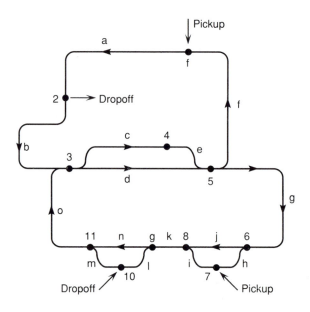

Link	Number of zones	Zone length
a	3	60
b	5	40
c — staging	4	20
d	2	50
e	1	40
f	4	60
g	4	60
h	1	70
i	1	70

Link	Number of zones	Zone length
j	1	80
k	1	30
l	1	70
m	1	70
n	1	80
o	3	60

The AGVs travel at a speed of 150 feet per minute and are positioned at the staging link (link c) at the start of the simulation. When an AGV completes a drop-off task, it checks to see if there is a current pickup request. If there is a request, the AGV is sent directly to the pickup; otherwise, it is sent back to the staging area. If there are requests at both pickup points, the shortest-distance rule applies. Simulate the system for 3,000 minutes; collect statistics on the part flowtime, the AGV utilization, and the number of requests waiting at each pickup point.

Exercise 9.3

Alter the system map for Exercise 9.2 such that pickup at intersection 7 and drop-off at intersection 10 are on the main track with the bypass being the longer section. The changes are shown below in the following table.

Link	Number of zones	Zone length
h	1	40
i	1	40
j	1	140
l	1	40
m	1	40
n	1	140

a. Simulate the revised system without using the bypass sections.

b. Simulate the system by using the bypass sections when the AGV is not going to the associated pickup or drop-off point.

Exercise 9.4

The guided-vehicle system shown below transfers parts through a system. Parts arrive at the input area, which also serves as a staging area for the AGVs, according to an exponential distribution with a mean of five minutes. Each part is processed in the same sequence: machine 1, 2, 3, and 4. All operation times are normally distributed with a mean of five minutes and a standard deviation of one minute. After the operation at machine 4 is completed, the part leaves the system without requiring the AGVs. AGV load and unload times are each one minute. Assume that there is unlimited storage capacity at the input and at each

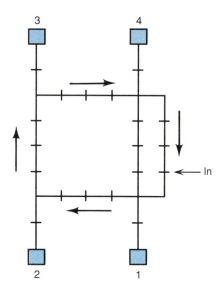

operation. Also assume that each of the zones shown in the figure left is 20 feet and that intersection lengths are 0.

Model this system such that all requests are handled on a first-come-first-served basis, regardless of the origin of the request. If there are no current requests when a vehicle completes its task, it is sent back to the staging area. There are four vehicles, which travel at 150 feet per minute, and they are positioned at the staging area at the start of the simulation. Simulate this system for 2,000 minutes; keep statistics on the busy AGVs, the total number of current requests, the machine utilizations, and the queues. Also record the flowtime for each part.

Exercise 9.5

The AGV system shown below serves four identical machines. An arriving part at the input area must first gain access to a free machine before it can be moved to the machine because there is no buffer space available. When a machine finishes an operation, an AGV is requested. Only after the part has been picked up by the AGV is the machine freed. Parts arrive according to an exponential distribution with a mean of 4 minutes. Operation times are normally distributed with a mean of 7 minutes and a standard deviation of two minutes. Load and unload times are each 0.5 minute. Finished parts are transferred to the output station, and the AGV is free to respond to other requests or is sent to the input area, which serves as a staging area. The AGVs move at a speed of 100 feet per minute. The zones shown in the diagram are 20 feet in length, and the intersections are zero feet in length. Simulate this system for 2,500 minutes.

a. How many AGVs are required if the track sections shown in dashes are not included?

b. Because of contamination problems, the clean operation shown in dashes has been added. Each time a part is picked up by an AGV (at either the input or at a machine) it must pass through this clean area (on its way to a machine or to the output station). It is not required to stop in the area. How many additional AGVs are required?

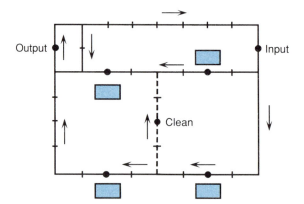

Exercise 9.6

The AGV system shown below is used to transfer parts from three receiving areas to two assembly areas. The parts arrive at a constant rate: every 10 minutes at intersection A, every 6 minutes at intersection B, and every 15 minutes at intersection C. Parts have an equal probability of going to assembly intersections Z and Y. At the assembly intersections, parts are removed at a constant rate of one every six minutes. A part remains on the AGV until it is removed. When the part has been removed, the AGV is free to respond to another request or is sent to the staging area, S, to await a request. Take link distances from the network, by using the number of zones shown. Assume that all zones are 10 feet and that intersections are of zero length. All links are unidirectional, and each AGV requires one zone with release-at-start control. The AGV speed is 120 feet per minute. Delay the start of the assembly operations for 30 minutes after parts start arriving to allow a buildup of parts. Simulate the system for 10,000 minutes. Determine the number of AGVs required to ensure that there is always a part available for the assembly operations.

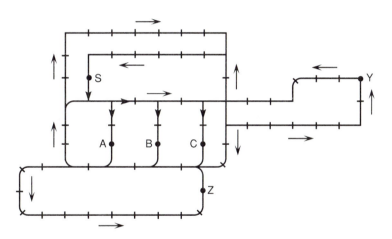

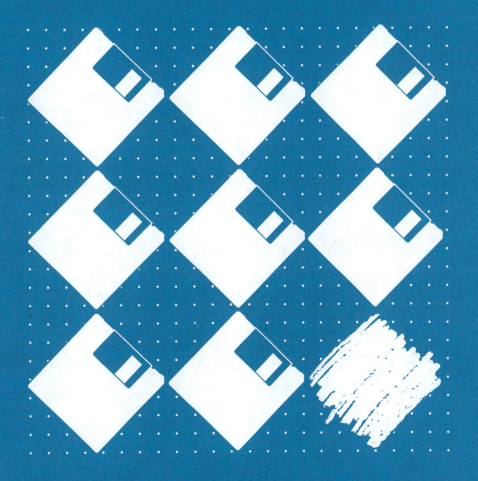

CHAPTER 10

Interfacing User-Written Subprograms

1. The Need for User-Written Subprograms

When modeling complex systems it is not uncommon to find situations in which it becomes difficult, if not impossible, to completely capture the system's logic by using the standard SIMAN block functions. You may also find that the model must interface with some type of data base or with the user through a set of menu options that allow a limited number of changes to model logic or data. Although most of these tasks can be performed by using the existing SIMAN blocks (e.g., READ and WRITE), some functions are easier to capture with user-written code in a lower-level language (e.g., FORTRAN or C). The user code option also provides the flexibility to develop discrete-event models for those who prefer modeling in this fashion or for systems best described in this manner.

The SIMAN language allows the user to include lower-level-language functions and routines in the simulation. Because the SIMAN simulation language is supported on a wide variety of computer platforms, the exact methods for including user code vary with the operating system. Complete information on these methods is contained in the system-specific SIMAN System Operation and Installation Guide. User code can be written in FORTRAN on all systems and with C, or other languages, on systems that provide an interface between the two languages.

The remaining portions of this chapter emphasize using the FORTRAN language but also provide examples using the C language. We begin with a general overview of the many possible applications of user code. Then we describe the various methods that can be employed to enter the code supplied by the user from the block model. Next we present the capabilities provided for interfacing with the SIMAN entities and variables from user code to the host model constructed with SIMAN blocks. Several examples illustrating these capabilities are provided. Note that the SIMAN language allows you to create a process model by using only blocks, to create a discrete-event model by using only user code, or to create a combined process/discrete-event model by using both. Continuous modeling, discussed in Chapter 11, can also be incorporated with any of these combinations.

All of the simulation modeling prior to this chapter has been performed by using SIMAN blocks and elements, the process-interaction mode. A model developed in this fashion allows you to view the system as being composed of a sequence of processes. The SIMAN blocks allow you to describe these processes and the logic that may be required to capture the activities occurring in the system being modeled. In this chapter we describe the use of user code to augment a process model or to develop a complete model through the use of the discrete event-scheduling mode.

User code can be entered from the SIMAN processor in a variety of ways. In most cases user code is called by an entity traveling through the model. Typical examples would be when an entity requires a decision by a user function, or when an entity enters an EVENT block. When an entity causes the call to user code, a pointer to the entity is passed by the SIMAN processor to the user code. This allows the user to query the SIMAN processor for any attribute values associated with that entity. While in user code it is possible to create and dispose of entities, place them in queues, or cause them to arrive at a station. While in user code the execution of the blocks is temporarily stopped, and no time advance is possible. When control is passed back to the SIMAN processor, the simulation continues. Only the calling entity can be returned to the Model Frame. If the calling entity is disposed of in user code, the SIMAN processor simply continues with the next normally occurring event.

User code can also be accessed without a calling entity. For example, standard routines are called at the start and at the end of each simulation run. You can also cause an event to occur through the SIMAN debugger. As with a calling entity, block processing is suspended until control is returned to the SIMAN processor.

User code is often employed at the start of a simulation to seed the system and to allow changes to selected values or options. The user code can, for example, open and read from a data file providing information on the current status of the system to be simulated, thereby creating and entering entities so that the system does not start in an empty state. The user code can then provide menu options that allow limited changes. Once the changes are completed, control passes back to the SIMAN processor, and the simulation starts.

The most common use of user code occurs when a simulation requires complex system control logic. Job priorities may, for example, periodically change based on system conditions, or complex logic may be required to determine the next set of job releases.

User code can also be applied to discrete-event modeling. Discrete-event modeling consists of modeling a system by describing the changes that occur in the system at discrete points in time. An instant in time at which the state of the system may change is called an *event time*, and the associated logic for processing the changes in the state is called an *event*. A discrete-event model is constructed by defining the events during which the system state changes and by then modeling the logic associated with each event. Events are scheduled to occur at specific instants in time during a simulation. Events can either reschedule themselves or schedule other events to occur. Because time doesn't advance within an event, changes in system behavior can only occur at event times. The system behavior is simulated by state changes that occur as events transpire.

Two basic types of events cause system changes. The first describes system changes that occur at the start of an activity, and the second describes changes that occur at the end of an activity. The system change and activities in a discrete-event model closely resemble those that occur in a process model. For example, consider the single-machine problem presented in Chapter 3, Sample Problem 3.1. This model consists of six SIMAN blocks: CREATE, QUEUE, SEIZE, DELAY, RELEASE, and COUNT. To model this problem in discrete-event code requires defining two events: a new part arriving and a part completing processing.

The event code for the arrival of a new part must first create the next part arrival, determine when it will arrive, and schedule it to occur as a future event. In the process mode, the CREATE block performs these activities automatically. The system status must then be checked to determine what happens to the arriving part. If the machine is busy, the part is placed in a queue to wait for the machine, and no other events are scheduled. If the machine is idle, its status is set to busy, the operation time is determined, and an event is scheduled to occur when part processing has been completed. In the process mode, these activities are automatically handled by the QUEUE-SEIZE-DELAY-RELEASE combination.

The event code for the second event, a part completing processing, counts the part and exits it from the system. In the process mode this sequence is accomplished with the COUNT block and the DISPOSE modifier. The system status must then be checked to see if the queue contains another job waiting for service. If the queue is empty, the machine is set to idle, and no other events are scheduled. If there is a job in the queue, it is removed, the operation time is determined, and an event for the part completing processing is scheduled. In the SIMAN process mode, these activities are automatically performed.

After the actions for an event have been completed, control is returned to the SIMAN processor, which advances the simulation time until the next scheduled event is to occur, i.e., another part arriving or completing processing. (This problem will be modeled in discrete-event code as one of the additional problems at the end of this chapter.)

Although the addition of user code provides a great deal of flexibility, it is generally advised that block constructs be used if the identical function can be achieved. Using block constructs eliminates the need to create a new SIMAN processor that includes the user code, and it also allows for more complete error-trapping.

3. Interfacing with the User Code

The user-written code and the SIMAN block model are interfaced when you incorporate your own routines(s) into a specialized executable version of SIMAN.

These routines must be written, compiled, and then linked to the SIMAN object and library files provided with the software. The SIMAN Systems Operation and Installation Guide that accompanies the software contains complete instructions. A complete list of available routines and functions can be found in Appendix C.

3.1 User-Written Routines

The routines with calling syntax shown in Figure 10-1 are automatically called by SIMAN. The C language routines correspond directly to the FORTRAN routines, although there is an additional argument for each routine. This argument, CMN, is used to identify the C structure that gives access to variables in SIMAN's FORTRAN common block SIM. The SIMAN Reference Guide describes how this structure can be used.

FORTRAN Language Syntax	C Language Syntax
PRIME	cprime(cmn)
WRAPUP	cwrap(cmn)
UCLEAR	cuclea(cmn)

Figure 10-1. SIMAN User-Written Routines

Routines PRIME and CPRIME are called by SIMAN at the start of each simulation replication. PRIME is most commonly used to initialize variables, to preload a system, or to access data from a user file or data base. Because this routine is called at the start of each replication, it allows you to set or change many of the variables or parameters for the entire simulation replication. These changes can be read from a user data file or can be entered interactively through a user-written menu system.

It may be helpful to understand how the calls to these routines are made. The standard SIMAN executable contains a dummy routine for each of the routines shown in Figures 10-1. For example, the dummy routine PRIME contains only a return statement as shown below. At the start of each simulation replication, this PRIME is called and, if a user routine is not included, no action is taken. A user-written routine PRIME replaces this dummy routine and performs the actions coded by the user. The remaining routines are included in SIMAN in the same fashion, with the functions returning a value of zero.

```
SUBROUTINE PRIME
RETURN
END
```

Routine WRAPUP is called at the end of each simulation replication. It is generally used for calculating and writing out special user statistics or the ending state of the system. It can also be used to write out the simulation results in a customized format that corresponds to reports obtainable from the real system.

Routine UCLEAR is called by SIMAN when the statistics for the simulation replication are cleared. It will be called, for example, if a WarmUp time for statistics is entered on the REPLICATE element. This routine is normally included if you are collecting special statistics that are not cleared automatically by SIMAN. It allows you to clear these statistics and the SIMAN statistics concurrently.

3.2 The Event Routine and User Functions

Unlike PRIME, WRAPUP, and UCLEAR, which are automatically called by SIMAN, a call to routine EVENT (Figure 10-2) must be user-initiated. The most common method for calling EVENT is to use the EVENT block, which is discussed in a later section. You can also call routine EVENT from the SIMAN debugger by using the command "EVENT Nev" (in which Nev is the specific event number to be called), or from any of the previously discussed routines (e.g., PRIME). You can also schedule a future event call with the ARRIVALS element. If the active entity calls routine EVENT, the record location pointer to that entity is passed by the first argument, Lent.

FORTRAN Language Syntax	C Language Syntax
EVENT(Lent,Nev)	cevent(Lent,Nev,cmn)

Figure 10-2. SIMAN User-Written EVENT Routine

Likewise, functions UF and UR are user-initiated with the syntax shown in Figure 10-3. Function UF is normally called from the block model by including the UF(Nuf) entry in an expression. Note that the calling form of the function used in the block model does not contain the argument Lent, the entity record location. This record location is automatically passed to the user-written routine. The argument Nuf is the function number to be called and allows you to reference this number in the user-written code when several functions are required. This function allows you to calculate a single value and return that value to evaluate the expression in the block model where it is referenced. An example of a user function for selecting among workstations is provided as an additional problem at the end of this chapter.

FORTRAN Language Syntax	C Language Syntax
UF(Lent,Nuf)	cuf(Lent,Nuf,cmn)
UR(Lent,Nur)	cur(Lent,Nur,cmn)

Figure 10-3. SIMAN User-Written Functions

Function UR allows you to include special rules for selecting a queue when using the PICKQ or QPICK blocks, for selecting a resource when using the SELECT block, or for selecting a transporter when using the REQUEST or ALLO-CATE block. This function is entered as UR(Nur) in the model; it returns the branch number of the SELECT, QPICK, or PICKQ block, or it returns the unit of transporter on a REQUEST or ALLOCATE block. The argument Nur is the specific user rule to be called and allows for the inclusion of several rules.

3.3 The EVENT Block

The EVENT block provides an interface from the block model to the user-written code; the symbol and statement for the EVENT block are shown below. When an entity arrives to an EVENT block, a call is made to routine EVENT with the event number given in the block. The entity pointer is passed as the first argument, Lent, and the event number as the second argument, Nev, in the routine call. Thus, the EVENT routine can be called from different places in the model, with each place having a different number.

EVENT
Number

    EVENT:Number;

When it returns to the block model, the status of the entity that entered the EVENT block depends directly on what actions are specified in the user-written code. In the most likely case the calling entity is returned to the model and is passed to the next block in the model. If, however, the user code causes the calling entity to be disposed of or to be redirected to some other place in the model (e.g., a queue), the calling entity is not returned.

For example, consider a model in which a job entering a different department in the model calls routine EVENT to establish its priority based on the system status. If the department status is such that the job cannot be completed on time, the user code schedules it for subcontract, which is not included in the model. In this case the job entity may be counted and disposed of, or it may be scheduled to arrive to the next department when the subcontracted work has been completed. In either case, the original entity entering the EVENT block in the model is redirected and is not returned to the EVENT block. SIMAN takes the next event entity from the event calendar and continues the simulation.

3.4 Special User-Written Routines

Several special routines are given in Figure 10-4. Routine KEYHIT is called by SIMAN whenever a keystroke is entered during execution of the simulation. Routine USAV is called when saving a snapshot, and URST is called when restoring a snapshot. The routine STATE is called only if you use continuous modeling constructs.

FORTRAN Language Syntax	C Language Syntax
KEYHIT(Icode)	ckeyhi(Icode,cmn)
USAV	cusav(cmn)
URST	curst(cmn)
STATE	cstate(cmn)

Figure 10-4. Special User-Written Routines

Routine KEYHIT allows you to access user code directly from the keyboard during execution of the simulation. Each time you press a key, the ASCII equivalent is determined, and routine KEYHIT is called with the resulting value. For example, if the key "a" is pressed, KEYHIT is called with the argument Icode set to 97. Pressing the key "S" results in Icode being set to 83. SIMAN fully supports this capability for the ASCII set of characters with values in the range of 1 to 127. On some systems, the extended character set (128 to 255) is supported as well as the function keys. Check the System Operation and Installation Guide for your system to determine if these options are available.

The use of KEYHIT allows real-time controlled entry into user code. For example, you can code a screen display of the current status of key variables in the system and prompt the display of this information with keyboard entry of the "S" or "s" key. Thus, by periodically pressing one of these keys you can monitor system status while the simulation is running. The FORTRAN code for this routine (shown below) assumes that a user routine called Status has been included to display the required information. KEYHIT can also be used to access a user menu that allows changes to data, or to any other user code. Note that the statement "simstr *sim;" is included in the C code listing to provide a pointer to the "sim" common block. The declaration statement "simint" is defined in the file "simlib.h" provided with SIMAN to ensure that the integer word sizes are consistent with the platform being used.

```fortran
c FORTRAN CODE
c
      SUBROUTINE KEYHIT(Icode)
      IF(Icode.EQ.ICHAR('S') .OR. Icode.EQ.ICHAR('s') THEN
        CALL Status
      ENDIF
      RETURN
      END
```

```c
/* C CODE */

void ckeyhi ( Icode,sim )

smint *Icode;
simstr *sim;
{
      if ((Icode=='\S')||(Icode=='\s'))
        status();
}
```

There are several keys that already cause SIMAN to react. For example, pressing the ESC, "D," or "d" key (codes 27, 68, and 100, respectively) during execution suspends the simulation run and returns control to the interactive debugger. The "Q" and "q" keys cause termination of the simulation run. Other keys are reserved by the Cinema version of the SIMAN processor. These ASCII codes are captured externally from routine KEYHIT; however, KEYHIT is always called first. Thus, if a "Q" (code 81) is entered, SIMAN first calls KEYHIT, at which time the user code can perform some function. If you do not want the simulation to terminate, the value of Icode to be returned to SIMAN from KEYHIT can be changed to a value (e.g., 0) that does not cause termination. If you do not change this value in KEYHIT, the simulation terminates.

The routine USAV is called when the SAVE command is used in the SIMAN interactive debugger. If user code is employed in a model containing local variables critical to the simulation, routine USAV can be used to write these values to a file so that they can be recalled when the RESTORE command is called from the interactive debugger. The routine URST is called when the RESTORE command is issued, thereby allowing the saved data to be read from the file and the local variables to be set to these saved values. Routine STATE is described in Chapter 11.

3.5 The Entity Identifier and Record Location

The entity identifier was first discussed in Section 2.5 of Chapter 4. This identifier, which provides a unique reference number for each valid entity, is given as part of a trace and is used in the interactive debugger. Each entity also has a corresponding record location pointer, which is used to reference the entity when in user code. The entity identifier can be obtained in the Model Frame by using the SIMAN function IDENT. This same value can be obtained in user code by using the corresponding FORTRAN function IDENT(Lent), which requires the entity record location as an argument.

When an entity is created in SIMAN, an entity record location is assigned to that entity. When the entity is disposed of, the record location remains, but it references an invalid entity. There are a finite number of possible record locations that correspond to the maximum number of entities allowed for a specific simulation model. You can think of these record locations as being divided in two sets: one referencing active or valid entities, and the other referencing invalid or not currently active entities. These record locations are reused and can move between the two sets many times during a simulation. The results of a call from user code that references an invalid record location are unpredictable; it may or may not produce a SIMAN termination error.

The value of the entity record location is passed as the first argument, Lent, of routine EVENT and functions UF and UR. Each currently valid entity has its own entity record location. This entity record location must be referenced whenever an action in user code is performed on a valid entity.

The entity record location allows you to manipulate any entity from user code. This manipulation includes creating new entities, disposing of valid entities, changing attribute values, etc. A relatively common error consists of using the wrong entity record location. Caution is suggested to ensure that you always use the correct record location. Also, you should never employ user code to dispose of or redirect the entity that calls either function UF or function UR. The use of this record location is illustrated in the following sections, which describe methods for interfacing user code and the model.

4. Interfacing from User Code to the Block Model

The previous sections described the ways of entering user-written code, either automatically or from the block model. Once you have entered user code, you must also be able to interface back to the block model and access the data specified in the Experiment Frame.

4.1 Accessing the SIMAN System Variables

All of the system variables, including the distributions, are directly available from user code in a format similar to that used in the Model Frame. These can be thought of as functions that return a value. Note that you cannot change the value by using these functions; you can only retrieve the current value. Thus, these SIMAN variables can only be used in the right-hand side of an expression in user-coded routines. (Special subroutines are provided to change the values of some system variables.) All entity-related attributes (e.g., M, IS, NS, etc.) must reference the entity record location; these are discussed in the next section.

Certain variables can be accessed, and new assignments can be made from within the user code. These variables are defined in a FORTRAN user common block labeled SIM. If any of these variables are to be referenced or assigned, this common block must be included, in the exact form shown below, in all FORTRAN user routines. If C routines are included, the common block SIM must be referenced by including it as the CMN argument.

```
Common /SIM/ D(50) , DL(50), S(50), SL(50),
& X(50), DTNOW, TNOW, TFIN , J , NUMREP
```

The variables S and D are the state variables and derivative, respectively. Variables DL and SL are the immediate past values of the D and S variables, respectively. DTNOW is the current integration step size. These variables are used for continuous modeling (see Chapter 11). The X variables are the SIMAN global variables. TNOW is the current simulation clock time, and TFIN is the ending time of the simulation replication. J is the integer index variable used by several of the advanced blocks. NUMREP is the current replication number.

All of these variables, except TNOW and NRUN, can be changed in user code. The ending time of the simulation can also be changed, although it should never be set to a time that is less than the current value of TNOW. For example, you may want the run length to be based on the results of a statistical test on key performance measures. In this case, you could terminate the simulation when these performance measures can be predicted with a stated confidence level. To do so, you default the simulation replication length time, Length, on the REPLICATE element (resulting in an infinite run time). You also periodically (based, perhaps, on a time loop in the Model Frame) call the EVENT routine with an event number of 1. This event performs the statistical test and, if it fails, returns control to the model. If it passes, the code sets TFIN equal to TNOW and returns control to the model, which then causes the replication to terminate. The abbreviated code for this routine is shown below.

```
c FORTRAN CODE

      Subroutine EVENT ( Lent, Nev )
      Common /SIM/ D(50) , DL(50), S(50), SL(50) ,
      Common /SIM/ X(50) , DTNOW , TNOW , TFIN , J , NRUN
c
c***perform statistical test here
c***if failed, set Ipass = -1 , else Ipass = +1
c
      IF ( IPASS .GT. 0 ) THEN
      TFIN = TNOW
      ENDIF
      RETURN
      END
```

```
/* C CODE */

void cevent ( Lent, Nev, sim )

smint *Lent, *Nev;
simstr *sim;
{
/* *** perform statistical test here
   *** if failed, set Ipass = -1, else Ipass = +1 */
   if (Ipass > 0)
     tfin = tnow;
   }
```

If other event calls were to be included in the model, the above routine could be modified to direct control based on the value of Nev, the event number, thereby allowing many events to be handled in the same routine. Examples of referencing other SIMAN variables in user code are provided in later sections.

4.2 Retrieving and Assigning Entity Attribute Values

References to entity attributes must include the entity record location, Lent. The FORTRAN functions shown in Figure 10-5 allow you to retrieve the attribute values of any entity. The naming convention used for the function names and arguments follow the normal FORTRAN convention for integer and real variables (i.e., i through n are integers, otherwise reals).

Function	Description
A(Lent,Natb)	Value of attribute number Natb
IS(Lent)	Value of attribute IS
M(Lent)	Value of attribute M
NS(Lent)	Value of attribute NS
IDENT(Lent)	Entity Identifier

Figure 10-5. Functions for Retrieving Attribute Values

The functions shown in Figure 10-6 allow you to access values on entities that have been grouped. Remember that there is a single entity that represents the group; the values for this entity can be obtained by using the functions shown in Figure 10-5. The Figure 10-6 functions allow you to retrieve the individual attributes of entities comprised in a group. The argument Nrnk identifies the entity's rank within the group. The function SAG returns the sum of a specified general-purpose attribute for all members of the group.

Function	Description
NG(Lent)	Number of entities in group
AG(Lent,Natb,Nrnk)	Value of attribute number Natb
ISG(Lent,Nrnk)	Value of attribute IS
MG(Lent,Nrnk)	Value of attribute M
NSG(Lent,Nrnk)	Value of attribute NS
LGRP(Lent,Nrnk)	Entity record location
SAG(Lent,Natb)	Sum of attribute number Natb for group

Figure 10-6. Functions for Retrieving Attribute Values of an Entity with Rank Nrnk

The routines given in Figure 10-7 allow you to assign new values to the attributes of an entity. The first four routines allow assignments to each individual attribute of the referenced entity. The next routine, ASSIGN, provides the means of assigning new values to all of the general-purpose attributes in a single routine. If this routine is used, the real array to be substituted for the second argument, Att, should be dimensioned to reflect the number of general-purpose attributes defined for each entity. This definition is made in the Experiment Frame with either the ATTRIBUTES or the DISCRETE element. The last routine listed in Figure 10-7, COPY, assigns the values currently in array Att to the attributes of the entity with record location Lent.

Routine	Description
SETA(Lent,Ntab,Val)	Set attribute Ntab to value Val
SETIS(Lent,Nval)	Set IS to value Nval
SETM(Lent,Nval)	Set M to value Nval
SETNS(Lent,Nval)	Set NS to value Nval
ASSIGN(Lent,Att)	Assigns attribute values to array Att
COPY(Lent,Att)	Assign values from array Att to attributes

Figure 10-7. Routines for Assign Entity Attribute Values

Consider a simple example in which each entity has five general-purpose attributes. We want an event that will check the value of each general-purpose attribute: if the value is greater than 2, double the value; otherwise set the value to 0. We also want to increase the value of M by 10. The code for this example is shown below. Note that the event number, Nev, is never referenced and that the common block, SIM, is not included because it is not necessary. The temporary attribute array, Att, has been dimensioned to 5. Note that we could have used routine SETA directly after the ENDIF to set each attribute individually instead of using routine ASSIGN, and we could have used routine COPY directly before the first DO loop instead of using function A.

```
c   FORTRAN CODE
c
      Subroutine EVENT(Lent,Nev)
      INTEGER Lent,Nev,Mstat,i
      REAL Att
      Dimension Att(5)
      DO 10 i = 1 , 5
        Att(i) = A(Lent,i)
        IF( Att(i) .GT. 2.0) THEN
          Att(i) = Att(i) * 2.0
        ELSE
          Att(i) = 0.0
        ENDIF
   10 CONTINUE
      Call ASSIGN(Lent,Att)
      Mstat = M(Lent) + 10
      Call SETM(Lent,Mstat)
      RETURN
      END
```

```
/* C CODE */

void cevent ( Lent, Nev, sim )
smint *Lent, *Nev;
simstr *sim;
{
      smint i, Mstat;
      float Att[5];
      for (i=0; i<=4; ++i)
        }
        Att[i]=A(Lent,&i);
        if( Att[i]>2.0)
          Att[i]=Att[i]*2.0;
        else
          Att[i]=0.0;
        }
      assign(Lent,&Att);
      Mstat=M(Lent)+10;
      setm(Lent,&Mstat);
}
```

As stated earlier, you can access most valid entities from user code. However, if routine EVENT or functions UR or UF are called from the block model, they only pass the record location for the calling entity. Also, if user code is entered through routines PRIME, WRAPUP, or KEYHIT, there is no calling entity. In order to have complete flexibility in user code a mechanism must be provided to allow the accessing of the record locations to other valid entities. These mechanisms are discussed in the next section.

4.3 Manipulating Entities

Valid entities in SIMAN can exist in several different states. There is at most one current active entity being processed. If control is currently in user code, then the entity being processed is the calling entity. This condition exists if routine EVENT or functions UR or UF are called from the block model. If routine PRIME or WRAPUP are called by SIMAN, there is no entity being processed.

Most valid entities in a simulation are either in some time delay (e.g., a ROUTE or a DELAY block) or in a queue. The record locations for these entities can be obtained by using the functions given in Figure 10-8.

The first four functions shown give you access to the SIMAN event calendar. Function LFCAL returns the record location of the first entity on the event calendar. The record locations for subsequent entities can be found by using function LSCAL. Repeated use of this function returns the record locations of all entities on the event calendar; if there are no more entities on the calendar, function LSCAL returns a value of 0. Function LFCAL always returns the record location of the next entity scheduled to become active. However, subsequent calls using LSCAL do not necessarily result in a time-ordered list. If there are multiple entities scheduled to come off the event calendar at the same time, the record locations are returned successively with LSCAL.

Function	Description
LFCAL	First entity on event calendar
LSCAL(Lent)	Successor entity to Lent
NEVENT(Lent)	Event number of entity Lent
TEVENT(Lent)	Event time of entity Lent
LFR(Nque)	First entity in queue Nque
LLR(Nque)	Last entity in queue Nque
LPRED(Lent)	Predecessor entity to Lent
LRANK(Nrnk,Nque)	Entity with rank Nrnk in Nque
LSUCC(Lent)	Successor entity to Lent

Figure 10-8. Functions for Retrieving Entity Record Locations

Function NEVENT returns the event number of the entity on the calendar. If the entity with record location Lent is scheduled to call routine EVENT, the value returned is the event number. Otherwise, a negative value is returned to indicate that there is no event number for this entity. Function TEVENT can be used to determine the event time, i.e., the time that the entity is scheduled to become active.

The last five functions listed in Figure 10-8 allow you to access entities in queues. LFR and LLR return the record locations of the first and the last entities in a queue. LRANK returns the record location of the entity at rank Nrnk in a queue. Functions LPRED and LSUCC can be used to find the predecessor and successor entities in a queue. If the referenced queue (Nque) is empty, or if there is no predecessor or successor, these functions return a value of 0.

These functions allow you to obtain the record location of most valid entities and some additional information about them. With this information, you can apply the previously described functions (see Figures 10-6 and 10-7) to obtain attribute values. Using the routines given in Figure 10-9 you can also manipulate entities.

The first two routines listed allow you to create and dispose of entities. Routine CREATE creates a new valid entity and returns the new record location. DISPOS releases the record location for later use. If the user code disposes of an entity and then creates a new entity, it is possible that the record location will be the same, even though the new and disposed of entities are considered to be separate. Also note that, unless initial values are entered in the ATTRIBUTES element, routine CREATE will return an entity that has all of its attributes set to 0.

Routine	Description
CREATE(Lent)	Create entity
DISPOS(Lent)	Dispose of entity
INSERT(Lent,Nque)	Insert entity in queue Nque
QUEUE(Lent,Nque)	Schedule entity to queue Nque
REMOVE(Lent,Nque)	Remove entity from queue Nque
ENTER(Lent,Nsta)	Send entity to station Nsta
SEND(Lent,Dt,Str,Len)	Send entity to block label in Dt time units
SCHED(Lent,I,Dt)	Schedule event I in Dt time units
SIG(Nsig)	Send signal Nsig
SIGNAL(Nsig,MaxRel)	Send signal Nsig to release maximum of MaxRel entities
CANCEL(Lent)	Remove entity from event calendar

Figure 10-9. Routines for Entity Manipulation

The next two routines listed in Figure 10-9 allow you to place valid entities in a queue. INSERT places the entity directly in the queue, and QUEUE schedules the entity to arrive to the queue in zero time units. Although these two routines are similar, the difference between them can be important. If the chosen queue precedes a SEIZE block with an available resource, using the INSERT routine simply places the entity in the queue; no other action occurs. The resource will not be allocated to the entity until the next entity arrives at the queue. Using the QUEUE routine causes the entity to arrive to the queue and to seize the available resource immediately. Routine REMOVE allows you to take an entity out of a queue. Its action is similar to routine CANCEL, which removes an entity from the event calendar.

Routine ENTER allows an entity to be sent to a STATION block in the model. This routine sets the attribute M to the destination station and then places the entity on the event calendar to arrive at the station zero time units later. An alternative method for entering entities in the block model is to use routine SEND. This routine allows you to send an entity to the block in the model with the attached label defined in character variable length Len. This routine also allows you to define an offset time for the arrival of the entity, Dt. Routine SCHED allows you to schedule a call to routine EVENT in Dt time units with a stated event number, I.

The last two routines listed in Figure 10-9 allow you to send signals to the SIMAN block model (see Section 7.1 in Chapter 8 regarding the SIGNAL block). SIG sends signal Nsig, where the number of entities to be released depends on the operands of the associated SIGNAL blocks in the model. Routine SIGNAL allows you to specify the maximum number of entities that can be released, MaxRel, although it is possible that the operands in the model may override this value. Using SIGNAL with the MaxRel argument set to −1 is equivalent to using routine SIG.

The last routine, CANCEL, removes the chosen entity from the event calendar. CANCEL does not dispose of the entity; it only removes it from the calendar. In general, caution is advised in removing entities from the event calendar.

The user code shown below illustrates a case in which job priorities are recalculated daily. If we assume that the time units are in hours and that this is a single-shift operation, a call to user code is made every eight hours. The job priority is recalculated based on its current slack, i.e., due date minus current time. The user code determines the number of entities in the queue and then enters a loop that removes the last entity from the queue, calculates the job slack (assume that attribute 2 is the due date), and determines the priority. That priority is then assigned to the entity's attribute 1, and the job is scheduled to arrive back at the same queue from which it was removed.

```
c   FORTRAN CODE
c
      INTEGER Num,Nqq,
      REAL Slack,Pri,
c
      Num = NQ(15)
      DO 11 i = Num, 1 , -1
        Nqq = LLR(15)
        CALL REMOVE(Nqq)
        Slack = (A(Nqq,2)-TNOW)/8.0
        IF(Slack.LE.1.0) THEN
          Pri = 1
        ELSEIF(Slack.LE.4) THEN
          Pri = 2
        ELSEIF(Slack.LE.10) THEN
          Pri = 3
        ELSE
          Pri = 4
        ENDIF
        CALL SETA(Nqq,1,Pri)
        CALL QUEUE(Nqq,15)
11      CONTINUE
```

```
/* C CODE */

main()
{
smint i, Num, Nqq, QNum=15, ANum=1;
float Slack, Pri;

for (Num=nq(&QNum); Num>=1; --Num)
    {
    Nqq=llr(&QNum);
    cremov(&Nqq);
    Slack=(a(&Nqq,&ANum)-(sim->tnow))/8.0;

    if(Slack<=1.0)
      Pri=1.0;
    elseif(Slack<=4.0)
```

```
    Pri=2.0;
elseif(Slack<=10.0)
    Pri=3.0;
else
    Pri=4.0;
      ANum=1;
      seta(&Nqq,&ANum,&Pri);
      queue(&Nqq,&QNum);
      }
```

Note that the entities are removed in reverse order because a last-in-first-out order rule determines the order for removing entities from the current events chain. We assume that entities in queue 15 are ranked using an LVF(1) rule. Removing them in reverse order retains a first-in-first-out tie-breaking rule.

4.4 Changing Status Variables and System Values

In constructing a SIMAN simulation model, much of the data used by the model is put into the Experiment Frame. Because the Model Frame must use this information, numerous functions have been described to allow access from the Model Frame. All of these functions can also be used in user code.

Functions for querying the transporter and conveyor data structures are given in Figure 10-10. The function ID returns the distance from the current station of the entity with record location Lent to station Nsta; it uses the distance set specified for the transporter set Ntrn. Function IDIST allows you to obtain the distance between any two stations, Nstb and Nste, for any valid distance set. The third function, ISGMT, returns the segment or conveyor length between two stations in the specified segment set, Nsgl.

Function	Description
ID(Lent,Ntrn,Nsta)	Distance from entity to station Nsta using distance set of transporter set Ntrn
IDIST(Ndst,Nstb,Nste)	Distance from station Nstb to Nsta using distance set Ndst
ISGMT(Nsgl,Nstb,Nste)	Segment length between stations Nstb and Nste in segment set Nsgl
IOFFST(Lent,Ioff)	Station number offset by Ioff from entity sequence set

Figure 10-10. Functions for Retrieving Transporter and Conveyor Information

The last function, IOFFST, allows you to query the sequences to determine past and future station numbers in the sequence that the referenced entity is following. This function determines the correct sequence, NS, for the entity with record location Lent and its current position in the sequence, IS; it then returns the station in the sequence, which is offset by Ioff. If you simply want the station in a sequence for a specified value of IS, we recommend using the SIMAN function MSQ.

The routines listed in Figure 10-11 allow you to reset a limited set of SIMAN system variables from user code. Routine SETMR allows you to change the capacity of a resource. This routine operates very much like the SCHEDULES element described in Chapter 8. Note that it does not perform an incremental change as does the ALTER block, but instead changes the capacity to the entered value, Ncap. If this new value is greater than the current value (function MR can be used to obtain the current value), then the increase occurs immediately. Like the SCHEDULES element and the ALTER block, if the new value results in a decrease, the capacity is decreased only when the resources become available.

Routine	Description
SETMR(Nres,Ncap)	Set resource number Nres to capacity Ncap
SETP(Nset,Np,Val)	Set parameter Np of set Nset to Val
SETTF(Ntab,Xval,Yval)	Set table Ntab value
SETVC(Ncnv,Vel)	Set conveyor Ncnv velocity to Vel
SETVT(Ntrn,Vel)	Set transporter Ntrn velocity to Vel
SETV(Index,Val)	Set global user variable with Index to Val

Figure 10-11. Routines for Changing System Variables

The next two routines, SETP and SETTF, allow you to change the values in the PARAMETERS and TABLES elements. Using SETP results in direct replacement with the new value. The arguments of the SETTF routine require that the independent, Xval, and the dependent, Yval, values be entered. If there is currently a value in the specified table, Ntab, for the independent argument, the new independent value is directly substituted. If there is no matching independent value, Xval, in the table, the closest corresponding X value that is less than Xval has its dependent value set to Yval.

The last two routines allow you to change the transporter velocities, SETVT, and conveyor velocities, SETVC.

A simple example of increasing the capacity of resource number 6 by a value of 2 is shown below. A similar example for increasing the value of parameter set 4, number 6, to twice its value is also included.

```
CALL SETMR( 7 , MR(7) +2 )
CALL SETP( 4 ,6 , 2.0 * P(4,6) )
```

The routines described in this section allow you to access entity and system information and to manipulate this information. The next section describes how you can access the statistical routines.

4.5 Performing Statistical Functions
Retrieving statistical information from user code is the same as retrieving from the block model. The complete list of functions available are listed in Appendix

C. In general, it is possible to retrieve the current average, standard deviation, number of observations, etc.

In addition to these functions, which allow you to obtain statistical information, several routines allow you to interact with statistical information. These routines are shown in Figure 10-12. The first routine, CLEAR, has no arguments and clears all statistical arrays. The next four routines listed allow you to clear individual statistics. If a negative argument is passed, the call causes all statistics of that type to be cleared. For example, a call of -1 using CLRTAL causes all tallies to be cleared. Note that the use of any of these routines does not change the reported time that statistics are cleared on the Summary Report. That time is taken from the REPLICATE element.

Routine	Description
CLEAR	Clear statistics
CLRCNT(Ncnt)	Clear counter Ncnt
CLRCST(Ncst)	Clear cstat Ncst
CLRDST(Ndst)	Clear dstat Ndst
CLRTAL(Ntal)	Clear tally Ntal
SUMRY	Create summary report
COUNT(Ncnt,Inc)	Increase counter Ncnt by Inc
TALLY(Ntal,Val)	Record value Val for tally Ntal

Figure 10-12. Statistical Routines

Routine SUMRY causes the complete SIMAN Summary Report to be generated and printed out. The last two routines allow you to include values in the observational statistics. Routine COUNT allows you to increase the counter, Ncnt, by a value, Inc. Routine TALLY allows you to include the value, Val, in the tally number, Ntal.

4.6 Avoiding Common Errors

The error-trapping and reporting provided by the SIMAN processor are not necessarily able to capture user-code errors. Recall that, if the SIMAN processor detects an error, it stops execution, reports the error, and places you in the interactive debugger. When you are in the debugger, you can inquire about the current state of the simulation and attempt to isolate the source of the error. For example, a termination error may result from an attempt to release more resources than are currently available.

The result of an error in user code is less predictable. It may cause a termination error with the only message being the FORTRAN or C termination error message. Many errors are captured by the SIMAN processor and reported; however, the exact point in the user code where the error occurred is not always obvious.

When using the SIMAN process mode, the interactive debugger provides an excellent vehicle for detecting the causes of errors. However, the debugger is not available when control of the simulation resides in user code. For example, when an entity passing through the block model enters an EVENT block, the debugger reports that it is about to call an event; no other information is reported until the entity re-enters the model or until control is returned to the SIMAN processor. However, some computer platforms do provide source-level debuggers, which can augment the SIMAN debugger.

In addition, you cannot access entities currently being conveyed by SIMAN. Nor can you necessarily access an entity that has had a resource preempted from it. Entities that are being transported can be found on the event calendar; however, manipulating these entities is not recommended.

Experience indicates that modelers often make similar types of errors. The entity record location is a common source of potential problems. As discussed earlier, reference to an invalid location or to the wrong location can yield unpredictable results. In using the routines provided with SIMAN, you must be careful to avoid argument mismatch — either in the number of arguments or in the argument type. Finally, you must also include the complete common block "SIM" if you are referencing any of these variables in user code.

5. Additional Sample Problems

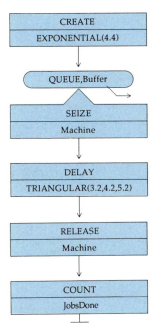

Figure 10-13. Block Diagram for Sample Problem 3.1

Although selected small examples on the use of user code have been provided, it is difficult to put together all the concepts without looking at complete models. The following three examples provide complete problems that should provide insight into applying user code. Sample problem 3.1, solved entirely in user code, illustrates the logic required for discrete-event modeling. The second problem illustrates how to read job descriptions from external data files and how to allow for decision making during a simulation run. Both of these problems can be modeled using only SIMAN blocks; they are presented here to illustrate the application of user code. The third problem illustrates the use of a user function. Although this problem can also be modeled strictly with SIMAN blocks, the model would be quite lengthy. This last problem is probably the best example of how user code can be applied in real-world models.

5.1 Sample Problem 10.1: The Single-Machine Problem

Let's take the single-machine problem as solved in Chapter 3, Sample Problem 3.1, and develop the solution by using the discrete-event portion of SIMAN. The block model for this problem is shown in Figure 10-13. The approach to this problem was briefly discussed in Section 2.0 of this chapter. It requires developing two events: an arrival (event 1) and an end of process (event 2).

Before we develop the logic for the two events, we must create the first arriving entity by using Routine PRIME, which is shown in Figure 10-14. Remember that PRIME is called at the start of each replication. The code shown below creates the first entity, which is given record pointer Lent by routine CREATE, schedules that entity (by using routine SCHED) to call event 1 zero time units later, and then returns control to the SIMAN processor. This entity becomes the first arrival to the system. Because there is no block model, the SIMAN processor causes the entity created by PRIME to call routine EVENT with an event number 1 at time 0; because there are no other entity creations, this is the first entity processed.

```
c         FORTRAN CODE
c
          SUBROUTINE PRIME
          INTEGER Lent,Nevt
          REAL Dtime
c
c           Create first arrival and schedule to arrive in
c           0 time units as an event 1
c
          CALL CREATE(Lent)
          Nevt = 1
          Dtime = 0.0
          CALL SCHED(Lent,Nevt,Dtime)
          RETURN
          END
```

```
/* C CODE */

#include "simlib.h"

void cprime ( sim )
simstr *sim;
{
        smint Lent, Nevt;
        float Dtime;

/*      Create first arrival and schedule to arrive at
        time 0 as an event 1 */

        create(&Lent);
        Nevt=1;
        Dtime=0.0;
        sched(&Lent,&Nevt,&Dtime);
}
```

Figure 10-14. Routine PRIME for Sample Problem 10.1

An arrival to the system, event 1, requires that the next arrival be scheduled and that the current arrival be placed in the queue to wait or to be processed by the machine, depending on the system status. The next arrival to the system needs to be created and scheduled to execute event 1 in the future (according to the time between arrivals). This action is accomplished in the process model with the CREATE block. In the user code for event 1, shown in Figure 10-15, we first create a new entity with record location Lent2. Note that we have used a different variable, Lent2, for the record location of the next arrival because we have not yet determined the action of the arrival that called event 1 with record location Lent. Having created the record location for the next arrival, we generate a sample from an exponential distribution, Otime, to represent the time between arrivals. We then schedule this next arrival to call event 1 in Otime time units by using routine SCHED.

```fortran
c   FORTRAN CODE
c
      SUBROUTINE EVENT(Lent,Nevt)
      INTEGER Lent,Nevt,Lent2,Istream,Nevt1,Nevt2,Nque,
     1        Nres,Ncap,Numc,Inc,job
      REAL Otime,Emean,Tmin,Tmode,Tmax,Ptime
      DATA Istream,Nevt1,Nevt2,Nque,Nres,Numc,Inc / 10,1,2,1,1,1,1/
      DATA Emean,Tmin,Tmode,Tmax / 4.4, 3.2, 4.2, 5.2/
c
c      Check for event type
c
      GOTO (1,2) , Nevt
c
c ****   Event 1: Arrival to system
c          Create next arrival and schedule
c
    1 CALL CREATE(Lent2)
      Otime { EXPO(Emean,Istream)
      CALL SCHED(Lent2,Nevt1,Otime)
c
c          Check for machine availability and place in
c          queue or schedule process delay
c
      IF(MR(Nres).GT.0) THEN
        CALL INSERT(Lent,Nque)
      ELSE
        Ncap = 1
        CALL SETMR(Nres,Ncap)
        Ptime = TRIA(Tmin,Tmode,Tmax,Istream)
        CALL SCHED(Lent,Nevt2,Ptime)
      ENDIF
      RETURN
```

```c
/* C CODE */

void cevent ( Lent, Nevt, sim )

smint *Lent, *Nevt;
simstr *sim;
{
      smint Lent2, Job, Ncap;
      float Otime, Ptime;
      static smint Istream=10, Nevt1=1, Nevt2=2, Nque=1, Nres=1, Numc=1, Inc=1;
      static float Emean=4.4, Tmin=3.2, Tmode=4.2, Tmax=5.2;
/*    Check for event type */
      if(*Nevt==1)
         {
/*    Event 1: Arrival to system.
      Create next arrival and schedule. */

         create(&Lent2);
         Otime=expo(&Emean,&Istream);
         sched(&Lent2,&Nevt1,&Otime);

/*    Check for machine availability and place in
      queue or schedule process delay. */

         if(mr(&Nres)>0)
           insert(Lent,&Nque);
         else
           {
           setmr(&Nres,&Ncap);
           Ptime=tria(&Tmin,&Tmode,&Tmax,&Istream);
           sched(Lent,&Nevt2,&Ptime);
           }
}
```

Figure 10-15. Event 1 for Sample Problem 10.1

Having scheduled the next arrival, the arriving entity then must check system status based on machine availability. In the block model this status check was performed automatically by the QUEUE-SEIZE combination, based on the availability of the resource Machine. However, in discrete-event code there is no mechanism for seizing or releasing a resource, which in SIMAN changes the corresponding value of the system variable NR. Therefore, we must provide a status variable that we can change to indicate the busy or idle status of a resource. We could use a SIMAN global variable or define a local variable in our EVENT routine. Instead, we define a resource with an initial capacity of 0, which indicates an idle state for our machine. When the machine becomes busy, we will change the resource capacity to 1 to indicate a busy state. Thus, if we want to define a SIMAN dstat that will give us the machine utilization, it will be a dstat on the system variable MR, rather than the variable NR.

With this logic the arriving entity checks system status based on the value of the function MR(Nres). If the machine is busy, this value will exceed 0, and the arriving entity with record location Lent will be placed in queue Nque with the routine INSERT. In this case there is no other action required, and control is returned to SIMAN, which determines the next action. If the variable MR(Nres) does not exceed 0, it will equal 0, meaning that the machine is idle. In this case the machine will be set to busy by calling routine SETMR, which causes the resource Nres to be set to a value of Ncap or 1. This occurrence equates to the entity's seizing the machine. The delay for processing, Ptime, is then obtained by taking a sample from a triangular distribution. This processing time becomes our offset when we schedule the entity with record location Lent to call event Nevt2, event 2, Ptime time units later by using routine SCHED. In our block model, this action was performed by the DELAY block. No other action is required for an arriving entity, event 1.

An end-of-service event, event 2, requires that the entity be counted and disposed of. And, if there are no waiting entities in the queue, the machine resource must be set to idle. If there are one or more entities in the queue, the first entity is removed, the process time delay is computed, and an end-of-service event is scheduled for this new entity. Figure 10-16 shows the code for this routine EVENT. The counter Numc is increased by the value Inc by calling routine COUNT, which corresponds to the COUNT block in our block model. The calling entity with record location Lent is then disposed of by using routine DISPOSE.

```
c   FORTRAN CODE
c
c **** EVENT 2" End of process delay
c
c       Count entity that has completed process
c       delay and dispose
c
    2 CALL COUNT(Numc,Inc)
      CALL DISPOSE(Lent)
c
c       Check queue for waiting entity
c         If there is a waiting entity, remove and
c           schedule process delay
c         Otherwise set machine to idle
c
```

```
              IF(NQ(Nque).GT.0) THEN
                Job = LFR(Nque)
                CALL REMOVE(Job,Nque)
                Ptime = TRIA(Tmin,Tmode,Tmax,Istream)
                CALL SCHED(Job,Nevt2,Ptime)
              ELSE
                Ncap = 0
                CALL SETMR(Nres,Ncap)
              ENDIF
              RETURN
              END
```

```
/* C CODE */

  else if(*Nevt==2)
    {
    /* EVENT 2: End of process delay.
       Count entity that has completed process
       delay and dispose. */

    count(&Numc,&Inc);
    dispos(Lent);
/* Check queue for waiting entity.
   If there is a waiting entity, remove and schedule process delay,
   Otherwise set machine to idle. */

    if(nq(&Nque)>0)
      {
      Job=lfr(&Nque);
      cremov(&Job,&Nque);
      Ptime=tria(&Tmin,&Tmode,&Tmax,&Istream);
      sched(&Job,&Nevt2,&Ptime);
      }
    else
      Ncap=0;
      setmr(&Nres,&Ncap);
    }
  }
```

Figure 10-16. Event 2 for Sample Problem 10.1

We then use the function NQ to check the system status by determining if there are waiting entities or jobs in queue Nque. If there are waiting entities, this value will exceed 0. We determine the record location (Job) of the first entity in the queue by using function LFR. We then remove this entity from queue Nque by using routine REMOVE. The process time, Ptime, is determined, and the entity with record location Job is scheduled as an event 2, Ptime time units later. If there are no entities in queue Nque, we change the machine status to idle by using routine SETMR to set the resource capacity to 0. In our block model these actions were performed automatically when the entity passed through the RELEASE block.

The completed discrete-event code required for our model can replace the six blocks in the process mode model. Thus, the Model Frame for the resulting discrete-event model contains only the BEGIN and END statements. Although there are no block statements in it, the Model Frame is required by SIMAN if the LINKER is to create a valid program file.

The corresponding experiment listing, given in Figure 10-17, is almost identical to that for Sample Problem 3.1. The single difference is that the Machine resource is initialized to 0 rather than defaulting to 1. This change is required because we are using the capacity of the resource to determine the status of the machine; a capacity of 0 indicates that the machine is to start in an idle state. The results from this simulation are identical to those obtained from Sample Problem 3.1.

```
BEGIN;
;              SAMPLE PROBLEM 10.1
PROJECT,      Sample Problem 10.1,SM;
QUEUES:       Buffer;
RESOURCES:    Machine,0;
COUNTERS:     JobsDone;
REPLICATE,    1, 0, 480;
END;
```

Figure 10-17. Experiment Listing for Sample Problem 10.1

5.2 Sample Problem 10.2: Reading from a Data File and User-Menu System

Assume a single-machine that processes jobs from a schedule file containing the time of arrival, the processing time, and the due date for each job. A sample portion of this job file ("JobList.Dat") is shown in Figure 10-18. Each line in this data file represents a single job. The first column contains the job arrival time, the second column the processing time, and the third column the due date of the job. Note that the jobs are ordered according to arrival time.

```
21.719100      7.339924      52.559330
33.059430      7.074973      85.305690
43.026400     10.875570     101.483700
52.075680      9.520042      78.905470
56.795830      8.989587     110.965200
70.086960      9.450091     144.105000
     .              .              .
     .              .              .
     .              .              .
739.739100      8.191173     813.107800
742.311500      5.279302     770.514200
742.522000      5.579456     753.890400
743.832500     11.759270     793.105900
748.083900     10.320550     828.850600
758.359700     12.600750     820.754300
761.544100      9.603547     814.860800
769.784500      9.530102     835.147800
     .              .              .
     .              .              .
     .              .              .
```

Figure 10-18. Sample Schedule File for Sample Problem 10.2

As long as there is no contention in the system, jobs are processed in a first-come-first-served order. However, when there is more than one job waiting to be processed, the user is to determine which job is serviced next. We are interested in collecting statistics on number of jobs in the system, machine utilizations, job flowtime, and job lateness. Although this problem can be developed with the SIMAN READ and WRITE blocks presented in Chapter 8, we will develop the model with SIMAN event code to read in the jobs and to provide the interaction with the user. The remaining portion of the model will be developed by using the SIMAN process mode.

The experiment listing for this sample problem is given in Figure 10-19. We have defined three attributes to carry the information on arrival, process, and due date time for each job. There is a single global variable, NumJobs, which is used to track the number of jobs currently in the system. The DSTATS and TALLIES elements include the information that we want to collect during the simulation run. Note that this listing contains no REPLICATE element. The simulation is designed to terminate when all jobs in the schedule file have been processed.

```
BEGIN;
PROJECT,        Sample Problem 10.2,SM;
ATTRIBUTES:     InTime:
                PTime:
                DueDate;
VARIABLES:      NumJobs;
RESOURCES:      Machine;
QUEUES:         MachQ:
                HoldQ;
TALLIES:        Flowtime:
                Lateness;
DSTATS:         NR(Machine),Machine Busy:
                NQ(HoldQ),Number in Queue:
                NumJobs,Number in System;
END;
```

Figure 10-19. Experiment Listing for Sample Problem 10.2

The model listing for our sample problem is given in Figure 10-20. Note that there is no CREATE block because all arriving jobs are entered from the user code. The first queue, HoldQ, is a detached queue, which provides a waiting area for all jobs entering the system. Jobs are placed in the second queue, MachQ, only when the machine resource is available. Therefore, the dstat on the number of waiting jobs references the first queue, HoldQ. Also notice that, after a job has finished processing at the DELAY block, it enters an EVENT block that calls event 2. This event determines the next action, if any, to be taken. After the machine resource is released, the job information is tallied, the number of jobs in the system (NumJobs) is decreased, and the entity is disposed of.

```
BEGIN;
;          Sample Problem 10.2
           QUEUE,HoldQ:DETACH;                  Job queue
           QUEUE,MachQ;                         wait for machine
           SEIZE:Machine;                       get machine
           DELAY:PTime;                         process time
           EVENT:2;                             check queue status
           RELEASE:Machine;                     release machine
           TALLY:Flowtime,INT(InTime);          tally flowtime
```

```
          TALLY:Lateness,TNOW-DueDate;          tally lateness
          ASSIGN:NumJobs=NumJobs-1:DISPOSE;      decrease job count
  END;
```

Figure 10-20. Model Listing for Sample Problem 10.2

Two routines must be developed for this problem. The first routine, PRIME, is shown in Figure 10-21. It opens the file called "JobList.Dat" and reads the information on the first job into the local array Att, which has been dimensioned to 3. It then creates a new record location for the entity and assigns the values in array Att to the three attributes of the newly created entity. Finally, it schedules the entity to call event 1 at the time of the first job arrival. For the first job the offset time to call event 1 is simply the arrival time of the first job, contained in Att(1). Control is then returned to the SIMAN processor.

```
c   FORTRAN CODE
c
      SUBROUTINE PRIME
      REAL Att(3)
      INTEGER Job,Nevt1
      DATA Nevt1/1/
c
c        open job data file, read in first job &
c        schedule arrival
c
      OPEN(11,file='JobList.Dat',status='OLD',Form='FORMATTED')
      CALL CREATE(Job)
      READ(11,*) Att
      CALL ASSIGN(Job,Att)
      CALL SCHED(Job,Nevt1,Att(1))
      RETURN
      END
```

```
/* C CODE */

#include "simlib.h"
#include <stdio.h>
#include <stdlib.h>
#include <ctype.h>

FILE *fp;

void cprime ( sim )

simstr~sim;
{
      smint Job;
      float Att[3];

      static smint Nevt1=1;

/*    Open job data file, read in first job &
      schedule arrival. */

      fp=fopen("joblist.dat","r");
      fscanf (fp,"%f %f %f",&Att[0],&Att[1],&Att[2]);
      create(&Job);
      assign(&Job,Att);
      sched(&Job,&Nevt1,&Att[0]);
}
```

Figure 10-21. Routine PRIME for Sample Problem 10.2

Because there is no CREATE block in the model, the entity scheduled by PRIME is the first entity to enter the simulation model. The EVENT routine code for event 1, which this entity will call, is given in Figure 10-22. The common block "SIM" has been included so that we can access the current simulation time, TNOW. Arriving entities, event 1, are directed to statement number 1 where the variable NumJobs is increased by 1 with routine SETV. Because there is only one global variable in the model, the index is obvious. However, if you include multiple variables, you must be sure to reference the correct index. The function V(1) returns the current value of NumJobs. We then determine what to do with the arriving entity. If the resource Machine is busy (i.e., NR(1) greater than 0), the entity is placed in HoldQ, queue number 2, by using routine INSERT. If the machine is idle, the entity is scheduled to enter queue 2, MachQ, by using routine QUEUE. When it enters queue MachQ, it immediately seizes the machine resource and enters the delay block for its processing time.

```
c   FORTRAN CODE
c
    SUBROUTINE EVENT(Lent,Nevt)
    common/sim/d(50),dl(50),s(50),sl(50),x(50),
   1          dtnow,tnow,tfin,j,numrep
    REAL Att(3),Vinc
    INTEGER Nevt,Nque1,Nque2,Job,Nevt1,Nvar,Nres,i,Nxtjob
    DATA Nque1,Nque2,Nevt1,Nvar,Nres / 1,2,1,1,1 /
    DATA Vinc / 1.0 /
c
    GO TO(1,2),Nevt
c
c      Event 1 : arrival to system-increase job count
c      variable, enter current arrival into system and
c      schedule next arrival
c
  1 CALL SETV(Nvar,V(Nvar)+Vinc)
    IF(NR(Nres).GT.0) THEN
      CALL INSERT(Lent,Nque2)
    ELSE
      CALL QUEUE(Lent,Nque1)
    ENDIF
    READ(11,*,ERR=999) Att
    CALL CREATE(Job)
    CALL ASSIGN(Job,Att)
    CALL SCHED(Job,Nevt1,Att(1)-TNOW)
999 RETURN
```

```
*/ C CODE */

void cevent ( Lent, Nevt, sim )

smint *Lent, *Nevt;
simstr *sim;
{
     smint i, j, idx, Job, NxtJob, at.end;

     float Att[3], Result;

     char chh[50];

     static smint Nque1=1, Nque2=2, Nevt1=1, Nvar=1, Nres=1;

     static float Vinc=1.0;

     if(*Nevt==1)
       {
       /* Event 1: arrival to system-increase job count
           variable, enter current arrival into system &
           schedule next arrival. */
       Result=v(&Nvar)+Vinc;
```

```
            setv(&Nvar,&Result);
    if(nr(&Nres)>0)
      insert(Lent,&Nque2);
    else
      queue(Lent,&Nque1);
    at.end=fscanf (fp,"%f %f %f",&Att[0],&Att[1],&Att[2]);
    if(at.end != EOF)
      {
      create(&Job);
      assign(&Job,Att);
      Result=Att[0]-(sim->tnow);
      sched(&Job,&Nevt1,&Result);
      }
    }
```

Figure 10-22. Event 1 for Sample Problem 10.2

After the new arrival enters the appropriate queue, the information for the next job arrival is read from the "JobList.Dat" file. A new entity record location is created, and the job values are assigned to its attributes. This entity is then scheduled to call event 1. Note that the offset time represents the time offset between the current time, TNOW, and the scheduled arrival time, Att(1). If this file is exhausted, no new entity is created, and the simulation terminates when all jobs have been processed. Recall that the Experiment Frame does not contain a REPLICATE element.

The above logic for event 1 results in the newly arrived job being sent directly to the MachQ if the Machine resource is idle; otherwise, it is sent to the HoldQ. Entities placed in the HoldQ can only be removed and sent to the Machine resource when event 2 is called. Remember that event 2 is called from the process model immediately after a job has finished processing but before the Machine resource is released.

The code for event 2 is shown in Figure 10-23. There are three possible conditions. The first occurs when the HoldQ, NQ(2), is empty. Under this condition, control is returned to the model where the resource is released, the job is tallied, the variable NumJobs is reduced, and the entity is disposed of. When this sequence occurs, the system is empty of all jobs. Time advances to the time of the next arrival, or, if there are no further arrivals, the simulation replication terminates.

```
c   FORTRAN CODE
c
c
c      Event 2 : end of service - check number in queue
c        if queue empty, return
c        if one in queue, schedule for service
c        if greater than one, write out job information and
c          request input from user
c
      2 IF(NQ(Nque2).LE.0) THEN
          RETURN
        ELSEIF(NQ(Nque2).EQ.1) THEN
c
c          only one job, schedule
c
```

```
            Job=LFR(Nque2)
            CALL COPY(Job,Att)
            CALL REMOVE(JOB,Nque2)
            WRITE(*',(//6x,A,F12.2/6x,A/6x,A/6x,A)')
     1      '*** Job Scheduled at Time :',TNOW,
     2      '        Arrival  Process  Due',
     3      '          Time     Time    Date  Slack',
     4      '        -------  -------   ----  -----'
            WRITE(*,'(12x,4F11.2)') Att,Att(3)-Att(2)-TNOW
            CALL QUEUE(Job,Nque1)
          ELSE
c
c         write out job status list
c
            WRITE(*,'(//6x,A,F12.2//6x,A/6x,A/6x,A)')
     1      '*** Simulation Time "',TNOW,
     2      'Queue  Arrival  Process  Due',
     3      ' Rank    Time     Time    Date  Slack',
     4      '-----  -------  -------   ----  -----
            DO 22 i=1,NQ(Nque2)
              IF(i.EQ.1) THEN
                Job=LFR(Nque2)
              ELSE
                Job=LSUCC(Job)
              ENDIF
              CALL COPY(Job,Att)
     22       WRITE(*,'(6x,I4,2x,4F11.2)') i,Att,Att(3)-Att(2)-TNOW
c
c         request choice from user
c
     23       WRITE(*,'(/10x,A)') 'Select next job by Queue Rank :'
            READ(*,*) Nxtjob
            IF(Nxtjob.EQ.0) THEN
              Nxtjob=1
            ELSEIF(Nxtjob.GT.NQ(Nque2)) THEN
              WRITE(*,'(10x,A)') '*** Invalid Queue Rank ***'
              GO TO 23
            ENDIF
            Job=LRANK(Nxtjob,Nque2)
            CALL REMOVE(Job,Nque2)
            CALL QUEUE(Job,Nque1)
          ENDIF
          RETURN
          END
```

```
/* C CODE */

  else if(*Nevt==2)
    {
    /* Event 2: end of service - check number in queue
       if queue empty, return
       if one in queue, schedule for service
       if greater than one, write out job information and
         request input from user */
    if(nq(&Nque2)<=0)
      ;
    else if(nq(&Nque2)==1)
      {
      /* only one job, schedule */
      Job=lfr(&Nque2);
      copy(&Job,Att);
      cremov(&Job,&Nque2);
      printf("\n\n\n*** Job Scheduled at Time' %9.2f",sim->tnow);
      printf("n\t\tArrival\t\tProcess\t\tDue");
      printf("n\t\t Time\t\t Time\t\tDate\t\tSlack");
      printf("n\t\t------\t\t-------\t\t----\t\t-----");
      printf("\n\t\t%6.2f\t\t%6.2f\t\t%6.2f\t\t%6.2f",Att[0],
        Att[1],Att[2], Att[2]-Att[1]-(sim->tnow));
```

```
            queue(&Job,&Nque1);
            }
        else
            {
            printf("n\n\n*** Simulation Time" %9.2f",sim->tnow);
            printf("n\nQueue\t\tArrival\t\tProcess\t\tDue");
            printf("nRank\t\t Time\t\t Time\t\tDate\t\tSlack");
            printf("n\t\t-------\t\t-------\t\t----\t\t-----");
            for (i=1; i<=nq(&Nque2); ++i)
                {
                if(i==1)
                    Job=lfr(&Nque2);
                else
                    Job=lsucc(&Job);
                copy(&Job,Att);
                printf("\n%d\t\t%6.2f\t\t%6.2f\t\t%6.2f\t\t%6.2f",
                    i,Att[0],Att[1],Att[2],Att[2]-Att[1]-(sim->tnow));
                }
            chh[idx=0]='\0';
            printf("n\n\tSelect next job by Queue Rank :");
            scanf("%s", chh);
            i=0;
            while(chh[i])
                {
                if (isdigit((int)chh[i])||(chh[i]=='\.')) /*
                    valid numerical input*/
                    ++i;
                else
                    {
                    printf("\n\n*** Input Error ***");
                    printf("\nchh[%d] = %c\n", i, chh[i]);
                    for(j=i; chh[j]; j++)
                        chh[j]=chh[j+1];
                    }
                }
            sscanf(chh, "%d", &NxtJob);
            if(NxtJob==0)
                NxtJob=1;
            Job=lrank(&NxtJob,&Nque2);
            cremov(&Job,&Nque2);
            queue(&Job,&Nque1);
            }
        }
    }
```

Figure 10-23. Event 2 for Sample Problem 10.2

The second condition occurs when there is exactly one job waiting in HoldQ. Because there is no decision, that job is removed from the HoldQ and sent to the MachQ where it seizes the released resource and delays for the processing time. Note that the user code for this condition includes write statements to the screen to inform the user that an entity has been scheduled.

The third and final condition covers situations in which there are two or more jobs awaiting service in HoldQ. In this case the user code writes a header to the screen and then performs the DO loop through statement number 22 for the number of entities in the HoldQ. The record location for the first entity in the queue is retrieved by using function LFR, and the remaining record locations are retrieved by using function LSUCC to find the successor to the previous entity. An alternative approach involves using function LRANK to find the record locations by referencing their ranks in the queue. After the record locations of these entities have been obtained, their attributes are copied by using routine COPY, to the local array Att. These attributes are then written to the screen. Note that the last number written to the screen represents the job slack time. This slack time is negative if the job is already late and positive if it can still be completed before its due date. The attributes for each job are referenced by the rank in the queue, and the user is asked to decide which job is next sent to the machine. An error check is provided in case a selected job rank is not on the list. If the error check were not included and the user were to enter an invalid number, SIMAN would terminate with an error message when the user code attempted to remove the job from the queue. Having identified a valid job, the record location is retrieved by using function LRANK, the job is removed from HoldQ by using routine REMOVE, and the job is sent to MachQ by using routine QUEUE. The calling entity is then returned to the block model.

Note that the entity entering the EVENT block in the model and calling the routine enters the user routine with its record location stored in local variable Lent. The value of this variable has not been changed because the entity will return to the block model where it will release the resource Machine, be tallied, and be disposed of. All record locations used to access information about entities in HoldQ are stored in a second local variable, Job.

The routine WRAPUP, given in Figure 10-24, closes the data file at the end of the replication before the SIMAN processor is exited.

```
c    FORTRAN CODE
c
     SUBROUTINE WRAPUP
c
     CALL CLOSE(11)
     RETURN
     END
```

```
/* C CODE */
void cwrap ( sim )
simstr *sim;
{
    fclose(fp);
}
```

Figure 10-24. Routine WRAPUP for Sample Problem 10.2

An example of the screen interaction is shown in Figure 10-25. The first activity indicates a job scheduled to start processing at time 593.76 without interaction from the user. Because the job arrival time, 590.52, precedes the scheduled time, the job is waiting in the HoldQ until the previous job is completed. The same is true for the next job, which is scheduled at time 601.29. Between the time when this job is scheduled (time 601.29) and the time when it is completed (time 625.34) three jobs enter the system. These jobs are displayed to the user at time 625.34, and in this case the user selects the job with the least slack, job 1. Upon completion at time 636.12, one additional job has entered the system, and again three jobs are listed. If we assume a least-slack decision rule, job 3 is selected.

```
*** Job Scheduled at Time : 593.76
        Arrival  Process    Due
         Time     Time     Date    Slack
        -------  -------    ----    -----
         590.52    7.54   631.80   30.51

*** Job Scheduled at Time : 601.29

        Arrival  Process    Due
         Time     Time     Date    Slack
        -------  -------    ----    -----
         594.13    7.39   627.96   19.27

*** Simulation Time : 625.34

Queue  Arrival  Process    Due
Rank    Time     Time     Date    Slack
-----  -------  -------    ----    -----
  1     615.18   10.78   650.91   14.79
  2     619.37    7.41   684.13   51.38
  3     624.24    8.52   668.48   34.63

   Select next job by Queue Rank : 1

*** Simulation Time : 636.12

Queue  Arrival  Process    Due
Rank    Time     Time     Date    Slack
-----  -------  -------    ----    -----
  1     619.37    7.41   684.13  40.60
  2     624.24    8.52   668.48  23.84
  3     626.96    9.45   651.22   5.65

   Select next job by Queue Rank : 3
```

Figure 10-25. Screen Interaction for Sample Problem 10.2

The Summary Report for this sample problem is given in Figure 10-26. The "JobList.Dat" file contains 100 jobs, and the user selects jobs by employing the least-slack decision rule.

```
Project:  Sample Problem 10.2
Analyst:  SM
Replication ended at time:  1142.18
                          TALLY VARIABLES
```

Identifier	Average	Variation	Minimum	Maximum	Observations
Flowtime	32.848	.79662	7.0750	113.14	100
Lateness	−15.08	−1.685	−72.94	30.91	100

```
                       DISCRETE-CHANGE VARIABLES
```

Identifier	Average	Variation	Minimum	Maximum	Final Value
Machine Busy	.78943	.51647	.00000	1.0000	.00000
Number in Queue	2.0864	1.1228	.00000	9.0000	.00000
Number in System	2.8759	.88876	.00000	10.000	.00000

Figure 10-26. Summary Report for Sample Problem 10.2

5.3 Sample Problem 10-3: A User-Defined Decision Rule

Consider a machining center that has 10 identical numerically controlled, NC, machines. This machining center services four different job types, each having a different processing time and requiring different tooling. A specific job type can only be processed on a given machine if it has the proper tooling. Jobs entering the system are directed to the machine that has the proper tooling and that can complete the job at the earliest time. If all machines are busy, ties are broken according to a defined machine priority, which differs for each job type. If more than one machine is available, ties are broken by sending the job to the machine that has been idle the longest.

The model listing for this sample problem is given in Figure 10-27. Arriving jobs are created and sent to the ASSIGN block where the job type, the processing time, and the machine are assigned. The processing time is generated from a normal distribution with parameters defined in global variables in the Experiment Frame. The machine assignment is made in a user function. The jobs then enter the queue for the assigned machine, seize the machine, undergo processing, get tallied, and leave the system.

```
BEGIN;
;        Sample Problem 10.3
         CREATE:EXPO(2):MARK(InTime);                      create arrivals
         ASSIGN:JobType=
            DISC(.2,1, .45,2, .75,3, 1,4):                 !set job type
          PTime=
            NORM(Mean(JobType),StD(JobType)):              !process time
          M=UF(JobType);                                   machine center
         QUEUE,M;                                          wait for machine
         SEIZE:Machine(M);                                 get machine
         DELAY:PTime;                                      process time
         RELEASE:Machine(M);                               release machine
         TALLY:JobType,INT(InTime);                        individual flowtimes
         TALLY:All FlowTimes,INT(InTime):DISPOSE;          all flowtimes
END;
```

Figure 10-27. Model Listing for Sample Problem 10.3

The experiment listing for this sample problem is given in Figure 10-28. The three attributes used in the model are defined, followed by the 10 numbered queues and the 10 identical machines. The VARIABLES element defines the means and standard deviations used to generate the processing times for the four different job types. The PARAMETERS element is used to identify which machines have the proper tooling for a given job type. The sequence in which these machine numbers are listed defines the priority if a tie exists. The last entry in each parameter set contains a negative number so that we know when the sequence of machines has ended. For example, a job type 3 can be processed on machine 8, 5, 4, 7, 3, or 10. If there is a tie, the first machine has the highest priority. There are four numbered tallies to provide the individual flowtimes by job type and a fifth tally to provide a flowtime for all jobs.

```
BEGIN;
PROJECT,     Sample Problem 10.3,SM;
ATTRIBUTES:  InTime:
             JobType:
             PTime;
QUEUES:      10;
RESOURCES:   Machine(10);
```

```
VARIABLES:   Mean(4),15,20,23,17:
             StD(4),3,4,4,3;
PARAMETERS:  1, 1,2,3,5,7,-1:
             2, 1,2,6,8,9,-1:
             3, 8,5,4,7,3,10,-1:
             4, 6,9,4,10,5,2,1,-1;
TALLIES:     1,Type 1 Flowtime:
             2,Type 2 Flowtime:
             3,Type 3 Flowtime:
             4,Type 4 Flowtime:
             All Flowtimes;
DSTATS:      NR(1),Machine 1:
             NR(2),Machine 2:
             NR(3),Machine 3:
             NR(4),Machine 4:
             NR(5),Machine 5:
             NR(6),Machine 6:
             NR(7),Machine 7:
             NR(8),Machine 8:
             NR(9),Machine 9:
             NR(10),Machine 10:
             NQ(1),Queue 1:
             NQ(2),Queue 2:
             NQ(3),Queue 3:
             NQ(4),Queue 4:
             NQ(5),Queue 5:
             NQ(6),Queue 6:
             NQ(7),Queue 7:
             NQ(8),Queue 8:
             NQ(9),Queue 9:
             NQ(10),Queue 10;
REPLICATE,   1,0,10000;
END;
```

Figure 10-28. Experiment Listing for Sample Problem 10.3

The user function that assigns a machine to each job is shown in Figure 10-29. Remember that this function is called when a new job enters the system in the first ASSIGN block in the model. The argument in the model call is the job type, which corresponds to the second argument, JobT, in the function statement. We define a local variable, Time, in which we maintain the time, by machine, at which the last scheduled job completes processing. We also include the named common block "sim" because we need the current simulation time, TNOW, in our function.

```
c   FORTRAN CODE
c
    FUNCTION UF(Lent,Jobt)
    common/sim/d(50),dl(50),s(50),sl(50),x(50),
  1          dtnow,tnow,tfin,j,numrep
    INTEGER Lent,Jobt,Index,Mbest,MachNum,Num3
    REAL Time(10)
    DATA Num3 / 3 /
c
c       assign Index into parameter set, get first machine number,
c       save min time and best machine number
c
    Index=1
    MachNum=P(JobT,Index)
 88 Tmin=Time(MachNum)
    Mbest=MachNum
c
c       increase machine Index, get new machine number
```

```
c
  99 Index=Index+1
     MachNum=P(JobT,Index)
     IF(MachNum.LE.0) THEN
c
c        negative number, at end of sequence, assign selected machine,
c        update time array to time job will be completed
c
         UF=Mbest
         Time(Mbest)=MAX(Time(Mbest),TNOW)+A(Lent,Num3b)
         RETURN
     ELSEIF(Tmin.LE.Time(MachNum)) THEN
c
c        new machine time not better than existing choice
c
         GO TO 99
     ELSE
c
c        new machine better, update choice at statement 88
c
         GO TO 88
     ENDIF
     RETURN
     END
```

```
/* C CODE */
#include "simlib.h"
#include "stdlib.h"
#include "stdio.h"
float cuf ( Lent, JobT, sim )
smint *Lent, *JobT;
simstr *sim;
{
smint Index=1, MachNum=0, Mbest=0, ithree=3;
float Tmin=3.2e21, Temp=0.0;
static float Time[10]={0,0,0,0,0,0,0,0,0,0};
MachNum=(int)p(JobT,&Index);
while(MachNum>0)
    {
    if(Tmin>Time[MachNum])
        {
        Tmin=Time[MachNum];
        Mbest=MachNum;
        }
    Index=Index+1;
    MachNum=(int)p(JobT,&Index);
    }
Temp=(float)Mbest;
Time[Mbest]=Max(Time[Mbest],sim->tnow)+a(Lent,&ithree);
return(Temp);
}
```

Figure 10-29. User Function For Sample Problem 10.3

When this function is called, we first initialize the index, Index, of our parameter set to 1. Then we retrieve the first machine number from the parameter set defined by the job type, JobT. We save the machine number and value from array Time as our current best. The code starting at statement number 99 increases the index of the parameter set and retrieves the next machine number. The subsequent IF statement determines the proper action to be taken. The first check determines whether all machines have been examined. If the machine number is negative, the selected machine, Mbest, is assigned to be returned as the function value, and the array time is updated. The intrinsic function MAX is used to determine whether the machine is busy or idle. If the value currently in the Time array is less than the current simulation time, TNOW, the machine is idle, and we want to add the processing time to the value of TNOW. Otherwise, the machine is busy, and we want to add the processing time to the value in the time array. Remember that we assigned the processing time to the third attribute, Ptime, in the model. After updating this array, we return control to the model where the selected machine is assigned to the entity's attribute M.

If the machine number is positive, the next check determines if the current best time is better than the time for the new machine. If the new machine time is not better, control is sent to statement number 99, which increases the index and starts the checks for the next machine. If the new time is better, control is sent to statement number 88, which saves the new best time and machine and then proceeds as before.

The Summary Report for this model is given in Figure 10-30. The results indicate that our system is quite busy with all machines being fairly evenly utilized.

```
Project:   Sample Problem 10.3
Analyst:   SM
Replication ended at time:   10000.0
```

TALLY VARIABLES

Identifier	Average	Variation	Minimum	Maximum	Observations
Type 1 Flowtime	39.136	.62079	8.0498	130.79	972
Type 2 Flowtime	43.020	.52385	6.5219	142.74	1271
Type 3 Flowtime	46.379	.50810	13.509	133.14	1472
Type 4 Flowtime	39.771	.60935	9.6219	131.93	1225
All Flowtimes	42.451	.56053	6.5219	142.74	4940

DISCRETE-CHANGE VARIABLES

Identifier	Average	Variation	Minimum	Maximum	Final Value
Machine 1	.95956	.20529	.00000	1.0000	1.0000
Machine 2	.96016	.20370	.00000	1.0000	1.0000
Machine 3	.94325	.24529	.00000	1.0000	1.0000
Machine 4	.94667	.23736	.00000	1.0000	1.0000
Machine 5	.95767	.21024	.00000	1.0000	1.0000
Machine 6	.94531	.24052	.00000	1.0000	1.0000
Machine 7	.94430	.24288	.00000	1.0000	1.0000
Machine 8	.96330	.19518	.00000	1.0000	1.0000
Machine 9	.94482	.24167	.00000	1.0000	1.0000
Machine 10	.94388	.24384	.00000	1.0000	1.0000
Queue 1	1.3283	1.0838	.00000	8.0000	2.0000
Queue 2	1.3064	1.0769	.00000	7.0000	3.0000
Queue 3	1.0988	1.1238	.00000	6.0000	2.0000
Queue 4	1.0709	1.1919	.00000	6.0000	2.0000
Queue 5	1.2103	1.1077	.00000	7.0000	2.0000
Queue 6	1.1280	1.1138	.00000	7.0000	2.0000
Queue 7	1.1335	1.1610	.00000	7.0000	3.0000
Queue 8	1.0422	1.0486	.00000	5.0000	2.0000
Queue 9	1.1879	1.1260	.00000	8.0000	2.0000
Queue 10	1.0547	1.1234	.00000	5.0000	3.0000

Figure 10-30. Summary Report for Sample Problem 10.3

This model can easily be expanded to include more machines and/or job types. Increasing the number of machines requires no changes to the Model Frame. In the Experiment Frame, however, the number of queues and resources must be increased, the new machines must be added to the appropriate parameter sets, and the size of the Time array in user code must be increased. Dstats could also be added. Increasing the number of part types requires adding processing time values, parameter sets, and tallies in the Experiment Frame and changing the discrete distribution in the Model Frame.

Exercise 10.1

Take the simple three-workstation flow line presented in Chapter 6, Sample Problem 6.1, and replace the block model with a discrete-event model.

Exercise 10.2

Modify the highway toll booth problem, Sample Problem 8.2, such that the decision as to which booth a vehicle uses is determined in a user function.

Exercise 10.3

Modify the production scheduling system problem, Sample Problem 8.4, by replacing the READ and WRITE blocks with user code.

Exercise 10.4

Modify the bank teller problem, Sample Problem 8.3, such that the reneging customer is determined in user code by examining the TellerQ once every minute.

Exercise 10.5

Modify the job shop problem, Sample Problem 8.1, by preloading one job on every machine at the start of the simulation. (Hint: Not all jobs go on every machine type.)

Exercise 10.6

Write a KEYHIT routine for Sample Problem 6.1 that displays the current Summary Report during the simulation whenever the "s" key is pressed.

Exercise 10.7

Modify Sample Problem 3.3 by adding user code to output utilizations by shift to the screen and run for 10 shifts. (Hint: You'll need to clear the dstats for these statistics every 480 time units after they are sent to the screen.)

Exercise 10.8

Modify Sample Problem 6.2 to include a stopping rule based on the quality of the estimate for flowtime. Use a warm-up time of 20,000 time units, and then accumulate 30 batches of 10,000 time units. After the 30 batches have been accumulated, calculate the half-width of the confidence interval (assume 95% confidence level) and, if that value is within 5% of the current mean, terminate the simulation.

Otherwise, continue the simulation for another batch of 10,000 time units. (Hint: You'll need two tallies — one containing the information on the current batch and another containing the information on the batch means. Also, remember to default the replication time on the REPLICATE element to infinity.)

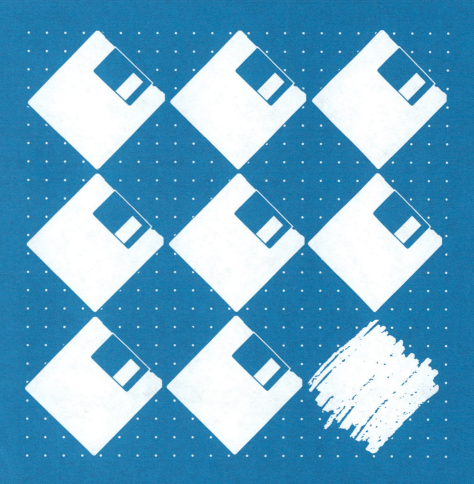

CHAPTER 11

CHAPTER 11

Continuous and Combined Models

1. Introduction

In previous chapters, we discussed only models with discrete-change-state variables, i.e., models in which the state of the system changed at isolated points in time called *events*. For example, the number of parts waiting in a machine's queue is a discrete variable that changes when either a new job arrives at the queue or an old job departs from the queue. Although models limited to discrete-change-state variables are sufficient for simulating a large class of systems (e.g., most discrete production processes), some systems require that we include one or more continuously changing variables. For example, in the model of a soaking pit furnace, the temperature of an ingot changes continuously as it cools when removed from the furnace. It may be necessary within our model to represent the ingot's temperature by a continuous-change-state variable. In this chapter we discuss concepts related to modeling continuously changing variables.

2. Continuous Modeling

We base our discussion of continuous modeling on an example involving the pumping of crude oil from a tanker into a storage tank. The oil is fed from the storage tank to a refinery for processing into gasoline, as shown in Figure 11-1. Note that two valves control the flow of oil into and out of this tank. Our task is to model the level of crude oil in this storage tank.

Figure 11-2 shows a discrete-variable response for the number of tankers waiting to unload oil over time. Note that the response remains fixed between the times corresponding to a tanker's arrival at and departure from the queue. We refer to models containing only discrete-change-response variables such as this as purely *discrete* models.

Now consider the corresponding plot shown in Figure 11-3, depicting the level of oil in the storage tank. Note that in this case changes in the state variable (i.e., the level of oil in the tank) occur continuously over time, not just at discrete events. When a tanker is unloading, the crude level in the tank continuously increases at a rate equal to the difference between the inward flow and the outward flow. When no tanker is unloading, the crude level continuously decreases at a rate

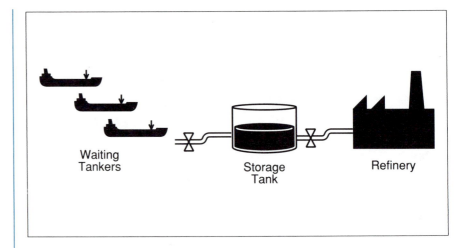

Figure 11-1. Schematic of Refinery System

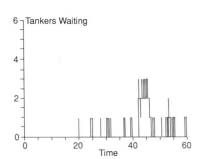

Figure 11-2. Number of
Tankers Waiting

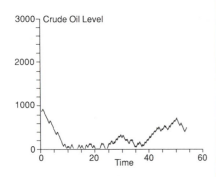

Figure 11-3. Crude Oil Level in the
Storage Tank

equal to the outward flow. We refer to models containing only continuously changing response variables as purely *continuous* models.

In some cases, our model contains response variables of each type. In the tanker example, we have both types of response variables present: a discrete-change-response variable for the queueing of tankers, and a continuous-change-response variable for the level of oil in the storage tank. We refer to models containing both types of response variables as *combined* models.

Note that the adjectives discrete, continuous, and combined as applied to simulation describe only the system's response variables. These terms in no way describe the nature of the independent variable, time.

Continuous and combined models typically reflect the continuous nature of the process being modeled. In particular, many physical processes, e.g., thermal, chemical, or electrical, are described by continuously changing response variables. In some cases, however, it is convenient to approximate a discretely changing variable by using a continuously changing variable. For example, in modeling the earth's population, the current population is actually a discrete-change variable that changes at event times corresponding to births and deaths; however, for convenience we may prefer to model population as a continuous-change variable.

2.1 Describing Systems in Terms of States and Rates

Continuous models are based on a defined relationship for the state of the system over time. Although the state is normally defined by a vector of values, we begin our discussion by looking at a simple case in which the state is defined by a single variable. If we denote the state of the system by the variable x, then our objective is to find a function f such that

$$x = f(t, \lambda, x_0)$$

where

    t denotes time,
    λ denotes parameters of the model, and
    x_0 denotes the initial conditions of the system.

This relationship is known as a *state equation*. Although our objective is to develop state equations that define the system's state explicitly over time in terms of its initial conditions and parameters, rarely are we able to do so. In most cases, we don't have enough insight into the complex interactions within the system's components for direct development of system state equations. Sometimes, however, we can develop a relationship for the rate of change of x with respect to time, called the *derivative* of x.

The derivative of x is denoted by dx/dt, commonly abbreviated by $\dot{x}$. Relationships involving derivatives of derivatives are also possible. We denote the nth-order derivative of x by $d^n x/dt^n$, or simply x with n dots above. Hence, $d^2 x/dt^2$ and $\ddot{x}$ each denote the second-order derivative of x.

A relationship involving one or more derivatives is known as a *differential equation*. The *order* of the equation is the highest order derivative in the equation. The differential equation is said to be *ordinary* if all of its derivatives relate to the same variable (typically time). A *partial* differential equation involves derivatives that relate to two or more variables (e.g., time and space). We restrict our attention to ordinary differential equations.

Therefore, each state variable can be defined directly by means of the state equation or indirectly by means of a differential equation. Although we prefer direct representation, we often must settle for an indirect representation that uses a differential equation.

Consider the problem of modeling an ingot's temperature as it cools to 70 degrees Fahrenheit after being removed from a soaking pit furnace at 2000 degrees Fahrenheit. In this case, the state variable is the ingot's temperature, denoted by Temp. According to Newton's law, the temperature of a body drops at a rate proportional to the difference between the temperature of the body and the temperature of the outside medium. Therefore, the rate of change of temperature, d/dt (Temp), is proportional to the difference between the temperatures of the ingot and ambient air, Temp −70. Because the temperature of the ingot is decreasing, we denote the constant of proportionality as (−k). The differential equation describing this process is

$$d/dt \ (\text{Temp}) = -k(\text{Temp}-70)$$

The development of the differential equation is not an end in itself; it is an intermediate step in obtaining the state equation. We want to be able to "solve" the differential equation to yield the state equation. For example, it can be shown that

$$\text{Temp} = 70 + 1930e^{-kt}$$

is a solution to the previous differential equation, and is therefore the state equation that we seek. In this example, the constant k is called the cooling constant and is a physical property of the ingot.

In general, a continuous or combined model contains one or more state or differential equations that define response variables in the system. If the model contains all state equations (our preference), then the state of the system is known for all time in terms of the model's initial conditions and parameters. We are rarely so fortunate, however, because, unlike the ingot example, the system of equations typically includes at least one differential equation that cannot be solved mathematically.

Except for certain special classes of problems, differential equations are very difficult to solve mathematically. For example, the seemingly simple equation

$$dx/dt = x^2 + t^2$$

has no easy solution and therefore must be left in the form of a differential equation. In these instances, we can use numerical techniques to obtain approximate numerical values for the state of the system over time.

2.2 Converting an Nth-Order Equation to N First-Order Equations

Numerical methods for integrating differential equations generally apply only to systems of first-order differential equations. In most of the continuous systems that we encounter, the differential equations are first-order equations; when they are not, we can mathematically convert any n^{th}-order ordinary differential equation to a system of n first-order equations by introducing n-1 new state variables. Consider, for example, the following second-order differential equation.

$$\ddot{x} = a\dot{x} + bx + c$$

By setting $\dot{x}$ equal to the new state variable, w, we can replace the previous equation with the following equivalent set of first-order equations.

$$\dot{x} = w$$
$$\dot{w} = aw + bx + c$$

Note that, because w is equal to $\dot{x}$, $\dot{w}$ is the second derivative of x with respect to t. By recursively applying this same idea to an nth-order equation, we can reduce it to a system of n first-order equations.

By replacing higher order derivatives as outlined above, all differential equations are reduced to expressions for the rate of change of the states in the system. For this reason sets of n first-order differential equations are often referred to as *rate* equations.

2.3 Solving Rate Equations by Euler's Method

Euler's method provides a simple numerical technique for solving a first-order ordinary differential equation. This method is based on the first two terms of the Taylor series expansion of x about t

$$x(t + \Delta t) = x(t) + \dot{x}(t)\, \Delta t + O(\Delta t^2)$$

where $O(\Delta t^2)$ indicates terms of order Δt^2 and higher. Given the value of x and x at time t, this equation allows us to approximate x at time $t + \Delta t$, as illustrated in Figure 11-4. Given the fact that we also know the initial state value, x_0, at time t_0, we can repeatedly apply the above relationship to determine x in tabular form at discrete times $t_0 + \Delta t$, $t_0 + 2\Delta t$, etc. The quantity Δt is called the *step size*, and the unknown quantity $O(\Delta t^2)$ in the Taylor series expansion is the *local truncation error* or *single step error* for the procedure.

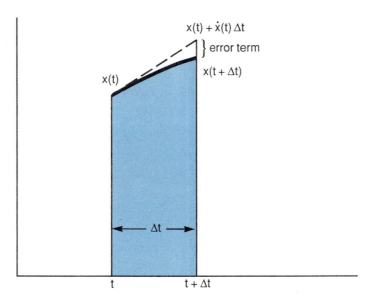

Figure 11-4. Illustration of Euler's Method

In general, we can improve our accuracy with this method at the expense of increased computation by reducing the step size Δt. Euler's method is not very effective in practice, however, because the step size needed to obtain the desired accuracy is often too small. Nevertheless, Euler's method is important because its basic idea provides the basis for a set of improved algorithms. These algorithms are collectively called Runge-Kutta methods.

2.4 Solving Rate Equations by Runge-Kutta Methods

All of the Runge-Kutta methods for solving differential equations have algorithms of the general form

$$x(t + \Delta t) = x(t) + \Phi \, \Delta t$$

where Φ is an estimate of dx/dt in the interval Δt. The estimate is computed as a weighted sum of two or more function evaluations for x within the interval Δt.

Although the Runge-Kutta methods use only first-order derivative evaluations, they can be shown to be equivalent in accuracy to higher-order Taylor-series expansions. The number of derivative terms in the Taylor-series expansion to which an algorithm is accurately equivalent is defined as the order of the method. For example, Euler's method is a first-order Runge-Kutta method, because its accuracy is equal to the first-order term in the Taylor-series expansion. The several higher-order Runge-Kutta methods developed can achieve more accuracy than Euler's method for the same number of function evaluations.

In contrast to Euler's method, Runge-Kutta methods often use a variable step size. The step size is automatically adjusted at each integration step such that a larger size is used in relatively flat portions of the response function, and a smaller size is used in other portions of the function, as required. In this way consistent accuracy can be maintained throughout the integration process. Variable step methods typically require that you specify a minimum and maximum allowable step size and a maximum single step error. The step size is adjusted between the minimum and maximum values as required to maintain the accuracy within the maximum single step error.

3. SIMAN's Continuous Framework

In SIMAN, we model continuous systems by coding the state and differential equations in FORTRAN or C. These equations, which define the model's state variables, are inserted into subroutine STATE, which is called by SIMAN during the simulation's execution. This subroutine computes the current value of either the state variable or the corresponding derivative value for each state variable in the model and returns these values to SIMAN. For those variables defined by derivatives, SIMAN automatically numerically integrates the derivative values by using a Runge-Kutta method, which yields values for the state variables over time.

3.1 Defining State and Rate Equations in Subroutine STATE

In writing subroutine STATE, you must assign a consecutive number, beginning with 1, to each continuous state variable in the model. For state variables defined directly by a state equation, the current value for the state variable is returned in $S(n)$, where n is the state variable's number. For those state variables indirectly defined by differential equations, the current value of the derivative is returned in $D(n)$, where n is the state variable's number. In the latter case SIMAN uses the current value of $D(n)$ to compute a new value for $S(n)$.

When numbering state variables, you first number all of the state variables defined by differential equations and then all of the state variables defined by state equations. For example, if you have two state variables defined by differential equations and one state variable defined by a state equation, the state variables defined by the differential equations should be numbered first. Subroutine STATE should return D(1) and D(2) (corresponding to the derivatives of the first two state variables defined by differential equations) and S(3) (corresponding to the value of the third state variable).

To illustrate this numbering convention, consider the following system of equations.

$$dw/dt = w + t$$
$$dz/dt = w + z$$
$$q = w + wz$$

In this case we have three state variables named w, z, and q. Both w and z are indirectly defined by differential equations, which SIMAN must integrate to obtain the current values of w and z. The variable q is directly defined by a state equation. Since the state variables defined by differential equations must be numbered first, we denote w as State Variable 1, z as State Variable 2, and q as State Variable 3. The coding for computing the current values of D(1), D(2), and S(3) is shown below.

```
D(1) - S(1) + TNOW
D(2) = S(1) + S(2)
S(3) = S(1) + S(1) * S(2)
```

Although the numbering of state variables must follow the convention discussed above, the ordering of equations within subroutine STATE is arbitrary, except for the ordering imposed by equation-coupling. For example, the three equations shown above can be arranged in any order without affecting the values returned for D(1), D(2), and S(3). However, the equations

```
D(1) = S(1)**2 + TNOW**2
D(2) = D(1) + S(1) + S(2)
```

must be entered as shown, because the current value D(1) is required to compute D(2). In some cases, the equations in a model can be coupled simultaneously. For example,

```
D(1) = S(1) + D(2)
D(2) = S(2)*D(1)
```

are simultaneously coupled because D(1) depends on D(2) and D(2) depends on D(1). In this case, you can either accept the small error introduced by using the previous value for D in one of the equations, or you can use an algorithm like the Gauss-Sidel method to solve the equations simultaneously.

In addition to the D and S arrays, SIMAN provides an array named X, which is in the SIM COMMON block and can be used for storing coefficients or flags associated with a differential equation. Although user-defined variables can be used for this same purpose, the X array is convenient because it provides an efficient method for passing data between the discrete and continuous components of the model. We will employ the X array in conjunction with the S and D arrays for defining differential equations in several sample problems throughout this chapter.

To illustrate coding subroutine STATE, we use a simple problem involving the population dynamics associated with the growth and decay of an infectious disease. The disease occurs within a single population, and recovery from the disease results in immunity. The population consists of three groups: (1) those who are well but susceptible, (2) those who are sick, and (3) those who are cured and therefore immune. Although the system's state actually changes discretely, we will assume that we can approximate the system with continuous-change variables describing the size of each group. We will use the state variables named Well, Sick, and Cured to denote each group's current size.

This system's dynamics are governed by the following system of differential equations.

$$d/dt \text{ (Well)} = -\text{RateInf} \times \text{Well} \times \text{Sick}$$
$$d/dt \text{ (Sick)} = \text{RateInf} \times \text{Well} \times \text{Sick}$$
$$-\text{RateRec} \times \text{Sick}$$
$$d/dt \text{ (Cured)} = \text{RateRec} \times \text{Sick}$$

In this example, RateInf is the rate of infection and RateRec is the rate of recovery. We will assume that RateInf is 0.001 and RateRec is 0.07.

Because all three state variables are defined by differential equations, they can be numbered in any order. We will assign numbers 1, 2, and 3 to the three state variables Well, Sick, and Cured, respectively. Subroutine STATE must be coded to return the rate of change of each of these state variables in D(1), D(2), and D(3). We will employ X(1) and X(2) to store the rate of infection and rate of recovery, respectively.

The FORTRAN code for the STATE subroutine is shown in Figure 11-5. The first statement in the subroutine is the FORTRAN COMMON block named SIM; this COMMON statement must always be included in FORTRAN versions of subroutine STATE as a mechanism for passing the values of S, D, and X between SIMAN and the subroutine. This statement should be entered exactly as shown.

```
        SUBROUTINE STATE
        COMMON/SIM/D(50),DL(50),S(50),SL(50),X(50),DTNOW,
    1            TNOW,TFIN,J,NRUN
        EQUIVALENCE (WellRate,D(1)) , (SickRate,D(2)) ,
          (CuredRate,D(3))
        EQUIVALENCE (Well,S(1)) , (Sick,S(2)), (Cured,S(3))
        EQUIVALENCE (RateInf,X(1)) , (RateRec,X(2))
c
        WellRate =-RateInf * Well * Sick
        SickRate = RateInf * Well * Sick -RateRec * Sick
        CuredRate = RateRec * Sick
```

```
c
      RETURN
      END
```

Figure 11-5. Sample FORTRAN Listing of Subroutine STATE

The EQUIVALENCE statements are used to associate the names WellRate, SickRate, and CuredRate with the variables D(1), D(2), and D(3); the names Well, Sick, and Cured, with the variables S(1), S(2), and S(3); and the names RateInf and RateRec with the variables X(1) and X(2). These statements allow these more descriptive names to be used in place of D, S, and X when coding the equations. Alternatively, the equations can be coded in terms of D, S, and X, in which case the EQUIVALENCE statements are omitted.

The declarative statements are followed by the code for the three differential equations. Each statement computes the state variable's rate of change and assigns this value to the appropriate derivative variable. These derivatives are passed to SIMAN as D(1), D(2), and D(3). SIMAN uses these values to compute the current values of S(1), S(2), and S(3), which are passed back to subroutine STATE on the next call.

3.2 Initializing S, D, and X Variables: The INITIALIZE Element

When developing a continuous model, the S, D, and X variables must be set to their initial conditions at the start of the simulation. For example, in the infectious disease model discussed above, we need to initialize the values of S(1), S(2), S(3), X(1), and X(2). This can be done by including the INITIALIZE element in the experiment.

The INITIALIZE element contains repeating groups of variable assignments of the form Variable = Value, where Variable can be any SIMAN-assignable variable (including S, D, and X). Value can be any constant numerical value. The format for this element is summarized below.

    INITIALIZE: Variable = Value :
               repeats;

Any variables not explicitly initialized are automatically assigned a default initial value of 0.

An example of the INITIALIZE element for the infectious disease model, which assigns initial values to S(1), S(2), X(1), and X(2), is shown below.

```
INITIALIZE: S(1) = 1000 :
            S(2) =   10 :
            X(1) = .001 :
            X(2) =   .07 ;
```

In this case, S(3) will assume a default initial value of 0.

3.3 Using the Continuous Time-Advance Mechanism

When the model contains one or more continuous-change variables, SIMAN must advance time to ensure that the continuous variables are appropriately updated. In this case, SIMAN can simply jump between events, as is done in a purely discrete model. This is particularly true when there exist differential equations that must be integrated within specified accuracy limits.

When there are one or more differential equations in a model, SIMAN modifies its time-advance mechanism to make a series of small steps between any normal, discrete events. SIMAN controls the size of each small step, denoted by the variable DTFUL, based on the parameters specified. Figure 11-6 shows the relationship between the variables SIMAN uses to perform each advance. At the beginning of each new step, all S and D values are copied into the arrays SL and DL, where the appended L denotes the last values. The value of TNOW at the beginning of the step is stored in TLAST. During a full step size of DTFUL (i.e., TNEW-TLAST), subroutine STATE is called by SIMAN six times with a varying partial step size given by the variable DTNOW. The current value of time within the step, given by TNOW, is equal to TLAST plus DTNOW. The D and S values returned by subroutine STATE are variables corresponding to the current partial step at time TNOW.

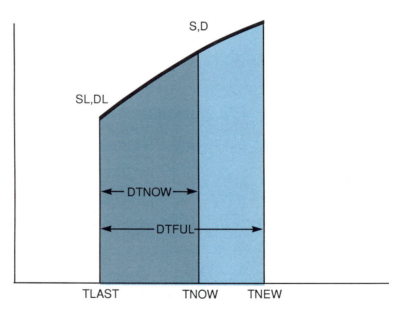

Figure 11-6. The Relationship of Variables Defining a Step

Based on the six separate calls to subroutine STATE, SIMAN computes an estimate for each S at time TNEW, an estimate of the error for this step, and a new proposed size for the next step. The procedure implemented in SIMAN for performing these calculations is the Runge-Kutta-Felhberg 4-5 procedure [Fehlberg,

1969]. If the estimated integration error is within user-specified limits, the full step is accepted, TLAST is moved to TNEW, the new S and D values are copied into the arrays SL and DL, and the process repeats for the new proposed step size. If the error is too large, SIMAN repeats the step but uses a starting time of TLAST and a smaller step size.

If subroutine STATE contains state equations but no differential equations, SIMAN employs a simpler time-advance strategy. In this case there is no integration required; therefore, a fixed-step time-advance procedure is used to call subroutine STATE once per step with DTNOW equal to DTFUL. No adjustment is made to the size of the step, because no integration error is computed.

Although the Runge-Kutta algorithm embedded in SIMAN is normally used to integrate any differential equation in the model, it is also possible to code different integration algorithms directly into subroutine STATE. To do so, you convert the differential equations into difference equations by using the variables SL, DL, and DTNOW. For example, you can replace the equation

```
D(2) = S(1) * S(2)
```

with the difference equation

```
S(2) = SL(2) + (S(1) * S(2)) *DTNOW
```

In the first case SIMAN computes the value of S(2) by using the embedded Runge-Kutta algorithm. In the second, the new value of S(2) is set to the value of S(2) at time TLAST plus the rate of change of S(2) multiplied by the time step, DTNOW. Note that this approach corresponds to the previously discussed Euler method.

3.4 Specifying Integration and Time-Advance Parameters: The CONTINUOUS Element

When a model contains continuous-change variables, you include the CONTINUOUS element in the experiment to specify the integration and time-advance parameters to be used by SIMAN. The format for this element is summarized below.

CONTINUOUS, NumDifEq, NumStateEq, MinStep, MaxStep,
                    Interval, AbsError,
                    RelError, Severity;

The first two operands on this element specify the number of differential and state equations included in subroutine STATE. If NumDifEq is greater than 0, then differential equations are included within the model. In this case, SIMAN integrates $D(n)$ over time to yield $S(n)$ by calling subroutine STATE six times per step. This integration is performed at each step for n between 1 and NumDifEq. If NumDifEq is 0, but NumStateEq is greater than 0, then subroutine STATE is called once per step to update the values of the state variables, but no integration is performed. If both NumDifEq and NumStateEq are 0, subroutine STATE is never called.

The MinStep and MaxStep values restrict the size used by SIMAN to values within this range. Although SIMAN may adjust the current step size based on the integration accuracy of the previous step, the new, full step size is always a value between MinStep and MaxStep. If no differential equations are included in the model (NumDifEq = 0), then a fixed step size is used, and DTFUL is set to MaxStep.

The Interval operand defines the time interval between successive points for recording the value of continuous-change variables. This value, also referred to as the *communication interval*, is used by the CSTATS element discussed in the next section.

The next two operands specify the per-step integration accuracy to be used by the Runge-Kutta algorithm embedded in SIMAN. The AbsError and RelError operands are the absolute and relative single-step integration errors. The total integration error allowed per step for state variable number n, denoted as TotError(n), is given by

$$TotError(n) = AbsError + RelError * S(n).$$

SIMAN automatically adjusts the full step size, DTFUL, to maintain the estimated integration error per step within this limit for each differential equation.

Although the values of AbsError and RelError control the single-step error, we are typically more interested in the accumulated or propagated errors across all steps in the simulation. Developing precise measures of this error is difficult; however, the accumulated error can be estimated roughly as one order of magnitude larger than the single-step error. Although this rule doesn't hold in all cases, it provides a basis for selecting values for AbsError and RelError.

The last operand on this element, Severity, determines what action should be taken by SIMAN if the requested single-step accuracy cannot be achieved without using a step size smaller than that specified by MinStep. The options are 1) F-end the run with an error message, 2) W-print a warning message and continue, or 3) N-continue the run without any message.

3.5 Recording Statistics on Continuous-Change Variables: The CSTATS Element

When our model includes continuous-change variables, we often want to use the Output Processor to record statistics about the variables or to save a history of the variable in an output file for plotting or further analysis. The CSTATS element provides this capability. The format for the CSTATS element is shown below.

CSTATS: Number, Variable, Name, OutFile:
       repeats;

The CSTATS element resembles the DSTATS element (used for discrete-change variables) in format and function. The primary difference in format is that, in the CSTATS element, the Variable operand must be specified as a continuous-change variable, i.e., as S(n) or D(n), where n is the number of the state variable. In terms of function, there are two differences in the CSTATS element.

The first difference involves the point in time when the values are observed. With discrete-change variables, a complete and accurate picture of the variables is obtained by examining the value following each event that updates the value. With continuous-change variables, however, we can't get an accurate picture because the variables are continuously changing over time. Instead, the variables are repeatedly observed as specified in the operand Interval, which is specified on the CONTINUOUS element.

The other functional difference is that the CSTATS element employs a trapezoidal integration rule in lieu of the DSTATS rectangular integration rule. Although the rectangular rule works well for discrete-change variables, the trapezoidal rule has much greater accuracy with continuous-change variables.

An example of the CSTATS element is shown below.

```
CSTATS: S(1),Heating Temp.,"Temp.dat":
        D(3),Cooling Rate;
```

The first CSTAT variable, S(1), is named Heating Temp; a history of this variable's values for time is saved in the output file named Temp.dat. The second CSTAT variable, D(3), is named Cooling Rate; only summary statistics are maintained for this variable.

4. Sample Problem 11.1: Cedar Bog Lake

To illustrate the concepts related to continuous modeling, we present a model developed by Williams [1971] of Cedar Bog Lake, Minnesota. As depicted in Figure 11-7, the model is a continuous representation of the lake ecosystem and consists of three species, solar energy input, organic lake-bottom sediment formation, and loss to the environment. These six components are measured by energy content in calories per square centimeters. The three species — plants, herbivores (fish that eat plants), and carnivores (fish that eat fish) — are denoted by the variables X_p, X_h, and X_c, respectively. The solar energy input, organic sediment formation, and environmental loss are denoted by the variables X_s, X_o, and X_e, respectively. The equations defining the interactions among these variables are

$$X_s = 95.9 \, (1.0 + 0.635 \, \sin(2\pi t))$$
$$\dot{X}_p = X_s - 4.03 \, X_p$$
$$\dot{X}_h = .48 \, X_p - 17.87 \, X_h$$
$$\dot{X}_c = 4.85 \, X_h - 4.65 \, X_c$$
$$\dot{X}_o = 2.55 \, X_p + 6.12 \, X_h + 1.95 \, X_c$$
$$\dot{X}_e = 1.00 \, X_p + 6.90 \, X_h + 2.70 \, X_c$$

where t is the time measured in radians, with a year equal to 2 π radians. These equations (which were developed by Williams) represent such processes as species predation, plant photosynthesis, etc.

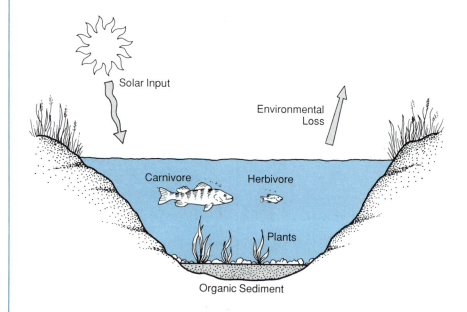

Figure 11-7. Schematic Diagram of Cedar Bog Lake Ecosystem: Sample Problem 11.1

We will simulate this system for a two-year period and record time-persistent statistics about the six state variables. We will use the following initial conditions for the model.

$$t = 0, X_p = .83, X_h = .003, X_c = .0001, X_o = 0.0, X_e = 0.0$$

The model for this system consists of five differential equations and one state equation (solar input). Although the solar input can be directly computed at each call to the subroutine by the state equation, the derivatives for the other five variables must be integrated by SIMAN to obtain the corresponding values for the state over time. Recall that SIMAN requires that continuous variables defined by differential equations be numbered before those defined by state equations. Therefore, we assign the numbers 1 through 5 to the state and derivative values representing plants, herbivores, carnivores, organic formation, and environmental loss, respectively, and we assign the number 6 to the state value representing solar input.

The FORTRAN coding for subroutine STATE for this example is shown in Figure 11-8. It contains the SIM COMMON block that passes the values of the S and D arrays between SIMAN and the subroutine. The DATA statement assigns the value 3.14159 to the variable PI for use in the state equation defining the solar input to the system. Note that the calculation of solar input, S(6), must precede the calculation of D(1) (plant growth rate) because S(6) appears to the right of the equation for D(1). (Readability of the routine would be improved by using EQUIVALENCE statements to assign symbolic names to the elements of the S and D arrays, e.g., Solar in place of S(6); we have decided not to use this approach, however, because we want to highlight the use of the S and D arrays in SIMAN.)

```
      SUBROUTINE STATE
      COMMON/SIM/D(50),DL(50),S(50),SL(50),X(50),
     1           DTNOW,TNOW,TFIN,J,NRUN
C
C     Sample Problem 11.1
C
      DATA pi / 3.14159/
      S(6) = 95.9 * (1. + .635 * SIN( 2. * pi * TNOW))
      D(1) = S(6)-4.03 * S(1)
      D(2) = .48 * S(1)-17.87 * S(2)
      D(3) = 4.85 * S(2)-4.65 * S(3)
      D(4) = 2.55 * S(1) + 6.12 * S(2) + 1.95 * S(3)
      D(5) = S(1¥ + 6.9 * S(2) + 2.7 * S(3)
      RETURN
      END
```

Figure 11-8. Subroutine STATE for Sample Problem 11.1

The experiment listing for this example is shown in Figure 11-9. The CONTINUOUS element specifies that the model uses five differential equations (numbered 1 through 5) and one state equation (numbered 6). Because five differential equations are specified for the model, SIMAN automatically integrates the values of D(1) through D(5) over time to obtain the values for S(1) through S(5). The minimum and maximum step sizes for the integration are 0.0025 and 0.025, respectively. An interval of 0.025 is specified, meaning that the values of the CSTAT variables are recorded every 0.025 years. The accuracy specification is defaulted, and a warning message is printed if the accuracy cannot be achieved with a minimum step size of 0.0025 years.

```
BEGIN;

PROJECT,         Sample Problem 11.1, SM;

CONTINUOUS,      5, 1, .0025, .025, .025;

CSTATS"          S(1), Plants, "P.dat":
                 S(2), Herbivores, "H.dat":
                 S(3), Carnivores, "C.dat":
                 S(4), Organic, "O.dat":
                 S(5), Environment, "E.dat":
                 S(6), Solar, "S.dat";

INITIALIZE:      S(1) = .83: S(2) = .003: S(3) = .0001:
                     S(4) = 0: S(5) = 0;

REPLICATE,       1, 0, 2;

END;
```

Figure 11-9. Experiment Listing for Sample Problem 11.1

The CSTATS element specifies that time-persistent statistics be recorded about the six continuous state variables. Specifying output files for the six CSTAT variables causes a history of the times for each variable to be saved in the indicated files. This history makes it possible to use the Output Processor to plot the response for these variables over time.

The INITIALIZE element establishes initial values for all continuous-state variables except solar input. The initial value for solar input is established based on TNOW at the first call by SIMAN to subroutine STATE. To execute this model, subroutine STATE must be linked to the SIMAN program by using the FORTRAN link facility on the host computer. In addition, the compiled experiment file (.e) must be linked to produce a program file (.p) by using the SIMAN-provided LINKER program. The exact procedures for accomplishing these steps are system-dependent.

The results for the simulation are summarized by the SIMAN Summary Report shown in Figure 11-10. A plot of the level of herbivores and carnivores over the two-year period, which was generated by using the Output Processor from the saved CSTATS files, is shown in Figure 11-11.

```
Project: Sample Problem 11.1
Analyst:  SM
Replication ended at time:  2.0
                    CONTINUOUS-CHANGE VARIABLES
Identifier   Average   Variation    Minimum      Maximum    Final Value
Plants       21.798    .30825      .83000        31.884     16.924
Herbivores    .57339   .33659      .30000E-02     .84387     .43784
Carnivores    .53701   .40285      .10000E-03     .79025     .56767
Organic      57.660    .64272      .00000        120.29     120.29
Environment  25.857    .64921      .00000         54.412     54.412
Solar        95.900    .44763      .00000        156.80     95.899
```

Figure 11-10. Summary Report for Sample Problem 11.1

As evident in this example, the difficult part of continuous modeling consists of developing the system's underlying equations. In this example, all of the hard work has been done by Williams, who developed the six equations describing the system. Once the equations are developed, it is relatively simple to code them into subroutine STATE by using the conventions required by SIMAN.

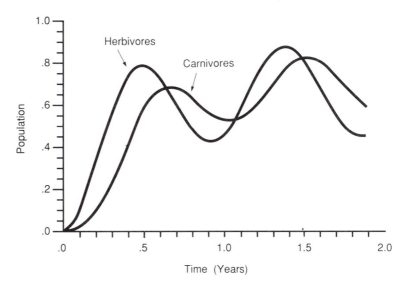

Figure 11-11. Plot of System Response for Cedar Bog Lake.

Combined discrete-continuous models incorporate both discrete- and con-
tinuous- change variables within the same model. For example, the crude oil storage tank system discussed earlier contains both discrete- and continuous-change-
response variables. The queueing of tankers at the unloading dock is a discrete
process, and the changing level of crude oil in the storage tank is a continuous
process. To model such systems, we must be able represent both the discrete and
continuous components of the system, as well as the interactions that may occur
among those components.

5.1 Modeling Combined Discrete-Continuous Interactions
Two fundamental interactions can occur between the discrete and the continuous
components of a combined model. The first are changes made to the continuous
component from the discrete component; examples include the instantaneous
increase in electrical energy because of power station activation and the instantaneous decrease in species population in a lake because of chemical spraying. This
type of interaction superimposes a discrete jump on a continuous-change-
response variable. The second type of interaction consists of changes made to the
discrete component from the continuous component. Examples include the completion of a chemical process when the concentration level of a reactant reaches a
prescribed value and the shutdown of a refinery when the level of crude oil falls
below a prescribed level.

    To model interactions involving changes to a continuous variable from the
discrete component, you change the value of the continuous variable from within
the discrete model by assigning a value to the state or derivative variable (S or D)

at an ASSIGN block. For example, we can represent a discrete increase of 10 units in the continuous-state variable, S(3), by the ASSIGN Block shown on the left.

This type of interaction requires no new modeling concepts; it simply combines ideas previously discussed. The ASSIGN block can be used anywhere within a discrete model to make this type of change in the value of a continuous variable.

5.2 Detecting State Events: The DETECT Block

Interactions involving changes made to the discrete component from the continuous component of a model are not as easy to model. In these cases, we must monitor the continuous variables and then take some action that causes a discrete change to occur when a continuous variable crosses a prescribed threshold. A *state event* provides the mechanism whereby the continuous component interacts with the discrete component.

State events are triggered by crossing a state or derivative variable against a *threshold* value. SIMAN automatically detects this crossing within a user-specified tolerance. When a crossing occurs within a continuous time advance, SIMAN automatically adjusts the full step size, DTFUL, so that the step ends with the specified state variable beyond the threshold but within some specified tolerance.

The direction of the targeted crossing can be specified as *positive*, *negative*, or *either*. If specified as positive or negative, then only crossings in the specified direction trigger an event, and all other crossings are ignored. If specified as either, then all crossings trigger a state event, regardless of the crossing's direction. An example of positive and negative crossings are shown in Figure 11-12.

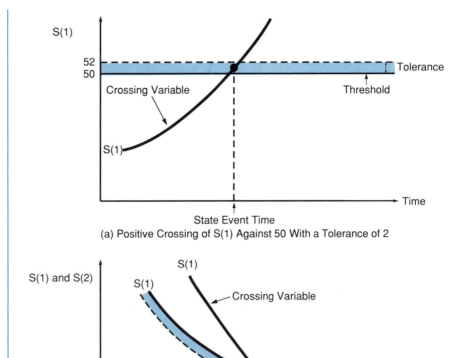

(a) Positive Crossing of S(1) Against 50 With a Tolerance of 2

(b) Negative Crossing of S(1) Against S(2) With a Tolerance of 2

Figure 11-12. Illustration of Positive and Negative Crossings

The value specified for the minimum step size, MinStep, in the CONTINU-OUS element sometimes prevents SIMAN from isolating the time of the crossing for a state event within the specified tolerance. This problem is illustrated in Figure 11-13, where the step size, DTFUL, has been reduced to MinStep, but the value of the state variable at the end of the step still exceeds the crossing's tolerance. When this occurs, the run ends with an error message, continues with a warning message, or continues with no message, as specified by the Severity operand on the CONTINUOUS element. Unless the run is terminated with an error message, the state event is processed, even if the crossing tolerance is not achieved.

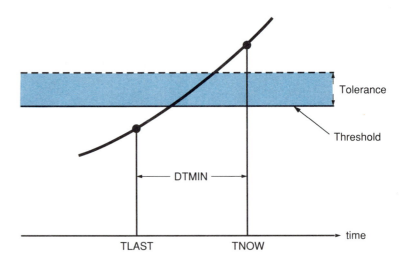

Figure 11-13. State Event Crossing Out of Tolerance

The value specified for the maximum step size, MaxStep, in the CONTINU-OUS element can also affect the processing of state events. If a large integration step is taken (because of a large value for MaxStep), a state variable can cross the threshold twice within a single step, as illustrated in Figure 11-14. Because SIMAN tests for state-event crossings between the start and end of a step, neither crossing will be detected in this case. To prevent this problem, MaxStep should be small enough to prevent the possibility of multiple crossings within a step.

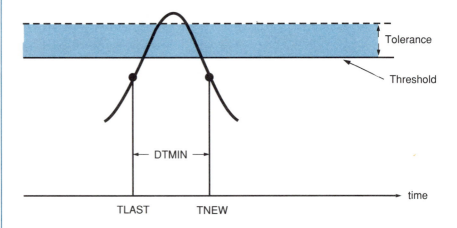

Figure 11-14. Multiple Crossings Within a Step

State events are defined in the discrete model by using the DETECT block shown below.

DETECT,BegStaID-EndStaID:Variable,Dir,Thresh,Tol;

```
DETECT,BegStaID-EndStaID
Variable,Dir,Thresh,Tol
```

The DETECT block, a type of Operation block, provides the primary interface between a model's continuous and discrete components. Whenever a DETECT block is included in the discrete component of the model, SIMAN automatically monitors the appropriate continuous variables at each continuous time advance in the simulation to detect the occurrence of a state event. The DETECT block creates and releases an entity at each occurrence of the block's defined state event. Hence, the DETECT block resembles the CREATE block, except that the creation of entities is triggered by the occurrence of state events, not by the passage of time.

The state-event condition associated with the DETECT block is prescribed by four operands: crossing variable, crossing direction, threshold value, and crossing tolerance. You specify the crossing variable as any continuous-state or derivative variable (S or D); the crossing direction as P (positive), N(negative), or E(either); the threshold value as any state or derivative variable, or as a constant; and the crossing tolerance as a constant.

When specifying the crossing variable or threshold value as S or D, you typically specify the variable's index as an integer, e.g., S(3). For developing generic submodels, SIMAN includes a special provision whereby the index can take the form M plus-or-minus k, where M is the station attribute and k denotes an integer. When entering the index of an S or D variable in this special form, you must also enter a beginning and an ending station on the block's top line segment to define a separate state event for each station number, M, within the specified range. When an entity is created at the DETECT block as the result of a state event, the associated value of M is assigned to the entity.

Entities created by the DETECT block are immediately released from the block and continue to the next block in the sequence. Entities arriving at the DETECT block from other blocks pass through the block with a time of 0.

Some examples of the DETECT block are shown on the left. The first DETECT block creates an entity whenever S(1) crosses the value 100 in the positive direction; the step size is adjusted to isolate the crossing within a tolerance of 1. The second DETECT block illustrates the use of this block in a generic-station submodel. In this case the block creates an entity with the station attribute M whenever S(M) crosses the threshold value contained in S(M+10) in the positive direction; the state-event specification is tested for M values in the range 1 through 10.

6.1 Sample Problem 11.2: A Soaking Pit Furnace

Steel ingots arrive to a soaking pit furnace in a steel plant where they are heated so that they can be rolled in the next stage of the process [Ashour and Bindingnavle, 1973]. There is space for 10 ingots in the soaking pit furnace. When an ingot arrives at the furnace, it is placed into the furnace if space is available; otherwise, it is placed in the cold ingot bank to wait for free space. The initial temperature of an arriving ingot is uniformly distributed between 400 and 500 degrees Fahrenheit. However, all ingots that are put into the cold ingot bank are assumed to have a temperature of 400 degrees on insertion into the soaking pit. A schematic diagram for this system is shown in Figure 11-15.

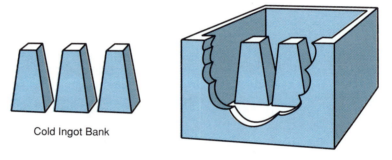

Cold Ingot Bank

Soaking Pit Furnace

Figure 11-15. Soaking Pit Furnace: Sample Problem 11.2

When an ingot is inserted into the furnace, it reduces the furnace temperature by the difference between the furnace temperature and the ingot temperature, divided by the number of ingots in the furnace. The furnace is heated according to the differential equation

$$dF/dt = .2 * (2600-F)$$

where F is the furnace temperature. The temperature change of ingots as they are heated by the furnace is described by the differential equation

$$dP_j/dt = h_j * (F-P_j)$$

where P_j is the temperature of the ingot in the jth position in the pit.

The variable h_j is the heating coefficient of the ingot in the jth position of the pit and is equal to 0.1 plus a sample from a normal distribution with a mean of 0.05 and a standard deviation of 0.01.

The ingots are heated in the furnace until the hottest ingot reaches 2,200 degrees, and then all ingots with a temperature greater than 2,000 degrees are removed.

The problem is to simulate this system for 200 hours and to record statistics on the utilization of the furnace, the heating time for the ingots, the temperature of the furnace, and the number of ingots in the cold bank. The initial furnace temperature is 1,100 degrees.

This example is modeled using the combined discrete/continuous features of SIMAN. The flow of ingots through the plant is modeled by using a Block Diagram, and the ingot and furnace temperatures are modeled as continuous state variables.

We begin the development of the continuous component of the model by making an equivalence between the problem variables and the SIMAN arrays S and D. We let S(j), for j = 1 through 10 represent the temperature of the ingot in the jth position in the pit, with a value of 0 indicating that the position is empty. The temperature of the furnace is represented by S(11), and the variable S(12) is the temperature of the hottest ingot. In addition, we let X(j) denote the heating coefficient for the ingot in position number j, with a value of 0 indicating that the position is empty.

The FORTRAN coding of subroutine STATE for this example is shown in Figure 11-16. Initially, S(12) is set to 0.0. Within the loop, the temperature of each ingot is tested against S(12), and for each case in which the temperature exceeds S(12), S(12) is reset to the ingot temperature. In this way, S(12) will be set to the maximum ingot temperature. The last statement in the loop computes the rate of change of the temperature for each ingot. Following the loop, the rate of change of the furnace temperature is computed.

```
      SUBROUTINE STATE
      COMMON/SIM/D(50),DL(50),S(50),SL(50),X(50),
     1            DTNOW,TNOW,TFIN,J,NRUN
C
C     Sample Problem 11.2
C
      S(12) = 0.0
      DO 10 i = 1,10
         IF(S(i) .GT. S(12)) S(12) ={ S(i)
         D(i) = X(i) * (S(11)-S(i))
10    CONTINUE
      D(11) = .2 * (2600.-S(11))
      RETURN
      END
```

Figure 11-16. Subroutine STATE for Sample Problem 11.2

The discrete component of the system is modeled by the block statements shown in Figure 11-17. The model consists of two segments, which will be described separately. The entities in the first model segment represent the ingots flowing through the system. The ingots are created at the CREATE block, and their arrival times to the system are marked in the attribute named TimeIn. The ingots wait in the queue named ColdBankQ for one unit of the resource named Pit. This resource is assigned a capacity of 10 and represents the 10 positions in the furnace. When a unit of Pit is seized, the index of the available position in the pit is determined by using the FINDJ block to test for X(j) equal to 0, which indicates that position number j is empty. The variable X(j) is then set to the heating coefficient for the ingot, and the variable S(j) is assigned the initial ingot temperature. A test is then made at the BRANCH block to determine if the ingot waited in the cold bank queue. If the current time, TNOW, is greater than the attribute TimeIn, the entity has waited in ColdBankQ, and the entity is branched to the block labeled ColdBank where the temperature of the ingot is reset to 400 degrees and TimeIn is re-marked with the current time. In either case, the ingots arrive at the ASSIGN block labeled Furnace where the furnace temperature, S(11), is reduced by the difference between the furnace temperature and the ingot temperature, divided by the number of ingots in the furnace. The ingot then enters the queue named SoakingPitQ where it waits to receive signal number j, where j is the position number. Following receipt of signal j, the resource Pit is released, and the heating time for the ingot is recorded.

The second model segment monitors the temperature of the ingots and releases ingots from the furnace by signaling an end of the heat-up operation, represented by the WAIT block in the first model segment. The DETECT block monitors the hottest ingot temperature, S(12), and detects crossings of this value in the positive direction against the threshold value of 2,200 degrees. When a crossing is detected, the DETECT block creates an entity that initiates a search over the index j from 1 to 10 to release all ingots having a temperature greater than 2,000 degrees. For each ingot released, a copy of the testing entity is sent to the block labeled EndSoak where a signal is sent to end the soaking for position number j, and the heating coefficient and ingot temperature for position number j are set to 0.

```
          BEGIN;

          ;           Sample Problem 11.2

                      CREATE: EXPO(2.25): MARK(TimeIn);    Create arriving ingots
                      QUEUE, ColdBankQ;                    Wait in the cold bank
                      SEIZE: Pit;                          Seize a position in the pit
                      FINDJ, 1, 10" X(J) == 0;             Find a free position
                      ASSIGN: X(J) = NORM(.05,.01) + .1:!  Assign the heating coeff.
                             S(J) = UNIF(400,500);         Assign the initial temp.
                      BRANCH,1:
                        IF, TNOW > TimeIn, ColdBank:
                        ELSE, Furnace;                     Test for ingot wait
          ColdBank    ASSIGN: S(J) = 400: MARK(TimeIn);    Reset temp to 400
          Furnace     ASSIGN: S(11) = S(11) -
                             (S(11)-S(J)) / NR(Pit);       Reduce furnace temp.
                      QUEUE, SoakingPitQ;                  Wait in soaking pit
                      WAIT: J;                             for end of soak signal
                      RELEASE: Pit;                        Release the pit position
                      TALLY:
                      HeatingTime, Int(TimeIn): DISPOSE;   Record the heating time

                      DETECT: S(12), P, 2200;              Detect max. temp. crossing
                      ASSIGN: J = 0;                       Initialize search index
          NextJ       ASSIGN: J = J + 1;                   Increment j
                      BRANCH:
                        IF, S(J) > 2000, EndSoak:
                        IF, J < 10, NextJ;                 Test for end of soak
```

```
EndSoak   SIGNAL: J;                        Signal end of soak
          ASSIGN: X(J) = 0: S(J) = 0: DISPOSE;  Reset pit variables
END;
```

Figure 11-17. Model Listing for Sample Problem 11.2

The experiment for this example is shown in Figure 11-18. Note that the CONTINUOUS element specifies that the model contain 11 differential equations and 1 state equation. The INITIALIZE element is used to initialize the furnace temperature to 1,100 degrees, and the CSTATS element is employed to record statistics on the furnace temperature.

```
BEGIN;
PROJECT,        Sample Problem 11.2, SM;
CONTINUOUS,     11, 1, .01, .1, .1;
ATTRIBUTES:     TimeIn;
INITIALIZE:     S(11) = 1100;
CSTATS:         S(11), Furnace Temp, "Temp.dat";
QUEUES:         ColdBankQ: SoakingPitQ;
RESOURCES:      Pit, 10;
DSTATS:         NQ(ColdBankQ), Cold Bank Queue, "NumCB.dat":
                NQ(SoakingPitQ), Furnace Util., "NumPit.dat";
TALLIES:        Heating Time;
REPLICATE,      1, 0, 200;
END;
```

Figure 11-18. Experiment Listing for Sample Problem 11.2

The SIMAN Summary Report for this example is shown in Figure 11-19. The report provides statistics on the number of ingots in the coldbank, the utilization of the furnace, and the furnace temperature. Plots of the number of ingots in the furnace and in the cold ingot bank and a plot of the furnace temperature over time are shown in Figure 11-20.

```
Project: Sample Problem 11.2
Analyst:  SM
Replication ended at time:  200.0

                      TALLY VARIABLES

Identifier      Average  Variation  Minimum  Maximum  Obs
Heating Time    21.923    .19155    12.026   31.341

                 DISCRETE-CHANGE VARIABLES

Identifier      Average  Variation  Minimum  Maximum    '
Cold Bank Queue  .24786   3.0141     .00000   4.0000
Furnace Util.   7.8615    .29988     .00000   10.000

                CONTINUOUS-CHANGE VARIABLES

Identifier      Average  Variation  Minimum  Maximum   ' .
Furnace Temp    2124.4    .12989    461.92   2533.0      23
```

Figure 11-19. Summary Report for Sample Problem 11.2

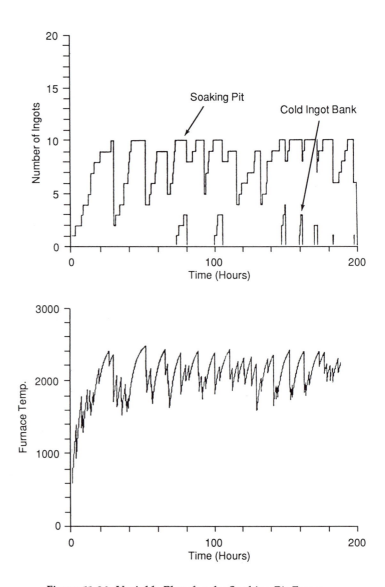

Figure 11-20. Variable Plots for the Soaking Pit Furnace

6.2 Sample Problem 11.3: A Chemical Reaction Process

A hydrogeneration reaction is conducted in four parallel reactors, with each reactor producing a different product [Hurst and Pritsker, 1973]. The reactors are supplied with hydrogen gas by a compressor through a surge tank with individual pressure valves for each reactor. The pressure valve connecting each reactor to the surge tank limits the pressure in each reactor to the minimum of the surge tank pressure and the critical pressure of 100 psia. A schematic diagram of the compressor, surge tank, pressure valves, and reactors is shown in Figure 11-21.

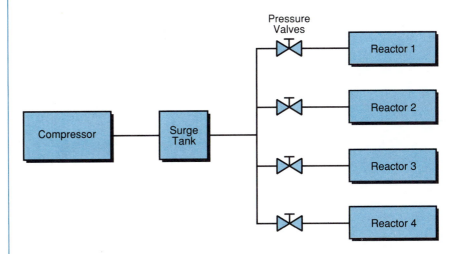

Figure 11-21. Schematic Diagram for Reactor Problem: Sample Problem 11.3

Each reactor may be started, stopped, discharged, and cleaned independently of the others. When a reactor is started, the concentration of the reactant is monitored until it reaches 10 percent of its initial value. At this time, the reactor is considered to have completed a batch, and is then turned off, discharged, cleaned, and recharged, and the process is repeated. The time to discharge a reactor is normally distributed with a mean of 1 hour and a standard deviation of 0.1 hour. The time required to clean and recharge a reactor is normally distributed with a mean of 1 hour and a standard deviation of 0.2 hour.

Before a reactor can be started, the surge tank pressure must be greater-than-or-equal-to the nominal pressure of 150 psia. In addition, when the surge tank pressure falls below the critical pressure of 100 psia, the operating policy prescribes that the last reactor started be turned off until the surge tank pressure reaches the nominal pressure of 150 psia. All other reactors that are on at that time will continue.

The reaction rate for reactor i is given as

$$P_e = \text{minimum } (P_t , 100)$$
$$dC_i/dt = -r_i s_i P_e C_i$$

where P_t is the surge tank pressure, P_e is the effective pressure to the reactor, C_i is the concentration of reactant in reactor i, r_i is the reaction constant for the product in reactor i, and s_i is a status flag equal to 1.0 if the reactor is on and to 0.0 if the reactor is off. The surge tank pressure is governed by the following equations.

$$f_i = -dC_i/dt \; v_i$$
$$dP_t/dt = k_1 - k_2 \sum_{i=1}^{4} f_i$$

where v_i is the volume of reactor i, and k_1 and k_2 are flow constants. The values for the model parameters are summarized below.

System Parameter	Model Variable	Definition	Initial Value
r_i	r(I)	Reaction constant for product in reactor i	.03466, .00866, .01155, .00770
v_i	v(I)	Volume of reactor i	10, 15, 20, 25
k_1	fk1	Compressor flow constant	500.
k_2	fk2	Reactor flow constant	120.
f_i	f(i)	Flow rate to reactor i	0.0
s_i	X(i)	Status of reactor i (1 is on, 0 is off)	0.0
C_i	S(i)	Concentrate of reactor i	.1, .4, .2, .5
dC_i/dt	D(i)	Reaction rate of reactor i	0.0
P_t	S(5)	Surge tank pressure	500
dP_t/dt	D(5)	Rate of change of surge tank pressure	0.
P_e	Peff	Effective pressure	100

The problem is to simulate the operation of the chemical reactors for 500 hours and to record statistics on the utilization of each reactor, the number of reactors on, the number of reactors halted because of low tank pressure, the concentration of reactant in each reactor, and the tank pressure. We will assume that each reactor is initially charged with a fresh batch of reactant and that the four reactors are scheduled to be turned on at half-hour intervals beginning with reactor 1 at time 0.0.

The model of this system uses a combined discrete/continuous state representation. The concentration of reactant in each reactor and the surge tank pressure are represented by continuous state variables. The remaining components of the system are modeled as discrete-change processes.

We begin the development of the continuous model by making an equivalence between the problem variables and the elements of the SIMAN arrays S and D. We denote the concentration of reactant in each of the four reactors by state variables S(1) through S(4), with the rate of reaction given by D(1) through D(4). The surge tank pressure and the rate of change of surge tank pressure are represented by S(5) and D(5), respectively.

The FORTRAN coding for subroutine STATE is shown in Figure 11-22. The parameters for the model, as defined earlier, are initialized in the DATA statements. Subroutine STATE begins by setting Peff to the minimum of the surge tank pressure and the critical pressure, and by setting SumF to 0. Within the loop, the rate of reaction is computed for each reactor, and the flow rate to each reactor is added to the variable SumF. When the loop is exited, the variable SumF equals the total flow rate from the surge tank. This value is then used to compute the rate of change of the surge tank pressure.

```
SUBROUTINE STATE
c
c     Sample Problem 11.3
c
      DIMENSION r(4), v(4), f(4)
      COMMON/SIM/D(50),DL(50),S(50),SL(50),X(50),
     1 DTNOW,TNOW,TFIN,J,NRUN
      DATA r(1),r(2),r(3),r(4) / .03466, .00866, .01155, .00770 /
      DATA v(1),v(2),v(3),v(4) / 10.0, 15.0, 20.0, 25.0 /
      DATA fk1,fk2 / 500., 120. /
      Peff = AMIN1(S(5), 100.)
      SumF = 0.0
      DO 10 i = 1,4
         D(i) { -r(i) * S(i) * X(i) * Peff
         f(i) { -D(i) * v(i)
  10  SumF = SumF + f(i)
      D(5) = fk1-fk2 * SumF
      RETURN
      END
```

Figure 11-22. Subroutine STATE for Sample Problem 11.3

The discrete processes of the system are modeled by the model statements shown in Figure 11-23. Entities representing batches enter the model at the STATION block via the ARRIVALS element in the experiment. Each entity proceeds through the two ASSIGN blocks where S(M) is set to the initial concentration for reactor number M and where S(M+5) is set to the threshold value defining the end of the reaction for reactor number M. Following the ASSIGN blocks, each entity proceeds to the BRANCH block where the surge tank pressure is tested to determine if the reactor can be started. If the pressure is at or above the nominal pressure, the entity is sent to the block labeled Start. Otherwise, the entity is sent to the block labeled LowTankP where it waits in the queue named ReactorOffQ for signal 0, which indicates that nominal pressure has been established. When the signal is received, the delayed entity is sent to the block labeled Start.

An entity arriving to the ASSIGN block labeled Start represents a batch ready to be started at reactor M. The variable X(M) is set to 1 to indicate that the reactor is on, and the entity is delayed in the queue named ReactorOnQ to wait for signal number M. This signal is sent whenever S(M) crosses S(M+5) in the negative direction, indicating that the batch in reactor M is complete. The entity then continues to the ASSIGN block where X(M) is reset to 0 to indicate that reactor M is now off. The entity proceeds through the DELAY block representing the discharge, cleanup, and recharge times. Following this delay, the entity is returned to the block labeled Charge where the process is repeated.

Three DETECT blocks are used in the model. The first DETECT block detects the negative crossing of S(M) against the threshold S(M+5), for M equal to station numbers between 1 and 4. When a crossing is detected, signal number M is sent to end the reaction for reactor number M. The second DETECT block detects the surge tank pressure decreasing to the critical value of 100. When this occurs, the last batch in the queue named ReactorOnQ is removed and is sent to the block labeled TurnOff where X(M) is set to 0. The batch is then sent to the block labeled LowTankP where it enters the queue named ReactorOffQ and waits for nominal pressure to be re-established.

The last DETECT block detects the surge tank pressure increasing to the nominal pressure of 150. When this occurs, signal number 0 is sent to release entities from the queue named ReactorOffQ.

```
BEGIN;

;           Sample Problem 11.3

            STATION, 1-4;
Charge      ASSIGN: S(M) = Concentration(M;:!        Assign initial concentration
                   S(M+5) = .1 * S(M);               Assign threshold concentration
            BRANCH, 1:
              IF, S(5) >= 150, TurnOn:
              ELSE, LowTankP;                         Test tank pressure
TurnOn      ASSIGN: X(M) = 1;                         Turn the reactor on
            QUEUE, ReactorOnQ;                        Wait in queue for
            WAIT: M;                                  end of reaction
            ASSIGN: X(M) = 0;                         Turn the reactor off
            DELAY:
            NORM(1,.1)+NORM(1,.2): NEXT(Charge);      Discharge, clean, and recharge

LowTankP    QUEUE, ReactorOffQ;                       Wait in queue for
            WAIT: 0: NEXT(TurnOn);                    nominal pressure

            DETECT, 1-4: S(M), N, S(M+5);             Detect threshold
            SIGNAL: M: DISPOSE;                       Signal end of reaction

            DETECT: S(5), N, 100;                     Detect critical pressure
            REMOVE:
            NQ, ReactorOnQ, TurnOff: DISPOSE;         Remove the last reactor
TurnOff     ASSIGN: X(M) = 0: NEXT(LowTankP);         Turn the reactor off

            DETECT: S(5), P, 150;                     Detect nominal pressure
            SIGNAL: 0: DISPOSE;                       Signal pressure ok
END;
```

Figure 11-23. Model Listing for Sample Problem 11.3

The experiment for this problem is shown in Figure 11-24. The CONTINU-OUS element specifies five differential equations and four state equations. The ARRIVALS element is used to create the initial entity arrivals at stations 1 through 4 corresponding to each of the four reactors in the model.

```
BEGIN;

PROJECT,           Sample Problem 11.3, SM;

CONTINUOUS,  5, 4, .01, 1, 1,,, N;

STATIONS:    4;

INITIALIZE:  S(5) = 500;

CSTATS:      S(1), Reactor 1 Conc.,"React1.dat":
             S(2), Reactor 2 Conc.,"React2.dat":
             S(3), Reactor 3 Conc.,"React3.dat":
             S(4), Reactor 4 Conc.,"React4.dat":
             S(5), Tank Pressure,"Pressure.dat":

ARRIVALS:    STATION(1), 0:
             STATION(2), .5:
             STATION(3), 1.0:
             STATION(4), 1.5;

VARIABLES:   Concentration(4), .1, .4, .2, .5;

QUEUES:      ReactorOnQ: ReactorOffQ;

DSTATS:      X(1), Reactor 1 Util.:
             X(2), Reactor 2 Util.:
             X(3), Reactor 3 Util.:
             X(4), Reactor 4 Util.:
             NQ(ReactorOnQ), Reactors On:
             NQ(ReactorOffQ), Reactors Off;

REPLICATE,   1,0,500;

END;
```

Figure 11-24. Experiment Listing for Sample Problem 11.3

The SIMAN Summary Report for this problem is shown in Figure 11-25. This report shows the utilization of the reactors, as measured by DSTATS on the X variables, and the number of reactors on and off, as measured by DSTATS on the lengths of the queues named ReactorOnQ and ReactorOffQ.

```
Project: Sample Problem 11.3
Analyst:  SM
Replication ended at time:  500.0
```

DISCRETE-CHANGE VARIABLES

Identifier	Average	Variation	Minimum	Maximum	Final Value
Reactor 1 Util.	.21104	1.9335	.00000	1.0000	.00000
Reactor 2 Util.	.51787	.96488	.00000	1.0000	.00000
Reactor 3 Util.	.42546	1.1621	.00000	1.0000	.00000
Reactor 4 Util.	.59097	.83195	.00000	1.0000	1.0000
Reactors On	1.7453	.43411	.00000	4.0000	1.0000
Reactors Off	.46843	1.3882	.00000	3.0000	.00000

CONTINUOUS-CHANGE VARIABLES

Identifier	Average	Variation	Minimum	Maximum	Final Value
Reactor 1 Conc.	.02757	1.0256	.00000	.10000	.97713E-02
Reactor 2 Conc.	.13469	.88407	.00000	.40000	.39823E-01
Reactor 3 Conc.	.07073	.90200	.00000	.20000	.19925E-01
Reactor 4 Conc.	.14493	.84321	.00000	.50000	.31645
Tank Pressure	184.42	.58462	48.530	843.96	148.80

Figure 11-25. SIMAN Summary Report for Sample Problem 11.3

A plot of the concentration of reactant in each of the four reactors is shown in Figure 11-26. This plot was generated by using the PLOTS command in the Output Processor.

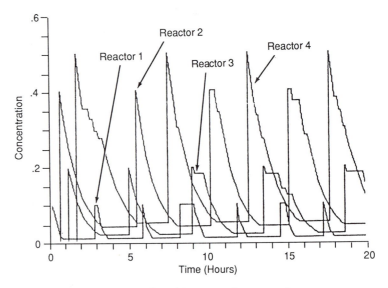

Figure 11-26. Plot of Reactant Concentration

Exercises

Exercise 11-1

Simulate the population dynamics involving the growth and decay of an infectious disease by using the equations presented in Section 3 of this chapter. Terminate the simulation when the size of the well group decreases to 20% of its original value.

Exercise 11-2

The vertical displacement of a mass suspended from a spring and a dashpot and subjected to a vertical force, f(t), is given by

$$m \, d^2x/dt^2 + k_1 \, dx/dt + k_2 \, x = f(t)$$

where

  m is the mass,
  x is the vertical displacement,
  k_1 is the dashpot constant, and
  k_2 is the spring constant.

Simulate the response of this system to a constant force f(t) = 1.0 for all t. Assume m = 1, k1 = 0.5, and k2 = 1.0. Run the simulation for one time unit and use the Output Processor to generate a plot of the mass displacement over time.

Exercise 11-3

Consider the following modifications to the Cedar Bog Lake problem (Sample Problem 11.1).

a. Stock the lake with herbivores by 0.2 calories/cm² every six months.

b. When the plant population reaches 15 calories/cm², spray the lake to reduce the plant population by 50 percent.

c. Stock the lake with carnivores by 0.2 calories/cm² whenever the herbivore population reaches 0.7 calories/cm².

Exercise 11-4

For the chemical reactor problem (Sample Problem 11-3), assume that a worker is required to discharge, clean, and recharge a reactor. Modify the model to incorporate the worker and compare the results obtained with one versus two workers.

Exercise 11-5

For the chemical reactor problem (Sample Problem 11-3), mathematically solve the differential equations and modify the SIMAN model to incorporate the derived solution.

Exercise 11-6

For the soaking pit furnace problem (Sample Problem 11-2), use the model to evaluate the performance improvement resulting from preheating arriving ingots such that their temperature is uniformly distributed between 600 and 700 degrees. Assume that the ingots waiting in the cold bank have a temperature of 600 degrees.

Exercise 11-7

A fleet of 15 tankers, each of which carries 150 thousand barrels (tb) of crude oil, travels from Valdez, Alaska, to an unloading dock near Seattle, Washington [Pritsker, 1974]. The time required for a tanker to travel from Seattle to Valdez, be loaded with crude, and then return to Seattle is normally distributed with a mean of 12 days and a standard deviation of 3 days. Loaded tankers arriving in Seattle wait their turn to be unloaded at an unloading dock. A tanker is emptied at the rate of 300 tb per day when the unloading dock is open. The unloading of a tanker is halted when the unloading dock closes at 12 P.M., and it then resumes the next morning at 6 A.M. A tanker is considered to be unloaded when its level of crude drops below 7.5 tb.

The crude from the tankers is pumped into a storage tank, which has a capacity of 2,000 tb. If the storage tank reaches its capacity, the unloading operation is halted until the level of crude in the storage tank drops below 1,600 tb. The storage tank is used to feed a refinery at the rate of 150 tb per day. The refinery operates 24 hours per day. However, if the level of crude in the storage tank drops below 5 tb, the refinery is shut down until the level reaches 50 tb.

a. Develop a SIMAN model to simulate this system for a one-year period and record statistics on the utilization of the unloading dock, the number of tankers waiting to unload, the average level of crude in the storage tank, and the percentage of time that the refinery operates. Assume an initial state in which the storage tank contains 1,000 tb of crude and loaded tankers are scheduled to arrive at the unloading dock equally spaced at three-day intervals starting with the first at time 0.

b. Use truncation and batching to develop a confidence interval on the level of crude in the storage tank. Compare the results to those obtained by using batching without truncating the initial condition bias.

Exercise 11-8

An expansion has been proposed for the refinery system described in Exercise 11-7. This expansion would increase the refinery capacity to 200 tb of crude per day. To handle this increased load, it has been suggested that either the unloading dock be kept open for 24 hours per day or an additional tanker be added to the fleet. Evaluate the impact of each of these alternatives on the utilization of the refinery.

References

ASHOUR, S. AND S. G. BINDINGNAVLE (1973), "An Optimal Design of a Soaking Pit Rolling Mill System," *Simulation*, Vol. 20, pp: 207-14.

FEHLBERG, E. (1969), "Low-Order Classical Runge-Kutta Formulas with Step-Size Control and Their Application to some Heat Transfer Problems," NASA Report TR R-315, Huntsville, Alabama.

HURST, N. R. AND A. A. B. PRITSKER (1973), "Simulation of a Chemical Reaction Process Using GASPIV," *Simulation*, Vol. 21, pp: 71-75.

PRITSKER, A. A. B. (1974), *The GASPIV Simulation Language*, John Wiley, New York, NY.

WILLIAMS, R. B. (1971), "Computer Simulation of Energy Flow in Cedar Bog Lake, Minnesota Based on Classical Studies by Lindeman," in *Systems Analysis and Simulation in Ecology*, B. C. Patten, Editor, Academic Press.

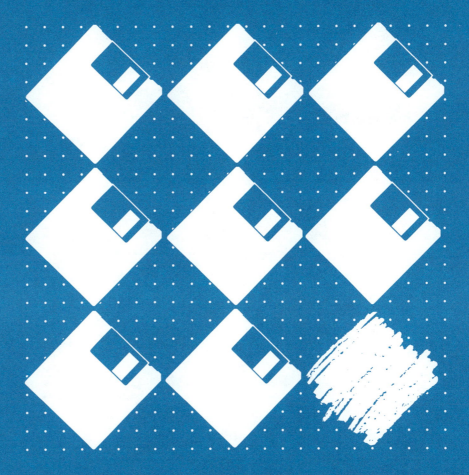

CHAPTER 12

CHAPTER 12
Variance Reduction Techniques

1. Introduction

When modeling large and complex systems, you may need substantial computer time to obtain precise estimates of the system's performance, particularly when you are simulating production systems on a personal computer. In some instances each replication of the model may require several hours of computer time. Therefore, an experimental design involving a large number of replications can require days to execute.

A number of methods have been developed that can produce equally precise estimates of the system's performance by using fewer model replications. These methods are collectively referred to as Variance Reduction Techniques (VRTs) because their aim is to reduce the variance in the point estimate for the mean response. These methods are essentially designed to improve the traditional methods of analysis presented in Chapter 5 by reducing the variance in the estimate of the response variable without introducing bias into its expected value. This reduction in variance gives a smaller confidence interval for the performance measure.

In general, the use of VRTs complicates analysis because, although these techniques can save computer time by reducing the required number of replications of the model, their proper use demands skill and judgement. Furthermore, there is generally no way to know in advance if the application of a VRT will actually reduce the variance. In some cases the use of VRTs can actually yield poorer results than straightforward analysis. However, in most cases these procedures are effective at reducing the variance of the estimator.

2. Classification of Methods

Various VRTs have been proposed over the years. We restrict our discussion to a subset of the four methods that we feel have the most practicality. For additional discussions of VRTs, refer to texts by Kleijnen [1974], Law and Kelton [1982], and Bratley, Fox, and Schrage [1986].

The four VRTs fall into two broad classes. The first class of methods incorporates a modeler's prior knowledge about the system when estimating the mean response; the result is a possible reduction in variance. The second class manipulates random numbers for each replication of the simulation, thereby inducing either a positive or a negative correlation between the mean response across replications. This induced correlation can lead to a reduction in the variance of the estimate of the overall mean response; one side effect, however, is that we can no longer assume independence between replications.

3. Methods Based on Prior Information

By incorporating prior knowledge about a system into our estimate of the mean, we hope to improve the reliability of the estimate. The two VRTs discussed in this section are based on this concept. In each case, you must have some prior knowledge of the system. Thus, the applicability of each of these methods depends on the system being modeled.

3.1 Indirect Measures

In some cases our prior knowledge about the system includes knowing an analytically derived relationship involving the performance measure. Indirect measures exploit this knowledge to obtain an indirect estimate of the performance measure, which has a smaller variance than the direct estimate of this same value.

Because many simulation models measure performance as related to queueing, we will use this class of models as a means of presenting this basic idea. At a given workstation within a queueing model, we frequently estimate the expected number of jobs in the queue (L_q), the expected waiting time in the queue (W_q), the expected total waiting time (W) at a station (including both the time in the queue and the processing time), and/or the expected number of jobs (L) at a station (including those jobs in the queue or being processed by the server).

According to general queueing theory, we know that, given some minor conditions, the variables L, Lq, W, and Wq are related to the arrival rate, λ, by Little's formula as shown below.

$$L = \lambda W$$

$$L_q = \lambda W_q$$

We also know that W and W_q are related according to the formula

$$W = W_q + S$$

where S is the time in the server.

If our objective is to estimate the average length of the queue (L_q), we can directly obtain statistics about the queue's length by using a DSTAT on NQ, or we can indirectly estimate L_q by using a TALLY block to collect statistics about the time that entities wait in the queue (W_q); then we can compute L_q from W_q by using Little's formula. Similarly, if our objective is to estimate the total time spent waiting at the station, we can directly estimate this quantity by marking arriving entities and tallying the intervals between arrival and departure, or we can indirectly estimate this quantity by tallying the time spent in the queue and then adding the known, expected processing time.

Because we have both a direct and an indirect method of estimating these quantities, the obvious question arises: Which estimate has the least variability and therefore provides the tighter confidence interval? In many cases the indirect measure provides a tighter confidence interval, often leading to a 30- to 40-percent reduction in the variance.

The indirect measure has less variability than the direct measure because we are replacing a random component by a known, fixed quantity. For example, the total time spent at the station is the sum of two random components: the time spent waiting in the queue and the processing time. In the indirect estimate, the second term is replaced by its known value, and it is therefore reasonable to expect a reduction in the variability of the overall estimate.

The use of indirect measures for estimating L, L_q, W, and W_q in $GI/G/s$ queueing systems (i.e., general independent arrival times, general service times, and s parallel servers) was studied by Law [1975], who showed that, when examining these systems, it is generally better to use indirect estimates of L, L_q, and W based on W_q than to use direct estimates. Therefore, during simulation we need only collect statistics about W_q, which can then be used to estimate W, L, and L_q.

Indirect measurement's main disadvantage is its dependence on the particular model being studied. We must find a theoretical relationship within the model involving a known parameter. Although Little's formula works for many queueing situations, the modeler may find it difficult to identify such a relationship in non-queueing situations. In addition, although Law provides proofs that variance reductions are generally obtained for the $GI/G/s$ queueing systems, the method is not guaranteed to work for other systems.

The main advantages of indirect measurement are its simplicity and its ability to obtain both direct and indirect measures from the same run. Using both direct and indirect estimates, we can compute the confidence intervals; then we can select the estimate with the smallest half-width. Hence, we use indirect measurement only when it helps us.

To illustrate the method of indirect measurement, consider a modified version of the restaurant model (Sample Problem 3.4) from Chapter 3. In this model we have marked the party arrival time to the restaurant in the attribute named SystemIn, and we have marked the party arrival time to the cashier in the attribute named CashierIn. In addition, we have added TALLY blocks to record the time in the table queue, the time in the cashier queue, and the total time in the system. This modified model is shown in Figure 12-1.

```
BEGIN;
        CREATE:     EXPO(1.6),Door:
                      MARK(SystemIn);              Create parties
        BRANCH,     1:
                    IF, TNOW <= 240, Open:
                    ELSE, Closed;                  Open or Closed ?
Closed  ASSIGN:     Door = 0: DISPOSE;             Set MaxBatches to 0
Open    ASSIGN:     PartySize=DISCRETE(.4,2,       !party size 2 (40%)
                                       .7,3,       !party size 3 (30%)
                                       .9,4,       !party size 4 (20%)
                                       1,5);       !party size 5 (10%)
        QUEUE,      TableQ, 5, Leave;              wait for table
        SEIZE:      Table,(PartySize+1)/2;         get tables
        TALLY:      Wtq, INT(SystemIn);            tally tableq wait
        DELAY:      TRIANGULAR(14,19,24)+          !delay by service
                      NORMAL(24,5);                delay by dining
        RELEASE:    Table,(PartySize+1)/2;         release tables

        QUEUE,      CashierQ: MARK(CashierIn);     wait for cashier
        SEIZE:      Cashier;                       seize cashier
        TALLY:      Wcq, INT(CashierIn);           tally cashierq wait
        DELAY:      NORMAL(1.5,.5);                delay to pay bill
        RELEASE:    Cashier;                       release cashier
        TALLY:      R, INT(SystemIn);              tally flowtime
        COUNT:      Served Parties:DISPOSE;        count served cust.

Leave   COUNT:      Lost Parties:DISPOSE;          count balked cust.
END;
```

Figure 12-1. Modified Restaurant Model

The expected time that a party spends in the restaurant, R, can be obtained by applying the queueing formulas to both the table and the cashier portions of the restaurant, as given by the following equation

$$R = W_{tq} + S_t + W_{cq} + S_c$$

where W_{tq} is the expected waiting time in the table queue, S_t is the expected service time at the table, W_{cq} is the expected waiting time at the cashier queue, and S_c is the expected service time at the cashier. From our prior knowledge of the system, we know that S_t is 43 minutes and S_c is 1.5 minutes. Substituting these values into the above equation yields

$$R = W_{tq} + W_{cq} + 44.5$$

This equation allows us to indirectly estimate the time in the restaurant, R, by estimating the waiting times in the table queue and the cashier queue. We can compare this estimate to the direct estimate obtained by recording the time in the restaurant at the last TALLY block in the model.

The following table summarizes direct and indirect estimates of time in the restaurant obtained from 10 independent model replications. The table also shows the sample mean and variance for both measures.

Replication	Flowtime (Direct)	Flowtime (Indirect)
1	49.317	49.306
2	48.359	48.665
3	48.573	48.938
4	45.194	46.964
5	46.784	46.757
6	48.405	48.092
7	50.980	51.056
8	48.536	48.933
9	48.860	48.975
10	50.197	50.145
mean	48.521	48.783
variance	2.637	1.698

In this case, the indirect estimate for flowtime has 36 percent less variance than does the direct estimate (1.698 versus 2.637). Hence, by using the indirect measure to estimate the flowtime, we are able to significantly improve our interval estimate of the actual flowtime through the restaurant. These interval estimates are shown graphically in Figure 12-2.

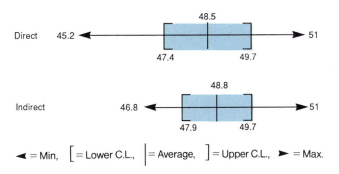

Figure 12-2. Confidence Interval based on Direct and Indirect Measures

3.2 Control Variates

The next method is based on the use of secondary variables, called *control variates*. Like indirect measurement, this method involves incorporating prior knowledge about a specific parameter within the model; it does not, however, require advance knowledge about a parameter's theoretical relationship within the model.

As an introduction to the use of control variates, consider the problem of estimating the expected number of parties served in the restaurant model (Sample Problem 3.4 from Chapter 3). Let us assume that we have replicated the system 10 times and obtained the number of served parties, x_i, for i corresponding to each of the 10 replications. The time between arrivals is also a random variable, which we will denote as C; based on our prior knowledge of the system, we know that $E(C) = 1.6$. Let us assume that we have also recorded the average time between arrivals for each replication, c_i. (This can be done by inserting a TALLY block with the BET option immediately following the CREATE block.) These values are summarized in the following table.

Replication	Time Between Arrivals (c_i)	Parties Served (x_i)
1	1.63	148
2	1.54	155
3	1.53	154
4	1.94	125
5	1.65	146
6	1.67	145
7	1.50	152
8	1.56	150
9	1.57	150
10	1.40	148

From replication to replication, the observed average time between arrivals, c_i, is larger or smaller than its expected value of 1.6. We expect that, when the observed interarrival time is larger than expected and fewer parties arrive, the throughput will be slightly lower than expected. Likewise, we expect that, when more parties than expected arrive, the throughput will be higher than expected. Therefore, the random variable C is said to partially control the random variable X, and hence it is called a control variate for X.

To use the method of control variates, we must assume that a relationship exists between the control variate, C, and the variable of interest, X. Unlike indirect measurement, however, this approach does not require that we know the exact mathematical relationship between the control variate and the variable of interest; we need only know that the values are related. We estimate this relationship by using the data recorded from the simulation. We then use this relationship to adjust the observed values of X.

We usually assume a simple linear relationship between the variable of interest and the control variate. We can then correct the observed values of the variable of interest, x_i, by using the observed values of the control variate, c_i, as follows:

$$x_{ci} = x_i - a\,(c_i - E(C))$$

where x_{ci} is the "corrected" observation, and the parameter a is a weighting factor.

If we treat the parameter as a known constant, the expected value and variance of X_c are given as follows:

$$E(X_c) = E(X) - a\,E(C - E(C)) = E(X)$$

$$\text{Var}(X_c) = \text{Var}(X) + a^2 \, \text{Var}(C) - 2a \, \text{Cov}(X,C)$$

Note that the expected value of X_c and X are the same, because $E(C-E(C)) = (E(C)-E(C)) = 0$. Also, the variance of X_c is smaller than the variance of X only if the covariance between X and C is non-zero and

$$a < 2 \, \text{Cov}(X,C) \, / \, \text{Var}(C) \text{ for any positive a,}$$

or

$$a > 2 \, \text{Cov}(X,C) \, / \, \text{Var}(C) \text{ for any negative a.}$$

This result shows that, when the control variate is correlated (either positively or negatively) and we appropriately select the parameter, a, we reduce the variance. The obvious question arises: How do we select the parameter in a way that maximizes the reduction? To obtain the optimal choice for the parameter, we differentiate the expression for the variance of X_c with respect to a, set the result equal to 0, and solve for a. The optimal value for a, denoted by a* obtained in this way is given as follows:

$$a^* = \text{Cov}(X,C) \, / \, \text{Var}(C)$$

Substituting the optimal value a* back into the expression for the variance of X_c yields the following expression for the minimum variance of X_c based on the use of the optimal coefficient a*

$$\text{Var}(X_c) = \text{Var}(X) - [\text{Cov}(X,C)]^2 \, / \, \text{Var}(C)$$

As we can see from the previous result, the corrected variable, X_c, will always have less variance than the directly observed variable, X, as long as we use the optimal weighting factor a* and as long as any correlation exists between X and C. Unfortunately, to compute a* we must know both the covariance between X and C and the variance of C. In any practical situation we do not know the covariance between X and C and therefore must estimate it from the observed values for X and C.

The most common method for estimating a* uses estimates for both the covariance between X and C and the variance of C — even though the latter is typically known. We compute an estimate for a* as follows:

$$s^2(c) = \sum_{i=1}^{n} (c_i - \bar{c})^2 / (n-1)$$

$$\text{C\^{o}v}(x,c) = \sum_{i=1}^{n} (x_i - \bar{x})(c_i - \bar{c}) \, / \, (n-1)$$

$$\hat{a}^* = \frac{\text{C\^{o}v}(x,c)}{s^2(c)}$$

We then generate the corrected observations by using the estimated value of a*

Continuing with our example, we compute a confidence interval on the number of parties served by first calculating $\hat{a}^*$ (which for this example is -51.85) and then by using this quantity to form the corrected estimates x_{ci} from our direct observations, x_i, of the number of parties served. The results of these calculations are shown below.

Replication	x_i	x_{ci}
1	148	149.2
2	155	151.8
3	154	150.4
4	125	142.5
5	146	148.5
6	145	148.5
7	152	146.7
8	150	148.0
9	150	148.4
10	148	137.4
mean	147.3	147.14
variance	71.79	17.69

Note that, in this case, the use of a control variate reduces the sample variance from 71.79 to 17.69.

Because the corrected observations have less variance, we use these observations to construct a 0.95 confidence interval with a half-width, h, as follows:

$$\bar{x}_c = 147.14$$
$$s(x_c) = 4.205$$
$$s(\bar{x}_c) = 1.33$$
$$t_{9,.975} = 2.262$$
$$h = 3.0$$
$$C.I. = [144.14, 150.14]$$

Compare this confidence interval with the one based on the direct observation, x_i, which is calculated as follows:

$$\bar{x} = 147.3$$
$$s(x) = 8.47$$
$$s(\bar{x}) = 2.68$$
$$t_{9,.975} = 2.262$$
$$h = 6.06$$
$$C.I. = [141.24, 153.36]$$

These confidence intervals are depicted in Figure 12-3. Note that, for this example, the variance based on the corrected observations, x_{ci}, compares favorably to the variance based on the direct estimates, x_i. In this case we use the control variate to obtain a 75 percent reduction in the variance and, consequently, a 50 percent improvement in the confidence interval width.

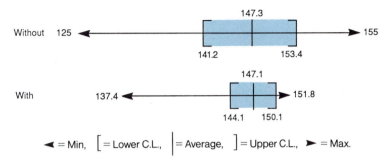

$$\blacktriangleleft = \text{Min,} \quad [= \text{Lower C.L.,} \quad | = \text{Average,} \quad] = \text{Upper C.L.,} \quad \blacktriangleright = \text{Max.}$$

Figure 12-3. Confidence Intervals With and Without the Use of Control Variates

Note that the calculation for estimating a^* outlined above is identical to the calculation of the least-square estimator of the coefficient, a, in the linear regression equation $X = a\,C + b + \varepsilon$, where a is the slope, b is the intercept, and ε denotes the random variation around the regression line. (Note that X corresponds to the regression-dependent variable, y, and C corresponds to the regression-independent variable, x.) As a result, you can use software packages or calculators that compute the linear regression coefficient, a, to compute the estimate of a^* for the control variate. Hence, this technique is sometimes referred to as *regression sampling*.

As discussed by Kleijnen [1974], when you estimate a^* from the observations as outlined above, the expected values of X_c and X are no longer equal, because a^* and c_i are not independent. Although Kleijnen presents a jackknife technique for eliminating the dependency between a^* and c_i, the bias is usually not substantial and is not a major factor in confidence-interval coverage; however, you should always regard the confidence intervals that result from using control variates as approximate.

The main advantage of control variates is that they are relatively easy to use. They only require that you identify an appropriate control variate, which has a known, expected value and is correlated to the response of interest. You must record statistics about the control variate and the variable of interest, and you must calculate the corrected observations, x_{ci}; however, as with indirect measures, you can use the same set of replications to calculate the variance with and without control variates. Hence, you eliminate the danger of producing less accurate results with a VRT.

For additional readings about control variates, refer to the text by Kleijnen [1974] and the excellent review paper by Lavenberg and Welch [1980]. For a discussion of the use of control variates in multi-population experiments, refer to the paper by Nozari, Arnold, and Pegden [1984].

4. Induced Correlation

A second general class of methods for reducing variance deliberately introduces a correlation between the response variables in successive replications of the simulation. We typically introduce this correlation by manipulating the seeds for the random-number generators. Under certain conditions, introducing a correlation reduces the variance of the mean response. We discuss two methods of variance reduction. The first, the method of common random numbers, only applies when we are comparing two or more systems. The second method, using antithetic variates, applies when we are estimating the response of a variable of interest.

Again, there is no guarantee that the procedures discussed here will actually produce a reduction in the variance; in fact, they can have the reverse effect. Unfortunately, inducing a correlation destroys the independence property across replications, so we cannot compute traditional estimates from the same set of replications for the purpose of comparison. Therefore, in practice we generally have no way of knowing how much variance we have gained or lost by using these methods. Despite these problems, these methods generally do work well and can yield substantial improvements in the reliability of our estimators.

4.1 Common Random Numbers

Although the method of common random numbers only applies when we are comparing two or more systems, it is probably the most commonly used VRT. Its relative popularity stems from its simplicity of implementation and general intuitive appeal. The method of common random numbers is based on the idea that, when we compare systems, we should do so under similar conditions. Our objective is to attribute any observed differences in performance measures to differences in the systems, not to random fluctuations in the underlying experimental conditions.

For example, let's consider the problem of comparing the FIFO (first-in-first-out) and SPT (shortest-processing-time) scheduling rules discussed in Chapter 5. Modified versions of the model and experiment for the SPT case are shown in Figure 12-4. If we simply make 10 independent replications of each system as we did in Section 6.2 of Chapter 5, some of the observed differences between the two cases may result from fluctuations in the random interarrival and service times. To eliminate this factor, we make matched pairs of replications, in which the interarrival times and service times for both the FIFO and SPT cases are the same within the pair. The interarrival and service times will differ, however, from one pair of replications to the next. Since the interarrival and service times within a FIFO — SPT pair are the same, the difference in the response between the two systems within the pair of replications will therefore result from differences in the underlying systems, not from chance variations in the random processes.

```
BEGIN;
        CREATE:    EXPONENTIAL(4.4,1):!         Enter the system
                   MARK(TimeIn);                Set arrival time
        ASSIGN:    ProcessTime=TRIA(3.2,4.2,5.2,2);  Set processing
        QUEUE,     Buffer;                      Wait for the machine
        SEIZE:     Machine;                     Seize the machine
        DELAY:     ProcessTime;                 Delay by the processing
        RELEASE:   Machine;                     Release the machine
        TALLY:     TimeInSystem,INT(TimeIn);    Tally time in system
        COUNT:     JobsDone:DISPOSE;            Count completed jobs
END;

BEGIN;

PROJECT,       Sample Problem 5.1,SM;

ATTRIBUTES:    TimeIn:
               ProcessTime;

QUEUES:        Buffer,LVF(ProcessTime);

RESOURCES:     Machine;

SEEDS:         1,12000,c:
               2,13000,c;

TALLIES:       TimeInSystem;

DSTATS:        NQ(BUFFER);

COUNTERS:      JobsDone;

OUTPUTS:       TAVG(TimeInSystem),"Tsys.dat";

REPLICATE,     10, 0, 480;

END;
```

Figure 12-4. Model and Experiment for the SPT Version

To demonstrate this concept, we use Chapter 5's notation for this example, where X_a denotes the response for system A (the FIFO case) and X_b denotes the response for system B (the SPT case). As before, let D equal the difference between the two systems, i.e., $D = X_a-X_b$. The lowercase equivalent of these random variables with an appended i denotes an observed value for the random variable on the ith replication of the simulation. The following equation gives the random variable D's variance.

$$Var(D) = Var(X_a) + Var(X_b) - 2Cov(X_a,X_b)$$

As you can see from this equation, if we make n independent pairs of replications (as was done in Chapter 5), the covariance term is 0, and the variance of D is the sum of the variances for X_a and X_b. On the other hand, if we introduce a positive covariance between X_a and X_b, we reduce D's variance by twice this amount.

The term "common random numbers" comes from the use of the same random numbers within pairs of replications as a means of inducing the needed positive covariance between the responses within a paired set of replications. Simply using the same random-number seed for each replication within the pair is usually not sufficient to induce covariance; we must also ensure that random numbers are synchronized, i.e., the random numbers are used at the same junction and for exactly the same purpose across systems. In our example, the random numbers are automatically synchronized because both the interarrival time and the service time for the job are assigned at arrival. As a result, the order in which the jobs are processed will not change the way that the random numbers are used within the model.

In more complicated situations we may need to use more involved modifications to ensure random-number synchronization across systems. SIMAN provides multiple random number streams which can be helpful for this purpose. In complex models we may avoid fully synchronizing all of the random processes in the model by restricting our attention to a small subset, such as the arrival process itself, and by not worrying about the remaining random processes. Although partial synchronization can reduce the correlation within the matched pairs of replications and thus weaken the variance reduction, in most cases it substantially reduces the effort needed to apply common random-number streams.

Statistical analysis based on common random numbers is founded on a single premise: Although we are introducing correlation between paired responses, the difference, D, across pairs of replications is independent. We achieve this independence by employing a different starting seed for each of the n pairs of replications. Consequently, we can use the method of analysis discussed in Chapter 5, Section 6.2, directly, even though we have introduced a correlation between the responses within the pairs of replications.

The easiest way to obtain the required independent pairs of correlated replications is to make two separate runs of n replications. In the first run we obtain n independent replications of System A; in the second, we obtain n independent replications of System B. To ensure that the jth replication within each of the two runs uses the same starting seed, we employ the SEEDS element to specify the same starting seed for the first replication within each run and for the reinitialization option "C," which denotes common random numbers. With these specifications, SIMAN uses a starting seed for the next replication that is exactly 100,000 observations away from the starting seed used on the previous replication. Thus, we are assured that the jth replication in each of the two runs starts with the same random number, even if the number of samples generated from replication to replication differs between the two systems.

We can use common random numbers to re-execute the example described in Chapter 5, Section 6.2, for comparing the system flowtime for the FIFO and SPT scheduling rules. We make two runs, of 10 replications each, with the SEEDS element as shown in Figure 12-4. In the first run, we default the queue ranking rule to FIFO. In the second run, we specify the rule as LVF(ProcessTime) corresponding to the SPT rule.

The results for these 10 pairs of replications are summarized in the following table.

Replication	Flowtime System A (FIFO)	Flowtime System B (SPT)	Difference
1	32.88	19.26	13.61
2	9.58	9.21	.38
3	23.42	21.39	2.03
4	37.09	22.15	14.94
5	32.02	16.82	15.20
6	26.22	17.57	8.65
7	16.28	15.07	1.21
8	16.15	13.19	2.96
9	26.57	20.04	6.54
10	28.26	19.50	8.76
		mean	7.43
		variance	32.95

As before, we then construct a confidence interval on the difference in response between the two systems, which yields the following results.

$\bar{d} = 7.43$
$s(d) = 5.74$
$s(\bar{d}) = 1.82$
$t_{9,.975} = 2.262$
$h = 4.11$
C.I. $= [3.32, 11.54]$

In Chapter 5 we analyzed this same problem without using common random numbers. That analysis yielded the following confidence interval.

C.I. $= [.6, 10.6]$

The confidence intervals for this problem, both with and without the use of common random numbers, are depicted in Figure 12-5. Note that the use of common random numbers reduces the sample variance of d from 48.4 to 32.95 (30 percent), which yields a 17 percent smaller confidence interval. In this example, incorporating common random numbers is a simple, highly effective technique.

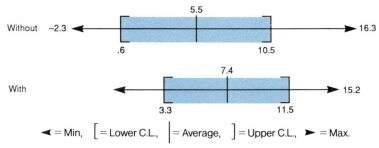

Figure 12-5. Confidence Intervals With and Without the Use of Common Random Numbers

Instead of using common random numbers to induce the required positive correlation within the paired replications, we can use an external data file to input the arrival and service times for the processed jobs. Note that both methods subject the systems to exactly the same sequence of arriving jobs and hence accomplish the same goal. Thus, whenever you use historical data to compare two systems, you use the method of common random numbers, even though the name is not really appropriate.

Unfortunately, there is no way to evaluate the increase or decrease in variance resulting from the use of common random numbers — other than to repeat the simulation runs without common random numbers. We cannot compute the confidence interval both with and without common random numbers from the same set of replications, as we can with other types of VRTs. In a practical application, therefore, we generally have no way of knowing whether our decision to use common random numbers is correct.

Although in most situations their use is effective, common random numbers can generate a negative covariance, which leads to less accurate results than those produced by independent runs. Although the likelihood of a negative covariance is small, Wright and Ramsey [1979] cite one such example involving the simulation of an inventory system.

4.2 Antithetic Variates

The last VRT that we discuss is antithetic variates. Like common random numbers, this technique reduces the variance by artificially inducing a correlation between replications of the model. Unlike common random numbers, the antithetic-variate technique applies when we are estimating a single system's performance.

The antithetic-variate method assumes that the recorded response of a simulation is a direct function of the random input to the model. For example, if a particular replication has lower-than-expected service times, the observed time spent waiting in the queue is also typically less than expected. To compensate for a replication with lower-than-expected service times we make a second, complementary replication with higher-than-expected service times — in the hope that, by averaging the results for these two replications, we will obtain a more representative estimate for the expected time spent waiting in the queue.

The antithetic-variate approach makes n independent pairs of correlated replications, where paired replications are for the same system. You create each pair of replications such that a smaller-than-expected observation in the first replication is offset by a larger-than-expected observation in the second, and vice versa. Assuming that this value is closer to the expected response than the value that would result from the same number of completely independent replications, you then average the two observations and use the result to derive the confidence interval.

We can present this idea more formally by letting the random variable X denote the response on the first replication within a pair, and by letting the random variable X' denote the response on the second replication within a pair. The random variable Y denotes the average of these two random variables, i.e., $Y = (X + X') / 2$. The lowercase of these variables with an appended i denotes observed values for these random variables on the ith pair of replications. The expected value of Y and the variance of Y are given as follows:

$$E(Y) = [E(X) + E(X')] / 2 = E(X) = E(X')$$

$$Var(Y) = [Var(X) + Var(X') + 2Cov(X,X')] / 4$$

From these equations we can see that Y has the same expected value as X and X' and that the variance of Y is reduced by a negative covariance between X and X'. The antithetic-variate technique exploits this property by inducing a negative covariance between X and X' and by using observations of Y to form the confidence interval on $\mu = E(X)$ as follows:

$$s^2(\bar{y}) = \sum_{i=1}^{n} (y_i - \bar{y})^2 / (n-1)\, n$$

$$h = t_{n-1,\, 1-\alpha/2}\, s(\bar{y})$$

$$u = [\bar{y} - h,\, \bar{y} + h]$$

We induce the negative covariance between replications within a pair by using the antithetics of the random numbers from the first replication in the pair as the random numbers in the second replication in the pair. In other words, if the jth random number in the first replication of the pair is $r_j \sim$ uniform(0,1), then the jth random number in the second replication of the pair is $r_j' = 1 - r_j$. Note that, because r_j is uniform(0,1), r_j' is also uniform(0,1).

Using antithetic random numbers to induce a negative covariance between the responses within a pair of replications assumes that the response is a monotonic function of the input random number. In other words, the response will always increase or always decrease as r_j increases. This requirement follows from the basic assumption that, by using r_j' on the second replication in a pair, we will generate a response opposite to that generated by using r_j on the first replication

545 Variance Reduction Techniques

in the pair. In a practical application we generally cannot be certain that this monotonic property is present, and we must simply rely on our general understanding of the system to determine whether our assumption is reasonable.

The antithetic-variate method of inducing a negative covariance between the paired replications requires that the random-number sequences within the two replications be synchronized, as with the common random-numbers method. To be synchronized, the random numbers must be used in exactly the same way in each replication within the pair. In other words, if in the first replication of the pair the jth random number determines the service time for the jth customer, then the complement of the jth random number must be used in the second replication of the pair for the same purpose.

The synchronization requirement frequently leads to the use of separate random-number streams for each of a model's random processes. As with common random numbers, in a practical application we are often content with a partial synchronization involving a few input variables (or possibly a single variable).

The SEEDS element enables us to make all of the necessary replications required by the antithetic-variate method in a single run of n replications by specifying the reinitialization option on the SEEDS Element as "A," which denotes antithetic sampling. With this specification, SIMAN generates odd-numbered replications (1, 3, etc.) from starting seeds that are spaced 100,000 observations apart from the initial starting seed. The even-numbered replications are generated from random numbers that are complements $(1-r_j)$ of the immediately preceding replication.

To illustrate the use of antithetic variates, we again consider Sample Problem 3.1 from Chapter 3, which we analyzed in Chapter 5, Section 6.1, to generate a confidence interval on the number of processed jobs. We again make a total of 10 replications of the model; however, this time we use antithetic variates to organize the run as five independent, correlated pairs of replications. The model and experiment for this example are shown in Figure 12-6. Note that we are employing antithetic variates involving only the arrival process, to which we have assigned a separate random-number stream (1). The "A" option in the SEEDS element for stream number 1 specifies the use of antithetic variates.

```
BEGIN;

        CREATE:    EXPONENTIAL(4.4,1);            Enter the system
        QUEUE,     Buffer;                        Wait for the machine
        SEIZE:     Machine;                       Seize the machine
        DELAY:     TRIANGULAR(3.2,4.2,5.2,2);     Delay by the
        RELEASE:   Machine;                       Release the machine
        COUNT:     JobsDone:DISPOSE;              Count completed jobs

    END;
```

```
BEGIN;
PROJECT,    Sample Problem 3.1,SM;
QUEUES:     Buffer;
RESOURCES:  Machine;
COUNTERS:   JobsDone;
SEEDS:      1, 12345, A:
            2, 56789;
REPLICATE,  10, 0, 480;
END;
```

Figure 12-6. Modified Model and Experiment for Sample Problem 3.1

The results for these 10 replications are shown below. Note that the even-numbered replications are the antithetic runs for the odd-numbered replications.

Replication	Jobs Done	Paired Average
1	103	
2	98	100.5
3	105	
4	107	106.0
5	91	
6	111	101.0
7	109	
8	107	108.0
9	94	
10	112	103.0
	mean	103.7
	variance	10.5

From these 10 values, we obtain five observations that we then use to form our confidence interval. These observations are formed by averaging the results for the paired replications (shown in the column labeled Paired Average). The calculations for the confidence interval based on these observations as follows:

$\bar{x} = 103.7$
$s(x) = 3.233$
$n = 5$
$s(\bar{x}) = 1.45$
$t_{4,.975} = 2.776$
$h = 4.0$
C.I. $= [99.7, 107.7]$

Compare these results to those from Chapter 5, where we solved the same problem based on 10 independent replications. These calculations produced the following confidence interval.

$$\bar{x} = 104.6$$
$$s(x) = 6.6$$
$$n = 10$$
$$s(\bar{x}) = 2.1$$
$$t_{9,.975} = 2.262$$
$$h = 4.7$$
$$\text{C.I.} = [99.9, 109.3]$$

These confidence intervals are depicted in Figure 12-7. Note that the use of antithetic variates has reduced the variance from 43.6 to 10.5 (76 percent), compared to the analysis based on independent replications. The variance of the mean reduced from 4.4 to 2.1. However, despite this large decrease in the variance, the half-width of the confidence interval has only decreased from 4.7 to 4.0 (15 percent) because of the decreased degrees of freedom (4 compared to 9). This finding illustrates an often overlooked problem in antithetic variates: *Even though you reduce the variance of the mean, the loss in half-width resulting from decreasing the degrees of freedom may more than offset the reduction.*

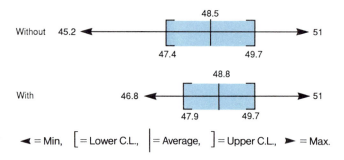

Figure 12-7. *Confidence Intervals With and Without Antithetic Variates.*

If we attempt to use the antithetic-variate method and fail to induce a negative covariance (e.g., by failing to synchronize the random numbers), our results are not as successful as those yielded by a more straightforward analysis based on independent replications. To minimize the impact of halving the degrees of freedom, we recommend 20 or more replications when using antithetic variates.

Unfortunately, the antithetic-variate and common-random-number methods suffer from the same disadvantage: There is generally no way in a practical application to determine whether the method has been successful. We cannot perform the analysis both with and without antithetic variates from the same set of replications. Thus, short of re-executing the simulations without using antithetic variates, we have no way of determining whether their use has been beneficial. We are able to make comparisons within our sample problem only because we have previously made independent replications of the same model.

5. Conclusions

As we have seen from the examples in this chapter, the use of VRTs can improve the reliability of our simulation results. It is not unusual for these methods to reduce the width of a confidence interval by as much as 50 percent. Note that, without the use of a VRT, we would need four times as many observations to achieve this same 50 percent reduction in the confidence interval width.

Despite these potential benefits, VRTs have been used infrequently in practical simulation applications. The reasons cited typically include the modeler's lack of understanding regarding VRT methods and a general unwillingness to complicate the analysis. Although their proper use demands skill and judgement, VRTs can be an effective method for significantly improving the reliability of simulation results.

Exercises

Exercise 12.1

Make 10 independent replications of the car wash model for Exercise 3.1 in Chapter 3 and collect statistics on the time spent by each car in the queue and in the system. Obtain an estimate for the expected time in the system by using an indirect measure based on the recorded waiting time in the queue and compare this to the direct estimate for this value.

Exercise 12.2

Make 20 independent replications of the model for Sample Problem 3.1 in Chapter 3. Repeat the 20 replications using antithetic variates. Compare the results to those obtained in Section 4.2 based on 10 replications of this same model.

Exercise 12.3

Make 10 replications of the car wash model for Exercise 3.1 in Chapter 3 and record statistics on time between arrivals to the car wash. Use this value as a control variate to form a confidence interval on the number of cars washed. Compare the results to those obtained without the use of the control variate.

Exercise 12.4

Consider the restaurant model (Sample Problem 3.4) presented in Chapter 3. Modify the model to record statistics on the time spent in service and dining, and use this value as a control variate to construct a confidence interval on the number of parties served. Compare the results to those obtained in this chapter based on using the time between arrivals as a control variate.

Exercise 12.5

Modify the model for Exercise 12.4 to record statistics on the time in the restaurant, and use the recorded time in service and dining as a control variate to construct a confidence interval on this value.

Exercise 12.6

Make 10 replications of the restaurant model (Sample Problem 3.4) by using common random numbers to compare the number of parties served at 50 versus 60 tables. Compare the results obtained with those obtained in Chapter 5 (Sample Problem 5.1).

Exercise 12.7

Perform an analysis of the results for Exercise 3.4 in Chapter 3 by using the method of replication. Base the analysis on 10 replications of each system and select a truncation point and replication length by examining the results for a pilot run of each model. Repeat the analysis by using common random numbers, and compare the results.

Exercise 12.8

Perform an analysis of the model results for Exercise 3.8b from Chapter 3, based on the method of replication with common random numbers, to evaluate the effectiveness of the proposed expediting strategy. If necessary, use a partial synchronization of the random-number streams. Compare the results to those obtained without common random numbers.

Exercise 12.9

Using antithetic variates, make 10 replications of the car wash model for Exercise 3.1 in Chapter 3. Compare the resulting confidence interval on the number of cars washed to the same interval based on 10 independent replications. Repeat the analysis using 20 replications.

Exercise 12.10

Repeat Exercise 12.8 but use the method of batching with common random numbers. (Hint: Use the REPLICATE element and specify the system initialization option as NO.)

References

BRATLEY, P., B. L. FOX, and L. E. SCHRAGE (1986), *A Guide to Simulation*, 2nd Edition, Springer-Verlag, New York.

KLEIJNEN, J. P. (1974), *Statistical Techniques in Simulation*, Part 1, Marcel Dekker, Inc., New York.

LAVENBERG, S. S. and P. D. WELCH, "A Perspective on the Use of Control Variates to Increase the Efficiency of Monte-Carlo Simulations," *Management Science*, Vol. 27, pp: 322-35.

LAW, A. M. (1975), "Efficient Estimators for Simulated Queueing Systems," *Management Science*, Vol. 22, pp: 30-41.

LAW, A. M. and W. D. KELTON (1982), *Simulation Modeling and Analysis*, McGraw-Hill, New York, NY.

NOZARI, A., S. ARNOLD, and C. D. PEGDEN (1984), "Control Variates for Multi-population Simulation Experiments," *IIE Transactions*, Vol. 16, No. 2, pp: 159-67.

WRIGHT, R. D. and T. E. RAMSAY (1979), "On the Effectiveness of Common Random Numbers," *Management Science*, Vol. 25, pp: 649-56.

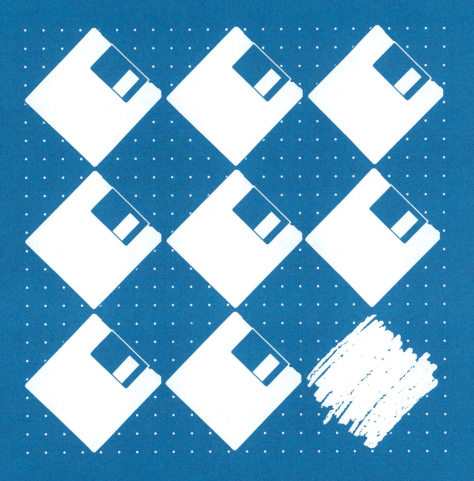

APPENDICES

APPENDIX A

Distributions

SIMAN contains a set of built-in functions for obtaining samples from the commonly used probability distributions. This appendix summarizes these distributions.

Each of the distributions in SIMAN has one or more parameter values associated with it. You must specify these parameter values to fully define the distribution. The number and meaning of the parameter values depend on the distribution. A summary of the distributions and parameter values is shown below.

Distribution	Parameter Values
Beta	$Alpha_1$, $Alpha_2$
Continuous	$CumP_1$, Val_1, $CumP_2$, Val_2, ...
Discrete	$CumP_1$, Val_1, $CumP_2$, Val_2, ...
Erlang	ExpoMean, K
Exponential	Mean
Gamma	Beta, Alpha
Lognormal	Mean, StdDev
Normal	Mean, StdDev
Poisson	Mean
Triangular	Min, Mode, Max
Uniform	Min, Max
Weibull	Beta, Alpha

The distributions can be specified by using one of two formats: you can select a single format, or you can mix formats within the same model. The format is determined by the name used to specify the distribution. The primary format is selected by using either the variable's full name or a four-letter abbreviation of the name consisting of the first four letters. For example, UNIFORM or UNIF specifies the uniform distribution in the primary format. The secondary format is selected by specifying the distribution with a two-letter abbreviation. For example, UN specifies the uniform distribution in the secondary format.

Continuous $(c_1,x_1,c_2,x_2,\dots)$	CONTINUOUS(CumP₁,Val₁,...) or CONT(CumP₁,Val₁,...) CP(ParamSet)

Density

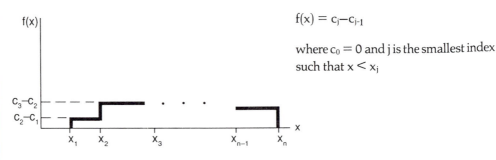

$f(x) = c_j - c_{j-1}$

where $c_0 = 0$ and j is the smallest index such that $x < x_j$

Distribution

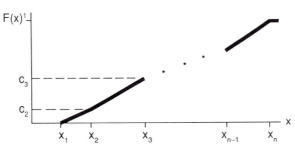

Parameters

The CONTINUOUS function in SIMAN returns a sample from a user-defined continuous probability distribution. All values between the smallest value (x_1) and the largest value (x_n) are possible. The distribution is defined by a set of n discrete values (denoted by $x_1, x_2, \dots, x_n$) and the cumulative probabilities (denoted by $c_1, c_2, \dots, c_n$) associated with these values. The cumulative probability (c_j) for x_j is defined as the probability of obtaining a value which is less-than-or-equal-to x_j. The distribution is assumed to be piecewise linear between the n discrete values. Because c_j is the cumulative probability, $c_1 = 0$ and $c_n = 1$.

Range

$[x_1, x_n]$

Mean

$$\int_x xf(x)dx$$

Variance

$$\int_x (x-\mu)^2 f(x)dx$$

Applications

The continuous probability distribution is used to incorporate empirical data for continuous random variables directly into the model. This distribution can be used as an alternative to a theoretical distribution that has been fit to the data.

| Discrete($c_1,x_1,c_2,x_2,\ldots$) | **DISCRETE(CumP$_1$,Val$_1$,...) or DISC(CumP$_1$,Val$_1$,...)**
DP(ParamSet) |

Density

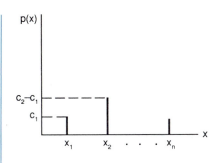

$$p(x_j) = c_j - c_{j-1}$$

where $c_0 = 0$

Distribution

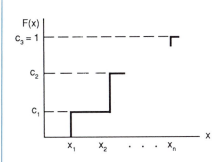

Parameters

The DISCRETE function in SIMAN returns a sample from a user-defined discrete probability distribution. The distribution is defined by the set of n possible discrete values (denoted by x_1, x_2, ... , x_n) that can be returned by the function and the cumulative probabilities (denoted by c_1, c_2, ... , c_n) associated with these discrete values. The cumulative probability (c_j) for x_j is defined as the probability of obtaining a value that is less-than-or-equal-to x_j. Hence c_j is equal to the sum of p_k for k from 1 to j, where p_k is the probability of obtaining the sample value x_k. By definition, $c_n = 1$.

Range

$[x_1, x_n]$

Mean

$\sum_k x_k p_k$

Variance

$\sum_k (x_k - \mu)^2 p_k$

Applications

The discrete probability distribution is used to incorporate discrete empirical data directly into the model. This distribution is frequently used for discrete assignments such as the job type, the visitation sequence, or the batch size for an arriving entity.

| Erlang(β,k) | ERLANG(ExpMean,k) or ERLA(ExpMean,k)
ER(ParamSet) |

Density

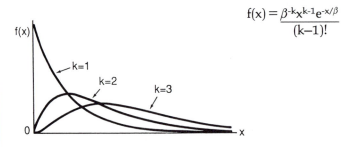

$$f(x) = \frac{\beta^{-k}x^{k-1}e^{-x/\beta}}{(k-1)!}$$

Parameters

If X_1, X_2, ... ,X_k are independent exponential samples, then the sum of these k samples has an Erlang-k distribution. The mean (β) of the exponential distribution and the number of exponential samples (k) are parameters of the distribution. The exponential mean is specified as a non-negative real number, and k is specified as a positive integer.

Range

$[0, +\infty]$

Mean

$k\beta$

Variance

$k\beta^2$

Applications

Erlang distribution is used in situations in which an activity occurs in phases and each phase has an exponential distribution. For large k the Erlang approaches the normal distribution. The Erlang distribution is often used to represent the time required to complete a task. The Erlang distribution is a special case of the gamma distribution in which the shape parameter, α, is an integer.

| Exponential(β) | EXPONENTIAL(Mean) or EXPO(Mean) |
| | EX(ParamSet) |

Density

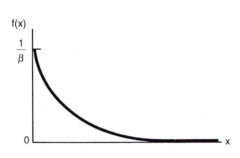

$$f(x) = \frac{1}{\beta} e^{-x/\beta} \text{ if } x > 0$$

$$0 \qquad \text{otherwise}$$

Parameters

The mean (β) specified as a non-negative real number.

Range

$[0, +\infty]$

Mean

β

Variance

β^2

Applications

This distribution is often used to model random arrival and breakdown processes, but it is generally inappropriate for modeling process delay times. The exponential distribution is used in situations in which the random quantities satisfy the memoryless property.

Gamma(β,α)	**GAMMA(Beta,Alpha) or GAMM(Beta,Alpha)** **GA(ParamSet)**

Density

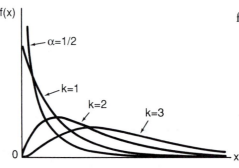

$$f(x) = \frac{\beta^{-\alpha} x^{\alpha-1} e^{-x/\beta}}{\Gamma(\alpha)} \quad \text{if } x > 0$$

$$\qquad\qquad 0 \qquad\qquad \text{otherwise}$$

where Γ is the gamma function

Parameters

Shape parameter (α) and scale parameter (β) specified as non-negative real values.

Range

$[0, +\infty]$

Mean

$\alpha\beta$

Variance

$\alpha\beta^2$

Applications

For integer shape parameters, the gamma is the same as the Erlang distribution. The gamma is often used to represent the time required to complete some task, e.g., a machining time or machine repair time.

| Lognormal(μ,σ) | LOGNORMAL(Mean,StdDev) or LOGN(Mean,StdDev) |
| | RL(ParamSet) |

Density

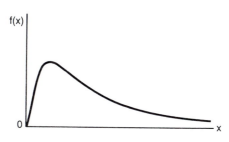

Let
$$\sigma^2_n = \ln(\sigma^2/\mu^2 + 1)$$
$$\mu_n = \ln(\mu) - \sigma^2_n/2$$
Then
$$f(x) = \frac{1}{\sigma x \sqrt{2\pi}}\ e^{-(\ln(x)-\mu)^2/2\sigma^2} \text{ if } x > 0$$
$$0 \qquad\qquad\qquad \text{otherwise}$$

Parameters

The mean (μ) and standard deviation (σ) specified as non-negative real numbers.

Range

$[0, +\infty]$

Mean

μ

Variance

σ^2

Applications

The lognormal distribution is used in situations in which the quantity is the product of a large number of random quantities. It is also frequently used to represent task times that have a non-symmetric distribution.

Normal(μ,σ)	NORMAL(Mean,StdDev) or NORM(Mean,StdDev) RN(ParamSet)

Density

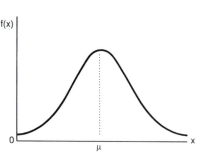

$$f(x) = \frac{1}{\sigma\sqrt{2\pi}}\, e^{-(x-\mu)^2/2\sigma^2}$$

Parameters

The mean (μ) specified as a real number, and the standard deviation (σ) specified as a non-negative real number.

Range

$[\infty, +\infty]$

Mean

μ

Variance

σ^2

Applications

The normal distribution is used in situations in which the central limit theorem applies — i.e., quantities that are sums of other quantities. It is also used empirically for many processes that are known to have a symmetric distribution and for which the mean and standard deviation can be estimated. Because the theoretical range is from $-\infty$ to $+\infty$, the distribution should only be used for processing times when the mean is at least three standard deviations above 0.

Poisson(λ)	POISSON(Mean) or POIS(Mean)
	PO(ParamSet)

Density

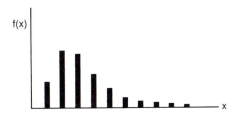

$$p(x) = \frac{e^{-\lambda}\,\lambda^x}{x!} \text{ if } x \varepsilon \{0,1,\ldots\}$$

$$0 \qquad \text{otherwise}$$

Parameters

The mean (λ) specified as a non-negative real number.

Range

$[0,1,2,\ldots,]$

Mean

λ

Variance

λ

Applications

The Poisson distribution is a discrete distribution that is often used to model the number of random events occurring in an interval of time. If the time between events is exponentially distributed, then the number of events that occur in a fixed time interval has a Poisson distribution. The Poisson distribution is also used to model random variations in batch sizes.

Triangular(a,m,b)	TRIANGULAR(Min,Mode,Max) or TRIA(Min,Mode,Max) TR(ParamSet)

Density

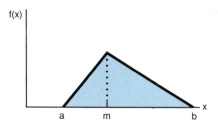

$$f(x) = \frac{2(x-a)}{(m-a)(b-a)} \quad \text{if } a \le x \le m$$

$$\frac{2(b-x)}{(b-m)(b-a)} \quad \text{if } m \le x \le b$$

Parameters

The minimum (a), mode (m), and maximum (b) values for the distribution specified as real numbers with $a < m < b$.

Range

[a, b]

Mean

$(a + m + b)/3$

Variance

$(a^2 + m^2 + b^2 - ma - ab - mb) / 18$

Applications

The triangular distribution is commonly used in situations in which the exact form of the distribution is not known, but estimates for the minimum, maximum, and most likely values are available. The triangular distribution is easier to use and explain than other distributions that may be used in this situation (e.g., the beta distribution).

| Uniform(a,b) | UNIFORM(Min,Max) or UNIF(Min,Max)
UN(ParamSet) |

Density

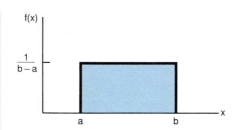

$$f(x) = \frac{1}{b-a} \quad \text{if } a \le x \le b$$

$$0 \quad \text{otherwise}$$

Parameters

The minimum (a) and maximum (b) values for the distribution specified as real numbers with a < b.

Range

[a, b]

Mean

(a + b)/2

Variance

$(b-a)^2/12$

Applications

The uniform distribution is used when all values over a finite range are considered to be equally likely. It is sometimes used when no information other than the range is available. The uniform distribution has a larger variance than other distributions that are used when information is lacking (e.g., the triangular distribution). Because of its large variance, the uniform distribution generally produces "worst case" results.

Weibull(β,α)

Weibull(Beta,Alpha) or WEIB(Beta,Alpha)
WE(ParamSet)

Density

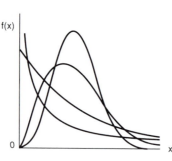

$$f(x) = \alpha\beta^{-\alpha}\, x^{\alpha-1}\, e^{-(x/\beta)^{\alpha}} \quad \text{if } x > 0$$

$$0 \qquad \text{otherwise}$$

Parameters

Shape parameter (α) and scale parameter (β) specified as non-negative real numbers.

Range

$[0, +\infty]$

Mean

$\dfrac{\beta}{\alpha}\, \Gamma\left(\dfrac{1}{\alpha}\right)$, where Γ is the gamma function

Variance

$$\dfrac{\beta^2}{\alpha}\left\{ 2\Gamma\left(\dfrac{2}{\alpha}\right) - \dfrac{1}{\alpha}\left[\Gamma\left(\dfrac{1}{\alpha}\right)\right]^2\right\}$$

Applications

The Weibull distribution is widely used in reliability models to represent the lifetime of a device. If a system consists of a large number of parts that fail independently, and if the system fails when any single part fails, then the time between failures can be approximated by the Weibull distribution. This distribution is also used to represent non-negative task times that are skewed to the left.

Critical Values

This appendix contains tables of critical values for the Kolmogorov-Smirnov and Chi-Squared goodness-of-fit tests and values of the student-t distribution.

Appendix B-1

Kolmogorov-Smirnov critical values

Degrees of Freedom N	$D_{0.10}$	$D_{0.05}$	$D_{0.01}$
1	0.950	0.975	0.995
2	0.776	0.842	0.929
3	0.642	0.708	0.828
4	0.564	0.624	0.733
5	0.510	0.565	0.669
6	0.470	0.521	0.618
7	0.438	0.486	0.577
8	0.411	0.457	0.543
9	0.388	0.432	0.514
10	0.368	0.410	0.490
11	0.352	0.391	0.468
12	0.338	0.375	0.450
13	0.325	0.361	0.433
14	0.314	0.349	0.418
15	0.304	0.338	0.404
16	0.295	0.328	0.392
17	0.286	0.318	0.381
18	0.278	0.309	0.371
19	0.272	0.301	0.363
20	0.264	0.294	0.356
25	0.24	0.27	0.32
30	0.22	0.24	0.29
35	0.21	0.23	0.27
Over 35	$\dfrac{1.22}{\sqrt{N}}$	$\dfrac{1.36}{\sqrt{N}}$	$\dfrac{1.63}{\sqrt{N}}$

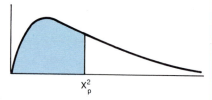

Percentile values (x^2) for the chi-square distribution, with v degrees of freedom (shaded area $= p$).

v	$x^2_{.995}$	$x^2_{.99}$	$x^2_{.975}$	$x^2_{.95}$	$x^2_{.90}$
1	7.88	6.63	5.02	3.84	2.71
2	10.60	9.21	7.38	5.99	4.61
3	12.84	11.34	9.35	7.81	6.25
4	14.96	13.28	11.14	9.49	7.78
5	16.7	15.1	12.8	11.1	9.2
6	18.5	16.8	14.4	12.6	10.6
7	20.3	18.5	16.0	14.1	12.0
8	22.0	20.1	17.5	15.5	13.4
9	23.6	21.7	19.0	16.9	14.7
10	25.2	23.2	20.5	18.3	16.0
11	26.8	24.7	21.9	19.7	17.3
12	28.3	26.2	23.3	21.0	18.5
13	29.8	27.7	24.7	22.4	19.8
14	31.3	29.1	26.1	23.7	21.1
15	32.8	30.6	27.5	25.0	22.3
16	34.3	32.0	28.8	26.3	23.5
17	35.7	33.4	30.2	27.6	24.8
18	37.2	34.8	31.5	28.9	26.0
19	38.6	36.2	32.9	30.1	27.2
20	40.0	37.6	34.2	31.4	28.4
21	41.4	38.9	35.5	32.7	29.6
22	42.8	40.3	36.8	33.9	30.8
23	44.2	41.6	38.1	35.2	32.0
24	45.6	43.0	39.4	36.4	33.2
25	49.6	44.3	40.6	37.7	34.4
26	48.3	45.6	41.9	38.9	35.6
27	49.6	47.0	43.2	40.1	36.7
28	51.0	48.3	44.5	41.3	37.9
29	52.3	49.6	45.7	42.6	39.1
30	53.7	50.9	47.0	43.8	40.3
40	66.8	63.7	59.3	55.8	51.8
50	79.5	76.2	71.4	67.5	63.2
60	92.0	88.4	83.3	79.1	74.4
70	104.2	100.4	95.0	90.5	85.5
80	116.3	112.3	106.6	101.9	96.6
90	128.3	124.1	118.1	113.1	107.6
100	140.2	135.8	129.6	124.3	118.5

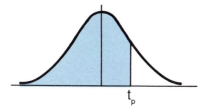

Appendix B-3

Values of students t distribution with v degrees of freedom (shaded area $= p$).

v	$t_{.995}$	$t_{.99}$	$t_{.975}$	$t_{.95}$	$t_{.90}$
1	63.66	31.82	12.71	6.31	3.08
2	9.92	6.96	4.30	2.92	1.89
3	5.84	4.54	3.18	2.35	1.64
4	4.60	3.75	2.78	2.13	1.53
5	4.03	3.36	2.57	2.02	1.48
6	3.71	3.14	2.45	1.94	1.44
7	3.50	3.00	2.36	1.90	1.42
8	3.36	2.90	2.31	1.86	1.40
9	3.25	2.82	2.26	1.83	1.38
10	3.17	2.76	2.23	1.81	1.37
11	3.11	2.72	2.20	1.80	1.36
12	3.06	2.68	2.18	1.78	1.36
13	3.01	2.65	2.16	1.77	1.35
14	2.98	2.62	2.14	1.76	1.34
15	2.95	2.60	2.13	1.75	1.34
16	2.92	2.58	2.12	1.75	1.34
17	2.90	2.57	2.11	1.74	1.33
18	2.88	2.55	2.10	1.73	1.33
19	2.86	2.54	2.09	1.73	1.33
20	2.84	2.53	2.09	1.72	1.32
21	2.83	2.52	2.08	1.72	1.32
22	2.82	2.51	2.07	1.72	1.32
23	2.81	2.50	2.07	1.71	1.32
24	2.80	2.49	2.06	1.71	1.32
25	2.79	2.48	2.06	1.71	1.32
26	2.78	2.48	2.06	1.71	1.32
27	2.77	2.47	2.05	1.70	1.31
28	2.76	2.47	2.05	1.70	1.31
29	2.76	2.46	2.04	1.70	1.31
30	2.75	2.46	2.04	1.70	1.31
40	2.70	2.42	2.02	1.68	1.30
60	2.66	2.39	2.00	1.67	1.30
120	2.62	2.36	1.98	1.66	1.29
∞	2.58	2.33	1.96	1.645	1.28

APPENDIX C
SIMAN Variables, Functions, and Routines

Attributes	A(Natb)	General purpose entity attribute Natb.
	IS	Integer entity sequence set index attribute.
	M	Integer entity station attribute.
	NS	Integer entity sequence set number attribute.
Conveyor Variables	CLA(Ncnv)	Length of accumulated entities on conveyor Ncnv.
	ICS(Ncnv)	Status of conveyor Ncnv. (0=Idle, 1=Moving, 2=Blocked, 3=Inactive)
	LC(Ncnv)	Number of cells conveying on conveyor Ncnv.
	LEC(Ncnv)	Length of entities conveying on conveyor Ncnv.
	MLC(Ncnv)	Length of conveyor Ncnv.
	NEA(Ncnv)	Number of accumulated entities on conveyor Ncnv.
	NEC(Ncnv)	Number of entities conveying on conveyor Ncnv.
	VC(Ncnv)	Velocity of conveyor Ncnv (user assignable).
Functions	ED(Nexp)	Returns a value from expression number Nexp.
	UF(Nuf)	Returns the value computed in user function Nuf.
	UR(Nur)	Returns an index computed in user rule Nur.
Group Variables	AG(Nrnk,Natb)	Attribute A(Natb) for entity Nrnk of the group.
	ISG(Nrnk)	Attribute IS for entity Nrnk of the group.
	MG(Nrnk)	Attribute M for entity Nrnk of the group.
	NG	The number of entities in the current entity's group.
	NSG(Nrnk)	Attribute NS for entity Nrnk of the group.
	SAG(Natb)	The sum of attribute A(Natb) from all group members.
Queue Variables	AQUE(Nque,Nrnk,Natb)	Attribute A(Natb) of the entity at rank Nrnk in queue Nque.
	ISQUE(Nque,Nrnk)	Attribute IS of the entity at Nrnk rank in queue Nque.
	MQUE(Nque,Nrnk)	Attribute M of the entity at rank Nrnk in queue Nque.
	NQ(Nque)	Number of entities in queue Nque.

	NSQUE(Nque,Nrnk)	Attribute NS of the entity at rank Nrnk in queue Nque.
	SAQUE(Nque,Natb)	Sum of attribute A(Natb) from all entities in queue Nque.
Resource Variables	MR(Nres)	Capacity of resource Nres (user assignable).
	NR(Nres)	Number of busy units of resource Nres.
Simulation Replication Variables	MREP	Number of replications to be executed.
	NREP	Current replication number.
	NUMENT	Current number of entities active in the model.
	TFIN	Ending time of the current replication (user assignable).
	TNOW	Current simulation time.
Special Purpose Variables	IDENT	The entity's identifier as it appears in the trace.
	NSYM(Name)	The number associated with the symbol name Name.
Station Variables	MSQ(Nseq,Iseq)	The station listed in sequence set Nseq, index Iseq.
	NE(Nsta)	Number of entities en-route to station Nsta.
Statistics Collection Variables	CAVG(Ncst)	Current time weighted average value of cstat Ncst.
	CMAX(Ncst)	Current maximum value of cstat Ncst.
	CMIN(Ncst)	Current minimum value of cstat Ncst.
	CSTD(Ncst)	Current standard deviation of cstat Ncst.
	CTPD(Ncst)	Current time period of cstat Ncst.
	DAVG(Ndst)	Current time weighted average value of dstat Ndst.
	DMAX(Ndst)	Current maximum value of dstat Ndst.
	DMIN(Ndst)	Current minimum value of dstat Ndst.
	DSTD(Ndst)	Current standard deviation of dstat Ndst.
	DTPD(Ndst)	Current time period of dstat Ndst.
	MC(Ncnt)	Maximum limit for counter Ncnt.
	NC(Ncnt)	Current count of counter Ncnt.
	TAVG(Ntal)	Current average value of tally Ntal.
	TMAX(Ntal)	Current maximum value of tally Ntal.
	TMIN(Ntal)	Current minimum value of tally Ntal.
	TNUM(Ntal)	Current number of observations of tally Ntal.
	TSTD(Ntal)	Current standard deviation of tally Ntal.
Storage Variable	NSTO(Nstr)	Number of entities in storage Nstr.
Table Look-Up	TF(Ntab,Xval)	The value of the dependent variable from table Ntab given the independent variable Xval.

Transporter Variables

ACC(Ntrn)	Acceleration of transporter set Ntrn.
DEC(Ntrn)	Deceleration of transporter set Ntrn.
IDSNET(Nnet,Ibx,Iex)	Length of travel between intersections Ibx and Iex in network Nnet.
ISZT(Ntrn,Nunit)	Size type of transporter unit Nunit of set Ntrn, (1=ZONE, 2=LENGTH). (See NSZT).
IT(Ntrn,Nunit)	Status (0=idle, 1=busy, 2=inactive), (user assignable).
LDL(Ntrn,Nunit)	Destination link of unit Nunit of set Ntrn.
LDX(Ntrn,Nunit)	Destination intersection of unit Nunit of set Ntrn.
LDZ(Ntrn,Nunit)	Destination zone of unit Nunit of set Ntrn.
LENZ(Nlnk)	Zone length of zones in link Nlnk.
LNKNUM(Ibx,Iex)	The link number connecting intersections Ibx and Iex.
LT(Ntrn,Nunit)	Location or destination of unit Nunit, set Ntrn.
LTL(Ntrn,Nunit)	Link location of unit Nunit, set Ntrn.
LTYP(Nlnk)	Link type (1=unidirectional, 2=bidirectional, 3=spur)
LTZ(Ntrn,Nunit)	Current zone number of unit Nunit of set Ntrn.
LX(Ninx)	Length of intersection Ninx.
MT(Ntrn)	Number of active units of transporter set Ntrn.
MZ(Nlnk)	Number of zones in link Nlnk.
NDX(Nlnk)	Destination intersection of vehicles on link Nlnk.
NEXTX(Nnet,Icx,Idx)	The next intersection of travel between intersection Icx and intersection Idx in network Nnet.
NL(Nlnk)	Number of occupied zones in link Nlnk.
NSZT(Ntrn,Nunit)	Size of transporter unit Nunit of set Ntrn.
NT(Ntrn)	Number of busy transporter units of set Ntrn.
NX(Ninx)	Status of intersection Ninx. (0=empty, 1=occupied)
NXB(Nln)	Beginning intersection of link Nlnk.
NXE(Nlnk)	Ending intersection of link Nlnk.
NZ(Nlnk,Nzon)	Zone status (1=occupied, 0=empty, −1=captured).
TAZNtrn,Nunit)	Time when unit Nunit arrived at its current location.
TVF(Ntrn)	Turning velocity factor of transporter set Ntrn.
TWZ(Ntrn,Nunit)	Accumulated time spent waiting for access to zones.
VL(Nlnk)	Link velocity factor of link Nlnk.
VT(Ntrn)	Velocity of transporter set Ntrn (user assignable).
VTU(Ntrn,Nunit)	Velocity of unit Nunit, set Ntrn (user assignable).
VX(Ninx)	Velocity factor of intersection Ninx.

User-Assignable Variables

D(N)	Derivative variable N, maximum of 50 available.
IT(Ntrn,Nuni)	Status of transporter unit Nunit of set Ntrn. (0=idle, 1=busy, 2=inactive).
J	General purpose integer variable.

MR(Nres)			Capacity of resource Nres.
P(I,J)			The value of parameter J in parameter set I.
X(N)			Global variable N, maximum of 50 available.
S(N)			State variable N, maximum of 50 available.
TFIN			Ending time of the current replication.
V(N)			Global user variable N.
VC(Ncnv)			Velocity of conveyor Ncnv.
VT(Ntrn)			Velocity of transporter set Ntrn.
VTU(Ntrn,Nunit)			Velocity of transporter unit Nunit, set Ntrn.

Built-In Functions

ABS(a)	Absolute value
ACOS(a)	Arc cosine
AINT(a)	Truncate
AMOD(a1,a2)	Real remainder, returns (a1−(aint(a1/a2)*a2))
ANINT(a)	Round to nearest integer
ASIN(a)	Arc sine
ATAN(a)	Arc tangent
COS(a)	Cosine
EP(a)	Exponential
HCOS(a)	Hyperbolic cosine
HSIN(a)	Hyperbolic sine
HTAN(a)	Hyperbolic tangent
MN(a1,a2,...)	Minimum value
MOD(a1,a2)	Integer remainder, same as AMOD except the arguments are truncated to integer values first.
MX(a1,a2,...)	Maximum value
LN(a)	Natural logarithm
LOG(a)	Common logarithm
SIN(a)	Sine
SQRT(a)	Square root
TAN(a)	Tangent

Queue, Resource, and Transporter Selection Rules

Queue	Resource	Transporter	Description
CYC	CYC	CYC	Cyclic priority
ER(Ner)	ER(Ner)	ER(NE)	Experimental rule Ner
LNQ			Largest number in queue
LRC	LRC		Largest remaining capacity
POR	POR	POR	Preferred order rule
RAN	RAN	RAN	Random
SNQ			Smallest number in queue
SRC	SRC		Smallest remaining capacity
UR(Nur)	UR(Nur)	UR(Nur)	Computed in user rule Nur
	LNB		Largest number busy

	SNB	Smallest number busy
	LDS	Largest distance to station
	SDS	Smallest distance to station

Subprogram Libraries, Subroutines

ASSIGN(Lent,A)	Assigns the values in real array A to the attributes of entity Lent.
CLEAR	Clears SIMAN system variable statistics.
CLRCNT(Ncnt)	Clear counter Ncnt
CLRCST(Ncst)	Clear cstat Ncst
CLRDST(Ndst)	Clear dstat Ndst
CLRTAL(Ntal)	Clear tally Ntal
CANCEL(Lent)	Remove entity Lent from the event calendar.
CHGPAG(Ipage)	Change the currently viewed page to Ipage in a Cinema animation. (0 = text page, 1 = graphics page).
COPY(Lent,A)	Copy the attributes of entity Lent to real array A.
COUNT(Ncnt,INC)	Increments counter Ncnt by integer value of INC.
CREATE(Lent)	Create an entity by assigning an entity record location to the integer variable Lent.
DISPOS(Lent)	Dispose an entity by returning the entity record location Lent to the pool of available records.
ENTER(Lent,Nsta)	Enter entity Lent into STATION block Nsta.
INSERT(Lent,Nque)	Insert entity Lent into queue Nque.
QUEUE(Lent,Nque)	Schedule entity Lent to arrive at queue Nque.
REMOVE(Lent,Nque)	Removes entity Lent from queue Nque.
SCHED(Lent,I,Dt)	Schedule event I to occur in Dt time units from the current time for entity Lent.
SEND(Lent,Dt,Str,Len)	Send entity Lent to the block label defined by character variable Str, length Len after Dt time units.
SETA(Lent,Natb,Val)	Set attribute Natb of entity Lent to the real value of Val.
SETIS(Lent,IS)	Set the sequence set index attribute for entity Lent to the integer value specified by the operand IS.
SETIT(Ntrn,Nunit,Ival)	Set the status of transporter unit Nunit, set Ntrn to the integer value specified by the operand Ival. (0 = idle, 1 = busy, 2 = inactive).
SETM(Lent,M)	Set the station number for entity Lent to the integer value specified as operand M.
SETMC(Ncnt,Ival)	Set the limit of counter Ncnt to the integer value specified by operand Ival.
SETMR(N,Ncap)	Set the capacity of resource number N to the integer value specified by the operand Ncap.
SETMSQ(Nseq,Iseq,Nsta)	Set the station number of index Iseq in sequence set Nseq to the value of Nsta.

SETNS(Lent,NS)	Set the sequence set attribute for entity Lent to the integer value specified by the operand NS.
SETP(N,Np,Val)	Set parameter number Np of parameter set N to the real value specified as the operand Val.
SETTF(Ntab,Xval,Yval)	Set the table pair to the real values specified by Xval and Yval in table number Ntab.
SETV(NVAR,Val)	Sets the value of user variable V having index NVAR to the real value specified as the operand Val.
SETVC(Ncnv,Vel)	Set the velocity of conveyor Ncnv to the real value specified by the operand Vel.
SETVT(Ntrn,Vel)	Sets the velocity of transporter Ntrn to the real value specified by the operand Vel.
SETVTU(Ntrn,Nunit,Vel)	Sets the velocity of transporter unit Nunit of set Ntrn to the real value specified by operand Vel.
SIGNAL(Nsig,Maxrel)	Send a signal specified by integer value of Nsig to all WAIT blocks, limit the number of entities released to Maxrel (set Maxrel=−1 for no limit).
SUMRY	Create a summary report.
TALLY(Ntal,Val)	Record the real value specified by the operand Val as an observation of tally Ntal.

Subprogram Libraries, Functions

A(Lent,Natb)	Value of attribute Natb for entity Lent.
AG(Lent,Nrnk,Natb)	Value of attribute A(Natb) for the entity at rank Nrnk of the group associated with entity Lent.
CONT(Vals,Numval,Is)	Value from a continuous distribution using random number stream Is. Real array Vals contains the list of probabilities and values, and Numval represents the number of elements in array Vals.
DISC(Vals,Numval,Is)	Value from a discrete distribution using random number stream Is. Real array Vals contains the list of probabilities and values, and Numval represents the number of elements in array Vals.
ICURPG(Ipage)	The current page number in a Cinema animation. (0=text page, 1=graphics page).
ID(Lent,Ntrn,Nsta)	Distance from station M of entity Lent to station Nsta using distance set of transporter Ntrn.
IDENT(Lent)	Entity identifier for entity with record location Lent.
IDIST(Ndst,Nstb,Nste)	The distance between stations Nstb and Nste in distance set Ndst.
IOFFST(Lent,Ioff)	The station number offset by Ioff from the current station in sequence set NS of entity Lent.
IS(Lent)	Value of attribute IS for entity Lent.

ISG(Lent,Nrnk)	Value of attribute IS for the entity at rank Nrnk of the group associated with entity Lent.
ISGMT(Nsgl,Nstb,Nste)	The segment length between stations Nstb and Nste in segment set Nsgl.
LFCAL	Record location of the first entity on the event calendar.
LFR(Nque)	Record location of the first entry in queue Nque.
LGRP(Lent,Nrnk)	The record location of the entity at rank Nrnk of the group associated with entity Lent.
LLR(Nque)	Record location of the last entry in queue Nque.
LPRED(Lent)	Record location of the predecessor to entity Lent.
LRANK(Nrnk,Nque)	Record location of entity ranked Nrnk in queue Nque.
LSCAL(Lent)	The location on the event calendar of the successor entity to entity Lent.
LSUCC(Lent)	Record location of the successor to entity Lent.
M(Lent)	Station number of entity Lent.
MG(Lent,Nrnk)	Value of station attribute M for the entity at rank Nrnk of the group associated with entity Lent.
NEVENT(Lent)	Event number of entity Lent when on event calendar.
NG(Lent)	Number of entities in entity Lent's group.
NS(Lent)	The value of the attribute NS for entity Lent.
NSG(Lent,Nrnk)	The value of sequence set attribute NS for the entity at rank Nrnk of entity Lent's group.
RLOGN(Rmn,Std,Is)	A value from a lognormal distribution with lognormal mean Rmn and lognormal standard deviation Std using random number stream Is.
RNORM(Rmn,Std,Is)	Value from a normal distribution with mean Rmn, standard deviation Std, random number stream Is.
SAG(Lent,Natb)	The sum of attribute A(Natb) from all members of the group represented by entity Lent.
TEVENT(Lent)	Time of event of entity Lent when on the event calendar.

User-Written Routines

The common block for use with user-written routines is shown below. DL and SL are the immediate past values of the corresponding D and S variables, and DTNOW is the current integration step size.

```
    COMMON /SIM/ D(50),DL(50),S(50),SL(50),
   &            X(50),DTNOW,TNOW,TFIN,J,NUMREP
```

EVENT(Lent,Nev)	Calls event Nev with entity Lent.
KEYHIT(Icode)	Sets Icode to the ASCII value of the key pressed during execution.
PRIME	Called at the beginning of each simulation replication.

STATE	Contains the state and differential equations used in a continuous simulation.
UCLEAR	Clears the user-defined statistics.
URST	Called just after recalling a snapshot.
USAV	Called just prior to saving a snapshot.
WRAPUP	Called at the end of each simulation replication.
UF(Lent,Nuf)	Value computed in user function Nuf using entity Lent.
UR(Lent,Nur)	Queue, resource, or transporter selection rule index computed in user rule Nur using entity Lent.

C calls
cevent(Lent,Nev,cmn)
ckeyhi(Icode,cmn)
cprime(cmn)
cstate(cmn)
cuclea(cmn)
curst(cmn)
cusav(cmn)
cwrap(cmn)
cuf(Lent,Nuf,cmn)
cur(Lent,Nur,cmn)

APPENDIX D
SIMAN Blocks

ACCESS: CnvName , Qty ;

CnvName	Name of conveyor to access [symbol name] {--}
Qty	Number of consecutive cells to access [expression truncated to an integer] {1}

ACTIVATE : TrnName ;

TrnName	Transporter unit to activate [TrnName, or TrnName(Unit)] {--}

ALLOCATE, Pr , AltPath : TrnName(Unit) , EntLoc ;

Pr	ALLOCATE block priority {1}
AltPath	Alternate path [VIA(StationID), VIA(STATION(StationID)), VIA(INTX(IntxID)), VIA(LINK(LinkID)), or VIA(LINK(LinkID,Zone))] {Follow System Map}
TrnName	Transporter name {--}
Unit	Transporter index [expression truncated to an integer; TSR; or TSR,AttributeID] {1}
EntLoc	Entity location [StationID, STATION(StationID) Value INTX(IntxID), or LINK(LinkID,Zone)] {Entity M}

ALTER: ResName , Qty :
repeats ;

ResName	Name of the resource to alter [ResName for simple resources, ResName(Index) for indexed resources] {--}
Qty	Capacity change [expression truncated to an integer capacity change] {1}

581   *SIMAN Blocks*

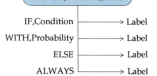

ASSIGN: Variable = Value :
      repeats ;

Variable	SIMAN variable or attribute {--}
Value	Value to be assigned [expression] {--}

BEGIN, Listing , ModelName ;

Listing	Option for generating a listing of model statements during model processing [Yes or No] {Yes}
ModelName	Model name associated with the statements in this model file [alphanumeric] {Blank}

BRANCH, MaxTake , Stream :
      IF, Condition , Label , Primary :
      WITH, Probability , Label , Primary :
      ELSE, Label , Primary :
      ALWAYS, Label , Primary ;

MaxTake	Maximum number of branches to take [expression truncated to an integer] {Infinite}
Stream	Random number stream to use with the WITH rule [integer] {10}
Condition	Branch condition [condition or expression] {--}
Probability	Probability of selecting branch [expression, $0 <=$ Probability $<= 1$] {--}
Label	Label of block to which copy of entity is routed [block label] {--}
Primary	Indicator that primary (incoming) entity can select this branch [Yes, No] {Yes}

CAPTURE: Qty , Dest ;

Qty	Number of forward zones or length of guided transporter track to capture [expression truncated to an integer] {--}
Dest	Travel destination [StationID, STATION(StationID) INTX(IntxID), or LINK(LinkID,Zone)] {--}

CLOSE, FileID ;

FileID	File to be closed [integer file number, or file symbol name] {--}

COMBINE

COMBINE
Qty,SaveCrit

COMBINE: Qty , SaveCrit ;

Qty	The number of entities to combine into a set [expression truncated to an integer] {--}
SaveCrit	Save criterion [FIRST, LAST, PRODUCT, SUM] {LAST}

CONVEY

CONVEY
CnvName,Dest

CONVEY: CnvName , Dest ;

CnvName	Name of the conveyor [symbol name] {Conveyor the Entity Accessed}
Dest	Destination Station [expression truncated to an integer station number, station symbol name, or SEQ] {SEQ{

COPY

COPY
Rank,QueueID,Label

COPY: Rank , QueueID , Label ;

Rank	Rank of the entity to be copied [expression truncated to an integer, or the keyword NQ] {--}
QueueID	Queue from which the entity is to be copied [queue symbol name, or expression truncated to an integer queue number] {--}
Label	Label of block to which the created entity copy is to be sent [block label] {--}

COUNT

COUNT
CounterID,Increment

COUNT: CounterID , Increment ;

CounterID	Counter number or name [expression truncated to an integer counter number, or counter symbol name] {--}
Increment	Counter increment [expression truncated to an integer] {--}

CREATE

CREATE,BatchSize,Offset
Interval,MaxBatches

CREATE, BatchSize , Offset : Interval , MaxBatches ;

BatchSize	Number of entities in each batch creation [expression truncated to an integer] {1}
Offset	Offset time from beginning of simulation replication for the first creation [expression] {0.0}
Interval	Time between batch creations [expression] {Infinite}
MaxBatches	Maximum number of batches to be created [expression truncated to an integer] {Infinite}

DELAY
Duration,StorID

DELAY: Duration , StorID ;

Duration	Length of the delay [expression] {0.0}
StorID	Storage associated with the DELAY block [expression truncated to an integer storage number, or storage symbol name] {No Storage}

DETECT,BegStaID-EndStaID
Variable,Dir,Thresh,Tol

DETECT, BegStaID — EndStaID : Variable , Dir , Thresh , Tol ;

BegStaID	Beginning station in range of station numbers [integer station number or station symbol name] {No Macro}
EndStaID	Ending station in range of station numbers [integer station number or station symbol name] {No Macro}
Variable	Crossing variable [S(N) or D(N)] {--}
Dir	Crossing direction [Positive, Negative, or Either] {--}
Thresh	Threshold value [S(N), D(N), or constant] {--}
Tol	Crossing tolerance [constant] {0.0}

DROPOFF,Rank,Qty
Label,Attributes

DROPOFF, Rank , Qty : Label , Attributes ;

Rank	Starting rank of entities to drop off [expression truncated to an integer] {1}
Qty	Number of entities to drop off [expression truncated to an integer] {1}
Label	Label to send entities which are dropped off [block label] {--}
Attributes	List of representative entity attributes that are assigned to the entities being dropped off [*, A(*), M, NS, IS, AttributeID] {--}

DUPLICATE
Qty,Label

DUPLICATE: Qty , Label :
repeats ;

Qty	Number of duplicate entities to be created [expression truncated to an integer] {0}
Label	Label to send duplicate entities to [block label] {Next Block}

EVENT
Number

EVENT: Number ;

Number	Event number [expression truncated to an integer] {--}

EXIT
CnvName,Qty

EXIT: CnvName , Qty ;

| CnvName | Name of the conveyor to exit [symbol name] {Conveyor the Entity Accessed} |
| Qty | Number of consecutive cells to release [expression truncated to an integer] {All Accessed Cells} |

FINDJ,BegJ,EndJ
Condition

FINDJ, BegJ , EndJ : Condition ;

BegJ	Start limit of index range to be searched [expression truncated to an integer] {--}
EndJ	End limit of index range to be searched [expression truncated to an integer] {--}
Condition	Search condition containing the index J [condition, Expression, MIN(Expression),or MAX(Expression)] {--}

FREE
TrnName

FREE: TrnName ;

| TrnName | Transporter unit to free [TrnName or TrnName(Index), Index is an expression truncated to an integer] {Transporter the Entity was Allocated} |

GROUP
Qty,SaveCrit

GROUP: Qty , SaveCrit ;

| Qty | Number of entities to be grouped into a set [expression truncated to an integer] {--} |
| SaveCrit | Save criterion [FIRST, LAST, PRODUCT, SUM] {LAST} |

HALT
TrnName

HALT: TrnName ;

| TrnName | Transporter unit to deactivate [TrnName or TrnName(Index), Index is an expression truncated to an integer] {--} |

INCLUDE: FileDesc ;

| FileDesc | File containing blocks to include in the model [system specific filename enclosed in double quotes] {--} |

INSERT: QueueLabel , Rank ;

INSERT	
QueueLabel,Rank	

QueueLabel	Label corresponding to the queue block where the entity will be inserted [block label] {--}
Rank	Queue rank to place the entity [expression truncated to an integer] {Queue Ranking Rule}

MATCH, AttributeID : QueueLabel , DestLabel : repeats ;

MATCH, AttributeID	
QueueLabel ──┬──> DestLabel	
QueueLabel ──┼──> DestLabel	
QueueLabel ──┴──> DestLabel	

AttributeID	Match attribute [integer attribute number, A(k), or attribute symbol name] {No Attribute}
QueueLabel	Label of the detached QUEUE block where entity resides [block label] {--}
DestLabel	Destination label for the entity [block label] {Dispose the Entity}

BlockID: Operands ... : Modifiers;

DETACH	Stop entity flow through the queue. The DETACH modifier may only be used with QUEUE blocks.
DISPOSE	Execute the block function, then remove the entity from the model.
MARK(AttributeID)	Assign the value of current simulated time (TNOW) to the entity's attribute specified by AttributeID, then execute the block function. Specify operand AttributeID as an integer attribute number, A(k), or as an attribute symbol name.
NEXT(Label)	Execute the block function, then send the entity to the block corresponding to Label.

MOVE , StorID , AltPath : TrnName , TrnDest , Vel ;

MOVE,StorID,AltPath	
TrnName,TrnDest,Vel	

StorID	Storage associated with the move block [expression truncated to an integer storage number, or storage symbol name] {No Storage}
AltPath	Alternate path [VIA(StationID), VIA(STATION(StationID)), VIA(INTX(IntxID)), VIA(LINK(LinkID)), or VIA(LINK(LinkID,Zone))] {Not Used}
TrnName	Transporter unit to move [TrnName or TrnName(Index)] {Unit the Entity was Allocated}

TrnDest	Transporter destination [StationID, STATION(StationID), INTX(IntxID), LINK(LinkID), LINK(LinkID,Zone), FIRSTX(StationID), FIRSTX(STATION(StationID)), FIRSTX(INTX(IntxID)), FIRSTX(LINK(LinkID)), or FIRSTX(LINK(LinkID,Zone))] {Entity M Value}
Vel	Velocity for MOVE [expression] {Current Velocity}

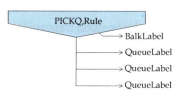

PICKQ, Rule , BalkLabel : QueueLabel : repeats;

Rule	Queue Selection Rule [CYC, ER(k), LNQ, LRC, POR, RAN, SNQ, SRC, UR(k)] {POR}
BalkLabel	Label to send balked entities to [block label] {Dispose the Entity}
QueueLabel	The label of each following QUEUE block [block label] {--}

PICKUP: QueueID , Rank , Qty ;

QueueID	Queue to pick entities up from [expression truncated to an integer queue number, or queue symbol name] {--}
Rank	Starting rank of the entities in queue QueueID to pick up [expression truncated to an integer] {1}
Qty	Number of entities to pick up [expression truncated to an integer] {1}

PREEMPT, Pr : ResName , AttributeID , Dest ;

Pr	PREEMPT priority number [expression truncated to an integer] {1}
ResName	Name of the resource to be preempted [ResName or ResName(Index), Index is an expression truncated to an integer] {--}
AttributeID	Attribute to store the remaining delay time in [integer attribute number, A(k), or attribute symbol name] {Stored Internally}
Dest	Destination of preempted entity after surrendering the resource [block label or STO(StorID), StorID is an expression truncated to an integer storage number, or a storage symbol name] {Held Internally for Reallocation}

SCAN : Condition ;

Condition	Scan condition [condition or expression] {--}

SEARCH, Set , BegJ , EndJ : Condition ;

Set	Set to be searched [GROUP, an expression truncated to an integer queue number, or a queue symbol name] {Search Current Entity's Group}
BegJ	Starting index rank for the search [expression truncated to an integer] {1}
EndJ	Ending index rank for the search [expression truncated to an integer] {Last Entity}
Condition	Search condition [condition, MIN(Expression), or MAX(Expression), Expression should contain one or more attributes] {--}

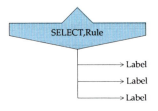

SEIZE, Pr : ResName , Qty :
repeats ;

Pr	Seize priority [expression truncated to an integer] {1}
ResName	Name of resource to seize [ResName or ResName(Index), Index is an expression truncated to an integer] {--}
Qty	Number of resource units required expression truncated to an integer {1}

SELECT, Rule : Label :
repeats;

Rule	Resource Selection Rule [CYC, ER(k), LNB, LRC, POR, RAN, SNB, SRC, or UR(k)] {POR}
Label	Label of each following SEIZE block [block label] {--}

SIGNAL: Code , TotalLimit ;

Code	Signal code [expression truncated to an integer] {--}
TotalLimit	Total number of entities to release [expression truncated to an integer] {Infinite}

SPLIT	
Attributes	

SPLIT: Attributes ;

Attributes   List of representative entity attributes that are assigned to members of the temporary set [*, A(*), M, NS, IS, AttributeID] {No Attribute Assignments}

START	
CnvName,Vel	

START: CnvName , Vel ;

CnvName   Name of the conveyor to activate [symbol name]   {--}

Vel   Conveyor velocity [expression] {Previous Velocity}

STATION,BegStaID-EndStaID

STATION, BegStaID — EndStaID ;

BegStaID   Lower limit of station range [integer station number or station symbol name] {--}

EndStaID   Upper limit of station range [integer station number or station symbol name] {No Range}

STOP	
CnvName	

STOP: CnvName ;

CnvName   Name of the conveyor to set deactivate [symbol name]{--}

SYNONYMS: NewString = OldString :
                repeats ;

NewString   Descriptive string [alphanumeric string] {--}

OldString   SIMAN string to replace [alphanumeric string] {--}

TALLY	
TallyID,Value	

TALLY: TallyID , Value ;

TallyID   Tally location to record variable [expression truncated to an integer tally number, or tally symbol name] {--}

Value   Value to be recorded [expression, INTerval(AttributeID), BETween(VariableID), or BETween] {--}

TRANSPORT,AltPath	
TrnName,EntDest,Vel,TrnDest	

TRANSPORT, AltPath : TrnName , EntDest , Vel , TrnDest ;

AltPath   Alternate path for transport [VIA(StationID), VIA(STATION(StationID)), VIA(INTX(IntxID)), VIA(LINK(LinkID)), or VIA(LINK(LinkID,Zone))] {Not Used}

TrnName	Transporter unit [TrnName or TrnName(Index), Index is an expression truncated to an integer] {Unit the Entity was Allocated}
EntDest	Entity destination station [expression truncated to an integer station number, station symbol name, or SEQ] {SEQ}
Vel	Velocity for TRANSPORT [expression] {Current Velocity}
TrnDest	Guided transporter destination [StationID, STATION(StationID), INTX(IntxID), LINK(LinkID), LINK(LinkID,Zone), FIRSTX(StationID), FIRSTX(STATION(StationID)), FIRSTX(INTX(IntxID)), FIRSTX(LINK(LinkID)), or FIRSTX(LINK(LinkID,Zone))] {Intersection Associated with EntDest Station}

WAIT: Code , WaitLimit ;

Code	Signal code [expression truncated to an integer signal code] {--}
WaitLimit	Maximum number of entities to release from this block when the signal code is received [expression truncated to an integer] {Infinite}

WRITE, FileID , Format , Rec : Variables ;

FileID	File to be written to [expression truncated to an integer file number, or file symbol name] {Standard Output}
Format	Format to use in interpreting data [exact FORTRAN format enclosed in double quotes and parenthesis, or FREE] {Format Specified in FILES Element, or FREE for Standard Output}
Rec	Record number to be written [expression truncated to an integer record number] {Next Record}
Variables	List of variables or expressions to write [an expression or any SIMAN attribute or variable] {No Variables}

APPENDIX E

SIMAN Elements

ARRIVALS: Number , Type , Time , BatchSize , Assignments :
repeats ;

Number	Arrival number [integer] {Sequential}
Type	Arrival type: STATION(StationID) QUEUE(QueueID) BLOCK(BlockID) EVENT(EventNumber) {--}
Time	Offset time from beginning of simulation replication for arrival to occur [constant] {0.0}
BatchSize	Number of entities in batch arrival [integer] {1}
Assignments	Initial values of general purpose attributes [ordered list of expressions separated by commas] {0.0}

ATTRIBUTES: Number , Name(Index) , Value , . . . :
repeats ;

Number	Attribute number (index into the A(k) array) [integer] {Sequential}
Name	Attribute name [symbol name] {Blank}
Index	Index into the named attribute array [constant] {No Array}
Value	Initial values upon entity creation [constant] {0.0 or Last Value}

BEGIN, Listing , Debugger ;

Listing	Generate experiment listing [Yes or No] {Yes}
Debugger	Invoke Interactive Debugger [Yes or No] {No}

CONTINUOUS, NumDifEq , NumStateEq , MinStep , MaxStep , Interval , AbsError , RelError , Severity , NumStateEv ;

NumDifEq	Number of differential equations [integer] {0}
NumStateEq	Number of state equation [integer] {0}
MinStep	Minimum allowable step size [constant] {1.0}
MaxStep	Maximum allowable step size [constant] {1.0}
Interval	Time between save points for recording values of CSTATS variables [constant] {Infinity}
AbsError	Absolute single step truncation error for the RKF algorithm [constant] {0.00001}
RelError	Relative single step truncation error for the RKF algorithm [constant] {0.00001}
Severity	Severity of an accuracy error when a step size smaller than MinStep is required [Fatal, Warning, No] {Warning}
NumStateEv	Number of state events [integer] {25}

CONVEYORS: Number , Name , SegmentSet , Vel , CellSize , Status , MaxPerEnt , Type , EntSize : repeats ;

Number	Conveyor number [integer] {Sequential}
Name	Conveyor name [symbol name] {--}
SegmentSet	Segment set number [integer] {--}
Vel	Conveyor velocity [constant] {1.0}
CellSize	Length of each conveyor cell [integer] {1}
Status	Initial status of the conveyor [Active or Inactive] {Active}
MaxPerEnt	Maximum number of cells occupied by any entity [integer] {1}
Type	Conveyor type [Accumulating or Non-accumulating] {Non-accumulating}
EntSize	Accumulation length of an entity [constant, attribute name, or attribute number] {Cell Size}

COUNTERS: Number , Name , Limit , InitOpt , OutFile : repeats ;

Number	Optional counter number [integer] {Sequential}
Name	Counter name and summary report identifier [symbol name] {Blank}

Limit	Counter limit [positive integer] {Infinite}
InitOpt	Initialize counter between simulation replications [Yes or No] {Yes}
OutFile	Output unit to which counter observations are written during the simulation run [integer unit number or system specific filename enclosed in double quotes] {No Save}

CSTATS: Number , Variable , Name , OutFile :
        repeats ;

Number	CSTATS number [integer] {Sequential}
Variable	Continuous variable to be recorded [S(k), D(k), k is an integer] {--}
Name	CSTATS name and identifier for labeling Summary Report [symbol name] {CSTATS Variable}
OutFile	Output unit to which CSTATS observations are written during simulation run [integer unit number or system specific filename enclosed in double quotes] {No Save}

DISCRETE, Entities , Attributes , Queues , Stations ;

Entities	Maximum number of concurrent entities in the system [integer] {Available Memory}
Attributes	Maximum number of general purpose attributes associated with each entity [integer] {0}
Queues	Largest queue number used [integer] {0}
Stations	Largest station number used [integer] {0}

Matrix form:

DISTANCES: Number , BegStaID − EndStaID , $D_{i,i+1}$, . . . , $D_{i,j}$ /
$$. . . /$$
$$D_{j-1,j} :$$

        repeats ;

Number	Distance set number [integer] {Sequential}
BegStaID	Beginning station identifier of distance matrix station range [integer station number, or station symbol name] {--}
EndStaID	Ending station identifier of distance matrix station range [integer station number, or station symbol name] {--}
$D_{i,j}$	Distance element of station range upper triangular matrix [positive integer] {0}

List form:

DISTANCES: Number , BegStaID — EndStaID — Distance , . . . :
            repeats ;

Number   Distance set number [integer] {Sequential}

BegStaID   Starting station identifier [integer station number, or station symbol name] {--}

EndStaID   Ending station identifier [integer station number, or station symbol name] {--}

Distance   Distance from BegStaID to EndStaID [positive integer] {0}

DISTRIBUTIONS: Number , Expression :
                repeats ;

Number   Distribution number [integer] {Sequential}

Expression   SIMAN expression {--}

DSTATS: Number , Expression , Name , OutFile :
          repeats ;

Number   DSTAT number [integer] {Sequential}

Expression   SIMAN expression on which time-persistent statistics are to be recorded {--}

Name   DSTAT name and label for the SIMAN Summary Report [symbol name] {DSTATS Expression}

OutFile   Output unit to which DSTATS observations are written during the simulation run [integer unit number or system specific filename enclosed in double quotes] {No Save}

EVENTS: Number , Variable , Direction , Thresh , Tol :
          repeats ;

Number   Event number [integer] {--}

Variable   Crossing variable [S(k), D(k), k is an integer] {--}

Direction   Crossing direction [P, N, or E] {--}

Thresh   Crossing threshold [constant, or S(k), D(k), k is an integer] {--}

Tol   Crossing tolerance [constant] {0.0}

FILES: Number , Name , FileDesc , Access , Structure , EndOpt , Comment , InitOpt , Unit :
  repeats ;

Number	File number [integer] {Sequential}
Name	File name used for identification on READ and WRITE blocks [symbol name] {Blank}
FileDesc	Operating system file name enclosed in double quotes [system-dependent] {Automatically Assigned}
Access	File type [SEQuential; or DIR(Length), direct access using record Length bytes] {SEQ}
Structure	File structure [UNFormatted; FREe; WKS; or "(Format)," exact FORTRAN format enclosed in double quotes and parentheses, Format must be 255 characters or fewer] {UNFormatted}
EndOpt	End-of-file action [ERRor, DISpose, REWind, or IGNore] {ERRor}
Comment	Character indicating comment record [character enclosed in double quotes, or No] {No}
InitOpt	Action to be taken at beginning of each simulation replication for sequential files [HOLD, REWind, or CLOSe] {HOLD}
Unit	FORTRAN unit number to be used for file I/O [integer] {Automatically Assigned}

INCLUDE: FileDesc ;

FileDesc	File containing elements to include in the model [system specific filename enclosed in double quotes] {--}

INITIALIZE: Variable = Value :
  repeats ;

Variable	Variable or integer attribute to be initialized [$D(k)$, IS, J, M, NS, $S(k)$, or $X(k)$, k is an integer] {--}
Value	Value to be assigned to the variable [constant (integer for IS, J, M, NS)] {--}

INTERSECTIONS: Number , Name , Length , Rule , VelChange :
  repeats ;

Number	Intersection number [integer] {Sequential}
Name	Intersection name [symbol name] {Blank}
Length	Travel length through intersection [integer] {0}

Rule	Link selection rule [FCFS, LCFS, LVF(AttributeID), HVF(AttributeID), CLOSEST, FARTHEST] {FCFS}
VelChange	Velocity change factor [constant] {1.0}

LAYOUTS: FileDesc , AnimAttrib , Scale , Frame , Key :
repeats ;

FileDesc	Cinema layout filename enclosed in double quotes [system-dependent] {Same as Program File}
AnimAttrib	Animation attribute [expression] {No Display of Entity Symbols}
Scale	Simulated time between screen updates [constant] {1.0}
Frame	Real time between screen updates [constant] {0.0}
Key	Key for recalling the layout during a run [alphanumeric character enclosed in double quotes] {No Key for Layout Recall}

LINKS: Number , Name , BegIntxID — BegDir , EndIntxID — EndDir , Zones , Length , Type , VelChange :
repeats ;

Number	Link Number [integer] {Sequential}
Name	Link Name [symbol name] {Blank}
BegIntxID	Beginning intersection [integer intersection number or intersection name] {--}
BegDir	Direction of link as it leaves the beginning intersection [integer] {0}
EndIntxID	Ending intersection [integer intersection number or intersection name] {--}
EndDir	Direction of link as it enters the ending intersection [integer] {BegDir}
Zones	Number of zones [integer] {1}
Length	Length of each zone [integer] {0}
Type	Link type [Unidirectional, Bidirectional or Spur] {Unidirectional}
VelChange	Velocity change factor [constant] {1.0}

NETWORKS: Number , Name , BegLinkID — EndLinkID , . . . :
repeats ;

Number	Network Number [integer] {Sequential}
Name	Network Name [symbol name] {Blank}

BegLinkID	Starting link in range of links to include [integer link number or link symbol name] {--}
EndLinkID	Ending link in range of links to include [integer link number or link symbol name] {No Range}

OUTPUTS: Number , Expression , OutFile , OutProcID :
repeats ;

Number	Output element number [integer] {Sequential}
Expression	SIMAN expression to be recorded {--}
OutFile	Output unit to which observations are written at the end of each replication [integer unit number or system specific filename enclosed in double quotes] {No Saving}
OutProcID	Identifier for labeling the output in the output processor and in the SIMAN Summary Report [alphanumeric] {Expression}

PARAMETERS: Number , Name , P_1 , ... , P_n :
repeats ;

Number	Parameter set number [integer] {Sequential}
Name	Parameter set name [symbol name] {Blank}
P_i	Parameter values [constant] {--}

PROJECT, Title , Analyst , Date ;

Title	Project title [alphanumeric] {Blank}
Analyst	Analyst name [alphanumeric] {Blank}
Date	Date in form of month/day/year {System-Specific}

QUEUES: Number , Name , Ranking :
repeats ;

Number	Queue number [integer] {Sequential}
Name	Queue name [symbol name] {Blank}
Ranking	Ranking criterion [FIFO, LIFO HVF(AttributeID), or LVF(AttributeID)] {--}

RANKINGS: QueueID , Ranking :
      repeats ;

QueueID   Queue identifier or lower limit of a queue range for which the ranking criterion applies [integer queue number, queue symbol name, or queue range] {--}

Ranking   Ranking criterion [FIFO, LIFO HVF(AttributeID), or LVF(AttributeID)] {--}

REDIRECTS: Number , Name , NetworkID ,
                BegIntxID — EndIntxID — NextIntxID , . . . :
      repeats ;

Number   Redirect Number [integer] {Sequential}

Name   Redirect Name [symbol name] {Blank}

NetworkID   Network Identifier [integer network number or network name] {--}

BegIntxID   Beginning Intersection ("from") [integer intersection number, or intersection symbol name] {--}

EndIntxID   Ending Intersection ("to") [integer intersection number, or intersection symbol name] {--}

NextIntxID   Intersection to go to Next [integer intersection number, or intersection symbol name] {--}

REPLICATE, NumReps , BeginTime , Length , InitSys , InitStats , WarmUp ;

NumReps   Number of simulation replications to execute [integer] {1}

BeginTime   Beginning time for the first replication [constant] {0.0}

Length   Maximum length of each replication [constant] {Infinite}

InitSys   Initialize system status between replications [Yes or No] {Yes}

InitStats   Discard previous observations between replications [Yes or No] {Yes}

WarmUp   Warm up time for system to reach steady state conditions [constant] {0.0}

RESOURCES: Number , Name(NumUnits) , Capacity , . . . :
      repeats ;

Number   Resource number [integer] {Sequential}

Name   Resource name [alphanumeric] {--}

NumUnits	Number of indexed units [integer] {Simple Resource}
Capacity	Initial capacity [integer or SCHED(k), k is integer] {1}

RULES: Number , Rule :
repeats ;

Number	Rule number [integer or range] {--}
Rule	Queue, Resource, or Transporter selection rule [CYC, LDS, LNB, LNQ, LRC, Max(Expression), MIN(Expression) POR, RAN, SDS, SNB, SNQ, SRC, or UR(k), k is integer] {--}

SCHEDULES: Number , Capacity * Duration ,...:
repeats ;

Number	Schedule number [integer] {--}
Capacity	Resource capacity [integer] {--}
Duration	Capacity duration [expression] {Infinite}

SEEDS: Stream , Seed , InitOpt :
repeats ;

Stream	Stream number to be initialized [integer between 1 and 10] {--}
Seed	Initial seed value [integer] {Machine-Dependent}
InitOpt	Reinitialize stream between replications [Yes, No, Common, Antithetic] {No}

SEGMENTS: Number , BegStaID , NextStaID — Length ,...:
repeats ;

Number	Segment set number [integer] {--}
BegStaID	Beginning station identifier [integer station number or station symbol name] {--}
NextStaID	Next station identifier [integer station number or station symbol name] {--}
Length	Distance from the previous station [integer] {--}

SEQUENCES: Number , BegStaID , Assignments & NextStaID , Assignments & ...:
repeats ;

Number	Sequence set number [integer] {Sequential}

BegStaID	Next station in visitation sequence [integer station number or station symbol name] {--}
Assignments	List of attributes or variables and their values upon entering the station {Leave Value}
NextStaID	Next station in the sequence [integer station number or station symbol name] {--}

STATIONS: Number , Name , IntxID :
repeats ;

Number	Station number [integer] {Sequential}
Name	Station name [symbol name] {Blank}
IntxID	Associated intersection [integer intersection number or intersection symbol name] {No Intersection}

STORAGES: Number , Name :
repeats ;

| Number | Storage number [integer] {Sequential} |
| Name | Storage name [symbol name] {Blank} |

SYNONYMS: NewString = OldString :
repeats ;

| NewString | Descriptive string [alphanumeric string] {--} |
| OldString | SIMAN string to replace [alphanumeric string] {--} |

TABLES: Number , Name , XLow , XInc , Y_1 ,..., Y_n :
repeats ;

Number	Table number [integer] {Sequential}
Name	Table name [symbol name] {Blank}
XLow	Low value for the independent variable [constant] {0.01}
XInc	Fixed increment between successive values of the independent variable [constant] {1.0}
Y_i	Dependent variable values corresponding to the independent variable [constants] {--}

TALLIES: Number , Name , OutFile :
         repeats ;

Number	Tally number [integer] {Sequential}
Name	Tally name and identifier for labeling Summary Report [symbol name] {Blank}
OutFile	Output unit or filename for saving observations [integer unit number, or system specific filename enclosed in double quotes] {No Save}

TRACE, BegTime , EndTime , Condition , Expression, . . . ;

BegTime	Time after the beginning time of the simulation at which the trace is to begin [constant] {0.0}
EndTime	Time after the beginning of the simulation at which the trace is to end [constant] {Infinite}
Condition	Trace condition [logical condition] {Trace ALL}
Expression	SIMAN expression to display during trace {No Values}

TRANSPORTERS: Number , Name , NumUnits , Map — Control ,
                    Vel — Accel — Decel — TurnVel ,
                    Position — Status — Size , . . . :
         repeats ;

Number	Transporter Number [integer] {Sequential}
Name	Transporter Name [symbol name] {--}
NumUnits	Number of available units [integer] {1}
Map	System Map [integer distance set, DISTANCE(k), or NETWORK(NetworkID)] {--}
Control	Type of zone control [Start, End, or k] {Start}
Vel	Velocity [constant] {1.0}
Accel	Transporter acceleration [constant] {0.0}
Decel	Transporter deceleration [constant] {0.0}
TurnVel	Turning velocity factor [constant] {1.0}
Position	Initial Position [StationID, INTX(IntxID), LINK(LinkID,Zone), or STATION(StationID)]
Status	Initial Status [Active or Inactive] {Active}
Size	Space vehicle occupies [LENGTH(k) or ZONE(k)] {1 Zone}

VARIABLES: Number , Name(Index) , Value ,...:
               repeats ;

Number   Variable number (index into the V(k) array) [integer] {Sequential}

Name   Variable name [symbol name] {Blank}

Index   Index into the named variable array [constant] {No Array}

Value   Initial values for variables at beginning of run [constant] {0.0 or Last Value}

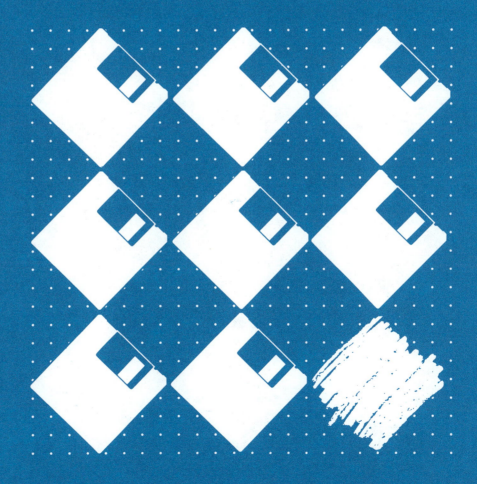

Index

A

A function 464
A(AttribID) 67
ACC(TrnID) 428
ACCESS block 261, 581
Accumulating conveyors 260, 275
ACTIVATE block 256, 581
Active entity 137, 143
Activity-scanning 24, 370
Advantages of simulation 9
AG function 465
AGV 235, 403
ALLOCATE block 249, 418, 581
Almost full-period generator 172
ALTER block 343, 581
Alternate paths 419
ALWAYS branch 105
Analyst name 86
Animation 305
Animation attribute 312
Antithetic variates 544
Applications 6
Arithmetic errors 151
Arnold, S. 539, 551
Array names 66
Arrays 100
ARRIVALS element 186, 372, 593
AS/RS 438
Ashour, S. 516, 528
ASSIGN block 102, 582
ASSIGN command 147
ASSIGN subroutine 465
Attributes 62
ATTRIBUTES element 99, 593
Auto-covariance stationary process 188
AutoCAD interface 311
Automated Guided Vehicles, see AGV
Average 166

B

Balci, O. 57, 158, 161
Balking 75
Bank teller 384
Banks, J. 158, 161
BARCHART command 195
Basic block types 63
Batch size selection 190, 199
Batching 189
BEGIN statement 83, 92
Behavior anomaly 159
Behavior comparison 159
Behavior prediction 159
Beta distribution 43, 49, 50, 557
BETA random variable 68
BETWEEN (BET) statistics 111
Bidirectional links 406
Binary files 365
Bindingnavle, S. 516, 528
Binomial distribution 49
Block comment 71, 83
Block diagram 62
Block function name 63
Block label 71, 83
Block modifiers 72
Block sequence number 71
Block statements 83
Blockage errors 151
Blocks 62
    ACCESS block 261, 581
    ACTIVATE block 256, 581
    ALLOCATE block 249, 418, 581
    ALTER block 343, 581
    ASSIGN block 103, 582
    BRANCH block 104, 582
    CAPTURE block 436, 582
    CLOSE block 368, 582
    COMBINE block 360, 583
    CONVEY block 262, 583
    COPY block 583

COUNT block 81, 583
CREATE block 74, 583
DELAY block 79, 584
DETECT block 512, 584
DROPOFF block 356, 584
DUPLICATE block 360, 584
EVENT block 456, 460, 584
EXIT block 262, 585
FINDJ block 371, 585
FREE block 239, 585
GROUP block 356, 585
HALT block 256, 585
INSERT block 586
MATCH block 354, 586
MOVE block 250, 418, 586
PICKQ block 349, 587
PICKUP block 356, 587
PREEMPT block 345, 587
QPICK block 349, 588
QUEUE block 75, 588
READ block 366, 588
RELEASE block 80, 588
RELINQUISH block 436, 589
REMOVE block 352, 589
REQUEST block 236, 418, 589
ROUTE block 221, 589
SCAN block 370, 386, 590
SEARCH block 352, 590
SEIZE block 77, 590
SELECT block 341, 590
SIGNAL block 369, 590
SPLIT block 356, 591
START block 270, 591
STATION block 220, 591
STOP block 270, 591
TALLY block 110, 591
TRANSPORT block 238, 591
WAIT block 369, 592
WRITE block 367, 592
BLOCKS editor 63

Bonferroni method 204
Boundary definition 34
BRANCH block 103, 582
Branches 105
Brately, P. 39, 44, 51, 57, 531, 550
Brazier, M. 26
Breakdowns 345
Breakpoints 139, 142

C

C 455
CANCEL BREAK command 142
CANCEL command 142
CANCEL INTERCEPT command 144
CANCEL subroutine 468
CANCEL TRACE CONDITION
    command 145
CANCEL TRACE ENTITY command 144
CANCEL TRACE EXPRESSION
    command 145
CANCEL WATCH /NOSTOP command 143
CANCEL WATCH command 143
CAPTURE block 436, 582
Carson, J. 158, 161
Cedar Bog Lake 507
Central Limit Theorem 48, 176
CEVENT function 459
Chemical reaction process 520
Chi-square table 570
Chi-Square test 51
Cinema 305
    animation attribute 312
    AutoCAD interface 311
    display point 311
    distance path object 319
    dynamic colors 318
    dynamic objects 309
    entity symbols 312
    frame delay 326
    frequencies object 318
    global symbols 317
    intersection object 322
    layout 309
    level object 317
    link object 322
    plots object 318
    queue object 313
    ragged queues 313
    ragged storages 316
    resource symbols 314
    ride point 322
    route path object 319
    rubberband mode 310
    scale factor 326
    segment path object 319
    seize point 315

skip-ahead 326
snap grid 311
staging area object 321
static objects 309
station object 319
storage object 315
straight queues 313
symbol libraries 311
time-advance parameters 325
variable object 316
Circuit board assembly system 283, 309
CKEYHI function 460
CLA(CnvID) 268
CLEAR subroutine 472
CLOSE block 368, 582
CLOSEST link rule 405
Closest to destination link rule, see CLOSEST
Closing files 368
CLRCNT subroutine 472
CLRCST subroutine 472
CLRDST subroutine 472
CLRTAL subroutine 472
Coefficient of variation 166
Colon (:) 84
COMBINE block 360, 583
Combined discrete-continuous models 495
Combined models 6
Combined process/discrete-event
    modeling 455
Commands 140
Commas (,) 84
Common block 463
Common random numbers 540
Communication interval 506
Comparing two systems 181, 203
    paired-t confidence interval 183
    two-sample-t method 183
COMPARISONS command 203
Compile-time errors 95
Compiling the model and experiment 93
Condition 69
Conditional branches 105
Confidence intervals (non-terminating
    systems) 168, 187, 201
    batch size selection 190, 199
    batching 189
    replication 188
    summing covariances 188
Confidence intervals (terminating
    systems) 168, 177, 201
    confidence level 178
    fixed sample-size procedure 179
    half-width 178
    student-t distribution 178
    t-value 178
    two-stage sampling procedure 179

Confidence level 178
Consistency 156
Continuity 156
CONTINUOUS (CONT) random variable
    68, 103
Continuous distribution 558
CONTINUOUS element 505, 594
Continuous modeling 6, 495
Continuous time-advance 504
Continuous time-advance parameters 505
Control variates 535
CONVEY block 262, 583
Conveyor Cells 261, 265
Conveyor Segments 265
Conveyor Variables 267
Conveyor variables 573
Conveyor, stopping and stopping 270
Conveyors 259
CONVEYORS element 265, 594
Conway, R. 35, 57
COPY block 583
COPY subroutine 465
Correcting errors 148
Correlation 176, 188
Correlogram 189
CORRELOGRAM command 197
COUNT block 81, 583
COUNT subroutine 472
Counters 81, 90
COUNTERS element 90, 594
CPRIME function 458
CREATE block 74, 583
CREATE subroutine 468
CSIMAN 309, 324
CSTATE function 460
CSTATS element 506, 595
Csum 189
CUCLEA function 458
CUF function 459
CUR function 459
CURST function 460
CUSAV function 460
CWRAP function 458
CYC 342, 350
Cycle length 172
Cyclic priority, see CYC

D

D array 501
Data errors 149
Data recording errors 152
DAVG(DstatID) 177
Deadlock errors 151
Debugger, see Interactive debugger
DEC(TrnID) 428
Decision maker 153

Degeneracy 156
DELAY block 79, 584
Department of Energy nuclear waste handling
    facility 330
DETACH modifier 351, 355
DETECT block 512, 584
Deterministic branches 105
Deterministic models 6
Differential equation 497
Direct-access file 364
Disadvantages of simulation 9
DISCRETE (DISC) random variable 68, 103
Discrete distribution 49, 559
DISCRETE element 87, 595
Discrete models 6
Discrete-event modeling 456
Discrete-event routines 465
    ASSIGN subroutine 465
    CANCEL subroutine 468
    CLEAR subroutine 472
    CLRCNT subroutine 472
    CLRCST subroutine 472
    CLRDST subroutine 472
    CLRTAL subroutine 472
    COPY subroutine 465
    COUNT subroutine 472
    CREATE subroutine 468
    DISPOS subroutine 468
    ENTER subroutine 468
    INSERT subroutine 468
    QUEUE subroutine 468
    REMOVE subroutine 468
    SCHED subroutine 468
    SEND subroutine 468
    SETA subroutine 465
    SETIS subroutine 465
    SETM subroutine 465
    SETMR subroutine 471
    SETNS subroutine 465
    SETP subroutine 471
    SETTF subroutine 471
    SETV subroutine 471
    SETVC subroutine 471
    SETVT subroutine 471
    SIG subroutine 468
    SUMRY subroutine 472
    TALLY subroutine 472
Display point 311
DISPOS subroutine 468
DISPOSE modifier 72
Distance matrix 245
Distance path object 319
DISTANCES element 244, 595
Distributions 555
    beta distribution 43, 49, 50, 557
    binomial distribution 49

continuous distribution 558
discrete distribution 49, 559
Erlang distribution 47, 50, 560
exponential distribution 41, 47, 561
gamma distribution 48, 50, 562
geometric distribution 49
lognormal distribution 48, 563
normal distribution 43, 48, 564
Poisson distribution 41, 49, 565
triangular distribution 41, 43, 47, 566
uniform distribution 41, 47, 567
Weibull distribution 48, 568
DISTRIBUTIONS element 374, 596
DMAX(DstatID) 177
DMIN(DstatID) 177
Documentation 23
Double period (..) 100
Doubting frame of mind 134
DROPOFF block 356, 584
DSTATS element 109, 596
DUPLICATE block 360, 584
Dynamic colors 318
Dynamic objects 309

E

Elements 85
    ARRIVALS element 186, 372, 593
    ATTRIBUTES element 99, 593
    CONTINUOUS element 505, 594
    CONVEYORS element 265, 594
    COUNTERS element 90, 594
    CSTATS element 506, 595
    DISCRETE element 87, 595
    DISTANCES element 244, 595
    DISTRIBUTIONS element 374, 596
    DSTATS element 109, 596
    EVENTS element 596
    FILES element 363, 597
    INITIALIZE element 503, 597
    INTERSECTIONS element 405, 597
    LAYOUTS element 323, 598
    LINKS element 406, 598
    NETWORKS element 407, 598
    OUTPUTS element 176, 599
    PARAMETERS element 376, 599
    PROJECT element 86, 599
    QUEUES element 87, 599
    RANKINGS element 600
    REDIRECTS element 434, 600
    REPLICATE element 91, 600
    RESOURCES element 89, 600
    RULES element 374, 601
    SCHEDULES element 343, 601
    SEEDS element 170, 173, 542, 546, 601
    SEGMENTS element 266, 601
    SEQUENCES element 233, 601

STATIONS element 224, 410, 602
STORAGES element 113, 602
TABLES element 375, 602
TALLIES element 112, 603
TRACE element 139, 603
TRANSPORTERS element 243, 411, 603
VARIABLES element 99, 604
ELSE branch 105
Empirical distributions 44
Empiricism 155
Empty and idle state 186
END command 193
END statement 83, 92
ENTER subroutine 468
Entities 62
Entity flow between blocks 72
Entity identifier 138, 462
Entity record location 462
Entity sets 355
Entity symbols 312
ERLANG (ERLA) random variable 68
Erlang distribution 47, 50, 560
Errors 149
    arithmetic errors 151
    blockage errors 151
    data errors 149
    data recording errors 152
    deadlock errors 151
    flow control errors 150
    initialization errors 150
    language conceptual errors 153
    overwriting errors 152
    units of measurement errors 150
Euler's method 499
Event 456
EVENT block 456, 460, 584
EVENT subroutine 459
Event time 456
Event-scheduling 24
EVENTS element 596
Exclamation point (!) 84
Existing data 44
EXIT block 262, 585
Experiment Frame 62
Experiment object file 94
Experiment source file 93
Experiment statement ordering 93
Experimental design 17
Experimentation 20
EXPMT processor 94
EXPONENTIAL (EXPO) random variable 68
Exponential distribution 41, 47, 561
EXPORTS command 205
Expression 69
Extended listings 95

F

Face validity 157
Farthest from destination link rule,
    see FARTHEST
FARTHEST link rule 405
FCFS link rule 405
Felhberg, E. 504, 528
FIFO 88
FILES element 363, 597
FILTER command 199
Final value 168
FINDJ block 371, 585
FIRST 357
First-come, first-served link rule, see FCFS
First-in-first-out, see FIFO
FIRSTX control option 433
Fisher, R. 51
Fishman, G. 187, 216
Fixed sample-size procedure 179
Flow control errors 150
Flow-line 222
Ford, D. 26
Ford, F. 6, 26
Forgionne, G. 6, 26
Formatted files 365
FORTRAN 455
Fox, B. 39, 44, 57, 531, 550
Frame delay 326
FREE block 239, 585
Free-path transporters 235
Frequencies object 318
From-to matrix 245

G

GAMMA (GAMM) random variable 68
Gamma distribution 48, 50, 562
Gass, S. I. 157, 161
General Motors truck assembly 327
General-purpose attributes 67
General-purpose variables 66
Generic station submodels 335
Geometric distribution 49
Global symbols 317
GO command 141
GO UNTIL command 141
Goodness-of-fit test 51
    Chi-Square test 51
    Kolmogorov-Smirnov test 54
GROUP block 356, 585
Group variables 573
Guided transporters 235, 403
Guided-transporter movement 412
Guided-transporter variables 428

H

Half-width 178

HALT block 256, 585
Heidorn, G. 19, 26
Help 148
HELP command 193
High-value-first, see HVF
Highest attribute value link rule,
    see HVF(AttribID)
Highway toll booth 382
Histogram 45, 196
HISTOGRAM command 195
Hold block 63, 75
Hospital emergency room 120, 211
Hurst, N. 520, 528
HVF 88
HVF(AttribID) link rule 405

I

Iconic models 5
ICS(CnvID) 268
ID function 470
IDENT function 464
IDIST function 470
IDSNET(NetID,IntxID1,IntxID2) 430
IF branch 105
Implementation 23
IMPORTS command 205
In-line comments 84
Indexed resources 337
Indirect measures 532
Information collection 32
Initial condition bias 186
Initial transient period 185
Initialization errors 150
INITIALIZE element 503, 597
Innis, G. 35, 57
Input 362
Input data 18
INSERT block 586
INSERT subroutine 468
Integer constant 65
Interactive debugger 139
    active entity 137, 143
    breakpoints 139, 142
    commands 140
    help 148
    intercepts 143
    prompt 140
    redirecting entity flow 147
    snapshots 147
    starting a debug session 140
    stopping a debug session 140
    watch variables 139, 143
Interactive debugger commands 140
    ASSIGN command 147
    CANCEL BREAK command 142
    CANCEL command 142

CANCEL INTERCEPT command 144
CANCEL TRACE CONDITION
    command 145
CANCEL TRACE ENTITY command 144
CANCEL TRACE EXPRESSION
    command 145
CANCEL WATCH /NOSTOP
    command 143
CANCEL WATCH command 143
GO command 141
GO UNTIL command 141
HELP command 193
NEXT command 147
RESTORE command 147
SAVE command 147
SET BREAK command 142
SET command 142
SET INTERCEPT command 143
SET TRACE CONDITION command 144
SET TRACE ENTITY command 144
SET TRACE EXPRESSION command 145
SET WATCH command 143
SHOW command 145
STEP command 141
VIEW command 145
VIEW COUNTERS command 145
VIEW DSTATS command 145
VIEW ENTITY command 143
VIEW QUEUE /BRIEF command 146
VIEW QUEUE command 146
VIEW SOURCE command 145
VIEW SUMMARY command 145
VIEW TALLIES command 145
Intercepts 143
Intersection object 322
Intersections 405
INTERSECTIONS element 405, 597
INTERVAL (INT) statistics 111
Interval estimate, see Confidence interval
INTERVALS command 201
Interviews 33
Intrinsic functions 576
INTX(IntersectionID) 419
IOFFST function 470
IS 229
IS function 464
ISG function 465
ISGMT function 470
ISZT(TrnID,Unit) 428
IT(TrnID,Unit) 247

J

J 352, 371
Jobshop 378
Johnson, Eric 307, 332

K

Kahneman, D. 40, 43, 58
Kelton, D. 44, 46, 50, 51, 57, 531, 550
KEYHIT subroutine 460
Kleijnen, J. 531, 539, 550
Kleine, H. 20, 27
Kolmogorov-Smirnov table 569
Kolmogorov-Smirnov test 54

L

Lag 189
Language conceptual errors 153
Largest Number Busy, see LNB
Largest Number in Queue, see LNQ
Largest Remaining Capacity, see LRC
LAST 357
Last-come, last-served link rule, see LCLS
Last-in-last-out, see LIFO
Lavenberg, S. 539, 550
Law, A. 46, 50, 51, 57, 531, 533, 550
Layout 309
LAYOUTS element 323, 598
LCLS link rule 405
LDL(TrnID,Unit) 429
LDX(TrnID,Unit) 429
LDZ(TrnID,Unit) 429
LEC(CnvID) 268
LENZ(LinkID) 430
Level object 317
LFCAL function 467
LFR function 467
LGRP function 465
LIFO 88
Line segments 65
Link object 322
Link selection rules 405
LINK(LinkID,Zone) 419
Link-time errors 95
LINKER processor 95
Linking model and experiment object files 95
Links 405
LINKS element 406, 598
Little's formula 532
LLR function 467
LNB 342
LNKNUM(IntxID,IntxID) 430
LNQ 350
Logical modeling framework 20
Logical variable 70
LOGNORMAL (LOGN) random variable 68
Lognormal distribution 48, 563
Lotus 123 363
Low-value-first, see LVF
Lowest attribute value link rule, see
    LVF(AttribID)
LPRED function 467

LRANK function 467
LRC 342, 350
LSCAL function 467
LSUCC function 467
LT(TrnID,Unit) 247, 250
LTL(TrnID,Unit) 429
LTV flexible machining cell 329
LTYP(LinkID) 430
LTZ(TrnID,Unit) 429
LVF 88
LVF(AttribID) link rule 405
LX(IntxID) 430

M

M 222, 336
M function 464
Manufacturing applications 8
MARK modifier 111
Markowitz, H. 41, 58
MATCH block 354, 586
Matching attribute 354
Material Requirements Planning, see MRP
Mathewson, S. 19, 27
Maximum likelihood estimates 50
Maximum number of entities 87
Maximum observation 166
MaxTake 104
McKay, K. 13, 27, 57, 58
Method of moments 50
MG function 465
Minimum observation 166
MLC(CnvID) 268
Model formulation 16
Model Frame 62
Model object file 94
MODEL processor 94
Model source file 83
Model translation 19
Model, definition 3
Modified flow-line 227
Modified flow-line revisited 338
Modified flow-line with accumulating
    conveyors 278
Modified flow-line with conveyors 259
Modified flow-line with finite buffers and
    conveyor failures 270
Modified flow-line with guided
    transporters 404
Modified flow-line with transporters 234
Modular modeling approach 220
Modulo value 172
MOVAVERAGE command 198
MOVE block 250, 418, 586
Moving average filter 187, 198
Moving between stations 221
MR(ResourceID) 77

MRP 389
MT(TrnID) 247
Multiplicative congruential method 171
Multiplier (16807) 172
Murray, K. 26
MZ(LinkID) 430

N

Nance, R. 20, 27, 57
Narrow aisle and transporter failures 249
NC(CounterID) 81, 177
NDX(LinkID) 431
NEA(CnvID) 268
NEC(CnvID) 268
Network information variables 430
Network status variables 431
Networks 407
NETWORKS element 407, 598
NEVENT function 467
Newton's law 497
NEXT command 147
NEXT modifier 72
Next-intersection matrix 410
NEXTX(NetID,IntxID1,IntxID2) 430
NG function 465
NL(LinkID) 431
No existing data 41
    mean value only 41
    range and most likely value 43
    range only 42
Non-accumulating conveyors 260
Non-terminating system 22, 174
Non-terminating system, analysis 185, 206, 211
    initial condition bias 186
        empty and idle state 186
        moving average filter 187, 198
        starting conditions 186
        truncation 186, 198, 199
        warm-up period, see initial transient period
    initial transient period 185
    steady-state behavior 185
    variance estimation, see Confidence intervals
        (non-terminating systems)
NORMAL (NORM) random variable 68
Normal distribution 43, 48, 564
Normalized random number 171
Nozari, A. 539, 551
NQ(QueueID) 76
NR(ResourceID) 77
NS 229
NS function 464
NSG function 465
NSTO(StorID) 79
NSZT(TrnID,Unit) 428
NT(TrnID) 247
Nth-order differential equation 498

Number of observations 166
NX(IntxID) 431
NXB(LinkID) 430
NXE(LinkID) 430
NZ(LinkID,Zone) 431

O

Object of a study 31
Observational data 109
One-Way Analysis of Variances Fixed
    Effects model 204
ONEWAYS command 204
Operands 65
Operation block 63
Operator priorities 70
Ordinary differential equation 497
Output 362
Output analysis 165
Output file 112
Output Processor 165, 191, 206
Output Processor commands 193
    BARCHART command 195
    COMPARISONS command 203
    CORRELOGRAM command 197
    END command 193
    EXPORTS command 205
    FILTER command 199
    HELP command 193
    HISTOGRAM command 195
    IMPORTS command 205
    INTERVALS command 201
    MOVAVERAGE command 198
    ONEWAYS command 204
    PLOTS command 194
    QUIT command 193
    SDINTERVALS command 204
    TABLES command 205
    VARTESTS command 204
OUTPUTS element 176, 599
Outside doubters 135
Overhead crane 443
Overwriting variables and attributes 152

P

Paired-t confidence interval 183
Parameter estimation 49
Parameter Value List 69
Parameters and relationships 157
PARAMETERS element 376, 599
Partial differential equation 497
Partitioning 35
Pearson, K. 51
Pegden, C. 539, 551
Permanent entity sets 356
Perriens, M. P. 136, 162
PERT 43

Phillips, D. 46, 58
PICKQ block 349, 587
PICKUP block 356, 587
Pilot runs 207
PLOTS command 194
Plots object 318
Point estimate 168
Poisson 41, 49
POISSON (POIS) random variable 68
Poisson distribution 41, 49, 565
Poorte, Jacob 307, 332
POR 342, 350
Positive economics 155
Power-and-free conveyor system 289
PREEMPT block 345, 587
Preempted entity queue 347
Preemption 345
Preferred Order Rule, see POR
Preparing data for analysis 208
Presentation of results 307
Primary entities 104
PRIME subroutine 458
Pritsker, A. 187, 216, 520, 527, 528
Probabilistic branches 105
Problem definition 13
Process 62
Process orientation 62
Process-interaction 25
PROD 357
Production runs 208
Production scheduling system 389
Program file 95
Project date 86
PROJECT element 86, 599
Project planning 13
Project title 86
Psuedo-random numbers 171

Q

QPICK block 349, 588
QUEUE block 75, 588
Queue object 313
Queue ranking rule 74
Queue selection rules 350
QUEUE subroutine 468
Queue variables 573
QUEUES element 87, 599
QUIT command 193

R

Ragged queues 313
Ragged storages 316
Ramsey, T. 544, 551
RAN 342, 350
Random number generation 171
    almost full-period generator 172

cycle length 172
modulo value 172
multiplicative congruential method 171
multiplier (16807) 172
normalized random number 171
psuedo-random numbers 171
random number stream 172
starting seed 171
unnormalized random number 171
Random number stream 172
Random priority, see RAN
Random sample generation 171
Random variable names 68
    BETA random variable 68
    CONTINUOUS (CONT) random variable
        68, 103
    DISCRETE (DISC) random variable 68, 103
    ERLANG (ERLA) random variable 68
    EXPONENTIAL (EXPO) random variable 68
    GAMMA (GAMM) random variable 68
    LOGNORMAL (LOGN) random variable 68
    NORMAL (NORM) random variable 68
    POISSON (POIS) random variable 68
    TRIANGULAR (TRIA) random variable 68
    UNIFORM (UNIF) random variable 68
    WEIBULL (WEIB) random variable 68
Random variables 68
    abbreviations 68
    parameter values 68
    primary format 68
    secondary format 68
Randomness, control of 170
RANKINGS element 600
Rate equation, see differential equation
Rationalism 155
READ block 366, 588
Reading data 366
Reading from a data file and user-menu
    system 478
Real constant 65
Redirecting entity flow 147
Redirects 434
REDIRECTS element 434, 600
Regression sampling 539
Relational operators 70
RELEASE block 80, 588
Release-at-end zone control 411
Release-at-start zone control 411
RELINQUISH block 436, 589
REMOVE block 352, 589
REMOVE subroutine 468
Removing entities from queues 352
REPLICATE element 91, 600
Replication 175, 188
Replication variables 574
Replications, number of 91

Representative entity 356
REQUEST block 236, 418, 589
Resource capacity 343
Resource priority 78
Resource selection rules 341
Resource symbols 314
Resource variables 574
Resources 77
RESOURCES element 89, 600
Restaurant 117, 209
RESTORE command 147
Rexstad, E. 35, 57
Ride point 322
ROUTE block 221, 589
Route path object 319
Rubberband mode 310
RULES element 374, 601
Run length control 81, 90, 91
Run-time errors 96
Runge-Kutta methods 499

S

S array 501
SAG function 465
Sample Problems
    AS/RS 438
    bank teller 384
    Cedar Bog Lake 507
    chemical reaction process 520
    circuit board assembly system 283, 309
    Department of Energy nuclear waste
        handling facility 330
    flow-line 222
    General Motors truck assembly 327
    highway toll booth 382
    hospital emergency room 120, 211
    jobshop 378
    LTV flexible machining cell 329
    modified flow-line 227
    modified flow-line revisited 338
    modified flow-line with accumulating
        conveyors 278
    modified flow-line with conveyors 259
    modified flow-line with finite buffers and
        conveyor failures 270
    modified flow-line with guided
        transporters 404
    modified flow-line with transporters 234
    narrow aisle and transporter failures 249
    overhead crane 443
    power-and-free conveyor system 289
    production scheduling system 389
    reading from a data file and user-menu
        system 478
    restaurant 116, 209
    single machine problem (discrete-event) 473

single workstation 73
soaking pit furnace 516
statistics on Queues, Resources, and time in
    system 108
two job types and a second workstation 97
United Parcel Service hub shifter
    simulation 328
user-defined decision rule 486
Westinghouse Just-In-Time fabrication
    shop 326
Sample trace 138
Sargent, R. G. 158, 161, 162
SAVE command 147
Save criterion 356
Scale factor 326
SCAN block 370, 386, 590
SCHED subroutine 468
SCHEDULES element 343, 601
Scheduling 389
Scheffee method 204
Schmeiser, B. 191, 216
Schrage, L. 39, 44, 57, 531, 550
Schriber, T. 42, 58
Schroer, B. 26
Schruben, L. 187, 204, 216
Scientific notation (E) 65
SDINTERVALS command 204
SDS 238
SEARCH block 352, 590
Searching entities in queues 352
Secondary entities 104
SEEDS element 170, 173, 542, 546, 601
Segment path object 319
Segment terminator 84
SEGMENTS element 266, 601
SEIZE block 77, 590
Seize point 315
SELECT block 341, 590
Semi-colon (;) 84
SEND subroutine 468
Sensitivity analysis 157
SEQ 229
SEQUENCES element 233, 601
Sequential flow connector 72
Sequential-access file 364
SET BREAK command 142
SET command 142
SET INTERCEPT command 143
SET TRACE CONDITION command 144
SET TRACE ENTITY command 144
SET TRACE EXPRESSION command 145
SET WATCH command 143
SETA subroutine 465
SETIS subroutine 465
SETM subroutine 465
SETMR subroutine 471

SETNS subroutine 465
SETP subroutine 471
SETTF subroutine 471
SETV subroutine 471
SETVC subroutine 471
SETVT subroutine 471
Shannon, R. 6, 26, 27
Sheppard, S. 13, 27
Shifts 343
Shortest-distance matrix 409
SHOW command 145
SIG subroutine 468
SIGNAL block 369, 590
Signals 369
SIM common block 463
SIMAN overview 25, 61
SIMAN Summary Report 166
    average 166
    coefficient of variation 166
    final value 168
    maximum observation 166
    minimum observation 166
    number of observations 166
Simplification and reduction 35
    aggregation 37
    impact on results 38
    omission 37
    substitution 37
Simulation process 12
Simulation, definition 3
Single machine problem (discrete-event) 473
Single workstation 73
Skip-ahead 326
Small-sample problem 307
Smallest Number Busy, see SNB
Smallest Number in Queue, see SNQ
Smallest Remaining Capacity, see SRC
Smallest-distance-to-station rule, see SDS
Smirnov, N. 54, 58
Snap grid 311
Snapshots 147
SNB 342
SNQ 350
Soaking pit furnace 516
Sources of data
Special characters (___, #, @, %, and $) 71
Special-purpose attributes 67
    A(AttribID) 67
    IS 229
    M 222, 336
    NS 229
Special-purpose variables 66
    ACC(TrnID) 428
    CLA(CnvID) 268
    DAVG(DstatID) 177
    DEC(TrnID) 428

DMAX(DstatID) 177
DMIN(DstatID) 177
ICS(CnvID) 268
IDSNET(NetID,IntxID1,IntxID2) 430
ISZT(TrnID,Unit) 428
IT(TrnID,Unit) 247
LDL(TrnID,Unit) 429
LDX(TrnID,Unit) 429
LDZ(TrnID,Unit) 429
LEC(CnvID) 268
LENZ(LinkID) 430
LNKNUM(IntxID,IntxID) 430
LT(TrnID,Unit) 247, 250
LTL(TrnID,Unit) 429
LTYP(LinkID) 430
LTZ(TrnID,Unit) 429
LX(IntxID) 430
MLC(CnvID) 268
MR(ResourceID) 77
MT(TrnID) 247
MZ(LinkID) 430
NC(CounterID) 81, 177
NDX(LinkID) 431
NEA(CnvID) 268
NEC(CnvID) 268
NEXTX(NetID,IntxID1,IntxID2) 430
NL(LinkID) 431
NQ(QueueID) 76
NR(ResourceID) 77
NSTO(StorID) 79
NSZT(TrnID,Unit) 428
NT(TrnID) 247
NX(IntxID) 431
NXB(LinkID) 430
NXE(LinkID) 430
NZ(LinkID,Zone) 431
TAVG(TallyID) 177
TAZ(TrnID,Unit) 429
TMAX(TallyID) 177
TMIN(TallyID) 177
TVF(TrnID) 428
TWZ(TrnID,Unit) 429
VC(CnvID) 268
VL(LinkID) 430
VT(TrnID) 247
VTU(TrnID,Unit) 247
VX(IntxID) 430
SPLIT block 356, 591
Spreadsheet 363
Spur link 416
SRC 342, 350
Staging area object 321
Standard normal distribution 189
Standardized time series 204
START block 270, 591
Starting a debug session 140

Starting conditions 186
Starting seed 171
State equation 497
State events 512
STATE subroutine 460, 500
Statement terminator 84
Static objects 309
Station attribute (M) 222
STATION block 220, 591
Station concept 220
Station number, 222, 336
Station object 319
Station ranges 336
Station submodels 219
Station variables 574
STATION(StationID) 419
Station-visitation sequences 228
STATIONS element 224, 410, 602
Statistical Summary Variables 177
Statistics collection variables 574
Statistics initialization 91
Statistics on Queues, Resources, and time in
    system 108
Status delay 75
Status functions 464
    A function 464
    AG function 465
    ID function 470
    IDENT function 464
    IDIST function 470
    IOFFST function 470
    IS function 464
    ISG function 465
    ISGMT function 470
    LFCAL function 467
    LFR function 467
    LGRP function 465
    LLR function 467
    LPRED function 467
    LRANK function 467
    LSCAL function 467
    LSUCC function 467
    M function 464
    MG function 465
    NEVENT function 467
    NG function 465
    NS function 464
    NSG function 465
    SAG function 465
    TEVENT function 467
Steady-state behavior 185
STEP command 141
Stochastic models 6
STOP block 270, 591
Stopping a debug session 140
Storage object 315

Storage variables 574
Storages 79, 113, 237
STORAGES element 113, 602
Straight queues 313
Structural and boundary verification 157
Student-t distribution 178
Submodels, see station submodels
Subscripts 66
SUM 357
Summing covariances 188
SUMRY subroutine 472
Suri, R. 26, 27
Symbol libraries 311
Symbolic models 5
Symbolic naming rules 70
Symptom generation 159
Synchronizing random numbers 542
System definition 16
System initialization 91
System map 243, 403

T
t-table 571
t-value 178
TABLES command 205
TABLES element 375, 602
TALLIES element 113, 603
TALLY block 111, 591
TALLY subroutine 472
TAVG(TallyID) 177
TAZ(TrnID,Unit) 429
Temporary entity sets 355
Terminating system, analysis 175, 206, 209
Terminating system, definition 174
Terminating systems 22
Test cases 136
Testing for model structure and data 157
Testing for reasonableness 156
Testing model behavior 158
TEVENT function 467
Time-advance parameters 325
Time-dependent data 109
TMAX(TallyID) 177
TMIN(TallyID) 177
Tomsicek, M. 26, 27
Trace 137
    active entity 137
    sample trace 138
TRACE element 139
    trace period 139
    trace condition 139
TRACE element 139, 603
Transporter size 434
Transporter variables 246
Transfer blocks 63, 221
Transferring data 204

TRANSPORT block 238, 591
Transporter breakdowns 256
Transporter variables 575
Transporters 235, 403
TRANSPORTERS element 243, 411, 603
TRIANGULAR (TRIA) random variable 68
Triangular distribution 41, 43, 47, 566
Truncation 186, 198, 199
Truncation of initial bias 92, 186, 198, 199
Tukey method 204
Turning-velocity factor 411, 428
Tversky, A. 40, 43, 58
TVF(TrnID) 428
Two job types and a second workstation 97
Two-sample-t method 183
Two-stage sampling procedure 179
TWZ(TrnID,Unit) 429
Type I and II verification errors 158

U

UCLEAR subroutine 458
UF function 459
Unformatted files 365
Unidirectional links 406
UNIFORM (UNIF) random variable 68
Uniform distribution 41, 47, 567
United Parcel Service hub shifter simulation 328
Units of measurement errors 150
Unnormalized random number 171
UR function 459
URST subroutine 460
USAV subroutine 460
User code 457
User-assignable variables 575
User-defined decision rule 486
User-written routines (C) 458
   CEVENT function 459
   CKEYHI function 460
   CPRIME function 458
   CSTATE function 460
   CUCLEA function 458
   CUF function 459
   CUR function 459
   CURST function 460
   CUSAV function 460
   CWRAP function 458
User-written routines (FORTRAN) 458
   EVENT subroutine 459
   KEYHIT subroutine 460
   PRIME subroutine 458
   STATE subroutine 460, 500
   UCLEAR subroutine 458
   UF function 459
   UR function 459
   URST subroutine 460
   USAV subroutine 460

WRAPUP subroutine 458

V

V(VariableID) 66
Validation 20, 133, 154
   decision maker 153
   rationalism 155
   empiricism 155
   positive economics 155
   testing for reasonableness 156
      absurd conditions 156
      consistency 156
      continuity 156
      degeneracy 156
   testing for model structure and data 157
      face validity 157
      parameters and relationships 157
      sensitivity analysis 157
      structural and boundary verification 157
      Type I and II errors 158
   testing model behavior 158
      behavior anomaly 159
      behavior comparison 159
      behavior prediction 159
      symptom generation 159
Variable object 316
Variables 66
VARIABLES element 99, 604
Variance estimation, see Confidence intervals
Variance reduction techniques 531
VARTESTS command 204
VC(CnvID) 268
Verification 20, 133
   animation as a verification aid 148
   correcting errors 148
   doubting frame of mind 134
   interactive debugger 139
   outside doubters 135
   test cases 136
   tracing model operation 137
VIA 419
VIEW command 145
VIEW COUNTERS command 145
VIEW DSTATS command 145
VIEW ENTITY command 143
VIEW QUEUE /BRIEF command 146
VIEW QUEUE command 146
VIEW SOURCE command 145
VIEW SUMMARY command 145
VIEW TALLIES command 145
Vincent, S. 46, 57
Visitation sequence, see station-visitation
   sequence
VL(LinkID) 430
VRT's, see variance reduction techniques
VT(TrnID) 247

VTU(TrnID,Unit) 247
VX(IntxID) 430

W

WAIT block 369, 592
Walkthroughs 135
Warm-up period, see initial transient period
Watch variables 139,143
WEIBULL (WEIB) random variable 68
Weibull distribution 48, 568
Weinberg, G. M. 4, 28, 135, 162
Welch, P. 187, 216, 539, 550
Westinghouse Just-In-Time fabrication
   shop 326
Wexelblat, R. 19, 28
Williams, R. B. 507, 528
Wilson, J. 187, 216
WITH branch 105
WKS spreadsheet file 363
World views 23
   activity-scanning 24
   event-scheduling 24
   process-interaction 25
Wright, R. 544, 551
WRITE block 367, 592
Writing data 367

X

X array 501

Z

Zeigler, B. 20, 25, 28
Zero-length zones 414
Zones 406